Why do you need this new edition?

If you're wondering why you should buy this new edition of the *Student's Book of College English*, here are a few great reasons!

W9-AHG-492

1. A new full-color book design makes finding the information you need much easier and makes reading a more user-friendly experience.

2. Instruction revised into smaller sections of text helps you scan for key ideas even as you read passages for more detailed instruction.

3. New Strategy Checklists show the steps involved in various processes to help you break down large assignments into manageable, productive tasks.

4. New outlines of chapter headings at the start of each chapter help you preview the content before you read.

5. Numerous word charts providing Tips for accomplishing writing goals.

6. New readings on engaging and current topics such as marketing on Facebook, Internet behavior, changes in marriage and the family, and immigration model the different writing assignments your instructor may assign.

7. Up-to-date, step-by-step instructions and illustrations of library and online research help you learn how to find sources for your assigned papers using computerized library catalogs, online databases, and the World Wide Web (Ch. 20).

8. New student essays include several that are based on sources to help you see how to use researched material in your writing and how to cite and document it.

9. New Source Samples show you where to find the information in your research sources that you need in order to cite and document those sources in college research papers (Ch. 21).

10. Up-to-date MLA and APA citation examples, including examples of the most recent electronic sources, show you how to correctly cite and document sources in your research papers.

11. A new Chapter 1 on critical reading skills provides different reading strategies when reading for different purposes, helping you practice college-level skills needed to read visual and textual elements in print documents and Web content.

PEARSON
Longman

Student's Book of College English

RHETORIC, READER, RESEARCH GUIDE, AND HANDBOOK

TWELFTH EDITION

DAVID SKWIRE
HARVEY S. WIENER
The City University of New York
LaGuardia Community College

Longman

New York San Francisco Boston
London Toronto Sydney Tokyo Singapore Madrid
Mexico City Munich Paris Cape Town Hong Kong Montreal

Acquisitions Editor: Lauren A. Finn
Development Editor: Marion Castellucci
Senior Supplements Editor: Donna Campion
Senior Marketing Manager: Sandra McGuire
Production Manager: Eric Jorgensen
Project Coordination, Text Design, and Electronic Page Makeup: Electronic Publishing
    Services Inc., NYC
Cover Design Manager: John Callahan
Cover Designer: Kay Petronio
Cover Image: © istock / Dra Schwartz
Photo Researcher: Anita Dickhuth
Senior Manufacturing Buyer: Dennis J. Para
Printer and Binder: Courier Kendallville
Cover Printer: Phoenix Color Corporation

For permission to use copyrighted material, grateful acknowledgment is made to the
copyright holders on pp. 723–727, which are hereby made part of this copyright page.

Library of Congress Cataloging-in-Publication Data
Student's book of college english : rhetoric, readings, research guide, and handbook /
    David Skwire, Harvey S. Wiener.—12th ed.
        p. cm.
    Includes bibliographical references and indexes.
    ISBN-13: 978-0-205-74178-6
    ISBN-10: 0-205-74178-9
    1. English language--Rhetoric. 2. English language--Grammar--Handbooks, manuals,
etc. 3. College readers. 4. Report writing. I. Wiener, Harvey S.

PE1408.S546 2008
808'.0427--dc22   2008041930

This book includes 2009 MLA guidelines.

Copyright © 2009 by Pearson Education, Inc.

All rights reserved. No part of this publication may be reproduced, stored in a retrieval
system, or transmitted, in any form or by any means, electronic, mechanical, photocopy-
ing, recording, or otherwise, without the prior written permission of the publisher. Printed
in the United States.

Longman
is an imprint of

PEARSON

www.pearsonhighered.com

2 3 4 5 6 7 8 9 1 0—CRK—12 11 10 09

ISBN-13: 978-0-205-74178-6
ISBN-10:   0-205-74178-9

Detailed Contents

9 EXAMPLE   174

GLOSSARY OF PROBLEM WORDS   670

ESL POINTERS: TIPS FOR NON-NATIVE WRITERS   707

Thematic Contents

The Natural World

Family Matters

Media, Arts, and Popular Culture

Love, Sweet Love

Gender Dynamics

Race, Equality, and Prejudice

Crime and Punishment

Portraits of People

Education, In School and Out

Fun and Laughs

On the Job

Preface to the Instructor

Changes give life; consistency sustains it. Although few traps are more insidious for an instructor than teaching a book—or a course—from memory, relying on a text's consistent philosophy from edition to edition has many rewards. Our twelfth edition has changed and improved, yet the basic appeal of *Student's Book of College English* remains unchanged: It provides in a coherent package thorough instruction on all the issues likely to face students within First Year English—and then supplements that instruction with numerous essays, poems, and works of fiction by student writers and professionals.

One of the special, possibly unique, features of *Student's Book* is the mix wherever practicable of readings for use as models and readings for use as subjects for compositions. We believe that this mix significantly increases the versatility of the book and helps account for its success. We maintain this principle in the twelfth edition. Users will find, for example, student and professional models of descriptive writing, but they will also find a short story that students can profitably analyze in writing their own descriptions.

We hope that clear prose and good sense also made their contributions to the success of earlier editions. We have tried to keep them constantly in mind while writing the current one.

What's New in the Twelfth Edition?

By making additions and improvements in the twelfth edition of *Student's Book*, we aim to keep the text fresh and timely. Outstanding features of this revision include:

- **Newly designed in full color**, the text now makes the utmost pedagogical use of color. Exercises are more clearly distinguished from instructional text; MLA and APA citations are easy to reference quickly; "to do" action steps stand out within each stage of the writing process—all to create a more inviting presentation and help students locate key elements at a glance.

- **Instruction has been revised into smaller sections of text** to better meet the needs of a new generation of readers and learners who want to be able to scan for key ideas even as they read passages of prose for more detailed instruction.

- **New Chapter 1 on Critical Reading** helps students recognize that there are different purposes for reading and understand that readers can use different strategies depending on the purpose. Specific attention helps develop skills for reading images, advertisements, charts, tables, graphs, and Web sites so that students learn to read visual information using a critical eye.

- **New Strategy Checklists** throughout the text combine a flowchart that shows a progression of steps with a checklist that organizes each step into a set of tasks, creating for students a specific action plan for different types of reading, stages of writing, methods of development, and research tasks.

- **Numerous word charts of "Tips"** for accomplishing specific writing goals. These include Tips for Reading Critically and Tips for Writing Essays, among many others, throughout the text.

- **New student essays include several that are source-based**. Not only will topics such as immigration, same-sex marriage, wolves in Yellowstone, citizenship, and television engage student interest, but source-based readings also model how to support theses with evidence and detail and how to integrate source material into one's own writing.

- **New professional essays on high interest topics** such as blogging and mixed marriages provide examples of how established writers use different patterns of development.

- **New chapter-opening outlines** help students practice reading skills introduced in Chapter 1 by previewing and anticipating new material as well as recognizing the hierarchy of main concepts and subtopics.

- **Updated research strategies and instruction in Chapter 20** help students cope with the vast array of research methods and sources now available.

  - **Searching an online library catalog** is explained with step-by-step illustrations of a key word search and the eventual resulting book entry.

  - **Searching a computerized periodical database** is explained and supported by another sequence of illustrations, from the initial key word search, to narrowing search terms, and finally to a journal article entry.

  - **The section on developing a working bibliography now** emphasizes the importance of gathering accurate source information and deemphasizes the particular technology used. It includes illustrations of bibliography records for a book, a journal article, and a Web source.

- **A reorganized and updated Chapter 21 on writing the research paper** retains an overview of the process as well as specific guidance on quoting and paraphrasing sources, avoiding plagiarism, citing and documenting sources in MLA and APA style, and preparing the final manuscript, but it is newly resequenced and redesigned to make topics easier to find, and newly updated to bring the content in line with developments in research writing.

- **Source samples** illustrate the original source material, whether a book, a journal article, or a Web page, in order to show students where in an original source they can cull information needed for citations in their research papers and Works Cited lists.
- **MLA and APA citations for electronic sources** have been expanded and updated.

Other Features of *Student's Book*

In preparing the twelfth edition, we have retained many time-tested features that help students improve their writing skills and produce good essays:

- **Comprehensive coverage of the writing process** addresses all aspects of writing, from prewriting and outlining to drafting and revising, while examples and annotations of student drafts help demystify writing.

- **A practical chapter on outlining** (Chapter 4), unique in rhetorics organized by rhetorical patterns, offers students a reliable strategy to help them progress from prewriting and their thesis statements into their rough drafts, helping them build coherence in their papers from the very first draft. Furthermore, in Chapter 20, *Student's Book* features outlining as a key part of the process of planning a research paper.

- **Two or more sample student essays in each modes chapter** offer twice as many student readings per rhetorical pattern than most other comparable rhetorics and expose students to a variety of options to consider as they plan and develop their own papers.

- **Over 85 readings** that include both classic and contemporary essays, photographs, cartoons, and Web-based writing provide students with material for response in their own writing as well as models for different rhetorical strategies.

- **Annotated professional samples** illustrate for students how active readers interact with texts.

- **Argument writing prompts, "Having Your Say,"** throughout the text ask students to think about a high-interest or controversial topic about which they have read and argue a position, strengthening their argumentation skills as a component of each chapter's writing assignments.

- **Photo-based writing assignments, "From Image to Words,"** encourage students to read photographs critically as texts and write essays in response to clear and pointed questions.

- **Critical Thinking activities, "Crosscurrents,"** at the end of the readings in each chapter in Part Two, encourage students to connect themes, ideas, and issues.

- **"Collaborative Learning" activities** create opportunities for students to learn in groups as they discuss reading selections and student samples.

- **Step-by-step, detailed treatment of the research paper** includes tips and Strategy Checklists for doing research and writing the research paper. "Frequently Asked Questions" about writing the research paper, coverage of MLA and APA documentation styles, and a fully annotated student research paper effectively help students solve some of their most troublesome research problems and learn the skills needed for research writing across the curriculum.

- **The Handbook** and **Glossary of Problem Words** in Part Six also offer **over 25 Self Test exercises** (with answers) that allow students to practice and evaluate their progress.

- **"ESL Pointers: Tips for Non-Native Writers,"** a dedicated section in the Handbook, features helpful instruction and exercises in key trouble spots for students learning English as a second language.

- **The alternate thematic table of contents** for readings, visual texts, and student writing supports instructors who want another way to approach the reading selections.

Plan of the Book

In **Part One, "Getting Started: The Principles of Good Reading and Writing,"** we explore critical reading, prewriting strategies, drafting, and revising, and provide extensive practice on drafting and developing a thesis. We show student writing at various stages of development and offer commentary to guide a reader's appreciation of how a paper progresses from start to finish. We continue our full coverage of outlining and instruction in the use of computers as an aid to writing and in peer evaluations.

Part Two, **"Methods of Development,"** contains ten chapters, one devoted to each of the key rhetorical modes, beginning with description and narration, working through example, process, comparison and contrast, classification and division, cause and effect, definition, and argumentation. Each of these chapters contains a discussion of how to write in the particular mode, professional and student examples ("Models of Writing"), readings intended to inspire writing ("Readings for Writing"), and a large number of analytical and generative exercises ("For Writing or Discussion" questions follow every selection). Many readings in Part Two are new. We've tried to incorporate new readings that reflect the interests of today's student body. As a culminating chapter in Part Two, we provide full instruction in using mixed modes so that students see and practice how to integrate different rhetorical strategies in a single paper.

To add to the practicality of the book, all chapters in Part Two end with suggested writing topics and with strategy checklists to serve as reminders and chapter summaries. Another popular feature in Part Two, "Crosscurrents," points out even more possibilities for writing topics by directing students' attention to thematic parallels between and among writing selections in different parts of the book.

Part Three, "Special Writing," includes a chapter on literary analysis and a chapter on writing essay exams, as well as an overview of business writing.

Part Four, "Research," gives considerable attention to essential research instruction. We include research with online databases, computerized card catalogs, and the Web, as well as significant coverage of the writing process, incorporating sources into one's own writing, avoiding plagiarism, and revising. The *MLA Style Manual and Guide to Scholarly Publishing*, Third Edition, the *Publication Manual of the American Psychological Association*, Fifth Edition, and the *APA Style Guide to Electronic References* (2007) guide our instruction in citation and documentation. Illustrated source samples of a book, a journal article, and a Web page help students see where to find citation information.

Part Five, "Style," includes three chapters: Chapter 22 helps students understand how to choose the right words to convey their meaning; Chapter 23, on effective sentences, highlights those stylistic issues directly involved with creation of effective sentences; and Chapter 24 on stylistic problems and solutions offers students practical writing advice, including guidelines for avoiding sexist language. The style chapters are especially noteworthy, we believe, for the great number and variety of exercises.

Part Six, "Handbook, Glossary, and ESL Pointers," is easily accessible through alphabetical arrangement of entries, a colored bar at the edge of all Part Six pages, and tabs with symbols that correspond to the list of Correction Symbols and Abbreviations on the inside front cover. The inside back cover contains guides to the text's planning, writing, and revising coverage, and a guide to the Handbook and Glossary, for quick reference. Student writers can find answers to most questions they have about grammar, sentences, punctuation, and mechanics in the Handbook and Glossary. Extensive exercises in Part Six enable students to demonstrate their command of the basics. A section called "ESL Pointers: Tips for Non-Native Writers" addresses many stumbling blocks faced by English-as-a-second-language student writers.

Supplements for Students and Instructors

- **Instructor's Manual**. The *Instructor's Manual*, revised by Angela R. Morales of Glendale College, features additional discussion on teaching strategies, including sample syllabi, portfolio instruction, and collaborative activities. In addition, the new manual contains an updated and expanded analysis of each essay.

    LONGMAN / PRENTICE HALL
    mycomplab
    where writing and research help is just a click away!

    - **The New MyCompLab Website**. The new MyCompLab integrates the market-leading instruction, multimedia tutorials, and exercises for writing, grammar, and research that users have come to identify with the program with a new online composing space and new assessment tools. The result is a revolutionary application that offers a seamless and flexible teaching and learning environment built specifically for writers. Created after years of extensive research and in partnership with composition faculty and students across the country, the new MyCompLab provides help for writers in the context of their writing, with instructor and peer commenting functionality, proven tutorials and exercises for writing, grammar, and research, an e-portfolio, an assignment-builder, a bibliography tool, tutoring services, and a gradebook and course management organization created specifically for writing classes. Visit www.mycomplab.com for more information.

- **Interactive E-book**. An e-book version of *Student's Book of College English* is also available in MyCompLab. This online version integrates the many resources of MyCompLab into the text to create an enriched, interactive learning experience for writing students.

- **Other Supplements**. Pearson English has a wide array of other supplementary items—some at no additional cost, some deeply discounted—that are available for packaging with this text. Please contact your local Pearson representative to find out more.

Acknowledgments

We are proud and grateful for the more than thirty years that our textbook has served college writers over the country. Our deepest thanks go to the faculty, students, and, we are certain, some of those students' children who have honored us with their trust and attention.

The planning and preparation of this edition, as well as earlier editions, have benefited enormously from the essential insights of Lauren A. Finn, our editor, and the wise counsel of Eben W. Ludlow, our former editor, now retired. We want to express special appreciation to Marion B. Castellucci, our development editor, whose wide-ranging experience and attention to detail kept us focused. We also thank Janice Wiggins-Clarke, whose good sense and good humor lifted us over the usual (and not so usual!) hurdles in the previous revision. And we owe a special debt of thanks to Scott Hitchcock, who guided us over the rough spots of production with calm and intelligence.

We are also grateful for the helpful advice of the reviewers of this edition: Michael Allen, North Central State College, and many of his students; Stephen Calatrello, Calhoun Community College; Dawn Copeland, Motlow State Community College; Rita Delude, Nashua Community College; Michael Keathley, Ivy Tech Community College; Robert T. Koch, Jr., University of North Alabama; Georgia Kreiger, Allegany College of Maryland; Leigh A. Martin, Community College of Rhode Island; Keflyn X. Reed, Bishop State Community College; Melanie Whitebread, Luzerne County Community College.

DAVID SKWIRE

HARVEY S. WIENER

Preface to the Student

We have written this book for you. We don't say that simply to win your confidence or to make you think well of us. We've felt for a long time that most textbooks are written for your instructor.

Writing textbooks for your instructor instead of for you is natural enough, in a way. Instructors, after all, must teach from the books, and no book that makes them unhappy is going to find its way into the classroom. Still, this book is written for you. Its purpose is to help you become a better writer and a more thoughtful reader than you are now. We believe that if you read this book carefully and ask questions in class whenever there are points you don't understand, you can improve your writing significantly. Neither we nor anyone else knows how to teach you to be a great writer, but—with your active participation—we think we can teach you to manage competently any writing assignment you're likely to get.

We've tried to write this book in a straightforward, unfussy fashion. We've concentrated as much as possible on being helpful about writing situations that you'll really face in class. We understand the ups and downs of drafting papers, and we try to guide you through the writing process. We've tried to pick reading selections that will interest you, as they have interested our own students, and that demonstrate writing principles you can apply to your own work. We've included a number of student writings, too, because we feel that comparing your work solely to that of experienced professionals is unprofitable and unfair. These writings were prepared by college students for classes similar to the one you're taking. Most of them are solid, honest pieces of work—but that's all. They are not intended to dazzle you with their genius, and they didn't all get A's in class either. We hope you'll use them as general points of reference, not as supreme models of excellence. We hope that you'll often outdo them in your own writing.

First Lesson

Now for your first lesson.

Although this book will give you a great deal of information about writing, almost all of that information grows out of five simple ideas—ideas that are sufficiently important and usable to be thought of as rules. We're not peddling magic formulas, however, and we're not suggesting that a ready-made list of rules and regulations can substitute for the experiences and discoveries and sheer hard work by which writers educate themselves. No list ever made the pain of having nothing to say less painful. And people—not lists—write dramatic first sentences, come up with fresh insights, and choose the perfect word. Any rules we set down here or elsewhere are useful only because they can give direction and control to the inevitable hard work and thus increase the chances that the hard work will be worth the effort.

Don't approach the five simple ideas that follow, therefore, as representing more than important guidelines. They're starting points, but they're not eternal truths. George Orwell, our lead essayist (Chapter 1), once drew up a list of rules for writing, the last of which was, "Break any of these rules rather than say anything outright barbarous." As a more immediate example, this book will advise you to write well-developed paragraphs and avoid sentence fragments. That's excellent advice, and we take it seriously, but in the first paragraph of this section of the preface we deliberately wrote a five-word paragraph that also happened to be a sentence fragment. Enough said.

Here are the five ideas on which we base much of this book:

1. Except for a few commonsense exceptions such as recipes, technical manuals, encyclopedia articles, and certain kinds of stories, poems, and plays, *writing should state a central idea*. (We call that central idea—or position, or stand, or proposal, or contention—the *thesis*.)

2. *The primary function of writing is to prove or support its thesis.*

3. *The most effective and interesting way to prove or support the thesis is to use specific details presented in specific language.*

4. *Writing requires organization. Every statement must connect logically to the thesis.*

5. *Good writing is the result of an ongoing process*. First thoughts and first drafts should lead to second thoughts and second drafts, sometimes third ones and fourth ones. *Revise, revise, revise.*

We'll be repeating and expanding and sometimes strongly qualifying these ideas throughout the book, but they are the heart of what we have to say. They are not obscure secrets or brand new discoveries. They are the assumptions about writing that nearly all good writers make. They are the principles that nearly all good writers try to put into practice in their own work.

In the chapters that follow, we will discuss in detail the full meaning and implications of these ideas and try to show you the most effective ways of applying them to common classroom writing assignments.

DAVID SKWIRE

HARVEY S. WIENER

About the Authors

David Skwire, with degrees from the University of Wisconsin–Madison and Cornell University, taught composition, creative writing, and American literature at Cuyahoga Community College for twenty-five years. He also served on the faculties at Tufts University and Temple University. He acknowledges, however, that his job of most interest to students was a two-year stint as a writer of humorous greeting cards. In addition to his coauthorship of *Student's Book of College English*, he is author of the successful *Writing with a Thesis*. Now retired, Skwire lives near Cleveland.

Harvey S. Wiener taught for many years as professor of English at LaGuardia Community College. He has served in a variety of administrative positions, most recently as Vice President at Marymount Manhattan College. Dr. Wiener has directed the basic writing program at Pennsylvania State University and has taught at Teachers College, Columbia University, Brooklyn College, Queensborough Community College, and the State University of New York at Stony Brook. A Phi Beta Kappa graduate of Brooklyn College, Wiener holds a Ph.D. in Renaissance literature from Fordham University. He was founding president of the Council of Writing Program Administrators and was chair of the Teaching of Writing Division of the Modern Language Association.

Wiener is the author of many books on reading and writing for college students and their teachers, including *The Writing Room*. His book for parents, *Any Child Can Write*, was a Book-of-the-Month Club alternate. His most challenging writing assignment was a test to qualify as Chief Writer for a network soap opera by developing the content for six weeks of episodes. He does not regret having lost the job to someone else.

PART ONE

Getting Started: The Principles of Good Reading and Writing

Among the first things you'll do in your college English course is read an essay and write a paper, and the chapters in Part One of *Student's Book of College English* provide important information on how to accomplish those ends with maximum efficiency and success. We look with particular attention at the writing process from start to finish.

- **Chapter 1** explains how to read an essay intelligently and what to look for as you read. Recognizing the qualities of good writing in your readings will help you become a better writer—one of your main goals for the course. Here we also explore how to read visual images such as advertisements, photographs, cartoons, and graphs.
- **Chapter 2** shows you how to get started with writing an essay of your own by using a variety of prewriting strategies for identifying a topic, organizing your ideas, limiting your topic appropriately, and considering your purpose and audience. A sample draft paper offers a concrete example of how one student put his ideas on paper. The chapter also includes a section on writing with a computer.
- **Chapter 3** focuses on the all-important thesis; you'll see how to develop a thesis for the topic that interests you and how to support it with details.
- **Chapter 4** deals with planning a paper by showing how to outline your written work.
- **Chapter 5** gives you an overview of the parts of a typical paper—the introduction, the body, and the conclusion—and explores paragraph development.
- **Chapter 6** explains and demonstrates how to revise and edit a paper. It includes a student's intermediate draft accompanied by an example of a peer evaluation as well as the student's final draft with his teacher's comments; the chapter also provides tips for revising and proofreading.

CHAPTER 1

Critical Reading

- Why Read?
- Reading for Best Results
- Critical Reading in Action
- Reading Visual Images
- Reading Web Sites
- Models of Writing

Why Read?

Even a few decades ago, the question "Why read?" would rarely have crossed anyone's mind. The essential way to wisdom and enlightenment, to understanding issues and reacting wisely to world events, to filling time with pleasurable activity, was to read books, magazines, journals, and newspapers. Reading brought knowledge; reading brought delight; reading brought comfort and self-awareness.

In an age of multimedia, however, the question "Why read?" has urgency. After all, televisions, DVD players, computers, video game consoles, MP3 players, and cell phones all compete to fill our time with exciting visual and auditory presentations. We can watch and listen to an extraordinary range of information without turning a page of paper.

So, why read? One set of responses to this question is obvious, of course. We read traffic signs and warning signs. We read recipes and directions for putting together a toy or installing an air conditioner. We read menus and sales brochures. Furthermore, we also read in various electronic media. Television images frequently include words that we have to read. Text messaging on a cell phone involves reading and writing. E-mail, instant messages, blogs, and Web sites usually require us to decode written language. So, reading skills such as dealing with new vocabulary, figuring out the meaning of a message, and using inference regularly come into play. At the very least, being an attentive reader is important for survival as we go about our daily lives.

But beyond these practical instances, why should you try to improve your reading competence, especially in college, where you can address innumerable topics and questions through nonbook sources? First, the skills involved in reading print material clearly apply to modern media, too. For example, if you're checking the U.S. Fish and Wildlife Service's Web site, http://www.fws.gov/ endangered, to write a paper on endangered species, you're going to have to read what the site has to say. You may also have to read magazine articles and scholarly papers online on the subject of endangered species. Technology, reading, and college learning are clearly intertwined.

Much of the world's collected knowledge still resides in print that dwells in non-cyber libraries and bookstores. To maximize your learning experience, you'll have to read books handed down across centuries, do required textbook reading in your courses, and research newspapers and magazines that may not be online. These print media have a permanence that cyberspace often lacks. (How many times have you checked a site you've visited before only to find it no longer exists or has not been updated to address recent incidents and developments?)

What we have to say about reading in this chapter will help you read in any of the media demanded by your college programs. To be a successful college reader, you have to be a critical reader. Critical reading means reading actively.

Many college students are passive readers. They start reading with little advanced thought. They expect the words and sentences on a page to produce meaning without the reader's help. Passive readers do little to build a partnership with the writer and the text in order to understand what the writer says.

Active readers, critical readers, on the other hand, know that they have to work at getting meaning from words and sentences. They take conscious steps to engage what they read. The writer and the reader together create meaning.

Reading for Best Results

Critical readers interact with a text. That is, they raise questions about word use and content, consider aspects of style and essay structure, and examine the facts and ideas a selection conveys. They check the writer's observations and conclusions against their own thoughts and experiences. Critical readers use many of the following strategies when reading.

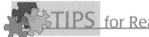 TIPS for Reading Critically

■ **Have a reason for reading.** Your reason shouldn't simply be "my teacher made me do it." Instead, you need to think in advance about what you expect to gain from your reading. Try to connect your purpose with the intellectual demands of the reading material and your expectations from it. You can read to learn new concepts and vocabulary. You can read to prepare for a class lecture or discussion or to learn someone's opinions on a controversial topic. You can read to stimulate your own writing for a required essay, to explore essential scholarship for a research paper, or to examine rhetorical and other writing strategies as an aid to honing your own skills. Without a purpose—or purposes—in bringing eye to paper, you risk a passive stance as a reader, and that puts you at risk of never truly interacting with the words before you.

■ **Explore what you know about the topic before you read.** Prior knowledge dramatically influences a reader's response to a text, in terms of both understanding and appreciation. Before you read anything below the title, look long and hard at it. Try to connect the title with any related information you may have seen or heard. Look at any subtitles, photographs, illustrations, graphs, charts—and all the accompanying captions—before you begin reading. Think a moment about the author's name and about any information provided about the author. When you start reading, stop after you complete the first paragraph or two. Think again about how you can relate what you already know to the topic the writer is investigating.

■ **As you read, record your responses.** Write down what the selection makes you think of or what it makes you feel. Write out any questions you have. Copy out phrases that stimulate, challenge, annoy, thrill, puzzle, or ignite you. Make notes in the margins of books you own.

■ **Establish the writer's thesis.** All good readers try to determine the main point of a reading. Sometimes the writer will tell you very directly what the thesis is, and before the end of the first few paragraphs—sometimes at the end of the very first sentence—you'll know exactly what the piece is about. But in other cases, no single statement or statements will tell you the thesis precisely. Here you have to state the writer's thesis in your own words. The various sentences and paragraphs in an essay will contribute information that you must use to define the thesis yourself.

■ **Pay attention to the words the writer chooses.** As you know, words are alive with both denotative (the dictionary definition) and connotative (the implied or suggested definition) meanings. Consider for a moment that a writer naming a person of about thirteen years old can use one of these words that, roughly speaking, would do the job: youngster, child, adolescent, teenager, kid, eighth grader, prepubescent, young adult. Critical readers always consider the implications of word choice and think about why a writer selects one word instead of another.

■ **Determine the writer's purpose and audience.**   Writers have many reasons for writing: to inform, to entertain, to challenge, to complain, to convince, to describe, to tell a story, to call for action—there are others certainly. Don't expect a "This is why I'm writing" sentence. But as you read, you should be able to figure out the intended purpose. Related to the writer's purpose is the audience the writer has in mind for the essay. The intended audience influences the writing markedly. For example, to write about steps for preventing the spread of AIDS, a writer would use wholly different strategies if writing for eighth-grade kids in a suburban classroom, for social workers in Chicago, or for health care workers in Africa.

■ **Consider the way that the writer has constructed the essay.**   Look at the sentences to see if they relate to the main point. Look at elements like introductions and conclusions, the essay's opening and closing doors, so to speak. Do they achieve their ends? Do they satisfy you? How do the parts of the essay hold together? Do all the ideas seem to relate to the central point? Do the sentences connect smoothly with each other? And how has the writer accomplished these near-magical feats? Attending to the structure of what you read will help you learn strategies for your own writing.

■ **Be aware of the writer's tone.**   Simply stated, *tone* is the writer's attitude toward the subject. For example, one writer writing about the high incidence of guns in schools could approach the topic with shock and horror; another, with anger; another, analytically, seeking only to understand motives; another, clinically, simply describing or chronicling events; another, sentimentally, longing for the good old school days with no weapons and with well-behaved kids. Thoughtful readers always keep an eye on the tone; like purpose and audience, it influences word choice, sentence structure, and style.

Critical Reading in Action

Look at the following selection and note in the margins the questions and comments that show how a critical reader might treat the piece "The Shy, Egg-Stealing Neighbor You Didn't Know You Had." Note the steady interaction between the student and the essay regarding language and content—the student reader cross-examines the piece, acknowledges important or difficult words, and makes comments on the writing. In short, these comments reflect many of the strategies outlined in the previous section of this chapter.

Answer the questions after you read.

LAWRENCE DOWNES

The Shy, Egg-Stealing Neighbor You Didn't Know You Had

Odd title— whose neighbor steals eggs? And if it's a neighbor, how could you not know you had it?

1   The suburbs, pretty as they may be, are <u>nobody's idea</u> of nature in balance. Sure, they are lush, green places where people and their vehicles get along with flowers, vegetables, songbirds and the littler mammals. But this harmony is enforced with an iron fist. It takes lots of chemicals, artificial irrigation and gas-powered trimming and mowing to keep such an arbitrary ecosystem under control.

True? Nobody's idea?

Fair? Urban "ecosystems" also arbitrary and must be controlled.

2   Leave it to nature to mount an <u>insurgency</u> against the tranquility of the <u>grass-and-pavement grid</u>. Canada geese and white-tail deer are the most brazen intruders, multiplying beyond all reason and refusing to be subdued. The best-equipped predators, people, sidestepped the job, finding it distasteful. Instead they adjust their garden netting, check for ticks and brood about the tendency of their fallen Eden to keep collapsing into chaos.

Nice word! implies conscious uprising, people on the attack!

Writer's view of suburbs. Good image—"grass-and-pavement grid."

Here, "insurgency" is by geese and deer!

People refuse to control the intruders. "Distasteful" because we'd have to kill them somehow.

3   But what if that didn't always happen? What if Mother Nature decided not to run amok but to tidy up?

Questions raised: Expect writer to answer them.

4   Just such an amazing circumstance appears to be happening on the outskirts of Chicago. Research biologists there announced last month that they had stumbled across a possible answer to the problem of the proliferating suburban goose: the proliferating suburban coyote.

Good image: "Mother" Nature tidying up.

Coyotes are keeping goose population in check. How?

5   The researchers belong to the <u>Cook County Coyote Project</u>, which has spent nearly six years studying the habits of more than 200 coyotes in the northern and western Chicago suburbs. Among other things, they tried to determine what the growing numbers of these beasts might have had to do with another puzzling development: the <u>sudden end of the goose explosion</u>. The local population of Canada geese had soared in the 1980's and 90's, but by 2000 the increase had slowed to about only 1 percent a year. An unknown predator was assumed to be the reason.

Sounds responsible. Google this?

Coyotes grow in numbers. Geese stop populating. What's the reason?

Repetition of word "proliferating" —good balancing. One proliferation is a problem, the other a solution.

6   The coyote was not an obvious suspect, being small and skulky and unlikely to stand up to a <u>wrathful Canada goose</u>. Examinations of coyote scat had seldom found damning traces of eggshell. But then infrared cameras exposed the coyote as a nest robber, one that carefully cracks open a goose egg and licks it clean.

Canada geese have mean tempers.

This is how it's done! Coyote cracks egg and sucks out insides— leaves no evidence.

7   Evidence like this bolsters the conclusion that coyotes, in their own wily way, have become <u>keystone predators</u> in a land long emptied of wolves and mountain lions. The Cook County project's principal investigator, Prof. Stanley Gehrt of Ohio State University, speaks admiringly of his subjects, who have withstood more than 200 years of hunting, trapping and poisoning and are more entrenched in North America than ever. Every state but Hawaii has them.

Wily means cunning.

No wolves or mountain lions left to do the job.

Expert testimony— professor knows the issues as project head.

Resourceful creatures!

Check on coyotes here in this state Goes back to title "Shy, Egg-Stealing Neighbors."

They have spread into suburbs and cities, forcing biologists to revise their definition of coyote habitat to this. Basically anywhere.

Here is what is really strange: <u>Humans have barely noticed</u>. Egg-rustling, night-howling varmints are raising litters in storm drains, golf courses, parks and cemeteries. They are sometimes heard but seldom seen. In cities, they keep to <u>themselves and work nights</u>. There are coyotes, Professor Gehrt says, living in the Chicago Loop.

8   Transition refers to previous paragraph.

You could <u>call that sneaky</u>. Or you could call it discreet. Professor Gehrt said that one surprising discovery of the study was how little danger the coyote poses to his unwitting human neighbors. "The risk is quite low, as long as we don't monkey with their behavior," he said. If you assert yourself when you see one—by yelling, cursing and throwing sticks—it will respect your space and lie low. The coyote's tendency to avoid people—and more importantly, raccoons—has made rabies a nonissue, Professor Gehrt said, with only one case of coyote-to-human transmission ever recorded.

9

"Sneaky" and "discreet"—words for human activity contribute to coherence of essay.

Coyotes will behave, he said, as long as people do not feed them. Leave nothing tasty outside in an open trash can or food dish, and definitely <u>nothing small and fluffy</u> at the end of a leash. Professor Gehrt says with confidence that the sensible suburban toddler has little to fear from the suburban coyote, but he will not say the same for the suburban Shih Tzu.

10

Obviously a cat or dog—coyotes will go after them.

Shih Tzu is a small dog, once a favorite of the Imperial Chinese court, now a favorite of wealthy suburbanites.

The Cook County Coyote Project is the largest and most comprehensive of its kind, but it is just one study. It is probably not the time to call for coyote subsidies and captive-breeding programs for goose-plagued subdivisions. But any effort to learn more about these creatures—like a four-year coyote study being done in Westchester County by New York State and Cornell University—is highly welcome. It is intriguing to consider the possibility that such a shunned, <u>maligned</u> animal may be a misunderstood hero. The suburbs could use well-mannered, responsible predators, and house cats are clearly not up to the job.

11

Maligned means badly treated.

Why maligned? What is coyote's history?

A little humor here. More use of "people" words ("well-mannered," "responsible").

FOR WRITING OR DISCUSSION

1. What is the main point of Downes' piece?

2. How do the marginal notes demonstrate critical reading?

3. Where does the reader call attention to issues of language? Why does the reader raise these issues?

4. How does the comment about the title show an application of prior knowledge? Now that you've read the selection, how would you answer the question that the reader raised about the title?

5. What additional comments or questions would you raise about this piece?

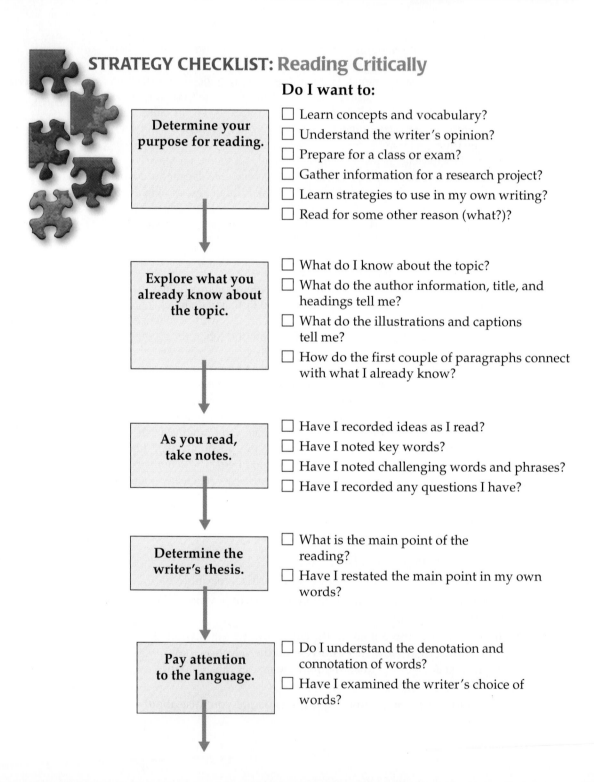

STRATEGY CHECKLIST: Reading Critically

Do I want to:

Determine your purpose for reading.

- ☐ Learn concepts and vocabulary?
- ☐ Understand the writer's opinion?
- ☐ Prepare for a class or exam?
- ☐ Gather information for a research project?
- ☐ Learn strategies to use in my own writing?
- ☐ Read for some other reason (what?)?

Explore what you already know about the topic.

- ☐ What do I know about the topic?
- ☐ What do the author information, title, and headings tell me?
- ☐ What do the illustrations and captions tell me?
- ☐ How do the first couple of paragraphs connect with what I already know?

As you read, take notes.

- ☐ Have I recorded ideas as I read?
- ☐ Have I noted key words?
- ☐ Have I noted challenging words and phrases?
- ☐ Have I recorded any questions I have?

Determine the writer's thesis.

- ☐ What is the main point of the reading?
- ☐ Have I restated the main point in my own words?

Pay attention to the language.

- ☐ Do I understand the denotation and connotation of words?
- ☐ Have I examined the writer's choice of words?

| Determine the writer's purpose and audience. | ☐ Why has the writer written the piece?
☐ Who is the writer's intended audience? |

| Consider the structure of the piece. | ☐ How do the introduction and conclusion serve the essay?
☐ Do all sentences relate to the main idea?
☐ Do sentences follow one another logically? |

| Pay attention to the writer's tone. | ☐ What is the writer's attitude to the subject?
☐ How does the language contribute to the tone? |

EXERCISE

Using what you have learned here about critical reading, examine the essay on pages 12–16, "A Hanging," by George Orwell (1903–1950). Orwell was a British citizen who at one point worked as a police officer in Burma, a colony in the British Empire and a province of India. A renowned essay writer, journalist, and social critic, Orwell searingly examines the relations between individual rights and oppressive governments in his novels *Animal Farm* and *1984*. Answer the questions below.

Before You Read

1. What purpose have you set for yourself before you read the text?
2. Before reading the entire essay, look at the note above about the author, look at the title of the selection, and read only the first two paragraphs. What thoughts are stimulated in your mind? What do you think this essay will be about? Where else have you read about or discussed similar issues?

During and After Your Reading

3. Keep pen and paper handy and write down thoughts as they occur to you. Use the margins, keeping in mind the notes in the margins of the piece by Lawrence Downes on pages 8–9. Underline, highlight, or copy challenging phrases and sentences. Raise questions.

4. What is the writer's thesis? State it in your own words. Where in the essay does the writer himself come closest to stating what you think is the thesis?

5. What is your view of the writer's use of language? Where do you find indelible images, snapshots of people and places through the use of color, sound, and action? What is the effect on the reader of the images in the first paragraph? the first sentence?

6. Why does Orwell never directly criticize capital punishment? Nonetheless, you are left with a very clear idea of where Orwell stands on the issue. How does he achieve that end? How does paragraph 10 serve the essay?

7. What is Orwell's purpose? How can you tell? Who do you believe is his intended audience? How can you tell?

8. Comment on the introduction (the first couple of paragraphs). Are they effective in bringing you into the scene as well as in revealing the topic of the essay? Why or why not? What is your reaction to the last paragraph? How does it provide dramatic closure to the essay? What strategies has Orwell used to connect the ideas smoothly from one sentence to the next, from one paragraph to the next?

9. What is the tone of the essay—Orwell's attitude to his subject? Is he indifferent, humorous, melodramatic, astonished, saddened, ironical, sentimental, imperialistic, liberal—or something else? Defend your choice.

GEORGE ORWELL

A Hanging

1   It was in Burma, a sodden morning of the rains. A sickly light, like yellow tinfoil, was slanting over the high walls into the jail yard. We were waiting outside the condemned cells, a row of sheds fronted with double bars, like small animal cages. Each cell measured about ten feet by ten and was quite bare within except for a plank bed and a pot of drinking water. In some of them brown silent men were squatting at the inner bars, with their blankets draped round them. These were the condemned men, due to be hanged within the next week or two.

One prisoner had been brought out of his cell. He was a Hindu, a puny wisp of a man, with a shaven head and vague liquid eyes. He had a thick, sprouting moustache, absurdly too big for his body, rather like the moustache of a comic man on the films. Six tall Indian warders were guarding him and getting him ready for the gallows. Two of them stood by with rifles with fixed bayonets, while the others handcuffed him, passed a chain through his handcuffs and fixed it to their belts, and lashed his arms tight to his sides. They crowded very close about him, with their hands always on him in a careful, caressing grip, as though all the while feeling him to make sure he was there. It was like men handling a fish which is still alive and may jump back into the water. But he stood quite unresisting, yielding his arms limply to the ropes, as though he hardly noticed what was happening.

Eight o'clock struck and a bugle call, desolately thin in the wet air, floated from the distant barracks. The superintendent of the jail, who was standing apart from the rest of us, moodily prodding the gravel with his stick, raised his head at the sound. He was an army doctor, with a grey toothbrush moustache and a gruff voice. "For God's sake hurry up, Francis," he said irritably. "The man ought to have been dead by this time. Aren't you ready yet?"

Francis, the head jailer, a fat Dravidian in a white drill suit and gold spectacles, waved his black hand. "Yes sir, yes sir," he bubbled. "All iss satisfactorily prepared. The hangman iss waiting. We shall proceed."

"Well, quick march, then. The prisoners can't get their breakfast till this job's over."

We set out for the gallows. Two warders marched on either side of the prisoner, with their files at the slope; two others marched close against him, gripping him by arm and shoulder, as though at once pushing and supporting him. The rest of us, magistrates and the like, followed behind. Suddenly, when we had gone ten yards, the procession stopped short without any order or warning. A dreadful thing had happened—a dog, come goodness knows whence, had appeared in the yard. It came bounding among us with a loud volley of barks, and leapt round us wagging its whole body, wild with glee at finding so many human beings together. It was a large woolly dog, half Airedale, half pariah. For a moment it pranced round us, and then, before anyone could stop it, it had made a dash for the prisoner, and jumping up tried to lick his face. Everyone stood aghast, too taken aback even to grab at the dog.

"Who let that bloody brute in here?" said the superintendent angrily. "Catch it, someone!"

A warder, detached from the escort, charged clumsily after the dog, but it danced and gambolled just out of his reach, taking everything as part of the game. A young Eurasian jailer picked up a handful of gravel and tried to stone the dog away, but it dodged the stones and came after us again. Its yaps echoed from the jail walls. The prisoner, in the grasp of the two warders, looked on incuriously, as though this was another formality of the hanging. It was several minutes before someone managed to catch the dog. Then we put my handkerchief through its collar and moved off once more, with the dog still straining and whimpering.

2

3

4

5
6

7

8

9   It was about forty yards to the gallows. I watched the bare brown back of the prisoner marching in front of me. He walked clumsily with his bound arms, but quite steadily, with that bobbing gait of the Indian who never straightens his knees. At each step his muscles slid neatly into place, the lock of hair on his scalp danced up and down, his feet printed themselves on the wet gravel. And once, in spite of the men who gripped him by each shoulder, he stepped slightly aside to avoid a puddle on the path.

10   It is curious, but till that moment I had never realised what it means to destroy a healthy, conscious man. When I saw the prisoner step aside to avoid the puddle, I saw the mystery, the unspeakable wrongness, of cutting a life short when it is in full tide. This man was not dying, he was alive just as we were alive. All the organs of his body were working—bowels digesting food, skin renewing itself, nails growing, tissues forming—all toiling away in solemn foolery. His nails would still be growing when he stood on the drop, when he was falling through the air with a tenth of a second to live. His eyes saw the yellow gravel and the grey walls, and his brain still remembered, foresaw, reasoned—reasoned even about puddles. He and we were a party of men walking together, seeing, hearing, feeling, understanding the same world; and in two minutes, with a sudden snap, one of us would be gone—one mind less, one world less.

11   The gallows stood in a small yard, separate from the main grounds of the prison, and overgrown with tall prickly weeds. It was a brick erection like three sides of a shed, with planking on top, and above that two beams and a crossbar with the rope dangling. The hangman, a grey-haired convict in the white uniform of the prison, was waiting beside his machine. He greeted us with a servile crouch as we entered. At a word from Francis the two warders, gripping the prisoner more closely than ever, half led, half pushed him to the gallows and helped him clumsily up the ladder. Then the hangman climbed up and fixed the rope round the prisoner's neck.

12   We stood waiting, five yards away. The warders had formed in a rough circle round the gallows. And then, when the noose was fixed, the prisoner began crying out on his god. It was a high, reiterated cry of "Ram! Ram! Ram! Ram!," not urgent and fearful like a prayer or a cry for help, but steady, rhythmical, almost like the tolling of a bell. The dog answered the sound with a whine. The hangman, still standing on the gallows, produced a small cotton bag like a flour bag and drew it down over the prisoner's face. But the sound, muffled by the cloth, still persisted, over and over again: "Ram! Ram! Ram! Ram! Ram!"

13   The hangman climbed down and stood ready, holding the lever. Minutes seemed to pass. The steady, muffled crying from the prisoner went on and on, "Ram! Ram! Ram!" never faltering for an instant. The superintendent, his head on his chest, was slowly poking the ground with his stick; perhaps he was counting the cries, allowing the prisoner a fixed number—fifty, perhaps, or a hundred. Everyone had changed colour. The Indians had gone grey like bad coffee, and one or two of the bayonets were wavering. We looked at the lashed, hooded man on the drop, and listened to his cries—each cry another second of life; the same thought was in all our minds: oh, kill him quickly, get it over, stop that abominable noise!

Suddenly the superintendent made up his mind. Throwing up his head he made a swift motion with his stick. "Chalo!" he shouted almost fiercely.

There was a clanking noise, and then dead silence. The prisoner had vanished, and the rope was twisting on itself. I let go of the dog, and it galloped immediately to the back of the gallows; but when it got there it stopped short, barked, and then retreated into a corner of the yard, where it stood among the weeds, looking timorously out at us. We went round the gallows to inspect the prisoner's body. He was dangling with his toes pointed straight downwards, very slowly revolving, as dead as a stone.

The superintendent reached out with his stick and poked the bare body; it oscillated, slightly. "*He's* all right," said the superintendent. He backed out from under the gallows, and blew out a deep breath. The moody look had gone out of his face quite suddenly. He glanced at his wristwatch. "Eight minutes past eight. Well, that's all for this morning, thank God."

The warders unfixed bayonets and marched away. The dog, sobered and conscious of having misbehaved itself, slipped after them. We walked out of the gallows yard, past the condemned cells with their waiting prisoners, into the big central yard of the prison. The convicts, under the command of warders armed with lathis, were already receiving their breakfast. They squatted in long rows, each man holding a tin pannikin, while two warders with buckets marched round ladling out rice; it seemed quite a homely, jolly scene, after the hanging. An enormous relief had come upon us now that the job was done. One felt an impulse to sing, to break into a run, to snigger. All at once everyone began chattering gaily.

The Eurasian boy walking beside me nodded towards the way we had come, with a knowing smile: "Do you know, sir, our friend (he meant the dead man), when he heard his appeal had been dismissed, he pissed on the floor of his cell. From fright—Kindly take one of my cigarettes, sir. Do you not admire my new silver case, sir? From the boxwallah, two rupees eight annas. Classy European style."

Several people laughed—at what, nobody seemed certain.

Francis was walking by the superintendent, talking garrulously: "Well, sir, all hass passed off with the utmost satisfactoriness. It was all finished—flick! like that. It iss not always so—oah, no! I have known cases where the doctor wass obliged to go beneath the gallows and pull the prisoner's legs to ensure decease. Most disagreeable!"

"Wriggling about, eh? That's bad," said the superintendent.

"Ach, sir, it iss worse when they become refractory! One man, I recall, clung to the bars of hiss cage when we went to take him out. You will scarcely credit, sir, that it took six warders to dislodge him, three pulling at each leg. We reasoned with him. 'My dear fellow,' we said, 'think of all the pain and trouble you are causing to us!' But no, he would not listen! Ach, he wass very troublesome!"

I found that I was laughing quite loudly. Everyone was laughing. Even the superintendent grinned in a tolerant way. "You'd better all come out and have a drink," he said quite genially. "I've got a bottle of whisky in the car. We could do with it."

14

15

16

17

18

19
20

21
22

23

24   We went through the big double gates of the prison, into the road. "Pulling at his legs!" exclaimed a Burmese magistrate suddenly, and burst into a loud chuckling. We all began laughing again. At that moment Francis's anecdote seemed extraordinarily funny. We all had a drink together, native and European alike, quite amicably. The dead man was a hundred yards away.

COLLABORATIVE LEARNING

One of the best ways to develop a critical reading style is to engage regularly in conversation about text—text you read and text you write, and we provide a series of collaborative exercises where you can benefit from the thoughts and ideas of fellow classmates. Collaboration requires an effort to reach consensus on an issue. *Consensus* is collective agreement or accord—a general concurrence after conversational give and take—with necessary acknowledgment of dissenting opinions. Through collaboration, you can benefit from the interactions in a group of people wrestling with a challenging topic or question.

Try this collaborative effort after reading "A Hanging." Form groups of five students and discuss the issue of capital punishment. Using Orwell's essay as a springboard for thinking and conversation, make a list of the pros and cons of taking the lives of accused criminals in the name of the state. As a group, try to reach consensus: If your group had the power, would it sustain or eliminate capital punishment? One person from each group should report back to the whole class. What is the general feeling of the class about this issue?

As your instructor directs, after you have heard all the groups' reports, look ahead to "Perspectives on the Death Penalty" in Chapter 15 and write an essay about capital punishment.

Reading Visual Images

Surely you've heard the saying "A picture is worth a thousand words." People use this saying not only to indicate the power and impact of a visual image, but also to suggest that words are a liability, that they cannot communicate as well as a single picture can. To sketch a scene verbally, the saying implies, we must use an endless supply of language (a thousand words!) to capture what a real-life scene, a photograph, a drawing, or an illustration can do much more simply through visual appeal.

But there is another way to understand the saying. Pictures without the viewer's use of words to explain, analyze, and interpret the image are pretty much worthless. Visual literacy—that is, the ability to understand and analyze images—depends on making meaning from what you see. When you look at a photograph, a pen-and-ink drawing, a cartoon, an illustration, an advertising promotion, you can't fully understand and appreciate it without language—the thousand-word part of the saying. "What am I seeing?" something in your brain asks. That's an old woman asking for a handout. The sun on that canvas is too bright. There's Snoopy lying on the roof of his doghouse again.

Always try to put thought into words when you read a visual image. Our powers as thinking, word-using human beings give us the ability to take as much as possible from a pictorial representation. A picture may be worth a thousand words—but think of the word *worth* in the adage to mean *valued at* or *deserving of* and you'll understand the point. (Don't go off thinking that this book advocates an excessive use of words here! The thousand-word part of the saying is a metaphor for "words needed for the task.")

 TIPS   for Understanding Visuals

- **Translate what you see into language.**   Tell yourself what you think the image means. If it has a caption or title, use the words presented as a springboard to interpret what you see.

- **Look at the whole image as well as its parts.**   Be sure to examine the parts as well as the whole to get the overall effect of a visual representation. Determine the relations among the people or places or events shown in the picture.

- **Consider the purpose and techniques used by the image creator.**   Like good writers, photographers, painters, illustrators, and producers of advertisements all use particular strategies to create intended responses from viewers. How close is the camera to its subject? What facial expression does the visual aim to capture? Is the scene natural or staged? How does the cartoon exaggerate its subject to produce a positive or negative image? Is the visual a composite, where pieces from several pictures are cut and pasted together to form a new image—and what does it mean if the image is, in fact, a composite?

- **Pay particular attention to advertisements.**   The creators of ads not only want to convince you of something, they also want you to take an action— buy this product, join this association, vote for this candidate. Be aware of the elements used to convince you. Does the ad appeal to your emotions, fears, goals, dreams, or desires? Who is its intended audience? How does the language in the ad interact with the visual elements?

■ **Examine carefully all visuals that accompany text.** Visual images present important content, and you should include them as part of your careful reading. Look thoughtfully at graphs, charts, statistical tables, photographs, maps, drawings, diagrams, and other illustrations. How do they help you better understand the material you're reading?

Reading a Photograph, Drawing, or Advertisement

Photos and drawings often accompany readings, and you want to be sure that you understand them fully. Advertisements use words and images to sell. Once again, you have to read actively—examine the details, ask yourself questions about what you see, and try to put your responses into language. Accompanying captions can help significantly, so read them carefully.

Examining a Photo

Look at the picture below. In a sentence explain the point of the picture—that is, what you think the picture is about.

Photo Courtesy: Chris Graythen/Getty Images

You probably said something like, "A young person is carrying three cats in a large plastic container." But certainly there is more to the photograph than that, and only careful observation can help you flesh out other important information. The person is stepping through water with shoes and socks on: that implies some kind of urgent departure, perhaps the result of a flood or a hurricane. Trees immersed in water support that observation. The expression on the person's face is one of worry, even fear; and although you might identify the person as a young male, there is little evidence in the photograph about the gender of the person. The writing on the T-shirt suggests other key elements, or at least helps you raise other questions. Is the word "Jesuit" merely a T-shirt decoration? Or does the word imply a religious or charitable commitment that might explain an apparently selfless act of animal rescue in a dangerous situation?

If this photograph accompanied some text, you might expect to find some answers to these questions in the language of the selection. In any case, looking carefully at the visual will help you extract meanings you might have missed and, through your active engagement with the photograph, will contribute to your growth as a critical reader. In the "Strategy Checklist: Reading and Interpreting Visuals" are some questions you should ask when you see a photo.

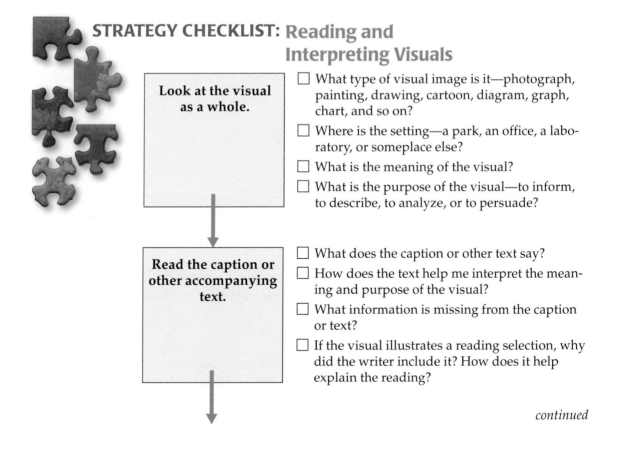

STRATEGY CHECKLIST: Reading and Interpreting Visuals

Look at the visual as a whole.

☐ What type of visual image is it—photograph, painting, drawing, cartoon, diagram, graph, chart, and so on?

☐ Where is the setting—a park, an office, a laboratory, or someplace else?

☐ What is the meaning of the visual?

☐ What is the purpose of the visual—to inform, to describe, to analyze, or to persuade?

Read the caption or other accompanying text.

☐ What does the caption or other text say?

☐ How does the text help me interpret the meaning and purpose of the visual?

☐ What information is missing from the caption or text?

☐ If the visual illustrates a reading selection, why did the writer include it? How does it help explain the reading?

continued

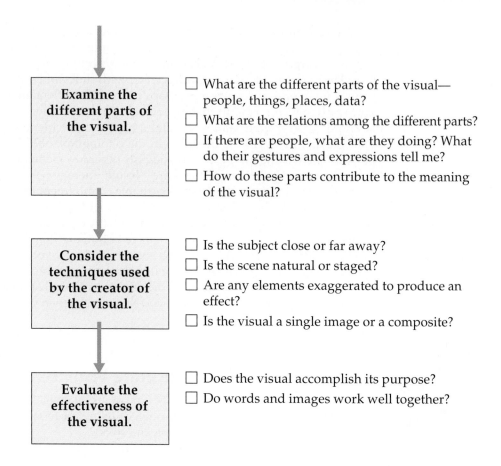

Examine the different parts of the visual.	☐ What are the different parts of the visual—people, things, places, data?
	☐ What are the relations among the different parts?
	☐ If there are people, what are they doing? What do their gestures and expressions tell me?
	☐ How do these parts contribute to the meaning of the visual?

Consider the techniques used by the creator of the visual.	☐ Is the subject close or far away?
	☐ Is the scene natural or staged?
	☐ Are any elements exaggerated to produce an effect?
	☐ Is the visual a single image or a composite?

| **Evaluate the effectiveness of the visual.** | ☐ Does the visual accomplish its purpose? |
| | ☐ Do words and images work well together? |

FOR WRITING OR DISCUSSION

1. Reexamine the photograph on page 18. Where do you think it was taken? How do you know?
2. What details of the scene best capture the sense of the moment?
3. Write a paragraph or two to tell the story that you think emerges from the picture.

Examining Advertisements

Advertisements use images and words to persuade us to buy a product, admire a company, or support a point of view on an issue. Use some of the strategies shown in the "Strategy Checklist: Reading and Interpreting Visuals" on pages 19–20 to answer questions about the following advertisements.

DODGE, "NITRO DRIVERS ALWAYS MAKE NEW 'FRIENDS'"

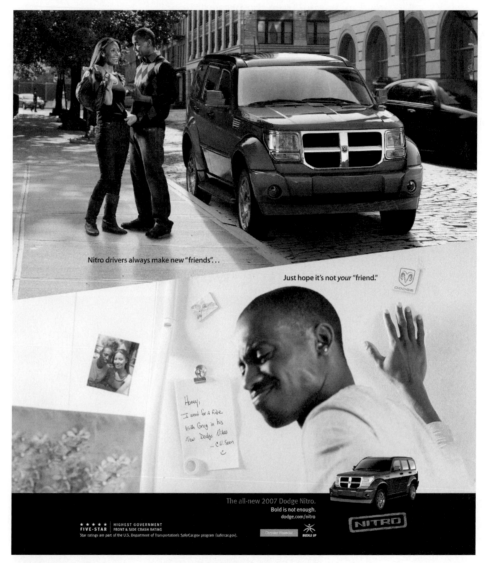

FOR WRITING OR DISCUSSION

1. Who are the people portrayed in the Dodge Nitro ad? How old are they? How do you know?

2. What do the captions under each photo mean? How do they relate to the photographs themselves? What does the slogan "Bold is not enough" at the bottom of the ad mean? How is the slogan supposed to affect consumers?

3. Obviously the ad aims for humor. Does it succeed? Why or why not?

4. Which of these would you say is the overall meaning that the ad wants readers to take from the presentation:

   ■ New cars help guys meet girls.

   ■ The Dodge Nitro handles well on the road.

   ■ If you don't have a new car, you may lose your girlfriend to a new car owner.

   ■ Girls are fickle.

   ■ Boys are desperate to own cars.

   ■ The Dodge Nitro is a safe, economical car.

5. The ad appeared in *Vibe,* a magazine focused on teenagers and young adults. It provides coverage of urban music and fashion, cars, and electronic gadgets. Why would the Chrysler Corporation, makers of Dodge automobiles, place an ad in this magazine? And why this particular ad?

6. Would you think of buying a Dodge Nitro as a result of this advertisement? Write an essay in which you analyze the ad and explain its appeal—or lack of appeal—to you.

NESTLÉ, "WANT A LITE BABY RUTH?"

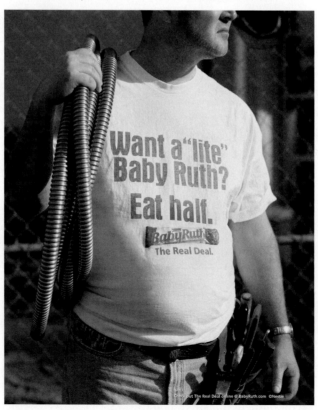

FOR WRITING OR DISCUSSION

1. Whom does the Baby Ruth ad portray? What kind of job does the man in the ad have?

2. Why does the ad present such a person—an overweight laborer—instead of a teenager or a more glamorous figure? What assertion does the visual image intend?

3. What is the meaning of the words on the man's T-shirt? Why is the word "lite" in quotation marks? Where else have you seen the word "lite" in product advertisements? What other "lite" product is the man in the picture not apt to use? How do you know?

4. This ad appeared in *Rolling Stone*, a magazine dedicated to music, bands, and recording artists and directed at a young teenage and post-teenage audience. Why would Nestlé, the makers of the candy bar, place an ad in this magazine? And why this particular ad?

5. Would you buy a Baby Ruth as a result of this advertisement? Write an essay in which you analyze the ad and explain its appeal—or lack of appeal—to you.

EXERCISE Trace the elements of a long-term advertising campaign, such as the campaign for milk ("Got milk?"), diamonds ("A diamond is forever"), insurance (Geico's Gekko), Camel cigarettes (Joe Camel), cereal (Tony the Tiger), or some other that has caught your eye over the years. Follow the guidelines on pages 19–20 to analyze the visual image you have chosen.

1. What does the campaign mean? Describe it and analyze it. What message is the advertiser attempting to convey?

2. Report on the total image as well as its parts. How do the parts of the image relate to the message the ad is attempting to convey?

3. What is the purpose of the advertising campaign—other than simply to get you to buy the product? What techniques has the creator of the image used? To whom is the campaign targeted? How do the words in the ads support the purpose and intended audience?

COLLABORATIVE LEARNING

Brainstorm in groups about the role of advertisements in our lives. Ask members of your group to share positive and negative views of advertising. What is the general consensus in each group: Have ads had an unquestionably positive or negative impact on our lives? After one person from each group reports to the full class, write a paper in which you explore the effects of advertisements in your life.

Reading Charts, Graphs, Tables, and Cartoons

To support their positions on a variety of topics across the disciplines, academic writers are making increasing use of visuals. As a reader, you need to pay close attention to visuals embedded in written texts since they often strengthen the writer's position. A writer explaining the inconsistencies in estimating the number of illegal aliens in the United States, for example, would have to provide written evidence. But think about the added impact of the following chart that the writer could insert into the essay:

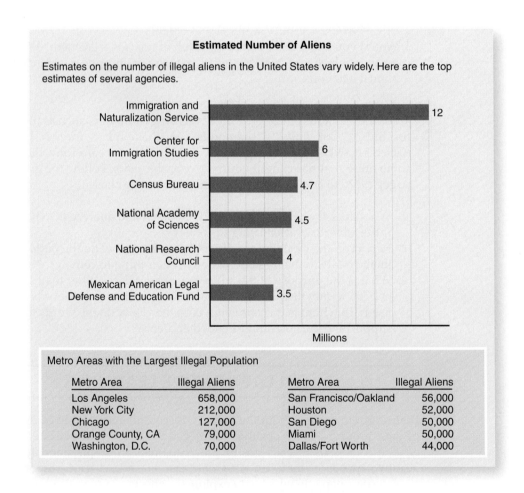

Estimated Number of Aliens

Estimates on the number of illegal aliens in the United States vary widely. Here are the top estimates of several agencies.

Agency	Millions
Immigration and Naturalization Service	12
Center for Immigration Studies	6
Census Bureau	4.7
National Academy of Sciences	4.5
National Research Council	4
Mexican American Legal Defense and Education Fund	3.5

Millions

Metro Areas with the Largest Illegal Population

Metro Area	Illegal Aliens	Metro Area	Illegal Aliens
Los Angeles	658,000	San Francisco/Oakland	56,000
New York City	212,000	Houston	52,000
Chicago	127,000	San Diego	50,000
Orange County, CA	79,000	Miami	50,000
Washington, D.C.	70,000	Dallas/Fort Worth	44,000

Note how the graph and the table beneath it put important data in visual and verbal form. The horizontal bars show readers the relations among the various estimates of illegal aliens in our country; the labels to the left of the bars identify the various organizations providing these estimates; and the numbers to the right of the bars indicate the millions of people in each estimate. The table lists in declining order the cities with the largest illegal alien populations and provides the estimated numbers of aliens in each city.

Graphs and tables show numeric information in a visual form that readers easily can grasp. A writer wishing to appeal to the reader's emotions and condition the response to an argument about the imagined threat of illegal aliens in this country can enhance her position by using an editorial cartoon:

"Well, they look pretty undocumented to me."

© The New Yorker Collection 2006. J. B. Handlesman from cartoonbank.com. All Rights Reserved.

The cartoon makes a humorous point about illegal immigration by using current language to show the arrival of European settlers to our shores when only Native Americans dwelled in America. No one on the *Mayflower* was a documented alien; in this view, the Pilgrims were illegal aliens. The cartoonist's negative view of our documentation demands on immigrants comes across subtly but powerfully in this visual representation.

HAVING YOUR SAY

What is your view on the issue of illegal immigration in the United States? Some policymakers favor strict laws and punishment for any immigrants found to have entered the country illegally. Others support a program of amnesty, allowing people who are already here to stay, work and pay taxes, and eventually become citizens. Using the chart and cartoon—and any other sources, including your own experience—write a few paragraphs on how you believe we should deal with undocumented aliens.

Reading Web Sites

As the World Wide Web continues to grow in content and complexity, Web sites have become important resources for finding information, exploring topics, and doing basic research. Combining vibrant visual images, lively graphics, color reproductions, and sound bytes along with print, Web sites are enticing resources for anyone with a computer. Yet the ease of setting up a site and making it widely available is both the strength and essential weakness of Internet sources. Just how reliable are they? Spammers—those who inundate your e-mail in-box with unwanted messages—no doubt have linked you to many sites of questionable value and authenticity that offer everything from weight-loss programs and cheap prescription medicine to home refinancing and obscene photographs. You already know that suspicious Web sites take up too much space on the Internet.

Usefulness and Reliability

The key question for anyone who uses the Internet is how to determine whether a site is reliable and its information valid. Perhaps even more than with conventional print sources, you have to bring sharp powers of observation and evaluation to Web sites in order to find information and determine their dependability. Teachers, librarians, and researchers have suggested a range of items to take into account when you evaluate a Web site. These items focus on currency, reliability, and authority. When you call up a Web site, keep in mind these principles for evaluating it.

TIPS for Reading and Evaluating Web Sites

■ **Don't assume that all information found on the Internet is reliable.**   Check to see if the information comes from a dependable source. For example, Web site addresses that end with abbreviations like *.gov* (government body), *.org* (nonprofit organization), and *.edu* are often reliable and can serve as good starting points for online research. Many *.com* sites are not reliable.

■ **Look carefully at the author or sponsor of the Web site.** Check the sponsor's and author's credentials. Identify the author's connection to any organization, lobbying group, or commercial enterprise, or to some association with a political, social, or economic agenda that can influence the site.

■ **Examine visual as well as verbal elements.** Web designers integrate words and graphics, so you need to think about how they interact to give you information.

■ **Read sidebars, banners, and tabs for more information and related links.** These additional elements can help you find further information on the topic.

■ **Use your prior knowledge as a barometer of the information you find on the site.** The online information should seem consistent with your other reading.

■ **Determine the purpose of the site and its intended audience and point of view.** If these elements are hidden or not easily accessible, treat the site with skepticism.

■ **Look for an indication of the dates the site was prepared and revised.** You want to certify that information is current. Even if the preparation and revision dates seem recent, be sure that the material itself is as well.

■ **Be sure that the site indicates its sources of information.** You want to be able to validate the information at similar sources and assure that facts seem reasonable, reliable, and truthful.

■ **Check the site for an appropriate level of breadth and range.** Unfortunately, superficial approaches to important topics are abundant on Web sites, and you want to be certain that any site you use shows an understanding of the issues' complexity.

■ **Be sure that the site provides adequate evidence to corroborate assertions made.**

Examining a Web Site

Examine the Web site on page 28, paying particular attention to the labels in the margin that point to important features of the site. Then, using the "Tips for Reading and Evaluating Web Sites" and the Strategy Checklist (page 29) answer the questions below.

Name of site

Sponsors

Skip navigation

MedlinePlus®
Trusted Health Information for You

A service of the U.S. NATIONAL LIBRARY OF MEDICINE
and the NATIONAL INSTITUTES OF HEALTH

About MedlinePlus | Contact Us FAQs | Site Map | Search MedlinePlus   Search box

Alternate
language
opton   español

Health Topics
Start here with 750 topics on conditions,
diseases and wellness

Links to
sections
of site   **Drugs & Supplements**
About your prescription and over-the-
counter medicines, herbs and supplements

Medical Encyclopedia
Includes pictures and diagrams

Dictionary
Spellings and definitions of medical words

News
Current health news and press
announcements

Directories
Find doctors, dentists and hospitals

Go Local
A service for finding local resources for
health-related issues

Other Resources
Local health services, libraries,
organizations, international sites and more

Current Health News
▸ Gene Changes May Predict Prostate
Cancer
▸ Adult Drug Effective in Treating
Psoriasis in Children
▸ Researchers Hone in on Cancer Stem
Cells for Melanoma
▸ More news

—

Featured Site

**Watch a live surgical
webcast of** surgery for
hearing loss **on January
17 at 6:00 p.m. EST.**

—

In the Spotlight

Need information on health
services? Go Local!
Find health services in your
hometown in:
▸Michigan
▸Minnesota

Interactive Tutorials
Over 165
slideshows with
sound and pictures

Links

ClinicalTrials.gov
Studies for new
drugs and treatments

NIHSeniorHealth
Health information
for older adults

Surgery Videos
Videos of surgical
procedures

NEW What's New

Director's Comments

NIH MedlinePlus
Magazine

E-mail Updates and
RSS

Date of last
update

Copyright | Privacy | Accessibility | Quality Guidelines
U.S. National Library of Medicine, 8600 Rockville Pike, Bethesda, MD 20894
National Institutes of Health | Department of Health & Human Services
Freedom of Information Act | USA.gov

Page last updated: 17 January 2008
URL for this page: http://medlineplus.gov

URL address

STRATEGY CHECKLIST: Reading and Evaluating Web Sites

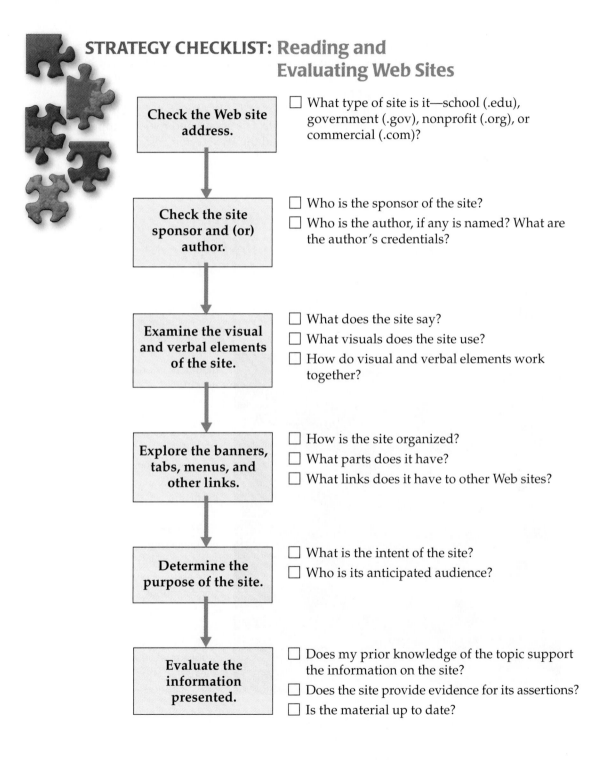

Check the Web site address.	☐ What type of site is it—school (.edu), government (.gov), nonprofit (.org), or commercial (.com)?
Check the site sponsor and (or) author.	☐ Who is the sponsor of the site? ☐ Who is the author, if any is named? What are the author's credentials?
Examine the visual and verbal elements of the site.	☐ What does the site say? ☐ What visuals does the site use? ☐ How do visual and verbal elements work together?
Explore the banners, tabs, menus, and other links.	☐ How is the site organized? ☐ What parts does it have? ☐ What links does it have to other Web sites?
Determine the purpose of the site.	☐ What is the intent of the site? ☐ Who is its anticipated audience?
Evaluate the information presented.	☐ Does my prior knowledge of the topic support the information on the site? ☐ Does the site provide evidence for its assertions? ☐ Is the material up to date?

Models of Writing

Try critical reading on your own. Read the following selection and, using what you have learned in this chapter, draw on the various skills that will help you understand the piece fully. Take notes as you read. Note the use of visuals and the way that they support the text.

Christopher Caldwell is a senior editor at *The Weekly Standard*. He is a regular contributor to the *Financial Times* and *Slate*. His essays and reviews appear in *The New York Times*, the *Wall Street Journal*, and the *Washington Post*.

Answer the questions after you read.

CHRISTOPHER CALDWELL

Intimate Shopping: Should Everyone Know What You Bought Today?

1   **"Information,"** the apostles of cyberspace have been singing for more than a decade, "wants to be free." Well, maybe *your* information does. But in late November, the social networking Web

Michael Lewis/GalleryStock

site Facebook discovered that many of its 58 million members don't feel that way. On social networks, people can exchange photos, letters and information with people they know, and "friend" people they don't. Facebook has grown so big, so rich (its market value is estimated at $15 billion) and so addictive because it offers its users new ways to exchange information and intimacies with people they care about. In early November, Facebook's 23-year-old C.E.O., Mark Zuckerberg, rolled out an advertising program called Beacon. It would track users onto the sites of Facebook's commercial partners—Coca-Cola, the N.B.A., *The New York Times* and Verizon, among others—and keep their friends posted about what they were doing and buying there.

Did it ever. A Massachusetts man bought a diamond ring for Christmas for his wife from overstock.com and saw his discounted purchase announced to 720 people in his online network. What if it hadn't been for his wife? What if he had been buying acne cream? Pornography? A toupee? You could go on. Researchers at Computer Associates, an information-technology firm, discovered that Beacon was more invasive than announced. MoveOn.org started a petition movement against Beacon that rallied 75,000 Facebook subscribers.

Facebook designed Beacon so that members would be able to "opt out" by clicking in a pop-up window. But these windows were hard to see and disappeared very fast. If you weren't quick on the draw, your purchases were broadcast to the world, or at least to your network. Since people, too, sometimes want to be free, privacy advocates urged that Beacon be made an "opt in" program, which members would have to explicitly consent to join. In early December, Facebook agreed to this approach.

The Beacon fiasco gives a good outline of what future conflicts over the Internet will look like. Whether a system is opt-in or opt-out has an enormous influence on how people use it. He who controls the "default option"—the way a program runs if you don't modify it—writes the rules. Online, it can be tempting to dodge the need to get assent for things that used to require it. This temptation is particularly strong in matters of privacy. For instance, the "default option" of the pre-Internet age was that it was wrong to read others' mail. But Google now skims the letters of its Gmail subscribers, in hopes of better targeting them with ads, and the N.S.A. looks for terrorists not only in the traditional manner—getting warrants for individual wiretaps— but also by mining large telecommunications databases.

So it is with Facebook's Beacon. We used to live in a world where if someone secretly followed you from store to store, recording your purchases, it would be considered impolite and even weird. Today, such an option can be redefined as "default" behavior. The question is: Why would it be? The price in reputation for overturning this part of the social contract is bound to be prohibitively high.

For the owners of social-networking sites, it may be a price worth paying. Thanks to data-collection technology, your shopping choices and preferences have

---

NOTHING SACRED?

Percentage of Americans who ...

do not know that charities are allowed to sell their names to other charities without permission.

| 72% |

do not know that supermarkets are allowed to sell information about purchases to other companies.

| 64% |

believe that this (false) statement is true: "If a Web site has a privacy policy, it means the site won't share my information with other Web sites and companies".

| 75% |

Source: Annenberg Public Policy Center, 2005
Chart by Charles M. Blow

2

3

4

5

6

value. Who owns those choices? Common sense says that you do. If a company wants to use you to advertise its products, it can pay you, just as Nike pays Tiger Woods. But the idea that your preferences (not to mention your conversations about them) are your property rests on an implicit social contract. And the thing about implicit contracts is that people who can figure out ways to break them can often make a lot of money.

7   The concept of "implicit contracts" was developed in a landmark 1988 paper by the economists Andrei Shleifer and Lawrence Summers. Their subject—hostile corporate takeovers—seems far from cyberprivacy, but it is not. Shleifer and Summers showed that increases in share price following takeovers were not due to gains in efficiency, as the defenders of those buyouts claimed. There often were such gains, but they were not the source of the profits. The profits came from reneging on implicit contracts—like the tradition of overpaying older workers who had been overworked when young on the understanding that things would even out later. These contracts, because implicit, were hard to defend in court. But the assets they protected were real. To profit from them, buyout artists had only to put someone in place who could, with a straight face and a clean conscience, say, "I didn't promise nothin'!"

8   As commerce moves from Main Street to the Web, lots of businessmen are in that position. All bets are off, and entrepreneurs are seeking new ways to make money by trial and error. Sometimes they do so by adding value to the economy. Sometimes they do so by abrogating implicit contracts. Like managers newly seated after a hostile takeover a quarter-century ago, today's online innovators are not always skilled at telling the difference: "Your friendships are your own business? Golly, I wasn't here when they negotiated *that*."

9   Beacon was a clumsy attempt to reset the default on the common-sense understanding of discretion and to profit off the resetting. As in the 1980s, technological sophistication, entrepreneurial genius and gains to efficiency are a part of this story—but a larger part was the attempt to monetize and sell a vulnerable implicit contract. Facebook was thwarted, as the corporate raiders of years past were not, because it aimed not at pension plans and seniority-based pay scales but at something considerably more valuable—the unwritten rules of privacy that make civilized human interaction possible.

FOR WRITING OR DISCUSSION

1. What did your prior knowledge contribute to your approach to the selection before reading it? How did the title help? The brief statement about what the essay deals with? The information about the author? The photo? The graph?

2. What is the main point of the selection? State it in your own words.

3. What notes or marginal comments did you write as you read the piece?

4. What was the writer's purpose in writing this piece? Who do you think was his intended reader?

5. How well do the introduction and conclusion serve the selection?

6. What does the photograph add to the selection? The graph? Why did the writer include these visuals with his essay?

For additional writing, reading, and research resources, go to **www.mycomplab.com** <http://www.mycomplab.com/> and choose Skwire/Wiener's *Student's Book of College English*, Twelfth Edition.

CHAPTER 2

Active Writing

- Choosing a Good Topic
- Determining Your Purpose and Audience
- Prewriting
- Writing Drafts
- Writing at a Computer
- One Student Writing: First Draft

Writing comes alive when it is the product of active engagement. Getting into the habit of a lively exchange with yourself and others about writing tasks will mean the difference between writing that is vital to you and your readers and writing that is mechanical and tedious, done just to finish an assignment.

In this chapter we will explore methods of getting started that many writers find extremely helpful when they have to produce a piece of work. And the first step for every writer is limiting the topic to a reasonable degree so that the task is not overwhelming and is possible to achieve, given the resources of time, word limitations, and available information.

Choosing a Good Topic

Choosing a subject isn't usually a big problem. If you choose to write about something on your own, you do so because you are interested in it and you want to share your thoughts with others. If you don't actually choose to write but are told to do so, your instructor will usually give you a general subject. For example, your history professor probably won't tell you simply to write a paper; he will assign a paper on the effects of Islamic culture on the Western world. Even when your assignment is an essay based on a personal experience, your instructor will give you a general subject: a memorable journey, an influential person, a goal, a hobby, a favorite magazine or newspaper.

Setting Limits on a Topic

Most subjects need to be limited, and that can create a problem. You need to decide what part of the subject you will write about. Consider the assignment about the effects of Islamic culture on the Western world. The topic is vast, and so you must limit it. Prewriting efforts (see pages 39–41) can help you identify one or two groups of ideas or facts that dominate your early thinking. You could choose one of them as your limited subject.

You can let your special interests determine how you limit the subject. If, for example, you have a good understanding of architecture, you may decide to explain how Islamic culture, contributed to modern architecture by exploring geometric forms. Or you might write about the influence on modern sculpture of geometric form as design. If you're a nursing or pre-med student, you could trace the contributions of the Islamic world to medical science. If you're interested in politics, you might discuss the effects on early Islamic cultures of the lack of a centralized government, comparing these cultures with others of the same period that were governed by a pope or emperor. Your interests could lead to other subjects—from military strategies to love poems—and still fulfill the assignment. Any subject, then, can and must be limited before you begin to write, and your personal interests can often determine the way you limit it.

Much of the writing you will do for your college courses, in a wide range of disciplines, will require research. In Chapter 21 you'll learn how to use sources appropriately. You know how to use a few citation systems so that you can adapt your writing and documentation to your teacher's instructions. But remember, all good writing and all good research must begin with a limited topic.

Narrowing a Topic in Stages

Some writers find it useful to narrow a broad topic to a manageable one through a series of three or four steps, each step contracting the topic a little more. By moving from a general topic to more and more specific ones, the writer can shape the subject to suit her interests and meet the requirements of the assignment.

Suppose you wanted to write about the topic *crime in America*. Clearly the topic is too broad. Note how the writer moved progressively to more specific subject matter.

TOO GENERAL	→	MORE LIMITED	→	LIMITED ENOUGH
Crime in America		Girls' suburban crime		Shoplifting among teenage girls in an affluent Los Angeles suburb

The topic *crime in America* is much too general to address in an essay; even an expert on crime would have trouble writing an entire book about the topic as stated. The student narrowed the topic further by limiting the issue of crime to crimes committed in the suburbs by girls. That still is too general and raises many questions that the student writer must address before settling on the topic—what age group of girls, what kinds of crimes, in which suburbs? Finally, the writer produced a controllable topic that she could address to meet the terms of her assignment in the time allotted to her for writing. She could produce an essay that dealt effectively with teenage shoplifters in a prosperous Los Angeles suburb. The limited topic allows her to proceed efficiently.

In the following examples you can see how student writers limited their topics in stages.

TOO GENERAL	→	MORE LIMITED	→	LIMITED ENOUGH
Sports		High school football		What makes a good high school football coach
Women's fashions		New trends in women's fashions		Body decorations—body paint, body jewelry, removable tattoos—in women rock stars
Politics		The policies of the Democratic party		Why I am a Democrat
Concerts		Promoting concerts		Promoting "nostalgia" concerts to the over-thirty set

EXERCISE

Limit the following broad topics, drawn from a wide variety of college courses.

Example

Broad topic	More limited	Still more limited
The Middle East	Peace negotiations in the Middle East	Anwar Sadat's efforts to make peace between Egypt and Israel in the 1970s

1. Rock concerts
2. Hurricanes
3. An embarrassing moment
4. The Bill of Rights
5. American's role in Iraq
6. Surgery
7. Olympic games
8. Women's magazines
9. Domestic violence
10. Driving lessons

Determining Your Purpose and Audience

Once you've limited your subject, you need to set your purpose and determine what audience you will write for, and doing so involves some related choices.

What is Your Purpose?

You must decide how you will treat your limited subject—that is, being clear about your purpose in writing. What will you do with it? Writing about your summer vacation, will you explain a process—for example, how to pitch a tent? Will you compare two campsites? Will you report an event—what happened when you unwittingly pitched your tent in a cow pasture? Will you argue that one can have an enjoyable yet inexpensive vacation by camping in state parks?

Each of these approaches will help you determine what to include and what to leave out of your essay and each will produce a different paper.

Who is Your Audience?

You also must determine what kind of reader you are writing for. The answer to that question will affect the style and content of your paper, because the words a writer chooses and the facts a writer selects are largely determined by the audience, the people who will read the material.

In a paper about pitching a tent, just imagine how different the paper would look if you wrote it for Cub Scouts planning to sleep in the backyard, troopers training in unfamiliar terrain, sporting goods sales clerks who have to explain a new product to potential buyers, or out-of-shape senior citizens camping for the first time.

You may now be thinking that any discussion of audience is pointless because you know who your reader is—your English professor. In one sense, that's true, of course. But you'll write better papers if, instead of thinking of your English professor every time you begin to write, you imagine other specific kinds of readers. Define a reader. Are you writing for a group of experts on your subject? for your classmates? for the president of your company? for readers of the editorial page of the morning paper? for readers of *Maxim*? *Vanity Fair*? *People*? for the "general reader"? Defining the reader not only helps you decide the style and exact content of your paper but also makes for livelier reading.

Your treatment of the subject and your sense of the audience help determine the purpose of your paper. And the purpose controls the style and content of the paper—its organization, its facts, its diction, its tone.

EXERCISE   For each topic listed here, indicate the purposes a writer might have for writing about it. Look at the example. You may wish to limit the topic first.

Example

   Topic: Teenage drivers

Possible purposes

1. To describe a harrowing drive with "wild man Bob," my sixteen-year-old cousin.
2. To explain how teenagers can save money on driving costs by following a few simple steps.
3. To compare and contrast male and female teenage drivers.
4. To classify types of sports car drivers I've observed in my job as a gas station attendant.
5. To argue in favor of allowing fourteen-year-olds to drive under special circumstances.
6. To convince teenagers of the dangers of drinking and driving.

Topics

1. Charities
2. Election reform
3. Job hunting
4. Fever
5. Drug testing for athletes

COLLABORATIVE LEARNING

Divide the class into three groups and examine the topic and audience sets below. Beside each topic is a list of possible audiences a writer could address. What demands do you think each audience would make on the writer? What different issues would the writer have to address for each audience?

Topic	Possible audience
1. Relaxation techniques	a. Sixth graders in an inner-city public school
	b. High-pressured business executives
	c. Recovering heart attack patients
2. Baking chocolate chip cookies	a. Students at a training school for chefs
	b. First-time homemakers
	c. Kindergarteners
3. The advantages of swimming in improving fitness	a. Home swimming pool manufacturers
	b. Physical therapists
	c. Overweight, sedentary college students

Prewriting

Experienced writers use many strategies to limber up, so to speak, well before they start producing the connected sentences and paragraphs that make up a first draft. The convenient label for these warm-up activities—**prewriting**—is a useful term: The prefix *pre-* reminds you that you have a good deal to do in advance of writing your paper. Many inexperienced writers fail because they leap too soon into producing their papers and do not take enough time with the various steps that can lead to successful writing.

By practicing prewriting strategies—thinking and talking about your ideas, free association, list-making, brainstorming, keeping a journal, reporters' questions, subject trees or maps—you'll uncover a surprising number of possibilities for your topic. For example, if you're trying to get started on a paper about your summer vacation topic, your prewriting exercises might stimulate memories of dancing all night and then going for a swim at sunrise, or the day your old Toyota broke down on a muddy road, or eating your first fiery salsa, or meeting a village character, or watching the sun set over the ocean, or sleeping out under the stars, or being confined to a tent for two hours amid torrential rain at a campsite one evening. Any one of these memories could make a good paper.

Before committing to a topic, always return to your warm-up activities and examine them. You may see that one or two groups of ideas or facts dominate your thinking—that is, you may have jotted down more points about, say, the town oddball you met than about any other highlight of your vacation. In that case, your topic choice should be clear: Write about the village character. If you discover that you have a number of limited subjects you could write about, flip a coin and settle on one so that you can get on with writing the paper. You will probably have other opportunities to write about your other subjects.

Use the strategies described in the "Strategy Checklist: Prewriting" to get started on ideas for your essay.

STRATEGY CHECKLIST: Prewriting

| Discuss your ideas. | ☐ What can I tell others about my topic? |
| | ☐ What ideas do my friends and family have? |

Explore your topic on the Internet.	☐ What information can I find about my topic?
	☐ How credible is the information I've found (see the Strategy Checklist on page 29)?
	☐ What ideas have I found that might be useful?

continued

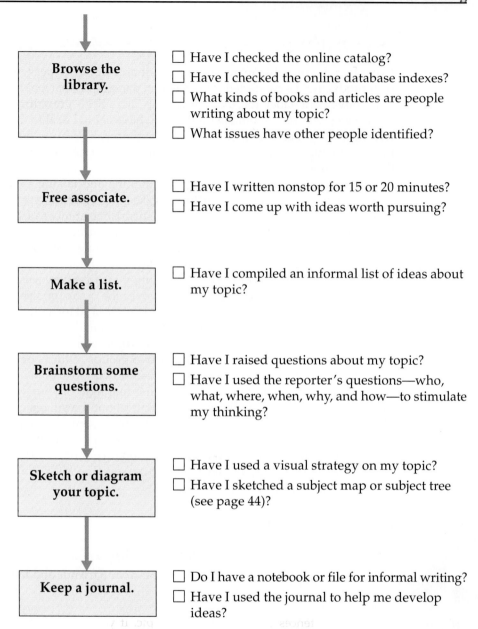

Browse the library.	☐ Have I checked the online catalog?
	☐ Have I checked the online database indexes?
	☐ What kinds of books and articles are people writing about my topic?
	☐ What issues have other people identified?

| Free associate. | ☐ Have I written nonstop for 15 or 20 minutes? |
| | ☐ Have I come up with ideas worth pursuing? |

| Make a list. | ☐ Have I compiled an informal list of ideas about my topic? |

| Brainstorm some questions. | ☐ Have I raised questions about my topic? |
| | ☐ Have I used the reporter's questions—who, what, where, when, why, and how—to stimulate my thinking? |

| Sketch or diagram your topic. | ☐ Have I used a visual strategy on my topic? |
| | ☐ Have I sketched a subject map or subject tree (see page 44)? |

| Keep a journal. | ☐ Do I have a notebook or file for informal writing? |
| | ☐ Have I used the journal to help me develop ideas? |

Organizing Ideas

Try to organize your thinking somewhat. You've identified and limited your topic; and you have considered your *audience* and *purpose*. Now, as you zero in on your central idea (Chapter 3 deals with the all-important thesis statement), look at your written thoughts and eliminate any that seem off target. Cluster the thoughts that seem to go together. You might even try a rough outline of main topics as headings and subtopics numbered beneath them. Or you might draw arrows and make circles to join related ideas, or use scissors and paste to lay connected impressions near each other.

Writing with a computer enables you to move words, sentences, and paragraphs and to keep at hand many versions of your efforts. You can refer to often, and perhaps even salvage, thoughts you may have rejected.

Your attempts at grouping related material are important because they can help you develop an outline (Chapter 4), a key organizing strategy for many writers. Outlining is especially important when you deal with complex topics or with lots of research materials. Like a road map, your outline can help you find your way through new territory.

Bear in mind that the prewriting activities described here are not rigid prescriptions. They vary from writer to writer, and they do not necessarily follow each other in an exact sequence. Prewriting is a loosely defined process that you should adapt freely to your own needs as a writer and to the elements of the writing task at hand.

Writing Drafts

Here are some suggestions for writing a rough draft.

TIPS for Writing a Rough Draft

- **Use your prewriting.** To begin the all-important drafting stage, use your prewriting. Read over your ideas on paper and your efforts at grouping your thoughts.

- **Write a first draft.** Then, without worrying about spelling, grammar, or punctuation, try to get your ideas down. Remember that you're only exploring here; you're not aiming for perfection. Your first draft is a rough copy that you will revisit later to make changes, additions, and deletions. Cross out words and phrases that are dead ends. Insert new thoughts in the margins. Don't worry here about being neat or correct. Your goal at this stage is to write clear, connected sentences that address your topic. If you're working on a computer, your first draft may look like a finished copy when you print it out. But don't let a neat, clean page lull you into thinking that you've finished working!

- **Show it around.** Once you've produced a draft, show it to a friend, your roommate, or another member of your writing class. Drawing on peer review (see pages 114–115) can provide very useful guidance from fellow writers in your class. Sometimes your instructor will read and comment on an early draft to help you think about possible approaches to your next draft.

■ **Revise.** Use the comments made on your papers to help you think about your revision and create your next draft. (Look ahead to Chapter 6.) You don't have to follow all the recommendations you receive or answer all the questions raised—but you must consider them.

■ **Write more drafts.** As you revise your paper, developing intermediate drafts, you want to change any sentences that are off base, add necessary details to support a point, and fix key errors. Don't concentrate on grammatical errors in early drafts; do address these errors as you move closer to a final copy.

By the time you're ready to share your final copy as a completed product, you will have shaped and reshaped your topic many times. Chapter 6 looks at revision and editing in more detail.

Writing at a Computer

Here are some tips for using a computer when you write.

 TIPS for Writing on a Computer

■ **Learn the ins and outs of your computer program and take advantage of all the features.** Be sure you know how to move sentences and paragraphs, insert and delete words, and copy portions of your paper. Use the delete function thoughtfully as you draft because you may want to return to early versions of your sentences. It's often best to *move* unwanted sentences rather than delete them.

■ **Evaluate your writing closely when using the Delete and Move functions.** In removing words and sentences or in shifting text around within your draft, reread your work to be sure that what you have moved fits sensibly in its new place. Check for jumbled sentences, incorrectly inserted passages, or empty spaces where words once stood, all of which will easily distract a reader. Remember to proofread your text carefully for these irritants.

■ **Remember two key words.** Print *and* Save. Before you leave the computer terminal always print out a draft of your work and be sure to save what you have written. Generating hard copy, or the printed version of your work, allows you to make changes and revisions when you are away from the computer. Storing (saving) your writing allows you to return to the document without having to start writing from scratch.

■ **Follow your instructor's guidelines about using special word processing features.** Your writing instructor may have strong feelings about computer dictionaries (spell checkers) or thesauruses and grammar or style programs—especially if you're in a course designed to teach spelling, vocabulary, grammar, and style. These computer devices do have limitations. A spell checker wouldn't detect omitted words or incorrectly used but correctly spelled words, for instance. Style checkers—that is, programs that read your pages for repeated words, excessively long or short sentences, too many adjectives, and other stylistic quirks—lack creative capacity and the ability to reason. And the style checkers may offer advice contrary to your instructor's advice.

■ **When printing your final document for submission to others, follow the conventions of manuscript preparation.** Remember to leave adequate margins—top, bottom, and sides. Avoid using a variety of typefaces—printing in roman, italics, boldface, small and large print—in one paper. Readers find multiple typefaces distracting. You should resist justifying the right-hand margin in the papers submitted for evaluation because this can result in unusual and distracting spacing within the paper itself.

One Student Writing: First Draft

In this chapter and in Chapter 6, you'll see how one student, John Fousek, went about limiting a subject and developing and revising a paper. Having been told to write a short paper on the topic "a friend," John did lots of advance thinking before he wrote. To explore his thoughts, he made a subject map about the topic (see page 44). As he considered this preliminary effort, he finally chose to write about his roommate, Jim, and began jotting down impressions about him. Because he knew his roommate well, however, John soon found that he would have too much material for a short paper and would have to limit his subject to one of Jim's characteristics. That was easy to do because John had argued with his roommate that morning and, still annoyed, could readily identify his major interest of the day: his roommate's irritating habits.

Next, John began to make a list of any of those habits that happened to occur to him. He ended up with quite a list:

doesn't empty ashtrays	doesn't tighten cap on shampoo
doesn't put out cigarettes	uses my printer paper without
doesn't take out garbage	replacing
slams doors on mornings	leaves wet towels on bathroom
I can sleep	floor

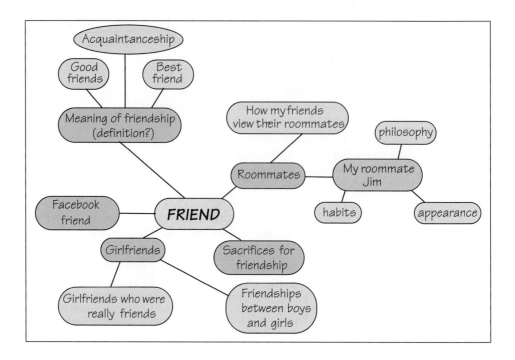

doesn't rinse dirty dishes	opens bathroom door when
uses my after-shave lotion	I'm showering
wears my socks	leaves drawers open
doesn't write down	never closes closet door
telephone messages	never hangs up his coat
doesn't do his share of	doesn't remove muddy boots
cooking	never empties dishwasher
plays stereo when I'm	reads my mail
studying	

After studying the list, John saw that he could not develop every point; he had to eliminate some items. He concluded that two of Jim's shortcomings bothered him most: Jim's failure to close things and his failure to dispose of things.

He eliminated all items on the list that did not pertain to those two failures and could now group his ideas:

Not closing	Not disposing
doesn't tighten cap on shampoo	doesn't put out cigarettes
doesn't close bathroom door	doesn't empty ashtrays
doesn't close drawers	doesn't empty dishwasher
doesn't close closet door	doesn't rinse dishes

Then John realized that even this limiting left him with too much to cover; finally, he decided to discuss in his paper only his roommate's failure to close things.

As John thought about how to organize his paper, he produced this rough outline:

<u>Intro:</u>

1. how much I like Jim—his personality, sharing, funny, honest
2. what I don't like: never closes things

<u>Drawers</u>

1. kitchen drawer always messy and left open
2. bedroom drawers and closets
3. I'm embarrassed by it all

<u>Bathroom</u>

1. leaves door open—shower area gets freezing cold
2. forgets to close shampoo bottle—shampoo spills all over me, much wasted down drain

Note how the informal outline builds on the preceding grouped list titled "Not closing." The rough outline provides a working plan for the first draft of John's essay.

With his outline and prewriting as resources, John was able to arrange his ideas and write a draft of his paper. His first draft appears on page 46.

John's rough draft is a good start. He states a thesis early in the paper. He presents concrete examples to support his irritation with Jim. He seems to have a good grasp of his topic. The paper has a beginning, a middle, and an end, and its ideas are related to each other. Note how John has raised questions for himself in the margins and spaces between lines.

FIRST DRAFT

my roommate   John Fousek

My friend Jim really irritates me with his habbit of ~~not~~ never closing

things that he opens up. Don't get me wrong. As roommates for the last

couple of years Jim and I get along real well in our small apartment. As

students we don't get to see each other a whole lot. We also both work

and this cuts down on the time we spend together too. We share

check spelling   *has a*
Thesis responsibilities in the apartment. I clean and Jim cooks. He's generous, ∧
statement *We had a good relationship over the last two years.*
OK? good sense of humor and is honest. ∧ But boy his shortcoming of not

                                                            Its?
closing things up burn∧s me up. It's a real pain.

                                                          because
For example never closing a drawer. This embarasses me a lot, ∧ I am

compulsive about being neat, Jim is a slob. He never thinks of organizing

Show his drawers. He just <u>dumps everything</u> into his drawers and closets. In
what's in
drawers the kitchen everything is just <u>dumped into the drawers</u> and he's

constantly banging silverware before every meal. This is when I'm usually

studying and I prefer peace and qui∧te to rattling kitchen items.

Of course he leaves the kitchen drawers open along with the clothing

                                              If he'd only organize the drawer
drawers. Our apartment always looks like a bomb hit it ∧ The appearance
                                                                          Trite?
check spelling
irritates my neat soul. I'm embarassed when friends visit us.
                                                         in the first place he
I get even madder at Jim's failure to close things in the bathroom he *wouldn't be*
            one sentence?   *bothering*
never closes the shampoo cap. This makes me lose my cool composure *me with his*
                                                    comma?   *noise and*
more than anything. ~~I always~~ When I'm in the shower/I always grab the

Fix this? shampoo bottle by the cap a loose cap results in the agravation of *check spelling*
Sounds
funny shampoo on my toes instead of my hair. And because I am economically

minded, moneywise, watching shampoo go down the drain really bothers

me.

Jim also often fails to close the bathroom door after using the facilities

while I shower. Since the bathroom has become warm and steamy during

                                              chills
the couse of my shower, the cold air annoys me, the idea that Jim has

been so thoughtless bothers me.

I try to overlook Jim's bad habbits but when he doesn't close things up

Conclusion
too short? especially when I get a cold blast of morning air in the shower it really
Expand?
irritates me.

But John's paper still needs revising and editing. John notes in the margin some issues he wants to think about when he revises, but there are many others he'll have to consider. His sentences are sometimes rambling and repetitive, and the writing is much too informal in spots. The ideas should be more smoothly connected, and some of the paragraphs should be joined. You no doubt noted errors in spelling and sentence structure. John must address all these issues as he develops successive drafts.

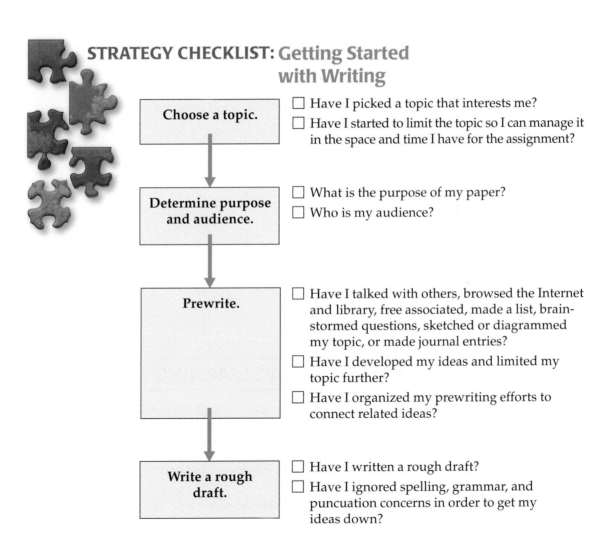

STRATEGY CHECKLIST: Getting Started with Writing

Choose a topic.
- [ ] Have I picked a topic that interests me?
- [ ] Have I started to limit the topic so I can manage it in the space and time I have for the assignment?

Determine purpose and audience.
- [ ] What is the purpose of my paper?
- [ ] Who is my audience?

Prewrite.
- [ ] Have I talked with others, browsed the Internet and library, free associated, made a list, brainstormed questions, sketched or diagrammed my topic, or made journal entries?
- [ ] Have I developed my ideas and limited my topic further?
- [ ] Have I organized my prewriting efforts to connect related ideas?

Write a rough draft.
- [ ] Have I written a rough draft?
- [ ] Have I ignored spelling, grammar, and puncuation concerns in order to get my ideas down?

EXERCISE Examine John Fousek's prewriting activities and his first draft and then answer the following questions.

1. How did John's subject map help him limit his topic?
2. How does John's first list compare and contrast with his second list (see page 44)? What specific features of the first list has John eliminated in the second? Why has he dropped so many details from the first list?
3. How does John's rough outline build on the list that he prepared, "Not closing"?
4. How does John's rough draft compare with his rough outline?

EXERCISE Use the prewriting techniques explained on pages 39–40 for one of the following topics that interests you. From these warm-up activities, determine how you would limit the subject.

1. Batman films
2. The environment
3. Friendship
4. The homeless
5. Television preachers
6. Volunteer work
7. Elections
8. Cell phones
9. Welfare-to-work programs
10. Being a politician

COLLABORATIVE LEARNING

Bring to class your prewriting efforts developed from the exercise above. Form groups of three students. In each group examine each other's prewriting. Answer the following questions for each student's work:

- In what ways does the prewriting show evidence of uncensored thought on the topic?

- Has the writer used the prewriting strategies to explore the topic effectively? How?

- What recommendations could you make so that the writer could get even better results from the prewriting effort?
- How does the prewriting activity help the writer limit the subject?

EXERCISE   Using your prewriting efforts, develop a first draft of your paper.

For additional writing, reading, and research resources, go to **www. mycomplab.com** <http://www.mycomplab.com/> and choose Skwire/Wiener's *Student's Book of College English*, Twelfth Edition.

CHAPTER 3

Finding and Supporting a Thesis

- Understanding the Thesis
- Elements of a Good Thesis
- Stating Your Thesis
- Supporting Your Thesis: Details
- Student Writing: Thesis and Details
- Models of Writing

Once you have narrowed your topic and identified your audience and purpose, you have to develop a thesis, a statement of the main point of your essay. Your reader should know as early as possible in your paper just what main point you are trying to make about your topic.

Understanding the Thesis

To be sure that you have the kind of central idea that will lead to an interesting and unified paper, you have further steps to take in the process of thinking as you write: You must state a thesis, and you must consider how to present appropriate and logical support for it.

A **thesis** is the position a writer takes on an arguable point—one on which more than one opinion is possible. It is the main idea the paper will support. The writer must convince the reader that this position or idea is valid.

Remember that your topic is not your thesis. Instead, your thesis is what you have to say about your topic. It is an opinion about, or an attitude toward, the topic, which you will attempt to support in your essay. It is a one-sentence summary of the idea the writer will defend. Here are two examples:

Topic	Thesis
Graduation requirements	Technical programs should require students to take some courses in the humanities.
Registration	A few simple changes would improve the registration procedure on our campus.

With few exceptions, the papers your instructors will ask you to write in college will benefit enormously from a thesis. A professor of American literature, for example, won't ask you to summarize *Huckleberry Finn*. She wants to know what conclusions you reached after reading the novel: *Mark Twain's* Huckleberry Finn *is an indictment of slavery*, let's say; or *Mark Twain, in* Huckleberry Finn, *criticizes the violence of the pre–Civil War South*. Until you can make that kind of statement, you aren't ready to write effectively because you don't have clearly in mind the point you will make. And if you aren't certain of what your idea is, you stand little chance of convincing a reader of its validity. It's important, therefore, to spend time thinking your idea through before you start writing. This will save time and grief in the long run.

Elements of a Good Thesis

There are several characteristics of a good thesis. When you are writing, you can use these tips to evaluate your thesis statements.

 TIPS for Evaluating a Thesis

- **A good thesis usually can be stated in one complete sentence.**   Even though you may find that you want to devote a paragraph or more to presenting the idea of your paper, until you can state your main idea in one sentence, you may not have it under control.

- **A good thesis makes a statement—that is, it gives an opinion or attitude about the facts.**   To say that Brutus stabbed Shakespeare's Julius Caesar on the Ides of March is to state a fact. A thesis, a statement *about* the fact, might read, *Brutus succeeded in killing Caesar on the Ides of March because Caesar had grown too arrogant and proud to protect himself.*

- **A good thesis is limited.**   The idea stated must be one that can be clearly explained, supported, and illustrated in the space called for. A long magazine article might have this as its thesis:

  > Although, as a result of a controversial and aggressive promotional campaign, women professional golfers now make more money and receive greater recognition than they did ten years ago, they still do not make as much money, receive as much media coverage, or command as much respect as men professional golfers.

  But this won't do for a thousand-word paper; the writer could not develop the thesis fully in so short a space. A better thesis for a short paper might read, *The promotional campaign for the Women's Professional Golf Association has attracted money and attention for professional female golfers.* An even better thesis would be, *The promotional campaign for the Women's Professional Golf Association will offend members and fans who oppose commercialism in women's athletics.*

■ **A good thesis is appropriately focused.**   Consider this thesis: *The reports in* Time *are entertaining and informative, but* Time *slants its reports to suit its political bias, and the vocabulary used by* Time *requires constant trips to the dictionary.* This thesis says three things about *Time*: the magazine's reports are entertaining and informative; the reports are slanted; the vocabulary of *Time* requires constant use of the dictionary. A writer who begins with such a thesis runs the risk of writing a three-part paper that has no central focus. The point of emphasis is not clear. To emphasize that the magazine's reports are entertaining and informative, the writer must subordinate the other points to that idea:

> Although the vocabulary used in *Time* requires constant trips to the dictionary and the reports are often slanted to suit a political bias, the reports are entertaining and informative.

To emphasize the shortcomings of the magazine, the writer should subordinate the entertaining and informative nature of the reports:

> Although the reports in *Time* are entertaining and informative, their vocabulary makes them hard to read, and the material is often slanted to suit a political bias.

■ **A good thesis is precise.**   It lets the reader and the writer know exactly what the paper will contain. Words such as *good, interesting, impressive,* and *many* are too vague to do the job. They say nothing about the subject: What is interesting or good to one person may appear dull or offensive to another. Don't say, "Agatha Christie's detective stories are good." Say, instead, "Agatha Christie's detective stories appeal to those who enjoy solving puzzles." Don't say, "My history class is interesting." Say, "My professor makes history easy to understand."

Stating Your Thesis

Rules for a good thesis are one thing; applying them is another. You may well ask how one arrives at that perfectly stated thesis. The methods may vary according to the circumstances.

TIPS for Developing a Thesis

■ **Answer a question.**   Sometimes, especially in essay examinations, the thesis statement is suggested by the question. Often, all you have to do is think of a one-sentence answer to the question, and you have your thesis statement.

Example question:	What is job enrichment? Is job enrichment an attempt by management to exploit workers?
Sample thesis statement:	Job enrichment, an effort to increase productivity by making the job more attractive, is an attempt by management to exploit laborers by motivating them to work harder.

In this thesis statement, the writer has both defined *job enrichment* and stated an opinion about the practice. The rest of the essay will give the reasons job enrichment, in this writer's opinion, is an attempt to exploit laborers.

■ **Think about your subject.**   Frequently, you have to work with a large-scale subject. As you know, it is up to you to limit the subject and decide what point you want to make about it (see pages 35–36). On some subjects—subsidizing college athletics, for example—you may already have a strong opinion. If you have information to back up that opinion, you have no problem. Just state your opinion and then begin thinking about how you can back it up. On other subjects, though, you may at first think you have no opinion. But you may have a question. You might have wondered why, for example, Japan seemed in years past to outdistance the United States in the production of everything from television sets to automobiles. Go to the library and the Web and read up on the subject. You may then decide that one reason Japan became a major industrial power is that the economy had not, since the end of World War II, had to support a military machine. Now you have a thesis.

■ **Review your prewriting activities.**   A valuable way to produce a thesis statement is to review your prewriting activities—free association, brainstorming, lists, and subject maps (see Chapter 2)—with an eye toward a central issue that may be brewing somewhere in your early, unedited thinking on a topic. Suppose that you're considering a paper on the subject of children's toys. It's near holiday time, you're a parent, and you've been giving lots of thought to toys lately. You've used free association to jot down any-thing that comes to mind on the topic. Your list might look like this:

Topic: Toys

1. Expense of toys
2. Shoddy construction: plastic parts don't fit together
3. Focus on violence: guns, destructive images
4. Too many batteries required
5. Sexist toys
6. Difficulty in putting together the parts of toys
7. Unclear, misleading assembly instructions

Considering your list, you note that three items (6, 7, and part of 2) relate to your frustrations with toy assembly. Putting together that kiddie gym really irritated you, didn't it? The more you think about that experience and others like it, the more you realize that item 7 on your list is the heart of the matter. The reason assembling toys is so difficult is that the instructions are unclear and misleading. There's your thesis statement: *Instructions accompanying disassem-bled toys are misleading.*

Here is the important message: You must have a thesis statement clearly in mind as you plan the rest of the paper.

It should be clear by now that a thesis is different from a topic. A topic is simply the subject of your paper, whereas a thesis makes an assertion about the subject. For the topic *toys*, you saw how the writer developed the thesis state-ment. Having a topic in mind helps you produce a thesis. Merely placing a title on top of your page to reflect your topic does not mean you have provided a thesis statement.

EXERCISE   Look at the thesis sentences below. What is the topic of each? What is the writer's main point—what does the writer want to say about the topic? How do you think each writer will go about supporting the thesis?

1. The costs of prescription drugs have skyrocketed, creating problems for consumers of all ages.
2. People use the label "terrorist" indiscriminately and therefore make unfair judgments based on race, color, or religion.

3. Some parents will do, say, or pay anything to get their children into the "right" nursery school.
4. Innovation in American automobile manufacturers has taken a back seat to advances by foreign competitors.
5. Through a variety of creative programs and police vigilance, it is possible to cut down dramatically on drunk driving among teens.

EXERCISE   Look at the topics in the exercise on page 38. What thesis could you develop about each of them?

EXERCISE   Determine which of the following items are thesis statements and which are not. Also determine which thesis statements are too general or too lacking in unity to make a good paper. How does each statement meet the specifications for a thesis, as explained on pages 51–52? Revise the unacceptable thesis statements accordingly.

1. In a weak economy, employers do not hire quality workers.
2. Teenage drivers are a menace!
3. Americans are saving less and less money each year.
4. Curtailing drug use begins with education.
5. Readers now can download from their home computers many complete texts, including short stories, novels, and works of nonfiction.

EXERCISE   Return to the exercise on page 36. For any five topics you limited there, develop thesis statements that could be used successfully in a paper.

Supporting Your Thesis: Details

Once you've stated your thesis clearly, you need to consider how you will support it. The best way to convince a reader that your idea is worth considering is to offer details that back up your point and to present these details logically.

Chapter 15 presents the important topic of logic, and you no doubt will examine it fully later on. Here, it is important to know that logic involves the relation between the particulars and generalities as you present them in your paper. Logic is the process of reasoning inherent in your writing, and all readers expect a kind of clarity and intelligence that make the points and arguments understandable and easy to follow. Logical writing avoids what we call *fallacies*—that is, false notions, ideas founded on incorrect perceptions. We'll consider logic and logical fallacies in greater depth later in your course.

Using Sensory Details

In presenting details to support your point, you have many options. If you're drawing on your own personal experience, you can *provide examples* that illustrate your point. Examples drawn from experience rarely prove anything; however, they point out why you've made the generalization put forth in your thesis. When you use personal experiences to support a thesis, you should rely on **concrete sensory details**—colors, actions, sounds, smells, images of taste and touch. Details rooted in the senses make what you've experienced come alive for the reader. If you are narrating an event or describing a scene, concrete imagery will help your readers see things your way. Thus, if you're writing about the misleading instructions for assembling toys, you might show your frustration by describing your efforts to put together the offending kiddie gym—the hunt for an orange plastic tube, the pungent smell of epoxy glue, the rough silver hooks that don't fit the holes made for them, and the diagram labeled in Japanese characters and no English words. George Orwell's "A Hanging" is a brilliant example of how concrete sensory details can support a thesis. You read Orwell's essay on pages 12–16. In the two paragraphs repeated below, note the rich imagery that the writer creates through sensory detail:

> It was in Burma, a sodden morning of the rains. A sickly light, like yellow tinfoil, was slanting over the high walls into the jail yard. We were waiting outside the condemned cells, a row of sheds fronted with double bars, like small animal cages. Each cell measured about ten feet by ten and was quite bare within except for a plank bed and a pot of drinking water. In some of them brown silent men were squatting at the inner bars, with their blankets draped round them. These were the condemned men, due to be hanged within the next week or two.
>
> One prisoner had been brought out of his cell. He was a Hindu, a puny wisp of a man, with a shaven head and vague liquid eyes. He had a thick, sprouting moustache, absurdly too big for his body, rather like the moustache of a comic man on the films. Six tall Indian warders were guarding him and getting him ready for the gallows. Two of them stood by with rifles with fixed bayonets, while the others handcuffed him, passed a chain through his handcuffs and fixed it to their belts, and lashed his arms tight to his sides. They crowded very close about him, with their hands always on him in a careful, caressing grip, as though all the while feeling him to make sure he was there. It was like men handling a fish which is still alive and may jump back into the water. But he stood quite unresisting, yielding his arms limply to the ropes, as though he hardly noticed what was happening.

Using Data: Statistics, Cases, and Expert Testimony

Other kinds of supporting details draw on **data**—statistics and cases that demonstrate a point. For example, if your thesis is *Driver education courses have had a dramatic effect on improving the car safety record of young teenagers*, you'd need to cite comparative data of teens who took the course and those who didn't. You also would need to show the decrease, let us say, in speeding violations, drunk driving, and fatal accidents. Your analysis of the data would help readers see how you interpret the details. You might focus on a particularly illuminating case—the record of a young driver, say, before and after a driver's education course.

In supporting your thesis, you also might want to present expert testimony as supporting details. **Expert testimony** means the words and ideas of respected thinkers on your subject. Depending on your topic, you'll find an array of experts, thoughtful researchers, and other authorities who have considered the same issue and who have shared their observations in a variety of sources. Thus, the books and magazines you read, the films and television programs you watch, the Web sites you visit, the radio stations you listen to, and the lectures and recitations in which you participate at school are all rich sources for details in an essay. For that thesis on assembling toys at home, for example, you might cite a Taiwanese manufacturer whom you saw on a business news film clip on the Public Broadcasting System and who talked about the problems in producing clear instructions for home toy assembly. You'd certainly want to quote from one or more sets of instructions to highlight their inadequacies. Perhaps an article in your local paper reported on a toy buyers' revolution, where dozens of angry parents dumped parts from unassembled kiddie gyms on the doorstep of a toy store because the parents couldn't figure out how to put the expensive toys together. Citing that article would strengthen your thesis.

Without adequate support, your thesis is merely an assertion—an opinion. Unsupported assertions never win readers' respect.

Note how the writer uses particular cases, relevant data, and expert testimony in these paragraphs:

> Most people view traffic with a mixture of rage and resignation: rage because congestion wastes valuable time, resignation because, well, what can anyone do about it? People have places to go, after all; congestion seems inevitable.
>
> But a surprising amount of traffic isn't caused by people who are on their way somewhere. Rather, it is caused by those who have already arrived. Streets are clogged, in part, by drivers searching for a place to park.
>
> Several studies have found that cruising for curb parking generates about 30 percent of the traffic in central business districts. In a recent survey conducted by Bruce Schaller in the SoHo district in Manhattan, 28 percent of drivers interviewed while they were stopped at traffic lights said they were searching for curb parking. A similar study conducted by Transportation Alternatives in the Park Slope neighborhood in Brooklyn found that 45 percent of drivers were cruising.
>
> When my students and I studied cruising for parking in a 15-block business district in Los Angeles, we found the average cruising time was 3.3 minutes, and the average cruising distance half a mile (about 2.5 times around the block). This may not sound like much, but with 470 parking meters in the district, and a turnover rate for curb parking of 17 cars per space per day, 8,000 cars park at the curb each weekday. Even a small amount of cruising time for each car adds up to a lot of traffic.

Over the course of a year, the search for curb parking in this 15-block district created about 950,000 excess vehicle miles of travel—equivalent to 38 trips, around the earth, or four trips to the moon. And here's another inconvenient truth about underpriced curb parking cruising those 950,000 miles wastes 47,000 gallons of gas and produces 730 tons of the greenhouse gas carbon dioxide. If all this happens in one small business district, imagine the cumulative effect of all cruising in the United States.

—Donald Shoup

Shoup, a professor of urban planning at the University of California Los Angeles, asserts that significant pollution derives from people's driving around looking for parking spots. He supports his thesis with a variety of data, and by presenting in detail a study conducted by a colleague in Manhattan, Bruce Schaller, Shoup brings outside expert authority to the argument. (Schaller is president of a consulting firm widely known for its knowledge of transportation issues.) And Shoup cites the case of the Los Angeles business district that he and his students studied.

COLLABORATIVE LEARNING

Form five groups. Ask each group to propose the kinds of details a writer might provide to support the following theses. Have each group report to the whole class.

1. Hispanic Americans have contributed substantially to economic growth in our southern cities.
2. Madonna's personal life, offensive as it may be, should not enter into judgments about her music.
3. Textbooks across the elementary school curriculum present women in passive roles.
4. Dawn on the desert is a haunting display of light and shadow.
5. Caring for an aging parent can drain a family's resources.

EXERCISE For any three thesis statements that you developed for the exercise on page 55, indicate the kinds of details you might use to support them.

Student Writing: Thesis and Details

Now let's look at a student's paper that illustrates a carefully defined thesis. As you read, see how the writer establishes the thesis and supports it in the essay. Marginal comments highlight important points.

Title: a phrase
from the essay's
dialog

Generalization in
first sentence
draws reader's
attention.

Thesis sentence
states writer's
opinion, is well
limited, well
focused, and
precise.

Concrete sensory
details support
point of the
paragraph.

Realistic dialog
enlivens essay.

Strong sensory
details further
support thesis.

Thomas Healey

"You Must Be Crazy!"

It's easy to note the behavioral dark spots in those around us. My father is a skinflint; when I need a loan or simply extra cash, he turns a deaf ear to my pleading hysterics. Mom is excessively moody. When something bothers her she sulks for hours, never revealing what set her off, and we just have to wait until she gets over it. However, as a fairly normal teenager, I never thought of myself as having any particular character flaws. Yet, as I faced my brother Matthew at his bedroom door one spring afternoon last year, I became aware of the ugly features of anger and temper in my personality.

Though he's two years younger than I am, Matt and I share many things, including our clothes sometimes. But this time he had borrowed my new tan sweater and had returned it to my drawer with big grease stains on the sleeve and near the collar. "How did this happen?" I shouted, pointing to a large black spot. "Oh," he said casually, looking up from the *Sports Illustrated* he was reading on the brown rug near his bed, "I was fooling around with the Chevy. Oil dripped on everything."

I couldn't believe my ears. "You wore my good sweater to work on your stupid car? I don't believe you." My neck tightened and my hands grew wet and cold. I felt my eyelid twitch. Matt rubbed the arch of his left foot covered in a white sweat sock. Then he shrugged his shoulders. "Those are the breaks," he said, looking down again at his magazine.

It was probably that lack of concern that drove me wild. Lunging at him, I pushed him down to the floor. The more I pushed against him, the angrier I felt. Some strange power had overtaken my body and mind. When I looked at Matt's face suddenly, I heard him choking, and I realized that I had my elbow pressed against his throat. What was I doing? I jumped up as Matt lay sputtering. "You must be crazy!" he gasped in a voice I could barely hear. His frightened blue eyes stared at me in amazement. "You could have killed me."

1

Introduction
builds up to
the thesis;
Healey will
not write
about his
mother and
father
anywhere in
the essay
other than
here in the
introduction.

2

Transition:
Words "Matt
and I"
remind
readers of
previous
paragraph
content.

3

Descriptive
details help
reader
envision
Matt.

4

Transition:
"that lack of
concern"

Words "drove
me wild"
establish
frame for
supporting
detail in
paragraph.

5   I remember looking at my hands and then back at Matt. He was right. I was crazy—crazy with anger. If rage could turn me into such a monster with my own brother, imagine what it could do under other conditions. "I'm sorry," I said. "I'm really sorry."

Conclusion connects to ideas expressed in thesis sentence.

6   At that moment I realized the full meaning of anger. It was a strong and dangerous emotion that could easily overpower a person who did not work to keep it under control.

FOR WRITING OR DISCUSSION

1. What is the writer's topic? What is his thesis? What is the relation between the topic and the thesis? In what ways is the thesis limited, focused, and precise? What is the writer's opinion or attitude as expressed in the thesis?

2. How do the sentences in the introduction build to the thesis?

3. How has the writer used descriptive detail to advantage? Which sensory images do you find most convincing? How does the description of Matthew contribute to the thesis?

4. What is the writer's purpose in this essay?

5. What is your opinion of the conclusion—the last paragraph of the essay? How might you expand it from its two-sentence structure? Or do you find it satisfying as is? Why, or why not?

6. Write a paper in which you explore anger or some other "dark spot" in your personality or in the personality of someone you know well.

HAVING YOUR SAY

Is sibling rivalry—the competition between brothers and sisters in the same family for attention and approval by parents and others—an inescapable consequence of living together in a family unit? Write an essay in which you argue for one side or the other on this question. Support your point of view with appropriate detail.

Now let's look at another student's paper. As you read, consider the thesis, and notice how the writer's choices of supporting detail and audience contribute to the development of the paper. Also, before you read, review the "Strategy Checklist: Reading Critically" on pages 10–11.

Clifford Wendell

The Computer and I

Computers were designed to make our lives easier, or so I'm told. Easier?   1
Not in my experience. They tend to put some challenge into my ordinarily dull life.

For example, upon receiving my usual monthly statement from a local   2
department store, I was a trifle surprised to find that the ten-dollar gift
certificate I had charged had suddenly turned into a generous one-
hundred-dollar gift. Tucked into the envelope along with my inflated bill was a
gentle reminder from the credit department informing me that they were
happy to serve me but my last charge had put my balance well above my
meager limit. My charge card was temporarily suspended, and my account was
turned over to their nasty little collection department. I telephoned to inquire
about this error that was ruining my credit rating and was informed by a crisp,
high-pitched voice that it knew I had purchased a one-hundred-dollar gift
certificate because that's what the computer said. I was also informed that the
computer rarely made an error. I told the owner of the high-pitched voice that I
am usually the exception to any rule and that her electronic co-worker had, in fact,
made an error on my bill. "Impossible," she said coldly. "The balance is owing."

"And that's exactly how it will remain—owing," I snapped in return. It's cash   3
from now on.

Another example of how the computer has made life more interesting   4
happened at the bank last week. It was a sunny Friday afternoon, and I was
looking forward to a relaxing but productive weekend. It seemed that nothing
could spoil my light, contented mood. I went into the drab, dark branch to
transfer money from my savings account to my checking account because I
had just realized that my automobile insurance was due the next day, the rent
the following day, and I desperately needed to put some groceries in the bare
cupboards. I finally made it to the caged teller and slid my pink withdrawal slip
in her direction. Her fat fingers flew over the keyboard of her terminal, and then

with a smug smile she said that I did not have the funds to cover my withdrawal. Patiently I showed her my receipt for a deposit made just the day before, my bankbook, and my displeasure at not being able to get at my own money. I explained that I would starve, my auto insurance would be canceled, and I would surely get into an accident the hour after it was no longer in effect, and I would probably be evicted from my home. "So," I said, "please check your records; there's some mistake." She smirked and said that I would have to wait until Monday for all the transactions to be processed. I wanted to process her. Instead, I withdrew fifteen of the twenty dollars she said remained in my account, went to McDonald's instead of the grocery store, took the bus instead of driving my uninsured car, and didn't answer the door when the landlord stopped by to collect the rent.

5   Then there was the time. . . . But I won't go into that; it's too depressing. Sometimes I think computers don't like me.

FOR WRITING OR DISCUSSION

1. What is the writer's thesis? Does he state it? If so, where and how? If not, how can you tell what his thesis is?
2. What is the difference here between the thesis and the topic?
3. How does the writer's description of the Friday afternoon as sunny, his mood as light and contented, and the bank as drab and dark (paragraph 4) contribute to the thesis? to the development of the paper?
4. The writer's descriptions of the clerk in the collection department and of the bank teller are not flattering (". . . a crisp, high-pitched voice"; "it knew"; "her fat fingers"; "she smirked"). Do you think he intended these phrases as personal insults? Why, or why not?
5. What is the effect of referring to the computer as "her electronic co-worker"?
6. Who is the audience for this paper? How do you know?
7. What author image does Wendell present? On what specific qualities of the paper do you base your judgment?

COLLABORATIVE LEARNING

Brainstorm in groups about the role of computers in our lives. Ask members of your group to share positive and negative computer experiences. What is the general consensus in each group: Have computers had an unquestionably positive impact on our lives? After one person from each group reports to the full class, write a paper in which you explore computers in your life.

Models of Writing

Read the pieces that follow, in which the writers provide convincing details to support the thesis, and then answer the questions that follow each selection. Examine "Strategy Checklist: Reading Critically" on pages 10–11 before you begin.

NICHOLAS D. KRISTOF
Love and Race

In a world brimming with bad news, here's one of the happiest trends: Instead of preying on people of different races, young Americans are falling in love with them.   1

Whites and blacks can be found strolling together as couples even at the University of Mississippi, once the symbol of racial confrontation.   2

"I will say that they are always given a second glance." acknowledges C.J. Rhodes, a black student at Ole Miss. He adds that there are still misgivings about interracial dating, particularly among black women and a formidable number of "White Southerners who view this race-mixing as abnormal, frozen by fear to see Sara Beth bring home a brotha."   3

Mixed-race marriages in the U.S. now number 1.5 million and are roughly doubling each decade. About 40 percent of Asian-Americans and 6 percent of blacks have married whites in recent years.   4

Still more striking, one survey found that 40 percent of Americans had dated someone of another race.   5

In a country where racial divisions remain deep, all this love is an enormously hopeful sign of progress in bridging barriers. Scientists who study the human genome say that race is mostly a bogus distinction reflecting very little genetic difference, perhaps one-hundredth of 1 percent of our DNA.   6

Skin color differences are recent, arising over only the last 100,000 years or so, a twinkling of an evolutionary eye. That's too short a period for substantial genetic differences to emerge, and so there is perhaps 10 times more genetic difference within a race than there is   7 between races. Thus we should welcome any trend that makes a superficial issue like color less central to how we categorize each other.

8   The rise in interracial marriage reflects a revolution in attitudes. As recently as 1958 a white mother in Monroe, N.C., called the police after her little girl kissed a black playmate on the cheek; the boy. Hanover Thompson, 9, was then sentenced to 14 years in prison for attempted rape. (His appeals failed, but he was released later after an outcry.)

9   In 1963, 59 percent of Americans believed that marriage between blacks and whites should be illegal. At one time or another 42 states banned intermarriage, although the Supreme Court finally invalidated these laws in 1967.

10   Typically, the miscegenation laws voided any interracial marriages, making the children illegitimate, and some states included penalties such as enslavement, life imprisonment, and whippings. My wife is Chinese-American, and our relationship would once have been felonious.

11   At every juncture from the 19th century on, the segregationists warned that granting rights to blacks would mean the start of a slippery slope, ending up with black men marrying white women. The racists were prophetic.

12   "They were absolutely right." notes Randall Kennedy, the Harvard Law School professor and author of a dazzling new book, "Interracial Intimacies," to be published next month. "I do think [interracial marriage] is a good thing. It's a welcome sign of thoroughgoing desegregation. We talk about desegregation in the public sphere: here's desegregation in the most intimate sphere."

13   These days, interracial romance can be seen on the big screen, on TV shows, and in the lives of some prominent Americans. Former Defense Secretary William Cohen has a black wife, as does Peter Norton, the software guru. The Supreme Court justice Clarence Thomas has a white wife.

14   I find the surge in intermarriage to be one of the most positive fronts in American race relations today, building bridges and empathy. But it's still in its infancy.

15   I was excited to track down interracial couples at Ole Miss, thinking they would be perfect to make my point about this hopeful trend. But none were willing to talk about the issue on the record.

16   "Even if people wanted to marry [interracially], I think they'd keep it kind of quiet," explained a minister on campus.

17   For centuries, racists warned that racial equality would lead to the "mongrelization" of America. Perhaps they were right in a sense, for we're increasingly going to see a blurring of racial distinctions. But these distinctions acquired enormous social resonance without ever having much basis in biology.

FOR WRITING OR DISCUSSION

1. What is Kristof's thesis? State it in your own words. How does paragraph 14 reinforce the thesis?

2. What are the varied cases that the writer presents to support his point? How do the data in paragraph 9 help support the thesis?

3. Where does Kristof use expert testimony to good effect?

4. Write an essay in which you explore interracial dating and (or) interracial marriage as it appears in your community—on campus or in your home town. What are the prevalent attitudes among your friends and family toward "love and race," to quote Kristof's title. What are your own attitudes toward the phenomenon?

LANGSTON HUGHES

Salvation

I was saved from sin when I was going on thirteen. But not really saved. It happened like this. There was a big revival at my Auntie Reed's church. Every night for weeks there had been much preaching, singing, praying, and shouting, and some very hardened sinners had been brought to Christ, and the membership of the church had grown by leaps and bounds. Then just before the revival ended, they held a special meeting for children, "to bring the young lambs to the fold." My aunt spoke of it for days ahead. That night I was escorted to the front row and placed on the mourners' bench with all the other young sinners, who had not yet been brought to Jesus. 1

My aunt told me that when you were saved you saw a light, and something happened to you inside! And Jesus came into your life! And God was with you from then on! She said you could see and hear and feel Jesus in your soul. I believed her. I had heard a great many old people say the same thing and it seemed to me they ought to know. So I sat there calmly in the hot, crowded church, waiting for Jesus to come to me. 2

The preacher preached a wonderful rhythmical sermon, all moans and shouts and lonely cries and dire pictures of hell, and then he sang a song about the ninety and nine safe in the fold, but one little lamb was left out in the cold. Then he said: "Won't you come? Won't you come to Jesus? Young lambs, won't you come?" And he held out his arms to all us young sinners there on the mourner's bench. And the little girls cried. And some of them jumped up and went to Jesus right away. But most of us just sat there. 3

A great many old people came and knelt around us and prayed, old women with jet-black faces and braided hair, old men with work-gnarled hands. And the church sang a song about the lower lights are burning, some poor sinners to be saved. And the whole building rocked with prayer and song. 4

5   Still I kept waiting to see Jesus.

6   Finally all the young people had gone to the altar and were saved, but one boy and me. He was a rounder's son named Westley. Westley and I were surrounded by sisters and deacons praying. It was very hot in the church, and getting late now. Finally Westley said to me in a whisper: "God damn! I'm tired o' sitting here. Let's get up and be saved." So he got up and was saved.

7   Then I was left all alone on the mourners' bench. My aunt came and knelt at my knees and cried, while prayers and songs swirled all around me in the little church. The whole congregation prayed for me alone, in a mighty wail of moans and voices. And I kept waiting serenely for Jesus, waiting, waiting—but he didn't come. I wanted to see him, but nothing happened to me. Nothing! I wanted something to happen to me, but nothing happened.

8   I heard the songs and the minister saying: "Why don't you come? My dear child, why don't you come to Jesus? Jesus is waiting for you. He wants you. Why don't you come? Sister Reed, what is this child's name?"

9   "Langston," my aunt sobbed.

10   "Langston, why don't you come? Why don't you come and be saved? Oh, Lamb of God! Why don't you come?"

11   Now it was really getting late. I began to be ashamed of myself, holding everything up so long. I began to wonder what God thought about Westley, who certainly hadn't seen Jesus either, but who was now sitting proudly on the platform, swinging his knickerbockered legs and grinning down at me, surrounded by deacons and old women on their knees praying. God had not struck Westley dead for taking his name in vain or for lying in the temple. So I decided that maybe to save further trouble, I'd better lie, too, and say that Jesus had come, and get up and be saved.

12   So I got up.

13   Suddenly the whole room broke into a sea of shouting, as they saw me rise. Waves of rejoicing swept the place. Women leaped in the air. My aunt threw her arms around me. The minister took me by the hand and led me to the platform.

14   When things quieted down, in a hushed silence, punctuated by a few ecstatic "Amens," all the new young lambs were blessed in the name of God. Then joyous singing filled the room.

15   That night, for the last time in my life but one—for I was a big boy twelve years old—I cried. I cried, in bed alone, and couldn't stop. I buried my head under the quilts, but my aunt heard me. She woke up and told my uncle I was crying because the Holy Ghost had come into my life, and because I had seen Jesus. But I was really crying because I couldn't bear to tell her that I had lied, that I had deceived everybody in the church, that I hadn't seen Jesus, and that now I didn't believe there was a Jesus any more, since he didn't come to help me.

FOR WRITING OR DISCUSSION

1. What is the thesis of this selection? State it in your own words.

2. What specific sensory details help support the thesis?

3. Why does the narrator not stand as he was expected to early in the narrative?

4. Why at the end does he in fact rise? How do the people around him react when he finally stands? Why? Why does the narrator cry at night?

5. Write an essay about how people pressured you (or someone you know) to do something you weren't sure was right. Or, perhaps you would prefer to write about a religious experience that you had. Be sure to support your thesis with concrete sensory detail.

W. MICHAEL COX AND RICHARD ALM

Scientists Are Made, Not Born

Do women have what it takes to become scientists?   1

The national debate on the issue—touched off by the unfortunate comments of Harvard's president. Lawrence Summers[1]—has so far missed the central point: scientists are made, not born. Athletic talent or musical genius may be gifts of the gods (or genes), but scientific knowledge requires years of education at the college level and beyond. So in our efforts to create more female scientists, what matters are the choices and opportunities open to young women at our universities.   2

Until the last 30 or so years, few women studied the sciences, so there was little mystery about why most people in those professions were men Over the past generation, however, our research shows, there has been a truly stunning change. As an illustration of the gains by women in historically male disciplines, consider how the percentages of women receiving bachelor's degrees in the sciences increased from 1970 to 2002 (the last year for which we have complete data).   3

Clearly, debating whether women are intellectually equipped for sciences makes little sense. Women themselves have already settled the issue, one degree at a time. The younger generations within the science professions are decidedly more female than the older ones.   4

---

[1]Summers suggested that biological makeup may disincline women from science and mathematics careers.

The "femininization" of the ranks will take place as a matter of simple math because the older, male-dominated groups will retire.

5   And, in terms of women's roles, the sciences aren't much different from many other occupations that require education. In the early 1970's, women received less than 10 percent of all graduate degrees in law, medicine, dentistry and veterinary medicine. They were below 20 percent in pharmacy.

BACHELOR'S	1970–71	2001–02
Engineering	0.8	18.9%
Physics	6.7	22.6%
Geology	11.0	44.7%
Computer Science	13.6	27.6%
Chemistry	18.4	48.4%
Biological Sciences	29.1	60.8%
Mathematics	37.8	46.7%
Health Sciences	77.1	85.5%

Also in master's degrees:

And in doctorates:

MASTER'S	1970–71	2001–02
Engineering	1.1	21.4%
Physics	6.9	20.9%
Geology	9.7	39.7%
Computer Science	10.3	33.2%
Chemistry	21.4	45.6%
Biological Sciences	33.6	57.8%
Mathematics	27.1	42.4%
Health Sciences	55.4	77.5%

DOCTORATES	1970–71	2001–02
Engineering	0.6	17.3%
Physics	2.9	15.5%
Geology	3.4	28.5%
Computer Science	2.3	22.8%
Chemistry	8.0	33.9%
Biological Sciences	16.3	44.3%
Mathematics	7.6	29.0%
Health Sciences	16.5	63.3%

Percent Share of Professional Degrees Awarded to Women

Legend:
- – – Veterinary
- —— Pharmacy
- – – Law
- ····· Medical
- —— M.B.A.
- ····· Dentistry

However, as the chart above indicates, today women earn about two-thirds of the degrees in veterinary medicine and pharmacy. They're approaching 50 percent in law, and they've topped 40 percent in medicine. More than a third of new dentists are women.

6

Likewise, women's share of master's degrees from business schools rose from 3.6 percent in 1970 to 41.1 percent in 2002.

7

Women have also greatly expanded their presence in the social sciences, including economics, political science and sociology. Overall, women earned 46.3 percent of the doctorates awarded in 2002, up from 13.3 percent in 1970.

8

Women themselves deserve credit for this extraordinary migration into higher education. They made different choices, perhaps because of the feminist movement's consciousness-raising, perhaps because the growing economy offered new opportunities while barriers to entry fell in many professions.

9

Women also changed how they expected to spend their adult lives. Back when most intended to leave the labor force after marrying and having children, it hardly

10

made economic sense for them to invest time and money in demanding academic pursuits. But as more women contemplated longer, uninterrupted careers, academic effort began to pay off.

11   Labor-force participation rates bear this claim out: From 1950 to 1968, less than 40 percent of women age 20 and older were working or looking for jobs. But that rate has been rising for decades, passing 50 percent in 1984 and nearing 60 percent today. (Men's labor force participation, although declining over the past two decades, is still higher, around 75 percent.)

12   There are of course still a few hot-button issues concerning gender and employment: equality in pay, maternity leave, flexible time for family commitments. But in terms of education and opportunity, women are getting ever closer to a level playing field.

13   If nothing else, the debate set off by Mr. Summers's remarks gives us a chance to recognize this remarkable change.

FOR WRITING OR DISCUSSION

1. The first paragraph asks a question. How does the essay answer it?

2. What is the writers' thesis?

3. What do the charts show? the graph?

4. How have the writers interpreted the data for readers in order to support the thesis?

5. Select a particular professional field that interests you—medicine, psychology, small businesses, or performing arts, for example—and investigate the changing opportunities available to women in that field over the last several years. Then write an essay in which you state your thesis clearly and back it up with statistical data. You may wish to draw charts or tables to accompany your essay.

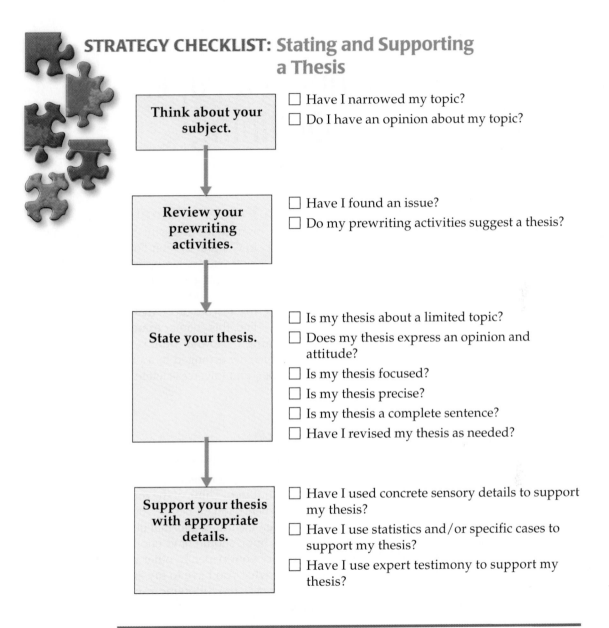

STRATEGY CHECKLIST: Stating and Supporting
a Thesis

Think about your subject.	☐ Have I narrowed my topic? ☐ Do I have an opinion about my topic?
Review your prewriting activities.	☐ Have I found an issue? ☐ Do my prewriting activities suggest a thesis?
State your thesis.	☐ Is my thesis about a limited topic? ☐ Does my thesis express an opinion and attitude? ☐ Is my thesis focused? ☐ Is my thesis precise? ☐ Is my thesis a complete sentence? ☐ Have I revised my thesis as needed?
Support your thesis with appropriate details.	☐ Have I used concrete sensory details to support my thesis? ☐ Have I use statistics and/or specific cases to support my thesis? ☐ Have I use expert testimony to support my thesis?

For additional writing, reading, and research resources, go to **www. mycomplab.com** <http://www.mycomplab.com/> and choose Skwire/Wiener's *Student's Book of College English*, Twelfth Edition.

CHAPTER 4

Planning a Paper: Outlining

- Creating a Rough Outline
- Making a Formal Outline
- One Student Writing: From Prewriting to Essay
- Preparing Your Formal Outline

Proper planning is a key to writing a successful paper. As we saw in Chapter 2, John Fousek's two planning efforts—grouping related materials in lists and a rough outline—helped him to produce his drafts. In addition to a discussion on making a rough outline, this chapter examines a more rigorous kind of planning, **formal outlining**. A formal outline requires clearly defined headings and subheadings, which are arranged in a prescribed format of Roman and Arabic numbers and upper- and lowercase letters.

Creating a Rough Outline

When you arrange your prewriting ideas in some kind of order, you have pretty much created a rough, or informal, outline. Linking related ideas, for example, and creating labels for them make good rough outlines. Think of the rough outline as an informal list, which you create as a convenience to you before you begin the more advanced aspects of developing your paper, including a formal outline. The rough outline does not follow a prescribed form, but it should have enough detail so that you can see the early shape and direction of your paper. In other words, the rough outline can help you decide preliminarily what you have to say and how to say it.

From prewriting notes, one student made the following rough outline for a paper on the value of television in today's society.

Rough Outline

THESIS: Television makes a valuable contribution in today's society.

1. **Introduction:** Why do people watch so much TV?

    Convenient and easy to use

Addictive

Little required effort

2. Television as excellent source of information

Up-to-date news as it happens: wars, weather disasters, business news, science and medicine advances

In-depth investigations: NOVA, 60 Minutes, etc

3. Television as entertainer

Comedy Central

Concerts, dance programs, drama, movies (all appealing to different tastes)

4. Television teaches

Children and Sesame Street

College courses via television

High school subjects review

5. **Conclusion:** Critics wrongly oppose television watching in the home.

This informal outline can guide the writer in producing his rough draft. The writer includes a thesis, which makes an assertion about the topic. Undoubtedly, the thesis will change more than once, and some of the items under the numbered headings will change as the writer produces the first and subsequent drafts. Therefore, as the paper progresses, the rough outline itself will change—a good thing, to be sure. You should view any outline as a dynamic product, a work in progress, just as your drafts are works in progress. Even if you don't follow your original plan exactly, your outline is a first stab at unifying your thoughts and presenting them coherently.

Another less detailed but equally helpful rough outline appears on pages 82–83 as thought blocks and labels for them. Your rough outline might include the following items.

TIPS for Making a Rough Outline

Include:

■ **Linked and labeled thought blocks.**

■ **A thesis statement.**

■ **An introduction or opening.**

■ **Ideas or main points in numbered sequence.**

■ **Possible supporting information for each main point.**

■ **A conclusion.**

EXERCISE   For any topic on page 36, develop a rough outline that you could use to write a paper on the subject.

Making a Formal Outline

A formal outline is a schematic presentation of your paper—a procedural diagram, if you will, in which you show the order of your topics and how they relate to each other. A formal outline gives a picture of the logical relations between the separate parts of the paper and the thesis or purpose. After your preliminary thinking on your topic and with your prewriting in hand, consider the formal outline as a road map to a territory you have just begun exploring but need clearer directions to navigate.

When you produce a formal outline, follow the conventions of its format, as presented on pages 75–77. After your prewriting, you should have an idea of your thesis. Thus, always begin your outline by stating your thesis or purpose. As we have pointed out before, you may want to modify your thesis as your outline takes shape, so don't be concerned if you haven't stated your thesis exactly the way you want it.

Establishing Main Divisions

After you state your thesis, your next task is to determine the main divisions of the paper as suggested by the thesis. In many cases, your choice of method of development (Part Two of this book) will determine the major sections. For example, if you wanted to write about why your brother decided not to go to college, what he is doing instead, and how his decision affected his personality, the sections of the paper seem clear, and you would use them as main headings in the outline format. Yes, you would still have to decide on what order to use in order to present the points in the paper, and what order to use for the supporting details under each point, but the three major parts of the paper are clear simply from the way you want to develop it.

In other papers, main divisions may not suggest themselves so clearly at the outset. As you examine your prewriting, try to see how some of what you've written falls into large blocks of thought. If you've written preliminary thoughts by hand, circles and arrows or marks in different colored pens or pencils can help you make visual links among related ideas that may be spread out over the page. If you write by computer, you can experiment by grouping thoughts into blocks, saving your effort, and trying yet another plan. Some word-processing programs have templates for outlining.

As the related thoughts come together, look at them as main points. If you can create a label for each thought block, you then can convert the label into a main heading. The main headings in your outline should match the number of blocks you have identified. If you see that your outline has more than five or so main points, reexamine it: You may be trying to do too much in your paper.

Adding Supporting Details

With thought blocks identified and labeled, you need then to think about the supporting details to place under each heading. The supporting points, of course, will pertain clearly to the main thought you stated in the heading. As you group these supporting points—some of which will appear in your prewriting, others to be invented as you produce the outline—they will become subheadings in your outline.

Once you've settled on your thought blocks, you will have to decide how to organize them. In a descriptive essay (Chapter 7), you generally move the reader from one place to the next, and once you decide where to begin (in a room, for example, front, back, sides, or middle), logic of place will assert itself. But for most other essays, the arrangement of thought blocks is strictly the writer's option, with logic the prevailing factor for appropriate decisions.

Formatting a Formal Outline

Begin by stating the thesis or purpose. Then indicate all major divisions of the paper with Roman numerals. Mark the support for the major divisions with capital letters and additional support for those major divisions with Arabic numerals. If you are planning a very long paper, you may want to make further subdivisions. To do so, next use small letters—*a, b, c*—and then arabic numerals in parentheses—*(1), (2)*—then lowercase letters in parentheses—*(a), (b)*.

A standard formal outline for a complex paper has the following format.

Complex Paper Formal Outline

Thesis or Purpose: [State the thesis or purpose of your paper here.]

    I. Major division

       A. First-level subdivision

     1. Second-level subdivision

     2. Second-level subdivision

       a. Third-level subdivision

       b. Third-level subdivision

         (1) Fourth-level subdivision

         (2) Fourth-level subdivision

  B. First-level subdivision

     1. Second-level subdivision

     2. Second-level subdivision

II. Major division

  A. First-level subdivision

     1. Second-level subdivision

     2. Second-level subdivision

  B. First-level subdivision

     1. Second-level subdivision

       a. Third-level subdivision

       b. Third-level subdivision

     2. Second-level subdivision

       a. Third-level subdivision

       b. Third-level subdivision

         (1) Fourth-level subdivision

         (2) Fourth-level subdivision

           (a) Fifth-level subdivision

           (b) Fifth-level subdivision

An outline for a short paper usually includes several major divisions and sometimes two or three subdivisions for each major topic. Remember that a word or a phrase in an outline can be expanded into a sentence—even a paragraph—in your essay.

A typical outline format for a short paper looks like this:

Short Paper Formal Outline

Thesis or Purpose: [State the thesis or purpose of your paper here.]

  I. Major division

    A. Subdivision

    B. Subdivision

II. Major division

    A. Subdivision

    B. Subdivision

    C. Subdivision

III. Major division

    A. Subdivision

    B. Subdivision

    C. Subdivision

Writing Topic and Sentence Outlines

Formal outlines are of two types, *topic outlines* and *sentence outlines*. A **topic outline** is one in which the writer uses just a few words or phrases to indicate the topics and subtopics that the paper covers. Topic outlines are sufficient for many short papers, especially those that classify or present a process. Longer papers and those that develop theses often profit from sentence outlines.

Here is a topic outline for a short paper on how to change automobile license plates.

Topic Outline

Purpose: To show how to change auto license plates.

I. Assemble materials

    A. Find screwdriver

    B. Find household oil

    C. Buy plastic screws

II. Remove old plates

    A. Oil screws to loosen rust

    B. Unscrew plates

    C. Discard metal screws

III. Mount new plates

    A. Position plate with screw holes

    B. Screw on plate using plastic screws

IV. Break and discard old plates

EXERCISE

1. What is the first major division of the license plate outline? The second? The third?
2. What supporting information does the outline indicate as subdivisions for the major division "Remove old plates"?
3. Why does the fourth major division not have any subdivisions?
4. What thesis could you propose for the essay that this outline suggests?
5. In what order has the writer chosen to arrange the thought blocks indicated as major divisions?

Longer papers and those that develop theses often benefit from sentence outlines. To write a **sentence outline**, you must sum up in one sentence what you want to say on each topic and subtopic. The sentence doesn't merely indicate the topic; it states what you intend to say about the topic. This kind of outline forces you to think through exactly what you want to say before you begin to write. By constructing a sentence outline, you will find out whether you really have support for your position. Look at the sentence outline below.

Sentence Outline

<u>Thesis</u>: My attitude toward the English language has changed from loathing to acceptance.

I. At first, I hated the English language.   *First major division*

  A. Knowing very little English, I felt isolated.   *First-level subdivision*

    1. I could not understand what people said to me.   *Second-level subdivisions*

    2. I could not tell others what I thought or felt.

  B. The isolation I felt made me want to return to Greece.   *First-level subdivision*

II. Now, six months later, I like the English language very much.   *Second major division*

  A. The support of the Greek family I live with has helped me to accept English.   *First-level subdivision*

    1. They gave me courage to try to use the language.

      a. They proved to me that they had learned the language.   *Second-level subdivision*

      b. They proved to me that they could talk with others in English.   *Third-level subdivision*

2. They held conversations with me in English.

B. The teachers in my English classes have helped me to accept the language.

   1. They are approachable and helpful outside of class.

   2. They are good instructors in class.

      a. They explain material clearly.

      b. They discuss a variety of subjects.

         (1) The variety increases my vocabulary.

         (2) The discussions improve my comprehension and speech.

Fourth-level subdivisions

III. I go out of my way now to assure my continuous contact with English.

A. I study English regularly.

   1. I work with a tutor for one hour every day.

   2. I study grammar and vocabulary two hours every night.

B. Since I meet few Greeks, I must speak English every day.

   1. I go to the supermarket to read and pronounce the names of consumer products.

      a. I love to say the weird names of candies and cereals.

         (1) Have you ever eaten Fiddle Faddle?

         (2) I have lots of fun with Captain Crunch, Sugar Frosted Flakes, and Count Chocula.

      b. I made friends with one of the stock boys who helps me when my English fails me.

   2. I always accept solicitation calls on the telephone just to practice my English.

EXERCISE

1. What are the major divisions of the outline? Put a checkmark beside each one. How do the major divisions relate to the thesis as stated as the first outline entry?
2. How do the items in I. A. 1. and 2. relate to the item in I. A.? To the item in I.? To the thesis?
3. Look at the various items connected to III in the outline. Label each item appropriately as major division and first-, second-, third-, and fourth-level subdivisions. Be prepared to explain why you chose the labels you did.
4. Using any one of the thought blocks labeled as a major division as well as the various subdivisions beneath it, try your hand at writing the paragraph that the outline suggests.

One Student Writing: From Prewriting to Essay

In an English class, one student, Alan Benjamin, received this assignment: Discuss the implications of the inscription on the pedestal of the statue in Shelley's poem "Ozymandias." We'll have more to say about approaches to literary analysis in Chapter 17; here we want to examine how the student developed a formal outline and how that outline led to the production of his essay.

First, read the brief poem "Ozymandias" so you'll know what stimulated the assignment.

PERCY BYSSHE SHELLEY

Ozymandias

I met a traveller from an antique land
Who said: Two vast and trunkless legs of stone
Stand in the desert. Near them, on the sand,
Half sunk, a shattered visage lies, whose frown,
And wrinkled lip, and sneer of cold command,
Tell that its sculptor well those passions read

Which yet survive, stamped on these lifeless things,
The hand that mocked them, and the heart that fed:[1]
And on the pedestal these words appear:
"My name is Ozymandias, king of kings:
Look on my works, ye Mighty, and despair!"
Nothing beside remains. Round the decay
Of that colossal wreck, boundless and bare
The lone and level sands stretch far away.

---

[1]The passions stamped on the broken face of the statue survive the hand (of the sculptor) that mocked them and the heart (of Ozymandias) that fed them.

Initial thinking about the assignment led the student to this prewriting effort.

Prewriting

Such arrogance! Ozy's inscription then and now

Statue meant to challenge all who saw it—I am mighty, the rest of you puny

How was statue built in the first place?

People today who think they're powerful can learn from Ozy's fate—not from envy

"King of Kings"—Ozymandias thinks a lot of himself

"Sneer of cold command"—poet shows vanity and arrogance in having statue built in
the first place

Ozy believes no one else will be able to match the magnificence of
his works

Is Ozy a real figure in history?

Vanity today too—all material things crumble and yield disappointment if you put your faith in the material things

Where was Ozymandias' statue erected? Maybe at the gates of his capital city? Where is this "antique land"?

Time eats away buildings and statues—look what's left of Ozymandias' vain effort to preserve his reputation and instill fear in people

"Despair"—Ozymandias' idea of despair comes from petty and foolish reasons. Now we have more realistic reasons for the origin of despair

Using his prewriting as a record of his preliminary thinking, Alan Benjamin tried to link related ideas visually using lines and boxes. As he considered the thought blocks suggested by his prewriting, he weighed how to organize them. He numbered related points so that he could see their interconnections. He did not link thoughts that seemed unrelated.

The next step on the road to preparing the outline and then writing the paper was to label the numbered blocks of thought. What words and phrases would best identify each cluster of information? The labels developed are preliminary and subject to considerable change as the outline takes shape; but you can see the first efforts below. The numbers correspond to the numbered thought blocks Benjamin grouped (see page 83).

Labels for Thought Blocks

1. Meaning of despair different now from Ozymandias' day
2. Meaning of the statue to Ozymandias and his contemporaries
3. Meaning now
4. The petty and foolish vs. realistic reasons for despair

GROUPING THOUGHT BLOCKS

Such arrogance! Ozy's inscription then and now. ①

Statue meant to challenge all who saw it–I am mighty, the rest of you puny ②

How was statue built in the first place?

People today who think they're powerful can learn from Ozy's fate–not from envy ③

Kin g of Kings"--Ozymandias thinks a lot of himself ②

"Sneer of cold command"–poet shows vanity and arrogance in having statue built in first place ②

Ozy believes no one else will be able to match the magnificence of his works ②

Is Ozy a real figure in history?

Vanity today too–all material things crumble and yield disappointment if you put your faith in the material things ③

Where was Ozymandias' statue erected? Maybe at the gates of his capital city? ②

Where is this "antique land"?

Time eats away buildings and statues–look what's left of Ozymandias' vain effort to preserve his reputation and instill fear in people ③

"Despair"–Ozymandias' idea of despair comes from petty and foolish reasons. Now we have more realistic reasons for the origin of despair ④

These labels and the thought blocks themselves serve as a rough outline and provide a good start for developing a formal outline. As the writer examined the labels and blocks of thought, he could identify the purpose he had in writing his paper. He wanted to contrast Ozymandias' views of despair as expressed in the poem with the meanings we bring to that word today. And as he weighed his purpose and the thought blocks he produced, he realized that the numbered clusters suggested the order that he would use. First he would present the king's notion of despair; then he would present the views we have of the term today based on the poem's assertions.

Here is the outline developed from the preliminary materials you just examined.

Outline

Purpose: To contrast Ozymandias' view of the word <u>despair</u> with the meanings we bring to the word as a result of the passage of time.

I. In the poem "Ozymandias" by Percy Bysshe Shelley, the inscription "My name is Ozymandias, king of kings: / Look on my works, ye Mighty and despair!" appears on a broken statue in the desert.

A. King Ozymandias had one thing in mind with that inscription.

B. Today the words take on a dramatically different meaning.

II. Vanity and arrogance motivated Ozymandias to build the statue of himself.

A. The features of his face assert his self-importance.

1. His "wrinkled lip and sneer of cold command" are apparent.

2. The size of the statue is "colossal."

3. He describes himself as "king of kings."

B. We can imagine the site of the statue at the gates of the capital or its central square and people's reactions to it.

1. Marble buildings gleam in the sunlight.

a. We can visualize the palace, the treasury, and the temples.

b. There are monuments to military victories.

2. "Mighty" people come to see the wonders of Ozymandias's kingdom.

3. "Look on my works, ye Mighty, and despair" the statue sneers.

a. Despair because your creations will never equal mine.

b. Despair because my works will make you see the insignificance of your own.

III. The passage of time has given a new dimension to Ozymandias's statement.

A. Ozymandias's kingdom is now a desert.

  1. Time eats away marble.

  2. Buildings and statues crumble.

    a. Little remains of the statue of Ozymandias.

      (1) Two grotesque stone legs stick up in the air.

      (2) The statue has a "shattered visage."

    b. What remains is sand and desolation.

B. The inscription on the pedestal takes on new significance.

  1. In one sense, it is meaningless.

    a. There are no more "works" left to look on.

    b. Ozymandias was silly in his pomposity.

  2. In another sense, the words have stronger and truer meaning than Ozymandias dreamed.

    a. Powerful people today can still despair as they look at Ozymandias' works.

    b. The despair people face will not be based on envy, however.

      (1) They will despair because they can see the fate of their own works.

      (2) They will despair because no matter how great their works are, the works won't matter.

      (3) They will despair because those who put their faith in material things are doomed to disappointment.

IV. With these contrasting views, there is more than enough despair to go around.

The paper developed from the formal outline appears next. As you read it, consider how the two relate to each other—and to the prewriting. How has the outline influenced the essay? What differences do you note?

Alan Benjamin
Enough Despair to Go Around

1   In Percy Bysshe Shelley's "Ozymandias," the poet reveals that these words are inscribed on the pedestal of a broken statue in the desert: "My name is Ozymandias, king of kings: / Look on my works, ye Mighty, and despair!" What King Ozymandias had in mind when he chose those words is dramatically different from the meaning they have now. The new meaning comes not from Ozymandias but from the passage of time.

2   The still visible "wrinkled lip and sneer of cold command" suggest the vanity and arrogance that motivated Ozymandias to have his statue built in the first place. The "colossal" size of the statue and Ozymandias' description of himself as "king of kings" add to the impression that he thought a great deal of himself and wanted others to do the same. We can imagine the statue being erected at the gates or in the central square of King Ozymandias' great capital city. Marble buildings gleam in the sunlight: the palace, the treasury, the temples, the monuments to military victories. Powerful and "mighty" people from all over the known world come to see the wonders of Ozymandias' kingdom. "Look on my works, ye Mighty, and despair," sneers Ozymandias: Despair because your creations, your works, will never be able to equal the magnificence of mine; despair because when you look at my works, you can only feel a sense of the pitiful insignificance of your own.

3   Time passes. Time eats away marble. Buildings and statues crumble. The glorious, thriving kingdom of Ozymandias is now a desert. Two grotesque stone legs stick up in the air, and together with a "shattered visage" they are all that is left of the statue. Everything else is sand and desolation. In one sense, the inscription on the pedestal has now become meaningless, for there are no more "works" left to look on, and we can think only of how silly Ozymandias must have been. In another sense, the words are filled with a strong new meaning, stronger and far more true than Ozymandias ever dreamed. Powerful and mighty people today can look at Ozymandias' works and still despair. This time, however, they will despair not because of envy, but because they can see the eventual fate of all their own works. They will despair because, even if their own works surpass those of Ozymandias, it won't make any difference. They will despair now because they can see that all material

things crumble to dust and that people who put their faith in such things are doomed to futility and disappointment.

Ozymandias originally hoped that the despair would come from petty and foolish reasons. Today it can come from more intelligent and realistic reasons. But there is still more than enough despair to go around as "the lone and level sands stretch far away." 4

EXERCISE

1. How do both the outline and the essay fulfill the writer's statement of purpose? What is the writer's thesis in this essay? Where does the writer state it most clearly?
2. How did the labels for the blocks of thought in the prewriting influence the outline?
3. What three items in the prewriting did Alan Benjamin not include in the thought blocks? Why do you think he excluded these items?
4. The outline is obviously a sentence outline, yet in two places we read not sentences but only fragments. Where? Why does the writer use fragments here? How do the items appear in the essay itself?
5. Look at the four major headings and the various subheadings in the outline. How do they relate to the essay itself? What similarities do you note? How does the essay differ from the section of the outline to which it corresponds?

HAVING YOUR SAY

What do you think the inscription on the pedestal means in Shelley's poem "Ozymandias"? Reread the poem on pages 80–81. Then make an assertion about the inscription and argue for your point with specific detail.

Preparing Your Formal Outline

Whether your outline is a topic or a sentence outline, it should include a statement of the thesis or purpose of the paper (depending on your teacher's instructions) and an indication by means of Roman numerals of the main points to be covered in the paper. Major and minor subdivisions, indicated by letters and Arabic numerals, respectively, should show how the main points will be developed.

Here are other points to observe in preparing an outline:

TIPS for Writing a Formal Outline

- **Do not make single subdivisions.** If you decide to subdivide a point, you must have at least two subdivisions. If there is a I, there must be a II; if there is an A, there must be a B. If you cannot think of two divisions, rephrase the heading so no division is necessary.

- **Use parallel grammatical forms for headings of equal importance.** Parallel forms help show the relation of headings to one another. If heading I reads "Assembling the ingredients," heading II should read "Mixing the ingredients," not "Mix the ingredients."

- **Make sure the divisions of an outline do not overlap and that you stick to a single principle of division.** You should not, for example, discuss books in terms of fiction, nonfiction, and novels because novels are logically a subdivision of fiction. You should not discuss the branches of government in terms of legislative, judicial, executive, and crooked politicians because one might find crooked politicians in any of the branches. You should not discuss people in terms of overweight, underweight, normal weight, and handsome. Obviously, the topic *handsome* does not belong in a division based on a principle of weight.

- **Make sure headings and subheadings show a proper logical relation.** In discussing athletes, you should not establish Babe Ruth as one major division and baseball players as a second. You might, however, treat great home-run hitters as a major division and Babe Ruth and Hank Aaron as subdivisions.

One final note about outlines: They can be as helpful after you've written your paper as they are during the early stages of development. For example, if you choose to use only your prewriting activities or a rough outline as a guide to writing your first draft, a formal outline at this stage provides a visual scheme of how your ideas relate to each other logically.

As you develop your outline, ask yourself the questions in the "Strategy Checklist: Preparing a Formal Outline." Your answers to these questions can provide guidance as you write and revise your draft. You can determine if your major divisions relate logically to your thesis, and you can shift subdivisions or add new ones as necessary.

STRATEGY CHECKLIST: Preparing a Formal Outline

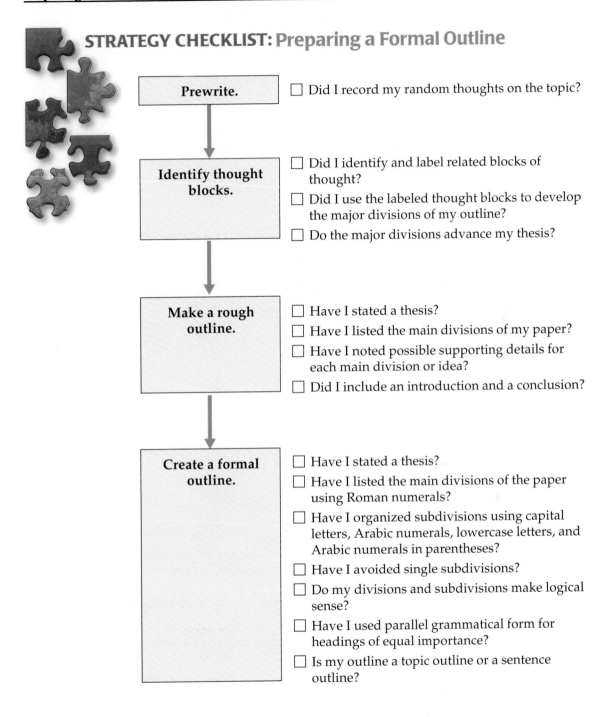

Prewrite.

☐ Did I record my random thoughts on the topic?

Identify thought blocks.

☐ Did I identify and label related blocks of thought?

☐ Did I use the labeled thought blocks to develop the major divisions of my outline?

☐ Do the major divisions advance my thesis?

Make a rough outline.

☐ Have I stated a thesis?

☐ Have I listed the main divisions of my paper?

☐ Have I noted possible supporting details for each main division or idea?

☐ Did I include an introduction and a conclusion?

Create a formal outline.

☐ Have I stated a thesis?

☐ Have I listed the main divisions of the paper using Roman numerals?

☐ Have I organized subdivisions using capital letters, Arabic numerals, lowercase letters, and Arabic numerals in parentheses?

☐ Have I avoided single subdivisions?

☐ Do my divisions and subdivisions make logical sense?

☐ Have I used parallel grammatical form for headings of equal importance?

☐ Is my outline a topic outline or a sentence outline?

EXERCISE

Comment on the following topic outlines. What are their successes? their faults?

1. *Thesis:* All my teachers make me think.

   I. My English teacher
     A. Challenges logic of papers
     B. Relates reading assignments to everyday life
     C. Wears pretty clothes

   II. My history teacher
     A. Gives lectures

   III. My music teacher
     A. Speaks three languages
     B. Has great sense of humor

2. *Purpose:* To classify the divisions of the federal government.

   I. The executive
     A. President

   II. Legislative
     A. House of Representatives
     B. Senate
     C. Lawyers
     D. Committees

   III. Judicial
     A. Supreme Court
     B. Judges
     C. Clerks

EXERCISE

What strengths and weaknesses do you see in the following sentence outlines? Revise them so that they are more suitable to the writer's needs.

1. *Thesis:* Nationalism swept two major countries in Europe through the strength of dynamic leaders.

   I. In the last half of the nineteenth century, nationalism surfaced in Germany and Italy.

   II. Bismarck in Germany, and Cavour, Garibaldi, and Mazzini in Italy were the four key figures in nineteenth-century nationalism.
     A. Cavour, Garibaldi, and Mazzini combined their talents to unify Italy.
       1. Cavour was the "brains" of unification.

    2. Garibaldi was the "sword."
    3. Mazzini was the "spirit" of the revolution.
   B. Otto von Bismarck was the creator of a unified German state.
    1. He used "blood and iron" to unify the separate German states.
    2. He suppressed liberalism and democracy.
    3. His militaristic policies contributed to the outbreak of World War I.

2. *Thesis:* Getting a broken appliance repaired by sending it to a service center requires careful packing and mailing.

  I. Broken appliances can be repaired by service centers.
    A. It's generally easy to bring the appliance to a service unit if one exists in your city.
    B. Often, no such centers exist nearby.
      1. The manufacturer's center may be out of state.
      2. Local repair shops cannot do the work.
      3. Each company has its own designs and required parts.

  II. Mailing the appliance requires attention to important details.
    A. You can find the mailing address easily.
      1. Check the literature that accompanied the object.
      2. Telephone the store where you purchased the object to find out the address.
    B. The biggest job is packing up the object and mailing it off.
      1. Find a strong cardboard box and pack the appliance well in order to prevent shifting and breakage.
      2. Close the carton with strong tape.
      3. Print mailing and home addresses carefully.
      4. Write a letter providing essential information.
        a. Tell what is wrong with the appliance and where you bought it.
        b. Address the envelope correctly and enclose the letter.
        c. Tape the envelope to the outside of the carton.
      5. The post office will weigh the package and tell you costs for mailing and insurance.

EXERCISE Put the following information into a sentence outline that follows the suggested form.

- *First main heading:* Travel throughout America is increasing in popularity with people of all age groups.
- *Subheadings:* College and high school students find travel adds to their education. People with young families feel that their children should

experience people in different settings. Old people find travel gives life a sense of purpose.

- *Second main heading:* There are several popular methods of travel.
- *Subheading:* Hitchhiking is frequently used among teenagers.
- *Further divisions:* It allows inexpensive travel. It allows the traveler to meet many people. It is dangerous, however.
- *More subheadings:* Young families still choose small automobiles and camping equipment. Older people often take planes or trains.

EXERCISE   One student jotted down the following information for an essay entitled "Linking Atlantic and Pacific: The Panama Canal." Read all of her data and then choose the two facts that represent the main headings (I and II). Then group the related facts under these headings in order to fill in the outline.

Disease, corruption, and lack of equipment caused the company to go bankrupt.

Actual construction cost $320 million.

The United States government eventually built the canal.

De Lessep's company dug 76 million cubic yards of dirt.

Sanitation cost $20 million.

A French company owned by Ferdinand De Lesseps was the first to try to dig a canal through the Isthmus of Panama.

The United States government removed over 211 million cubic yards of earth.

The original French companies received $40 million.

The canal cost the United States about $390 million.

Ten million dollars was paid to Panama for rights.

EXERCISE   Write a formal topic or sentence outline of

1. John Fousek's paper on his roommate's irritating habits (see Chapter 2; page 46).
2. Hugh Nicholes' paper "The Mechanics of Backyard Mechanics" on pages 101–102.

EXERCISE   For the topic you limited in the exercise on page 48, prepare an outline that will help you develop a draft paper.

EXERCISE   Look ahead to the formal outline (page 521) for the research paper. What does the outline tell you about how the writer will develop the paper?

COLLABORATIVE LEARNING

Bring to class the outline you produced for the previous exercise, an outline to help you develop a draft of a paper. Form groups of three or four and comment on each other's outlines. As you discuss the work of members in the group, address these questions:

- Does the outline indicate a clear thesis? If not, how can the writer improve it?
- Do the main categories indicate appropriate divisions for the paper?
- Do the subcategories logically support the main categories under which the writer has placed them?
- Does the outline follow the conventions of outline form?

For additional writing, reading, and research resources, go to **www. mycomplab.com** <http://www.mycomplab.com/> and choose Skwire/Wiener's *Student's Book of College English*, Twelfth Edition.

CHAPTER **5**

Writing Your Paper: An Overview

- Writing a Strong Introduction
- Writing the Body Paragraphs
- One Student Writing: Topic Sentences
- Writing a Strong Conclusion

Before we proceed in Part Two to developing different kinds of papers—comparison, classification, process, and others—we first need to discuss the characteristics common to almost all types of papers.

Writing a Strong Introduction

To start, you need a beginning, or an **introduction**. The introduction consists of one or more paragraphs that set the stage for the essay.

Stating the Thesis

The simplest introduction identifies the subject and states the thesis. This is not to say that the thesis statement you produced in your prewriting or placed at the top of your outline must necessarily appear in the same form in the actual introduction. For example, John Fousek's original thesis in Chapter 2, *My friend Jim really irritates me with his habit of never closing things that he opens up*, is stated differently in the introductory paragraph of his final draft in Chapter 6:

> But Jim has one shortcoming that irritates me: He doesn't close things.

Turn to Fousek's paper on pages 122–123 and note how his introduction builds to the thesis with interesting and pertinent information about his roommate, Jim, that sets the stage for the main point of the paper.

For yet another example, look ahead to the paper, "The Beginning of the End" (pages 420–422). Harriet McKay's original thesis statement in her outline for that paper was:

Although the ending of "Charles" by Shirley Jackson is a surprise, the author subtly presents clues throughout the story that enable one, on a second reading, to see that Jackson does prepare for the ending.

As you can see, in the final paper, she writes instead:

Until the last sentence of Shirley Jackson's "Charles," I had no idea that Charles, the terror of kindergarten, was an imaginary person created by Laurie and that Charles's little monster antics were really Laurie's own antics. The author fooled me completely, but I have to admit that she played fair. She gave her readers all the clues they needed to make a sensible guess about how the story would end.

What matters is to present the idea of the thesis in the most interesting manner possible.

Forecasting the Paper

Sometimes, in addition to identifying the subject and stating the thesis, the introduction lists the divisions of the rest of the paper.

Amid the growing pressure to study hard and make good grades, any student who admits to attending college to catch a mate risks alienation, hostility, and ridicule. I'm not sure that's fair. Although I firmly believe that students, while they are in college, should get the best education possible, I see no harm in their looking for a spouse at the same time. I believe college is an ideal place for an intelligent man or woman to look for a mate. For one thing, it's easy to meet eligible members of the opposite sex in college. Also, college provides a setting in which friendships can grow freely and naturally into love. Besides, an educated person surely wants a mate who shares his or her interests and tastes. What better place to find such a person than in college?

Here, the introduction identifies the subject—finding a mate while in college—and then states the thesis—*College is an ideal place for an intelligent man or woman to look for a mate.* The sentences following the thesis statement let you know how the writer will advance the argument in the body of the paper. You are prepared to expect the three reasons to be developed in such a way as to prove that college is an ideal place to find a mate.

Using Different Introductory Strategies

Although in short papers the one-paragraph introduction is most common, you are not limited to only one paragraph. Consider this four-paragraph introduction:

> "I don't like to do my Christmas shopping early. I enjoy the bustle of last-minute crowds."
>
> "Why should I start research for my term paper this early? I work best under pressure."
>
> "I'll replace the washer on the bathroom sink Saturday when I have time to do it properly."
>
> We recognize such statements for what they are—excuses for procrastination. We have, of course, been told from childhood that putting off until tomorrow what we can do today is bad practice, and we feel guilty about not following such good advice, so we make up excuses to justify our tendency to delay performing unpleasant tasks. But away with guilt. Away with excuses. Procrastination, far from being evil, can, in many cases, have positive effects.

The first three paragraphs give examples of the subject—procrastination. The fourth paragraph discusses the examples and then, about the time the reader probably expects a humdrum list of ways to avoid putting off tasks, offers a surprising thesis: *Procrastination may be a good thing.*

Many other kinds of introductions can start an essay effectively. You might, for example, occasionally try dramatizing a situation:

> Sheila felt light-headed: Her eyes would not focus and there was a slight hum in her ears. Her hands, wet and clammy, shook so that she could hardly write. She could not concentrate. She wanted only to run, to be away from that terrible scene.
>
> Sheila had not just witnessed some horrible accident that she must report. She is a freshman composition student who has been told to write her first in-class

composition. Many students will recognize Sheila's symptoms. Perhaps the following tips about writing a composition under pressure will help alleviate their pain.

The scene described in the first paragraph attracts the reader's attention. The second paragraph explains the situation and anticipates the rest of the paper, which offers tips on writing under pressure. Another option is to use an anecdote to illustrate the subject:

Mrs. Peters was busily talking to a neighbor over the telephone one afternoon when she experienced the sudden fear that her baby son had been hurt. She told her neighbor and ran to check the baby, supposedly napping in his crib upstairs. To her horror, she found the child unconscious on the floor. Evidently he had tried to climb out of the crib but, in the attempt, had fallen on his head. Mrs. Peters's "knowing" her baby was in danger is the kind of experience many of us have had at one time or another. Yesterday, for example, I dialed a friend, and just before his telephone could ring, he picked up the receiver to call me. Both of these incidents are illustrations of the kind of thought transference known as *telepathy*.

The two anecdotes in this introduction show how telepathy, the subject of the paper, functions. The remainder of the paper explains how telepathy works.

As you can see, introductions take various forms. In many cases, as in the preceding paragraph, the thesis sentence appears at the end of the introduction. The examples here by no means exhaust the possibilities, but they do illustrate some ways of approaching a subject. Whatever form you choose, it's important to remember that the introduction must interest your readers—after all, you do want them to read the remainder of the paper—and it should in some way prepare readers for what follows.

 ## TIPS for Writing a Strong Introduction

Consider these options as you plan to write an introduction for your paper.

■ **Build to your thesis.** When you have a tentative thesis in place, you can build to it with a series of sentences. Your introduction should present the thesis in the most interesting manner possible. Spark your readers' interest and set a context for the thesis in your introduction.

■ **Identify the paper's divisions.** Let the reader know how you will treat the subject in the body of your paper.

■ **Seek variety with more than one paragraph.**   Some topics benefit from a multi-paragraph introduction that builds to the thesis.

■ **Tell an anecdote.**   A story relevant to your topic can appeal to readers and engage their interest.

■ **Deal with the opposition.**   If you're writing about why sixteen-year-olds should have the right to vote, build to your thesis by explaining why some people oppose such a plan.

■ **Ask a challenging question.**   You can stimulate your readers' interest with a thought-provoking question or series of questions that you will address in your essay.

■ **Inject some humor.**   Often a humorous statement can win readers over as you prepare to build to the serious topic at hand.

■ **Quote a statement relevant to your topic.**   Use a quote from books or current periodicals. *Bartlett's Familiar Quotations* or online quotation sites can be helpful resources.

■ **Provide dramatic data or statistics.**   You can give important background to your topic by citing data. Consider the introductory data in the first sentence of this brief introduction to a paper about presidential campaign contributions on college campuses:

At three major universities, Harvard, Stanford, and Columbia, more than 80 percent of the dollars in 2008 presidential campaign donations went to Democratic candidates. But these figures mask a strong conservative Republican base on college campuses.

Writing the Body Paragraphs

The **body** of a paper provides support for the thesis presented in the introduction. Body paragraphs develop the writing plan or outline and should lead readers logically from one section to another without causing confusion.

Writing Topic Sentences

One method of leading your reader is to write clear topic sentences for each paragraph. A **topic sentence** is to a paragraph what a thesis is to a paper: It expresses the central idea of the paragraph. The remainder of the paragraph gives support for the topic sentence.

Stated Topic Sentences

Topic sentences generally appear at the beginning of a paragraph, but they can appear anywhere in a paragraph.

Topic Sentence at the Beginning

Mrs. Jackson, my landlady's mother, is very nosy. Living on the first floor of the building affords her easy knowledge of the comings and goings of everyone living there. No matter how many times I descend the stairs in one day, I always find Mrs. Jackson peeking out of her front door. Usually she makes some statement or asks some question: "You really get around a lot. I guess you're going to the grocery now, huh?" I must give an explanation, denial, or confirmation of her guess—rather loudly, I might add, because of her hearing problem. Whenever company calls, they too are detained and cross-examined on the first floor. "Who are you going to see?" "Are you a relative?" "I guess you've known her a long time." Never does a visitor get up the stairs without first conversing with Mrs. Jackson.

Topic Sentence at the End

He drank noisily and chewed with his mouth open. He stuffed food into his mouth with his fingers and wiped his chin with the sleeve of his coat. He made loud, vulgar comments to the waitress, who had difficulty hiding her anger as other customers turned to stare. His idea of conversation was to regale his date with statistics about the World Series or facts about his expensive new car—especially its expense. *An hour with Bruce in the city's most costly restaurant made Jane wish she had dined at home alone on a tuna fish sandwich.*

Topic Sentence in the Middle

A fire-warning detector will "smell" smoke and sound an alarm; a guided missile will "see" and pursue a radar echo or the hot engines of a bomber; a speed governor will "feel" when a shaft is spinning too fast and act to restrain it. *But . . . quotation marks are appropriate in all such cases, because these machines do not have minds and they do not perceive the world as human beings do.* Information from our eyes, ears, and other senses goes to our brains, and of some of it (by no means all) we are aware as a vivid part of our conscious experience, showing us the world we inhabit.

—Nigel Calder, *The Mind of Man*

On rare occasions, writers do not state the topic sentence directly at all; instead, they imply it:

Implied Topic Sentence

Often when I find some passage in a book especially impressive—especially bright, say, or especially moving—I find myself turning to the dust jacket, if the author's picture is there, to communicate, to say a kind of "Well done." Coretta Scott King's photograph, soft, shadowed, and lovely, is on the jacket of her book *My Life with Martin Luther King, Jr.* I must have turned to it a dozen times in the reading of this book.

Here, the paragraph's central idea—that Coretta Scott King's book *My Life with Martin Luther King, Jr.* is especially impressive—is so clear that a statement of it is unnecessary; indeed, to state it directly would mar the grace of the paragraph. Implied topic sentences are tricky, though; use them cautiously. An idea that seems quite clear to you may not be as clear to your reader.

In summary, a topic sentence states the central idea of the paragraph. Wherever you decide to put your topic sentence, keep your readers in mind. They should not experience any confusion in following your thought. The central idea of every paragraph must be clear enough to lead readers easily from one point of your paper to another.

One Student Writing: Topic Sentences

In the following student paper, Hugh Nicholes classifies a group of his friends. Notice how the topic sentences move the classification along.

Hugh Nicholes

The Mechanics of Backyard Mechanics

Introduction states similarities among friends and sets frame for thesis.

Among my circle of friends and acquaintances, whose ages range from twenty to thirty-five, there is a general point of similarity. They are all short of funds and they depend on cars for transportation. Consequently, they all attempt to maintain and repair their own cars when possible. These backyard mechanics fall into three amusing categories: the putterer, the gas station mechanic, and the gadgeteer.

1

Thesis sentence: Friends who repair their own cars ("backyard mechanics") fall into three categories.

Topic sentence of second paragraph: introduces first kind of backyard mechanic that this paragraph will present. Note effective link between topic sentence and thesis sentence.

The putterer, as his title suggests, approaches his work in an aimless, often ineffective manner. Although he will undertake almost any job and stick with it until it is completed, he does so with considerable trepidation, and for good reason. It generally takes him ages to complete a job unless he gets help. His almost complete ignorance of machinery is well balanced by an insufficiency of tools. He works on the theory that if he makes no major alterations, he can do no major damage, and he may accomplish something while fooling around. He may be identified by his conversation: "Say, good buddy, why don't you drop over and have a beer or two with me? By the way, I'm doing a little work on my car. You used to do this sort of thing; maybe you've got some ideas?"

2

Supporting details establish qualities of the "putterer."

Topic sentence of third paragraph.

The gas station mechanic replaces components; he never tries to repair anything that can be unbolted and forced off a more general assembly. Often he replaces many components before he finds the one that was actually defective. This technique frequently costs more money than he can afford. He has a fair number of tools and some mechanical knowledge. He works on the theory that anything can be replaced by reversing the process of removal. His typical comment on his repairs is, "Damn! I guess the problem wasn't electrical. Can you lend me twenty bucks? I think I need a new carburetor."

3

Supporting details explain the category "gas station mechanic."

Supporting details explain the "gadgeteer."

The gadgeteer is a study in improvisation. His command of theory is good, his experience is adequate, but his application is dubious. He generally has a nearly sufficient number of tools, but he relies on tape, string, and wire. His

4

Topic sentence of fourth paragraph.

basic theory of operation reads as follows: "If something doesn't work, it may as well be experimented upon; the worst that can happen is it gets broken, which is what is wrong in the first place. A car will run without many of its components." His generally does. When speaking of his repairs, he usually sounds slightly doubtful: "All I did was twist this strut around so this thing off an old Ford truck would fit, and now it runs like a top. I think." Of the three groups, this type has the most fun with his car.

5   My best friend, Robert, has gone through all three stages, which shows that placement in a category is not permanent. In fact, one may change categories at any time for any reason, and, in the case of the putterer and the gas station mechanic, that would be a good thing to do.

Topic sentence of final paragraph. Note important link to thesis sentence.

FOR WRITING OR DISCUSSION

1. What is the thesis of the paper?
2. Do the topic sentences give you a good idea of the nature of each type of mechanic? Why, or why not?
3. Which type of mechanic is the best? In what paragraph is this type described? Should he have been described earlier? Why, or why not?
4. Does the audience for the paper need to know much about cars to appreciate the descriptions of each type? Why, or why not?
5. What does the topic sentence of the last paragraph contribute to your impression of the three types?

COLLABORATIVE LEARNING

Form groups and examine the following short paragraphs, all of which lack a topic sentence. As a group, develop a logical topic sentence for each. Then, report your topic sentence and compare it with those written by other groups.

1. Jason's room is always in a shambles because he never bothers to pick up after himself. His clothes, schoolbooks, and other papers are on the floor, on his bed, and every place else. He never bothers to take dishes back to the kitchen. He just lets them pile up, and he won't lift a finger

to tidy up his room until he is literally threatened. Jason is so lazy that when he is watching television, rather than change the channel, he'll just watch the same station all evening, even if he doesn't like the programs. He even walks around with his shoes untied because he is too lazy to bend over and tie them. Sometimes I think he may be too lazy to breathe.

2. Bigfoot, for example, has unusual eating and drinking habits. Instead of eating his own dry cat food, he eats the dog's food. He eats my mother's plants and gets on top of the table to drink tea from a cup when he thinks no one is looking. Besides his peculiar eating and drinking habits, Bigfoot has weird physical features. He has six toes on each of his front paws. He's also cross-eyed. And talk about crazy behavior! Bigfoot behaves more strangely than any other cat I've met. He chases dogs off the porch, wrestles with the family dog, and bites and chases his own tail. The crazy cat can't even climb a tree.

3. Many students enter college with poor reading and writing skills. During their first year of college they need special courses designed to elevate their language competence, although they should have achieved a reasonably high level in high school. In addition, teachers often criticize first-year college students for their inability to think critically. What, college teachers wonder, have students done during four years of high school? What books have they read? What writing have they done? Have they not analyzed books, films, events?

Writing Transitions

Another way to help readers follow your thoughts is to use **transitions**, words or phrases that show the logical connections between ideas. Transitional words like *and, but, however, therefore, next,* and *finally* act as signals. They say to a reader, "Here's an additional point," or "A contrast is coming up," or "Now, I'm drawing a conclusion." Transitions make connections between ideas clear and therefore easy to follow. Consider, for example, the following pairs of sentences.

Awkward: My nephew is a brat. I love him.

Better: My nephew is a brat, *but* I love him.

Awkward: The magician showed the audience that the hat was empty. He pulled a rabbit from it.

Better: *First* the magician showed the audience that the hat was empty. *Then* he pulled a rabbit from it.

Here are some examples of transitions.

Common Transitional Expressions

To show space relations

above, adjacent to, against, alongside, around, at a distance from, at the, below, beside, beyond, encircling, far off, forward, from the, in front of, in the rear, inside, near the back, near the end, nearby, next to, on, over, surrounding, there, through the, to the left, to the right, up front

To show time relations

afterward, at last, before, earlier, first, former, formerly, further, furthermore, immediately, in the first place, in the interval, in the meantime, in the next place, in the last, later on, latter, meanwhile, next, now, often, once, previously, second, simultaneously, sometime later, subsequently, suddenly, then, therefore, third, today, tomorrow, until now, when, years ago, yesterday

To indicate something added to what has come before

again, also, and, and then, besides, further, furthermore, in addition, last, likewise, moreover, next, nor, too

To give examples or to intensify points

after all, as an example, certainly, for example, for instance, indeed, in fact, in truth, it is true, of course, specifically, that is

To show similarities

alike, in the same way, like, likewise, resembling, similarly

To show contrasts

after all, although, but, conversely, differ(s) from, difference, different, dissimilar, even though, granted, however, in contrast, in spite of, nevertheless, notwithstanding, on the contrary, on the other hand, otherwise, still, though, unlike, while this may be true, yet

To indicate cause and effect

accordingly, as a result, because, consequently, hence, since, then, therefore, thus

To conclude or summarize

finally, in brief, in conclusion, in other words, in short, in summary, that is, to summarize

I do not need to tell you how important the election is. *Nor* do I need to remind you to vote tomorrow.

Laura is always on one kind of diet or another. *Yet* she never seems to lose any weight.

Medicare can be a blessing to elderly people. The difficulty of filling out all the required forms, *however*, sometimes makes them wonder how blessed they are.

I have been a thrifty stay-at-home most of my life. It was a surprise to my children, *therefore*, when I went off to Europe first class last summer.

Avoiding Too Many Transitions

Used sensibly, transitions contribute to the smoothness of your paper. However, too many transitions can be as distressing to a reader as too few. This example overuses transitional words:

The children wanted to see the animals in my woods. *However*, they made too much noise. *In the first place*, all twenty of them shouted. *Moreover*, they screamed. *Furthermore*, they threw rocks into the streams. *Therefore*, birds, frogs, even bugs went rushing to the hills. *As a result*, the children saw no animals. *Nor* should they have expected to see animals after making so much noise. *Nevertheless*, I was sorry that they thought they might see what only hours of silence and days of watching ever bring to sight.

Now look at how the paragraph actually appears in *The Inland Island* by Josephine Johnson:

"Where are all your animals?" the little children cried, running . . . through the woods—twenty little children, panting, shouting, screaming, throwing rocks into the streams. Birds, frogs, even bugs went rushing to the hills. How sad that the children thought they might see what only hours of silence, days of watching ever bring to sight.

Clearly, Johnson's paragraph is far better. All those transitions in the first paragraph do not help it flow; rather, they get in the way. Use transitions, then, but use them only to signal a logical connection that would not otherwise be obvious.

Using Sentences and Paragraphs as Transitions

In making connections between ideas, you are not limited to single words and short phrases. Often the topic sentence serves both as a transition and as an indicator of the central idea of a paragraph.

Besides making life difficult for his parents, Charles sent his first-grade teacher home with a nightly headache.

Although the Puritans observed a strict code of behavior, their lives were often filled with great joy.

In sentences of this kind, the introductory adverbial phrase or clause (shown here in italics) points back to the preceding paragraph to provide a transition. At the same time, the rest of the sentence points forward to the subject matter of the paragraph for which it is the topic sentence.

Occasionally, an entire paragraph may serve as a transition. It's sometimes a good idea to stop—at a logical point, of course—and sum up what you've said so far before going on to another point. The good **transitional paragraph**, like the transitional topic sentence, points back to what has gone before and points forward to what is yet to come. Note the successful use of these transitional paragraphs:

> Thus, granting Professor Maly time to do a thorough and conscientious new edition of her book will add to her professional standing, bring a bit of valuable attention and some money to the college, and result in a book more helpful than ever in teaching students how to write clear English. These considerations are, I think, justification for the professional leave she has requested, but I have other reasons for recommending that her request for leave be granted.

> So much for the preparation of the surface. Now we are ready to paint.

> Thus, Jackie Robinson had to confront a long tradition of bigotry in the major leagues. How did he meet this challenge?

> With all these arguments in favor of state-run lotteries, opponents of such lotteries can still raise some valid points.

EXERCISE   See the excerpt from John Fousek's paper on page 118. How would you revise the over-coordinated sentence?

Developing Paragraphs: Unity and Coherence

In addition to leading your reader from one paragraph to another, you need to be certain that the paragraphs themselves are logically and adequately developed. A **paragraph**—a group of related sentences developing a single topic—must be unified, coherent, and complete.

Paragraph Unity

A paragraph must be **unified**—that is, all the sentences in the paragraph must develop one idea, the one contained in the topic sentence. Anything that doesn't contribute to the idea should be omitted from the paragraph. One of the following two paragraphs appears exactly as it was written by Lewis Thomas, a skilled essayist whose paragraphs are beautifully unified. Which paragraph do you think Thomas wrote?

Paragraph 1

[1]Viewed from the distance of the moon, the astonishing thing about the earth . . . is that it is alive. [2]The photographs show the dry, pounded surface of the moon in the foreground, dead as an old bone. [3]Aloft, floating free beneath the moist, gleaming membrane of bright blue sky, is the rising earth, the only exuberant thing in this part of the cosmos. [4]If you could look long enough, you would see the swirling of the great drifts of white cloud, covering and uncovering the half-hidden masses of land. [5]If you had been looking for a very long, geologic time, you could have seen the continents themselves in motion, drifting apart on their crustal plates, held afloat by the fire beneath. [6]It has the organized, self-contained look of a live creature, full of information, marvelously skilled in handling the sun.

Paragraph 2

[1]Viewed from the distance of the moon, the astonishing thing about the earth . . . is that it is alive. [2]The great technological advances that made it possible for man to walk on the moon also made it possible to send photographs back to earth. [3]Such are the miracles of modern science that you sat in your living room and watched the astronauts romp, enjoying their gravity-less freedom. [4]Soon, however, you saw something much more important, the photographs of the moon. [5]The photographs show the dry, pounded surface of the moon in the foreground, dead as an old bone. [6]It is so dead you marvel that poets for centuries have hymned its praises. [7]On the other hand, aloft, floating free beneath the moist, gleaming membrane of bright blue sky, is the rising earth, the only exuberant thing in this part of the cosmos. [8]If you could look long enough, you would see the swirling of the great drifts of white cloud, covering and uncovering the half-hidden masses of land. [9]If you had been looking for a very long, geologic time, you could have seen the continents themselves in motion, drifting apart on their crustal plates, held afloat by the fire beneath. [10]It has the organized, self-contained look of a live creature, full of information, marvelously skilled in handling the sun.

The first paragraph is the paragraph taken from Lewis Thomas. In the second—and longer—one, sentences 2, 3, 4, and 6 obviously do not advance Thomas's idea that the earth is alive. Instead, they distract the reader, and the paragraph loses its central idea in the confusion.

TIPS for Achieving Paragraph Unity

■ **Give each paragraph a controlling idea by means of a topic sentence.**

■ **Check each sentence in a paragraph to see that it supports the main idea.**

■ **Revise or eliminate any sentence that distracts from the main idea.**

Paragraph Coherence

A paragraph must have **coherence**; it must stick together. This means the sentences must be smoothly integrated. You can't expect your readers to follow your thought if the sentences do not follow some intelligible order. Is the following paragraph orderly? Can you follow the writer's thought?

> Yesterday was one big disaster. When I found my right rear tire flat as a board, I laid my head on the steering wheel and wept. The burned bacon didn't help, either; especially after that cold shower, I needed a hot meal. I had worked so hard on my paper I didn't think it was fair that the professor gave me a "D" on it. Sleeping through the alarm always starts my day off wrong. And now I've got to write a 20-page term paper for history. I should have stayed in bed.

Using a simple **chronological order** can make this paragraph coherent:

> Yesterday was one big disaster. I slept through the alarm. Late, I rushed to the bathroom. No more hot water. Teeth chattering from a cold shower, I decided to cook a hot breakfast—and burned the bacon. I gulped down some cold shredded wheat and dashed to my car. By running two traffic lights, I made it to my English class on time and eagerly waited for the professor to return our papers. I had worked hard and was sure I had made at least a "B," if not an "A." Then I saw a big red "D" at the top of my paper. It didn't seem fair. I went on to my history class, and the professor assigned a 20-page term paper. I decided to cut my remaining classes and go home. When I got to my car and found the right rear tire flat as a board, I laid my head on the steering wheel and wept. I should have stayed in bed.

You can achieve order in a number of other ways as well. One of these lies in the use of **space order**—from left to right, from top to bottom, or, as in the following example, from near to far.

> It was a rimy morning, and very damp. I had seen the damp lying on the outside of my little window, as if some goblin had been crying there all night, and using the window for a pocket-handkerchief. Now I saw the damp lying on the bare hedges and spare grass, like a coarser sort of spiders' webs; hanging itself from twig to twig and blade to blade. On every rail and gate, wet lay clammy, and the marsh-mist was so thick, that the wooden finger on the post directing people to our village—a direction which they never accepted, for they never came there—was invisible to me until I was quite close under it. . . . The mist was heavier yet when I got out upon the marshes, so that instead of my running at everything, everything seemed to run at me. . . .
>
> —Charles Dickens, *Great Expectations*

You can sometimes **enumerate reasons** by listing them in regard to an action or belief (italics added):

> I have sought love, *first*, because it brings ecstasy—ecstasy so great that I could often have sacrificed all the rest of life for a few hours of this joy. I have sought it,

next, because it relieves loneliness—that terrible loneliness in which one shivering consciousness looks over the rim of the world into the cold unfathomable lifeless abyss. I have sought it, *finally*, because in the union of love I have seen, in a mystic miniature, the prefiguring vision of the heaven that saints and poets have imagined. That is what I sought, and though it might seem too good for human life, that is what—at last—I have found.

—Bertrand Russell, "What I Have Lived For"

You can give coherence to a paragraph by means of **cause and effect**:

This sentiment of retaliation is, of course, exactly what impels most offenders to do what they do. Except for racketeers, robbers, and professional criminals, the men who are arrested, convicted, and sentenced are usually out to avenge a wrong, assuage a sense of injury, or correct an injustice as they see it. Their victims are individuals whom they believe to be assailants, false friends, rivals, unfaithful spouses, cruel parents—or symbolic figures representing these individuals.

—Karl Menninger, *The Crime of Punishment*

Perhaps one of the most useful logical relations you can use to achieve coherence within a paragraph is the **comparison** of one thing to another:

In science fiction, which is the literature of extrapolation, there is to be found the recurrent theme of the omniscient computer which ultimately takes over the ordering of human life and affairs. Is this possible? I believe it is not; but I also believe that the arguments commonly advanced to refute this possibility are the wrong ones. . . . It is said, for example, that computers [unlike humans] "only do what they are told," that they have to be programmed for every computation they undertake. But I do not believe that I was born with an innate ability to solve quadratic equations or to identify common members of the British flora; I, too, had to be programmed for these activities, but I happened to call my programmers by different names, such as "schoolteacher," "lecturer," or "professor."

—W. T. Williams, "Computers as Botanists"

You can achieve coherence by using **parallel structure**. Note the use of semicolons to achieve parallelism in this paragraph, all written to support the word *black* at the beginning.

Black: the dead locust limb that scrapes my bedroom window; crows, hundreds of them, perched like clothespins in the branches of a bare tree; the crooked lines of tar that fill the cracks on a concrete highway; the tip of Buddy's nose when it is wet; seven black swans, floating on a leaf-flecked pond; twisted Italian tobies in a yellow box; leeches squirming in a white earthen jar; burned gunpowder from my shotgun on the flannel cleaning rag; the lacquered Eaglerock biplane at Rogers Field; tiny cloves stuck in a baked Virginia ham; licorice in elastic sticks and lozenges and squares; cloud shadows on fields of ripening grain.

Another strategy for achieving coherence is **repetition**. In the paragraph below by Mark Twain, the words "I know" help integrate the sentences smoothly.

I know how a prize watermelon looks when it is sunning its fat rotundity among pumpkin vines and "simblins"; I know how to tell when it is ripe without "plugging" it; I know how inviting it looks when it is cooling itself in a tub of water under the bed, waiting; I know how it looks when it lies on the table in the sheltered great floor space between house and kitchen, and the children gathered for the sacrifice and their mouths watering; I know the crackling sound it makes when the carving knife enters its end, and I can see the split fly along in front of the blade as the knife cleaves its way to the other end; I can see its halves fall apart and display the rich red meat and the black seeds, and the heart standing up, a luxury fit for the elect; I know how a boy looks behind a yard-long slice of that melon, and I know how he feels; for I have been there. I know the taste of the watermelon which has been honestly come by, and I know the taste of the watermelon which has been acquired by art.

—Mark Twain, *Autobiography*

Pronouns help achieve coherence. They refer readers to a previously idetified noun (the antecedent) and help the writer connect the ideas without having to name the nouns again and again.

The Deadbeat Dad has emerged as our principal cultural model for ex-fathers, for obviously failed fathers. As a cultural category, the Deadbeat Dad has become our primary symbol of the growing failure of fatherhood in our society. We demonize him in part because he reminds us of our fatherlessness. He represents loss. He forces us to reduce our expectations. Consequently, we vilify him, we threaten him—we demand that he pay—largely because he so clearly embodies the contemporary collapse of good-enough fatherhood.

—David Blankenhorn, *The Deadbeat Dad*

Use any of these methods—or any others that work—to achieve coherence. The important thing is to achieve it—to make the relation between and among sentences clear to the reader.

 TIPS   for Achieving Paragraph Coherence

■ **Be sure that your sentences follow each other logically.**

■ **Use appropriate—but not excessive—transitions.**

■ **Order details appropriately through chronological or spatial order or though a list.**

■ **Show causes and effects clearly.**

■ **Compare one thing to another.**

■ **Use parallel structure.**

■ **Use repetition.**

■ **Link ideas with pronouns.**

Writing a Strong Conclusion

A good **conclusion** gives a sense of finality, which you can achieve in one of several ways.

The easiest way to conclude a paper is to mention again its major ideas. The following example concludes a paper in which the writer explains membership in a book club:

> Interesting reading, the exchange of ideas, and new friends—these were my reasons for joining a book club. I have not been disappointed.

Some conclusions merely restate the thesis, although in different words to avoid monotony.

> There's an explanation for everything, it's true, but some explanations are more readily acceptable than others. That's the way it is.
>
> —George E. Condon

Some conclusions interpret the significance of the material presented in the body of the paper.

> Since these personality characteristics depend on the growth of the layers of the little egg from which the person developed, they are very difficult to change.
>
> Nevertheless, it is important for the individual to know about these types, so that he can have at least an inkling of what to expect from those around him, and can make allowances for the different kinds of human nature, and so that he can become aware of and learn to control his own natural tendencies, which may sometimes guide him into making the same mistakes over and over again in handling his difficulties.
>
> —Eric Berne

An anecdote sometimes effectively concludes a paper. Following is the conclusion to a paper about the rewards given Dr. Jonas Salk for his polio vaccine:

> Probably the greatest tribute Dr. Salk received was unwittingly paid by a small boy whose father, having shown his son the research center, told him that Dr. Salk invented the polio vaccine. The boy, looking puzzled, said, "Daddy, what's polio?"

Quotations and questions can serve to conclude papers. Both devices are used in this conclusion to a paper urging support of the United Torch Drive:

> Samuel Johnson defined a patron as "one who looks with unconcern on a man struggling for life in the water, and when he has reached ground encumbers him with help." Shall we be merely patrons of the needy?

Some of the most effective conclusions attempt to set a broader, more general context for the topic. Such a conclusion helps the reader see that the limited topic you have advanced has relevance beyond your immediate concerns in the paper. By developing a larger application for the topic, you provide a new significance for it.

A student writer produced this thesis sentence in an effort to show the different shades of meaning for the word "excitement":

> <u>Excitement means one thing to a seven-year-old and something quite different to a girl in her teens</u>.

In the first body paragraph the writer tells of the excitement she felt on a day her whole third grade class visited her house to see the backyard cherry tree in bloom. In the next paragraphs she tells of a political demonstration she participated in and the excitement and fear of being jostled in a crowd and then knocked to the ground by people fleeing the police. Here is the conclusion to the essay:

> In both instances I experienced excitement; one moment simple and innocent, and the other complex and explosive. Since such different situations aroused the same kind of emotion, I wonder if our emotions are reliable at all until we have a full chance to test them with time and experience. I have to laugh when I hear my thirteen-year-old neighbor say she loves her high school boyfriend. Does she have any idea of what the word means? How does she know it will mean the same for her next week? Love is an emotion, and to rely on an early or untested experience for the definition for me is ridiculous. Still, many young people marry at seventeen or eighteen, claiming deep love for their partners. Then, of course, in too many cases, the divorce courts spring into action just a short time after. It seems to me that decisions based on emotions must be very carefully made so that we understand the full range of meaning we attach to any special feeling.
>
> *—Sarah Fogel*

The conclusion establishes a new, general context; the writer's experiences lead her to believe that only maturity allows us true perspective on emotion. The essay itself is about excitement; the conclusion deals with an altogether different emotion, love; yet the example in the conclusion works very well to help the writer make her larger point.

 TIPS for Writing a Strong Conclusion

- ■ **Refer to the major ideas in the paper.**
- ■ **Restate the thesis in different words.**
- ■ **Interpret the significance of the ideas presented.**
- ■ **Use a lively anecdote.**
- ■ **Present a quotation.**
- ■ **Raise a question.**
- ■ **Establish a new context for the topic.**

Forms of conclusions, like forms of introductions, vary. All conclusions, however, should relate to what has gone before. Furthermore, all conclusions should be consistent in tone with the body of the paper. Don't let a strong argument dwindle away because of a weak conclusion. If Patrick Henry, for example, had concluded his speech to the House of Burgesses with, "Thus, gentlemen, now that you have heard my arguments, I am sure you will agree with me that we should oppose the British crown," his words would not have been remembered. Instead, he said:

> Is life so dear, or peace so sweet, as to be purchased at the price of chains and slavery? Forbid it, Almighty God! I know not what course others may take; but as for me, give me liberty or give me death!

Brevity is essential in good conclusions. Make the important points in the body of your paper. The conclusion should briefly drive the points home.

EXERCISE For the draft of your own paper, examine the introduction, body, and conclusion in light of the guidelines explored in this chapter. What changes, additions, or deletions should you make in the draft? Revise your paper and submit it to your instructor and classmates for their comments and suggestions.

CHAPTER 6

Revising, Editing, and Proofreading Your Paper

- Peer Review: Learning from Other Students
- One Student Writing: Revising and Editing
- Proofreading
- Putting It All Together
- One Student Writing: Final Draft
- A Brief Note on Style

As good as John Fousek's first draft is (see Chapter 2, page 46), like all papers, it needs revising and editing. These two interrelated terms identify critical stages in the development of a successful paper.

When you **revise**, you rethink the ideas and concepts in your paper and change them to reflect your new thoughts. Revision means literally *looking again*. In revising your paper, you want to present and explore any fresh insights you've developed, make necessary changes in focus and direction for your topic, and add essential details. When you **edit**, you make changes in language and expression. You reshape sentences for clarity and emphasis, you improve the style, you attend to appropriate word choice, diction, and sentence structure. As a specialized part of editing, **proofreading** (see pages 119–121) allows you to concentrate on often overlooked errors in spelling, grammar, and punctuation. Frequently, the efforts work hand in hand, especially as you draw closer to your final draft; you revise and edit at the same time.

In your first effort to produce another draft, focus on the content of your essay. Try to make your paper as clear as possible. Check on organization and development of ideas. Examine your introduction and conclusion. Consider the unity, coherence, and completeness of your paragraphs. Where should you add information? What unexplored feature of your topic could you open for your readers' advantage? How could you connect related thoughts in different parts of your paper?

Peer Review: Learning from Other Students

John shaped his first draft by working first with another student in a peer-critiquing session in class.

Some teachers build peer review sessions into regular writing instruction. In **peer review**, you and your classmates comment on each other's drafts. Sometimes you work in small groups and offer comments and suggestions orally. Or, you can write comments directed at specific questions posed by fellow writers or by your teacher on a peer-response checklist.

Following the instructor's guidelines for using a peer-response guide or checklist, the person who read John's paper gave him this written evaluation.

Peer Evaluation Guide and Student Response

1. What is the main point of the paper?

   You are trying to show what annoys you about your roommate, that he doesn't close things.

2. What is the best part of the paper?

   The bathroom examples—funny! I've had toe shampoos, too! I also like the open drawers part.

3. What recommendations for improvement can you make?

   a. *Add more details. Show some of the stuff in the drawers—how they're dumped in. Maybe describe the bathroom, too?*

   b. *I agree with your question—watch trite and slang words. "Like a bomb hit it" must go!*

These comments from one of John's classmates will be very helpful as John attends to the next draft. Certainly, the paper could benefit from more precisely stated details. And, as the student reviewer suggests, the writing is too conversational. John thought more about his topic and the comments and suggestions his classmate provided. Another friend and John's teacher offered further insights about the first draft.

COLLABORATIVE LEARNING

Exchange drafts with another student in the class and write comments about the student's paper. Ask the other student to write comments on your paper as well. The purpose of your comments is to help the writer produce the next draft. Focus most of your comments on the questions about thought, content, and essay form. Do not make extensive comments about errors in grammar, spelling, and punctuation.

One Student Writing: Revising and Editing

Back at the computer, John developed his next draft, shown following.

INTERMEDIATE DRAFT

My Roommate

1   Jim and I have been sharing an apartment for the last two years and we get along pretty well. We are both students. We both work. We don't spend a lot of time together. When we are together, we cooperate with chores. Jim does the cooking because he's good at it, *and* I do the cleaning. Jim is fun to be with and he has many good qualities. He is honest, generous, and a fun guy. We had a good relationship over the last two years. I like Jim very much but he has one habit that I see as an annoying shortcoming. Jim doesn't close things.

2   For example, he never, or almost never, *needed?* closes drawers or closet doors. I may be compulsive about being neat but he's a complete slob. It never seems to have entered his mind to organize a drawer.

3   His clothes closet is just as messy, he does the same thing in the kitchen when he's cooking. If he'd organize the drawer in the first place the noisy silverware wouldn't bother me. Spoons and knives clink together as he pokes through the nearest open drawer looking for things in the mess. Our apartment usually looks like a messy rummage sale. I really get embarrassed when any of my friends visit and they see the place looking so messy.

4   I'm bothered even more by Jim's failure to close bathroom objects, for example, he never closes the shampoo cap. This makes me lose my ~~cool~~ composure more than anything. When I'm showering, I always grab the shampoo bottle by the cap. *a* loose cap always results in shampoo on my toes and not in my hair, which at this point is soaking wet. Because I am economically minded, moneywise watching a green puddle of shampoo going down the drain wasted every day really upsets me. Jim forgets to close the bathroom door after using the facilities while I shower. The bathroom has grown warm and steamy during the cou*r*se of my shower, the cold morning air chills me. Jim's thoughtlessness is very annoying.

5   Jim is such a great guy, and I know his failure to close things is a minor bad habbit, and I try to overlook it. However, it does tend to irritate me, especially when cold air hits me right after I'm out of the shower.

EXERCISE

1. How does the revised first paragraph compare and contrast with the first paragraph in the earlier draft on page 46? What improvements has John made? What further suggestions would you make for revision and editing?
2. Where else in the essay has John made significant changes from first draft to intermediate draft? What other recommendations would you make?

No doubt you noted the advances in John's paper. He tightened the introduction and sharpened the thesis sentence. (See Chapter 5, pages 94–98, and Chapter 3, pages 52–55.) He eliminated some colloquial expressions. He provided some concrete language; "a green puddle of shampoo" is a good image.

Improvements aside, you probably saw as well several areas for John to explore in further revision and editing. John's paper would benefit significantly from even more sensory language (see page 56). In paragraph 1, better coordination and subordination would link related thoughts and eliminate the bumpy ride from sentence to sentence. In addition, some of John's sentences still ramble a bit and ideas are repeated, as in the last few sentences of the third paragraph. Note how many times John refers to messy conditions; the repetitive language needs revision and editing here. Some of the ideas throughout the essay should be reordered or more smoothly connected (or both), and some of the paragraphs should be joined. John's first and last paragraphs, vital elements in any paper, could be strengthened (see Chapter 5).

Although John made handwritten changes to correct some mistakes, his sentences contain many structural errors—particularly run-ons and fragments. In the revision process, some of these errors may disappear simply because new or reorganized sentences will replace some of those with mistakes. Nevertheless, a pattern of errors emerges here, and John must address them as he revises, edits, and proofreads in successive drafts. The "Strategy Checklist: Revising and Editing Your Drafts" on pages 120–121 will help you consider revising and editing strategies as you develop your paper.

Learning from Your Instructor's Comments

Your instructor may read an early draft of your writing and (or) your final copy. In either case, she no doubt will use a system of marking symbols (like those at the end of this book), as well as marginal comments and final summary remarks to suggest changes and corrections for you to consider. Pay careful attention to any comments you receive. When you revise your work again, think through your instructor's suggestions as you make the changes and corrections your instructor indicates. If you are responding to comments on a final draft, you should answer any questions and rewrite any segments you've been asked to.

Reproduced on page 118 are the last two paragraphs of John Fousek's intermediate draft, together with his teacher's marginal comments and symbols. Note especially his instructor's summary comments at the end of the paper.

INTERMEDIATE DRAFT WITH INSTRUCTOR'S COMMENTS

cs

I'm bothered even more by Jim's failure to close bathroom objects, for example, he never closes the shampoo cap. This makes me lose my good composure more than anything. When I'm showering. I always grab the shampoo bottle by the cap. A loose cap always results in shampoo on my toes and not in my hair, which at this point is soaking wet. Because I am economically minded, moneywise watching a green puddle of shampoo going down the drain wasted every day really upsets me. Jim forgets to close the bathroom door after using the facilities while I shower. The bathroom has grown warm and steamy during the course of my shower, the cold morning air chills me. Jim's thoughtlessness is very annoying. *cs*

frag sp
The "wise" ending is questionable in making adjectives. Do you need "moneywise" at all here?

Too much coordination in this sentence. Revise?

Good! You corrected a run-on

Jim is such a great guy, and I know his failure to close things is a minor bad habit, and I try to overlook it. However, it does tend to irritate me, especially when cold air hits me right after I'm out of the shower.

You've certainly made Jim's habits real for us. Everybody knows an "I don't close things" person. (I admit it —I'm one myself!) Limiting the topic to one specific shortcoming focuses the paper well. I like sensory images like "banging silverware" (par. 2) and "warm and steamy" (next-to-last par.).

Consider these points as you revise:

1. Provide more details in par. 2. Show us the mess in the drawers. What's in them? What do they look like?

2. Slang and colloquial expressions can be bothersome. Don't get too stuffy now, but do strive for a slightly more formal writing style. Look especially at "pretty well "and "fun guy."

3. Smooth out transitions and logic as I've indicated in the margin.

4. Proofread carefully for those run-ons, comma splices, and fragments— these can be major problems on a final draft. See relevant sections in the Handbook (at the end of <u>Student's Book</u>) for review and practice.

5. The conclusion lacks impact. Can you interpret the significance of your experience with Jim? Go beyond the immediate experiences you share with the readers here.

Good try for an intermediate draft, John. Revise! Revise! Revise!

EXERCISE   Read the excerpt from John Fousek's paper on page 118 and make the grammatical and spelling changes that respond to the marginal symbols written by John's teacher.

Proofreading

Proofreading is the part of the editing process in which you reread your paper particularly for errors. This step in the writing process is best accomplished at two stages.

First, proofread your draft after you make revisions and edit before you produce the final copy for submission. At this point, check for problems in grammar, syntax, spelling, and usage. Proofread the paper a second time just before you turn it in to catch mistakes you may have overlooked. At this stage, you can make minor revisions neatly on the final copy. However, if you discover major problems that require extensive reworking, you should produce another copy. Do not submit for evaluation a paper containing numerous changes and corrections.

You'll find the following pointers useful as you proofread.

TIPS   for Careful Proofreading

- **When you proofread, read slowly.**   Your purpose is to check for errors, and quick readings make errors hard to find.

- **Proofread after you have made revisions and editing changes.**   Do not try to revise and proofread at the same time. Except for glaring errors, which you should correct as you find them, revision and editing call for concentration on thought and meaning. If you attend to errors when you revise, you won't be focusing on issues related to the content and clarity of your paper. Thus, treat proofreading as a separate activity, after you're satisfied with your writing and revising.

- **Be familiar with the types of errors that you tend to make and keep them in mind as you proofread.**   If you tend to write run-on sentences or fragments, proofread your paper for those mistakes especially. Thoughtful students keep a record of their own errors and consult it before proofreading. At the very least, you should look over any comments and corrections that your instructor or your peers have written on other papers you wrote.

- **If you use a computer, be sure to remove wrong words or extra letters when you make spelling changes.**   Also remember to reformat your text if necessary and to examine your paragraphing: All paragraphs must be indented. Use the cursor as a proofreading aid by moving it from word to word as you proofread; this step will help you slow down your reading.

- **If you must make minor revisions on a final copy, use blue or black ink, not pencil.**   Cross out errors neatly with one line and insert changes directly above the mistake or in the margin, if you need more room. Remember, extensive changes on a draft mean that you must do another draft before submitting it. Use a caret (^) for insertions.

She admonished _^brother for being late.
                      her

Putting It All Together

In Part One, you've examined many key features in developing a paper for your writing course and have done numerous exercises designed to help you produce and revise a draft. Since your revised copy will be the draft you submit for evaluation, take time to review the following checklist as you rework your drafts. The tips are stated as general questions to ask yourself as you revise, edit, and proofread.

We've devised similar checklists, more specific for the focused writing task at hand, for each chapter in Part Two, "Methods of Development."

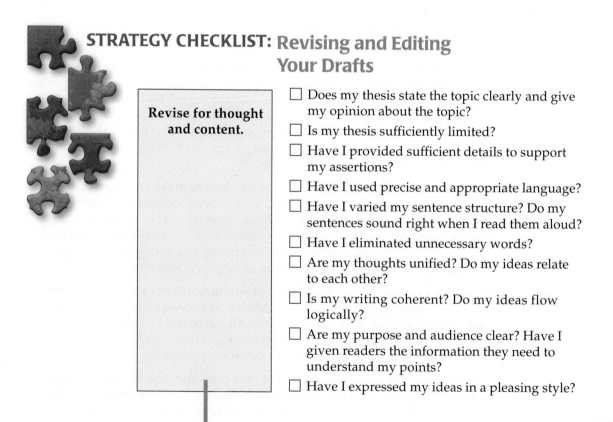

STRATEGY CHECKLIST: Revising and Editing Your Drafts

Revise for thought and content.

☐ Does my thesis state the topic clearly and give my opinion about the topic?

☐ Is my thesis sufficiently limited?

☐ Have I provided sufficient details to support my assertions?

☐ Have I used precise and appropriate language?

☐ Have I varied my sentence structure? Do my sentences sound right when I read them aloud?

☐ Have I eliminated unnecessary words?

☐ Are my thoughts unified? Do my ideas relate to each other?

☐ Is my writing coherent? Do my ideas flow logically?

☐ Are my purpose and audience clear? Have I given readers the information they need to understand my points?

☐ Have I expressed my ideas in a pleasing style?

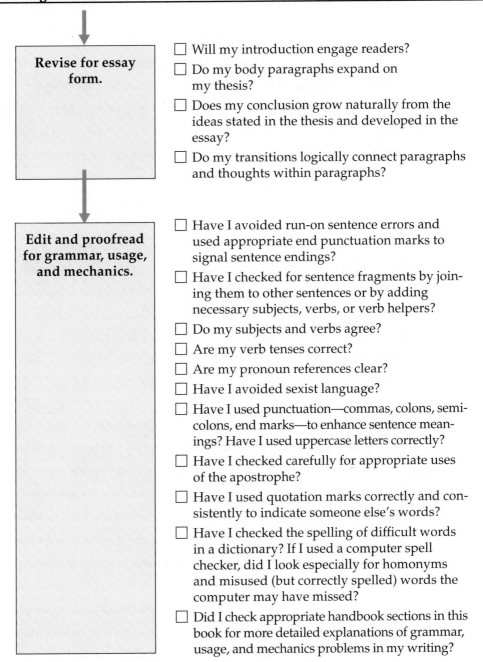

Revise for essay form.

☐ Will my introduction engage readers?

☐ Do my body paragraphs expand on my thesis?

☐ Does my conclusion grow naturally from the ideas stated in the thesis and developed in the essay?

☐ Do my transitions logically connect paragraphs and thoughts within paragraphs?

Edit and proofread for grammar, usage, and mechanics.

☐ Have I avoided run-on sentence errors and used appropriate end punctuation marks to signal sentence endings?

☐ Have I checked for sentence fragments by joining them to other sentences or by adding necessary subjects, verbs, or verb helpers?

☐ Do my subjects and verbs agree?

☐ Are my verb tenses correct?

☐ Are my pronoun references clear?

☐ Have I avoided sexist language?

☐ Have I used punctuation—commas, colons, semi-colons, end marks—to enhance sentence meanings? Have I used uppercase letters correctly?

☐ Have I checked carefully for appropriate uses of the apostrophe?

☐ Have I used quotation marks correctly and consistently to indicate someone else's words?

☐ Have I checked the spelling of difficult words in a dictionary? If I used a computer spell checker, did I look especially for homonyms and misused (but correctly spelled) words the computer may have missed?

☐ Did I check appropriate handbook sections in this book for more detailed explanations of grammar, usage, and mechanics problems in my writing?

One Student Writing: Final Draft

After reading his paper over several times, discussing it with friends and his writing teacher, making revisions, and producing new drafts, John finally submitted the following paper to his instructor.

FINAL DRAFT

My Roommate, Jim

1   My roommate, Jim, and I have shared a small apartment for the past two years. On the whole, we get along very well. We are both students, and we both work, so we don't spend much time together; but when we do, we cooperate. Jim, who is good at it, does most of the cooking; I do most of the cleaning. We find the arrangement satisfactory. And I like Jim. He is generous, witty, honest. Our two-year association has, for the most part, been a good one. But Jim has one shortcoming that irritates me: He doesn't close things.

2   Jim, for example, almost never closes a drawer or a closet door, and his failure to do so is often a source of embarrassment to me. The problem is that I am compulsively neat, and Jim, I'm sorry to say, is a slob. It seems never to have occurred to him that the contents of a drawer could be organized. When he does his laundry, he just empties his bag of clean clothes into a drawer—white socks, underwear, a rainbow of t-shirts with college crests, pajamas, graying handkerchiefs. When the drawer is full, he begins filling the next one. Then when he needs clean socks or a shirt, he rolls the contents of the drawer around until he finds what he wants, often leaving rejected items hanging over the edge of the drawer. His clothes closet is just as messy as the drawers. He does the same kinds of things in the kitchen. Spatulas, flatware, eggbeaters, knives clink together as he pokes through the nearest open drawer to find his favorite tool for beating eggs or mincing onions. If he'd organized the drawer in the first place, the rattle of kitchenware wouldn't disturb my study time before every meal. Since Jim doesn't close drawers or closets, our apartment usually looks like the site of a rummage sale at closing time. The appearance offends my neat soul and embarrasses me when friends visit us.

3   The irritation I experience because of open drawers and closets, however, is nothing compared with the irritation that Jim's failure to close things in the bathroom produces. Jim's failure to tighten the cap on the shampoo bottle, for example, causes me to completely lose my composure when I am showering. Because I am in the habit of grasping the shampoo bottle by its cap, a loose cap results in the annoyance of shampoo on my toes instead of in

my hair. And because I am a frugal sort, I hate seeing a green puddle of unused shampoo oozing down the drain each day. Jim also often fails to close the bathroom door after using the facilities while I shower. Since the bathroom has become warm and steamy during the course of my shower, the cold draft of morning air chills and distresses me, and the idea that he has been so thoughtless bothers me.

When that frigid air blasts my wet body, my irritation with Jim reaches its peak. Nevertheless, because he is such a great guy and because I know his failure to close things is, in the scheme of human problems, just a minor bad habit, I try to overlook it. I shut my mouth and take a deep breath. In fact, by learning to deal with this annoyance I think I've learned a little about how to handle the frustrations of some of my friends' strange habits in general. I keep a good sense of humor and I hold my temper. After all, I'd rather have opened closets and drawers than a door closed on friendship.

4

EXERCISE How does John's intermediate draft compare and contrast with the first draft? What advice did he take from the peer critique? What other changes did he make?

EXERCISE How does John's final draft compare and contrast with his intermediate draft? What additions has he made? How has he improved the level of detail in the intermediate draft? How has he improved the structure of his paragraphs? Where has he eliminated unnecessary words and sentences? How has he corrected grammatical errors?

A Brief Note on Style

Your paper should be readable. Of course, a polished style doesn't just happen when some English teacher calls for it, and Part Five of this book focuses on style at some length. You might find it helpful to look at that section now.

PART TWO

Methods of Development

In Part One we considered the general requirements for a good paper: It must have a limited subject, a purpose, and a thesis; it must support the thesis; and it must be organized. In Part Two we look at the requirements for particular kinds of papers.

Many writing assignments call for specific methods of development. In a psychology class, for example, you might have to **compare and contrast** psychosis and neurosis. In a history class, you might have to trace the **process** by which the Bolsheviks took power after the Russian Revolution. In a sociology class, you might have to **classify** the groups that make up a community, taking into consideration the level of income, education, taste, and social practices of each group. Each of these assignments requires a specific method of development, and Part Two of the text shows you how to meet these requirements.

Other writing assignments, though they may not call for specific methods, profit from an intelligent combination of the methods of development explored in Part Two. A definition, for instance, might require the use of comparisons, examples, and cause-and-effect methods. Thus, even though we have, for the purposes of discussion, arbitrarily established separate methods, we recognize that, more often than not, writers regularly combine these approaches. Chapter 16 examines strategies for integrating methods of development.

We also recognize that our "rules" about methods of development are not sacred, even though we often deliver them as if we believe they are. But we have discovered from our own students that at least some clearly stated guidelines are helpful. As you gain practice, you will discover the exceptions to these guidelines that work for you.

Description

When most students receive an assignment like "Write a **description** of a person, place, or thing" (a car, a wedding, a painting, or a temper tantrum), their first impulse is often to describe what the person, place, or thing looks like. Although many excellent descriptions do just that, in deciding on your subject and how to treat it, you don't need to limit your choices so severely. Most good descriptive writing appeals to the reader's senses, and sight is only one of our five senses. For example, an essay titled "Good Old Franks and Beans" would describe taste; "Nighttime Noises" would describe sound; "Real Men Don't Use Cologne" would describe smell; and "Kids Need Cuddling (and So Do I)" would stress how good it feels to be cuddled—the sense of touch. A piece of descriptive writing generally will explore more than one of the senses: The glories of franks and beans could involve sight and smell as well as taste, for example. Strong specific writing (see pages 55–58) is filled with life, and sensory appeal is likely to be built right in.

Writing Your Descriptive Paper

The following guidelines for descriptive writing should be helpful.

TIPS for Writing a Descriptive Essay

- **Don't take inventory. You must have a thesis.** Periodically, shopkeepers need to take inventory. The procedure is vital to business survival, but if you try to include every piece of information you have on your subject in a descriptive essay, you are inviting disaster.

The writer who takes inventory may begin this way:

> My friend Judy is twenty years old. She is a solid C student. She has black hair, brown eyes, and weighs 115 pounds. Her family is comfortably middle class. Judy is very nearsighted but is vain about her appearance and often does not wear her glasses. She's been my friend for many years, and I like her.

This paragraph is simply a random collection of stray descriptive facts. No logic, no principle, seems to be at work here except the desire to get everything in—to take inventory. But getting everything in is a task that has no end; if the writer feels Judy's grades are worth mentioning, why decide not to mention the titles of the books she has read over the past year? Why decide that her grades are worth mentioning in the first place—or her weight, or her eyesight, or her family? Why are twenty thousand other facts about Judy not in the paper—the presents she received on her last birthday, her height, the name of her optometrist? If the writer is only taking inventory, all facts are of equal importance, which means, in effect, that no facts are of any importance.

A descriptive essay needs a thesis. You must think of your paper not as "A Description of Judy" but as an attempt to prove that "Judy is terribly vain," or "Many people think that Judy is self-centered, but she has many fine qualities," or "Judy has no remarkable traits of any kind, and I wonder why she has been my best friend for so many years." Therefore, you must choose only the descriptive details that are connected to your thesis; if it will break your heart to omit a colorful but irrelevant detail, you must change your thesis to make the detail relevant. Sometimes, of course, a simple change in phrasing can turn a seemingly irrelevant detail into something significant, and your thesis can remain unchanged. Notice how a thesis and a few additional phrases can transform the mess about Judy into a coherent start for a potentially effective paper.

> There is nothing at all special about my friend Judy. Judy is such a completely ordinary twenty-year-old woman that I often wonder how our friendship has lasted so long and stayed so warm.
>
> Just for starters, consider these totally ordinary facts about her. Physically, she has absolutely undistinguished black hair and brown eyes, stands an average 5 feet 4 inches, and weighs an average 115 pounds. Scholastically, she is a solid C student. By solid I *mean* solid. In two years at college, I can't recall her once getting a daring C– or an exciting C+. Her family—you guessed it—is comfortably middle class, not too rich and not too poor. Even in her little flaws, Judy is just what you'd expect. Like so many people of her age, she tends to be vain about personal appearance and all too frequently tries to get by without her glasses, even though she's very nearsighted.

The important thing to remember here, then, is don't describe simply to describe. Description always serves the broader purpose identified in your thesis.

■ **Use lively, specific details.** The most effective way of communicating an immediate sense of your subject is to use specific details rooted in sensory language—color, action, sound, smell, touch, taste. Don't tell your reader that a room is old and neglected: Indicate the squeaky floorboard next to the door, the lint collected in the coils of the radiator, the window propped up with a sooty stick of wood. If you do the job with details, the sense of age and neglect will come through. The more precise the detail, the greater its potential for arousing the attention of your reader. Nothing should be beneath your notice. The condition of a man's fingernails, the name of the store where a woman buys her clothes, or a broken traffic light on a street corner can convey as much information about a man, a woman, or a neighborhood—and convey it more interestingly—than any number of generalized comments.

■ **Choose a principle of organization that presents the descriptive details in a logical sequence.** This suggestion means that you should have some way of determining what comes first and what comes next. The particular organizing principle you select makes little difference as long as it helps create a coherent paper. In describing a snowstorm, for instance, you might organize by **time,** presenting the storm from the first hesitant flakes through the massive downfall to the Christmas-card quietness at the end of the storm. In describing a landscape, you might organize by **space,** beginning with the objects farthest from the observer and working your way closer. A physical description of a person could go from top to bottom or bottom to top.

Fortunately, not all principles of organization have to be this rigid. You could build a landscape description by progressing from the most ordinary details to the least ordinary details. If the top-to-bottom approach to a description of a person strikes you as dull or inappropriate, you might organize the paper by unattractive features and attractive features or first impressions and second impressions. The important consideration is that you provide some clear principle to give structure to the paper.

Student Writing: Description

In the selection below, a student uses description to explore the relation between his father's working life and his own. Annotations in the margin point to key features of the essay, particularly the elements of description that enhance the writing.

Nick Fiscina

Dad's Disappointment

1   As a kid of fifteen, I'll never forget the first time I worked along with my father in the attic of our old house one hot summer afternoon. Dad spent most

of his life as a construction worker, and I saw then how disappointing this existence was to him.

As we worked together to finish the attic by putting up insulation on the bare wooden beams of the roof, the smell of dust and perspiration filled the air. In the large gray room bits of paint and plaster hung loose on the walls. As if in another world, Dad lifted a large black bag of insulation onto his left shoulder and lumbered to the wooden ladder. Climbing it, he raised up the insulation in his large hands, brown and scarred, and waited without a word for me to staple the substance in place. His fingers held the material firmly as the staples clicked loudly, joining the insulation to the roof beams. Dad's nails were broken and dirty and small freckles spread beneath the graying hairs on the backs of his hands. As he held the insulation without talking, streams of burning dust fell on us, covering our arms and faces, and in the curly strands of black hair that hung on Dad's forehead there was a snowy-white layer of fine powder. Although it burned and scratched me, nothing bothered Dad's toughened, tanned skin.

As I watched his grim, silent efforts, it passed through my mind that my father had a teaching degree from a university in the old country, Italy. I asked him, maybe too harshly as I think about this moment so many years ago, why he got into construction work if he had qualifications as a teacher. He remained silent for a long time. His massive arms hung at his sides and circles of sweat stained his brown shirt. After a while a voice filled with defeat broke into the dust-filled air. "Well, you see, Nicola," he said, "in life you make the best you can with what you have. I have to work with my hands to keep the family going." It really surprised me that my father should have such an attitude. This man I often hated for his angry temper and harsh words seemed very human to me. When I looked into his hard brown eyes gazing sadly past me, and watched the crow's feet at the corners wrinkle in a squint, I saw that he had accepted the life of a construction worker with disappointment in spite of success at it.

A family man myself with two young boys of my own, I've now had my fill of construction work. I earn a living at it, but I too feel its

2

Sensory details. Examples:
Sight: bare wooden beams; large hands, brown and scarred; snowy-white powder
Sound: staples clicked loudly
Smell: dust and perspiration
Touch: burned and scratched

3

4

disappointments. The conditions are harsh, the work is hard, and there is no security. I shudder to think of my sons writing an essay like this about me fifteen years from now. I can't accept my father's view of things: simply making the best you can with what you have. I want something better and more challenging, and I'm willing to sacrifice what I have to achieve it. That's why I'm enrolled in this community college course for medical technology, which, I believe, will be a more fulfilling career. Though I still nail insulation to roofbeams and do other jobs with my hands, I look forward to a better life for my family and me.

Conclusion links to introduction and thesis sentence.

FOR WRITING OR DISCUSSION

1. What is the writer's thesis? Does he keep the thesis in mind through the body of the paper? How do you know?

2. What details of the writer's father do you find particularly compelling and original? To which senses do the images you like seem to appeal?

3. How has the writer managed to convey his father's disappointment other than in the direct statement in the opening paragraph?

4. How is this essay an example of descriptive detail arranged chronologically?

5. The closing paragraph moves off the topic of the writer's father and focuses on the writer himself. What is your reaction to this conclusion? Does it violate the thesis, or does it apply the thesis to a new frame of reference? Support your opinion.

6. Write a short descriptive paper focusing on some relative who, through his or her words or actions, gave you some special insight into that person's character. Use concrete sensory detail to give the reader a snapshot of your relative.

    The student essay that follows describes a memorable place. Answer the questions after you read.

Gwendolyn Wellington

A Birth Room

At General Hospital there I lay on stark white sheets in a stark white room, only a large
white clock with black hands, a worm-eaten chair and a window in my view, as I waited with
fear for the arrival of my first born.

While the snowy January dawn rolled lazily through the window, I could see the wind
making snow drifts outside and could feel it blow crystals through the rotting window sill.
Overhead loomed a menacing light pressed to a vast white ceiling. In front of me an orderly in a
green-nylon gown cheerily imprisoned my ankles in metal stirrups. "Don't fret none honey," she
said. "You ain't the first to have a baby." I forced a smile, but then a sharp pain in my back made
me twitch. It passed in a moment although I swore I saw black spots growing on the walls.

I looked to my left as I ran my fingers over the worn leather straps that held my
wrists. The thin second hand moved swiftly on the clock near the door. It was five after
seven. Behind me the anesthetist, all in white with mask in hand, fussed with some metal
tools, and I saw his intense black eyes darting swiftly. The sudden smell of alcohol
nauseated me.

In the distance I heard moans reverberating down the corridors—moans of women in
labor. I felt reassured about this, for I was one step higher. I was in the delivery room; they
still suffered in the labor rooms. To my right Dr. Kassop paced inaudibly, his rubber shoes
sliding on the polished green tiles. Then he moved close and with warm fingers touched my
brow. How such a small thing can be so comforting! Near my feet Nurse Day bustled about
adjusting the tubes from a bottle hanging upside down on a metal stand

No sympathy for a frightened person from her, I thought. To her it was just another birth.

Then as I stared at those erupting black spots on the wall, I heard a liquid splashing.
Suddenly I felt the icy coldness of antiseptic between my thighs as a cry of "Oye!" from a
Spanish woman far off rang in my ears. A great pain made me scream and the stark white
room reeled. Was that my new baby's cry? That's all I remember. The anesthetist covered
my nose with the sharp smell of his medicine as everything went blank, my fears and the
white birth room lost in sleep.

FOR WRITING OR DISCUSSION

1. What principle of organization (see pages 108–111) has the writer followed to present the descriptive details?

2. Where are the details most effective? Where are they least effective?

3. Wellington describes an event as well as a place. What sensory details dramatize the birth of her baby?

4. What has the exact quote in paragraph 2 contributed to the essay?

5. Write a descriptive paper on a memorable place. You may choose to describe a house, a block, a school, a neighborhood, or some similar topic.

Critical Reading: Description

As with any piece that you read, you want to engage in critical reading (see Chapter 1). Observe the marginal notes in this selection. They show how the reader stayed alert to the various issues of language and content, raising questions and making comments that helped her understand the brief essay. Let the comments guide you as you think through the selections in this chapter on description.

ESMERALDA SANTIAGO

A Blanco Navidad for New Yorikans

Spanish for "White Christmas."

Sad.
Another sound. The room is alive!

Three Kings Day on January 6—major holiday in PR.

1 It's Christmas Eve in my sister Alicia's apartment in the Parkchester section of the Bronx. In the living room, her stereo plays the brassy, conga-driven rhythms of *salsa and merengue*, or the plaintive strains of Puerto Rican *aguinaldos*. The music is loud, and, unable to hold a conversation, I ask my brother to dance. Charlie leads me to the left, to the right, in circles, avoiding the other couples and our two-year-old nephew, who stands in the middle of the room bawling for his mother.

2 When it gets too hot, we step out to the sidewalk. The snow Americans write songs about seems imminent. A white Christmas is pretty, but for me it brings to mind my other life in Puerto Rico. There, the air doesn't force me to hunch my shoulders and draw my head, turtle-like, into my coat. There, Christmas Eve is for midnight mass and small gifts. The big gifts will come later, when the Three Magi have made their way to the island upon their trusty camels.

3 But I'm here now, in the land of Santa Claus and overnight delivery of presents bought over the Internet. I, 4 of my 11 siblings, and our mother, live in New York. None of our spouses is Puerto Rican, and our children and grandchildren have been born and raised in the United States. In our New York–based family there are

"New Yorikans"—a newly coined word for Puerto Ricans who live in New York.
Image of sound. Spanish dance music.
What does *aguinaldos* mean? Some kind of song or singer?
It's going to snow.

Some differences between Christmas in NY and PR.

Christmases

"translucent
jiggle of a
honey-colored
flan"—original
picture!
Spanish words.

Foods help bring
Puerto Rican
Christmas to NY.
Old custom
in PR.

A thick rice
soup.

Again PR in the
U.S.

Good visual
images.
Snow brings the
writer back fully
to NY from her
Puerto Rican
Navidad.

Big family,
assimilated
into American
culture
in NY.
4

Good
images—
color,
sound,
smell,
taste,
touch.

5

Adapted
American
custom
against
backdrop of
Spanish
version of
"Silent
Night."
6

7
Same image
as in
paragraph 2.
Weather
differences
are
important to
Santiago.

25 people, with whom we celebrate our American Christmas by trying to recreate *Las Navidades* as we knew them on the island.

And here, as there, we cook. Spicy ginger and cloves embedded in coconut rice. Oregano and garlic crusted over a pork shoulder, its crunchy skin smoky and brown. We evoke *Las Navidades* in the translucent jiggle of a honey-colored flan, in the sugar syrup that hardens into a crackle over the top and down the sides of the custard. It's in the fresh, unhulled pigeon peas and in the bunches of spiny, fragrant recao leaves bought at the marketa. It's in the banana leaves roasted over the open flame of a gas burner until they're the color of Spanish olives. When Mami spoons grated plantain on the leaf, and Delsa tops it with a dollop of ground meat and spices, *Las Navidades* are in every grain of salt they've poured, in every garlic clove they've mashed.

The gift-giving that used to take place on Jan. 6 now happens at the stroke of midnight on Christmas Eve. The children, who have fallen asleep curled up on the sofa or an easy chair, are roused and placed in front of the tree. One of us passes over the packages to eager hands. No one opens a gift until everything has been distributed. Then the sound of paper tearing, the squeals of delight, the hugs and hand-slapping and laughter drown out the sounds of the stereo, where someone has thought to put on the Spanish version of "Silent Night."

Afterwards, the presents are put in piles in the corners so we can continue the celebration. We're hungry again, so Mami makes a chicken *asopao* while the sisters tidy the kitchen. Those of us not cleaning up huddle in small groups, talking. Mostly, we make plans for the next party, on New Year's Eve, because for us, like in Puerto Rico, *Las Navidades* doesn't end on Dec. 25.

The *asopao* eaten, the sleepy children are gathered, the presents are stuffed into shopping bags, and we scatter to our individual homes. The street is deserted and quiet, every surface covered in white. Within minutes, the sidewalk bears the traces of our footsteps heading in different directions. Before I climb into my car, I stare at the flakes dancing under the street lamp. Then I hunch my shoulders and pull my head into my coat, astonished that, while I wasn't looking, my *Navidad* in New York has become Christmas, dusted with snow.

FOR WRITING OR DISCUSSION

1. What is the thesis of this piece? How do the marginal comments help you arrive at the thesis, which the writer does not state in the essay?
2. How does the title help set up the purpose of the selection?
3. Where has Santiago made effective comparisons?
4. Which images do you find most original? Which help you best appreciate this Puerto Rican Christmas in America?
5. In your opinion, which elements of descriptive writing outlined on pages 126–128 does the selection best demonstrate?
6. Write an essay on a holiday that you celebrate with your family. Make the scene come alive with concrete sensory details of color, sound, smell, taste, and touch.

Models of Writing

The examples of description that follow show professional writers at work. Note how description never becomes merely a piece of pretty writing but communicates insights and ideas.

ROGER ANGELL

On the Ball

1   It weighs just over five ounces and measures between 2.86 and 2.94 inches in diameter. It is made of a composition-cork nucleus encased in two thin layers of rubber, one black and one red, surrounded by a hundred and twenty-one yards of tightly wrapped blue-gray wool yarn, forty-five yards of white wool yarn, fifty-three more yards of blue-gray wool yarn, a hundred and fifty yards of fine cotton yarn, a coat of rubber cement, and a cowhide (formerly horsehide) exterior, which is held together with two hundred and sixteen slightly raised red cotton stitches. Printed certifications, endorsements, and outdoor advertising spherically attest to its authenticity. Like most institutions, it is considered inferior in its present form to its ancient archetypes, and in this case the complaint is probably justified: on occasion in recent years it has actually been known to come apart under the demands of its brief but rigorous active career. Baseballs are assembled and hand-stitched in Taiwan (before this year the work was done in Haiti, and before 1973 in Chicopee, Massachusetts), and contemporary pitchers claim that there is a tangible variation in the size and feel of the balls that now come into play in a single game; a true peewee is treasured by hurlers, and its departure from the premises, by fair means or foul, is secretly mourned. But never mind: any baseball is beautiful. No other small package comes as close to the ideal in design and utility. It is a perfect object for a man's hand. Pick it up and it instantly suggests its purpose; it is meant to be thrown a considerable distance—thrown hard and with precision. Its feel and heft are the beginning of the sport's critical dimensions; if it were a fraction of an inch larger or smaller, a few centigrams heavier or lighter, the game of baseball would be utterly different. Hold a baseball in your hand. As it happens, this one is not brand new. Here, just to one side of the curved surgical welt of stitches, there is a pale-green grass smudge, darkening on one edge almost to black—the mark of an old infield play, a tough grounder now lost in memory. Feel the ball, turn it over in your hand; hold it across the seam or the other way, with the seam just to the side of your middle finger. Speculation stirs. You want to get outdoors and throw this spare and sensual object to somebody, or, at the very least, watch somebody else throw it. The game has begun. . . .

FOR WRITING OR DISCUSSION

1. What are the two meanings of the essay's title, "On the Ball"?
2. When were you certain that the subject being discussed is a baseball?

3. Notice the number of facts in the first two sentences. What purpose do the facts serve in the development of the description?

4. What is meant by the sentence that begins, "Like most institutions, it is considered inferior in its present form . . ."? What does the sentence show about the author's attitude toward contemporary manufacturing techniques? How does the sentence telling where baseballs were once made support that attitude?

5. What is the thesis of the selection?

6. At what point does the selection cease to be factual and become a matter of opinion?

7. At what point does the writer bring the reader into the description? Why does he do so?

8. Do the sentences beginning with "Hold a baseball in your hand" make you feel the ball? Why or why not?

9. Write a paper describing a single small object—for example, a football, an ashtray, a kitchen utensil, a wristwatch. Try to use both factual and personal details to make your reader see or feel the object as you do.

JOAN DIDION

Marrying Absurd

To be married in Las Vegas, Clark County, Nevada, a bride must swear that she is eighteen or has parental permission and a bridegroom that he is twenty-one or has parental permission. Someone must put up five dollars for the license. (On Sundays and holidays, fifteen dollars. The Clark County Courthouse issues marriage licenses at any time of the day or night except between noon and one in the afternoon, between eight and nine in the evening, and between four and five in the morning.) Nothing else is required. The State of Nevada, alone among these United States, demands neither a premarital blood test nor a waiting period before or after the issuance of a marriage license. Driving in across the Mojave from Los Angeles, one sees the signs way out on the desert, looming up from that moonscape of rattlesnakes and mesquite, even before the Las Vegas lights appear like a mirage on the horizon: "GETTING MARRIED? Free License Information First Strip Exit." Perhaps the Las Vegas wedding industry achieved its peak operational efficiency between 9:00 p.m. and midnight of August 26, 1965, an otherwise unremarkable Thursday which happened to be, by

Presidential order, the last day on which anyone could improve his draft status merely by getting married. One hundred and seventy-one couples were pronounced man and wife in the name of Clark County and the State of Nevada that night, sixty-seven of them by a single justice of the peace, Mr. James A. Brennan. Mr. Brennan did one wedding at the Dunes and the other sixty-six in his office, and charged each couple eight dollars. One bride lent her veil to six others. "I got it down from five to three minutes," Mr. Brennan said later of his feat. "I could've married them en masse, but they're people, not cattle. People expect more when they get married."

2 What people who get married in Las Vegas actually do expect—what, in the largest sense, their "expectations" are—strikes one as a curious and self-contradictory business. Las Vegas is the most extreme and allegorical of American settlements, bizarre and beautiful in its venality and in its devotion to immediate gratification, a place the tone of which is set by mobsters and call girls and ladies' room attendants with amyl nitrite poppers in their uniform pockets. Almost everyone notes that there is no "time" in Las Vegas, no night and no day and no past and no future (no Las Vegas casino, however, has taken the obliteration of the ordinary time sense quite so far as Harold's Club in Reno, which for a while issued, at odd intervals in the day and night, mimeographed "bulletins" carrying news from the world outside); neither is there any logical sense of where one is. One is standing on a highway in the middle of a vast hostile desert looking at an eighty-foot sign which blinks "Stardust" or "Caesar's Palace." Yes, but what does that explain? This geographical implausibility reinforces the sense that what happens there has no connection with "real" life; Nevada cities like Reno and Carson are ranch towns, Western towns, places behind which there is some historical imperative. But Las Vegas seems to exist only in the eye of the beholder. All of which makes it an extraordinarily stimulating and interesting place, but an odd one in which to want to wear a candlelight satin Priscilla of Boston wedding dress with Chantilly lace insets, tapered sleeves and a detachable modified train.

3 And yet the Las Vegas wedding business seems to appeal to precisely that impulse. "Sincere and Dignified Since 1954," one wedding chapel advertises. There are nineteen such wedding chapels in Las Vegas, intensely competitive, each offering better, faster, and, by implication, more sincere services than the next: Our Photos Best Anywhere, Your Wedding on a Phonograph Record, Candlelight with Your Ceremony, Honeymoon Accommodations, Free Transportation from Your Motel to Courthouse to Chapel and Return to Motel, Religious or Civil Ceremonies, Dressing Rooms, Flowers, Rings, Announcements, Witnesses Available, and Ample Parking. All of these services, like most others in Las Vegas (sauna baths, payroll-check cashing, chinchilla coats for sale or rent), are offered twenty-four hours a day, seven days a week, presumably on the premise that marriage, like craps, is a game to be played when the table seems hot.

4 But what strikes one most about the Strip chapels, with their wishing wells and stained-glass paper windows and their artificial bouvardia, is that so much of their business is by no means a matter of simple convenience, of late-night liaisons between show girls and baby Crosbys. Of course there is some of that. (One night about eleven o'clock in Las Vegas I watched a bride in an orange minidress and masses of flame-colored hair stumble from a Strip

chapel on the arm of her bridegroom, who looked the part of the expendable nephew in movies like Miami Syndicate. "I gotta get the kids," the bride whimpered. "I gotta pick up the sitter, I gotta get to the midnight show." "What you gotta get," the bridegroom said, opening the door of a Cadillac Coupe de Ville and watching her crumple on the seat, "is sober.") But Las Vegas seems to offer something other than "convenience"; it is merchandising "niceness," the facsimile of proper ritual, to children who do not know how else to find it, how to make the arrangements, how to do it "right." All day and evening long on the Strip, one sees actual wedding parties, waiting under the harsh lights at a crosswalk, standing uneasily in the parking lot of the Frontier while the photographer hired by The Little Church of the West ("Wedding Place of the Stars") certifies the occasion, takes the picture: the bride in a veil and white satin pumps, the bridegroom usually in a white dinner jacket, and even an attendant or two, a sister or a best friend in hot-pink *peau de soie*, a flirtation veil, a carnation nosegay. "When I Fall in Love It Will Be Forever," the organist plays, and then a few bars of Lohengrin. The mother cries; the stepfather, awkward in his role, invites the chapel hostess to join them for a drink at the Sands. The hostess declines with a professional smile; she has already transferred her interest to the group waiting outside. One bride out, another in, and again the sign goes up on the chapel door: "One Moment please—Wedding."

I sat next to one such wedding party in a Strip restaurant the last time I was in Las Vegas. The marriage had just taken place; the bride still wore her dress, the mother her corsage. A bored waiter poured out a few swallows of pink champagne ("on the house") for everyone but the bride, who was too young to be served. "You'll need something with more kick than that," the bride's father said with heavy jocularity to his new son-in-law; the ritual jokes about the wedding night had a certain Pangiossian character, since the bride was clearly several months pregnant. Another round of pink champagne, this time not on the house, and the bride began to cry. "It was just as nice," she sobbed, "as I hoped and dreamed it would be."

5

FOR WRITING OR DISCUSSION

1. What is the significance of Didion's title for this essay? How does the title relate to her thesis? Do you agree with the title? Is marriage in Las Vegas absurd?

2. Why does the writer provide information about August 26, 1965?

3. This piece appeared in the 1960s. In what ways is it still relevant? What do you know about marriage ceremonies in Las Vegas today? Do the wedding chapels as Didion described them still exist? You might research the topic using a search engine like Google.

4. Didion calls Las Vegas "bizarre and beautiful in its venality." Which images in the essay support her view? Where do you find original uses of sensory language?

5. Write an essay about a wedding you attended. If you noted any absurd elements, use them as supporting detail for a thesis built around what you consider absurd activity, even at a conventional wedding. Be sure to use concrete sensory details.

Readings for Writing

Use the essay by Dick Feagler and the excerpt from Maxine Hong Kingston's book *The Woman Warrior* as potential topics for descriptive papers of your own.

DICK FEAGLER

Willie

1   What do you want to do with Willie Sommervil? His life is in your hands. Obviously, you ought to know a little bit about him before you decide. So let me help you out.

2   Willie is 36. A black man. A churchgoer. In fact, he sings in the choir. He has three children. They are not with him, but that isn't his fault. That's because of circumstances beyond his control. He sends them as much money as he can. He hasn't got a lot and sometimes he works a 15-hour-day to make it.

3   His work is seasonal. If you want to get fancy about it, you can call him a landscape architect. He cuts lawns and plants flowers. He rakes leaves. He'll do a little painting for you. He'll clean your gutters. Wash your windows if you want him to.

4   Most of this is fair-weather work. In the winter, things are leaner for Willie. He'll shovel your driveway or your walk. When he runs short of money, there's a restaurant that will hire him to wash dishes. Willie won't take a dime of welfare.

5   He pays his taxes and his Social Security. In the high summer, when work is plentiful, he hires neighborhood kids to help him out. Oh, and he worked himself up from total poverty. He started his business with a borrowed lawn mower. Now he owns a pickup truck, three lawn mowers and a house.

6   I feel I'm losing you. Virtue does not hold an audience. The little devices we use to capture your attention are not present, so far, in Willie's story.

7   So I'll tell you that Willie is in danger. Real and immediate danger. Since I told you he is black, you might be tempted to make certain stereotypical assumptions about the kind of danger he is in. Stray bullet danger, perhaps. Drug gang danger. And it is true that once Willie was beaten and burned on the face. But the people who beat him and burned him are not his worst enemies at the moment.

8   You are.

9   Maybe you think I'm being melodramatic? Think again. The biggest threat to Willie's future is you and the power you have reposed in the . . . federal immigration judge.

10   Willie Sommervil is a Haitian refugee. Why didn't I say so in the first place? Because, if I had, you might have said, "The hell with him, then."

11   Say the words "Haitian refugee" and a little movie starts playing in the mind. A little movie that shows crowds of people, packed in a boat like sardines, some of them AIDS infected. Threatening to spill out on our shores and jam the welfare rolls and spread disease and clutter up some vision of what America should be.

Willie Sommervil is all that an American should be and more than many are. When he lived   12
in Haiti, he befriended American missionaries and U.S. Coast Guardsmen. That's why he was
beaten and burned on the face. Government-sanctioned thugs did it because he was a friend to
America.

A Methodist clergyman got him out seven years ago and brought him to the community of   13
Lakeside on Marblehead in Ottawa County [Ohio]. That's where Willie pulled himself up by his
bootstraps—just like we Americans are always telling the poor to do.

I've got a cottage at Lakeside and that's how I happen to know Willie. I happen to be writing   14
this in a room he painted. I see him at least once a week. His English is pretty good and he's
working to make it better. Sometimes, in church on Sunday, I watch him in the choir and suspect he's just moving his lips during some of the more arcane passages of the old Wesley
hymns.

But his spirit is articulate. And when he prays, he prays to stay here. And to bring over   15
his children.

I want Willie to stay here. He's the kind of American America needs. So I will be in the   16
federal court at 9 a.m. April 20, along with a lot of my Lakeside neighbors, to urge [the
judge] to allow Willie to keep being what he already is. A good American.

The problem is you. You don't want him. I admit you probably didn't know that until now.   17
But your government, acting on your behalf, has already denied Willie's earlier request for asy-
lum and ordered him deported. Sent back to the people who burned him and beat him and
who still have his name on their list.

Karen Meade is Willie's lawyer. She specializes in immigration law. Her case files, she says,   18
are full of deserving people who ought to be allowed their chance at America. People who are
working hard and paying taxes and ought to be permitted to stay. People whom we ignore,
brush off, because their skin is chocolate brown like Willie's, but who are sweating to
make the battered old promise of America live. The way the Irish made it, and the Poles, and
the Germans.

You hear Meade say that and you ignore it. It is easy to ignore pieces of paper in a file.   19
When you reduce human beings to file folders, they cease to be human. You can issue orders
that collapse their worlds and send them off to fates unknown. And assume the country is better
for it.

I've told you about Willie Sommervil, the man. Willie Sommervil is also a file number. He is   20
an "A" with eight digits after it. He is in a drawer in the immigration office. Probably, these days,
he is also in a computer. A couple of key strokes and his American dream will vanish. Maybe
there will be one last message on the screen asking if you wish the data to be saved.

How about it? Do you?   21

FOR WRITING OR DISCUSSION

1. The essay begins and ends with questions. Which, if any, are traditional questions
   with the author wondering what the answer will be? Which, if any, are rhetorical

questions used primarily for effect with the author knowing what answer he expects or wants?

2. The author has a more important purpose than simply to describe Willie. What is that purpose?

3. Where does the writer attack stereotyped conceptions that he feels his readers are likely to have?

4. "Virtue does not hold an audience," Feagler complains. It's hard to make goodness and decency as interesting as evil. Try it. Write a description of a person characterized by unspectacular, everyday goodness and decency. Make the goodness come alive through specific details.

MAXINE HONG KINGSTON
"My Mother Has Cooked for Us"

1 My mother has cooked for us: raccoons, skunks, hawks, city pigeons, wild ducks, wild geese, black-skinned bantams, snakes, garden snails, turtles that crawled about the pantry floor and sometimes escaped under refrigerator or stove, catfish that swam in the bathtub. "The emperors used to eat the peaked hump of purple dromedaries," she would say. "They used chopsticks made from rhinoceros horn, and they ate ducks' tongues and monkeys' lips." She boiled the weeds we pulled up in the yard. There was a tender plant with flowers like white stars hiding under the leaves, which were like the flower petals but green. I've not been able to find it since growing up. It had no taste. When I was as tall as the washing machine, I stepped out on the back porch one night, and some heavy, ruffling, windy, clawed thing dived at me. Even after getting chanted back to sensibility, I shook when I recalled that perched everywhere there were owls with great hunched shoulders and yellow scowls. They were a surprise for my mother from my father. We children used to hide under the beds with our fingers in our ears to shut out the bird screams and the thud, thud of the turtles swimming in the boiling water, their shells hitting the sides of the pot. Once the third aunt who worked at the laundry ran out and bought us bags of candy to hold over our noses; my mother was dismembering skunk on the chopping block. I could smell the rubbery odor through the candy.

2 In a glass jar on a shelf my mother kept a big brown hand with pointed claws stewing in alcohol and herbs. She must have brought it from China because I do not remember a time when I did not have the hand to look at. She said it was a bear's claw, and for many years I thought bears were hairless. My mother used the tobacco, leeks, and grasses swimming about the hand to rub our sprains and bruises.

Just as I would climb up to the shelf to take one look after another at the hand, I would hear my mother's monkey story. I'd take my fingers out of my ears and let her monkey words enter my brain. I did not always listen voluntarily, though. She would begin telling the story, perhaps repeating it to a homesick villager, and I'd overhear before I had a chance to protect myself. Then the monkey words would unsettle me; a curtain flapped loose inside my brain. I have wanted to say, "Stop it. Stop it," but not once did I say, "Stop it."

3

"Do you know what people in China eat when they have the money?" my mother began. "They buy into a monkey feast. The eaters sit around a thick wood table with a hole in the middle. Boys bring in the monkey at the end of a pole. Its neck is in a collar at the end of the pole, and it is screaming. Its hands are tied behind it. They clamp the monkey into the table; the whole table fits like another collar around its neck. Using a surgeon's saw, the cooks cut a clean line in a circle at the top of its head. To loosen the bone, they tap with a tiny hammer and wedge here and there with a silver pick. Then an old woman reaches out her hand to the monkey's face and up to its scalp, where she tufts some hairs and lifts off the lid of the skull. The eaters spoon out the brains."

4

Did she say, "You should have seen the faces the monkey made"? Did she say, "The people laughed at the monkey screaming"? It was alive? The curtain flaps closed like merciful black wings.

5

"Eat! Eat!" my mother would shout at our heads bent over bowls, the blood pudding awobble in the middle of the table.

6

She had one rule to keep us safe from toadstools and such: "If it tastes good, it's bad for you," she said. "If it tastes bad, it's good for you."

7

We'd have to face four- and five-day-old leftovers until we ate it all. The squid eye would keep appearing at breakfast and dinner until eaten. Sometimes brown masses sat on every dish. I have seen revulsion on the faces of visitors who've caught us at meals.

8

"Have you eaten yet?" the Chinese greet one another.

9

"Yes, I have," they answer whether they have or not. "And you?"

10

I would live on plastic.

11

FOR WRITING OR DISCUSSION

1. What is Kingston's main point? Although the selection is rich in acutely observed details, Kingston is not writing description for its own sake. How do the details support the main idea?

2. What instances of sensory language do you find most vivid and original? What details make you see the scene exactly as Kingston sees it?

3. What does Kingston suggest about her mother by means of the descriptions of what she cooked for the family?

4. What is your reaction to the monkey feast description?

5. Write a descriptive essay about an unusual meal you have eaten. Make the details you record serve a clearly stated thesis.

Reading and Writing About Poetry

Use this poem by a contemporary writer to stimulate your thinking about descriptive language and to help you write description.

MARK STRAND

Black Sea

One clear night while the others slept, I climbed
the stairs to the roof of the house and under a sky
strewn with stars I gazed at the sea, at the spread of it,
the rolling crests of it raked by the wind, becoming
like bits of lace tossed in the air. I stood in the long
whispering night, waiting for something, a sign, the approach
of a distant light, and I imagined you coming closer,
the dark waves of your hair mingling with the sea,
and the dark became desire, and desire the arriving light.
The nearness, the momentary warmth of you as I stood
on that lonely height watching the slow swells of the sea
break on the shore and turn briefly into glass and disappear ...
Why did I believe you would come out of nowhere? Why with all
that the world offers would you come only because I was here?

5

10

FOR WRITING OR DISCUSSION

1. What is the main point of Strand's poem?

2. What does the sea make him think of? How does it stimulate his thoughts?

3. Which appeals to the senses can you identify here? How do the comparisons in lines 5 and 12 contribute to the meaning of the poem?

4. In what ways is this a love poem? A poem about nature?

5. Write a descriptive essay in which you show how some phenomenon in nature reminds you of an important person in your life—a friend, a parent, a love, a child.

6. Write your own poem about nature and how it connects to a person in your life.

STRATEGY CHECKLIST: Writing and Revising Your Descriptive Paper

Plan the paper.	☐ Have I used prewriting to explore ideas for a subject?
	☐ Will I describe a person, a place, or an object?
	☐ How can I limit the topic so that it is focused and meaningful?
	☐ Have I thought about the kinds of details I can use?
	☐ Have I thought carefully about my purpose in writing?
	☐ Do I have my audience clearly in mind?
	☐ Have I considered using an outline to organize my ideas?
Write a first draft.	☐ Have I established a clear thesis that states the topic and expresses an opinion?
	☐ Have I supported my thesis with sensory detail—appeals to sight, hearing, taste, smell, and touch?
	☐ Have I organized details logically—in space or time order or by some other principle that gives structure to my description?
Revise and edit the paper.	☐ Have I avoided taking inventory of a random collection of facts?
	☐ Have I established the topic in a lively introduction to capture and hold the reader's attention?
	☐ Have I used transitions when necessary to link ideas?
	☐ Does my conclusion tie together the points of the description?

continued

☐ Have I proofread for grammar, spelling, and mechanics?

WRITING TOPICS

If you cannot easily decide on a topic for your description paper, you might want to try one or more of these suggestions.

1. An office party
2. A religious leader
3. A loyal pet
4. A street corner
5. An afternoon schoolyard
6. People waiting in a line
7. Sloppy eaters
8. Doctor's waiting room
9. Restaurant waiters
10. Bad drivers
11. A school cafeteria
12. An amusement park
13. A hospital room
14. The contents of a wallet or pocketbook
15. Summer nights
16. A natural disaster
17. A morning at the beach
18. My best friend
19. The biology lab
20. A favorite food

CROSSCURRENTS

Esmeralda Santiago in "A Blanco Navidad for New Yorikans" (pages 132–133) and Maxine Hong Kingston in "My Mother Has Cooked for Us" (pages 140–141) both describe their family's food. What similar strategies have the writers used to present their descriptions? How do their strategies differ?

COLLABORATIVE LEARNING

Form groups of five students and discuss the student models: "Dad's Disappointment" (pages 128–130) and "A Birth Room" (page 131). How do the papers demonstrate the principles of descriptive writing? What recommendations would you make for improving the essays? Discuss your group's conclusions with the rest of the class.

From **IMAGE** to **Words**: A Reading and Writing Assignment

Photo courtesy: Rose Hartma/Corbis

1. What is the scene of the picture? How do you know?
2. What is the purpose of the complicated structure on the man's shoulders? Why is it so colorful?
3. Use the photograph above as the basis for a short descriptive paper. Be sure to establish a thesis and make the description come alive with sensory detail. Expand the single visual dimension of the photograph by imagining and recording colors, sounds, smells, and sensations of touch.

For additional writing, reading, and research resources, go to **www.mycomplab. com** <http://www.mycomplab.com/> and choose Skwire/Wiener's *Student's Book of College English*, Twelfth Edition.

CHAPTER **8**

Narration

- ■ Writing Your Narrative Paper
- ■ Student Writing: Narration
- ■ Models of Writing
- ■ Readings for Writing
- ■ Reading and Writing About Poetry

"Last night, as I was driving home from work, I stopped for the light at Fifty-fifth and Main. I was just sitting there minding my own business when, all of a sudden. . . ."

"You'll never guess what the kids did today."

"That reminds me of the time. . . ."

Think of how often during a conversation you say something like "That reminds me of the time. . ." and then tell a story.

We all tell stories, and for many reasons. Usually we tell stories just to share our daily experience with others. Frequently, however, we tell stories to make a point. Sometimes the point is simply, "Yes, I've had an experience like that, too. I know how you feel." That kind of story helps establish a bond between people. At other times, we tell stories that illustrate ideas. A pastor, for example, does not merely say that repentance will bring forgiveness; he reads the story of the prodigal son from the Bible. Or we tell stories to make people laugh: "Once there was a person named Mike who had a friend named Pat, and. . . ." Whatever the case, we enjoy telling and hearing stories, and you have been telling and hearing them all your life. So the assignment to write a narrative paper should be one you will enjoy.

A **narrative** is a story. To *narrate* means "to tell, to give an account of." Narratives take many forms. A novel is a narrative. So is a short story. A biography is a narrative because it tells the story of a person's life. Historical narrative traces events over time. Often a narrative is a brief story included in a longer work to illustrate an idea. (An argument calling for the enforcement of safety standards in steel mills, for example, might include a story about a worker who lost two fingers because a hot steel bar fell on her.) A **narrative paper** tells a story, usually of a personal experience, that makes a point or supports a thesis. The purpose of a narrative paper is to recreate an experience in such a way that your readers can imaginatively participate in it and share it with you.

Writing Your Narrative Paper

As you plan and write your paper, keep the following principles in mind.

TIPS for Writing a Narrative Essay

■ **Limit the subject.** Almost any experience you have had can serve as subject matter for a narrative paper. You've had thousands of experiences in your life, and any one of them—from getting lost on your way to school to moving into your first apartment—can make good subject matter for a paper if you tell the story well.

But you must limit the subject, and, in a narrative paper, time usually determines the limits of your subject. Your goal is to tell a story so dramatically and so completely that your readers can share the experience. A subject such as your summer as a camp counselor, therefore, is too broad—unless you want to write a book. But you could tell about the time a skunk got into your RV. Even one day in the city provides too much material for a complete and dramatic story. But some part of that day—the hour you spent watching a pair of cardinals in the park teach their baby how to fly—can make a good story. It's probably no exaggeration to say that the subject cannot be too limited.

■ **Have a thesis.** The experience you narrate is not as important as its significance to you. Why did the experience matter to you? Why do you want to tell about it? Did it change you in some way? Did it embarrass you? Did it make you happy? Sad? Was it thrilling? Frustrating? Did it lead to a decision? Did you learn something about yourself or about others or about the world around you? Were you disappointed? Any little event in your life—even taking out the garbage—can make good subject matter for a narrative paper if you determine the significance of the experience and tell the story well.

The student essay "The Death of Santa Claus" on pages 152–154, for example, tells of the painful way one little girl learned the truth about Santa. As you read the story, you'll surely find it touching, amusing, and sad. You may feel that the older brother, Clay, was unnecessarily cruel. The reason you have these feelings is that the author saw the significance of her experience and narrated it so skillfully that you share it with her. No matter how ordinary the experience may seem to you, if you determine its significance, your readers will be able to share it with you and will find it interesting.

The significance of your experience—your interpretation of it, what it meant to you—is your thesis. The thesis of "The Death of Santa Claus," for example, is *Because of the manner in which I discovered that there is no Santa Claus, Christmas lost its joy and sense of magic.* You don't have to state the thesis directly in your paper all the time, but you should certainly know what it is, because the significance of the experience is exactly what you want to convey to your audience.

The thesis is important, too, because it controls the content of the paper. It helps you decide what to put in the paper and what to leave out. We tolerate rambling spoken narratives, when we must, out of consideration for a speaker's feelings. Even so, we wish the person would get to the point. But we won't tolerate written narratives that ramble because we don't have to. We can always put the book or paper down. So have a thesis; it helps keep the narrative under control.

To see how a thesis keeps the narrative under control, turn again to "The Death of Santa Claus." Notice that the writer does not tell everything that happened on Christmas Eve. She doesn't tell her readers that she brushed her teeth, or ate breakfast, or put together a jigsaw puzzle. Such facts do not contribute to her point. But other facts do: Clay is accustomed to deference from the younger children (and they are accustomed to giving it); everyone in the house is irritable, which leads to the writer's challenge of her brother's authority and the mother's uncharacteristic rebuke of the boy; and the mother forces Clay to take his little sister with him to the grocery. These facts explain why Clay wants to hurt his sister, and what better way to hurt a seven-year-old on Christmas Eve than to tell her the truth about Santa Claus? These are the facts developed in the narrative, and the thesis determines them.

■ **Use specific details.**   In every chapter of this book, we urge you to use specific details because they give life to your writing, and the narrative paper is no exception. If your story is about being frightened out of your wits the first time you spent a night alone in your aunt's hundred-year-old house, it matters that the dark red living room curtains were made of velvet so thick that no light could penetrate them, that cobwebs hung from the ceiling, that no lamp in the room was bright enough to illuminate the corners, that the stairs creaked and the wind moaned. Remember, a narrative re-creates an experience for your readers. In most cases, you can make your readers feel what you felt if you use specific details. What you learned in the last chapter about descriptive writing will help you considerably here and elsewhere when you need to marshal concrete sensory language.

A word of caution, however. The details you use, like everything else in your paper, should support your thesis. Extraneous details, no matter how vivid, always feel like padding and frustrate readers.

■ **Use language that sounds natural.**   Your readers should feel that an intelligent, articulate friend is telling them a story. The language of a narrative, therefore, should sound conversational, which means you should avoid two extremes—the pompous and the inarticulate.

As, for the first time, I entered the portals of the edifice that housed my new employer and donned the attire specified for my position, I felt apprehensive.

Like, man, that first day, ya know, was like. . . well, when I put that waiter's jacket on, ya know, I was scared.

Try, instead, something like this:

> I was nervous that first day on the job. When I put on my white waiter's jacket, my hands trembled.

These sentences sound natural, and they give a conversational tone to the narrative.

Another way to give a natural sound to your narrative is to use direct quotations when appropriate (see "Quotation Marks," pages 641–642).

> "Are you having a good time?" she asked.
> "Not really," I replied, "but I don't want to spoil the party for you and the kids."

Direct quotations give a sense of reality to the narrative, sometimes by helping set a scene, as they do in "Champion of the World":

> "I ain't worried 'bout this fight. Joe's gonna whip that cracker like it's open season."
> "He's gone whip him till that white boy call him Momma."
> —Maya Angelou, "Champion of the World"

These comments, which follow the description of the crowd that has gathered at the general store to hear the broadcast of a boxing match, continue to set the scene of the exciting event.

Direct quotations are also good for revealing the personality and feelings of the characters in your narrative:

> "Get lost," he growled.

> "I'm not your doormat!" she screamed.

> Her voice filled with sympathy, the teller said, "I'm very sorry, but the computer is down. I'm afraid you'll have to come back tomorrow."

Direct quotations, then, are useful in developing a narrative. Don't feel, however, that you must fill your paper with them. For example, "Foul Shots" (see pages 161–163) contains only one short direct quotation, but the narrative sounds natural and tells a powerful story.

■ **Give order to the narrative.** Like the descriptive paper discussed in Chapter 7, most papers contain, first, an introduction, which includes the thesis statement; next, a body, which supports the thesis and is organized according to the principle of time, space, or logic; and, finally, a conclusion, which restates the thesis and gives a sense of finality to the paper. A narrative paper also should contain these three parts, but the development of each part is somewhat different from that of other papers.

■ **Introduce your narrative.**   The introduction does not necessarily include a thesis statement. Instead, it may set the scene for the narrative:

> It was in Burma, a sodden morning of the rains. A sickly light, like yellow tinfoil, was slanting over the high walls into the jail yard. We were waiting outside the condemned cells, a row of sheds fronted with double bars, like small animal cages. Each cell measured about ten feet by ten and was quite bare within except for a plank bed and a pot of drinking water. In some of them brown silent men were squatting at the inner bars, with their blankets draped round them. These were the condemned men, due to be hanged within the next week or two.
>
> —George Orwell, "A Hanging"

Sometimes the introduction gives the background—the facts that led to the experience being narrated:

> In 1969, I was a senior on the Luther Burbank High School basketball team. The school is on the south side of San Antonio, in one of the city's many barrios. After practice one day our coach announced that we were going to spend the following Saturday scrimmaging with the ball club from Winston Churchill High, located in the city's rich, white north side.
>
> —Rogelio R. Gomez, "Foul Shots"

Indeed, sometimes a narrative paper doesn't even have an introduction. In this case, the writer simply begins with the first event of the story:

> "There's a gun at your back. Raise your hands and don't make a sound," a harsh voice snarled at me. I raised my hands.

■ **Sequence your body paragraphs.**   The body of the narrative paper also differs from that of most other papers in that its organization only can be chronological. It is possible to begin with the present and then portray an earlier episode:

> As I sit in my soft leather easy chair that I keep in front of the fireplace this time of year and gaze at brightly burning pine logs, I remember a Christmas ten years ago when I was not so comfortable.

But the heart of the narrative—what happened ten years ago—should proceed chronologically. Since you want your readers to share the events as you experienced them, you must present the events in the order that they occurred: First this, then that, and later something else. And you should let your readers know, by means of transitions, what the chronology is. Transitions are, of course, important to any piece of writing, but the kinds of transitions that indicate the passage of time are essential to a narrative paper:

> then, next, soon, later
> at four o'clock, a few minutes later, on the way back, the next morning

After I removed the bullets . . .

I must have been asleep a couple of hours when a shout awakened me.

■ **Conclude your narrative.**   Finally, the narrative's conclusion as well is different from other conclusions. In some narratives, the thesis of the paper appears for the first time in the conclusion. The writer tells a good story in the introduction and body and then states the significance of the story at the end of the paper:

> At last I admitted to myself that the raccoons had won. I was tired of getting up in the middle of the night to gather the garbage they scattered about the backyard. I was tired of trying to find a garbage can that they could not open. I was, in fact, tired of the country. As I crept wearily back to my bedroom, I knew *the raccoons had taught me a valuable lesson: I did not belong in the country; I belonged in a high-rise apartment in the heart of the city.* And that's just where I moved two weeks later.

At other times, when the main point of the narrative is sufficiently clear within the piece, the conclusion may imply the thesis without restating it, or it may take up other ideas stated or hinted at in the narrative. In the essay "Foul Shots" (pages 161–163), you might state writer Rogelio R. Gomez's thesis like this: *Our failure to respond to an insult at a basketball game that we thought would assert our racial superiority instead made us feel worthless and inferior.* The essay's conclusion reads:

> Two decades later, the memory of their gloating lives on in me. When a white person is discourteous, I find myself wondering what I should do, and afterward, if I've done the right thing. Sometimes I argue when a deft comment would suffice. Then I reprimand myself, for I am no longer a boy. But my impulse to argue bears witness to my ghosts. For, invariably, whenever I feel insulted I'm reminded of that day at Churchill High. And whenever the past encroaches upon the present, I see myself rising boldly, stepping proudly across the years and crushing, underfoot, a silly bag of Fritos.

Since the essay narrative makes the point, Gomez has no need to belabor the obvious. But note how his conclusion reminds readers of the ideas presented in the introduction and helps unify the essay.

In any event, the conclusion for a narrative paper should do what all good conclusions do: Give the paper a sense of completeness.

Student Writing: Narration

Read the following narrative by a student writer. Annotations highlight narrative strategies and essay development.

Alycia Hatten

The Death of Santa Claus

Limited subject: "that heart-breaking Christmas Eve" confines topic in time and establishes narrative sequence.

Introduction: brief (one sentence long), yet clearly implies thesis, which controls contents of paper.

1   I will never forget that heartbreaking Christmas Eve when my oldest brother murdered Santa Claus.

2   Clay was eleven that year; I was seven, Brian five, and Kevin four. Clay had always been the leader. Brian, Kevin, and I had always done everything he told us to do, and we always believed everything he said: If Clay said it, then it was the gospel truth. Clay, naturally, had come to expect us to look up to him.

Important background details.

Narrative chronology begins here.

3   That Christmas Eve was cold and rainy, so we children had been in the house all day. Although we tried to be good so Santa would visit us that night, we grew restless and irritable as the day wore on. Our mother, too, became irritable because, in addition to answering our questions and trying to think of ways to keep us amused, she had worked all day preparing for the Christmas feast our three uncles and four aunts would share with us the next day.

4   I don't know where I got the nerve, but that afternoon, for the first time in my life, I challenged Clay's authority. It was about four o'clock, and, at my mother's suggestion, I had turned to my coloring book. I had almost finished coloring the picture of a little girl, and I was especially proud of the costume I had given her. At that time, I believed pink and purple to be the two loveliest colors possible, and I had given the little girl a pink dress and purple shoes.

Time transition: "that afternoon"; "about four o'clock."

Specific details appeal to sense of sight: "pink dress and purple shoes."

5   Just as I was putting the finishing touches on the shoes, Clay came into the den from the kitchen and began to inspect my work. "That's dumb," he said. "Who ever heard of purple shoes?" And picking up a black crayon, he began coloring my beautiful purple shoes black.

6   "Mommie," I screamed, "Clay's messin' up my picture and he says I'm dumb! You can, too, have purple shoes, can't you?"

7   My mother could usually settle an argument so gently that we were seldom aware it had been settled. This time, however, she rushed into the den from the kitchen, wiping flour dust from her hands, and snapped, "Clay, put

Sharp image of mother: Sensory details appeal to sight, sound, and touch.

that crayon back where you found it and leave your sister alone!" To me she said, "There's nothing to cry about. I've always liked purple shoes."

Clay dropped the black crayon and, turning on the TV, sat down to watch. Since my mother had confirmed my taste in colors, I finished my picture and forgot about the incident.

8

A few minutes later, my father came home, and we all had an early supper. My mother resumed her baking and discovered that she would need more candied citrus to finish her last batch of cookies. Perhaps because she knew Clay was hurt and she wanted us to become friends again, she told Clay and me to put on our raincoats and go to the corner store to get the citrus.

9

Transitions continue to advance the chronological sequence: "A few minutes later."

"Why does <u>she</u> have to go with me?" Clay whined.

10

Direct quotations throughout give sense of reality to narrative.

"It'll be good for your sister to get out of the house for a while. Besides, she's getting to be a big girl, and you can teach her to count the change," my mother replied.

11

Clay and I set out on our journey. I babbled all the way. Clay said hardly a word, but I was too happy to be going to the grocery with him to notice. On the way back I said to Clay, "Let's run home so we won't miss any of the 'Santa Claus Is Coming to Town' special."

12

Clay said, "No, I'm not runnin' home to see that stupid program, and there ain't a Santa Claus anyway."

13

I stopped dead in my tracks and said, "What do you mean there ain't a Santa Claus? Mommie just took us to Halle's yesterday to see him and we have pictures of him at home, and Mommie and Daddy don't tell lies, and I'm gonna tell on you when we get home." I could hardly wait to get home so I could tell my mother about Clay's awful lie.

14

"Your brother's just teasing you, and if he doesn't stop, Santa's going to leave him a big bag of ashes," my mother reassured me. Brian, Kevin, and I laughed with relief! I went into the den and started watching "Santa Claus Is Coming to Town."

15

16   When the commercial came on, Clay said, "Come on, I'll prove it to you." He went to Daddy's desk and got his flashlight. Then we went downstairs to the basement. Clay said, "Come over here to this big locker and I'll show you your toys."

Sharp visual details at key moment in the narrative.

17   We went to the locker, and Clay pulled open the door while I looked in with the flashlight. And there they were: Most of the toys I had asked Santa for were in the locker!

18   I went to bed that night heartbroken. I felt as if someone had died. The next morning, even the presence of the bicycle I had dreamed of couldn't cheer me up. I didn't feel the sense of magic and the happiness that I had come to associate with Christmas morning. And I haven't ever again, not since Clay killed Santa Claus.

Conclusion captures the pain of the moment and gives the paper a sense of completeness.

FOR WRITING OR DISCUSSION

1. Do the title and the first paragraph of the narrative reveal too much of the story? Why, or why not?

2. The writer uses strong words like *murdered, died,* and *killed* to suggest the way she felt when learning the truth about Santa. What do these words reveal about her understanding of her brother's behavior?

3. The thesis of the narrative is not directly stated. Should it be?

4. Identify four expressions that indicate the passage of time.

5. What do the direct quotations reveal about Clay and his sister?

6. How do the following details serve the narrative?

   "That Christmas Eve was cold and rainy . . . ." (paragraph 3)
   "I had given the little girl. . .purple shoes." (paragraph 4)
   ". . .[S]he rushed into the den. . . , wiping flour dust from her hands. . . ."
      (paragraph 7)

7. Write a narrative paper about the time you learned the truth about some myth (Santa Claus, the Easter bunny, the tooth fairy) of your childhood. Or, write a narrative about the difficulty you have or had in giving up some cherished belief.

Here is another student narrative. Note the use of concrete detail.

Jarrett David Lee Jackson
My Father's House

When I walk into my father's house every day, I always wonder if my parents should have stayed together and how my life would have changed because of it. It just seems funny to me that seven years ago my parents and my sister and I were one big happy family. 1

My father still lives at our old house with his new wife. I still think of all the memories I have in that house, and I also think about all the memories that he's making with a new family. I remember falling <u>up</u> the stairs for some reason. My sister found it amusing to see me bleeding and crying. It hurts every time I walk up to the door, knowing I have to knock instead of just using my key to get in. I don't even have a key to my father's house. Maybe he's just forgetful, or maybe he just doesn't want me to have one. Every time I come to the house, I remember that horrible night. 2

The date was July 14, 1994. It's strange after all these years that I can remember the exact date. I remember to read all that day to keep my mind off of the past. I usually stay alone, too, choosing to isolate myself. 3

I remember cooking dinner that night. It had been a long, bad day at school, and I remember only wanting to go outside. I asked my mother if I could go outside and play. She gave me a hurt, empty look, like she didn't know what to say. Her face was full of hurt and disgust for something, but I didn't know what. She told me no and also to ask my father when he got home. She turned her back to me and rubbed her forehead and eyes as if she wanted to cry but was holding it in. 4

I'd never seen my mother that bothered by something, but I didn't know what it was. I went to my older, wiser sister to see if she knew what was wrong with our mother. I knew she didn't really know *everything*, but it always made me feel better if my sister and I both didn't know what was going on. My sister got me through many, many problems in my life, but even she couldn't help me through this one. 5

6   My father walked through the door at about 6:30. Usually he was home by 5:30. I had seen him late about three times in my whole life. I greeted him at the door with a hello. He said hello back with a very serious face. I was scared to ask him what was wrong, so I just told him that dinner was ready. He said okay, but it was like he wasn't even talking to me. After he hung up his coat, he walked right past me like I wasn't even there.

7   About 8:00, I went to my room to watch television and play a game or two. My mother was in the shower. My mother usually takes her nightly shower about nine or ten o'clock, so she was kind of early. My father entered the room and sat down on my bed. He told me to pause the game and come to their bedroom. I would have asked why, but I was looking in his face and he looked dead serious, so I just followed orders and went to their bedroom. My sister immediately followed. She pushed me, and we started playing, but then I caught a glimpse of my father's face and stopped. My sister sat down on the other side of the bed. I tried to think what I might have done in the past couple of days that I might have gotten into serious trouble for.

8   My father sat on the bed and said he loved us, but he got real nervous for some reason. Then my mother came in from the shower with her robe on. Her eyes showed that she was hurt or had been crying. She sat down in a chair next to the bed, but far away from my father. He tried to let us down easy about the situation. He explained how people fall out of love with one another, but still care for one another. I didn't understand. Who was he talking about? Was this some sort of life lesson I had to learn that day? I got scared and sick to my stomach as I feared the worst.

9   *"We're getting a divorce."* The most devastating words I have ever heard. Out of my father's mouth? My heart dropped down to my feet. I couldn't move from off of the bed. My sister was crying so hard I couldn't hear anything else. My mother grabbed hold of me, trying to say she was sorry between her sobs. Everyone was crying but my father and me. I maintained eye contact with him. I couldn't break contact with him for fear I would look weak in one of those situations where I must not appear weak.

"How could you do this to us?" I asked, fighting back tears. 10

"Well, son, it can't be explained. It just happened," he answered in a mellow tone. 11

My father is a strong, stony man, and I really didn't expect too much emotion to pour forth. 12
He was also a loud man, but he maintained his hushed, mellow tone. He explained that he was moving out and that I would have to become the man of the house. It was a responsibility I knew I wasn't ready for, but I had to accept. I knew I would try to be a man to the best of my boyish abilities.

My father slept on the couch that last night together. The house was extremely 13
silent. I didn't hear any snoring or even breathing. I was in my room thinking about being the man of the house, of remaining strong for what remained of our family. I got up to talk with my father, but when I got to the top of the stairs I stopped. A dead silence filled the house as I realized I couldn't ask him for any help again. I felt that he was taking the easy way out by divorcing my mother. I right then promised myself that I would be a better father and man than he was. I would always try my hardest and at eleven years old I would step up and become a better man than my father.

I'll never forget that day because while it was the lowest point in my life, it was 14
also a breakthrough for me. It was *my day*, an enlightenment of some sort. Oddly enough, I still love my father, but in my heart I know I will be a better man than he has been, a better husband, father, and man. I understand that love is forever and can never be "divorced."

FOR WRITING OR DISCUSSION

1. What is the writer's thesis? Where in the essay do you find it stated most clearly?
2. Where does the writer use sensory language most vividly?
3. Write a narrative paper about a personal discovery after you experienced an intense moment with your parents or other family members.

Models of Writing

These professional examples of narration are typical of the narratives you will have to write, stories that come directly from the writers' personal experiences. Notice as you read how each selection tells a good story but also makes a significant point.

CAROL K. LITTLEBRANDT

Death Is a Personal Matter

1   My father sleeps. I sit writing . . . trying to get something on paper I know is there, but which is as elusive and slippery as the life that's ending before me.

2   My father has cancer. Cancer of the sinuses, and as the autopsy will show later, of the left occipital lobe, mastoid, cerebellum.

3   His head lies at an awkward angle on the pillow because of a lump on his neck grown to grapefruit size—the visible sign that, for some reason, was not considered worthy of biopsy for ten doctor-to-doctor-running months. The invisible is worse.

4   My imagination enters the chamber of horrors of overgrown sinus passages, and I wince at the thought of the excruciating pain my father has borne for so long. Occasionally the pain rips through the veil of drugs and, still asleep, he reaches out a skinny white arm and grips the bed railing with a hand, gnarled, but still warm and amazingly strong.

5   I watch his rickety body shudder from the bombarding agonies. I cry and pray and gently wipe the glistening sweat from his forehead, sit again and watch, not quite sure what I am watching for. I have no measure of previous days and nights. I have only been here a few hours.

A Painful Burden

6   When I came in, he didn't know me. I wrote my name on a card with the words, "I'm here, Dad." And he tried to understand, but couldn't. Later, when a friend arrived, he managed introductions of the lovely lady "who looks just like my daughter" to "my good friend, Oskar." Then, joking and being gracious, he made Oskar and me laugh, enjoy ourselves and feel comfortable. And we felt love. Now it is night, and I do not know whether the fitful sleep is appropriate and whether tomorrow he will wake and have time to joke and be gracious again.

7   I have not seen my father for nine months, when the lump was still a secret below his ear. A few months later I heard about it and headaches, and then from time to time all the

diagnoses of arthritis, a cyst, sinusitis . . . even senility. Then finally—the lump now a painful burden to be carried—he was subjected to nine days of tests of bowels, bladder, blood. And on the last day a hollow needle was inserted into the growth; the cells gathered, magnified, interpreted and pronounced cancer. Immediate surgery and/or cobalt treatment indicated.

They were told, my mother and father, the day after his 75th birthday party. Then, after panic and the trauma of an old World War I rifle that would not fire, with my mother—ordered outside the bedroom—hearing click, click, click . . . and a plastic bag, tucked around my father's face in one last act of stricken, singular loyalty and cooperation by my mother, to be clawed away at the last moment . . . and spilled pills . . . and falling . . . and weeping ... and holding each other . . . and finally giving in, my father reluctantly left his own bed and was taken to the hospital.　　8

"Let Me Alone"

And after the trauma of no dentures, no hearing aid and one unexpected cobalt treatment, triumphant that his mind functioned and his voice was firm, he state unfalteringly: "Let me alone. No more treatments. I am 75. I have had an excellent life. It is time for me to die in my own way." His decision was not met with approval.　　9

These things I learned later, but now I hear him moan and watch his face contort and his bony fingers press his forehead. And I go down the night corridors of the hospital and ask for another shot for my father. All the nurses look at me, and I at them. We do not speak. It is not necessary. The air is filled with the serene mystery of tacit agreements. Another doctor is in charge now, and the orders written on the chart are clear and kind.　　10

After the shot is given, my father's breathing changes. There are longer intervals between each breath. I time them with my own breathing, and feel the suspense as I wait to exhale and take another breath. But even now I do not know I am here for the end. I am not familiar with dying. I pray again he will not suffer long. I anticipate weeks because his heart is that of a lion.　　11

I pet him, and hold his hand and kiss it. I wipe away the urine from between his wasted legs, knowing he would be terribly embarrassed if he knew. But I am grateful to minister to him with love at the end of his life.　　12

In the morning, another friend comes in to relieve me. I go for breakfast. A head nurse severely scolds me for wearing a cotton nightgown smock over my slacks as certainly not appropriate to wear in my father's room. I shrug and order coffee.　　13

Later on, washed and clean, my father rests peacefully on his side. I take his hand. He wakens, and now with only one eye functioning, but it blue and clear, he smiles a sweet gentle smile, and says, "Holy smokes . . . it's Carol." The last child has come and he is happy. Then for a moment he looks puzzled . . . Carol all the way from Buffalo? . . . and then he understands. He tells me he would like to rest now and squeezes my hand. His eyes　　14 close, and as though a shade were being pulled back from his face, the pain moves from chin to nose to forehead and disappears. He sleeps and breathes softly. I smile at his peace. I leave.

15　　My mother returns to the hospital to take my place. The phone rings 30 minutes later. Gently and quietly my father has died with her last kiss upon his lips.

Joyous Freedom

16　　As the family drives back to the hospital, I sense a great elation as if someone were flying with arms flung out in total freedom. I chuckle because the joyous, almost gleefully alive, feeling, is so strong. Yes, old man . . . Pop . . . I'm glad for you. Enjoy, enjoy and Godspeed.

17　　Death is not easy under any circumstances, but at least he did not suffer tubes and IVs and false hope, and we did not suffer the play-acting, the helpless agonies of watching a loved one suffer to no purpose, finally growing inured to it all or even becoming irritated with a dying vegetable that one cannot relate to any longer. In the end, I have learned, death is a very personal matter between parent and offspring, husbands and wives, loving neighbors and friends, and between God or symbols of belief and the dying ones and all who care about them.

18　　There comes a point where it is no longer the business of the courts, the American Medical Association, the government. It is private business. And I write now publicly only because it needs to be said again, and my father would have agreed.

19　　So, Pop, I say it for you, for all of us still here. Wish us well and God bless.

FOR WRITING OR DISCUSSION

1. What is the thesis of this piece?

2. Littlebrandt is writing about a complex and controversial subject. Where does she seem to give serious consideration to the position of those who may differ with her views?

3. What is the writer's attitude toward the medical profession? In what ways are her views both positive and negative?

4. What purposes do the many details about the nature of the father's illness serve in the essay?

5. Explain the meaning of "Wish us well . . ." in paragraph 19.

6. We all celebrate or commemorate the landmarks in our lives—births, marriages, deaths. Write a narrative showing how a person or group of people faced one of these major events.

ROGELIO R. GOMEZ
Foul Shots

Now and then I can still see their faces, snickering and laughing, their eyes mocking me. And   1
it bothers me that I should remember. Time and maturity should have diminished the pain,
because the incident happened more than 20 years ago. Occasionally, however, a smug smile
triggers the memory, and I think, "I should have done something." Some act of defiance could
have killed and buried the memory of the incident. Now it's too late.

In 1969, I was a senior on the Luther Burbank High School basketball team. The school is   2
on the south side of San Antonio, in one of the city's many barrios. After practice one day our
coach announced that we were going to spend the following Saturday scrimmaging with the
ball club from Winston Churchill High, located in the city's rich, white north side. After the
basketball game, we were to select someone from the opposing team and "buddy up"—talk
with him, have lunch with him and generally spend the day attempting friendship. By telling
us that this experience would do both teams some good, I suspect our well-intentioned coach
was thinking about the possible benefits of integration and of learning to appreciate the differences of other people. By integrating us with this more prosperous group, I think he was
also trying to inspire us.

But my teammates and I smiled sardonically at one another, and our sneakers squeaked   3
as we nervously rubbed them against the waxed hardwood floor of our gym. The prospect
of a full day of unfavorable comparisons drew from us a collective groan. As "barrio boys,"
we were already acutely aware of the differences between us and them. Churchill meant
"white" to us: It meant shiny new cars, two-story homes with fireplaces, pedigreed dogs
and manicured hedges. In other words, everything that we did not have. Worse, traveling
north meant putting up a front, to ourselves as well as to the Churchill team. We felt we
had to pretend that we were cavalier about it all, tough guys who didn't care about
"nothin'."

It's clear now that we entered the contest with negative images of ourselves. From   4
childhood, we must have suspected something was inherently wrong with us. The evidence
wrapped itself around our collective psyche like a noose. In elementary school, we were
not allowed to speak Spanish. The bladed edge of a wooden ruler once came crashing
down on my knuckles for violating this dictum. By high school, however, policies had
changed, and we could speak Spanish without fear of physical reprisal. Still, speaking
our language before whites brought on spasms of shame—for the supposed inferiority of our
language and culture—and guilt at feeling shame. That mixture of emotions fueled our
burning sense of inferiority.

After all, our mothers in no way resembled the glamorized models of American TV   5
mothers—Donna Reed baking cookies in high heels. My mother's hands were rough and
chafed, her wardrobe drab and worn. And my father was preoccupied with making ends
meet. His silence starkly contrasted with the glib counsel Jim Anderson offered in "Father

Knows Best." And where the Beaver worried about trying to understand some difficult homework assignment, for me it was an altogether different horror, when I was told by my elementary school principal that I did not have the ability to learn.

6   After I failed to pass the first grade, my report card read that I had a "learning disability." What shame and disillusion it brought my parents! To have carried their dream of a better life from Mexico to America, only to have their hopes quashed by having their only son branded inadequate. And so somewhere during my schooling I assumed that saying I had a "learning disability" was just another way of saying that I was "retarded." School administrators didn't care that I could not speak English.

7   As teenagers, of course, my Mexican-American friends and I did not consciously understand why we felt inferior. But we might have understood if we had fathomed our desperate need to trounce Churchill. We viewed the prospect of beating a white, north-side squad as a particularly fine coup. The match was clearly racial, our need to succeed born of a defiance against prejudice. I see now that we used the basketball court to prove our "blood." And who better to confirm us, if not those whom we considered better? In retrospect, I realize the only thing confirmed that day was that we saw ourselves as negatively as they did.

8   After we won the morning scrimmage, both teams were led from the gym into an empty room where everyone sat on a shiny linoleum floor. We were supposed to mingle—rub the colors together. But the teams sat separately, our backs against concrete walls. We faced one another like enemies, the empty floor between us a no man's land. As the coaches walked away, one reminded us to share lunch. God! The mere thought of offering them a taco from our brown bags when they had refrigerated deli lunches horrified us.

9   Then one of their players tossed a bag of Fritos at us. It slid across the slippery floor and stopped in the center of the room. With hearts beating anxiously, we Chicanos stared at the bag as the boy said with a sneer, "Y'all probably like 'em"—the "Frito Bandito" commercial being popular then. And we could see them, smiling at each other, giggling, jabbing their elbows into one another's ribs at the joke. The bag seemed to grow before our eyes like a monstrous symbol of inferiority.

10   We won the afternoon basketball game as well. But winning had accomplished nothing. Though we had wanted to, we couldn't change their perception of us. It seems, in fact, that defeating them made them meaner. Looking back, I feel these young men needed to put us "in our place," to reaffirm the power they felt we had threatened. I think, moreover, that they felt justified, not only because of their inherent sense of superiority, but because our failure to respond to their insult underscored our worthlessness in their eyes.

11   Two decades later, the memory of their gloating lives on in me. When a white person is discourteous, I find myself wondering what I should do, and afterward, if I've done the right thing. Sometimes I argue when a deft comment would suffice. Then I reprimand myself, for I am no longer a boy. But my impulse to argue bears witness to my ghosts. For, invariably, whenever I

feel insulted I'm reminded of that day at Churchill High. And whenever the past encroaches upon the present, I see myself rising boldly, stepping proudly across the years and crushing, underfoot, a silly bag of Fritos.

FOR WRITING OR DISCUSSION

1. What specific evidence in the narrative shows that the white teammates stereotyped their Hispanic opponents? What was the "Frito Bandito" commercial that Gomez mentions in paragraph 9?

2. What specific details are used to embody the white world of the north side of town? Is the author guilty of stereotyping?

3. Why is it significant that the events written about happened "more than 20 years ago"?

4. The good intentions of the coaches appear only to have made matters worse. Write a narrative showing the failure of good intentions.

Readings for Writing

The essay and short story that follow can provide you with strong subjects for your own narrative paper.

GREG SARRIS

"You Don't Look Indian"

I have heard that someone said to American Indian writer Louise Erdrich, "You don't look   1
Indian." It was at a reading she gave, or perhaps when she received an award of some kind for her writing. Undoubtedly, whoever said this noted Erdrich's very white skin, her green eyes and her red hair. She retorted, "Gee, you don't look rude."

You don't look Indian.   2

How often I too have heard that. But unlike Erdrich, I never returned the insult, or challenged   3
my interlocutors. Not with words anyway. I arranged the facts of my life to fit others' conceptions of what it is to be Indian. I used others' words, others' definitions. That way, if I didn't look Indian, I might still be Indian.

4   Well, I don't know if I am Indian, I said, or if I am, how much. I was adopted. I know my mother was white—Jewish, German, Irish. I was illegitimate. Father unknown. It was back in the fifties when having a baby without being married was shameful. My mother uttered something on the delivery table about the father being Spanish. Mexican maybe. Anyway, I was given up and adopted, which is how I got a name. For awhile things went well. Then they didn't. I found myself with other families, mostly on small ranches where I milked cows and worked with horses. I met a lot of Indians—Pomo Indians—and was taken in by one of the families. I learned bits and pieces of two Pomo languages. So if you ask, I call myself Pomo. But I don't know . . . My mother isn't around to ask. After she had me, she needed blood. The hospital gave her the wrong type and it killed her.

5   The story always went something like that. It is true, all of it, but arranged so that people might see how I fit. The last lines—about my mother—awe people and cause them to forget, or to be momentarily distracted, from their original concern about my not looking Indian. And I am illegitimate. That explains any crossing of borders, anything beyond the confines of definition. That is how I fit.

6   Last year I found my father. Well, I found out his name—Emilio. My mother's younger brother, my uncle, whom I met recently, remembered taking notes from his sister to a "big Hawaiian type" on the football field. "I would go after school while the team was practicing," my uncle said. "The dude was big, dark. They called him Meatloaf. I think his name though was Emilio. Try Emilio."

7   To have a name, even a nickname, seemed unfathomable. To be thirty-six years old and for the first time to have a lead about a father somehow frightened me. You imagine all your life; you find ways to account for that which is missing, you tell stories, and now all that is leveled by a name.

8   In Laguna Beach I contacted the high school librarian and made arrangements to look through old yearbooks. It was just after a conference there in Southern California, where I had finished delivering a paper on American Indian education. I found my mother immediately, and while I was staring for the first time at an adult picture of my mother, a friend who was with me scanned other yearbooks for an Emilio. Already we knew by looking at the rows and rows of white faces, there wouldn't be too many Emilios. I was still gazing at the picture of my mother when my friend jumped. "Look," she said. She was tilting the book, pointing to a name. But already, even as I looked, a dark face caught my attention, and it was a face I saw myself in. Without a doubt. Darker, yes. But me nonetheless.

9   I interviewed several of my mother's and father's classmates. It was my mother's friends who verified what I suspected. Emilio Hilario was my father. They also told me that he had died, that I missed him by about five years.

10   I had to find out from others what he couldn't tell me. I wanted to know about his life. Did he have a family? What was his ethnicity? Luckily I obtained the names of several relatives, including a half-brother and a grandfather. People were quick about that, much more so than about the ethnicity question. They often circumvented the question by telling stories about my father's athletic prowess and about how popular he was. A few, however, were more candid. His father, my grandfather, is Filipino. "A short Filipino man," they said. "Your father got his height from his mother. She was fairer." Some people said my grandmother was Spanish, others said she was Mexican

or Indian. Even within the family, there is discrepancy about her ethnicity. Her mother was definitely Indian, however. Coast Miwok from Tomales Bay just north of San Francisco, and just south
of Santa Rosa, where I grew up. Her name was Rienette.

During the time my grandmother was growing up, probably when her mother—Rienette—   11
was growing up too, even until quite recently, when it became popular to be Indian, Indians in
California sometimes claimed they were Spanish. And for good reason. The prejudice against
Indians was intolerable, and often only remnants of tribes, or even families, remained to face
the hatred and discrimination. My grandmother spoke Spanish. Her sister, Juanita, married a
Mexican and her children's children are proud *Chicanos* living in East Los Angeles. Rienette's
first husband, my grandmother and her sister's father, was probably part Mexican or Portuguese—I'm not sure.

The story is far from complete. But how much Indian I am by blood is not the question   12
whose answer concerns me now. Oh, I qualify for certain grants, and that is important. But
knowing about my blood heritage will not change my complexion any more than it will
my experience.

In school I was called the white beaner. This was not because some of my friends happened   13
to be Mexican, but because the white population had little sense of the local Indians. Anyone
with dark hair and skin was thought to be Mexican. A counselor once called me in and asked if
my family knew I went around with Mexicans. "Yes," I said. "They're used to it." At the time, I
was staying with an Indian family—the McKays—and Mrs. McKay was a mother to me. But I
said nothing more then. I never informed the counselor that most of my friends, the people she
was referring to, were Indian—Pomo Indian. Kashaya Pomo Indian. Sulfur Bank Pomo Indian.
Coyote Valley Pomo Indian. Yokaya Pomo Indian. Point Arena Pomo Indian. Bodega Bay
Miwok Indian. Tomales Bay Miwok Indian. And never mind that names such as Smith and
Pinola are not Spanish (or Mexican) names.

As I think back, I said nothing more to the counselor not because I didn't want to cause trouble   14
(I did plenty of that), but because, like most other kids, I never really knew a way to tamper with
how the authorities—counselors, teachers, social workers, police—categorized us. We talked
about our ethnicity amongst ourselves, often speculating who was more or less this or that. So
many of us are mixed with other groups—white, Mexican, Spanish, Portuguese, Filipino. I know
of an Indian family who is half Mexican and they identify themselves as Mexicans. In another family of the same admixture just the opposite is true. Yet for most of the larger white community, we
were Mexican, or something.

And here I am with blue eyes and fair skin. If I was a white beaner, I was, more generally, a   15
kid from the wrong side of the tracks. Hood. Greaser. Low Brow. Santa Rosa was a much smaller
town then, the lines more clearly drawn between the haves and the have-nots, the non-colored
and the colored. Suburban sprawl was just beginning; there was still the old downtown with its
stone library and old Roman-columned courthouse. On the fringes of town lived the poorer
folk. The civil rights movement had not yet engendered the ethnic pride typical of the late sixties
and early seventies.

I remember the two guys who taught me to box, Manuel and Robert. They said they were   16
Portuguese, Robert part Indian. People whispered that they were black. I didn't care. They
picked me out, taught me to box. That was when I was fourteen. By the time I was sixteen, I beat

heads everywhere and every time I could. I looked for fights and felt free somehow in the fight. I say I looked for fights, but really, as I think about it, fights seemed to find me. People said things, they didn't like me, they invaded my space. I had reason. So I fought. And afterwards I was somebody. Manny said I had a chip on my shoulder, which is an asset for a good fighter. "Hate in your eyes, brother," he told me. "You got hate in your eyes."

17   I heard a lot of "Indian" stories too. We used to call them old-time stories, those about Coyote and the creation. Then there were the spook stories about spook men and women and evil doings. I knew of a spook man, an old guy who would be sitting on his family's front porch one minute and then five minutes later, just as you were driving uptown, there he'd be sitting on the old courthouse steps. The woman whose son I spent so much time with was an Indian doctor. She healed the sick with songs and prayer; she sucked pains from people's bodies. These are the things my professors and colleagues wanted to hear about.

18   I was different here too. I read books, which had something to do with my getting into college. But when I started reading seriously—about the middle of my junior year in high school—I used what I read to explain the world; I never engaged my experience to inform what I was reading. Again, I was editing my experience, and, not so ironically, I found meaning that way. And, not so ironically, the more I read the more I became separated from the world of my friends and what I had lived. So in college when I found people interested in my Indian experience as it related to issues of ecology, personal empowerment, and other worldviews, I complied and told them what I "knew" of these things. In essence I shaped what I knew to fit the books and read the books to shape what I knew. The woman who was a mother to me came off as Castaneda's Don Juan. Think of the "separate reality" of her dream world, never mind what I remember about her—the long hours in the apple cannery, her tired face, her clothes smelling of rotten apples.

19   Now, as I sort through things, I am beginning to understand why I hated myself and those people at the university; how by sculpting my experience to their interests, I denied so much of my life, including the anger and self-hatred that seeps up from such denial. I wanted to strike back, beat the hell out of them; I imagined them angering me in some way I could recognize— maybe an insult, a push or shove—so that I could hurt them. Other times I just wanted them to be somewhere, perhaps outside the classroom, on a street, in a bar, where they came suddenly upon me and saw me fighting, pummelling somebody. Anger is like a cork in water. Push it down, push it down, and still it keeps coming to the surface.

FOR WRITING OR DISCUSSION

1. How does the writer's illegitimacy explain "any crossing of borders, anything beyond the confines of definition"?

2. What stereotypes did Sarris have to endure as he was growing up?

3. What steps does the writer take to uncover his personal family history? How do you explain his efforts?

4. Assume that Sarris could have one meeting with his father or mother. Write a narrative about that meeting. Or, as an alternate assignment, write a narrative about the first meeting between a child and a long-lost parent.

KATE CHOPIN
The Story of an Hour

Knowing that Mrs. Mallard was afflicted with a heart trouble, great care was taken to break to her as gently as possible the news of her husband's death. 1

It was her sister Josephine who told her, in broken sentences; veiled hints that revealed in half concealing. Her husband's friend Richards was there, too, near her. It was he who had been in the newspaper office when intelligence of the railroad disaster was received, with Brently Mallard's name leading the list of "killed." He had only taken the time to assure himself of its truth by a second telegram, and had hastened to forestall any less careful, less tender friend in bearing the sad message. 2

She did not hear the story as many women have heard the same, with a paralyzed inability to accept its significance. She wept at once, with sudden, wild abandonment, in her sister's arms. When the storm of grief had spent itself she went away to her room alone. She would have no one follow her. 3

There stood, facing the open window, a comfortable, roomy armchair. Into this she sank, pressed down by a physical exhaustion that haunted her body and seemed to reach into her soul. 4

She could see in the open square before her house the tops of trees that were all aquiver with the new spring life. The delicious breath of rain was in the air. In the street below a peddler was crying his wares. The notes of a distant song which some one was singing reached her faintly, and countless sparrows were twittering in the eaves. 5

There were patches of blue sky showing here and there through the clouds that had met and piled one above the other in the west facing her window. 6

She sat with her head thrown back upon the cushion of the chair, quite motionless, except when a sob came up into her throat and shook her, as a child who has cried itself to sleep continues to sob in its dreams. 7

She was young, with a fair, calm face, whose lines bespoke repression and even a certain strength. But now there was a dull stare in her eyes, whose gaze was fixed away off yonder on one of those patches of blue sky. It was not a glance of reflection, but rather indicated a suspension of intelligent thought. 8

There was something coming to her and she was waiting for it, fearfully. What was it? She did not know; it was too subtle and elusive to name. But she felt it, creeping out of the sky, reaching toward her through the sounds, the scents, the color that filled the air. 9

Now her bosom rose and fell tumultuously. She was beginning to recognize this thing that was approaching to possess her, and she was striving to beat it back with her will—as powerless as her two white slender hands would have been. 10

When she abandoned herself a little whispered word escaped her slightly parted lips. She said it over and over under her breath: "free, free, free!" The vacant stare and the look of terror that had followed it went from her eyes. They stayed keen and bright. Her pulses beat fast, and the coursing blood warmed and relaxed every inch of her body. 11

12   She did not stop to ask if it were or were not a monstrous joy that held her. A clear and exalted perception enabled her to dismiss the suggestion as trivial.

13   She knew that she would weep again when she saw the kind, tender hands folded in death; the face that had never looked save with love upon her, fixed and gray and dead. But she saw beyond that bitter moment a long procession of years to come that would belong to her absolutely. And she opened and spread her arms out to them in welcome.

14   There would be no one to live for her during those coming years; she would live for herself. There would be no powerful will bending hers in that blind persistence with which men and women believe they have a right to impose a private will upon a fellow-creature. A kind intention or a cruel intention made the act seem no less a crime as she looked upon it in that brief moment of illumination.

15   And yet she had loved him—sometimes. Often she had not. What did it matter! What could love, the unsolved mystery, count for in face of this possession of self-assertion which she suddenly recognized as the strongest impulse of her being!

16   "Free! Body and soul free!" she kept whispering.

17   Josephine was kneeling before the closed door with her lips to the keyhole, imploring for admission. "Louise, open the door! I beg; open the door—you will make yourself ill. What are you doing, Louise? For heaven's sake open the door."

18   "Go away. I am not making myself ill." No; she was drinking in a very elixir of life through that open window.

19   Her fancy was running riot along those days ahead of her. Spring days, and summer days, and all sorts of days that would be her own. She breathed a quick prayer that life might be long. It was only yesterday she had thought with a shudder that life might be long.

20   She arose at length and opened the door to her sister's importunities. There was a feverish triumph in her eyes, and she carried herself unwittingly like a goddess of Victory. She clasped her sister's waist, and together they descended the stairs. Richards stood waiting for them at the bottom.

21   Some one was opening the front door with a latchkey. It was Brently Mallard who entered, a little travel-stained, composedly carrying his grip-sack and umbrella. He had been far from the scene of accident, and did not even know there had been one. He stood amazed at Josephine's piercing cry; at Richards' quick motion to screen him from the view of his wife.

22   But Richards was too late.

23   When the doctors came they said she had died of heart disease—of joy that kills.

FOR WRITING OR DISCUSSION

1. What is Chopin's main point here? What does the title contribute to the story?

2. How do you account for Mrs. Mallard's feelings toward her husband? Chopin's story was written in 1892. What might the period suggest in terms of attitudes of married men and women toward each other?

3. How do the paragraphs that come before paragraph 11 prepare you for the exultant "free, free, free!" uttered by Mrs. Mallard? For example, what do paragraphs 3–6 contribute to the story?

4. What do the doctors think killed Mrs. Mallard? What really killed her? What is the irony, then, in the last line of the story?

5. What narrative strategies do you identify here? How does the sequence of events play a particularly important role in the story?

6. How would the story turn out, do you think, if it were Mr. Mallard who incorrectly learned of the death of his wife? How, given the basic premise of "The Story of an Hour," do you think he would react? How might he react upon seeing his wife alive?

7. Write an essay in which you analyze and explain Mrs. Mallard's feelings toward her husband.

Reading and Writing About Poetry

In this brief poem, Countee Cullen presents an unforgettable narrative. Answer the questions that follow it.

COUNTEE CULLEN

Incident

Once riding in old Baltimore
    Heart-filled, head-filled with glee,
I saw a Baltimorean
    Keep looking straight at me.

Now I was eight and very small,
    And he was no whit bigger,
And so I smiled, but he poked out
    His tongue, and called me, "Nigger."
I saw the whole of Baltimore

5

10   From May until December;
         Of all the things that happened there
         That's all that I remember.

FOR WRITING OR DISCUSSION

1. How well does the title serve the poem? Why did the poet choose this title, do you think?

2. What is the mood of the narrator in stanza one? How do you account for it? How do you account for what the boy says to the narrator in stanza two?

3. What is your reaction to the last stanza? How do you account for its power?

4. Write a narrative essay in which you tell about a moment in which someone said something to you that has stayed in your memory for a long time.

STRATEGY CHECKLIST: Writing and Revising Your Narrative Paper

Plan the paper.

☐ Have I used prewriting to explore ideas for a subject?

☐ Have I thought about my purpose for writing—that is, will my narrative make a point?

☐ Do I have my audience clearly in mind?

☐ Have I limited my topic?

☐ Have I considered using an outline to organize my ideas?

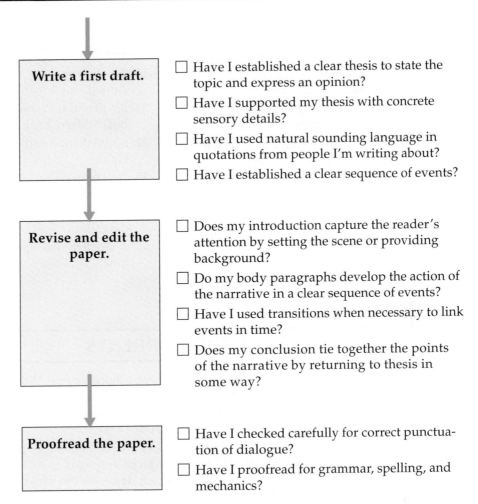

Write a first draft.

- ☐ Have I established a clear thesis to state the topic and express an opinion?
- ☐ Have I supported my thesis with concrete sensory details?
- ☐ Have I used natural sounding language in quotations from people I'm writing about?
- ☐ Have I established a clear sequence of events?

Revise and edit the paper.

- ☐ Does my introduction capture the reader's attention by setting the scene or providing background?
- ☐ Do my body paragraphs develop the action of the narrative in a clear sequence of events?
- ☐ Have I used transitions when necessary to link events in time?
- ☐ Does my conclusion tie together the points of the narrative by returning to thesis in some way?

Proofread the paper.

- ☐ Have I checked carefully for correct punctuation of dialogue?
- ☐ Have I proofread for grammar, spelling, and mechanics?

WRITING TOPICS

If you are having trouble deciding on a topic for your narrative paper, you might find it helpful simply to choose one of the following proverbs, quotations, or commonsense statements and then write a narration supporting or attacking it.

1. Money can't buy happiness.

2. Money is the root of all evil.

3. I never met a man I didn't like.

4. If you can't take the heat, get out of the kitchen.

5. When the going gets tough, the tough get going.

6. You can't tell a book by its cover.

7. If at first you don't succeed, try, try again.

8. There's no such thing as a bad boy.

9. Nobody knows the trouble I've seen.

10. A penny saved is a penny earned.

11. Small children, small problems; big children, big problems.

12. Spare the rod and spoil the child.

13. Hell hath no fury like a woman scorned.

14. Good fences make good neighbors.

15. A stitch in time saves nine.

CROSSCURRENTS

1. Prejudice is a central element in both "Foul Shots" (pages 161–163) and "Incident" (pages 169–170). Write an essay in which you discuss these two selections together. How does each writer approach the issue of prejudice? Provide specific examples to support your views.

2. Both "'You Don't Look Indian'" by Greg Sarris (pages 163–166) and "My Father's House" by Jarrett David Lee Jackson (pages 155–157) deal with relations between parents and children. How do the ideas in the selections relate to each other? What do you think Sarris would have said to Jackson?

COLLABORATIVE LEARNING

In groups of five students each, compare and contrast the two student pieces "The Death of Santa Claus" (pages 152–154) and "My Father's House" (pages 155–157) as models of narrative essays. Use the "Strategy Checklist: Writing and Revising Your Narrative Paper" as a touchstone for your comments.

From **IMAGE** To **WORDS**: A Reading and Writing Assignment

Photo courtesy: Bruce Ely/Newhouse News Service/Landov

1. Where is this scene set? How do you know?

2. What details of the photograph capture the crisis of the moment?

3. Using the photograph write a short narrative paper to tell the story that to your mind emerges from the picture. Be sure to write a thesis that establishes both the topic and your opinion about it. Make the narrative come alive with sensory detail. Be sure that the sequence of events that you propose is clear to your readers.

For additional writing, reading, and research resources, go to **www. mycomplab. com** <http://www.mycomplab.com/> and choose Skwire/Wiener's *Student's Book of College English*, Twelfth Edition.

CHAPTER 9

Example

- Writing Your Example Paper
- Student Writing: Example
- Researched Student Writing: Example
- Critical Reading: Example
- Models of Writing
- Readings for Writing
- Reading and Writing About Poetry

An **example**—or **illustration**—represents, or sometimes shows, the primary nature of the larger group to which it belongs: A rattlesnake is an example of a reptile; kidnapping is an example of crime; a Cadillac is an example of General Motors products. An **example paper** relies almost solely on examples to support the thesis, and learning to manage this kind of paper well will help prepare you for all the varieties of papers you will have to write.

Nearly all good writing depends heavily on examples or illustrations as an important means of supporting ideas—and for sound reasons. Examples give concreteness and, therefore, clarity to ideas. A writer may say, for instance, that going to school can be frustrating, and, as a student, you nod your head in agreement. But how can you be sure that you and the writer have the same understanding of frustration? When the writer goes on to tell stories about the causes of her frustration—when she writes about her inability to stand on her head in her physical education class, or her ineptness at dissecting a cat in her anatomy class, or her habitual failure to recharge the batteries of her calculator before going to her math class—you understand what the writer means by frustration. The examples give to the abstract idea *frustration* not only clarity but also concreteness, and the concreteness does much to make the idea interesting.

Because concreteness and clarity are essential to good writing, example often shapes even the smallest sentence sequence:

> To convince a reader, good writers usually offer support for their generalizations. In the Declaration of Independence, for example, Thomas Jefferson cited twenty-eight violations of basic human rights to support his assertion that George III was a tyrant.

Similarly, examples can develop an entire paragraph:

> History and legend tell us that some of the greatest scientific discoveries are the result of inspirations caused by chance occurrences. Three brief examples can demonstrate this point. First, Archimedes' noticing the rise of the water level as he

submerged himself in a tub led to the formulation of the laws of liquid displacement, the foundation of many of the laws of modern physics. Second, Sir Isaac Newton discovered the law of gravity because an apple fell on his head while he was sitting under a tree. Third, after being caught in a strong current of hot rising air while flying his gas balloon, George Alexander Whitehead thought about the occurrence and developed the fundamental principles of meteorology. These and other incidents show that many of the greatest scientific developments spring from lucky accidents that stimulate work in a specific direction.

Writing Your Example Paper

Writers can shape sentences and paragraphs by means of example, but our concern in this chapter is to look at an entire paper developed by example. In such a paper, the writer offers well-developed examples to support a thesis. The success of the paper will depend largely on the quality of these illustrations and on their arrangement. We have some suggestions.

 TIPS   for Writing an Example Essay

- **Be specific.**   Remember, the purpose of an example is to give concreteness and clarity to an idea, and you won't get either with vague language (see pages 546–550). Notice the concrete language and the specific details in the following passage:

> I spent a good part of my life close to nature as a migratory worker, lumberjack, and placer miner. Mother Nature was breathing down my neck, so to speak, and I had the feeling that she did not want me around. I was bitten by every sort of insect, and scratched by burrs, foxtails and thorns. My clothes were torn by buck-brush and tangled manzanita. Hard clods pushed against my ribs when I lay down to rest, and grime ate its way into every pore of my body. Everything around me was telling me all the time to roll up and be gone. I was an unwanted intruder. I could never be at home in nature the way trees, flowers and birds are at home . . . in the city. I did not feel at ease until my feet touched the paved road.
>   The road led to the city, and I knew with every fiber of my being that the man-made world of the city was man's only home on this planet, his refuge from an inhospitable nonhuman cosmos.
>   —Eric Hoffer, "Cities and Nature"

Now, consider how much less vivid and therefore less interesting is the following version of Hoffer's passage:

> I lived and worked outdoors for several years, and the experience taught me that the city is the preferable habitat for man. In nature, I always felt dirty and uncomfortable. Nature was inhospitable to me. I was an alien

there and never felt comfortable until I turned again toward the city, the only appropriate environment for man.

Obviously, good examples use specific details expressed in concrete language.

■ **Make certain that your examples are examples, and that your generalization, or thesis, is one that examples can support.**   As noted earlier, an example is a single item selected from many to show the nature or character of the group, or it is one of many specific instances in which a generalization proves to be true. If Maria is the only woman in your school who has dyed her hair green, you cannot generalize that green hair is a fad in your school and then cite the one case as an example, no matter how vividly you describe Maria's new hair color. You can, however, use Maria's green hair as an example of her eccentricity if she really is eccentric—if she exhibits several other odd characteristics. An example is one of many, and a generalization is that which is usually or frequently or generally true of its subject.

■ **Play fair.**   When the subject allows, you should try to select examples that represent an honest cross-section of your subject. If you want to show, for instance, that most of the teachers in a particular school are boring lecturers, try to find examples of some who are young, some who are middle-aged, and some who are nearing retirement. Again, some of your examples should be women and some men, some perhaps single and some married. Your examples should also indicate a fair distribution among departments. You don't want your examples to suggest that all boring lecturers are middle-aged, married men who wear glasses and teach English. Rather, you want to show that boring teachers pop up everywhere and too often in this particular school, reflecting many backgrounds and subject areas—and even ways of being boring.

Of course, you don't always have to use several examples to make your point. Often, a good way to develop a thesis is to use one **extended example.** Even so, you should select the example according to the same rules of fairness that apply to the selection of numerous examples. It must truly represent an honest cross-section of the subject.

The following passage from Sasha Abramsky's essay "When They Get Out" for *Atlantic* does just that. In it, the writer illustrates the painful effects of incarceration on the lives of ex-prisoners.

> Recently I met several ex-prisoners in New York City who were putting their lives back together under the auspices of the Fortune Society, a non-profit organization that runs one of the country's most successful and intensive post-release programs. Some of the people I met had done terrible things; others

had merely taken foolish wrong turns. Regardless, talking with them gave each one a human face. It helped me to understand that most of these ex-cons are damaged people with hopes and fears and dreams that perhaps can be coaxed out of them in a nurturing environment like Fortune's.

The most extraordinary of the people I met was a thirty-nine-year-old named Edmond Taylor, who had served a total of eighteen years in a variety of New York's toughest prisons for crimes ranging from drug dealing to violent assault. Out of prison for the past couple of years, Taylor has dedicated himself to change; he works full time as a counselor, helping other prisoners to adjust to life on the outside, and he is regarded by Fortune's executive director, JoAnne Page, as one of her great success stories. Taylor came to meet me straight from counseling a distraught woman who'd been told at a job interview that the company wouldn't hire her because she had a felony conviction. He said, "If I can save just one person a year, I'm happy."

A highly articulate man, more capable than most of understanding what led him into violence and helped to destroy half his life, Taylor explained that he had spent nearly four years in "the box"—some of that time in Clinton Dannemora prison, near the Canadian border, for being what he described as "a vocal critic" of conditions within the prison. Describing his reaction to being released from isolation back into the general prison population, he said, "First there's fear, then there's anger, and the anger takes over. It's violent anger. Very quick. No thought of the magnitude of the consequence of the violence. An individual bumped me, rushing to get to the gym. And I rushed up behind him and hit him with a pipe. He went into coma." Taylor went straight back into the box. I asked how long it had taken him to recover from isolation. He looked surprised by the question, and said, "Honestly, I've still not recovered. I've been out of isolation five and a half years. Ms. Page is my boss. If she was to confront me when I had a lot on my mind, anger would come up before rational thought. Anger. Strike back. Now it's not so much physical as verbal. In another situation it would cause me to lose my job." Then Taylor told me a shameful secret. Shortly after he got out of prison, he was living with his brother. His brother criticized him for some of the attitudes he'd brought out of prison with him. "I felt fed up, and I attacked him." Taylor said. "I grabbed him, choked him, lifted him off his feet, threw him to the ground. I pummeled him causing him to get several stitches above the eye. I grabbed a kitchen knife—I don't remember any of this; he told me afterward—and put it to his neck and said. 'I should kill you. I hate you.' The realization that I put my hands on my baby brother— the only person at that time who'd ever been in my corner . . . "

—Sasha Abramsky, "When They Get Out"

On reading this passage, we accept Abramsky's generalization not only because he tells the story of Edmond Taylor so vividly but also because it illustrates the uncontrollable anger of prisoners kept in isolation and then released into the general prison population. The writer uses one extended example to make his point: He focuses on the violent reactions of a single prisoner and his efforts to keep his own anger in check as he attempts to help others.

One extended example, then, can serve to support a thesis if the example is fully and convincingly developed. More often than not, however, you can build a stronger argument with several short examples. In this case, you need to give order to your examples, and this brings us to our last tip on writing an example paper.

■ **Think about the arrangement of your examples.** Sometimes the best arrangement is chronological. The examples in the paragraph on pages 174–175 about scientific discoveries, for instance, are presented in chronological order—from the ancient to the modern world. At other times, a spatial order works best. In supporting a thesis about the restaurants in your town, you might offer examples from several sections of the town, and those examples could be arranged geographically from north to south, east to west.

Or consider this: Many writers like to save their best example for last in order to achieve a dramatic conclusion. Others like to use their best example first to awaken interest. Certainly, the first and last are likely to get the most attention from a reader. Since some examples are more dramatic and convincing than others, you would do well to bury the weaker ones in the middle of the paper. Of course, if all your examples are equally excellent, you have nothing to worry about.

Student Writing: Example

See what you think of the quality and arrangement of examples in the following student papers. Annotations for the first paper will help focus your attention on key elements in writing example essays.

Monica Branch

Keep It Simple

1   I have eaten some incredible food in my time. My family has always liked to celebrate important occasions by going out to fancy restaurants, so

Introduction: Provides background information that builds to the thesis. Paper is not about "incredible food," yet with this information writer establishes reason for choosing her thesis.

graduations, engagements, college acceptances, anniversaries, and so on are times to try venison with cranberry gravy, or lobster Newburg, or pasta with a cream sauce and seven different kinds of unpronounceable mushrooms. So, I have eaten some fabulous meals over the years, and I have loved virtually all of them. But the more gourmet food I sample, the more I become convinced that the very best food is the simplest.

Consider barbecued spareribs. They are simple, unassuming, messy finger food. But purchased from the smoke-filled corner rib joint, served over a slice of white bread to catch the sauce, with a side of crisp fries and a paper cup of soggy coleslaw, dripping with fat, calories, and character, there is absolutely nothing better.

There is nothing better except for maybe real, homemade macaroni and cheese (not the kind that comes in a box with a packet of orange powder). Give me a brutally cold winter day. Let me feast my eyes on that beautiful, crunchy, brown top, fresh from the oven. We're talking joy. We're talking peace. We're talking love.

And then there's the fluffernutter! A huge glob of peanut butter and a huger glob of marshmallow fluff on the softest white bread around—it sounds like nothing, but it is the perfect sandwich. It wraps sweet, salty, crunchy, and smooth into one convenient package. The incredible stickiness is a delight as well.

There are Oreo cookies, ants on a log (celery sticks decorated with cream cheese and raisins), packaged chicken soup with ring-shaped noodles, southern fried steak, cold leftover pizza, bright orange French dressing, cinnamon toast, oatmeal with brown sugar, dill pickles, and a thousand other marvelous, simple foods. I love them all.

So, the next time my family and I have something special to celebrate, I will happily go to the fanciest restaurant they can find, but my love and respect for simple, ordinary, better-than-anything foods will never cease. And I'll be down at the rib joint when they're ready to go.

Margin notes:

Thesis presents generalization that examples can illustrate.

Transition: "Consider . . ." links first body paragraph to thesis.

Sensory appeals to sight and sound.

More specific language to provide images for reader.

Last body paragraph lists other examples to supplement three examples developed in previous body paragraphs.

2
First example to support thesis. Concrete details provide sensory image for reader.

3
Second example.

4
Third example: Examples represent a good cross-section of the subject.

5

6
Conclusion: Returns to the idea of the thesis and reminds reader of "incredible food" introduction.

FOR WRITING OR DISCUSSION

1. Where does the writer first present the thesis statement? Where does she repeat it?
2. Instead of providing an additional lengthy example, the next-to-last paragraph lists a number of short examples. What does the writer gain by this change in strategy?
3. Where are definitions provided for foods with which some readers may be unfamiliar?
4. Use the title "Keep It Simple" for an example paper of your own celebrating simplicity in a subject of your choice, such as clothing, cars, weddings, laws, music, movies, and so on.

Laura Zager
A True Tale of a Family

1   I imagine that I'm one of the few American youths who happily wear the sweaters made by their grandmothers. I probably also qualify for the minority of teenagers who freely elect to spend most evenings cross-stitching and watching "Beavis and Butt-head" with their parents. Sickly enough, I can even identify positive qualities in my mother and father, an opinion which, if voiced too loudly, would automatically revoke my membership in the "Sulky, Post-Adolescent Union."

2   As a good daughter does, I love my family. Yet more importantly, I truly like my family. Fundamentally, they are a seemingly random, odd assortment of people connected by an unspoken desire to know and take care of each other. Like the British Royal Family, I was born into this circle and consider it a privilege to be a member. Unlike the British Royal Family, taped episodes of "South Park," gallons of delicious, smooth eggnog at Christmas, gun shows and karate demonstrations are standard fare for us. Each member of my family is supremely individual and brings his or her own experiences and viewpoints to the table.

From each of them, I've picked up qualities which have made me the person I am and will shape the person I will become.

My grandmother taught me to love glue. If it isn't working, add more glue. When I was younger, we'd attach goggly eyeballs to pieces of paper, tack felt to Popsicle sticks, cover lumps of cardboard with glitter. Today, my grandmother wraps ribbons around toilet seat covers, papers cardboard boxes, and affixed a smiley sticker to her computer monitor. She taught me to want to cook. Like the magnificent casseroles, glorious biscotti, and divinely inspired stuffed shells she makes, tuna fish slapped on a stale cracker by her hand becomes the ambrosial nectar of the gods. For my grandmother, there are always improvements to be made, family to be fed, missions to be conquered.

I'd like to be that way, too.

My mother taught me to "get it done now." At the slightest breath of a request, she is on the phone, calling whoever needs to be called, be it pizza delivery or the secretary-general of the United Nations. Several years ago, I mumbled something under my breath about "maybe, possibly" wanting to get my hair just a little bit trimmed, and, faster than I could voice a coherent statement, scissors were flying and bits of hair were showering the ground. That's fast. She is always ready with an aspirin and water to take it with for headaches, and can clairvoyantly tell just when a hot bath is necessary for recovery. For her children, she will climb Kilimanjaro, march on Washington or raise general hell.

I'd like to be that way, too.

My father taught me that it's good to know as much as possible. He spends his lunch hours searching reference books for the point at which two obscure geographical marking lines cross, can rattle off the name and principal actors of every gunslinging television program of his youth, and managed to clear up an entire year's worth of trigonometry haze in several hours. He was one of the first people to realize that the Internet is useful for very little else than searching for song lyrics. My father taught me to try to make things last. We own a small white towel with our last name, "ZAGER," printed on it in permanent marker. The way my father tells it, he was born into that towel, used it throughout his youth, and dried himself through college and graduate school with it. There are photographs of my father at Sesame Place holding me as a toddler, wearing the same sneakers he wore yesterday. Seventeen-year-old sneakers.

8   I'd like to be that way, too.

9   I will be that way. Day by day, I see myself slowly morphing into my grandmother, my mother, my father, the rest of my family. At this rate, their composites will produce a liberal, pet-collecting carpenter in flashy shoes who carries a large rifle around in a knitted bag. This is a fate I will merrily succumb to. My family is my core, my constant, my favorite people. They're me, inextricably, and I am eternally attached to them.

FOR WRITING OR DISCUSSION

1. What is the writer's thesis?
2. What is the writer's tone in the essay? How does the last line of the first paragraph contribute to the tone? (See page 180.)
3. What is the effect of Zager's repeating the sentence "I'd like to be that way, too"?
4. What examples does Zager provide in paragraph 2? In what ways does the rest of the essay expand on these examples?
5. Which examples do you find most convincing as support for the writer's thesis?
6. Write an essay about the effect of close family members on your life or the life of someone you know. Use examples to support your thesis.

Researched Student Writing: Example

In this student essay, note the effective integration of electronic and print sources as supporting examples for the writer's thesis.

Laura Merkner

Children of Television

The topic of children and television has been controversial for years. Many people   1
worry that children will be affected negatively by television messages that involve violence,
drugs, and sexuality. But, is all TV bad for children? Viewing experts say television programs
could be deemed appropriate for a younger viewing audience if there is educational value in
the program, if the program promotes non-violent behavior, and if the parent is monitoring
what their child is watching. These three factors could lead to children watching more
appropriate programs on television.

Children between the ages of four and sixteen are usually the most influenced by   2
what they watch on television. According to TV Turnoff Network, an organization that
promotes "More Reading, Less TV," when children between the ages of four and six
were asked if they would rather watch TV or spend time with their fathers, more than
fifty percent of the youngsters opted for the TV ("Facts and Figures"). These figures
might be appalling, but the survey doesn't say *what* the young children would rather
watch on TV. Some television programs for children could actually be considered
beneficial for them. Some shows such as *Sesame Street* and *Mr. Rogers'
Neighborhood* are considered educational since they help children learn fundamental
skills such as counting, colors, and friendship. The Federal Communications
Commission (FCC) has even identified for television networks what programs are
considered educational. According to the FCC, educational, or core programs, must be
"at least 30 minutes in length, be aired between the hours of 7:00 a.m. and 10:00
p.m., and be a regularly scheduled weekly program." Each television station must also
"air at least three hours of their core programming per week, must provide parents and
consumers with advance information about core programs being aired, and define the
type of programs that qualify as core programs" ("Children's"). For example, the
popular children's cartoon *Dragon Tales*, is on for thirty minutes at 1:30 p.m. every
day, so this wholesome show does qualify as a core program for PBS. So, if parents

monitor what their children watch and are looking for educational programs, the FCC has laid out some basic guidelines to make this process easier.

3   Another guideline to make children's viewing habits safer is to not allow them to watch shows that promote violence. In 1966, Rosemary Lee Potter made a rather surprising discovery concerning a violent television show. Potter was working on a National Defense Educational Act for her graduate school program and was observing a first-grade class and teacher. The teacher gave the children puppets in order to help them with their verbal behavior. The children used the puppets to act out scenes, but what was surprising was that the children were usually narrating scenes from the popular *Batman* program that was aired weekly on the television set at home. Because of the increased enthusiasm in reading and speaking prompted by this show, the teacher developed reading material related to the caped crusader and his adventures. When the teacher tried out this reading material, Potter observed that "The children paid unusually close attention to detail, listened more closely to other readers, read complex sentences, and attacked unknown and difficult words with great confidence." The reason why this is such a surprising discovery is because the *Batman* series could be considered a rather violent television show. Each week Batman must face an adversary and must physically, and sometimes mentally, beat his opponent in order to triumph as the victor. In each episode, there are often many kicks and punches used while Batman defeats his adversary. The program itself involves violence, but it does seem to promote a non-violent attitude. Batman typically only uses violence when it is necessary. Even though this could be considered a very violent television show, the kids were able to take something positive out of it. The teacher was able to use the fun and adventurous nature of Batman in order to help her students become excited about learning. Nothing that makes children excited about learning could be considered bad.

4   Some people, however, would disagree with that statement. Some believe that if a child is watching television, then nothing good can come of it. The TV Turnoff Network

gives us another astonishing figure: In 1961, five percent of American children were obese, but in 2003, this percentage increased by over ten percent ("Facts and Figures"). This tells us that the obesity in children is increasing, and we already know that weight gain is linked to inactivity of the body. If children are watching TV many hours a day, then their body is inactive for just as many hours, and then the child will more than likely be gaining weight. The TV Turnoff Network also informs us that television "slows the metabolism and promotes an unhealthy lifestyle" ("Give TV"). So, if a child is gaining weight because he is watching too much TV, then yes, TV is a problem. However, if the child is watching an excessive amount of TV, then the problem might go deeper than his TV habits. Obesity in America is a growing epidemic but it is the parents' job to police what their kids are doing. If parents believe that their child is taking too much time watching TV and sitting on the couch, then the parent may want to suggest a healthier alternative for entertainment.

5

It is frightening to think about how teenage violence has progressed throughout the years, but TV should not be considered the only culprit. The programs on television can positively affect the younger generation if the program is educational, if the program is not excessively violent, and if the parents monitor what their kids are watching. Television can be a positive tool, since as Potter points out, "One of the best ways to offset the difficulties TV poses to children is to intervene in their viewing process by making constructive use of the massive TV experience" (Potter iv). If television is used in a positive and constructive manner, then there is no reason why parents should worry about their children sitting down and watching some television.

Works Cited

"Children's Educational Television." *Federal Communications Commission.* Federal Communications Commission, 1990. Web. 1 Dec. 2005.

"Facts and Figures about Our TV Habit." *TV Turnoff Network.* TV Turnoff Network Real Vision, 2003. Web. 1 Dec. 2005.

"Give TV the Hiking Boot." *TV Turnoff Network*. TV Turnoff Network Real Vision, 2001.
      Web. 7 Dec. 2005.

Potter, Rosemary Lee. *The Positive Use of Commercial Television with Children*. Columbus:
      Avon, 1976. Print.

FOR WRITING OR DISCUSSION

1. What is the thesis of Merkner's essay?
2. Which data do you find particularly effective? Why?
3. How does the case of Potter's observations of a first-grade class support the writer's thesis? How is it an instance of an extended example?
4. Other than convenience, why do you think Merkner may have chosen mostly electronic sources for her research? What does the Web offer that books do not? What do books offer that Web sites do not?
5. Write an essay in which you consider the statement at the end of the third paragraph: "Nothing that makes children excited about learning could be considered bad." Use specific examples to support the thesis.

HAVING YOUR SAY

What do you think is responsible for the increased violence shown by many teenagers across the country? What role do television and the movies play? Home environment? Neighborhood? Genetic makeup? Write an example essay in which you treat only those elements that you think contribute to teenage violence. Be sure to do some research in the library and on the Web. Cite your sources as your teacher instructs. You might want to look ahead to Chapter 20.

Critical Reading: Example

Look at the marginal notes in this selection. They point to content and language issues to which an active critical reader pays attention. Note how the reader raises questions and makes comments that build understanding of the essay. You should apply thinking like this as you read the various selections in this book—and in your other courses. Answer the questions after you have read the piece and the surrounding commentary.

Mind's Eye:
Phrase for
the
imagination,
what you see
in your head
as you think.

Repetition
asserts
importance
of phrase to
the thesis.

He means a
visual
imagination
—but he
can't lay out
drawings of
these
highways in
a scrapbook.

Different
kinds of
roads have
different
effects on
his mind.

Even
familiar
routes fade
from the
memory.

Another
example of
"familiar
stretch of
highway."

The area is
changing but
the roads
remain
constant.

VERLYN KLINKENBORG

Inside <u>the Mind's Eye</u>, a Network of Highways

It occurred to me the other day, on an <u>old familiar stretch</u> of highway out West, to think of all the <u>old familiar stretches</u> of highway in my life. Not as a <u>metaphor</u> or a way of seeing where I've gotten in life—the answer, in asphalt, being exactly nowhere—but just for the fun of it. 1

If I had a <u>more graphic imagination</u>, I would draw all those strips of road side by side in an oversized scrapbook or cut them out of the folding maps and glue them into a single discontinuous journey. For a while, for instance, I drove across Massachusetts and back again every week to teach. I did the same up the border of New York and Vermont. These days, I drive two routes through the Hudson Valley every week. 2

These roads I can see in my mind if I just close my eyes. They are so <u>grooved</u> into me that I doubt they will ever fade. Other roads—regular routes once upon a time—still come back to me in patches, like parts of the highway between Keams Canyon, on the Hopi Reservation, and Flagstaff, Ariz. 3

But some deeply familiar routes have long since worn away almost completely, leaving behind only the feeling of what it's like to be a child pressed against the door as the car makes a right-angle turn. That always happened somewhere on the drive to my grandparents' house in northwest Iowa. Was it in Boyden or Cherokee? 4

I drove <u>that old route</u> a year ago, and it seemed to me as though I had never seen it before, though to be fair, my family last made that trip more than 40 years past, in a 1963 white Ford Galaxy. 5

The thought of all these highways occurred to me somewhere between Crow Agency, Mont, and the Wyoming border, part of a longer drive from Billings to Sheridan. In the last dozen years, <u>I've driven that stretch of highway—I90—dozens of times</u>. It's a daydreamer's road, a <u>big, wide freeway</u> cutting through a <u>big, wide country</u>. 6

The road rolls up out of the lowland along the Yellowstone River—<u>past the refineries</u> and the <u>Billings live-stock auction</u>—into a great sweep of <u>wheat land, across the Crow Reservation</u> over a shoulder of the <u>Rosebud Mountains</u> and down into the <u>Tongue River</u> drainage. 7

Whenever I think of that road, that's usually the direction I'm heading, north to south, always surprised to find the Wyoming welcome sign farther off than I remember; always surprised <u>to see how little has changed</u> in a West where everything is changing as fast as it can. 8

There are times on that highway when I feel motionless even at 80 miles an hour. Often, the car begins to buck whenever it gets crosswise to the wind, which has no impediments out there. When I first began making that trip, it still had the feel of a <u>mythic journey</u>, pushing backward in time. 9

Metaphor
means
comparison:
Writer won't
compare
highway
travel with
travel down
the road of
life's
achievements.
He wants to
look at roads
he's traveled
simply for the
fun of it.

"grooved"—
powerful
word shows
permanence
of image.

"That old
route":
transition.

Repetition
again—
emphasizes
the point.

The route of
this drive and
examples of
what he
sees.

Mythic
means
imaginary or
like a myth.
The words
echo the first
four words in
the title.

The land creates and then erodes the myths.

10   It wasn't the Crow Reservation that made me feel that way or the signs for Little Bighorn. <u>It was the lay of the land, the rimrock, the grasses, the antelope racing across the plains.</u> And there have been night drives when it felt as if every mile had to be won against my own fatigue. But if I spend enough time in the West the <u>myths erode, and what I'm left with is an actual landscape</u>.

11   In a dry year, a vast swath of wheat burns black. Another year, the radio is suddenly full of Christian stations, a mixture of salvation rock and hometown choirs coming over the air. One trip, a <u>golden eagle nearly lands on the hood of the car</u>. On another, I wake up from my daydream and find myself closing in fast on a sugar-beet truck headed for Western Sugar in Billings, a single light flashing slowly on its tail. The <u>beets look</u> prehistoric, <u>like lumps of</u> matter waiting to be formed.

Examples of "actual landscape."

Similar phrase in par. 11: "Wheat burns black."

12   I'm still only an occasional traveler on this road, of course. I've missed the blizzards that shut it down from time to time, though I've caught more than enough of the thunderstorms, <u>black as a burned wheatfield</u> in the sky, that scour the ridges and the flats. A couple of months ago, I drove all the way from Hardin to Garryowen under the arc of the most violent rainbow I've ever seen, a dense wall of color shimmering overhead.

More examples of "land elements" creating a myth in his mind—"the illusion of frozen beasts."

13   <u>This last time</u>, I left Sheridan after a hard autumn frost. In the pastures along the highway, the horses seemed to have frozen solid overnight. They held themselves absolutely motionless, broadside to the rising sun, in all of the classic postures available to their kind. One stood with eyes closed, ears pricked backward. Another lay with front legs folded under, its neck arched so that only its muzzle touched the ground. Some stood clumped together in frozen bands amid frozen herds of cattle.

Transition.

14   There was no breeze to sweep their tails of manes. Mile after mile; pasture after pasture, the illusion held, as if I were driving through a land of <u>cryogenic</u> beasts.

The sun dismisses the illusion.

15   Then the morning sun took hold, and they all came to life again.

FOR WRITING OR DISCUSSION

1. What is Klinkenborg's thesis?
2. How has he used examples to make his point? Which examples do you find most visual?
3. Which marginal comments did you find most helpful? Why? What other comments might you have added?
4. Read "Childhood Transgressions," following, by John Updike. Make your own marginal comments to demonstrate your active critical reading of the selection.
5. Write a brief essay on roads, streets, or highways that you have traveled by car, bicycle, or foot. Write a thesis about these roadways and use examples to support your point.

Models of Writing

The three selections that follow demonstrate how writers can use effective examples to make a point.

JOHN UPDIKE
Childhood Transgressions

In a sense, all of life—every action—is a transgression. A child's undulled sensitivity picks up the cosmic background of danger and guilt. A child is in constant danger of doing something wrong. I was most severely punished, as I fallibly recall it, for being late in getting back home. At least once and perhaps several times my mother, her face red with fury, pulled a switch from the stand of suckers at the base of the backyard pear tree and whipped me on the backs of the calves with it, when I had been, let's say, a half-hour late in returning from the playground or some friend's house a few blocks away. Fear for my safety was, I suppose now, behind this stinging discipline, but at the time it seemed mixed up with her fear that, by playing late with some other boy, I would be on the road to homosexuality. She didn't like to see me wrestling with other boys, even on our own property. No doubt she was right, taking "homosexual" in its broadest meaning, about young male roughhousing, but to my pre-pubescent self her anxieties seemed exaggerated. She didn't like to see my father, a six-foot-two schoolteacher with, as far as I could see, normal tendencies, put his hand on his hip either. But whatever the psychological roots of her (as I saw it, with eyes full of tears) overreaction, it did its work on my superego. I have an unconquerable dread of being late for appointments or returning home later than promised, and what modest heterosexual adventures were mine in adulthood received the slight extra boost, from deep in my subconscious, of my mother's approval. Better this than one more game of Parcheesi over at Freddy Schreuer's, as the clock ticked sinfully toward five-thirty.

We were Lutherans, and, as American Protestant denominations go, Lutherans were rather soft on transgression. In Luther's combative, constipated sense of the human condition, there was not much for it but to pray for faith and have another beer. This side of the cosmic background and of my mother's sexual preferences, I didn't really think I could do much wrong. Normal childhood sadisms—bug torture, teasing, fishing—repelled me, and I was all too inclined to believe the best of my cultural-political context, from President Roosevelt down.

A child's transgressions are often, I believe, simple misunderstandings of how the world is put together. Once, attending a movie with my parents, I took the chewing gum from my mouth and put it on the seat where my father, a second later, sat, ruining forever (my impression was) the trousers of his new suit. The sense of a grievous financial mishap, verging on ruin, permeated the days afterward, and I had no answer to the question, *Why did I do it?* The answer seemed to be that I had wanted to get the chewing gum out of my mouth and had no sense of the consequences of my placing it on the seat beside me. I certainly meant my father no harm; he was mildness itself toward me, and an awareness of his financial fragility dominated our threadbare household.

Yet the other transgression that comes to mind also threatened him, though remotely, it appears now. Shillington, Pennsylvania, was a small town, where everything impinged. My father was a schoolteacher, and his domain began just beyond our backyard, across an alley and a narrow cornfield. The school grounds included the yellow brick high school, several accessory buildings, a football field encircled by a cinder track, a baseball diamond with grass and bleachers and wire backstop, and a softball field that was little more, off season, than a flat piece of dirt with a scruffy grass outfield. Early one spring, exulting perhaps in my March birthday, I was riding my fat-tired Elgin bicycle in this familiar terrain, alone, and thought to pedal across the dirt infield. I was stupidly slow to realize that the thawing earth was mud and that I was sinking inches down with every turn of the wheel. Within some yards, I could pedal no farther, and dismounted and walked the bike back to firmer *terra*; only then did I see, with a dull thud of the stomach, that I had left a profound, insolently wandering gouge in the infield, from beyond third base to behind the pitcher's mound. It looked as if a malevolent giant had run his thumb through the clay. I sneaked home, scraped the dried crust from my tires, and hoped it would all be as a dream. Instead, my father began to bring home from school news of this scandal, the vandalized softball field. The higher-ups were incensed and the search for the culprit was on. He would be fired, I reasoned, if the culprit were revealed as his son, and we would all go to the county poorhouse—which, conveniently, was situated only two blocks away.

5   I forget how it turned out—my best memory is that I never confessed, and that the atrocious scar remained on the softball field until the advent of dusty summer. How old was I? Old enough to propel a bicycle with some force, and yet so young that I did not grasp the elemental fact of spring mud. How blind we are, as we awkwardly push outward into the world! Such a sense of transgression and fatal sin clings to this (in its way, innocent) incident that I set down my confession with trepidation, fearful that the Shillington authorities will at last catch up to me, though I live hundreds of miles away, my father has been dead for over twenty years and the last time I looked at the softball field it was covered with Astroturf.

FOR WRITING OR DISCUSSION

1. What is the thesis of Updike's essay?

2. What examples does Updike provide to illustrate his point about transgression and punishment?

3. What is your response to the explanation Updike gives for his mother's anxieties about his lateness? In what ways is she merely being protective of her son's well-being? In what ways is she being homophobic? Looking back, is he tolerant or critical of her behavior? How do attitudes toward homosexuality today compare and contrast with the attitude Updike reveals in his mother?

4. Write an example paper about misdeeds and misbehaviors and the ensuing punishments, real or perceived, in your childhood or the childhood of someone you know. Develop a thesis that finds some central thread in or that proposes an interesting generalization from these examples.

BARBARA EHRENREICH
What I've Learned from Men

For many years I believed that women had only one thing to learn from men: how to get the attention of a waiter by some means short of kicking over the table and shrieking. Never in my life have I gotten the attention of a waiter, unless it was an off-duty waiter whose car I'd accidentally scraped in a parking lot somewhere. Men, however, can summon a maître d' just by thinking the word "coffee," and this is a power women would be well advised to study. What else would we possibly want to learn from them? How to interrupt someone in mid-sentence as if you were performing an act of conversational euthanasia? How to drop a pair of socks three feet from an open hamper and keep right on walking? How to make those weird guttural gargling sounds in the bathroom?

But now, at mid-life, I am willing to admit there are some real and useful things to learn from men. Not from all men—in fact, we may have the most to learn from some of the men we like the least. This realization does not mean that my feminist principles have gone soft with age: what I think women could learn from men is how to get *tough*. After more than a decade of consciousness-raising, assertiveness training, and hand-to-hand combat in the battle of the sexes, we're still too ladylike. Let me try that again—we're just too *damn* ladylike.

Here is an example from my own experience, a story that I blush to recount. A few years ago, at an international conference held in an exotic and luxurious setting, a prestigious professor invited me to his room for what he said would be an intellectual discussion on matters of theoretical importance. So far, so good. I showed up promptly. But only minutes into the conversation—held in all-too-adjacent chairs—it emerged that he was interested in something more substantial than a meeting of minds. I was disgusted, but not enough to overcome 30-odd years of programming in ladylikeness. Every time his comments took a lecherous turn, I chattered distractingly; every time his hand found its way to my knee, I returned it as if it were something he had misplaced. This went on for an unconscionable period (as much as 20 minutes); then there was a minor scuffle, a dash for the door, and I was out—with nothing violated but my self-esteem. I, a full-grown feminist, conversant with such matters as rape crisis counseling and sexual harassment at the workplace, had behaved like a ninny—or, as I now understand it, like a lady.

The essence of ladylikeness is a persistent servility masked as "niceness." For example, we (women) tend to assume that it is our responsibility to keep everything "nice" even when the person we are with is rude, aggressive, or emotionally AWOL. (In the above example, I was so busy taking responsibility for preserving the veneer of "niceness" that I almost forgot to take responsibility for myself.) In conversations with men, we do almost all the work: sociologists have observed that in male–female social interactions it's the woman who throws out leading questions and verbal encouragements ("So how did you *feel* about that?" and so on) while the man, typically, says "Hmmmm." Wherever we go, we're perpetually smiling—the on-cue smile, like the now-outmoded curtsy, being one of our culture's little rituals of submission.

We're trained to feel embarrassed if we're praised, but if we see a criticism coming at us from miles down the road, we rush to acknowledge it. And when we're feeling aggressive or angry or resentful, we just tighten up our smiles or turn them into rueful little moues. In short, we spend a great deal of time acting like wimps.

5   For contrast, think of the macho stars we love to watch. Think, for example, of Mel Gibson facing down punk marauders in "The Road Warrior" . . . John Travolta swaggering his way through the early scenes of "Saturday Night Fever" . . . or Marlon Brando shrugging off the local law in "The Wild One." Would they simper their way through tight spots? Chatter aimlessly to keep the conversation going? Get all clutched up whenever they think they might— just might—have hurt someone's feelings? No, of course not, and therein, I think, lies their fascination for us.

6   The attraction of the "tough guy" is that he has—or at least seems to have—what most of us lack, and that is an aura of power and control. In an article, feminist psychiatrist Jean Baker Miller writes that "a woman's using self-determined power for herself is equivalent to selfishness [and] destructiveness"—an equation that makes us want to avoid even the appearance of power. Miller cites cases of women who get depressed just when they're on the verge of success—and of women who do succeed and then bury their achievement in self-deprecation. As an example, she describes one company's periodic meetings to recognize outstanding salespeople: when a woman is asked to say a few words about her achievement, she tends to say something like, "Well, I really don't know how it happened. I guess I was just lucky this time." In contrast, the men will cheerfully own up to the hard work, intelligence, and so on, to which they owe their success. By putting herself down, a woman avoids feeling brazenly powerful and potentially "selfish"; she also does the traditional lady's work of trying to make everyone else feel better ("She's not really so smart, after all, just lucky").

7   So we might as well get a little tougher. And a good place to start is by cutting back on the small acts of deference that we've been programmed to perform since girlhood. Like unnecessary smiling. For many women—waitresses, flight attendants, receptionists—smiling is an occupational requirement, but there's no reason for anyone to go around grinning when she's not being paid for it. I'd suggest that we save our off-duty smiles for when we truly feel like sharing them, and if you're not sure what to do with your face in the meantime, study Clint Eastwood's expressions—both of them.

8   Along the same lines, I think women should stop taking responsibility for every human interaction we engage in. In a social encounter with a woman, the average man can go 25 minutes saying nothing more than "You don't say?" "Izzat so?" and, of course, "Hmmmm." Why should we do all the work? By taking so much responsibility for making conversations go well, we act as if we had much more at stake in the encounter than the other party—and that gives him (or her) the power advantage. Every now and then, we deserve to get more out of a conversation than we put into it: I'd suggest not offering information you'd rather not share ("I'm really terrified that my sales plan won't work") and not, out of sheer politeness, soliciting information you don't really want ("Wherever did you get that lovely tie?"). There will be pauses, but they don't have to be awkward for *you.*

It is true that some, perhaps most, men will interpret any decrease in female deference as 9
a deliberate act of hostility. Omit the free smiles and perky conversation-boosters and someone is bound to ask, "Well, what's come over *you* today?" For most of us, the first impulse is
to stare at our feet and make vague references to a terminally ill aunt in Atlanta, but we
should have as much right to be taciturn as the average (male) taxi driver. If you're taking a
vacation from smiles and small talk and some fellow is moved to inquire about what's "bothering" you, just stare back levelly and say, the international debt crisis, the arms race, or the
death of God.

There are all kinds of ways to toughen up—and potentially move up—at work, and I leave 10
the details to the purveyors of assertiveness training. But Jean Baker Miller's study underscores
a fundamental principle that anyone can master on her own. We can stop acting less capable
than we actually are. For example, in the matter of taking credit when credit is due, there's a
key difference between saying "I was just lucky" and saying "I had a plan and it worked." If you
take the credit you deserve, you're letting people know that you were confident you'd succeed
all along, and that you fully intend to do so again.

Finally, we may be able to learn something from men about what to do with anger. As a 11
general rule, women get irritated: men get *mad*. We make tight little smiles of lady-like exas-
peration; they pound on desks and roar. I wouldn't recommend emulating the full basso pro-
fundo male tantrum, but women do need ways of expressing justified anger clearly,
colorfully, and, when necessary, crudely. If you're not just irritated, but *pissed off*, it might
help to say so.

I, for example, have rerun the scene with the prestigious professor many times in my mind. 12
And in my mind, I play it like Bogart. I start by moving my chair over to where I can look the
professor full in the face. I let him do the chattering, and when it becomes evident that he has
nothing serious to say, I lean back and cross my arms, just to let him know that he's wasting my
time. I do not smile, neither do I nod encouragement. Nor, of course, do I respond to his bland-
ishments with apologetic shrugs and blushes. Then, at the first flicker of lechery, I stand up and
announce coolly, "All right, I've had enough of this crap." Then I walk out—slowly, deliberately, confidently. Just like a man.

Or—now that I think of it—just like a woman. 13

FOR WRITING OR DISCUSSION

1. Specifically, what changes in their usual behavior does the writer think would
   be beneficial for women?

2. Is the writer guilty of stereotyping men and women? Why or why not?

3. Why is the frequent use of humor so effective?

4. Write a paper using examples either to describe or to demonstrate the falsity of a
   common male or female stereotype (the "strong, silent type," the "jock," the
   "dumb blonde," the "schoolmarm," and so on).

Readings for Writing

These two selections will provide you with further instances of the use of examples in writing as well as possible subject matter for an example paper of your own. The first is the first section of a longer essay about the decline of reading in our age; the second is a well-known essay by a woman who wants a wife of her own.

CALEB CRAIN
Twilight of the Books

1   In 1937, twenty-nine percent of American adults told the pollster George Gallup that they were reading a book. In 1955, only seventeen percent said they were. Pollsters began asking the question with more latitude. In 1978, a survey found that fifty-five percent of respondents had read a book in the previous six months. The question was even looser in 1998 and 2002, when the General Social Survey found that roughly seventy percent of Americans had read a novel, a short story, a poem, or a play in the preceding twelve months. And, this August, seventy-three percent of respondents to another poll said that they had read a book of some kind, not excluding those read for work or school, in the past year. If you didn't read the fine print, you might think that reading was on the rise.

2   You wouldn't think so, however, if you consulted the Census Bureau and the National Endowment for the Arts, who, since 1982, have asked thousands of Americans questions about reading that are not only detailed but consistent. The results, first reported by the N.E.A. in 2004, are dispiriting. In 1982, 56.9 percent of Americans had read a work of creative literature in the previous twelve months. The proportion fell to fifty-four percent in 1992, and to 46.7 percent in 2002. Last month, the N.E.A. released a follow-up report, "To Read or Not to Read," which showed correlations between the decline of reading and social phenomena as diverse as income disparity, exercise, and voting. In his introduction, the N.E.A. chairman, Dana Gioia, wrote, "Poor reading skills correlate heavily with lack of employment, lower wages, and fewer opportunities for advancement."

3   This decline is not news to those who depend on print for a living. In 1970, according to *Editor & Publisher International Year Book*, there were 62.1 million weekday newspapers in circulation—about 0.3 papers per person. Since 1990, circulation has declined steadily, and in 2006 there were just 52.3 million weekday papers—about 0.17 per person. In January 1994, forty-nine percent of respondents told the Pew Research Center for the People and the Press that they had read a newspaper the day before. In 2006, only forty-three percent said so, including those who read online. Book sales, meanwhile, have stagnated. The Book Industry Study Group estimates that sales fell from 8.27 books per person in 2001 to 7.93 in 2006. According to the Department of Labor, American households spent an average of a hundred and sixty-three dollars on reading in 1995 and a hundred and twenty-six dollars in

2005. In "To Read or Not to Read," the N.E.A. reports that American households' spending on books, adjusted for inflation, is "near its twenty-year low," even as the average price of a new book has increased.

More alarming are indications that Americans are losing not just the will to read but even the ability. According to the Department of Education, between 1992 and 2003 the average adult's skill in reading prose slipped one point on a five-hundred-point scale, and the proportion who were proficient—capable of such tasks as "comparing viewpoints in two editorials"—declined from fifteen percent to thirteen. The Department of Education found that reading skills have improved moderately among fourth and eighth graders in the past decade and a half, with the largest jump occurring just before the No Child Left Behind Act took effect, but twelfth graders seem to be taking after their elders. Their reading scores fell an average of six points between 1992 and 2005, and the share of proficient twelfth-grade readers dropped from forty percent to thirty-five percent. The steepest declines were in "reading for literary experience"—the kind that involves "exploring themes, events, characters, settings, and the language of literary works," in the words of the department's test-makers. In 1992, fifty-four percent of twelfth graders told the Department of Education that they talked about their reading with friends at least once a week. By 2005, only thirty-seven percent said they did.

The erosion isn't unique to America. Some of the best data come from the Netherlands, where in 1955 researchers began to ask people to keep diaries of how they spent every fifteen minutes of their leisure time. Time-budget diaries yield richer data than surveys, and people are thought to be less likely to lie about their accomplishments if they have to do it four times an hour. Between 1955 and 1975, the decades when television was being introduced into the Netherlands, reading on weekday evenings and weekends fell from five hours a week to 3.6, while television watching rose from about ten minutes a week to more than ten hours. During the next two decades, reading continued to fall and television watching to rise, though more slowly. By 1995, reading, which had occupied twenty-one percent of people's spare time in 1955, accounted for just nine percent.

The most striking results were generational. In general, older Dutch people read more. It would be natural to infer from this that each generation reads more as it ages, and, indeed, the researchers found something like this to be the case for earlier generations. But, with later ones, the age-related growth in reading dwindled. The turning point seems to have come with the generation born in the nineteen-forties. By 1995, a Dutch college graduate born after 1969 was likely to spend fewer hours reading each week than a little-educated person born before 1950. As far as reading habits were concerned, academic credentials mattered less than whether a person had been raised in the era of television. The N.E.A., in its twenty years of data, has found a similar pattern. Between 1982 and 2002, the percentage of Americans who read literature declined not only in every age group but in every generation—even in those moving from youth into middle age, which is often considered the most fertile time of life for reading. We are reading less as we age, and we are reading less than people who were our age ten or twenty years ago.

There's no reason to think that reading and writing are about to become extinct, but some sociologists speculate that reading books for pleasure will one day be the province of a special "reading class," much as it was before the arrival of mass literacy, in the second half of the nineteenth century. They warn that it probably won't regain the prestige of exclusivity; it may just become "an increasingly arcane hobby." Such a shift would change the texture of society. If one person decides to watch "The Sopranos" rather than to read Leonardo Sciascia's novella "To Each His Own," the culture goes on largely as before—both viewer and reader are entertaining themselves while learning something about the Mafia in the bargain. But if, over time, many people choose television over books, then a nation's conversation with itself is likely to change. A reader learns about the world and imagines it differently from the way a viewer does; according to some experimental psychologists, a reader and a viewer even think differently. If the eclipse of reading continues, the alteration is likely to matter in ways that aren't foreseeable.

FOR WRITING OR DISCUSSION

1. What is the main point of this selection?
2. Which examples do you find most valuable in supporting Crain's point?
3. How does the use of data contribute to the selection? What sources does the writer use? Are they effective? Why or why not?
4. Why does the writer report on studies from the Netherlands?
5. The subtitle of this longer essay is "What will life be like if people stop reading?" Write an essay in which you answer the question.

HAVING YOUR SAY

Write an essay in which you argue for or against the importance of reading books in our modern society. You should consider some of the other available options for learning or entertainment—computer resources, television, audio books, movies, video games, and self-improvement videos—no matter which side of the argument you choose.

JUDY BRADY

I Want a Wife

1   I belong to that classification of people known as wives. I am A Wife. And, not altogether incidentally, I am a mother.

2   Not too long ago a male friend of mine appeared on the scene fresh from a recent divorce. He had one child, who is, of course, with his ex-wife. He is obviously looking for

another wife. As I thought about him while I was ironing one evening, it suddenly occurred to me that I, too, would like to have a wife. Why do I want a wife?

I would like to go back to school so that I can become economically independent, support myself, and, if need be, support those dependent upon me. I want a wife who will work and send me to school. And while I am going to school I want a wife to keep track of the children's doctor and dentist appointments. And to keep track of mine, too. I want a wife to make sure my children eat properly and are kept clean. I want a wife who will wash the children's clothes and keep them mended. I want a wife who is a good nurturant attendant to my children, who arranges for their schooling, makes sure that they have an adequate social life with their peers, takes them to the park, the zoo, etc. I want a wife who takes care of the children when they are sick, a wife who arranges to be around when the children need special care, because, of course, I cannot miss classes at school. My wife must arrange to lose time at work and not lose the job. It may mean a small cut in my wife's income from time to time, but I guess I can tolerate that. Needless to say, my wife will arrange and pay for the care of the children while my wife is working.

4

I want a wife who will take care of *my* physical needs. I want a wife who will keep my house clean. A wife who will pick up after me. I want a wife who will keep my clothes clean, ironed, mended, replaced when need be, and who will see to it that my personal things are kept in their proper place so that I can find what I need the minute I need it. I want a wife who cooks the meals, a wife who is a *good* cook. I want a wife who will plan the menus, do the necessary grocery shopping, prepare the meals, serve them pleasantly, and then do the cleaning up while I do my studying. I want a wife who will care for me when I am sick and sympathize with my pain and loss of time from school. I want a wife to go along when our family takes a vacation so that someone can continue to care for me and my children when I need a rest and change of scene.

I want a wife who will not bother me with rambling complaints about a wife's duties. But I want a wife who will listen to me when I feel the need to explain a rather difficult point I have come across in my course of studies. And I want a wife who will type my papers for me when I have written them.

6

I want a wife who will take care of the details of my social life. When my wife and I are invited out by my friends, I want a wife who will take care of the babysitting arrangements. When I meet people at school that I like and want to entertain, I want a wife who will have the house clean, will prepare a special meal, serve it to me and my friends, and not interrupt when I talk about the things that interest me and my friends. I want a wife who will have arranged that the children are fed and ready for bed before my guests arrive so that the children do not bother us. I want a wife who takes care of the needs of my guests so that they feel comfortable, who makes sure that they have an ashtray, that they are passed the hors d'oeuvres, that they are offered a second helping of the food, that their wine glasses are replenished when necessary, that their coffee is served to them as they like it.

And I want a wife who knows that sometimes I need a night out by myself.

I want a wife who is sensitive to my sexual needs, a wife who makes love passionately and eagerly when I feel like it, a wife who makes sure that I am satisfied. And, of course, I want a wife who will not demand sexual attention when I am not in the mood for it. I want a wife who assumes the complete responsibility for birth control, because I do not want more children. I want a wife who will remain sexually faithful to me so that I do not have to clutter up my intellectual life with jealousies. And I want a wife who understands that *my* sexual needs may entail more than strict adherence to monogamy. I must, after all, be able to relate to people as fully as possible.

9   If, by chance, I find another person more suitable as a wife than the wife I already have, I want the liberty to replace my present wife with another one. Naturally, I will expect a fresh, new life; my wife will take the children and be solely responsible for them so that I am left free.

10   When I am through with school and have a job, I want my wife to quit working and remain at home so that my wife can more fully and completely take care of a wife's duties.

11   My God, who *wouldn't* want a wife?

FOR WRITING OR DISCUSSION

1. What is the thesis of this essay?
2. How does Brady use the rhetorical strategy of example? Which examples do you find most compelling in support of Brady's argument?
3. What is the effect on the reader of the multiple examples Brady provides? How successful is she in supporting her argument?
4. How has the writer achieved a humorous effect in the essay? In what ways do you detect anger or frustration beneath the surface of the humor?
5. Write an essay called "I Want a Husband." Write the essay from the point of view of a *male* seeking a husband, and provide examples in the way Brady has. You can choose a humorous or a serious tone, based on your purpose.

HAVING YOUR SAY

Brady wrote this essay many years ago at the height of the women's movement in America. Have demands on women in our society changed or remained the same from those indicated in the essay? Select one side or the other and write an argumentative paper in which you support your point with specific details.

Reading and Writing About Poetry

In this poem, Edna St. Vincent Millay uses examples to build toward a dramatic point. Read "Lament" and then answer the questions that follow.

EDNA ST. VINCENT MILLAY

Lament

Listen, children:
Your father is dead.
From his old coats
I'll make you little jackets;
I'll make you little trousers   5
From his old pants.
There'll be in his pockets
Things he used to put there,
Keys and pennies
Covered with tobacco;   10
Dan shall have the pennies
To save in his bank;
Anne shall have the keys
To make a pretty noise with.
Life must go on,   15
And the dead be forgotten;
Life must go on,
Though good men die;
Anne, eat your breakfast;
Dan, take your medicine;   20
Life must go on;
I forget just why.

FOR WRITING OR DISCUSSION

1. What point is Millay trying to make about the death of a family member?
2. How does the poet use examples to make her point? What is the effect of the sensory details such as "Keys and pennies / Covered with tobacco"?
3. Which sensory images do you find most compelling and original?
4. What is the effect of the title? The last line of the poem?
5. Write an example essay in which you indicate how you or someone close to you explained difficult events to a child, such as a serious accident, the need to move to a different city or neighborhood, or the death of a loved one. Use concrete sensory details. Be sure to use more than one example.

STRATEGY CHECKLIST: Writing and Revising Your Example Paper

Plan the paper.	☐ Have I used prewriting to explore ideas for a subject? ☐ Have I limited my topic so that my examples will support it effectively? ☐ Have I concentrated on using specific examples to support my thesis? ☐ Have I thought carefully about my purpose in writing? ☐ Do I have my audience clearly in mind? ☐ Have I considered using an outline to organize my ideas?
Write a first draft.	☐ Have I established a clear thesis that my examples support? ☐ Have I supported my thesis with honest examples that represent a cross-section of my subject? ☐ Have I arranged the examples in logical order—in space or time order or by order of importance?
Revise and edit the paper.	☐ Does my introduction capture and hold the reader's attention? ☐ Have I used transitions when necessary to link ideas? ☐ Does my conclusion tie the examples together?
Proofread the paper.	☐ Have I proofread for grammar, spelling, and mechanics?

WRITING TOPICS

If you are having difficulty deciding on a topic for your example paper, you might find some help among our suggestions. Use examples to support or attack one of the following statements.

1. Watching the news does not guarantee that you get the whole story.
2. Students on college campuses are turning more and more conservative in their politics.
3. Some television commercials are more entertaining than most of the scheduled programs.
4. The senior year in high school is more fun than hard work.
5. Many dangers await the desert hiker.
6. Teenagers do not know how to manage money.
7. Student government teaches important values.
8. Religion leaves many serious problems unsolved.
9. The United States has become the world's police force.
10. Computer dating is more popular now than ever.
11. Hazing rituals are unfortunate features of high school sports.
12. The chores on a farm are endless!
13. Not all problems can be solved—we just have to live with them.
14. Some modern conveniences have turned out to be very inconvenient.
15. Affirmative action has (has not) benefited America.

CROSSCURRENTS

One of the main premises in Barbara Ehrenreich's "What I've Learned from Men" (pages 191–193) is that what women could learn from men is "how to get tough" and that the tough guy's attraction is that he seems to have, or does have, "an aura of power and control." How would Ehrenreich react to John Updike in "Childhood Transgressions" (pages 189–190)? Does the kind of trepidation he shows in confessing his sins make him weak, or does he maintain "an aura of power and control"? Are Updike's comments related to gender or to something else, do you think? Could a woman have written a piece like "Childhood Transgressions"? Explain your answer.

COLLABORATIVE LEARNING

In groups of five, discuss the student essays "Keep It Simple" (pages 178–179) and "A True Tale of a Family" (pages 180–182) as models of example essays. Comment on the thesis, the quality of the examples (are they specific, fair, and arranged in a clear and effective order, for instance), the introduction and the conclusion, and any other elements that draw your attention. Also consider the audiences to whom the writers have directed their papers. Do thesis, purpose, and details make the point successfully? What recommendations could you make to improve the essays?

From **IMAGE** To **Words**: A Reading and Writing Assignment

Photo Courtesy: Jeff Greenberg/PhotoEditInc.

Use the photograph above as the basis of an essay that you develop by examples. First, decide on a topic that the photograph suggests and your attitude towards it. For example, you might propose a thesis like one of these:

- It's easy to tell the sure signs of spring.
- A Saturday morning in June at the park is filled with people having a good time.

Feel free to use one of these; or develop a thesis sentence of your own. Whatever your thesis sentence, be sure to support it with examples drawn from the photograph. Feel free to expand and embellish details through concrete sensory language.

CHAPTER **10**

Process

- Writing Your Process Paper
- Student Writing: Process
- Researched Student Writing: Process
- Models of Writing
- Readings for Writing
- Reading and Writing About Poetry

The **process** paper indicates a series of actions, changes, or functions that bring about an end or a result. The most familiar kind of process paper is the "how-to" paper, a step-by-step set of instructions on how to do or make something—how to change a tire, how to bake a cake, how to do aerobic exercise, how to assemble a bicycle. Some process papers explain how something is done, not necessarily a procedure the reader or even the writer can perform—how viruses attack cells, how a cellular phone works, how companies design video games, for example.

Writing Your Process Paper

Follow these guidelines for writing process papers:

TIPS for Writing a Process Essay

- **Choose carefully the kind of process you will write about—showing how to carry out a process or explaining a process that you don't expect a reader to carry out.** If you're an expert at some task like baking a rhubarb pie or setting up a tank for saltwater tropical fish or making the best coffee your side of the Mississippi, you can draw on your personal experiences to explain the process. But don't be fooled into a complacent attitude about it: Because you're an expert doesn't mean that your reader will easily understand the materials you need, the language of the activity, or even the appropriate sequence of events. In most cases you have to state the obvious, as Michael Wollan does in his process paper "Coffee Time" (pages 207–208): You will note that he reminds his readers to wash the percolator (a term he defines) before beginning. Experienced coffee makers might dismiss this as needless advice, but someone who has never perked coffee before had better acknowledge and follow the step. The point here is that if you're writing for an audience who may not know how to carry out the process you're explaining and is looking to you for careful guidance, you have to make sure that you omit no important steps.

On the other hand, you might choose to explain a process that you don't expect someone to carry out, and that explanation requires additional strategies. If you know from experience how to take apart a clock, for example, and want to explain how it's done without expecting someone to perform the intricate task, you'll need to follow the suggestions in the previous paragraph, of course. Leave nothing out. Assume that your readers have little knowledge of the task at hand. But you may be interested in a process whose steps you yourself do not know—how plants carry out photosynthesis, how double-entry bookkeeping works, what steps we can take to reduce greenhouse gases, for instance. In these cases, you'll need to do research in the library or on the Web so that you understand the process fully enough to explain it to someone else. And here, too, you must make a thorough go of it so readers don't come away puzzled about any steps.

■ **Make certain that the explanation is complete and accurate.**   If, for example, you want to describe the process for baking a cake, you would mislead your reader if you omitted the instruction to grease and flour the pan. It's surprisingly easy to leave out important steps. You will be writing about a process you know extremely well, and you probably perform some steps—such as greasing a pan—without consciously thinking about them.

■ **Maintain strict chronological order.**   Tell your reader what to do first, what to do second, and so on. Once the cake is in the oven, it is too late to say that one must stir walnuts into the batter.

■ **If a particular kind of performance is called for in any part of the process, indicate its nature.**   Should the batter be stirred vigorously or gently? Should an applicant for a job approach the interviewer humbly, aggressively, nonchalantly? Besides indicating the nature of the action, you should also tell the reader why such action is called for. Readers are more likely to follow instructions if they understand the reasons for them.

■ **Group the steps in the process.**   A process may include many steps, but you usually can group them in their chronological order, under logical headings.
Suppose you want to explain how to make a favorite dish—stir-fried shrimp, for example. You could develop paragraphs around two headings as part of a rough outline as shown following. Because they often require such precise steps in strict order, process papers lend themselves to outlining. You should develop an outline (see Chapter 4) as a check on the accuracy of your presentation.

    A.   Assembling ingredients
        1. Raw shrimp
        2. Oil
        3. Red and green peppers
        4. Almonds
        5. Hot chiles
        6. Orange rind
        7. Orange juice
        8. Cornstarch

    B.   Assembling utensils
        1. Wok
        2. Sharp kitchen knife with small blade
        3. Cooking fork
        4. Wooden spoon
        5. Measuring cup and measuring spoons

Other headings to organize steps logically for this topic might include "C. Mixing ingredients" and "D. Cooking ingredients." A number of steps may be involved in each of the divisions A, B, C, and D, but reading the steps in paragraphs that address the groups separately is far less overwhelming and confusing to readers than beginning with step 1 and ending with step 19. What steps would you include under the "C" and "D" headings for a process paper on making stir-fried shrimp?

■ **Pay careful attention to your audience.** Who will read your process paper? Who do you anticipate as your main audience? For example, a paper explaining a quick way to change the oil in a car would use one approach to address a group of experienced auto mechanics but quite another one to address car owners eager to save on repair costs but unfamiliar with the parts of an automobile.

■ **Define terms that might be unfamiliar to the reader or that have more than one meaning.** To most of us, *conceit* means extreme self-love, but to a literary scholar, it means an elaborate and extended metaphor. The scholar, when writing instructions for first-year students on analyzing a poem, would have to define the term for readers.

■ **Have a thesis.** It's possible just to present a clear set of instructions and stop. But the most interesting process papers do have theses. Few of us read car manuals or recipe books for pleasure, but we might well read the student paper "Coffee Time" (pages 207–208) more than once, just for the fun of it. Part of the fun comes from the thesis, which gives the paper focus and charm. It's a good idea, then, to try for a thesis.

■ **Anticipate difficulties.**   One way to prevent difficulties for your readers is to warn them in advance when to expect problems:

> This step requires your constant attention.
>
> Now you will need all the strength you can muster.
>
> You'd better have a friend handy to help with this step.

Another way to anticipate difficulties is to give readers advice on how to make the process easier or more pleasant. Wearing old clothes isn't essential to the process of shampooing a carpet, of course, but you've learned from experience that dirty suds can fly and soil clothing, and you want to pass that information on. Similarly, it's possible to apply organic garden insecticides without using a face mask, but you've learned that the unpleasant odors can cause severe coughing and sneezing even if the products are considered harmless. Naturally, you want to warn your readers about how to avoid possible side effects.

■ **Tell the reader what to do if something goes wrong.**   In many processes, one can follow the instructions faithfully and still encounter problems. Prepare your reader for such cases.

> If, at this point, the pecan pie is not firm when you test the center, reduce the heat to 250 degrees and cook it 15 minutes longer.
>
> If, even after careful proofreading, you find a misspelled word at the last minute, carefully cross out the word and neatly print the correction by hand.

■ **Use other rhetorical strategies as needed.**   It's hard to write a process paper without drawing on some of the other writing strategies explored in this book. Narrative, for example, will help you frame the chronological sequence of steps to take in the process you're explaining. You may need to use descriptive details to identify some object. If you look ahead to the chapters on cause and effect (13) and definition (14), you might find explanations there that will help you develop your topic. The point is that you should mix rhetorical approaches as needed to write the best process paper that you can.

■ **Weigh your options for an introduction and a conclusion.**   An introduction to a how-to paper, in addition to presenting the thesis, might state when and by whom the process would be performed. It could also list any equipment needed for performing the process, and it might briefly list the major headings or divisions of the process. Don't forget about the need for a conclusion. You want the last thought in your reader's mind to be about the process as a whole, not about the comparatively trivial final step.

Student Writing: Process

Following are process papers by student writers. How has the writer given clear instructions on performing the task? Annotations on the first paper highlight features of this process essay. Answer the questions after you read.

Michael Wollan

Coffee Time

Drip coffee is all the rage nowadays. Pour some water into a drip coffeemaker, put ground coffee in a filter below the water, flip a switch, and watch some hot stuff pretending to be coffee dribble into a glass container. That's not real coffee. And that brown fluid you're drinking from a McDonald's paper cup and have filled from a big urn, that's not real coffee either. Neither is the hot drink that bubbles on a heating unit at even the best restaurants, nor the bitter, lemon peel-tainted thimbles of muddy liquid called espresso. And the stuff made from a spoonful of crystals added to boiling water—how could anybody call that coffee?

1

Introduction: Negatives help set up thesis in next paragraph.

As a passionate coffee drinker, I know that only one kind is truly worthy of the name. It's percolated coffee, and I'm going to tell all you confused and deceived coffee drinkers just how to make it. In case you don't know, a percolator is a metal pot with a spout and a lid that contains a glass bubble on the top. A tube fits inside the pot; on it will sit a round metal container that holds the coffee. A cover with multiple tiny holes encloses the container.

2

Clearly stated thesis.

Definition of *percolator*, key term in essay, for readers unfamiliar with the object.

Some people think that perked coffee is hopelessly out of date (you probably don't even have a percolator in your kitchen), but it's really so retro that it's avant garde. Brewing good coffee in a percolator requires patience and skill, but the first sip tells you it was all worth the effort. To begin, wash the

3

Transition: "To begin" starts chronological arrangement.

percolator thoroughly to remove any bits of used black grounds from the last brew that can ruin this one. Next, decide on how many cups you want to make. For each cup of coffee, use two level tablespoons of ground coffee and six ounces of cold water. (Some stubborn coffee lovers will add salt or eggshells to the ground coffee in order to improve the taste, but these are unneeded additions, mostly for showoffs who swear that even the best grinds need help from human tinkering.) Pour the water into the pot and put the coffee into the small basket with the hole in the center. Cover the basket with the perforated lid. Attach the basket to the metal stand; then place the whole assembly into the water-filled percolator. Put the lid with the small glass dome on top of the coffee pot. Finally, place it on the stove.

Specific details support the steps and enliven the explanation.

Transition: "Finally,"

4   The best way to brew coffee is with a medium gas flame, not electric heat. When boiling begins, the percolator will groan and rumble like distant thunder. The heat forces liquid up the tube. The liquid hits the glass slowly at first and then with rhythmic plop-plop-plops. The water falls downward through the perforated lid, through the ground coffee, and back into the base of the pot. Lower the flame as soon as you hear the first tiny noises against the glass, or the liquid will splatter all over the stove. Or, it could quickly boil down, and the resulting swill could serve only as black paint for your backyard fence. Over a small flame the coffee will perk gently, gradually turning brown. The rich, intoxicating aroma of coffee beans now will hang in the air. In exactly seven minutes after the boil, your perked coffee will be ready.

Next step in process. Transition sentence "The best way to brew coffee . . ." moves process along.

Simile: "groan and rumble like distant thunder" helps reader see process through concrete sensory detail.

Simile: "swill could serve only as black paint."

Writer explains potential problems: Liquid could splatter or boil down.

5   Don't contaminate it with milk or cream or sugar or tiny pink envelopes of artificial sweetener or by using a weird concoction made from vanilla or almond or raspberry (ugh!) flavored beans. Drink your coffee black, full strength. Some people think that it helps to treat yourself to this magnificent potion as a reward after a great event, like the end of finals week, or getting a date with the dark-haired gem in your bio class, or passing your driver's test after three flunks. But it really doesn't matter when you drink freshly brewed percolated coffee. For those in the know, it is its own reward.

Conclusion maintains light and humorous mood and returns to the thesis by reinforcing excellence of brewed coffee.

FOR WRITING OR DISCUSSION

1. What is the thesis of this essay? How does it relate to the title?

2. The essay is clearly more than just a step-by-step guide to making coffee. What was the writer's purpose in writing this essay? Who is his intended audience?

3. What elements make this a strong process paper? Could you make coffee from the way Wollan tells how to do it? Why or why not?

4. How has the writer used sensory detail to advantage? Where does humor come into play? What other rhetorical strategies does the writer draw on to explain the process?

5. Choose a simple task performed in the kitchen or some other room of your house or apartment and write a paper to explain how to do it. Decide on your audience and purpose before you begin writing, and make the process come alive so that your readers can duplicate it. Use sensory details and, if appropriate to your thesis and purpose, try your hand at some humor.

Researched Student Writing: Process

As you will see in Part 4 of this book, one of the key assignments your instructors will require is the formal research paper, and *Student's Book of College English* explores in depth the steps you need to take to prepare your research paper effectively. But even at this early stage in your developing skills as a writer, you know that using source material to support your thesis is an excellent way to strengthen your point.

In the paper that follows, note how the writer integrates quotations and paraphrases into the essay. Note further how the writer cites sources directly in the essay and how those sources appear fully in a list of works cited at the end of the paper. When you finish reading, answer the questions.

Ayoko Folikoue

Installation Art: Umbrellas Spread Across the Landscape

I have always thought that a work of art is something that has to be preserved from generation to generation and kept not only because of its beauty but also its originality. I

1

believe that, as time passes, any work of art gains more value, and I think that is what art is all about. It is always fascinating to visit a museum or a gallery to admire a work of art. But I realize these days that art has gone far beyond the confined space of a gallery and has conquered a larger space in the environment in order to be in some way part of this environment. This new innovation in the artistic world is called Installation Art. The term itself may sound unusual for some people and bring them to ask themselves this question: what is Installation Art? After gathering much information, I now think that the Installation Art even if it started at a certain period of time is more a newly renovated form of art than a period of art. The couple Christo and Jeanne-Claude are the artists who reflect the ideas in this period.

2   In the late 60's a new form of art appeared; nature became an element of the artistic world. Installation Art is made for a specific space, which explains the first term given to the new form of art, Site Specific. The term became widely used between 1970 and 1980. Because it is recent, it seems to have different meanings. Nicholas De Oliveira writes in the preface of his book *Installation Art*, "Perhaps because Installation is of such recent pedigree, it seems to enjoy a certain mobility of meaning" (8).

3   Installation Art is used as a communication tool that gives the artist or the viewer a medium that in some ways goes beyond language and provides more ideas in cases of conflict or situations that occurred in the society, by exaggerating it visually. Installation Art places many objects in nature to create a special idea. It seeks to modify the way we experience art in a particular space by exploiting certain qualities of the space. Installations may be temporary or permanent, but most will be remembered in posterity only through documentation.

4   One of the first artists working in this new medium was the Frenchman Marcel Duchamp (1887–1968). He chose to use many ready-made products in the gallery to create a work of art (De Oliveira 11). This type of art existed but was more commonly called "assemblage" or "Environment" because the artist brought many materials together to fill a space of a gallery. Later the term changed and became Installation Art, which suits the idea of this type of art better.

Now, there is a large range of artists who chose this kind of medium. Among them are Ann Hamilton, Walter De Maria, Nancy Holt, and many more. However, the most famous artists creating Installation Art are probably the couple mentioned before, Christo and Jeanne-Claude. Both were born on June 13, 1935. They have lived in the United States since 1964 but have worked worldwide. They are known as pioneers of Installation Art. One of their first works is the *Running Fence* (1972–1976). It was 18 feet high and 240,000 square yards of heavy woven white nylon fabric along 24.5 miles extending from East to West near Highway 101 north of San Francisco in Sonoma and Marin Counties (Bersson 628). This kind of project demands a big investment, and Christo and Jeanne-Claude had to pay the expenses by selling the drawings, collages, scales models and original lithographs. They also had to go through social, political and artistic negotiations to bring the project into execution. This took years of patience and planning.

5

Their most recent project was *The Gates* in Central Park, New York City, 1979–2005. It was on display from February 12 to 27, 2005. It is a combination of some 7,500 frames hung with orange colored panels and installed along 23 miles (Harper 55).

6

In 1991, Christo and Jeanne-Claude finally executed one of their projects started since 1984. It was *The Umbrellas*, a Japanese and American project. The project was to link the United States and Japan by a series of massive yellow and blue umbrellas which opened and closed. The yellow umbrellas for the United States were placed in California and signified the dryness of the California hills. The blue for Ibaraki Valley in Japan symbolized the omnipresence of water in Japan. They chose the sites; Ibaraki Valley, 72 miles north of Tokyo, and the California site, 60 miles north of Los Angeles, located in similar valley formations (Chernow 316–17).

7

All *The Umbrellas* are octagonal with pointed tops. They are made from 4.6 million square feet of heavy yellow and blue fabric and were fixed alongside roads and rivers crossing rural areas, fields and intersections in suburban areas in both countries. The frames of *The Umbrellas* were made with aluminum and steel. They are 19 feet tall and 28 feet in diameter, but light enough to be carried by 10 people. Burt Chernow writes

8

in *Christo and Jeanne-Claude*, "*The Umbrellas* needed to be both lightweight and able to withstand winds" (323). They stand vertically in sometimes uneven terrain. They are sometimes arranged in clusters, then in a line or spaced apart from each other according to the slope of the terrain on which they rested. The shape is both geometric because of the umbrellas and organic because of the landscape. With a three-dimensional shape they are smooth when touched and could endure winds blowing up to 65 miles per hour when opened, and 100 miles per hour when closed (Chernow 325). The unity lies in the yellow and blue color of *The Umbrellas* and their shape. The variety stems from the uneven landscape. The contrast between the golden yellow and blue color of *The Umbrellas*, with the green color of the landscape, especially in the sunlight, offers the viewer a stunning sight. 1,340 umbrellas were installed in Ibaraki Valley and 1,760 yellow umbrellas in California. The plan was to open the umbrellas in both sites simultaneously in October, 1991. On October 9, all *The Umbrellas* were opened. The blue and yellow umbrellas looked like dots spreading across the opened landscape. Because of the large scale of the work, it is hard to describe the emphasis or focus of the artwork. Despite the extravagance and cost of their projects, Christo and Jeanne-Claude decided to preserve their artistic freedom by accepting support from no one but themselves.

9   Today, a work of art can be assimilated beautifully in nature and can be part of the landscape without destroying it. Installation Art has gone far beyond the confined space of a gallery to conquer wider spaces. As humans, we experience and contemplate this new form of art. The way we experience art has changed over time, and maybe ten years from now, we will get to experience other forms of artistic work.

Works Cited

Bersson, Robert. *Responding to Art: Form, Content and Context*. New York: McGraw, 2004. Print.

Chernow, Burt. *Christo and Jeanne-Claude*. New York: St. Martin's, 2000. Print.

De Oliveira, Nicholas. *Installation Art*. New York: Smithsonian Inst. P, 1994. Print.

Harper, Paula. "Financing the Gates." *Art in America* Sept. 2000: 55. *Academic Search Premier*. Web. 11 Oct. 2005.

FOR WRITING OR DISCUSSION

1. What is the writer's thesis? Which details best support it?
2. Where does the writer explain a process most clearly?
3. What do the citations from other sources add to the material?
4. Where has the writer defined terms? Indicated materials?
5. Choose some aspect of the arts and, narrowing your topic, explain a process using external sources and citations. Some possibilities: How to produce animation for movies; how stunt men and women train for the job; how a music video is made.

Models of Writing

The selections that follow can help you to develop your process paper. As you read them, keep in mind the guidelines that you examined on pages 203–206. For example, are the explanations clear, complete, and accurate, and how do the writers achieve these goals? Is the order of activities easy to follow? How do the writers group the steps in the process for easier understanding? What terms do the writers define? What terms should they have defined? And, perhaps most important, what is the thesis in each case? What does the writer intend for the instructions to demonstrate? The questions after each reading ask you to address these issues.

The selections are good examples of process writing by professionals. The first writer takes a straightforward, no-nonsense, how-to-do-it approach. The next writer reminisces about Monday chores on an Iowa farm. See which selection you like better. Answer the questions after each selection.

R. R. KAUFFMAN
How to Survive a Hotel Fire

1   As a firefighter, I have seen many people die in hotel fires. Most could have saved themselves had they been prepared. . . .

2   Contrary to what you have seen in the movies, fire is not likely to chase you down and burn you to death. It's the byproducts of fire—smoke and panic—that are almost always the causes of death.

3   For example, a man wakes up at 2:30 a.m. to the smell of smoke. He pulls on his pants and runs into the hallway—to be greeted by heavy smoke. He has no idea where the exit is, so he runs first to the right. No exit. Where is it? Panic sets in. He's coughing and gagging now; his eyes hurt. He can't see his way back to his room. His chest hurts; he needs oxygen desperately. He runs in the other direction, completely disoriented. At 2:50 a.m. we find him . . . dead of smoke inhalation.

4   Remember, the presence of smoke doesn't necessarily mean that the hotel will burn down. Air-conditioning and air-exchange systems will sometimes pick up smoke from one room and carry it to other rooms or floors.

5   Smoke, because it is warmer than air, will start accumulating at the ceiling and work its way down. The fresh air you should breathe is near the floor. What's more, smoke is extremely irritating to the eyes. Your eyes will take only so much irritation, then they will close and you won't be able to open them.

6   Your other enemy, panic—a contagious, overpowering terror—can make you do things that could kill you. The man in the foregoing example would not have died if he had known what to do. Had he found out beforehand where the exit was—four doors down on the left—he could have gotten down on his hands and knees close to the floor, where the air is fresher. Then, even if he couldn't keep his eyes open, he could have felt the wall as he crawled, counting doors.

7   Here are my rules for surviving hotel fires:

8   *Know where the exits are.* As soon as you drop your luggage in your room, turn around and go back into the hallway to check for an exit. If two share a room, both should locate the exit. Open the exit door. Are there stairs or another door beyond? As you return to your room, count the doors you pass. Is there anything in the hallway that would be in your way—an ice machine, maybe? This procedure takes very little time and, to be effective, it must become a habit.

9   *Become familiar with your room.* See if your bathroom has an exhaust fan. In an emergency you can turn it on to help remove smoke. Check the window. If it opens, look outside. Do you see any ledges? How high up are you?

10   *Leave the hotel at the first sign of smoke.* If something awakens you during the night, investigate it before you go back to sleep. In a hotel fire near Los Angeles airport, one of the guests was awakened by people yelling but went back to bed thinking it was a party. He nearly died in bed.

Always take your key. Don't lock yourself out of your room. You may find conditions elsewhere unbearable. Get in the habit of putting the key in the same place. The night stand, close to the bed, is an excellent spot. 11

Stay on your hands and knees. If you do wake up to smoke, grab your key from the night stand, roll off the bed and crawl toward the door. Even if you could tolerate the smoke when standing, don't. Save your eyes and lungs for as long as possible. Five feet up, the air may already be full of carbon monoxide. If the door isn't hot, open it slowly and check the hallway. 12

Should you decide to leave, close the door behind you. Most doors take hours to burn. They are excellent fire shields, so close every one you go through. 13

Make your way to the exit. Stay against the wall closest to the exit, counting doors as you pass. 14

Don't use the elevator. Elevator shafts extend through all floors of a building, and easily fill with smoke and carbon monoxide. Smoke, heat, and fire do odd things to elevator controls. Several years ago a group of firemen used an elevator in responding to a fire on a 20th floor. They pushed No. 18, but the elevator shot past the 18th floor and opened on the 20th—to an inferno that killed the firemen. 15

If you can't go down, go up. When you reach the exit stairwell and begin to descend, hang on to the handrail as you go. People may be running and they could knock you down. 16

Sometimes smoke gets into the stairwell. If it's a tall building, the smoke may not rise very high before it cools and becomes heavy, or "stacked." You could enter the stairwell on the 23rd floor and find it clear, then as you descend, encounter smoke. Do not try to run through it; people die that way. Turn around and walk up. 17

When you reach the roof, prop open the door. (This is the *only* time to leave a door open.) Any smoke in the stairwell can now vent itself. Find the windward side of the building (the side that the wind is blowing *from*) and wait until the firefighters reach you. Don't panic if you can't get out onto the roof because the door is locked. Many people have survived by staying put in the stairwell until the firefighters arrived. Again, don't try to run through the smoke. 18

Look before you leap. If you're on the ground floor, of course, just open the window and climb out. From the next floor you might make it with only a sprained ankle, but you must jump out far enough to clear the building. Many people hit windowsills and ledges on the way down, and cartwheel to the ground. If you're any higher than the third floor, chances are you won't survive the fall. You would probably be better off staying inside and fighting the fire. 19

If you can't leave your room, fight the fire. If your door is too hot to open or the hallway is completely filled with smoke, don't panic. First, open the window to help vent any smoke in your room. (Don't break the window; if there is smoke outside, you may need to close it.) 20

If your phone is still working, call the fire department. (Do not assume it has been notified. Incredibly enough, some hotels will not call the fire department until they verify whether there is really a fire and try to put it out themselves.) 21

22   Flip on the bathroom fan. Fill the tub with water. Wet some sheets or towels, and stuff them into the cracks around your door to keep out smoke. Fill your ice bucket or waste-basket with water from the bathtub and douse the door and walls to keep them cool. If possible, put your mattress up against the door and secure it with the dresser. Keep every-thing wet. A wet towel tied around your nose and mouth can be an effective filter of smoke particles. Swing a wet towel around the room; it will help clear the smoke. If there is fire outside the window, remove the drapes, move away as much combustible material as you can, and throw water around the window. Use your common sense, and keep fight-ing until help arrives.

FOR WRITING OR DISCUSSION

1. What is the thesis of this selection?
2. Regarding the possibilities of fire, what does the writer believe are the most important steps to take when checking into a hotel?
3. What can a person do to avoid the toxic effects of smoke? Why is climbing up the exit stairwell sometimes a better strategy than climbing down? What should you do if you're trapped in your hotel room?
4. Why may this essay be called a process paper? How does the writer address the issues identified on pages 203–206?
5. Who is the specific audience whom Kauffman has in mind? How do you know?
6. Why does the writer provide the example of the man who awakens to the smell of smoke? What other examples appear here?
7. How does the writer establish his credentials for writing this piece? Why does he establish them?
8. Write a paper in which you outline the process to follow in meeting some other emergency—choking, an automobile accident, a robbery, or a flood or blizzard, for example.

MILDRED ARMSTRONG KALISH

Wash Day

1   Nowadays, with computerized washing machines and automatic water temperature controls, we don't give the family wash a second thought. I note that my children and grandchildren

change clothing from the skin out every single day and throw every item, including the bath towel used only once, into the hamper. I'm sure they would be amazed to learn that in my day men, women, and children put on clean clothes on Monday morning and were expected to wear them for the entire week, because laundering those clothes was a major undertaking, with every member of the family called upon to contribute.

Though Monday was the official wash day throughout the farm community and in the town of Garrison, preparations usually started Sunday night, when all of the dirty clothes were collected, sorted, and given special scrutiny. The boys were expected to empty the pockets of their shirts and "overhauls"—the ubiquitous bibbed pants made of blue denim. All men and boys wore them; women and girls almost never did. Mama would turn the pant and shirt pockets inside out and brush away the chaff, dirt, alfalfa seeds, and barley beards. All the clothes were then put to soak in a large galvanized tub of cool water.

If we were in Garrison, the next step was for a couple of the Big Kids to bring the copper oval-shaped boiler up from the cellar and place it on the Monarch kitchen range. Here was where real cooperation began. We Little Kids would pump cistern water into three-gallon galvanized buckets and the boys would carry them, two at a time, to fill both the boiler and the reservoir that was permanently attached to the kitchen range. We used cistern water— which is rainwater collected and stored in a cistern usually thirty to forty feet deep and lined with stones—because rainwater, unlike well water, is soft. In fact, there is a saying in Iowa that the well water is so hard you have to bite it out of the cup. Everyone uses it for drinking and for cooking, because it tastes fabulous and makes great coffee. But since it doesn't allow suds to form and is harsh on the skin, hair, and clothing, soft cistern water is always used for washing.

The laundry soap was also prepared on Sunday night. Using a tin cabbage slicer, Grandpa shredded one and a half bars of P&G, Fels Naphtha, or our own homemade brown soap into a green marbleized graniteware pan kept exclusively for this purpose. After adding a little water to the pan, he placed it on the back of the warm kitchen range and by morning we would have plenty of soft soap ready for the washing machine.

Since the stove had to be kept fired up to heat the wash water, wash day always meant beans for supper, because we could leave them to cook untended on the back of the hot stove. So while Grandpa made the soap, Grandma and I picked over a couple of pounds of navy beans. After discarding the tiny rocks and shriveled beans that we always found, we placed the remainder in a big iron pot. The next morning we would throw in a couple of carrots, an onion, a small slab of bacon or a ham hock, and a few potatoes. Except for an occasional stir, the bean pot required no further attention.

Once the wash water was brought to a boil Monday morning, the heavy, awkward, round wooden washing machine was moved into the kitchen and Grandpa filled it with the water from the boiler and added the soft soap. All the clothes were washed in the same water, and were washed in order of whiteness and cleanliness: white clothes and bed linens first, followed by hand and dish towels, then the colored clothes, and finally the men's work socks, shirts, and overalls. In order to operate the washing paddles, once a batch of clothes was put in, someone alternately pushed and pulled a shoulder-high lever which was attached under the tub by some intricate arrangement of worm gears. Push-pull, push-pull, push-pull: fifteen minutes for every load. We all took turns at this task until it was time to leave for school, and then Grandpa manned the lever.

7   Sometime around 1936 when Roosevelt's Rural Electrification Act made life easier for farmers, Grandpa purchased a Maytag washing machine. We were thrilled to have it. Of course, we still washed all of the clothes in a single tub of water, but the chore of push-pull, push-pull was eliminated. That square, brushed aluminum Maytag did duty in our family for over twenty years (though for the last half dozen it was used only to wash dog beds).

8   Once the clothes were clean, using a wooden wash stick—best described as an unpainted broomstick—we lifted them out of the steaming water and put them through the hard rubber rollers of the hand-turned wringer, from whence they fell into a tub of cool rinse water. After being rinsed, they had to be wrung out again. Rinsing and wringing was a two-person activity. One person turned the handle of the wringer, while another rinsed the clothes by hand and fed them through the rubber rollers which ejected them into the wicker wash basket below.

9   Then the whole process started over again with the next load of clothes, which was placed in that same wash water, followed by the third, fourth, and fifth loads, until all were washed, rinsed, and wrung out.

10   A much-admired accomplishment in those days was the ability to make smooth starch. Here is how you made and used it. First of all, you prepared a paste by adding cold water to the dry, powdery starch and stirred it until it had the consistency of thin toothpaste. Then you stirred this mixture constantly while you poured boiling water into it. If you stopped stirring or pouring, even briefly, you created a lumpy, unusable mess. For the final step, after pouring this starchy liquid into a dishpan half filled with cool water, you dipped the freshly washed shirt fronts, collars and cuffs, aprons, blouses, dresses, and tablecloths into it and hung them out to dry.

11   We considered it a badge of honor to get all the wash on the line by ten o'clock in the morning, and to hang the clothes according to the strict method dictated by the housewives of the community. Sheets and pillowcases, handkerchiefs and towels had to be hung just so, the edges pulled taut between thumbs and forefingers. We called this procedure pressing by hand, for if done properly, it saved a lot of ironing later. We turned all the colored clothes inside out to discourage fading. We hung shirts, blouses, and undershirts by the tails; we hung pants and shorts from the belt line; we pinned all socks in pairs by the toes; and we hung all like items together.

12   Is there any sense in trying to make the modern-day reader understand the immense satisfaction we experienced in viewing our bright, clean wash arranged in such a meticulous fashion on the clothesline? Heaven knows we had more than enough to do without this added display of superhousewifery. But the whole ritual was a matter of pride.

13   There was a rumor in Garrison that a wily housewife, whose husband drove a long-haul semitruck, resulting in frequent and erratic absences, chose the clothesline method for signaling her handsome, blond lover. When her husband was in residence, she pinned the belt of his pants to the line; when he was absent, she pinned the legs of the pants to the line

so they hung upside down. I never knew whether this was true or not, but it did make for good gossip.

There were a few years when the women in Garrison hung their panties and bras inside a pillowcase to conceal them from the eyes of any lascivious males who happened to pass by while these unmentionables were drying. But people made fun of the practice and it was soon abandoned. I don't recall that we ever engaged in that bit of silly primness on the farm.   14

In the summertime the clothes would sometimes dry so fast that by the time we got the second basket out to the line, the first batch was already dry. We removed the clothes from the line as soon as they dried, being careful not to wrinkle the sweet-smelling, deliciously warm, sundried garments. We, meaning Grandma, Mama, my little sister, and I, would immediately put the sheets and pillowcases back on the beds, looking forward to the time when we could lie down on them. To crawl between crisp sheets, warm and fresh from the sun and air, at the end of a bone-wearying day, is one of the true soul-restoring luxuries of life, which hardly anyone of the current generation will ever know.   15

If the weather presented us with a quick drying day, we did the ironing as soon as we brought the clothes indoors, using the three heavy flatirons that had been heating on the back of the stove. Otherwise, we dipped a small vegetable brush in water, sprinkled the clothes to be ironed, rolled them tightly, placed them in the wash basket, and ironed them on Tuesday.   16

In the winter, to limit our exposure to the freezing weather, we carefully folded the wet sheets, pillowcases, and towels, shook the wrinkles out of the shirts and blouses, and warmed the clothespins in the oven before dashing outdoors to hang the clothes on the line. Sometimes the clothes would freeze stiff before we ever got the clothespins on them. However, we pinned them on the line anyway, for the wind usually evaporated the ice and they would flap fairly dry before too long. If they didn't dry, however, the great heater that served the living and dining rooms had to be stoked with chunks of oak, and then we had to remove the frozen items from the line and dry them on long wooden sticks placed on the backs of wooden chairs. These two-by-two-inch sticks were twelve feet long and did double duty as frames for quilting at another time. Sometimes it would take two days to get the whole wash dry.   17

At the end of wash day we had to drain and clean the washing machine and move it back to its proper place. But if it was summer, we emptied the wash water into buckets and took them out to the outhouse where we used the dirty but soap-laden water to scrub down the oak seats and the floor. Remember: Waste not; want not.   18

FOR WRITING OR DISCUSSION

1. What is the writer's thesis in this selection? How does the last sentence comment on the thesis?

2. How does the first paragraph establish an appropriate context for the rest of the selection?

3. Kalish identifies a number of processes that she explains to readers. Which one do you find most interesting or engaging? Which specific details make the process especially clear for you?

4. Where does the writer define terms? Why does she take time to provide these definitions?

5. Write an essay about a process in which some of your family participates together—cooking a meal, cleaning the house, raking leaves, visiting the supermarket.

Readings for Writing

The selections that follow are useful in stimulating your thinking about process analysis. The first is about racism on college campuses. The second deals with restrictions for a child at a television set.

NIKKI GIOVANNI

Campus Racism 101

1   There is a bumper sticker that reads: TOO BAD IGNORANCE ISN'T PAINFUL. I like that. But ignorance is. We just seldom attribute the pain to it or even recognize it when we see it. Like the postcard on my corkboard. It shows a young man in a very hip jacket smoking a cigarette. In the background is a high school with the American flag waving. The caption says: "Too cool for school. Yet too stupid for the real world." Out of the mouth of the young man is a bubble enclosing the words "Maybe I'll start a band." There could be a postcard showing a jock in a uniform saying, "I don't need school. I'm going to the NFL or NBA." Or one showing a young man or woman studying and a group of young people saying, "So you want to be white." Or something equally demeaning. We need to quit it.

2   I am a professor of English at Virginia Tech. I've been here for four years, though for only two years with academic rank. I am tenured, which means I have a teaching position for life, a rarity on a predominantly white campus. Whether from malice or ignorance, people who think I should be at a predominantly Black institution will ask, "Why are you at Tech?" Because it's here. And so are Black students. But even if Black students weren't here, it's painfully obvious that this nation and this world cannot allow white students to go through higher education without interacting with Blacks in authoritative positions. It is equally clear that predominantly Black colleges cannot accommodate the numbers of Black students who want and need an education.

Is it difficult to attend a predominantly white college? Compared with what? Being passed over for promotion because you lack credentials? Being turned down for jobs because you are not college-educated? Joining the armed forces or going to jail because you cannot find an alternative to the streets? Let's have a little perspective here. Where can you go and what can you do that frees you from interacting with the white American mentality? You're going to interact; the only question is, will you be in some control of yourself and your actions, or will you be controlled by others? I'm going to recommend self-control.

3

What's the difference between prison and college? They both prescribe your behavior for a given period of time. They both allow you to read books and develop your writing. They both give you time alone to think and time with your peers to talk about issues. But four years of prison doesn't give you a passport to greater opportunities. Most likely that time only gives you greater knowledge of how to get back in. Four years of college gives you an opportunity not only to lift yourself but to serve your people effectively. What's the difference when you are called nigger in college from when you are called nigger in prison? In college you can, though I admit with effort, follow procedures to have those students who called you nigger kicked out or suspended. You can bring issues to public attention without risking your life. But mostly, college is and always has been the future. We, neither less nor more than other people, need knowledge. There are discomforts attached to attending predominantly white colleges, though no more so than living in a racist world. Here are some rules to follow that may help:

4

Go to class. No matter how you feel. No matter how you think the professor feels about you. It's important to have a consistent presence in the classroom. If nothing else, the professor will know you care enough and are serious enough to be there.

5

Meet your professors. Extend your hand (give a firm handshake) and tell them your name. Ask them what you need to do to make an A. You may never make an A, but you have put them on notice that you are serious about getting good grades.

6

Do assignments on time. Typed or computer-generated. You have the syllabus. Follow it, and turn those papers in. If for some reason you can't complete an assignment on time, let your professor know before it is due and work out a new due date—then meet it.

7

Go back to see your professor. Tell him or her your name again. If an assignment received less than an A, ask why, and find out what you need to do to improve the next assignment.

8

Yes, your professor is busy. So are you. So are your parents who are working to pay or help with your tuition. Ask early what you need to do if you feel you are starting to get into academic trouble. Do not wait until you are failing.

9

Understand that there will be professors who do not like you; there may even be professors who are racist or sexist or both. You must discriminate among your professors to see who will give you the help you need. You may not simply say, "They are all against me." They aren't. They mostly don't care. Since you are the one who wants to be educated, find the people who want to help.

10

Don't defeat yourself. Cultivate your friends. Know your enemies. You cannot undo hundreds of years of prejudicial thinking. Think for yourself and speak up. Raise your hand in class.

11

Say what you believe no matter how awkward you may think it sounds. You will improve in your articulation and confidence.

12   *Participate in some campus activity.* Join the newspaper staff. Run for office. Join a dorm council. Do something that involves you on campus. You are going to be there for four years, so let your presence be known, if not felt.

13   You will inevitably run into some white classmates who are troubling because they often say stupid things, ask stupid questions—and expect an answer. Here are some comebacks to some of the most common inquiries and comments:

14   **Q:** What's it like to grow up in a ghetto?
15   **A:** I don't know.

16   **Q:** (from the teacher): Can you give us the Black perspective on Toni Morrison, Huck Finn, slavery, Martin Luther King, Jr., and others?
17   **A:** I can give you *my* perspective. (Do not take the burden of 22 million people on your shoulders. Remind everyone that you are an individual, and don't speak for the race or any other individual within it.)

18   **Q:** Why do all the Black people sit together in the dining hall?
19   **A:** Why do all the white students sit together?

20   **Q:** Why should there be an African-American studies course?
21   **A:** Because white Americans have not adequately studied the contributions of Africans and African-Americans. Both Black and white students need to know our total common history.

22   **Q:** Why are there so many scholarships for "minority" students?
23   **A:** Because they wouldn't give my great-grandparents their forty acres and the mule.

24   **Q:** How can whites understand Black history, culture, literature, and so forth?
25   **A:** The same way we understand white history, culture, literature, and so forth. That is why we're in school: to learn.

26   **Q:** Should whites take African-American studies courses?
27   **A:** Of course. We take white-studies courses, though the universities don't call them that.

28   **Comment:** When I see groups of Black people on campus, it's really intimidating.
29   **Comeback:** I understand what you mean. I'm frightened when I see white students congregating.

30   **Comment:** It's not fair. It's easier for you guys to get into college than for other people.
31   **Comeback:** If it's so easy, why aren't there more of us?

32   **Comment:** It's not our fault that America is the way it is.
33   **Comeback:** It's not our fault, either, but both of us have a responsibility to make changes.

34   It's really very simple. Educational progress is a national concern; education is a private one. Your job is not to educate white people; it is to obtain an education. If you take the racial world on your shoulders, you will not get the job done. Deal with yourself as an individual

worthy of respect, and make everyone else deal with you the same way. College is a little like playing grown-up. Practice what you want to be. You have been telling your parents you are grown. Now is your chance to act like it.

FOR WRITING OR DISCUSSION

1. The title is an immediate shock to most readers. Why? What is the effect of the "101" in the title?

2. Giovanni establishes her credentials (paragraph 2). Why does she do this? How does it contribute to the point of the essay?

3. Why does she make a comparison between prison and college? Is this an effective comparison—or do you think it a bit over-the-top? Explain your position.

4. What rules does the writer propose for black students who attend white colleges? Could these rules apply to any students, no matter what their race, or do you think they are particularly race-based? Why?

5. What is the effect on the essay of the recommended responses to "stupid" questions and comments black students may hear on campus?

6. Write a process essay in which you give advice to white students attending a predominantly black college, or any other college in which they are a minority.

SUSAN DOUGLAS

Remote Control: How to Raise a Media Skeptic

"Mommy, Mommy, come here now! Hurry, you're gonna miss it. It's Barbie's High-Steppin' Pony, and its legs really move! Hurreeeeeey!"   1

"No!" I bark, as I'm wiping the dog barf up from the carpet, stirring the onions again so they don't burn, and slamming the phone down on a caller from Citibank who wants to know how I'm doin' today. It is 5:56 p.m., and I'm in no mood. "I don't come for commercials, and besides, the horse doesn't really move—they just make it look that way."   2

"Oh yeah?" demands my daughter, sounding like a federal prosecutor. "It can too. It's not like those old ones where you told me they faked it—this one really does move."   3

So now I have to go see and, indeed, the sucker takes batteries, and the stupid horse moves—sort of. "See, Mommy, the commercials don't always lie."   4

Moments like this prompt me to wonder whether I'm a weak-kneed, lazy slug or, dare I say it, a hypocrite. See, I teach media studies, and, even worse, I go around the country lecturing   5 about the importance of media literacy. One of my talking points is how network children's programming is, ideologically, a toxic waste dump. Yet here I am, just like millions of parents during that portion of the day rightly known as hell hour—dinnertime—shoving my kid in front of Nickelodeon so my husband and I can get dinner on the table while we whisper sweet nothings like "It's your turn to take her to Brownies tomorrow" and "Oh, I forgot to tell you that your mother called three days ago with an urgent message."

6   We let her watch Nickelodeon, but I still pop in to ridicule Kool-Aid commercials or to ask her why Clarissa's parents (on *Clarissa Explains It All*) are so dopey. I am trying to have it both ways: to let television distract her, which I desperately need, and to help her see through its lies and banalities. I am very good at rationalizing this approach, but I also think it isn't a bad compromise for overworked parents who believe Barbie is the anti-Christ[1] yet still need to wash out grotty lunch boxes and zap leftovers at the end of the day.

7   It's best to be honest up front: My house is not media proofed. I am not one of those virtuous, haloed parents who has banished the box from the home. I actually believe that there are interesting, fun shows for my daughter to watch on TV. (And I'm not about to give up *ER*.)

8   But I'm also convinced that knowing about television, and growing up with it, provides my daughter with a form of cultural literacy that she will need, that will tie her to her friends and her generation and help her understand her place in the world. So instead of killing my TV, I've tried to show my daughter basic nonsense-detecting techniques. Don't think your choices are either no TV or a zombified kid. Studies show that the simple act of intervening—of talking to your child about what's on television and why it's on there—is one of the most important factors in helping children understand and distance themselves from some of the box's more repugnant imagery.

9   I recommend the quick surgical strike, between throwing the laundry in and picking up the Legos. Watch a few commercials with them and point out that commercials lie about the toys they show, making them look much better than they are in real life. Count how many male and female characters there are in a particular show or commercial and talk about what we see boys doing and what we see girls doing. Why, you might ask, do we always see girls playing with makeup kits and boys playing with little Johnny Exocet missiles? Real-life dads change diapers, push strollers, and feed kids, but you never see boys doing this with dolls on commercials. Ask where the Asian and African-American kids are. Point out how most of the parents in shows geared to kids are much more stupid than real-life parents. (By the way, children report that TV shows encourage them to talk back to their folks.) Tell them that all those cereals advertised with cartoon characters and rap music (like Cocoa Puffs and Trix) will put giant black holes in their teeth that only a dentist with a drill the size of the space shuttle can fix.

10   One of the best words to use when you're watching TV with your kids is *stupid*, as in "Aren't Barbie's feet—the way she's always forced to walk on her tiptoes—really stupid?" or "Isn't it stupid that Lassie is smarter than the mom on this show?" (My favorite Barbie exercise: Put your kitchen timer on for a minute and make your daughter walk around on her tiptoes just like Barbie; she'll get the point real fast.) *Cool*—a word that never seems to go out of style—is also helpful, as in "Isn't

---

[1]In the days before the return of Christ to the world, the Christian religion believes, an evil person, the *Antichrist*, will appear.

it cool that on *Legends of the Hidden Temple* (a game show on Nickelodeon) the girls are as strong and as fast as the boys?" Pointing out what's good on TV is important too.

See, I think complete media-proofing is impossible, because the shallow, consumerist, anti-intellectual values of the mass media permeate our culture. And we parents shouldn't beat ourselves up for failing to quarantine our kids. But we can inoculate them—which means exposing them to the virus and showing them how to build up a few antibodies. So don't feel so guilty about letting them watch TV. Instead, have fun teaching them how to talk back to it rather than to you.

11

FOR WRITING OR DISCUSSION

1. What process is Douglas trying to explain? How successful is she in accomplishing her goal?

2. What is Douglas's thesis? How does she use an introduction to build to the thesis? What do the words in the title, "Remote Control," contribute to the essay?

3. What specific techniques does the writer offer her daughter in order to help the child develop a critical eye for television viewing?

4. What is your reaction to such words and phrases as, "indeed, the sucker takes batteries," "toxic waste dump," "hell hour," and "zap leftovers at the end of the day"? Why does Douglas use such informal, even slang, expressions? Who do you think is her intended audience?

5. Write a process essay in which you indicate how you would explain to a child how to be cautious about some essentially pleasure-giving act—riding a bicycle or a horse, playing in the street, or eating junk food, for example. Or, write a process paper on how you would help a child learn to be critical about watching television.

HAVING YOUR SAY

Television: Is it good or bad for children? Write an essay in which you argue one side or the other of this controversial topic.

Reading and Writing About Poetry

How will the world end? Robert Frost builds on contemporary theories to create a deceptively simple poem. Read "Fire and Ice" and answer the questions that follow.

ROBERT FROST

Fire and Ice

Some say the world will end in fire,
Some say in ice.

5

From what I've tasted of desire
I hold with those who favor fire.
But if it had to perish twice,
I think I know enough of hate
To say that for destruction ice
Is also great
And would suffice.

FOR WRITING OR DISCUSSION

1. What scientific notions of the possible destruction of the world does Frost draw on? What does fire symbolize? Ice? What emotions does Frost connect to each of these states of temperature?

2. In the last line, how does the understatement—saying something less than the writer really means or less strongly than the situation calls for—contribute to the poem?

3. What role do comparison and contrast play in the poem? (See Chapter 11.)

4. Why do you think Frost takes five lines to explain destruction by ice and only two lines to explain destruction by fire?

5. Write a process essay that is opposite to Frost's point. That is, write a paper to explain how the world will survive and avoid destruction.

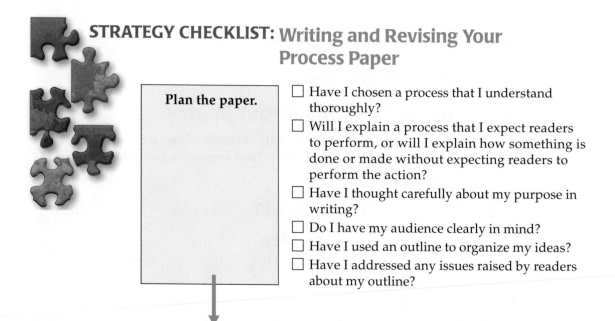

STRATEGY CHECKLIST: Writing and Revising Your Process Paper

Plan the paper.

☐ Have I chosen a process that I understand thoroughly?

☐ Will I explain a process that I expect readers to perform, or will I explain how something is done or made without expecting readers to perform the action?

☐ Have I thought carefully about my purpose in writing?

☐ Do I have my audience clearly in mind?

☐ Have I used an outline to organize my ideas?

☐ Have I addressed any issues raised by readers about my outline?

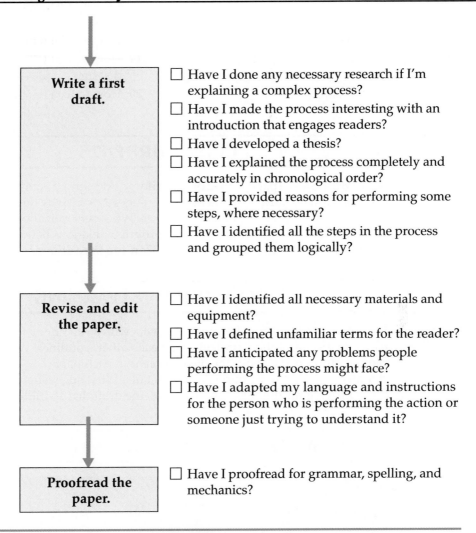

Write a first draft.	☐ Have I done any necessary research if I'm explaining a complex process? ☐ Have I made the process interesting with an introduction that engages readers? ☐ Have I developed a thesis? ☐ Have I explained the process completely and accurately in chronological order? ☐ Have I provided reasons for performing some steps, where necessary? ☐ Have I identified all the steps in the process and grouped them logically?
Revise and edit the paper.	☐ Have I identified all necessary materials and equipment? ☐ Have I defined unfamiliar terms for the reader? ☐ Have I anticipated any problems people performing the process might face? ☐ Have I adapted my language and instructions for the person who is performing the action or someone just trying to understand it?
Proofread the paper.	☐ Have I proofread for grammar, spelling, and mechanics?

WRITING TOPICS

If you cannot easily decide on a topic for your process paper, you might want to use one of these suggestions as a topic idea:

1. How to be a working mother
2. How to use the Internet
3. How to achieve peace in the Middle East
4. How to teach math concepts to preschoolers
5. How to adopt a child in your city or state
6. How a steam engine works
7. How to get an A in English
8. How to make your favorite sandwich
9. How to prevent juvenile crime
10. How to manage stress
11. How to read a book
12. How a light bulb works
13. How to enjoy a concert
14. How to waste time

15. How to listen to music

16. How World War II began

17. How to help a candidate win an election

18. How to deal with terrorists

19. How to deal with natural disaster

20. How to fix a flat tire

CROSSCURRENTS

Both "Wash Day" (pages 216–219) by Mildred Armstrong Kalish and "Remote Control: How to Raise a Media Skeptic" (pages 223–225) by Susan Douglas provide snapshots of children and parents. What generalizations can you draw from the two pieces about the appropriate relations between parents and children? How are the selections alike? How are they different?

COLLABORATIVE LEARNING

Develop an outline for the topic that you will write about for your process paper. In groups of three students, read each other's outlines. What suggestions can the group make about the development of each paper? Use the outlines to comment on the thesis, purpose, and details. What suggestions can you make for improving the outlines and, therefore, the draft that should follow?

From **IMAGE** To **WORDS**: A Reading and Writing Assignment

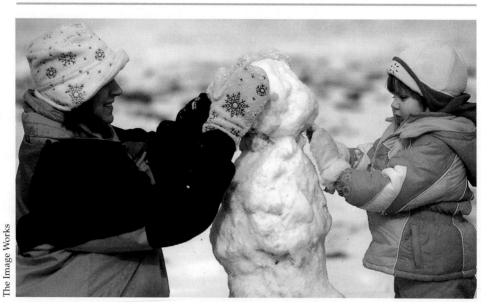

Photography: © Syracuse Newspapers/G. Wells / The Image Works

In the photograph on page 228, what process are the two figures engaging in? What, if anything, do you find striking or unusual about the photograph? Who do you think is helping whom in carrying out the process? Where do you think this activity takes place? Write a brief paper in which you explain the photo by answering some of the questions above. Be sure to identify the two figures as well as the process they are attempting to carry out.

For additional writing, reading, and research resources, go to **www. mycomplab. com** <http://www.mycomplab.com/> and choose Skwire/Wiener's *Student's Book of College English*, Twelfth Edition.

CHAPTER 11

Comparison and Contrast

- Writing Your
  Comparison–Contrast Paper
- Student Writing:
  Comparison–Contrast
- Models of Writing
- Readings for Writing

A *comparison* shows the similarities between two or more things; a *contrast* shows the differences between two or more things. Used interchangeably, if imprecisely, each term often includes the other. Asked to compare, you'll probably contrast automatically as well. Asked to contrast, you can't escape comparing too. Many teachers use the unambiguous term **comparison–contrast** to signal the task of showing likenesses and differences. No matter what the term, the most common kind of essay question on examinations calls for comparison and contrast. It is important, then, to master the techniques of this method of development.

Writing Your Comparison–Contrast Paper

Everyone uses comparisons, sometimes to explain the unfamiliar, and sometimes just to establish a superficial similarity: "He is as slow as a snail," for example. But to produce a good comparison–contrast paper, the writer must apply logical principles to the consideration of similarities and differences.

TIPS for Writing a Comparison–Contrast Essay

- **Compare and contrast according to a single principle.** You might compare automobiles and airplanes as means of transportation, or you might compare them as causes of air pollution. The principle in the first instance might be ease of travel; in the second, pollution. In each case, the principle determines the similarities and differences discussed in the paper. If you're concerned with ease of travel, you won't mention the variety of colors that both airplanes and automobiles can be painted. If you're concerned with pollution, you won't mention the comfort of adjustable seats.

  In a sense, this means developing a thesis. However, you usually must establish a principle for comparison–contrast before you can arrive at a thesis: The meaning of the similarities and differences. Having examined the similarities and differences according to the principle of ease of travel, you might establish as a thesis that travel by air is more convenient than travel by automobile.

■ **Compare and contrast according to a single purpose.** One useful purpose is to clarify. For an audience that knows little about soccer, for example, you could make the game understandable by comparing it to football, a game with which more American audiences are familiar. A foreign student might explain the courtship and wedding customs of his or her country by contrasting them to their American equivalents.

A second purpose of comparison–contrast is to show the superiority of one thing over another: Spiffy Peanut Butter is a better buy than Spunky Peanut Butter, say; or living in a high-rise apartment is easier than living in a house; or travel by air is more convenient than travel by automobile.

A third purpose of comparison–contrast is to use the two items as examples of a generalization. Toni Cade Bambara and Toni Morrison show in their writings that African-Americans want to be thought of as individuals rather than as stereotyped representatives of causes or groups.

■ **Be fair with your comparison–contrasts.** If you see an exception to the comparison you have made, mention it. This is known as *qualification*, and often it can win the reader's respect and confidence.

■ **Follow an established pattern of organization.** A comparison–contrast paper can be organized in one of three ways: subject by subject, point by point, or a combination of the two.

Student Writing: Comparison–Contrast

Subject-by-Subject Pattern

For short papers, one of the clearest patterns of organization—for comparison *or* contrast—is the **subject-by-subject pattern** or **block method**. If you select this pattern, you first discuss one side of the subject completely, and then you discuss the other side. You must, of course, stress the same points in discussing each side of the subject; otherwise there will be no comparison. The diagram on the next page will help you visualize the block method.

The following student outline and paper use the subject-by-subject pattern of organization.

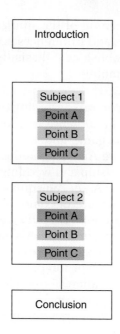

Subject-by-Subject Pattern

Lea Fasolo
Outline for Life after Death

<u>Thesis</u>: Mrs. Caruso's character underwent a dramatic change for the worse after the death of her husband.

I. Before husband's death

    A. Neighborhood children

    B. Grandsons

    C. Shopping

    D. Church

II. After husband's death

    A. Neighborhood children

    B. Grandsons

    C. Shopping

    D. Church

Lea Fasolo

Life after Death

The death of one's spouse can sometimes bring about severe personality changes, particularly in the elderly.

1

I've lived in the house next to the Carusos for twenty years, since I was three. I remember fondly the sweet old couple who used to live next door. George Caruso was a shy, quiet man who kept mostly to himself. His wife, Assunta, on the other hand, was full of life and great fun to be around. And we were around quite a bit. Many an afternoon there would be half a dozen kids in her backyard, helping her pull weeds, pick grapes, or shell peas. We used to take turns mowing her lawn and trimming her hedges. On days when her grandsons, Rodney and David, would visit, she'd have us all in the kitchen for homemade pizza and lemonade. She never seemed to get tired of us, and we felt the same about her. In fact, she got along great with all the neighbors. There were a lot of old couples on the street then, and they used to walk to church together on Sundays. The women often took shopping trips together to Shaker Square. Mrs. Caruso was always involved with some activity in the neighborhood. But most important in her life was Mr. Caruso, her silent partner.

2

George died suddenly one day in 2003. From that time on, Mrs. Caruso was like a different woman. For a while, she simply shut herself off from everyone around her. But soon she became known as the "Witch of East 115th Street."

3

All of a sudden, or so it seemed, the kids were like poison to her. Even when they offered help, she just yelled at them to get away from her yard. She was very self-sufficient now. She mowed the lawn and pulled the weeds with a devilish passion. Not even in the dead of winter would she let her grandsons help her. They used to come over and volunteer to do her shopping and shovel the walk. She would send them away and go out herself and shovel until the concrete shone through. As one would guess, visits from her family became less and less frequent.

4

It was about this time that she also began doing her own shopping alone, ignoring the long friendships she had with the other elderly women on the street, who were now, like herself, widows also. She no longer went to church, either. She had grown bitter and cold, but most of all she just wanted to be alone.

5

And that's how she died last fall—alone. It was a Tuesday evening, and her garbage cans weren't out front. That's when I got suspicious. She was very meticulous about her trash,

6

hauling it from her garage to the lawn every week without fail. I ran to her back porch to find only the screen door closed. I yelled and banged, then went home and called her on the phone. After five tries and no answer, I called the police. They arrived just as her daughter was making her biannual visit. Minutes later, Lydia's screams confirmed my suspicions. And I cried, because once I had loved Mrs. Caruso as if she were my grandmother, and it hurt to remember the day I began to hate her.

Point-by-Point Pattern

A second pattern of development is the **point-by-point** or **alternating pattern**. Although this pattern is most frequently used in writing long papers, it is by no means restricted to them. In this pattern, the writer establishes one or more points of comparison or contrast and then applies those points to each side of a subject. We can represent this pattern in a diagram.

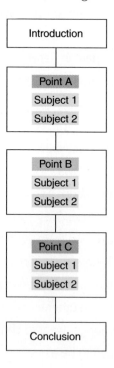

Point-by-Point Pattern

The following student outline and essay use the point-by-point method of organization.

Barry Barnett

Outline for Smarter But

<u>Thesis</u>: Over the past ten years, I have become smarter but not happier.

   I.   Food
- A.   Ten years ago
- B.   Today

  II.   Exercise
- A.   Ten years ago
- B.   Today

 III.   Money
- A.   Ten years ago
- B.   Today

Barry Barnett

Smarter But

1   I'm thirty-two, and I finally had the sense to go to college. All my courses may still have the words "Introduction to" in them, but at least I'm getting decent grades. Yes, I'm a lot smarter than I was at twenty-two, that's for sure. I'm a lot smarter, but . . .

2   For instance, I'm a lot smarter about food. When I was twenty-two, I was eating my way to an early grave and an even earlier pot belly. Fat and cholesterol were the only things that tasted good. The perfect breakfast consisted of fried eggs, bacon, English muffins lavishly coated with butter, and home fries. For lunch, a king-size corned beef sandwich and a chocolate milkshake would usually be enough. The perfect dinner would be either sirloin steak or barbecued spare ribs—French fries on the side, of course. I could take care of any between-meal hunger pangs with a can of beer and a few fistfuls of peanuts. Today I plan to live forever because today it's Total and skim milk for breakfast, a salad with diet dressing for lunch. Dinner is a glorious festival of choices—broiled fish or broiled chicken (no skin, please) or pasta primavera or a microwave special (two whole plastic bags and less than 300 calories). Snack time means veggies and diet Coke. I'm a lot smarter about food, but . . .

3   I'm a lot smarter about exercise, too. When I was twenty-two, exercise generally was limited to unavoidable physical chores like climbing stairs, washing the car, and carrying out the trash. Once in a while I'd engage in a rousing game of ping-pong. Now that I'm ten years older, I try to jog every other day. When it's too cold or wet for jogging, I get on my in-place bicycle and pedal for a half hour. I may easily die of boredom but never of a circulatory disease. I'm a lot smarter about exercise, but . . .

4   Finally, I'm a lot smarter about money than I was at twenty-two. Why have a bad time when I could always buy a good time? All that food and liquid refreshment cost money. Concerts and athletic events cost money. I had a job, and life was for living, and you only go around once. Today I budget my money, and most of it gets spent on rent and utilities and the wife and child who have become the biggest part of my life. I still have a job, but I know too many people who have been laid off, and most of what's left of my money goes to the bank, not to living it up. I'm a lot smarter about money, but . . .

5   So I'm smarter about eating, but eating's no real fun anymore. I'm smarter about exercise, but exercise is a bore. I'm smarter about money, but managing money is a major burden. How much have I gained from becoming so smart? Are there any courses on the advantages of staying young and stupid?

HAVING YOUR SAY

Write an essay in which you argue about the advantages of "staying young and stupid" over "becoming so smart." Or, reverse the terms and argue about the advantages of "becoming so smart" over "staying young and stupid."

Combined Pattern of Comparison–Contrast

The point-by-point pattern and the subject-by-subject pattern are most useful for stressing only the similarities between two items *or* only the differences between two items. Sometimes, however, you may want to give weight to similarities *and* differences. To do so, you can combine the two patterns, as in the following student examples.

The diagram following represents the combined pattern visually.

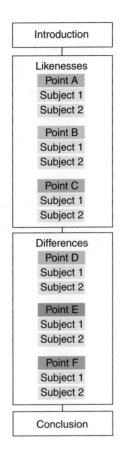

Combined Pattern

5

Stacy Kissenger

Outline for Birds of a Feather?

<u>Thesis</u>: My two friends Laurie and Tammy have sharply different dispositions.

- I.   Similarities
    - A.   Farms preferred to city life
    - B.   Interest in sports
    - C.   Fun-loving natures
- II.   Differences
    - A.   Laurie's temperament always cheerful
    - B.   Tammy moody and not even-tempered

Stacy Kissenger

Birds of a Feather?

1   Despite their close relationship, my two friends Tammy Smith and Laurie Potter provide striking contrasts in their dispositions.

2   Granted, there are many ways in which these friends are similar. Both born on farms, Tammy and Laurie prefer fields of corn to buzzing city streets. Their love for farming unites them as together they lecture their city slicker friends like me about Guernseys and Holsteins or about the uses of cultivators. Both girls also share an interest in athletics. The two of them played on the high school basketball team and by their senior year had developed the flawless "Smith-Potter" rebounding method, which included elbowing and stomping on anyone separating them and the ball. Off the basketball court their fun-loving natures further reinforce each other as they tease and joke, often to the dismay of those around them. Once they convinced the shop teacher's daughter that rubber crowbars and metric screwdrivers really existed.

3   But the personality differences between these two friends are much more outstanding than the likenesses. Laurie is carefree and easygoing, with a well of cheerfulness within her. Her sapphire eyes twinkle brightly and the corners of her lips curl upward into a smile as she chats with her friends in the college hallways. When I am feeling miserable, she jokes and giggles to chase away the depression. Her own anger rarely surfaces. When everyone else rages, Laurie rarely shows hostility, except perhaps in her face. Angry, she retreats within herself. Her chatter ceases as the twinkle disappears from her eyes. Her jaw locks tightly, and every muscle tenses. The soft brown crop of curls and the light sprinkling of freckles across her nose suddenly make her face look sharp. But the anger passes quickly, and Laurie once again radiates warmth and excitement.

4   Tammy, in contrast, is much less even-tempered. Though she is a warm and generous person, her moods often change drastically. Frequently she grows depressed and sulks for days at a time. Her forehead wrinkles with anxiety; her hazel eyes glare disgustedly, even at best friends. If Laurie or I try to find out why she is so angry, she growls, "Just leave me alone!" and stalks away. Once I watched her face flush with crimson as she snatched a phone book and hurled it, its pages flapping before it thudded against the floor like a dead

bird. At another time I saw her kick the wall beside her bed, leaving a black heel mark just above her pillow. Neither people nor things are safe when one of her famous moods transforms Tammy into a monster!

Despite some likenesses, then, these two contrasting personalities have convinced me   5
that being birds of a feather is not essential for friendship; although their dispositions differ widely, Laurie and Tammy are each other's best friends.

Models of Writing

As you read the selections that follow, notice the comparison–contrast patterns at work in each one.

MARK TWAIN (SAMUEL L. CLEMENS)
The Professional

The face of the water [of the Mississippi River, where the author was a steamboat pilot] in   1
time became a wonderful book—a book that was a dead language to the uneducated passenger but which told its mind to me without reserve, delivering its most cherished secrets as clearly as if it uttered them with a voice. And it was not a book to be read once and thrown aside, for it had a new story to tell every day. Throughout the long twelve hundred miles there was never a page that was void of interest, never one that you could leave unread without loss, never one that you would want to skip, thinking you could find higher enjoyment in some other thing. There never was so wonderful a book written by man, never one whose interest was so absorbing, so unflagging, so sparklingly renewed with every reperusal. The passenger who could not read it was charmed with a peculiar sort of faint dimple on its surface (on the rare occasions when he did not overlook it altogether) but to the pilot that was an *italicized* passage; indeed it was more than that, it was a legend of the largest capitals with a string of shouting exclamation-points at the end of it, for it meant that a wreck or a rock was buried there that could tear the life out of the strongest vessel that ever floated. It is the faintest and simplest expression the water ever makes, and the most hideous to a pilot's eye. In truth, the passenger who could not read this book saw nothing but all manner of pretty pictures in it, painted by the sun and shaded by the clouds, whereas to the trained eye these were not pictures at all, but the grimmest and most dead-earnest of reading matter.

2   Now when I had mastered the language of this water, and had come to know every trifling feature that bordered the great river as familiarly as I knew the letters of the alphabet, I had made a valuable acquisition. But I had lost something, too. I had lost something which could never be restored to me while I lived. All the grace, the beauty, the poetry, had gone out of the majestic river! I still keep in mind a certain wonderful sunset which I witnessed when steamboating was new to me. A broad expanse of the river was turned to blood; in the middle distance the red hue brightened into gold, through which a solitary log came floating, black and conspicuous; in one place a long, slanting mark lay sparkling upon the water; in another the surface was broken by boiling, tumbling rings, that were as many-tinted as an opal; where the ruddy flush was faintest, was a smooth spot that was covered with graceful circles and radiating lines, ever so delicately traced; the shore on our left was densely wooded, and the somber shadow that fell from this forest was broken in one place by a long, ruffled trail that shone like silver; and high above the forest wall a clean-stemmed dead tree waved a single leafy bough that glowed like a flame in the unobstructed splendor that was flowing from the sun. There were graceful curves, reflected images, woody heights, soft distances; and over the whole scene, far and near, the dissolving lights drifted steadily, enriching it every passing moment with new marvels of coloring.

3   I stood like one bewitched. I drank it in, in a speechless rapture. The world was new to me, and I had never seen anything like this at home. But as I've said, a day came when I began to cease from noting the glories and the charms which the moon and the sun and the twilight wrought upon the river's face; another day came when I ceased altogether to note them. Then, if that sunset scene had been repeated, I should have looked upon it without rapture, and should have commented upon it, inwardly, after this fashion: "This sun means that we are going to have wind tomorrow; that floating log means that the river is rising, small thanks to it; that slanting mark on the water refers to a bluff reef which is going to kill somebody's steamboat one of these nights, if it keeps on stretching out like that; those tumbling 'boils' show a dissolving bar and a changing channel there; the lines and circles in the slick water over yonder are a warning that that troublesome place is shoaling up dangerously; that silver streak in the shadow of the forest is the 'break' from a new snag, and he has located himself in the very best place he could have found to fish for steamboats; that tall dead tree, with a single living branch, is not going to last long, and then how is a body ever going to get through this blind place at night without the friendly old landmark?"

4   No, the romance and beauty were all gone from the river. All the value any feature of it had for me now was the amount of usefulness it could furnish toward compassing the safe piloting of a steamboat. Since those days, I have pitied doctors from my heart. What does the lovely flush in a beauty's cheek mean to a doctor but a "break" that ripples above some deadly disease? Are not all her visible charms sown thick with what are to him the signs and symbols of hidden decay? Does he ever see her beauty at all, or doesn't he simply view her professionally and comment upon her unwholesome condition all to himself? And doesn't he sometimes wonder whether he has gained most or lost most by learning his trade?

FOR WRITING OR DISCUSSION

1. What pattern of development does Twain use to contrast the beginner's view of the river to the seasoned professional's view?

2. In paragraph 1, Twain uses *analogy*—a special kind of comparison—to describe the river as if it were a book. Identify the words and phrases used to show this analogy.

3. In which sentence or sentences does Twain first state the thesis? Where does he restate the thesis?

4. Do you agree with Twain that increased knowledge interferes with simple emotional pleasure? Why, or why not?

5. Write a paper about how you once felt about some person, place, or idea, emphasizing the contrast between past and present.

WILLIAM ZINSSER
Speaking of Writing

A school in Connecticut once held "a day devoted to the arts," and I was asked if I would come and talk about writing as a vocation. When I arrived I found that a second speaker had been invited—Dr. Brock (as I'll call him), a surgeon who had recently begun to write and had sold some stories to magazines. He was going to talk about writing as an avocation. That made us a panel, and we sat down to face a crowd of students and teachers and parents, all eager to learn the secrets of our glamorous work.

Dr. Brock was dressed in a bright red jacket, looking vaguely bohemian, as authors are supposed to look, and the first question went to him. What was it like to be a writer?

He said it was tremendous fun. Coming home from an arduous day at the hospital, he would go straight to his yellow pad and write his tensions away. The words just flowed. It was easy. I then said that writing wasn't easy and wasn't fun. It was hard and lonely, and the words seldom just flowed.

Next Dr. Brock was asked if it was important to rewrite. Absolutely not, he said. "Let it all hang out," he told us, and whatever form the sentences take will reflect the writer at his most natural. I then said that rewriting is the essence of writing. I pointed out that professional writers rewrite their sentences over and over and then rewrite what they have rewritten.

5   "What do you do on days when it isn't going well?" Dr. Brock was asked. He said he just stopped writing and put the work aside for a day when it would go better. I then said that the professional writer must establish a daily schedule and stick to it. I said that writing is a craft, not an art, and that the man who runs away from his craft because he lacks inspiration is fooling himself. He is also going broke.

6   "What if you're feeling depressed or unhappy?" a student asked. "Won't that affect your writing?"

7   Probably it will, Dr. Brock replied. Go fishing. Take a walk. Probably it won't, I said. If your job is to write every day, you learn to do it like any other job.

8   A student asked if we found it useful to circulate in the literary world. Dr. Brock said he was greatly enjoying his new life as a man of letters, and he told several stories of being taken to lunch by his publisher and his agent at Manhattan restaurants where writers and editors gather. I said that professional writers are solitary drudges who seldom see other writers.

9   "Do you put symbolism in your writing?" a student asked me.

10   "Not if I can help it," I replied. I have an unbroken record of missing the deeper meaning in any story, play or movie, and as for dance and mime, I have never had any idea of what is being conveyed.

11   "I *love* symbols!" Dr. Brock exclaimed, and he described with gusto the joys of weaving them through his work.

12   So the morning went, and it was a revelation to all of us. At the end Dr. Brock told me he was enormously interested in my answers—it had never occurred to him that writing could be hard. I told him I was just as interested in *his* answers—it had never occurred to me that writing could be easy. Maybe I should take up surgery on the side.

13   As for the students, anyone might think we left them bewildered. But in fact we gave them a broader glimpse of the writing process than if only one of us had talked. For there isn't any "right" way to do such personal work. There are all kinds of writers and all kinds of methods, and any method that helps you to say what you want to say is the right method for you. Some people write by day, others by night. Some people need silence, others turn on the radio. Some write by hand, some by word processor, some by talking into a tape recorder. Some people write their first draft in one long burst and then revise; others can't write the second paragraph until they have fiddled endlessly with the first.

14   But all of them are vulnerable and all of them are tense. They are driven by a compulsion to put some part of themselves on paper, and yet they don't just write what comes naturally. They sit down to commit an act of literature, and the self who emerges on paper is far stiffer than the person who sat down to write. The problem is to find the real man or woman behind the tension.

FOR WRITING OR DISCUSSION

1. What pattern of organization does Zinsser use to present the contrasting approaches to writing?

2. Where does the writer state his thesis?

3. Although Dr. Brock's approach to writing may be the best method for him, how does Zinsser indicate that he is skeptical of Brock's approach?

4. In paragraph 1, how would Zinsser define the difference between a vocation and an avocation? How does this difference help account for the different attitudes toward writing?

5. Choose some activity other than writing—anything from decorating for a holiday to studying for an examination—and write a paper contrasting the easygoing versus the more difficult approach to completing it.

SUZANNE BRITT
That Lean and Hungry Look

Caesar was right. Thin people need watching. I've been watching them for most of my adult 1 life, and I don't like what I see. When these narrow fellows spring at me, I quiver to my toes. Thin people come in all personalities, most of them menacing. You've got your "together" thin person, your mechanical thin person, your condescending thin person, your tsk-tsk thin person, your efficiency-expert thin person. All of them are dangerous.

In the first place, thin people aren't fun. They don't know how to goof off, at least in the 2 best, fat sense of the word. They've always got to be doing. Give them a coffee break, and they'll jog around the block. Supply them with a quiet evening at home, and they'll fix the screen door and lick S & H green stamps. They say things like "there aren't enough hours in the day." Fat people never say that. Fat people think the day is too damn long already.

Thin people make me tired. They've got speedy little metabolisms that cause them to bustle 3 briskly. They're forever rubbing their bony hands together and eyeing new problems to "tackle." I like to surround myself with sluggish, inert, easygoing fat people, the kind who believe that if you clean it up today, it'll just get dirty again tomorrow.

Some people say the business about the jolly fat person is a myth, that all of us chubbies 4 are neurotic, sick, sad people. I disagree. Fat people may not be chortling all day long, but they're a hell of a lot *nicer* than the wizened and shriveled. Thin people turn surly, mean and hard at a young age because they never learn the value of a hot-fudge sundae for easing tension. Thin people don't like gooey soft things because they themselves are neither gooey nor soft. They are crunchy and dull, like carrots. They go straight to the heart of the matter while fat people let things stay all blurry and hazy and vague, the way things actually are. Thin people want to face the truth. Fat people know there is no truth. One of my thin friends is always staring at complex, unsolvable problems and saying, "The key thing is. . . ." Fat people never say that. They know there isn't any such thing as the key thing about anything.

5   Thin people believe in logic. Fat people see all sides. The sides fat people see are rounded blobs, usually gray, always nebulous and truly not worth worrying about. But the thin person persists. "If you consume more calories than you burn," says one of my thin friends, "you will gain weight. It's that simple." Fat people always grin when they hear statements like that. They know better.

6   Fat people realize that life is illogical and unfair. They know very well that God is not in his heaven and all is not right with the world. If God was up there, fat people could have two doughnuts and a big orange drink anytime they wanted it.

7   Thin people have a long list of logical things they are always spouting off to me. They hold up one finger at a time as they reel off these things, so I won't lose track. They speak slowly as if to a young child. The list is long and full of holes. It contains tidbits like "get a grip on yourself," "cigarettes kill," "cholesterol clogs," "fit as a fiddle," "ducks in a row," "organize" and "sound fiscal management." Phrases like that.

8   They think these 2,000-point plans lead to happiness. Fat people know happiness is elusive at best and even if they could get the kind thin people talk about, they wouldn't want it. Wisely, fat people see that such programs are too dull, too hard, too off the mark. They are never better than a whole cheesecake.

9   Fat people know all about the mystery of life. They are the ones acquainted with the night, with luck, with fate, with playing it by ear. One thin person I know once suggested that we arrange all the parts of a jigsaw puzzle into groups according to size, shape and color. He figured this would cut the time needed to complete the puzzle at least by 50 percent. I said I wouldn't do it. One, I like to muddle through. Two, what good would it do to finish early? Three, the jigsaw puzzle isn't the important thing. The important thing is the fun of four people (one thin person included) sitting around a card table, working a jigsaw puzzle. My thin friend had no use for my list. Instead of joining us, he went outside and mulched the boxwoods. The three remaining fat people finished the puzzle and made chocolate, double-fudged brownies to celebrate.

10   The main problem with thin people is they oppress. Their good intentions, bony torsos, tight ships, neat corners, cerebral machinations and pat solutions loom like dark clouds over the loose, comfortable, spread-out, soft world of the fat. Long after fat people have removed their coats and shoes and put their feet up on the coffee table, thin people are still sitting on the edge of the sofa, looking neat as a pin, discussing rutabagas. Fat people are heavily into fits of laughter, slapping their thighs and whooping it up, while thin people are still politely waiting for the punch line.

11   Thin people are downers. They like math and morality and reasoned evaluation of the limitations of human beings. They have their skinny little acts together. They expound, prognose, probe and prick.

12   Fat people are convivial. They will like you even if you're irregular and have acne. They will come up with a good reason why you never wrote the great American novel. They will cry

in your beer with you. They will put your name in the pot. They will let you off the hook. Fat people will gab, giggle, guffaw, gallumph, gyrate and gossip. They are generous, giving and gallant. They are gluttonous and goodly and great. What you want when you're down is soft and jiggly, not muscled and stable. Fat people know this. Fat people have plenty of room. Fat people will take you in.

FOR WRITING OR DISCUSSION

1. Tell why you agree or disagree with this statement: "In 'That Lean and Hungry Look,' Britt is mostly contrasting fat and thin people just for laughs. She is a good deal more serious, however, about contrasting two opposing philosophies of life."
2. What pattern of organization does Britt use to make the contrasts?
3. Using the comparison–contrast technique of Britt's essay, write a paper in which you attempt to refute the author's position—that is, defend the thin person's view.

HAVING YOUR SAY

What is your view of the effects of being thin or being fat on a person's personality? Write a comparison–contrast essay, supporting your point with specifics.

BRUCE CATTON

Grant and Lee: A Study in Contrasts

When Ulysses S. Grant and Robert E. Lee met in the parlor of a modest house at Appomattox Court House, Virginia, on April 9, 1865, to work out the terms for the surrender of Lee's Army of Northern Virginia, a great chapter in American life came to a close, and a great new chapter began. 1

These men were bringing the Civil War to its virtual finish. To be sure, other armies had yet to surrender, and for a few days the fugitive Confederate government would struggle desperately and vainly, trying to find some way to go on living now that its chief support was gone. But in effect it was all over when Grant and Lee signed the papers. And the little room where they wrote out the terms was the scene of one of the poignant, dramatic contrasts in American History. 2

3　　　　They were two strong men these oddly different generals, and they represented the strengths of two conflicting currents that, through them, had come into final collision.

4　　　　Back of Robert E. Lee was the notion that the old aristocratic concept might somehow survive and be dominant in American life.

5　　　　Lee was tidewater Virginia, and in his background were family, culture, and tradition . . . the age of chivalry transplanted to a New World which was making its own legends and its own myths. He embodied a way of life that had come down through the age of knighthood and the English country squire. America was a land that was beginning all over again, dedicated to nothing much more complicated than the rather hazy belief that all men had equal rights and should have an equal chance in the world. In such a land Lee stood for the feeling that it was somehow of advantage to human society to have a pronounced inequality in the social structure. There should be a leisure class, backed by ownership of land; in turn, society itself should be keyed to the land as the chief source of wealth and influence. It would bring forth (according to this ideal) a class of men with a strong sense of obligation to the community; men who lived not to gain advantage for themselves, but to meet the solemn obligations which had been laid on them by the very fact that they were privileged. From them the country would get its leadership; to them it could look for the higher values—of thought, of conduct, or personal deportment—to give it strength and virtue.

6　　　　Lee embodied the noblest elements of this aristocratic ideal. Through him, the landed nobility justified itself. For four years, the Southern states had fought a desperate war to uphold the ideals for which Lee stood. In the end, it almost seemed as if the Confederacy fought for Lee; as if he himself was the Confederacy . . . the best thing that the way of life for which the Confederacy stood could ever have to offer. He had passed into legend before Appomattox. Thousands of tired, underfed, poorly clothed Confederate soldiers, long since past the simple enthusiasm of the early days of the struggle, somehow considered Lee the symbol of everything for which they had been willing to die. But they could not quite put this feeling into words. If the Lost Cause, sanctified by so much heroism and so many deaths, had a living justification, its justification was General Lee.

7　　　　Grant, the son of a tanner on the Western frontier, was everything Lee was not. He had come up the hard way and embodied nothing in particular except the eternal toughness and sinewy fiber of the men who grew up beyond the mountains. He was one of a body of men who owed reverence and obeisance to no one, who were self-reliant to a fault, who cared hardly anything for the past but who had a sharp eye for the future.

8　　　　These frontier men were the precise opposites of the tidewater aristocrats. Back of them, in the great surge that had taken people over the Alleghenies and into the opening Western country, there was a deep, implicit dissatisfaction with a past that had settled into grooves. They stood for democracy, not from any reasoned conclusion about the proper ordering of human society, but simply because they had grown up in the middle of democracy and knew how it worked. Their society might have privileges, but they would be privileges each man had won for himself. Forms and patterns meant nothing. No man was born to anything, except perhaps to a chance to show how far he could rise. Life was competition.

Yet along with this feeling had come a deep sense of belonging to a national community. The Westerner who developed a farm, opened a shop, or set up in business as a trader could hope to prosper only as his own community prospered—and his community ran from the Atlantic to the Pacific and from Canada down to Mexico. If the land was settled, with towns and highways and accessible markets, he could better himself. He saw his fate in terms of the nation's own destiny. As its horizons expanded, so did his. He had, in other words an acute dollars-and-cents stake in the continued growth and development of his country.

9

And that, perhaps, is where the contrast between Grant and Lee becomes most striking. The Virginia aristocrat, inevitably, saw himself in relation to his own region. He lived in a static society which could endure almost anything except change. Instinctively, his first loyalty would go to the locality in which that society existed. He would fight to the limit of endurance to defend it, because in defending it he was defending everything that gave his own life its deepest meaning.

10

The Westerner, on the other hand, would fight with an equal tenacity for the broader concept of society. He fought so because everything he lived by was tied to growth, expansion, and a constantly widening horizon. What he lived by would survive or fall with the nation itself. He could not possibly stand by unmoved in the face of an attempt to destroy the Union. He would combat it with everything he had, because he could only see it as an effort to cut the ground out from under his feet.

11

So Grant and Lee were in complete contrast, representing two diametrically opposed elements in American life. Grant was the modern man emerging; beyond him, ready to come on the stage, was the great age of steel and machinery, of crowded cities and a restless burgeoning vitality. Lee might have ridden down from the old age of chivalry, lance in hand, silken banner fluttering over his head. Each man was the perfect champion of his cause, drawing both his strengths and his weaknesses from the people he led.

12

Yet it was not all contrast, after all. Different as they were—in background, in personality, in underlying aspiration—these two great soldiers had much in common. Under everything else, they were marvelous fighters. Furthermore, their fighting qualities were really very much alike.

13

Each man had, to begin with, the great virtue of utter tenacity and fidelity. Grant fought his way down the Mississippi Valley in spite of acute personal discouragement and profound military handicaps. Lee hung on in the trenches at Petersburg after hope itself had died. In each man there was an indomitable quality . . . the born fighter's refusal to give up as long as he can still remain on his feet and lift his two fists.

14

Daring and resourcefulness they had, too: the ability to think faster and move faster than the enemy. These were the qualities which gave Lee the dazzling campaigns of Second Manassas and Chancellorsville and won Vicksburg for Grant.

15

Lastly, and perhaps greatest of all, there was the ability, at the end, to turn quickly from war to peace once the fighting was over. Out of the way these two men behaved at Appomattox came the possibility of a peace of reconciliation. It was a possibility not wholly realized, in the years to come, but which did, in the end, help the two sections to become one nation again . . . after a war whose bitterness might have seemed to make such a reunion wholly impossible.

16

No part of either man's life became him more than the part he played in their brief meeting in the McLean house at Appomattox. Their behavior there put all succeeding generations of Americans in their debt. Two great Americans, Grant and Lee—very different, yet under everything very much alike. Their encounter at Appomattox was one of the great moments of American history.

FOR WRITING OR DISCUSSION

1. What is Catton's thesis? Which sentence in the essay best states the thesis?

2. What pattern of organization does Catton use to advance the comparison and contrast? Point to specific paragraphs and sentences to support your view.

3. Which of Lee's qualities do you find most impressive? which of Grant's? Which leader would you rather spend an hour with? Why?

4. Comment on the introduction (paragraphs 1 and 2) and the conclusion (paragraph 16). How do they help create the important sense of unity in the essay?

5. Write a comparison–contrast essay in which you present two public figures—in the military, in government, in the arts, for example. Choose people who have something in common (perhaps their field of interest is enough of a linkage), and explain to readers what makes the two people similar to yet different from each other.

Readings for Writing

The selections that follow can provide you with subject matter for a comparison–contrast paper of your own. Questions and possible assignments appear after each set of selections.

Youthful Imagination: Two Stories for Comparison and Contrast

SHIRLEY JACKSON

Charles

The day my son Laurie started kindergarten he renounced corduroy overalls with bibs and began wearing blue jeans with a belt; I watched him go off the first morning with the older girl next door, seeing clearly that an era of my life was ended, my sweet-voiced nursery-school tot replaced by a long-trousered, swaggering character who forgot to stop at the corner and wave good-bye to me.

He came home the same way, the front door slamming open, his cap on the floor, and the voice suddenly become raucous shouting, "Isn't anybody *here*?"   2

At lunch he spoke insolently to his father, spilled his baby sister's milk, and remarked that his teacher said we were not to take the name of the Lord in vain.   3

"How was school today?" I asked, elaborately casual.   4

"All right," he said.   5

"Did you learn anything?" his father asked.   6

Laurie regarded his father coldly. "I didn't learn nothing," he said.   7

"Anything," I said. "Didn't learn anything."   8

"The teacher spanked a boy, though," Laurie said, addressing his bread and butter. "For being fresh," he added, with his mouth full.   9

"What did he do?" I asked. "Who was it?"   10

Laurie thought. "It was Charles," he said. "He was fresh. The teacher spanked him and made him stand in a corner. He was awfully fresh."   11

"What did he do?" I asked again, but Laurie slid off his chair, took a cookie, and left, while his father was still saying, "See here, young man."   12

The next day Laurie remarked at lunch, as soon as we sat down, "Well, Charles was bad again today." He grinned enormously and said, "Today Charles hit the teacher."   13

"Good heavens," I said, mindful of the Lord's name, "I suppose he got spanked again?"   14

"He sure did," Laurie said. "Look up," he said to his father.   15

"What?" his father said, looking up.   16

"Look down," Laurie said. "Look at my thumb. Gee you're dumb." He began to laugh insanely.   17

"Why did Charles hit the teacher?" I asked quickly.   18

"Because she tried to make him color with red crayons," Laurie said. "Charles wanted to color with green crayons so he hit the teacher and she spanked him and said nobody play with Charles but everybody did."   19

The third day—it was Wednesday of the first week—Charles bounced a see-saw on to the head of a little girl and made her bleed, and the teacher made him stay inside all during recess. Thursday Charles had to stand in a corner during story-time because he kept pounding his feet on the floor. Friday Charles was deprived of blackboard privileges because he threw chalk.   20

On Saturday I remarked to my husband, "Do you think kindergarten is too unsettling for Laurie? All this toughness, and bad grammar, and this Charles boy sounds like such a bad influence."   21

"It'll be all right," my husband said reassuringly. "Bound to be people like Charles in the world. Might as well meet them now as later."   22

On Monday Laurie came home late, full of news. "Charles," he shouted as he came up the hill; I was waiting anxiously on the front steps. "Charles," Laurie yelled all the way up the hill, "Charles was bad again."   23

"Come right in," I said, as soon as he came close enough. "Lunch is waiting."   24

"You know what Charles did?" he demanded, following me through the door. "Charles yelled so in school they sent a boy in from first grade to tell the teacher she had to make   25

Charles keep quiet, and so Charles had to stay after school. And so all the children stayed to watch him."

26   "What did he do?" I asked.

27   "He just sat there," Laurie said, climbing into his chair at the table. "Hi, Pop, y'old dust mop."

28   "Charles had to stay after school today," I told my husband. "Everyone stayed with him."

29   "What does Charles look like?" my husband asked Laurie. "What's his other name?"

30   "He's bigger than me," Laurie said. "And he doesn't have any rubbers and he doesn't ever wear a jacket."

31   Monday night was the first Parent-Teachers meeting, and only the fact that the baby had a cold kept me from going; I wanted passionately to meet Charles's mother. On Tuesday Laurie remarked suddenly, "Our teacher had a friend come to see her in school today."

32   "Charles's mother?" my husband and I asked simultaneously.

33   "Naaah," Laurie said scornfully. "It was a man who came and made us do exercises, we had to touch our toes. Look." He climbed down from his chair and squatted down and touched his toes. "Like this," he said. He got solemnly back into his chair and said, picking up his fork, "Charles didn't even do exercises."

34   "That's fine," I said heartily. "Didn't Charles want to *do* exercises?"

35   "Naaah," Laurie said. "Charles was so fresh to the teacher's friend he wasn't *let* do exercises."

36   "Fresh again?" I said.

37   "He kicked the teacher's friend," Laurie said. "The teacher's friend told Charles to touch his toes like I just did and Charles kicked him."

38   "What are they going to do about Charles, do you suppose?" Laurie's father asked him.

39   Laurie shrugged elaborately. "Throw him out of school, I guess," he said.

40   Wednesday and Thursday were routine; Charles yelled during story hour and hit a boy in the stomach and made him cry. On Friday Charles stayed after school again and so did all the other children.

41   With the third week of kindergarten Charles was an institution in our family; the baby was being a Charles when she cried all afternoon; Laurie did a Charles when he filled his wagon full of mud and pulled it through the kitchen; even my husband, when he caught his elbow in the telephone cord and pulled telephone, ashtray, and a bowl of flowers off the table, said, after the first minute, "Looks like Charles."

42   During the third and fourth weeks it looked like a reformation in Charles; Laurie reported grimly at lunch on Tuesday of the third week, "Charles was so good today the teacher gave him an apple."

43   "What?" I said, and my husband added warily, "You mean Charles?"

44   "Charles," Laurie said. "He gave the crayons around and he picked up the books afterward and the teacher said he was her helper."

45   "What happened?" I asked incredulously.

46   "He was her helper, that's all," Laurie said, and shrugged.

47   "Can this be true, about Charles?" I asked my husband that night. "Can something like this happen?"

"Wait and see," my husband said cynically. "When you've got a Charles to deal with, this may mean he's only plotting."   48

He seemed to be wrong. For over a week Charles was the teacher's helper; each day he handed things out and he picked things up; no one had to stay after school.   49

"The P.T.A. meeting's next week again," I told my husband one evening. "I'm going to find Charles's mother there."   50

"Ask her what happened to Charles," my husband said. "I'd like to know."   51

"I'd like to know myself," I said.   52

On Friday of that week things were back to normal. "You know what Charles did today?" Laurie demanded at the lunch table, in a voice slightly awed. "He told a little girl to say a word and she said it and the teacher washed her mouth out with soap and Charles laughed."   53

"What word?" his father asked unwisely, and Laurie said, "I'll have to whisper it to you, it's so bad." He got down off his chair and went around to his father. His father bent his head down and Laurie whispered joyfully. His father's eyes widened.   54

"Did Charles tell the little girl to say *that*?" he asked respectfully.   55

"She said it *twice*," Laurie said. "Charles told her to say it *twice*."   56

"What happened to Charles?" my husband asked.   57

"Nothing," Laurie said. "He was passing out the crayons."   58

Monday morning Charles abandoned the little girl and said the evil word himself three or four times, getting his mouth washed out with soap each time. He also threw chalk.   59

My husband came to the door with me that evening as I set out for the P.T.A. meeting. "Invite her over for a cup of tea after the meeting," he said. "I want to get a look at her."   60

"If only she's there," I said prayerfully.   61

"She'll be there," my husband said. "I don't see how they could hold a P.T.A. meeting without Charles's mother."   62

At the meeting I sat restlessly, scanning each comfortable matronly face, trying to determine which one hid the secret of Charles. None of them looked to me haggard enough. No one stood up in the meeting and apologized for the way her son had been acting. No one mentioned Charles.   63

After the meeting I identified and sought out Laurie's kindergarten teacher. She had a plate with a cup of tea and a piece of chocolate cake; I had a plate with a cup of tea and a piece of marshmallow cake. We maneuvered up to one another cautiously, and smiled.   64

"I've been so anxious to meet you," I said. "I'm Laurie's mother."   65

"We're all so interested in Laurie," she said.   66

"Well, he certainly likes kindergarten," I said. "He talks about it all the time."   67

"We had a little trouble adjusting, the first week or so," she said primly, "but now he's a fine little helper. With occasional lapses, of course."   68

"Laurie adjusts very quickly," I said. "I suppose this time it's Charles's influence."   69

"Charles?"   70

"Yes," I said laughing, "you must have your hands full in that kindergarten, with Charles."   71

"Charles?" she said. "We don't have any Charles in the kindergarten."   72

SAKI (H. H. MUNRO)
The Open Window

1   "My aunt will be down presently, Mr. Nuttel," said a very self-possessed young lady of fifteen; "in the meantime you must try and put up with me."

2   Framton Nuttel endeavored to say the correct something which should duly flatter the niece of the moment without unduly discounting the aunt that was to come. Privately he doubted more than ever whether these formal visits on a succession of total strangers would do much towards helping the nerve cure which he was supposed to be undergoing.

3   "I know how it will be," his sister had said when he was preparing to migrate to this rural retreat; "you will bury yourself down there and not speak to a living soul, and your nerves will be worse than ever from moping. I shall just give you letters of introduction to all the people I know there. Some of them, as far as I can remember, were quite nice."

4   Framton wondered whether Mrs. Sappleton, the lady to whom he was presenting one of the letters of introduction, came into the nice division.

5   "Do you know many of the people round here?" asked the niece, when she judged that they had had sufficient silent communion.

6   "Hardly a soul," said Framton. "My sister was staying here, at the rectory, you know, some four years ago, and she gave me letters of introduction to some of the people here."

7   He made the last statement in a tone of distinct regret.

8   "Then you know practically nothing about my aunt?" pursued the self-possessed young lady.

9   "Only her name and address," admitted the caller. He was wondering whether Mrs. Sappleton was in the married or widowed state. An undefinable something about the room seemed to suggest masculine habitation.

10   "Her great tragedy happened just three years ago," said the child; "that would be since your sister's time."

11   "Her tragedy?" asked Framton; somehow in this restful country spot tragedies seemed out of place.

12   "You may wonder why we keep that window wide open on an October afternoon," said the niece, indicating a large French window that opened on to a lawn.

13   "It is quite warm for the time of the year," said Framton; "but has that window got anything to do with the tragedy?"

14   "Out through that window, three years ago to a day, her husband and her two young brothers went off for their day's shooting. They never came back. In crossing the moor to their favorite snipe-shooting ground they were all three engulfed in a treacherous piece of bog. It had been that dreadful wet summer, you know, and places that were safe in other

years gave way suddenly without warning. Their bodies were never recovered. That was the dreadful part of it." Here the child's voice lost its self-possessed note and became falteringly human. "Poor aunt always thinks that they will come back someday, they and the little brown spaniel that was lost with them, and walk in at that window just as they used to do. That is why the window is kept open every evening till it is quite dusk. Poor dear aunt, she has often told me how they went out, her husband with his white waterproof coat over his arm, and Ronnie, her youngest brother, singing 'Bertie, why do you bound?' as he always did to tease her, because she said it got on her nerves. Do you know, sometimes on still, quiet evenings like this, I almost get a creepy feeling that they will all walk in through that window—"

15 She broke off with a little shudder. It was a relief to Framton when the aunt bustled into the room with a whirl of apologies for being late in making her appearance.

16 "I hope Vera has been amusing you?" she said.

17 "She has been very interesting," said Framton.

18 "I hope you don't mind the open window," said Mrs. Sappleton briskly; "my husband and brothers will be home directly from shooting, and they always come in this way. They've been out for snipe in the marshes today, so they'll make a fine mess over my poor carpets. So like you menfolk, isn't it?"

19 She rattled on cheerfully about the shooting and the scarcity of birds, and the prospects for duck in the winter. To Framton it was all purely horrible. He made a desperate but only partially successful effort to turn the talk on to a less ghastly topic; he was conscious that his hostess was giving him only a fragment of her attention, and her eyes were constantly straying past him to the open window and the lawn beyond. It was certainly an unfortunate coincidence that he should have paid his visit on this tragic anniversary.

20 "The doctors agree in ordering me complete rest, an absence of mental excitement, and avoidance of anything in the nature of violent physical exercise," announced Framton, who labored under the tolerably widespread delusion that total strangers and chance acquaintances are hungry for the least detail of one's ailments and infirmities, their cause and cure. "On the matter of diet they are not so much in agreement," he continued.

21 "No?" said Mrs. Sappleton, in a voice which only replaced a yawn at the last moment. Then she suddenly brightened into alert attention—but not to what Framton was saying.

22 "Here they are at last!" she cried. "Just in time for tea, and don't they look as if they were muddy up to the eyes!"

23 Framton shivered slightly and turned towards the niece with a look intended to convey sympathetic comprehension. The child was staring out through the open window with a dazed horror in her eyes. In a chill shock of nameless fear Framton swung round in his seat and looked in the same direction.

24   In the deepening twilight three figures were walking across the lawn towards the window; they all carried guns under their arms, and one of them was additionally burdened with a white coat hung over his shoulders. A tired brown spaniel kept close at their heels. Noiselessly they neared the house, and then a hoarse young voice chanted out of the dusk: "I said, Bertie, why do you bound?"

25   Framton grabbed wildly at his stick and hat; the hall door, the gravel drive, and the front gate were dimly noted stages in his headlong retreat. A cyclist coming along the road had to run into the hedge to avoid imminent collision.

26   "Here we are, my dear," said the bearer of the white mackintosh, coming in through the window, "fairly muddy, but most of it's dry. Who was that who bolted out as we came up?"

27   "A most extraordinary man, a Mr. Nuttel," said Mrs. Sappleton; "could only talk about his illnesses, and dashed off without a word of goodby or apology when you arrived. One would think he had seen a ghost."

28   "I expect it was the spaniel," said the niece calmly; "he told me he had a horror of dogs. He was once hunted into a cemetery somewhere on the banks of the Ganges by a pack of pariah dogs, and had to spend the night in a newly dug grave with the creatures snarling and grinning and foaming just above him. Enough to make anyone lose their nerve."

29   Romance at short notice was her speciality.

FOR WRITING OR DISCUSSION

1. In what ways could you classify these pieces as "surprise ending" stories? How does each writer achieve the surprise? What clues to the outcome do you notice in each case before you reach the ending?

2. In what ways are the children in the stories similar? Different? How do the adults affect the outcome—the parents in Laurie's case, the aunt and Mr. Nuttel (note the man's name!) in the niece's case?

3. The last line of each story is well known. How do the last lines capture the heart of the stories?

4. Write a paper comparing and (or) or contrasting Jackson's short story with Saki's. You may use one or more of the preceding questions to guide you in limiting your subject.

Legalizing Drugs: Two Web Sites for Comparison and Contrast

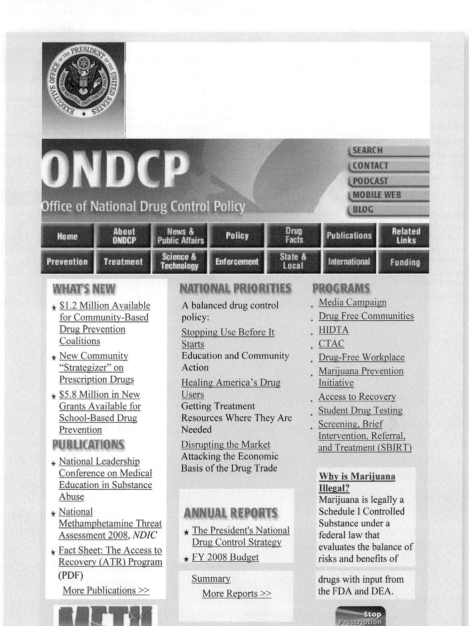

ONDCP
Office of National Drug Control Policy

SEARCH
CONTACT
PODCAST
MOBILE WEB
BLOG

| Home | About ONDCP | News & Public Affairs | Policy | Drug Facts | Publications | Related Links |
| Prevention | Treatment | Science & Technology | Enforcement | State & Local | International | Funding |

WHAT'S NEW

* $1.2 Million Available for Community-Based Drug Prevention Coalitions
* New Community "Strategizer" on Prescription Drugs
* $5.8 Million in New Grants Available for School-Based Drug Prevention

PUBLICATIONS

* National Leadership Conference on Medical Education in Substance Abuse
* National Methamphetamine Threat Assessment 2008, *NDIC*
* Fact Sheet: The Access to Recovery (ATR) Program (PDF)

More Publications >>

NATIONAL PRIORITIES

A balanced drug control policy:

Stopping Use Before It Starts
Education and Community Action

Healing America's Drug Users
Getting Treatment Resources Where They Are Needed

Disrupting the Market
Attacking the Economic Basis of the Drug Trade

ANNUAL REPORTS

* The President's National Drug Control Strategy
* FY 2008 Budget

Summary
More Reports >>

PROGRAMS

. Media Campaign
. Drug Free Communities
. HIDTA
. CTAC
. Drug-Free Workplace
. Marijuana Prevention Initiative
. Access to Recovery
. Student Drug Testing
. Screening, Brief Intervention, Referral, and Treatment (SBIRT)

Why is Marijuana Illegal?
Marijuana is legally a Schedule I Controlled Substance under a federal law that evaluates the balance of risks and benefits of

drugs with input from the FDA and DEA.

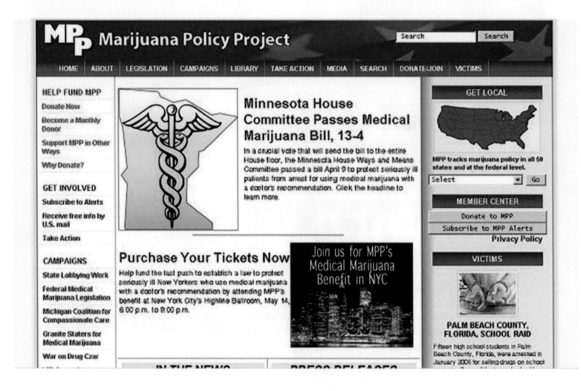

FOR WRITING OR DISCUSSION

1. Drug abuse in America has stimulated heated arguments on whether or not to make drugs like marijuana legal. What positions does each of these Web sites take on the argument? Which Web site makes its point more forcefully? Why do you think so?

2. How do visual elements contribute to each presentation?

3. Have you ever heard of the ONDCP or the MPP? How reliable are these Web sites as suppliers of accurate information? How do you know? How could you find out more about them?

4. Write an essay in which you compare and contrast these two Web sites. You may want to visit the sites before you write to view updated versions of what you see here. (We downloaded the material in early 2008.) If you find it helpful, use any of the preceding questions to guide you in limiting and developing your topic.

HAVING YOUR SAY

Do you believe that we should make the use of drugs like marijuana legal? Write an essay in which you argue one side or the other. You may wish to check library or online resources for more information.

Love, Sweet Love: Two Poems for Comparison and Contrast

The comparison–contrast paper is especially effective as a means of writing about literature. When you examine one literary work along with another, the comparison often provides fresh insights into both works. If, for example, you read the following two poems separately, you would probably not derive the same meaning from them as did the student who compares them in "Two Kinds of Love." The annotations on the student's essay will help you see the pattern at work.

WILLIAM SHAKESPEARE

Sonnet 29

When, in disgrace with Fortune and men's eyes,
I all alone beweep my outcast state,
And trouble deaf heaven with my bootless[1] cries,
And look upon myself and curse my fate,
Wishing me like to one more rich in hope,   5
Featured like him, like him with friends possessed,
Desiring this man's art, and that man's scope,
With what I most enjoy contented least;
Yet in these thoughts myself almost despising,
Haply[2] I think on thee, and then my state,

---

[1]Futile.
[2]By chance.

Like to the lark at break of day arising
From sullen earth, sings hymns at heaven's gate;
  For thy sweet love remembered such wealth brings
  That then I scorn to change my state with kings.

WILLIAM SHAKESPEARE

Sonnet 130

My mistress' eyes are nothing like the sun;
Coral is far more red than her lips' red;
If snow be white, why then her breasts are dun;
If hairs be wires, black wires grow on her head.
5 I have seen roses damasked, red and white,
But no such roses see I in her cheeks;
And in some perfumes is there more delight
Than in the breath that from my mistress reeks.
I love to hear her speak; yet well I know
10 That music hath a far more pleasing sound.
I grant I never saw a goddess go:
My mistress, when she walks, treads on the ground.
  And yet, by heaven, I think my love as rare
  As any she belied with false compare.

Julie Olivera

Two Kinds of Love

Introduction and thesis: Writer establishes framework for comparison–contrast.

Shakespeare's Sonnet 29, "When, in disgrace with Fortune and men's eyes," and Sonnet 130, "My mistress' eyes are nothing like the sun," both strike me as very fine love poems. Both offer great tributes to the loved person. Love comes in all shapes and sizes, however, and I think the

1

Purpose clear:
To show
superiority of
one poem over
the other.

Transition and
introduction to
first subject in
comparison.

Quotations from
poem advance
brief summary of
Sonnet 29.

Writer's
interpretation of
"When, in
disgrace."

Transition to
second subject
of comparison
and clear pattern
of organization.

feelings expressed in "My mistress' eyes" are more realistic and more trustworthy. I'd rather be the woman that poem was written for than the other woman.

"When, in disgrace," begins by describing a situation in which the poet feels totally depressed. Totally is no exaggeration. He hasn't had any good "fortune," people look down on him, he is jealous of other people, heaven is "deaf" to his prayers. He has little or no hope. He has few, if any, friends. The things he enjoys most mean nothing to him. He even comes close to hating himself. The second part of the poem very beautifully says that even in a foul mood like that if he just happens to "think on thee," he cheers up. He realizes, in fact, that he is one of the luckiest men in the world. He has her love, and her love makes him richer than a king in all that really matters. "For thy sweet love remembered such wealth brings / That then I scorn to change my state with kings."

Well, I'd be flattered, of course, and I might even wipe away a tear, but I'm not sure how much I would trust him. Love is a great inspiration to fall back on if one's life starts going to pieces, but it also has to exist on a day-to-day basis, through all the normal wear and tear, through all the boredom and nothing-special times. If I save a drowning person, he might say with complete sincerity that he loves and adores me, but that is no real basis for a lifelong relationship. If it takes bad times to make the poet realize how much he loves his lady, what starts happening to the love when times aren't so bad?

In "My mistress' eyes," the poet is not depressed, but confident and cheerful. He is in love just as much, but this time with a real person, not a goddess or miracle worker. If anything bothers him, it is people who have to depend on illusions and lies to make their loves seem worthwhile. He still wouldn't trade places with a king, yet he knows and gladly accepts that other women are better-looking, and that they have nicer voices, and even that they have sweeter-smelling breath. He doesn't have to turn his lady into something she isn't in order to love her.

2

Fair
explanations:
Writer
identifies
sonnet's
strengths
even though
she likes this
poem less
than the other
poem she will
discuss.

3

Analogy
helps writer
support her
point about
love as
defined in
the poem.

4

Summary
and
interpretation
of Sonnet
130.

In this paragraph, writer develops contrast between the two poems.

5   I think this expression of love is by far the more valid one. People want to be loved for what they are, imperfections and all. If someone says he loves me, I want to feel he loves me rather than an unrealistic mental image he has of me. If all he loves is the image, the love is an insult. In direct contrast, the poet in "When, in disgrace" seems to love the woman for what she does for him, while the poet in "My mistress' eyes" loves her simply for what she is.

Conclusion: A strong restatement of the thesis.

6   Between the stickiness and sweetness of the first poem and the realism of the second, I have to choose the second. Both poems are fine, but one is written for rare moods, and the other is written for a lifetime.

FOR WRITING OR DISCUSSION

1. What pattern of development does the writer use? How would you outline the paper?

2. Has the writer produced a unified comparison–contrast paper, or has she written two separate essays on two separate poems? Explain your answer.

3. In your view, do the poems present two opposing attitudes? The writer assumes they were written about two different women. Could they have been written about the same woman?

4. Write a paper in which you compare and contrast the two sonnets by Shakespeare. Follow the guidelines on writing a comparison–contrast essay explored in this chapter.

STRATEGY CHECKLIST: Writing and Revising Your Comparison–Contrast Paper

Plan the paper.	☐ Have I used prewriting to explore ideas for a subject?
	☐ Have I determined a single principle by which to compare and contrast?
	☐ Will I show similarities, or differences, or a combination of the two?

☐ Have I chosen a pattern of development that suits my subject?

☐ Have I thought carefully about my purpose in writing?

☐ Do I have my audience clearly in mind?

☐ Have I used an outline to organize my ideas?

Write a first draft.

☐ Have I developed a clear thesis?

☐ Have I provided enough support for my thesis?

☐ Have I used the patterns of development appropriately?

- Subject-by-subject (block) pattern: See page 231.
- Point-by-point (alternating) pattern: See page 234.
- Combined pattern: See page 236.

Revise and edit the paper.

☐ Does my introduction establish the purpose for my comparison?

☐ Do my points suit the purpose I have established?

☐ Have I cut any points that do not support my thesis?

☐ Should I add more points to support my thesis?

☐ Have I checked my paper against my outline to make sure it is arranged logically?

☐ Does my conclusion bring my paper to a logical ending?

Proofread the paper.

☐ Have I proofread for grammar, spelling, and mechanics?

WRITING TOPICS

If you are having difficulty deciding on a topic for your comparison–contrast paper, the following suggestions might be helpful. Bear in mind that the number of comparison–contrast topics is almost infinite, and ours just begin to scratch the surface. Our suggestions are intended more to start your own thoughts flowing than to be specific, final topics.

1. Any past-versus-present topic: cars, sports teams or athletes, places you've lived, girlfriends or boyfriends, movie stars, musical styles, clothes, ways of celebrating a holiday, a change in your attitude toward someone or something, attitudes before and after 9/11.

2. What you thought something was going to be like and what it was actually like: a country, a town, college life, a job, a book, a romantic attachment, a marriage, a divorce, a tourist attraction.

3. A which-is-better topic: two competing products, cultures, newscasters, restaurants, television sitcoms, business establishments, seasons of the year, cats versus dogs, breeds of dog, methods of disciplining children.

4. Two contrasting types of people: teachers, police officers, drivers, salespeople, political leaders, "dates," hairstylists, servers at restaurants.

5. Two contrasting (but sometimes confused) emotions or character traits: love and infatuation, courage and recklessness, pride and arrogance, snobbery and good taste, fear and terror.

6. Two contrasting views on a controversial issue: dealing with terrorists, compulsory drug testing for high school athletes, abortion, SUV drivers, censorship, pornography, to name a few possibilities.

CROSSCURRENTS

1. In a short essay, compare the views of writing and learning to write as indicated in Zinsser's "Speaking of Writing" (pages 241–242) and Mohan Sivanand's "Why I Write Wrong" (look ahead to pages 298–299).

2. Judy Brady and Barbara Ehrenreich present views on the relations between men and women and the differences between the sexes. Write an essay in which you compare and contrast the essential points in "I Want a Wife" (pages 196–198) and "What I've Learned from Men" (pages 191–193).

COLLABORATIVE LEARNING

In groups of three to five students, discuss the student essays "Life after Death" (pages 196–198), "Smarter But" (pages 235–236), and "Birds of a Feather?" (pages 238–239). Look particularly at the relations between the outlines presented and the essays themselves. In what ways did the writers use the outlines successfully in developing the papers? What suggestions can the group make for improving the outlines? the essays?

From **IMAGE** To **WORDS**: A Reading and Writing Assignment

Photography by Robert Brenner/PhotoEditInc.

Use the photograph above to write a brief essay that compares and contrasts the two people you see. Consider not only the obvious differences—their age, appearance, and so on—but also what you think both of their objectives are.

For additional writing, reading, and research resources, go to **www. mycomplab.com** <http://www.mycomplab.com/> and choose Skwire/Wiener's *Student's Book of College English*, Twelfth Edition.

CHAPTER 12

Classification and Division

Classification and division are among humanity's most advanced, yet most basic, modes of thought. These thinking skills allow us to see relations among parts and so make the world around us more comprehensible.

Classification and Division in Action

Saturday night is just around the corner, and you've decided to spend a quiet evening at home—cook some pasta, make a salad, rent a movie from the video rental shop, and pick up the latest Stephen King book for a little night-time terror before bed. If you're walking, biking, driving, or taking a bus, you're already plotting the most efficient route. Maybe it's Blockbuster video rental first, Pathmark Supermarket second, and the local library last.

At Blockbuster, signs direct you to different groups of films—new releases, comedies, adventure classics, romances, and others. You decide on *Knocked Up*—you've seen it at least twice before—but its antics seem to be the perfect antidote to Stephen King. So you head over to the comedies section and take what you want from the shelf. There's a two-for-one special tonight—well, maybe you'll be bored the third time around with Seth Rogan, Katherine Heigl, and Paul Rudd and company—so you head over to the adventure classics section; your friend Consuelo has been raving about *The Thin Red Line*, a World War II film set in the Pacific that she calls beautiful poetry, and you find your way to the right shelf for that film too.

At Pathmark, your first stop is at the produce area for the makings of a small salad, then to the boxes of macaroni and spaghetti piled high in the pasta section (it's linguine tonight, you've decided), and then over to the shelves marked "Sauces" for a jar of Ronzoni's meat sauce. Finally, you go to the frozen food section, check out the ice-cream bin, and pick Ben and Jerry's Cherry Garcia.

Off to the library then; inside this branch has a section called New Releases near the check out desk. You look for the King book and note that one copy is in the group of books to rent with a daily fee and another copy in the group of free books—from which you grab your copy and head home.

Using Division (or Analysis)

When you established your route for picking up the various items you needed for Saturday night at home, you used *division*, maybe even unconsciously. You considered the whole map of your town or neighborhood and divided it into separate units to make your trip easier. The video shop, the supermarket, the library—these are the sections of your larger surrounding geography. When you divide, you break down something (here, your town or neighborhood) into parts or sections. Your purpose in dividing was for ease of transport and so you divided the entity into units that served your purpose. Clearly, many other possibilities exist for dividing the neighborhood you live in, all depending on the purpose for the division. You could separate the neighborhood by the way people vote in elections; by the ethnic makeup of various sections; by the architectural varieties of buildings; by the lawns and flower gardens and what they look like; and by the school districts and the businesses—the options are numerous.

In the process of division—which, incidentally, many people call *analysis*—you break down an entity into its discrete parts, all based on some organizing principle. Division moves from the general to the specific; you look at a large category and try to understand it better by seeing what makes it up. When you analyze a Big Mac, a rock song, a television program, a magazine ad, or a poem, you divide it into distinct elements in order to understand the parts and how they contribute to the whole.

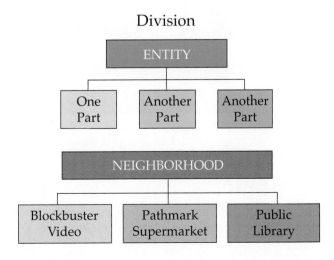

Division

Using Classification

As you scooted around town to the video shop, the supermarket, and the library, you used a different, but related, thinking skill. When you searched for movies, pasta, vegetables, ice cream, and a King thriller, you relied on *classification*. To locate specific items, you had to identify the large group into which someone had placed them. Classification creates large entities from discrete components.

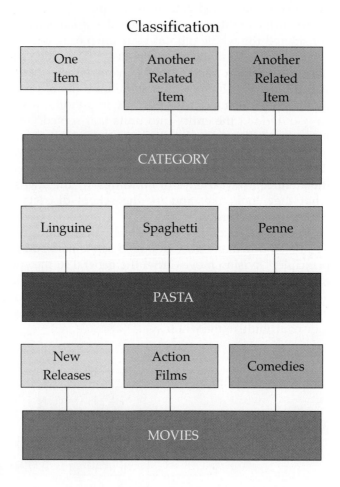

Classification

How Are Classification and Division Different?

Do you see the differences? *Division* moves from the larger group to the smaller parts. *Classification* moves from the smaller parts to the larger group. Division and classification as rhetorical strategies often work hand in hand and overlap considerably.

If you wanted to write about preparing for your Saturday night at home, as we've revealed it here, you might explain how you *divided* your neighborhood into entities that let you move easily from one stop to the other. Then you'd explain how *classification* at your various stops helped you set up an evening of leisure according to your own design.

To take another example, if you wanted to write about violence on television, you might *divide* the topic into news shows, daytime soap operas, and children's programs. Selecting one or more of these, you might then *classify* the soaps, for example. You might identify categories of violence that you saw on the soap operas, such as violence against children, violence among husbands, wives and lovers, and violence at the workplace. Each category would require supporting detail to make your classification stick—but we'll have more to say later about how to write your classification essay.

Reviewing Division Strategies

As you've seen, another name for division is *analysis*. When you analyze—a poem or short story, a process or procedure, or the reasons for some behavior or action—you divide the issue into components. In analysis by *division*, you break down a subject usually thought of as a single unit into each one of its parts. An analysis of a stereo system, for example, requires naming and describing each of its components. An analysis of a breakfast cereal requires a listing of the number of calories and the grams of protein, carbohydrates, fat, and sodium in a single serving. An analysis of a process—how to change a light bulb or how to make iron ore into steel—requires discussing the separate steps of the process. So, in fact, if you have written a process paper, you have already used one major form of division.

If you wrote a literary analysis using comparison–contrast strategies (see pages 258–260), you used division to break the piece of literature into the components that concerned you before you showed similarities and differences.

When you write a cause-and-effect paper, often called *causal analysis* (see Chapter 13), division will help you separate an entity—an event, an action, or a consequence—into components.

We deal, therefore, with analysis (division) in other sections of this book. This chapter focuses on *classification*.

Writing Your Classification Paper

As you have seen, **classification** is the process by which we categorize members of a large group—ideas, people, plants, animals, books, pasta, films, and so on—on the basis of a single principle. Classification enables us to cope with a large body of material by organizing it into smaller, more workable categories. Besides, we all like to classify. We do it naturally. Students classify their professors as boring or stimulating. Homemakers classify their cooking utensils, perhaps as those used often and those used occasionally, and place them in drawers and cupboards accordingly. But whether used for fun or for profit, classification has certain requirements, many of which you have already used in developing outlines.

 ## TIPS for Writing a Classification Essay

- **Determine the basis for classification and then apply it consistently.** To classify automobiles, you would not want to establish as the categories "foreign cars," "expensive cars," and "sedans" because these classes do not have the same basis of classification. The first class is based on country of origin, the second on price, and the third on body style. A member of one class would be likely to overlap into others. A Rolls-Royce or a Mercedes, for example, could fit into any of the three classes. Logic would require selection of a single basis of classification such as price and then sticking to the issue of price with subclasses like "expensive," "medium-priced," and "low-priced." Likewise, if you were going to classify the courses you are taking according to level of interest, you shouldn't establish as the categories "dull," "moderately interesting," and "difficult." The class "difficult" violates the principle of classification—level of interest, in this case.

- **Define terms that might be unfamiliar to your audience or that are used in a special way.** A writer using technical terms like *mesomorph, ectomorph*, and *endomorph* to describe human body types would need to define those terms. Even familiar terms like *mature* and *immature* or *realistic* and *unrealistic* may often require definitions because their interpretations can vary. Similarly, suppose you invent names for your categories. You might, for instance, classify joggers as red-faced wobblers, short-legged two-steppers, and long-legged striders. You must share with your reader your understanding of these made-up terms.

- **Decide whether you need only describe each category fully or whether you need to add clarifying examples.** A classification of people as overweight, underweight, and normal, for example, would require merely a complete description of each type. Readers could, on the basis of the description, decide which category the various people they meet belong to. On the other hand, a classification of the present Supreme Court justices as liberals or conservatives, besides giving the characteristics of liberal and conservative justices, should also give the names of the justices who belong to each category and some explanation of why they appear in each group.

■ **Have a thesis.**   In one sense, of course, the classification itself provides the basis for a thesis. If you assert that there are three classes of teachers or four classes of pet owners or five classes of social drinkers and can support your assertion, you have a thesis. But as usual, your thesis should express your opinion about or attitude toward your subject. You could show, for example, that one of the categories is preferable to the others, or that all the categories are silly or despicable or admirable. Having a thesis gives force and interest to your categories.

■ **Establish some kind of order.**   In some cases, you can order your categories according to time, from earliest to latest. Or, depending on your thesis, several other possibilities for ordering the categories present themselves. You might order the categories from worst to best, best to worst, least enjoyable to most enjoyable, or weakest to strongest, for example. In most listings, you may have more interesting comments to make about some classes than about others. Arrange your classes so that the less interesting ones are in the middle of your paper. Hook your readers with a strong first category and leave them satisfied with an even stronger last category. The practice of ordering categories will make an important contribution to your classification papers.

Student Writing: Classification

See what you think of this student's effort at classification; use the annotations to guide your reading.

Yvonne C. Younger

Tomorrow, Tomorrow

Introduction: Begins to establish the context for classification.

Up and at 'em. Make hay while the sun shines. Seize the bull by the horns. Never put off 'til tomorrow what can be done today. Just do it. There are scores of ways for people to tell others to get up, get out, and get going. Fortunately, there are just as many ways to completely avoid doing anything at all.

Topic divided; categories identified indicate basis for classification.

Over the past few years I have made a serious and concentrated study of the varied ways to procrastinate. I have discovered that there are as many ways to avoid work as there are people who wish to avoid working. Happily for the length of this essay, however, I have determined that all kinds of procrastination

1

2

Thesis includes writer's assertion and purpose.

can be divided into four major groups: the classic, the childish, the responsible, and the artistic.

3   The classic type of procrastination is particularly typical of teenagers. It involves lying face up on a flat surface of the procrastinator's choice—beds, sofas, and floors are popular. The procrastinator then proceeds to count ceiling tiles, trace the path of a wandering spider, or simply gaze at a fixed point off in the distance. The advantage of this procrastination style is that it requires no effort. The disadvantage is that there is nothing to distract the work-avoider from the guilt he or she feels at not doing what must be done.

First category includes example to explain "classic" procrastination.

4   Procrastinating in the childish style is standard for college students. Faced with an essay to write, a problem set to complete, or a stack of bills to pay, childish procrastinators are overcome with the desire to play. Video games, Legos, and Frisbees are some common tools of this method. The popularity of this style stems at least partly from its ability to convince others that deep down the procrastinator is amusing and energetic, not lazy. Its single drawback is the expense of equipping oneself with enough games and toys to have a really good time.

Second category and examples.

5   Those who procrastinate responsibly are liable to be adults with a reputation for being organized and "together." Their approach to avoiding work is to find other, different, less unappealing work to do. To put off filing their taxes, followers of this style will scrub floors, bake endless batches of cookies, alphabetize their CD collections, and even color-code their sock drawers. The advantage of this style is that one is simply too busy to be working at unpleasant chores. The grave disadvantage is that one ends up working anyway.

Third category: "responsible" procrastination with illustrative examples.

Last category: Most interesting group placed last in the essay.

6   Artistic procrastination is for the creative spirit. On the surface it resembles classic procrastination almost exactly. The work-avoider lies on the couch all day, staring into the distance. However, when accused of procrastinating, the artistic procrastinator looks offended and either explains that he or she is waiting for inspiration to strike, or looks tortured and complains that no one

understands artistic struggle and true suffering. The best part of this procrastination method is how impressive it can be if done properly. The worst part is that, no matter how convincingly it is done, one will always be suspected of simply lying on the couch.

Conclusion links to introduction and thesis.

Each type of procrastination has its advantages and disadvantages. Each style is also remarkably good for ignoring and avoiding work. Try them all; perfect your favorite, and never work again.

7

FOR WRITING OR DISCUSSION

1. What determines the order in which the first three classes are presented?
2. Should the fourth class have been saved for last, or should it have been presented earlier? Why or why not?
3. Which classes make most effective use of specific details? Which class uses specific details least effectively?
4. Where does the essay briefly turn to comparison–contrast writing? Why?
5. Does the author seem to favor any one class above the others? Is there a thesis?
6. Write a classification paper, choosing an undesirable type or person or practice as your subject: spoiled brats, incompetent parents, nags, worriers, bigots, drinkers, smokers, and so on.

HAVING YOUR SAY

Many cultures and societies view procrastination as evil, the devil's work. Yet doing nothing has a large group of followers in our age. What is your view of procrastination? Write an essay in which you take a position on one side or the other of this topic.

Models of Writing

As you read the following models of classification essays, consider how the writers have observed the strategies of classification discussed in this chapter.

JARED SANDBERG

A Brief, Handy Guide to Those Odd Birds in the Upper Branches

1 Bosses, like birds, come in a wide variety of colorful species, and learning how to identify yours can be instructive and fun. To assist you, I offer "A Field Guide to Bosses," with apologies to winged friends and special thanks to contributing boss-watchers.

2 *Time-Wasting Sapsucker*: This boss mistakes activity for productivity. Can be seen pounding head against the wall like a woodpecker and encouraging others to do same. A stickler for punctuality, he'll retaliate against latecomers with passive-aggressive scheduling. Can damage homes as well. Habitat: under your skin. Call: "I have a new project for you." Says one retired history professor: "No meaningful creative ability, poor social skills," but leaves a lot of droppings. Not to be confused with the Yellow-Bellied Fence Sitter, whose preferred habitat is uncertainty.

3 *Winking-Eyed Rooster*: A morning person, this cocky strutter manages by fear. He picks on everyone but favors young and weak. Prone to sarcastic clapping. Diets on negatives, pointless rules and supercilious displays of power. Greets friends by fake-boxing. Habitat: the spotlight. Call: "Whodda Man?" "Very easy to spot," says software engineer Robert Czarnecki. "Just listen for shouting."

4 *Pigeon-Toed Thrasher*: Common in all climes. Poor long-distance vision and weak sense of direction makes migration impossible. Flits from task to task. Multiple top priorities. Scatters e-mails when alarmed. Mimics every opinion to be right about something. Like other thrashers, "lots of commotion and precious little accomplishment," says ornithologist Charles Duncan. Habitat: thickets. Call: "I knew it!"

5 *Really Red-Faced Cardinal*: Ferocious in defense of his place in the pecking order, this boss is so territorial he'll attack his own reflection in windows. Still upset about something that happened decades ago. Prefers unthreatening cohorts and limits their contact with outsiders. Nostril flare and spitting distinguishes him from a Tanager (see below). Habitat: behind closed doors. Call: throaty, unpublishable exclamations.

6 *Micro-Tanager*: Common control freak that circles the floor and hovers over desks. Has firm, stifling grip. Hoards credit for herself. "She can't let go of things," says the professor. "She can't believe that any of us are going to do the job the way it needs to be done." Misdirects others to keep everyone guessing. Habitat: other people's business. Call: a clipped "I better do it."

7 *Sharp-Tongued Grouse*: Grumbler; displays permanent disappointment. Beaten down by superiors and unimpressed with staffers. Feathers always ruffled. "Nothing is ever good enough," says one research librarian. Stays low to the ground and makes no secret about how he'd run the place, but is too chicken to tell it to bosses. Thinks he's proved himself and shouldn't have to work for advancement. Makes you write your own performance review but never submits it. Habitat: pharmacies and ledges. Call: a plaintive, whining moan.

Puff-Chested Nuthatch: This boss is a nimble climber. Considered an excellent self-promoter who tells underlings to work hard so he can look good. Desperately tries to be chairman's wingman. Spends "all his time preening his personal image," says spotter Richard Clark. Distinguished from the similar Sharp-Elbowed Loon in that he's not good with names or hallway chatter and is more self-forgiving. Blames lapses on his secretary and thinks she doesn't know it. Habitat: the mirror on his office door. Call: overzealous laughter at CEO's bad jokes, interspersed with a rhythmic "Absolutely."   8

Eleven-Fingered Vulture: Loves to chew out people in public. Grabs prime office space from freshly fledged colleagues. Tiny head relative to his body. Tan and leathery, he winters in Boca time-share. "You wouldn't want one as a pet," says Mr. Duncan. Habitat: racquetball courts. Call: "Not much of an athlete, are ya?"   9

Two-Faced Snipe: This boss's courtship ritual involves huge promises that are never kept. He will abandon any toady under his wing he suspects is disloyal or ascending. Shows charm but often backstabs and sets up others for failure. Prefers cover of dense brush to open fields. "Virtually no one is safe," says the research librarian, "from verbal lacerations." Eats off of other people's plates. Habitat: mud. Call: a conspiratorial, "C'mere a minute . . ."   10

Once-Crested Bufflehead: Walks like a boss, talks like a boss but is really a quack. Had a great idea once and won't let you forget it. Coasts on his own hot air. Gathers periodicals for the men's room. Lengthy pauses during his long tales make you think he's a liar. Says one Los Angeles lawyer: "This boss has advanced as far as he will ever go." Habitat: threadbare laurels. Call: "Once, when I . . ."   11

Sage Dove: Tame and approachable, this variety nods while walking. Bright, gregarious and a touch irreverent, solicits opinions from his flock. Commands respect from and for his direct reports. Defers to their expertise. Habitat: out on a limb for you. Call: a reassuring coo. "I'd try to seek out folks like him," says Howard Karten, who last spotted one 30 years ago. "Sadly, they're few and far between—a true *rara avis*."   12

FOR WRITING OR DISCUSSION

1. What does Sandberg mean by "odd birds"? Why does he say that he is offering readers "'A Field Guide to Bosses"? He obviously builds his presentation around an extended metaphor—bosses as birds. Does the metaphor work? Explain your response.

2. What categories does the writer establish in his scheme of classification?

3. Many of the entries that provide supporting detail for each category are sentence fragments. Why has the writer used so many fragments?

4. Obviously, this is a humorous piece. How does the writer accomplish the humor? How does naming the groups after birds contribute to the comic effect?

5. The writer builds his comic presentation on real characteristics of people in charge. Where is Sandberg most accurate in his classification? What bosses do you recognize in these categories?

6. This piece, originally a column in the *Wall Street Journal*, obviously has no conclusion. Why? What would you write in a conclusion for this selection?

7. Write your own classification essay called "A Field Guide to _____" and fill in the blank with some entity you wish to classify—teachers, workers, movies, sports figures, fellow students, actors, for example. Try your hand at humor, using animals, plants, or some other natural phenomenon to help identify the groups you establish.

JOHN HOLT
Three Kinds of Disciplines

1   A child, in growing up, may meet and learn from three different kinds of disciplines. The first and most important is what we might call the Discipline of Nature or of Reality. When he is trying to do something real, if he does the wrong thing or doesn't do the right one, he doesn't get the result he wants. If he doesn't pile one block right on top of another, or tries to build on a slanting surface, his tower falls down. If he hits the wrong key, he hears the wrong note. If he doesn't hit the nail squarely on the head, it bends, and he has to pull it out and start with another. If he doesn't measure properly what he is trying to build, it won't open, close, fit, stand up, fly, float, whistle, or do whatever he wants it to do. If he closes his eyes when he swings, he doesn't hit the ball. A child meets this kind of discipline every time he tries to do something, which is why it is so important in school to give children more chances to do things, instead of just reading or listening to someone talk (or pretending to). This discipline is a great teacher. The learner never has to wait long for his answer; it usually comes quickly, often instantly. Also it is clear, and very often points toward the needed correction; from what happened he cannot only see that what he did was wrong, but also why, and what he needs to do instead. Finally, and most important, the giver of the answer, call it Nature, is impersonal, impartial, and indifferent. She does not give opinions, or make judgments; she cannot be wheedled, bullied, or fooled; she does not get angry or disappointed; she does not praise or blame; she does not remember past failures or hold grudges; with her one always gets a fresh start, this time is the one that counts.

2   The next discipline we might call the Discipline of Culture, of Society, of What People Really Do. Man is a social, a cultural animal. Children sense around them this culture, this network of agreements, customs, habits, and rules binding the adults together. They want to understand it and be a part of it. They watch very carefully what people around them are doing and want to do the same. They want to do right, unless they become convinced they

can't do right. Thus children rarely misbehave seriously in church, but sit as quietly as they can. The example of all those grownups is contagious. Some mysterious ritual is going on, and children, who like rituals, want to be part of it. In the same way, the little children that I see at concerts or operas, though they may fidget a little, or perhaps take a nap now and then, rarely make any disturbance. With all those grownups sitting there, neither moving nor talking, it is the most natural thing in the world to imitate them. Children who live among adults who are habitually courteous to each other, and to them, will soon learn to be courteous. Children who live surrounded by people who speak a certain way will speak that way, however much we may try to tell them that speaking that way is bad or wrong.

The third discipline is the one most people mean when they speak of discipline—the Discipline of Superior Force, of sergeant to private, of "You do what I tell you or I'll make you wish you had." There is bound to be some of this in a child's life. Living as we do surrounded by things that can hurt children, or that children can hurt, we cannot avoid it. We can't afford to let a small child find out from experience the danger of playing in a busy street, or of fooling with the pots on the top of a stove, or of eating up the pills in the medicine cabinet. So, along with other precautions, we say to him, "Don't play in the street, or touch things on the stove, or go into the medicine cabinet, or I'll punish you." Between him and the danger too great for him to imagine we put a lesser danger, but one he can imagine and maybe therefore wants to avoid. He can have no idea of what it would be like to be hit by a car, but he can imagine being shouted at, or spanked, or sent to his room. He avoids these substitutes for the greater danger until he can understand it and avoid it for its own sake. But we ought to use this discipline only when it is necessary to protect the life, health, safety, or well-being of people or other living creatures, or to prevent destruction of things that people care about. We ought not to assume too long, as we usually do, that a child cannot understand the real nature of the danger from which we want to protect him. The sooner he avoids the danger, not to escape our punishment, but as a matter of good sense, the better. He can learn that faster than we think. In Mexico, for example, where people drive their cars with a good deal of spirit, I saw many children no older than five or four walking unattached on the streets. They understood about cars, they knew what to do. A child whose life is full of the threat and fear of punishment is locked into babyhood. There is no way for him to grow up, to learn to take responsibility for his life and acts. Most important of all, we should not assume that having to yield to the threat of our superior force is good for the child's character. It is never good for *anyone's* character. To bow to superior force makes us feel impotent and cowardly for not having had the strength or courage to resist. Worse, it makes us resentful and vengeful. We can hardly wait to make someone pay for our humiliation, yield to us as we were once made to yield. No, if we cannot always avoid using the Discipline of Superior Force, we should at least use it as seldom as we can.

There are places where all three disciplines overlap. Any very demanding human activity combines in it the disciplines of Superior Force, of Culture, and of Nature. The novice will be told, "Do it this way, never mind asking why, just do it that way, that is the way we always do it." But it probably *is* just the way they always do it, and usually for the very good reason that it is a way that has been found to work. Think, for example, of ballet training. The student in a class is told to do this exercise, or that; to stand so; to do this or that with his head, arms, shoulders, abdomen, hips, legs, feet. He is constantly corrected. There is no argument. But behind these seemingly autocratic demands by the teacher lie many decades of custom and tradition, and behind that, the necessities of dancing itself. You cannot make the moves of classical ballet unless over many years you have acquired, and renewed every day, the needed strength and suppleness in scores of muscles and joints. Nor can you do the difficult motions, making them look easy, unless you have learned hundreds of easier ones first. Dance teachers may not always agree on all the details of teaching these strengths and skills. But no novice could learn them all by himself. You could not go for a night or two to watch the ballet and then, without any other knowledge at all, teach yourself how to do it. In the same way, you would be unlikely to learn any complicated and difficult human activity without drawing heavily on the experience of those who know it better. But the point is that the authority of these experts or teachers stems from, grows out of their greater competence and experience, the fact that what they do *works*, not the fact that they happen to be the teacher and as such have the power to kick a student out of the class. And the further point is that children are always and everywhere attracted to that competence, and ready and eager to submit themselves to a discipline that grows out of it. We hear constantly that children will never do anything unless compelled to by bribes or threats. But in their private lives, or in extracurricular activities in school, in sports, music, drama, art, running a newspaper, and so on, they often submit themselves willingly and wholeheartedly to very intense disciplines, simply because they want to learn to do a given thing well. Our Little-Napoleon football coaches, of whom we have too many and hear far too much, blind us to the fact that millions of children work hard every year getting better at sports and games without coaches barking and yelling at them.

FOR WRITING OR DISCUSSION

1. What are the names of the three kinds of disciplines?
2. Identify the topic sentence in each paragraph.
3. In what kind of discipline are parents and teachers least active? Why?
4. What kind of discipline does the author like least? What are the reasons for his dislike? Is he completely opposed to it?
5. What is the purpose of the last paragraph?
6. Choose some kind of behavior as your subject and write a classification paper titled "Three Kinds of _____." Possible subjects could be nervousness, exercise, studying, arguing, driving, shopping, praying, and so on.

Readings for Writing

The following essays will stimulate your thinking on division and classification. The first is a piece by a Nobel Prize–winning economist who complains about the way we classify people of the world because the categories rob us of our "plural identities." The second selection, written by a University of Chicago professor of law and political science, highlights a danger of the Internet, which permits people to become part of like-thinking groups.

AMARTYA SEN

A World Not Neatly Divided

When people talk about clashing civilizations, as so many politicians and academics do now, they can sometimes miss the central issue. The inadequacy of this thesis begins well before we get to the question of whether civilizations must clash. The basic weakness of the theory lies in its program of categorizing people of the world according to a unique, allegedly commanding system of classification. This is problematic because civilizational categories are crude and inconsistent and also because there are other ways of seeing people (linked to politics, language, literature, class, occupation, or other affiliations).

The befuddling influence of a singular classification also traps those who dispute the thesis of a clash: To talk about "the Islamic world" or "the Western world" is already to adopt an impoverished vision of humanity as unalterably divided. In fact, civilizations are hard to partition in this way, given the diversities within each society as well as the linkages among different countries and cultures. For example, describing India as a "Hindu civilization" misses the fact that India has more Muslims than any other country except Indonesia and possibly Pakistan. It is futile to try to understand Indian art, literature, music, food, or politics without seeing the extensive interactions across barriers of religious communities. These include Hindus and Muslims, Buddhists, Jains, Sikhs, Parsees, Christians (who have been in India since at least the fourth century, well before England's conversion to Christianity), Jews (present since the fall of Jerusalem), and even atheists and agnostics. Sanskrit has a larger atheistic-literature than exists in any other classical language. Speaking of India as a Hindu civilization may be comforting to the Hindu fundamentalist, but it is an odd reading of India.

A similar coarseness can be seen in the other categories invoked, like "the Islamic world." Consider Akbar and Aurangzeb, two Muslim emperors of the Mogul dynasty in India. Aurangzeb tried hard to convert Hindus into Muslims and instituted various policies in that direction, of which taxing the non-Muslims was only one example. In contrast, Akbar reveled in his multiethnic court and pluralist laws, and issued official proclamations insisting that no one "should be interfered with on account of religion" and that "anyone is to be allowed to go over to a religion that pleases him."

4   If a homogeneous view of Islam were to be taken, then only one of these emperors could count as a true Muslim. The Islamic fundamentalist would have no time for Akbar; Prime Minister Tony Blair, given his insistence that tolerance is a defining characteristic of Islam, would have to consider excommunicating Aurangzeb. I expect both Akbar and Aurangzeb would protest, and so would I. A similar crudity is present in the characterization of what is called "Western civilization." Tolerance and individual freedom have certainly been present in European history. But there is no dearth of diversity here, either. When Akbar was making his pronouncements on religious tolerance in Agra, in the 1590's, the Inquisitions were still going on; in 1600, Giordano Bruno was burned at the stake, for heresy, in Campo dei Fiori in Rome.

5   Dividing the world into discrete civilizations is not just crude. It propels us into the absurd belief that this partitioning is natural and necessary and must overwhelm all other ways of identifying people. That imperious view goes not only against the sentiment that "we human beings are all much the same," but also against the more plausible understanding that we are diversely different. For example, Bangladesh's split from Pakistan was not connected with religion, but with language and politics.

6   Each of us has many features in our self-conception. Our religion, important as it may be, cannot be an all-engulfing identity. Even a shared poverty can be a source of solidarity across the borders. The kind of division highlighted by, say, the so-called "antiglobalization" protesters—whose movement is, incidentally, one of the most globalized in the world—tries to unite the underdogs of the world economy and goes firmly against religious, national, or "civilizational" lines of division.

7   The main hope of harmony lies not in any imagined uniformity, but in the plurality of our identities, which cut across each other and work against sharp divisions into impenetrable civilizational camps. Political leaders who think and act in terms of sectioning off humanity into various "worlds" stand to make the world more flammable—even when their intentions are very different. They also end up, in the case of civilizations defined by religion, lending authority to religious leaders seen as spokesmen for their "worlds." In the process, other voices are muffled and other concerns silenced. The robbing of our plural identities not only reduces us; it impoverishes the world.

FOR WRITING OR DISCUSSION

1. Sen argues against classification, yet his essay does have a structure. What is it? How does he classify?

2. What, according to Sen, is the basic weakness of the thesis of clashing civilizations? What does "singular classification" mean? Why is classifying people in terms of their civilization "crude and inconsistent"?

3. Why does Sen worry particularly about the use of singular classification by political leaders?

4. Write an essay about "singular classifications" that you observe on your current campus, at your high school, or in your neighborhood.

CASS R. SUNSTEIN
How Polarizing Is the Internet?

In 1995 the technology specialist Nicholas Negroponte predicted the emergence of "the Daily   1
Me"—a newspaper that you design personally, with each component carefully screened and chosen in advance. For many of us, Negroponte's prediction is coming true. As a result of the Internet, personalization is everywhere. If you want to read essays arguing that climate change is a fraud and a hoax, or that the American economy is about to collapse, the technology is available to allow you to do exactly that. If you are bored and upset by the topic of genocide, or by recent events in Iraq or Pakistan, you can avoid those subjects entirely. With just a few clicks, you can find dozens of Web sites that show you are quite right to like what you already think.

Actually you don't even need to create a Daily Me. With the Internet, it is increasingly easy   2
for others to create one for you. If people know a little bit about you, they can discover, and tell you, what "people like you" tend to like—and they can create a Daily Me, just for you, in a matter of seconds. If your reading habits suggest that you believe that climate change is a fraud, the process of "collaborative filtering" can be used to find a lot of other material that you are inclined to like. Every year filtering and niche marketing becomes more sophisticated and refined. Studies show that on Amazon, many purchasers can be divided into "red-state camps" and "blue-state camps," and those who are in one or another camp receive suitable recommendations, ensuring that people will have plenty of materials that cater to, and support, their predilections.

Of course self-sorting is nothing new. Long before the Internet, newspapers and   3
magazines could often be defined in political terms, and many people would flock to those offering congenial points of view. But there is a big difference between a daily newspaper and a Daily Me, and the difference lies in a dramatic increase in the power to fence in and to fence out. Even if they have some kind of political identification, general-interest newspapers and magazines include materials that would not be included in any particular Daily Me; they expose people to topics and points of view that they do not choose in advance. But as a result of the Internet, we live increasingly in an era of enclaves and niches—much of it voluntary, much of it produced by those who think they know, and often do know, what we're likely to like. This raises some obvious questions. If people are sorted into enclaves and niches, what will happen to their views? What are the eventual effects on democracy?

To answer these questions, let us put the Internet to one side for a moment and explore   4
an experiment conducted in Colorado in 2005, designed to cast light on the consequences of self-sorting. About 60 Americans were brought together and assembled into a number of groups, each consisting of five or six people. Members of each group were asked to deliberate on three of the most controversial issues of the day: Should states allow same-sex couples to enter into civil unions? Should employers engage in affirmative action by giving a

preference to members of traditionally disadvantaged groups? Should the United States sign an international treaty to combat global warming?

5   As the experiment was designed, the groups consisted of "liberal" and "conservative" enclaves—the former from Boulder, the latter from Colorado Springs. It is widely known that Boulder tends to be liberal, and Colorado Springs tends to be conservative. Participants were screened to ensure that they generally conformed to those stereotypes. People were asked to state their opinions anonymously both before and after 15 minutes of group discussion. What was the effect of that discussion?

6   In almost every case, people held more-extreme positions after they spoke with like-minded others. Discussion made civil unions more popular among liberals and less popular among conservatives. Liberals favored an international treaty to control global warming before discussion; they favored it far more strongly after discussion. Conservatives were neutral on that treaty before discussion, but they strongly opposed it after discussion. Liberals, mildly favorable toward affirmative action before discussion, became strongly favorable toward affirmative action after discussion. Firmly negative about affirmative action before discussion, conservatives became fiercely negative about affirmative action after discussion.

7   The creation of enclaves of like-minded people had a second effect: It made both liberal groups and conservative groups significantly more homogeneous—and thus squelched diversity. Before people started to talk, many groups displayed a fair amount of internal disagreement on the three issues. The disagreements were greatly reduced as a result of a mere 15-minute discussion. In their anonymous statements, group members showed far more consensus after discussion than before. The discussion greatly widened the rift between liberals and conservatives on all three issues.

8   The Internet makes it exceedingly easy for people to replicate the Colorado experiment online, whether or not that is what they are trying to do. Those who think that affirmative action is a good idea can, and often do, read reams of material that support their view; they can, and often do, exclude any and all material that argues the other way. Those who dislike carbon taxes can find plenty of arguments to that effect. Many liberals jump from one liberal blog to another, and many conservatives restrict their reading to points of view that they find congenial. In short, those who want to find support for what they already think, and to insulate themselves from disturbing topics and contrary points of view, can do that far more easily than they can if they skim through a decent newspaper or weekly newsmagazine.

9   A key consequence of this kind of self-sorting is what we might call enclave extremism. When people end up in enclaves of like-minded people, they usually move toward a more extreme point in the direction to which the group's members were originally inclined. Enclave extremism is a special case of the broader phenomenon of group polarization, which extends well beyond politics and occurs as groups adopt a more extreme version of whatever view is antecedently favored by their members.

10   Why do enclaves, on the Internet and elsewhere, produce political polarization? The first explanation emphasizes the role of information. Suppose that people who tend to oppose nuclear power are exposed to the views of those who agree with them. It stands to reason that such people will find a disproportionately large number of arguments against nuclear

power—and a disproportionately small number of arguments in favor of nuclear power. If people are paying attention to one another, the exchange of information should move people further in opposition to nuclear power. This very process was specifically observed in the Colorado experiment, and in our increasingly enclaved world, it is happening every minute of every day.

The second explanation, involving social comparison, begins with the reasonable suggestion that people want to be perceived favorably by other group members. Once they hear what others believe, they often adjust their positions in the direction of the dominant position. Suppose, for example, that people in an Internet discussion group tend to be sharply opposed to the idea of civil unions for same-sex couples, and that they also want to seem to be sharply opposed to such unions. If they are speaking with people who are also sharply opposed to these things, they are likely to shift in the direction of even sharper opposition as a result of learning what others think.

11

The final explanation is the most subtle, and probably the most important. The starting point here is that on many issues, most of us are really not sure what we think. Our lack of certainty inclines us toward the middle. Outside of enclaves, moderation is the usual path. Now imagine that people find themselves in enclaves in which they exclusively hear from others who think as they do. As a result, their confidence typically grows, and they become more extreme in their beliefs. Corroboration, in short, reduces tentativeness, and an increase in confidence produces extremism. Enclave extremism is particularly likely to occur on the Internet because people can so easily find niches of like-minded types—and discover that their own tentative view is shared by others.

12

It would be foolish to say, from the mere fact of extreme movements, that people have moved in the wrong direction. After all, the more extreme tendency might be better rather than worse. Increased extremism, fed by discussions among like-minded people, has helped fuel many movements of great value—including, for example, the civil-rights movement, the antislavery movement, the antigenocide movement, the attack on communism in Eastern Europe, and the movement for gender equality. A special advantage of Internet enclaves is that they promote the development of positions that would otherwise be invisible, silenced, or squelched in general debate. Even if enclave extremism is at work—perhaps *because* enclave extremism is at work—discussions among like-minded people can provide a wide range of social benefits, not least because they greatly enrich the social "argument pool." The Internet can be extremely valuable here.

13

But there is also a serious danger, which is that people will move to positions that lack merit but are predictable consequences of the particular circumstances of their self-sorting. And it is impossible to say whether those who sort themselves into enclaves of like-minded people will move in a direction that is desirable for society at large, or even for the members of each enclave. It is easy to think of examples to the contrary—the rise of Nazism, terrorism, and cults of various sorts. There is a general risk that those who flock together, on the Internet or elsewhere, will end up both confident and wrong, simply because they have not been sufficiently exposed to counterarguments. They may even think of their fellow citizens as opponents or adversaries in some kind of "war."

14

15   The Internet makes it easy for people to create separate communities and niches, and in a free society, much can be said on behalf of both. They can make life a lot more fun; they can reduce loneliness and spur creativity. They can even promote democratic self-government, because enclaves are indispensable for incubating new ideas and perspectives that can strengthen public debate. But it is important to understand that countless editions of the Daily Me can also produce serious problems of mutual suspicion, unjustified rage, and social fragmentation—and that these problems will result from the reliable logic of social interactions.

FOR WRITING OR DISCUSSION

1. What is Sunstein's thesis? What is the significance of "the Daily Me"?
2. What two basic categories does the writer establish in regard to "personalization"?
3. In what ways does the Colorado experiment of 2005 contribute to the essay? How does the experiment classify modes of thinking?
4. How does the Internet help polarize people into groups?
5. What are "enclaves" and "niches"? How do they serve the strategy of classification?
6. What dangers does Sunstein see for self-sorting as permitted by the Internet?
7. What is the function of the conclusion in this essay? How does it serve to summarize two essential positions regarding the Internet?
8. Write an essay on what you see as the strengths or weaknesses of the Internet. Try to classify the elements in your position and then provide examples of each.

Reading and Writing About Poetry

Robert Frost writes playfully about a classification scheme that turns into an understated assertion of regard.

ROBERT FROST

The Rose Family

The rose is a rose,
And was always a rose.

But the theory now goes
That the apple's a rose,
And the pear is, and so's   5
The plum, I suppose.
The dear only knows
What will next prove a rose.
You, of course, are a rose—
But were always a rose.   10

FOR WRITING OR DISCUSSION

1. Frost has taken a literal classification system and used it to reach a larger assertion, which comes off as wonderful and humorous understatement. The botanical
   category Rosacaea includes the fruits named in lines 4–6. How does Frost use this
   fact to structure the poem?

2. What is the purpose of the last two lines? The title?

3. What do lines 7–8 mean?

4. In what ways is "The Rose Family" a love poem?

5. Write a classification essay in which you establish a broad category and explain
   what should and should not be included in the group. For example, you might
   want to classify teachers, cousins, rock music, film idols, or novels.

STRATEGY CHECKLIST: Writing and Revising Your Classification Paper

Plan the paper.

- ☐ Have I used prewriting to identify a topic for classification?
- ☐ Have I determined a basis for my classification that allows a logical grouping?
- ☐ Have I thought carefully about my purpose in writing the classification essay?
- ☐ Do I have my audience clearly in mind?
- ☐ Have I used an outline to identify groups and suggest examples in each group?

continued

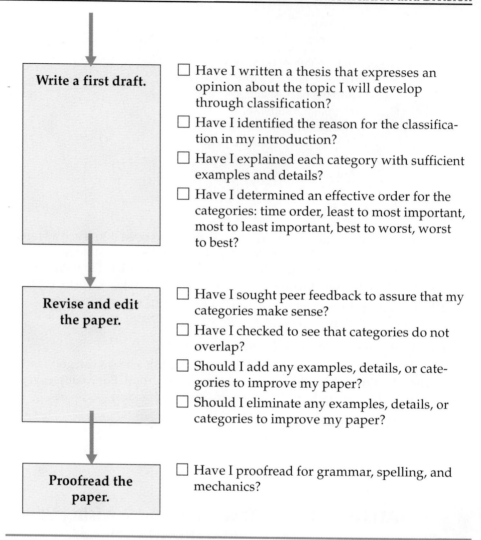

Write a first draft.	☐ Have I written a thesis that expresses an opinion about the topic I will develop through classification?
	☐ Have I identified the reason for the classification in my introduction?
	☐ Have I explained each category with sufficient examples and details?
	☐ Have I determined an effective order for the categories: time order, least to most important, most to least important, best to worst, worst to best?

Revise and edit the paper.	☐ Have I sought peer feedback to assure that my categories make sense?
	☐ Have I checked to see that categories do not overlap?
	☐ Should I add any examples, details, or categories to improve my paper?
	☐ Should I eliminate any examples, details, or categories to improve my paper?

| Proofread the paper. | ☐ Have I proofread for grammar, spelling, and mechanics? |

WRITING TOPICS

The following list of subjects may offer you some ideas for a topic for your classification paper. Notice how some subjects can easily be limited further than they are: "Summer jobs" could be limited to summer jobs at resorts, "outstanding teachers" to outstanding physical education teachers, and so on.

1. Tyrants
2. Attitudes toward Christmas
3. Campus parties
4. Outstanding teachers
5. Summer jobs
6. Major classes of love
7. Automobiles
8. Male or female chauvinists
9. Types of chili (or pizza or burgers)
10. Natural disasters
11. People at a sporting event

12. TV preachers

13. Good drugs

14. Concert goers

15. Voters

16. Holiday gifts

17. Terrorism

18. Shoppers

19. The contents of my handbag (or bookbag or briefcase)

20. Great leaders

CROSSCURRENTS

John Holt's "Three Kinds of Discipline" (pages 274–276) and John Updike's "Childhood Transgressions" (pages 189–190) both deal with treating the consequences of a youngster's doing something viewed as wrong. What would Holt say to Updike's parents? to Updike?

COLLABORATIVE LEARNING

Read or reread the professional essays included in this chapter: "A Brief Handy Guide to Those Odd Birds in the Upper Branches," "Three Kinds of Disciplines," "A World Not Neatly Divided," and "How Polarizing Is the Internet?" Which of the essays does your group think better embodies the principles of good classification papers? What elements do you point to as contributing to the success of the essays? In what ways does the best essay reflect the points on pages 268–269?

From IMAGE To WORDS: A Reading and Writing Assignment

Photography © Syracuse Newspapers/David Lassman/ The Image Works

To classify the elements of the scene in the photograph on page 285, what categories or groups could you establish? How many classification schemes could you suggest as a way of organizing the objects? Indicate at least two ways that you could classify the objects and list several items that you would include in each group. Create a chart and fill in your own responses.

Then, using one of the organizing schemes that you have identified, write a brief paper in which you classify the elements in the photograph. Be sure that you develop a thesis; make some assertion about the elements that you classify and provide details from the picture to support your point. Of course, you may expand on any details that the photograph suggests—colors, for example, or smells that are relevant to your classification scheme.

For additional writing, reading, and research resources, go to **www. mycomplab.com** <http://www.mycomplab.com/> and choose Skwire/Wiener's *Student's Book of College English*, Twelfth Edition.

CHAPTER **13**

Cause and Effect

- Writing Your Cause and Effect Paper
- Student Writing: Cause and Effect
- Researched Student Writing: Cause and Effect
- Models of Writing
- Readings for Writing
- Reading and Writing About Poetry

Many of the papers you write in college will require analysis of causes or circumstances that lead to a given result: Why does the cost of living continue to rise? Why do people with symptoms of cancer or heart disease put off consulting a doctor? In questions of this type, the **effect** or result is given, at least briefly. Your job is to analyze the causes that produce the effect.

Other assignments will require that you discuss the results of a particular case: What are the positive and negative effects of legalizing lotteries? What are the effects of giving direct legislative power to the people. What is the effect of noise pollution on our bodies? In questions of this type, the **cause** is given, and you must determine the effects that might result or have resulted from the cause.

Writing Your Cause and Effect Paper

Cause and effect papers do not call for the rigid structure demanded of classification and process papers. Nevertheless, writers must meet some logical demands.

TIPS for Writing a Cause and Effect Essay

- **Do not confuse cause with process.** A process paper tells *how* an event or product came about; a cause and effect paper tells *why* something happened.

- **Avoid the *post hoc* fallacy.** That a man lost his billfold shortly after walking under a ladder does not mean that walking under the ladder caused his loss. Similarly, that a woman lost her hearing shortly after attending a loud rock concert does not prove that her deafness is a direct result of the band's decibel level. (See the discussion of *post hoc* fallacies in Chapter 15 on page 341.)

■ **Do not oversimplify causes.**   Getting a good night's sleep before an exam doesn't cause a student to receive the highest grade in the class. The rest certainly won't do any harm, but familiarity with the material covered on the exam, intelligence, and an ability to write also have something to do with the grade. Almost all effects worth writing about have more than one cause.

■ **Do not oversimplify effects.**   Even though it may be true that many people lose money by gambling on lotteries, that does not mean legalizing lotteries will result in nationwide bankrutcy.

■ **Follow an established pattern of organization.**   Once you have determined the causes or effects that you wish to discuss, you can organize your paper in several ways. In a paper devoted primarily to cause, the simplest way to open is to identify the effect in the introduction, then to develop the reasons for that effect in the body of the paper. If, for example, you want to explain a recent rise in the cost of living, you might begin with an indication of the rise (effect)—the cost of living has risen dramatically during the past three years and promises to go even higher in the coming year—before dealing with the causes. Similarly, a paper devoted primarily to effect usually begins with a description of the cause. If your subject is the probable effects of a proposed tax increase, you might begin with a description of the proposal itself (cause) before discussing effects.

  In some cases, as when cause and effect are of approximately equal concern, you may want to present one dramatic instance of an effect to open the paper. For example, you might begin a paper on ocean pollution with a description of the infamous 1989 oil spill in Alaska, a striking example of oil pollution. The rest of the introduction would lead into the causes, or sources, of ocean pollution in general. The first major division of what follows might list several important causes other than oil spillage, and the second major division might detail the effects of those causes: extermination of sea life, danger to public health, and so on. Explaining causes and effects requires careful pruning of ideas. Given the length requirements of your paper, the time you have to complete it, and the demands of your topic, you want to be sure to cover enough—but not too much—territory.

Student Writing: Cause and Effect

Now let's take a look at two student papers and see how the writers manage the cause and effect strategy. Annotations on the first paper point to key features of this cause and effect essay.

Richard S. Smith

Cause for Failure

I was never a good student and never thought twice about it until I had to face the reality of putting together a life for myself. When I try now to understand my years of failure in school, I can come up with some answers, now that I'm finally in college and serious about my work. External factors as well as some bad personal decisions all contributed to my problems.

In the first place, things were not easy at home. I'm not trying to lay the blame of my past failures on my home life—I hate people who are constantly making excuses for themselves because other people created trouble for them. Nevertheless, I know that family tensions didn't help my school record. For much of my childhood five of us lived in a small, dark apartment on Sutter Avenue. My father died when I was five, and my mother's energy after a day of packing chemicals at a local factory was too low for her to keep after me. After dinner, her eyelids drooping with exhaustion, she would stretch out on an old brown sofa before the television, and my sisters and I would sit beside her. We never heard a word about doing homework or opening our books. At report card time she was always furious with our failures, but I think she knew that she just had no strength to push us forward. She couldn't even find the strength to push herself.

My friends were no help either. They certainly were not the studying kind. On spring afternoons we would cut high school classes regularly, smoking and rapping in my friend Jerry's old Ford or dribbling lay-ups at the basketball courts in Hillcrest Park. I read a survey by the U.S. Department of Education that showed that fewer than two-thirds of my generation's high school students ever graduated, but in my group of eight students not one of us received a diploma. And we couldn't have cared less!

1

Introductory paragraph presents thesis.

2

Transition "In the first place," opens second paragraph as writer states the first cause.

Cause developed with images and explanation.

Next cause introduced. Word "either" serves as transition that lends coherence to paper.

3

Cause developed with details.

Another cause
identified: "most
important
reason"
establishes
principle of
arrangement in
essay.

4   Perhaps the most important reason for my failures, though, was that I never saw (or maybe it's more accurate to say that I never allowed myself to see) a connection between what we did at our scratched wooden desks and what was waiting for us beyond our high school days. I don't think that I ever believed Mrs. Allen's pages of algebra homework or Mr. Delaney's boring lectures on the Civil War had any real meaning for me. What did this have to do with my life? I had no concept then of what an educated person was supposed to know or understand. Everything to me had to have an immediate payoff. What good would knowing an equation or the Emancipation Proclamation do for me?

Writer identifies
effects of his
failure in school
as he builds
toward
conclusion.

5   And then I tried to find a job. I worked for a few years as a stockboy without getting anywhere. Lugging up cartons of Coke and boxes of toilet tissue from the basement of Foodtown was not my idea of a future. I tried finding other jobs without success. In my case, I suppose it was both the lack of a diploma and the lack of an education that held me back. I started studying for the high school equivalency exam and passed it on the first try.

6   As a business major now at my community college, I know that there are no guarantees about my life from now on, but at least a college degree may open doors that people slammed in my face before. And I'm trying to see myself as getting educated. Maybe those courses in social science and literature will shape my thinking and help me later on.

FOR WRITING OR DISCUSSION

1. What is the thesis of Smith's paper?
2. What pattern of organization does the writer use in this essay?
3. Are the causes the writer gives reasonable explanations for his school failures? Defend your response.
4. What images does the writer provide to help you envision the scene?
5. Think of your own pattern of successes and failures at school and write a paper that analyzes its causes.

Researched Student Writing: Cause and Effect

Note how the writer uses details drawn from source materials to produce a forceful cause and effect essay.

Keely Cutts

Wolves in Yellowstone

Yellowstone National Park, part of the states of Wyoming, Montana, and Idaho, is   1
the center of a controversial issue. From 1872, when the park was founded, until the 1920s, the gray wolf was an integral part of Yellowstone ecology. But by 1926, the U.S. government had successfully eliminated all the wolves in Yellowstone National Park. But now legislation has been proposed to reintroduce the wolf to Yellowstone. The legislation would allow for a limited reintroduction of several packs of the Canadian gray wolf, which is very much like the wolf that was part of Yellowstone's original environment. The total number of wolves is not to exceed one hundred. On both sides of the issue—those for the return of the wolf into the park and those against it— emotions run high. But once the hyperbole surrounding the reintroduction of the wolves is swept away and one scrutinizes the advantages and disadvantages of the reintroduction, there is little reason to continue questioning the benefits of returning gray wolves to Yellowstone National Park.

One of the most compelling reasons for the return of the wolf to Yellowstone is that   2
human intervention led to the wolf's disappearance. Since humans created the ecological void, we have a responsibility to return the endangered animal to its original habitat. As a member of the federal government's endangered species list for twenty-four years, the gray wolf is the only endangered or threatened animal indigenous to the park not to have its own recovery program (Gallagher 39). Wolves were an integral part of the wilderness of the area now known as Yellowstone National Park for nearly two million years before the United States government sanctioned the program to eradicate the wolf population in the lower forty-eight states (Begley and Williams). Since 1926, when the last pair of indigenous gray wolves were killed in the Yellowstone area, the animal has not been seen

in its ancestral home (Plummer and Shaw 105). Without the human intervention that resulted from hundreds of years of misconceptions and biases, it is unlikely that wolves would have disappeared from the Yellowstone area.

3   Another reason that it is important to return the gray wolf to Yellowstone is the ecological imbalance caused by the wolf's disappearance. While many of the people near Yellowstone fear that the introduction of a new set of Canadian gray wolves will create an imbalance in the park's ecosystem, the truth is that their presence will actually improve the park environment (Gallagher 37). According to biologists, the wolf's absence has "caused a serious ecological imbalance" (Gallagher 37). Without the wolves to prey on the many elk, bison, and deer, the populations of those groups have expanded to such numbers that they are overgrazing and many die every winter from lack of food (Begley and Williams). The wolves will help keep the numbers of larger animals, such as deer, elk, moose, and bighorn sheep, in balance and remove the old and ill animals from the herds, creating a healthier gene pool. Also, with the natural reduction of grazing animals, the local flora, which has been reduced due to overgrazing, will have a chance to reestablish itself.

4   Opponents to the reintroduction argue that the wolves will kill large numbers of the animals in the park, which will have far-ranging effects. Many fear the drop in game will result in less profit from hunting licenses, meaning less revenue for the surrounding states ("NRA"). It is more likely that with the projected one hundred animals reintroduced into the park, the elk population in particular would drop from 3,329 to 3,165, a difference of only 164 animals (Williamson 58). The wolf predation should only involve the older and weaker of the herds, benefiting the herd population as a whole. The fear that the elk, bison, and deer population would disappear with the return of the wolves to the park seems to be unfounded. Wolf advocate and founder of the Wolf Fund, Renee Askins, notes "the only time that [she] can recall when one animal did in another with such a vengeance was the great turn-of-the-century wolf hunts" (qtd. in Dawidoff 44).

In addition to the issues of responsibility and ecology, the challenge of wildlife management is involved in the return of the wolves to Yellowstone. Because Yellowstone is a natural habitat for wolves, and since other areas in the United States where the gray wolf can be found are few, the return of the gray wolf to the park is essential. A total of only 1,250 gray wolves can be found in the states of Minesota, Wisconsin, and Michigan. The introduction of Canadian gray wolves to the park could significantly change the status of the endangered animal (Begley and Williams). In the event that some new disease should strike the wolf population in the lower United States, it is entirely possible that the only remaining wolves in the country would be found in Alaska (Begley and Williams). Opponents to the reintroduction argue that in Alaska there is a gray wolf population of nearly 5,000 and there is therefore no need to expand gray-wolf territory. Those wolves, however, are for the most part cut off from the lower forty-eight states, and even that territory is dwindling, as people continue to develop more and more of Alaska (Begley and Williams). Yellowstone, with 2.2 million acres, or 3,472 square miles (larger than the states of Delaware and Rhode Island combined), would provide the indigenous park animal sufficient area to increase and thrive, without infringing upon animals outside the park.

The most explosive and emotional aspect of reintroducing wolves to Yellowstone involves the wolves' impact on the lifestyle and livelihood of the people living near the park. Hunters and officials of surrounding state governments have their concerns, and ranchers who make a living herding cattle have fears for their livestock. Each of these issues causes concern for all involved, but even with these concerns, I believe the return of the gray wolf is still the best option.

Hunters believe reintroducing the wolves will reduce the populations of the elk, deer, and bison to such low levels that they will not be able to be hunted. The hunters further believe that because of the gray wolf's status on the endangered species list, hunters will be unable to hunt the predator, as they would hunt a non-endangered predator under similar circumstances (Williamson 58). Their concerns seem groundless,

5

6

7

for as I mentioned earlier, there is a minimal projected drop in herd populations, and in other wolf-populated areas, wolves contribute to only 6 percent of big-game deaths. In additions, once the wolf population has been firmly established, some licenses might be granted for wolf hunting (Gallagher 41).

8   People are also concerned with how the reintroduction of wolves will affect those states adjacent to the park, since some states depend on revenues from hunting licenses. With the reintroduction, the U.S. Fish and Wildlife Service would require the states around the park to survey the populations of elk, deer, and bison for two years without providing funding, and many feel the extra cost would detract from other wildlife programs already run by the states ("NRA"). While these concerns are valid, the small projected decrease in game populations would be unlikely to significantly decrease the demand for hunting licenses, and the non-subsidized survey would only be required for two years. Most states already conduct these surveys and would only need to conduct them sooner than they might otherwise.

9   Objections from ranchers near Yellowstone pose a more serious obstacle to reintroducing gray wolves to the park. Many ranchers believe the wolves pose a threat of tremendous financial losses. Jim Magagna said about the situation, "We can lose animals to bears, eagles, coyotes— and now they want to add one more factor. There are few old-timers left who can tell you harrowing tales of wolves" (qtd. in Satchell). Most ranchers hate the wolf passionately, expressing their feelings in comments like, "Why not invite the Mafia to move in next door?" (Plummer and Shaw 104). This hatred stems mostly from folklore about the damage caused by the original gray wolves of Yellowstone before their eradication more than seventy years ago.

10   The truth is that none of the 392 land allotments for grazing surrounding Yellowstone is directly linked to the park. Wolves rarely attack and kill livestock, except in the absence of their normal prey ("Local Heroes"). The numbers of cattle lost to wolf predation in areas such as Minnesota and Montana are one in every 8,000 and one in every 25,000 respectively. In the case that ranchers do have problems with wolves, a wildlife support group, Defenders of Wildlife, is developing a fund to help cover the costs of farmers and ranchers who lose money due to wolf attacks (Skow 13).

11   Finally, the fear of those surrounding the park that wolves will attack people should not keep wolves out of Yellowstone. In modern history, there has never been an unprovoked attack

on a person by a non-rabid wolf: in the ninety-seven-year history of the wolf in the Algonquin National Forest in Canada, "[o]nly one person has been injured by a wolf—a little girl who shone a flashlight in a wolf's eye and was scratched" (Plummer and Shaw 105–106).

The controversial reintroduction of the gray wolf into Yellowstone is more than just the return of a native animal to its original habitat; it will also involve overcoming misconceptions and releasing the wolf from its mythology (Askins 17). But while people's fears color their perceptions toward the reintroduction, the return of the wolf to the park will help create the environment that existed in 1872, when 2.2 million acres of land was declared Yellowstone National Park.

12

Works Cited

Askins, Renee. "Releasing Wolves from Symbolism: Congressional Testimony." *Harper's* Apr. 1995: 15–17. Print.

Begley, Sharon, and Elisa Williams. "Crying Wolf in Yellowstone." *Newsweek* 16 Dec. 1985: 74. Print.

Dawidoff, Nicholas. "One for the Wolves." *Audubon* July 1992: 38–45. Print.

Gallagher, Winifred. "Return of the Wild." *Mother Earth News* Sept. 1990: 34–41. Print.

"Local Heroes." *Good Housekeeping* July 1993: 51. Print.

"NRA Questions the Costs of Wolf Reintroduction." *American Hunter* Nov. 1994: 14. Print.

Plummer, William, and Bill Shaw. "Yellowstone's Neighbors Are Howling Mad over a Plan to Return Wolves to the Park." *People Weekly* 24 Sept. 1990: 104–106. Print.

Satchell, Michael. "The New Call of the Wild." *US News and World Report* 29 Oct. 1990: 29. Print.

Skow, John. "The Brawl of the Wild." *Time* 6 Nov. 1989: 13–16. Print.

Williamson, Lonnie. "The Big Bad Wolf?" *Outdoor Life* Nov. 1992: 57–58. Print.

FOR WRITING OR DISCUSSION

1. What is the writer's thesis? How does the introduction build effectively to the thesis?
2. What causes and effects does Cutts deal with to support her thesis? Has she concentrated more on causes or effects, do you think? Where is her argument most successful?

3. Where has the writer used expert testimony most successfully, do you think? Which quotation do you find most powerful? Why?

4. Look at the list of works cited. Why has Cutts drawn on materials from such a wide range of sources?

5. The federal government placed 66 wolves in Yellowstone National Park and part of Idaho in 1995–1996. By 2007, as many as 1,500 wolves were living in Idaho, Montana, and Wyoming. What were the consequences of the reintroduction? How did local citizens feel about it?

6. In February 2008 the United States removed the northern Rockies gray wolf from the list of species protected under the Endangered Species Act. (Gray wolves have had endangered species status since 1974.) What could have prompted this action? What do you think will be the consequences?

7. In July 2008, a judge in Mantana issued an injunction that restored Federal protections. What could have prompted *this* action?

8. Do some research on endangered species in your area and write an argumentative essay about steps that should be taken in order to preserve the plant or animal in today's world.

Models of Writing

The readings that follow illustrate different cause and effect combinations. Carll Tucker analyzes both causes and effects. Mohan Sivanand deals mainly with causes. As you read the selections, note the great diversity of subjects that lend themselves to the cause and effect pattern.

CARLL TUCKER

On Splitting

1   One afternoon recently, two unrelated friends called to tell me that, well, their marriages hadn't made it. One was leaving his wife for another woman. The other was leaving her husband because "we thought it best."

2   As always after such increasingly common calls, I felt helpless and angry. What had happened to those solemn vows that one of the couples had stammered on a steamy August afternoon three years earlier? And what had happened to the joy my wife and I had sensed when we

visited the other couple and their two children last year, the feeling they gave us that here, in this increasingly fractionated world, was a constructive union?

I did not feel anger at my friends personally: Given the era and their feelings, their decisions probably made sense. What angered me was the loss of years and energy. It was an anger similar to that I feel when I see abandoned foundations of building projects—piled bricks and girders and a gash in the ground left to depress the passerby.

When our grandparents married, nobody except scandalous eccentrics divorced. "As long as we both shall live" was no joke. Neither was the trepidation brides felt on the eves of their wedding days. After their vows, couples learned to live with each other—not necessarily because they loved each other, but because they were stuck, and it was better to be stuck comfortably than otherwise.

Most of the external pressures that helped to enforce our grandparents' vows have dissolved. Women can earn money and may enjoy sex, even bear children, without marrying. As divorce becomes more common, the shame attendant on it dissipates. Some divorcés even argue that divorce is beneficial, educational; that the second or third or fifth marriage is "the best." The only reasons left to marry are love, tax advantages, and, for those old-fashioned enough to care about such things, to silence parental kvetching.[1]

In some respects, this freedom can be seen as social progress. Modern couples can flee the corrosive bitterness that made Strindberg's marriages nightmares.[2] Dreiser's Clyde Griffiths might have abandoned his Roberta instead of drowning her.[3]

In other respects, our rapidly rising divorce rate and the declining marriage rate (as more and more couples opt to forgo legalities and simply live together) represent a loss. One advantage of spending a lifetime with a person is seeing each other grow and change. For most of us, it is not possible to see history in the bathroom mirror—gray hairs, crow's feet, yes, but not a change of mind or temperament. Yet, living with another person, it is impossible not to notice how patterns and attitudes change and not to learn—about yourself and about time—from those perceptions.

Perhaps the most poignant victim of the twentieth century is our sense of continuity. People used to grow up with trees, watch them evolve from saplings to fruit bearers to gnarled and unproductive grandfathers. Now, unless one is a farmer or a forester, there is almost no point to planting trees because one is not likely to be there to enjoy their maturity. We change addresses and occupations and hobbies and lifestyles and spouses rapidly and readily, much as we change TV channels. In our grandparents' day one committed oneself to certain skills and disciplines and developed them. Carpenters spent lifetimes learning their craft; critics spent lifetimes learning literature. Today, the question often is not "What do you do?" but "What are you into?" Macrame one week, astrology the next, health food, philosophy, history, jogging, movies, EST—we flit from "commitment" to "commitment" like bees among flowers because it is easier to test something than to master it, easier to buy a new

---

[1]Complaining.
[2]August Strindberg (1849–1912) was a Swedish dramatist.
[3]The reference is to Dreiser's 1925 novel, *An American Tragedy*.

toy than to repair an old one.

9   I feel sorry for what my divorced friends have lost. No matter how earnestly the former spouses try to "keep in touch," no matter how generous the visiting privileges for the parent who does not win custody of the children, the continuity of their lives has been broken. The years they spent together have been cut off from the rest of their lives; they are an isolated memory, no more integral to their past than a snapshot. Intelligent people, they will compare their next marriages—if they have them—to their first. They may even, despite not having a long shared past, notice growth. What I pray, though, is that they do not delude themselves into believing, like so many Americans today, that happiness is only measurable moment to moment and, in their pursuit of momentary contentment, forsake the perspectives and consolation of history.

10   There is great joy in watching a tree grow.

FOR WRITING OR DISCUSSION

1. What causes does Tucker give for the increase in divorce? Does the writer clearly approve or disapprove of any of these causes?

2. According to Tucker, what are the most negative effects of divorce? Are there any possible good effects?

3. Explain how the writer tries to link the rise in divorce rates to general trends in American lifestyles.

4. Explain what Tucker means in the last sentence of the essay.

5. Write a paper analyzing the effects of some major decision you've made in your life, such as marriage, divorce, or choice of school, job, or place of residence.

MOHAN SIVANAND

Why I Write Wrong

1   The day I discovered Grammar Check in my new word processor, I was delighted. Grammar Check (GC) is supposed to help you guard against making mistakes in English, including those that would make the best of writers blush.

Reprinted with permission from the April 2000 *Reader's Digest*. Copyright © 2000 by the Reader's Digest Assn., Inc.

Oops. I can already see a wiggly green line under *writers* in my previous sentence. That's Grammar Check at work. The green wiggly underline is the digital equivalent of a referee throwing a flag.

2

Let's see what's wrong. GC suggests that I change *writers* to *writer's*. As in *writer's block*, I suppose—and that's not much help, is it? Meanwhile, I spot a curvaceous red line under *wiggly* itself. This time it's GC's cousin Spell Check blowing the whistle. Suggested change: *wiggle*.

3

But back to the causes of writer's blush. Grammar Check is very precise. By pressing F7 on the keyboard and clicking on Options then Settings, you can instruct your machine to watch out for Commonly Confused Words, Clichés, Contractions, Jargon, Wordiness, Gender-Specific Words and much, much more.

4

Strange. Not a single wiggle line appeared in the previous sentence despite the wordiness and all those capitals. GC, however, is not happy with my beginning that paragraph with *But*, and recommends I change it to *Nevertheless*.

5

"If you're so smart," I say aloud to GC, "here's something you can't mess around with." I type in a well-known line from Shakespeare: "Friends, Romans, countrymen, lend me your ears; I come to bury Caesar, not to praise him."

6

Oh, dear! GC suggests I change *countrymen* to *fellow citizens*. Friends, Romans, fellow citizens? That is an unkind cut.

7

Maybe I've been unfair. Shakespeare, after all, was a poet. I try a line of prose: "Sorrow came—a gentle sorrow—but not at all in the shape of any disagreeable consciousness."

8

Problem again: wiggle line under *came*. "Verb confusion (no suggestions)," says GC's warning box. "You're the one who is confused," I type. "Jane Austen was the most clear-headed of writers, and she never needed no Grammar Check or Microsoft Word." (Know something? GC hasn't yet spotted my double negative. But cousin SC wants me to change *Austen* to *Austin*. Ah, man, that's smart!)

9

Wait a second. I see a new green wiggle line under *man*. "Gender-Specific Language," I'm warned. The alternatives suggested in place of *man* are *operate* or *staff*.

10

If grammar is a tricky thing, Grammar Check is a downright booby trap. GC must be at a very early stage in its evolution. Something like jellyfish on the scale of living things. ("Likes jellyfish," GC insists.)

11

Nevertheless—although you've paid good money for it—you can always switch off Grammar Check. Better still, throw it out the Windows.

12

FOR WRITING OR DISCUSSION

1. In what ways is this a cause and effect essay?

2. What is Sivanand's thesis?

3. What, according to the writer, is the effect of Grammar Check and Spell Check on his prose? What would result if the writer followed the instructions of these two language helpers that are part of his word processing program?

4. How does the writer achieve humor in his piece?

5. Write your own short, humorous cause and effect essay called "Why I _____ Wrong." Fill in the blank with a word or phrase of your choice. For example, you might consider using a word like *eat, sing, talk, dance, drive,* or *do homework.* Explain the cause of your "wrong" act and indicate some of the consequences of your behavior. Keep a light and humorous tone.

HAVING YOUR SAY

Have computers made our lives simpler or more complicated? Choose one side of the issue and write an essay to support your point of view.

Readings for Writing

The first selection below deals with the sorry state of the recording industry and the second with the effects on teenagers of their adventures online. The two pieces may provide you with subject matter for a cause and effect analysis.

TONY SACHS AND SAL NUNZIATO
Spinning into Oblivion

1   Despite the major record labels' best efforts to kill it, the single, according to recent reports, is back. Sort of.

2   You'll still have a hard time finding vinyl 45s or their modern counterpart, CD singles, in record stores. For that matter, you'll have a tough time finding record stores. Today's single is an individual track downloaded online from legal sites like iTunes or eMusic, or the multiple illegal sites that cater to less scrupulous music lovers. The album, or collection of songs—the de facto way to buy pop music for the last 40 years—is suddenly looking old-fashioned. And the record store itself is going the way of the shoehorn.

3   This is a far cry from the musical landscape that existed when we opened an independent CD shop on the Upper West Side of Manhattan in 1993. At the time, we figured that as far as business ventures went, ours was relatively safe. People would always go to stores to buy music. Right? Of course, back then there were also only two ringtones to choose from— "riiiiinnng" and "ring-ring."

Our intention was to offer a haven for all kinds of music lovers and obsessives, a shop that catered not only to the casual record buyer ("Do you have the new Sarah McLachlan and . . . uh . . . is there a Beatles greatest hits CD?") but to the fan and oft-maligned serious collector ("Can you get the Japanese pressing of 'Kinda Kinks'? I believe they used the rare mono mixes"). Fourteen years later, it's clear just how wrong our assumptions were. Our little shop closed its doors at the end of 2005.

    The sad thing is that CDs and downloads could have coexisted peacefully and profitably. The current state of affairs is largely the result of shortsightedness and boneheadedness by the major record labels and the Recording Industry Association of America, who managed to achieve the opposite of everything they wanted in trying to keep the music business prospering. The association is like a gardener who tried to rid his lawn of weeds and wound up killing the trees instead.

    In the late '90s, our business, and the music retail business in general, was booming. Enter Napster, the granddaddy of illegal download sites. How did the major record labels react? By continuing their campaign to eliminate the comparatively unprofitable CD single, raising list prices on album-length CDs to $18 or $19 and promoting artists like the Back-street Boys and Britney Spears—whose strength was single songs, not albums. The result was a lot of unhappy customers, who blamed retailers like us for the dearth of singles and the high prices.

    The recording industry association saw the threat that illegal downloads would pose to CD sales. But rather than working with Napster, it tried to sue the company out of existence—which was like thinking you've killed all the roaches in your apartment because you squashed the one you saw in the kitchen. More illegal download sites cropped up faster than the associa-tion's lawyers could say "cease and desist."

    By 2002, it was clear that downloading was affecting music retail stores like ours. Our reg-ulars weren't coming in as often, and when they did, they weren't buying as much. Our impulse-buy weekend customers were staying away altogether. And it wasn't just the indepen-dent stores; even big chains like Tower and Musicland were struggling.

    Something had to be done to save the record store, a place where hard-core music fans worked, shopped and kibitzed—and, not incidentally, kept the music business's engine chug-ging in good times and in lean. Who but these loyalists was going to buy the umpteenth Elton John hits compilation that the major labels were foisting upon them?

    But instead, those labels delivered the death blow to the record store as we know it by getting in bed with soulless chain stores like Best Buy and Wal-Mart. These "big boxes" were given exclusive tracks to put on new CDs and, to add insult to injury, they could sell them for less than our wholesale cost. They didn't care if they didn't make any money on CD sales. Because, ideally, the person who came in to get the new Eagles release with exclusive bonus material would also decide to pick up a high-speed blender that frappéed.

    The jig was up. It didn't matter that even a store as small as ours carried hundreds of titles you'd never see at Best Buy and was staffed by people who actually knew who Van Morrison was, or that Tower Records had the entire history of recorded music under one roof while Costco didn't carry much more than the current hits. A year after our shop closed, Tower went out of business—something that would have been unthinkable just a few years earlier. The customers who had grudgingly come to trust our opinions made the move to online shopping or lost interest in buying music altogether. Some of the most loyal fans had been soured into denying themselves the music they loved.

12   Meanwhile, the recording industry association continues to give the impression that it's doing something by occasionally threatening to sue college students who share their record collections online. But apart from scaring the dickens out of a few dozen kids, that's just an amusing sideshow. They're not fighting a war any more than the folks who put on Civil War regalia and re-enact the Battle of Gettysburg are.

13   The major labels wanted to kill the single. Instead they killed the album. The association wanted to kill Napster. Instead it killed the compact disc. And today it's not just record stores that are in trouble, but the labels themselves, now belatedly embracing the Internet revolution without having quite figured out how to make it pay.

14   At this point, it may be too late to win back disgruntled music lovers no matter what they do. As one music industry lawyer, Ken Hertz, said recently, "The consumer's conscience, which is all we had left, that's gone, too."

15   It's tempting for us to gloat. By worrying more about quarterly profits than the bigger picture, by protecting their short-term interests without thinking about how to survive and prosper in the long run, record-industry bigwigs have got what was coming to them. It's a disaster they brought upon themselves.

16   We would be gloating, but for the fact that the occupation we planned on spending our working lives at is rapidly becoming obsolete. And that loss hits us hard—not just as music retailers, but as music fans.

FOR WRITING OR DISCUSSION

1. What is Sachs's and Nunziato's thesis in this selection?

2. What major causes do they identify for the decline of the record business? How do their personal experiences as owners of a music shop help them make their point?

3. Do you agree that "CDs and downloads could have coexisted peacefully and profitably"? How did the record labels react to the illegal site Napster?

4. Write an essay in which you identify another new technology and how it has caused a change in an older method of behavior. Some possible topics: the computer vs. the typewriter, television vs. the radio, e-mail vs. the telephone—there are many others certainly.

BRENT STAPLES

What Adolescents Miss When We Let Them Grow Up in Cyberspace

My 10th-grade heartthrob was the daughter of a fearsome steelworker who struck terror into the hearts of 15-year-old boys. He made it his business to answer the telephone—and so always knew who was calling—and grumbled in the background when the conversation went on too long. Unable to make time by phone, the boy either gave up or appeared at the front door. This meant submitting to the first-degree for which the girl's father was soon to become famous. 1

He greeted me with a crushing handshake, then leaned in close in a transparent attempt to find out whether I was one of those *bad* boys who smoked. He retired to the den during the visit, but cruised by the living room now and then to let me know he was watching. He let up after some weeks, but only after getting across what he expected of a boy who spent time with his daughter and how upset he'd be if I disappointed him. 2

This was my first sustained encounter with an adult outside my family who needed to be convinced of my worth as a person. This, of course, is a crucial part of growing up. Faced with same challenge today, however, I would probably pass on meeting the girl's father—and out-flank him on the Internet. 3

Thanks to e-mail, online chat rooms and instant messages—which permit private, real-time conversations—adolescents have succeeded at last in shielding their social lives from adult scrutiny. But this comes at a cost. The paradox is that teenagers nowadays are both more con-nected to the world at large than ever, and more cut off from the social encounters that have historically prepared young people for the move into adulthood. 4

The Internet was billed as a revolutionary method of enriching our social lives and expanding our civic connections. This seems to have worked well for elderly people and oth-ers who were isolated before they got access to the World Wide Web. But a growing body of research is showing that the heavy use of the Net actually isolates younger socially connected people who are unwittingly allowing time online to replace face-to-face interaction with their families and friends. 5

Online shopping, checking e-mail and Web surfing—mainly solitary activities—have turned out to be more isolating than watching television, which friends and family often do in groups. Researchers have found that the time spent in direct contact with family members drops by as much as half for every hour we use the Net at home. 6

This should come as no surprise to two-career couples who have seen their domestic lives taken over by e-mail and wireless tethers that keep people working around the clock. But a startling body of research from the Human-Computer Interaction Institute at Carnegie Mellon has shown that heavy Internet use can have a stunting effect outside the home as well. Studies show that gregarious, well-connected people actually lose friends, and experience symptoms of loneliness and depression, after joining discussion groups and other activities. People who 7 communicated with disembodied strangers online found the experience empty and emotionally frustrating but were nonetheless seduced by the novelty of the new medium. As Prof. Robert Kraut, a Carnegie Mellon researcher, told me recently, such people allowed low-quality relationships developed in virtual reality to replace higher-quality relationships in the real world.

8   No group has embraced this socially impoverishing trade-off more enthusiastically than adolescents, many of whom spend most of their free hours cruising the Net in sunless rooms. This hermetic existence has left many of these teenagers with nonexistent social skills—a point widely noted in stories about the computer geeks who rose to prominence in the early days of Silicon Valley.

9   Adolescents are drawn to cyberspace for different reasons than adults. As the writer Michael Lewis observed in his book *Next: The Future Just Happened*, children see the Net as a transformational device that lets them discard quotidian identities for more glamorous ones. Mr. Lewis illustrated the point with Marcus Arnold, who, as a 15-year-old, adopted a pseudonym a few years ago and posed as a 25-year-old legal expert for an Internet information service. Marcus did not feel the least bit guilty, and wasn't deterred, when real world lawyers discovered his secret and accused him of being a fraud. When asked whether he had actually read the law, Marcus responded that he found books "boring," leaving us to conclude that he had learned all he needed to know from his family's big-screen TV.

10   Marcus is a child of the Net, where everyone has a pseudonym, telling a story makes it true and adolescents create older, cooler, more socially powerful selves any time they wish. The ability to slip easily into a new, false self is tailor-made for emotionally fragile adolescents, who can consider a bout of acne or a few excess pounds an unbearable tragedy.

11   But teenagers who spend much of their lives hunched over computer screens miss the socializing, the real world experience that would allow them to leave adolescence behind and grow into adulthood. These vital experiences, like much else, are simply not available in a virtual form.

FOR WRITING OR DISCUSSION

1. What does Staples mean in the title by the phrase "Grow Up in Cyberspace"? How is the phrase an example of a metaphor?

2. What is the purpose of the personal anecdote at the beginning of the essay?

3. How does the writer support his point that heavy Internet use "has a stunting effect" outside the home?

4. How does Staples use expert testimony in this essay? Are the cited sources reliable? How do you know?

5. Why, according to the writer, are adolescents drawn to cyberspace?

6. How does the last paragraph serve as a statement of Staples's thesis?

7. Write an essay on how cyberspace can be a *positive* influence on adolescents.

Consider the cause and effect implications in this illustration by a well-known cartoonist for popular magazines like the *New Yorker*, in which this cartoon appeared.

REASSIGNED PENDING
AN INVESTIGATION

© The New Yorker Collection 2003 Mike Twohy from cartoonbank.com. All rights reserved.

FOR WRITING OR DISCUSSION

1. What do the visual elements tell you about the setting of the cartoon? What is the man on the chair wearing? What kind of chair is it? What job is the man performing? What do the plants on the ground tell you?

2. How does the caption attempt to explain the absurdity of the scene? Does the caption in fact explain anything, or does it merely add to the absurdity?

3. What could the man have done to cause his reassignment? What is the apparent result of his actions?

4. In what other contexts have you heard the statement that appears as the caption in the cartoon? What kind of new job would you expect someone "reassigned pending an investigation" to have? How does the cartoonist meet (or challenge) your expectations?

5. In what ways does the cartoon reflect the reality of how businesses deal with high-level employees they want to protect? or how companies treat employees they cannot or will not dismiss? or how legislators deal with people caught in political problems?

6. Write a humorous cause and effect essay in which you explain why the man is on his current assignment and what the effects of the assignment are.

Reading and Writing About Poetry

You may find that, like the comparison–contrast strategy, cause and effect analysis also is a useful tool for writing about literature. You look at a character and say, "Why is he like that, exactly?" Then you examine the work to discover the causes for the character traits you have observed. Or you may trace the causes that lead to a crisis in a work of literature.

Following is a famous poem by Edwin Arlington Robinson, "Richard Cory." After you have read the poem, study the student paper that follows it.

EDWIN ARLINGTON ROBINSON
Richard Cory

Whenever Richard Cory went down town,
    We people on the pavement looked at him:
He was a gentleman from sole to crown,
    Clean favored, and imperially slim.

5   And he was always quietly arrayed,
    And he was always human when he talked;
But still he fluttered pulses when he said,
    "Good morning," and he glittered when he walked.

And he was rich—yes, richer than a king,
10   And admirably schooled in every grace:
In fine, we thought that he was everything
    To make us wish that we were in his place.

So on we worked, and waited for the light,
    And went without the meat, and cursed the bread;
15   And Richard Cory, one calm summer night,
    Went home and put a bullet through his head.

Craig Anders

We and He

What caused Richard Cory to "put a bullet through his head"? It is impossible, upon reading the last line of "Richard Cory" by Edwin Arlington Robinson, to say that the poem concludes with a clever surprise ending and then dismiss it from our minds. The poem does not end with the last line. Imagine the suicide of a friend or relative. Assuming the person did not suffer from a painful terminal illness, we would be stunned with surprise and sadness for a while, but we would soon begin to ask ourselves and each other the big question: Why? We will probably never get any certain answers, but with the knowledge of the suicide, we may think back to what we imagined were minor events or comments or moods of daily life and see some of them in a new light. We may, "in fine," be able to make an intelligent guess about the causes of the suicide. There are no certain answers about Richard Cory's death, either, but if we take every word of the poem seriously, we have a better basis for making an intelligent guess than we usually find in the world around us. 1

We certainly will not get very far if we settle for the most obvious explanation and say that Richard Cory killed himself because money can't buy happiness. First, the poem concentrates on more about Cory than money alone: his slimness, his manners, his way of talking, his way of dressing. Second, the poem makes it clear that poverty can't buy happiness any more than wealth can. The "people on the pavement" are extremely unhappy: They envy Cory, resent having to work, wish vainly for better times, "curse" the cheap things they have to make do with, and long for the expensive things they must do without. "Richard Cory" is no poem about the spiritual rewards of being poor. 2

At the same time, we need to recognize that with all their unhappiness, the poor people <u>are</u> better off than Richard Cory. Hating every minute of their lives—or thinking that they do—they still get up each morning. The simplest, most inescapable fact of the poem is that Cory killed himself and the people on the pavement went on living. What made their lives more worth living than his? 3

4   One possible answer is that the poor people's envy keeps them going. They have desires and they have hopes. They want to ride into town like Richard Cory instead of walking on the pavement. They want all that money can buy. It can't buy happiness, but the poor people don't know that yet. Until they find out, they have something to live for. Cory has all that life can offer. But isn't that just another way of saying that life can now no longer offer anything else to Cory? And if that is the case, what point is there to continuing one's life?

5   An even better answer is that what the poor people have that Cory does not have is each other. Cory is a man alone. At one point, the poem expresses amazement at Cory's even being human. When he is acknowledged to be human, he is seen as the most special, most isolated kind of human—a king. He is "richer than a king"; he is not merely slim but "imperially slim"; his head is not an everyday human head but a "crown." The people look up to Cory so much that he might as well inhabit another galaxy, and it's lonely being an alien. Cory comes to town and says, "Good morning," for example, perhaps hoping for a friendly conversation, a little human contact. But Cory does not get conversation. When he says, "Good morning," pulses flutter and hearts skip a bit. "Richard Cory talked to me today. Isn't that fantastic?"

6   The people on the pavement have each other. Cory has no one. The speaker in the poem is a "we," not an "I." We looked at him, we wished we were in his place, we "waited for the light, / And went without the meat, and cursed the bread." The speaker knows more deeply than any conscious thought that he is part of a "we"—that his feelings, his aspirations, his resentments are shared by others. It may not be a happy life or even a good life, but it is a life that is shared, a life of community and communion. Cory's money, manners, and position not only can't buy that but make it impossible for him to buy, no matter how "human" he may truly be or want to be.

7   Richard Cory dies of loneliness. The people on the pavement find the strength to go on living because loneliness is the only problem they do not have.

FOR WRITING OR DISCUSSION

1. What causes does the writer give for Richard Cory's suicide? Do you have some other explanation?

2. Where is the thesis of the paper stated?

3. Does the introduction clearly call for an analysis of causes? Explain.

4. Does the author's use of quotations from the poem help prove the thesis? Why or why not?

5. Write a paper on the causes of the "people on the pavement's" envy of Richard Cory or on the probable effects of his suicide on them.

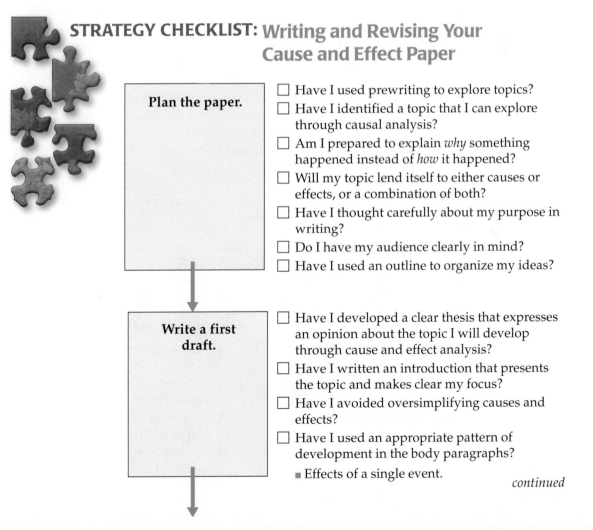

STRATEGY CHECKLIST: Writing and Revising Your Cause and Effect Paper

Plan the paper.

☐ Have I used prewriting to explore topics?

☐ Have I identified a topic that I can explore through causal analysis?

☐ Am I prepared to explain *why* something happened instead of *how* it happened?

☐ Will my topic lend itself to either causes or effects, or a combination of both?

☐ Have I thought carefully about my purpose in writing?

☐ Do I have my audience clearly in mind?

☐ Have I used an outline to organize my ideas?

Write a first draft.

☐ Have I developed a clear thesis that expresses an opinion about the topic I will develop through cause and effect analysis?

☐ Have I written an introduction that presents the topic and makes clear my focus?

☐ Have I avoided oversimplifying causes and effects?

☐ Have I used an appropriate pattern of development in the body paragraphs?

   ■ Effects of a single event.

continued

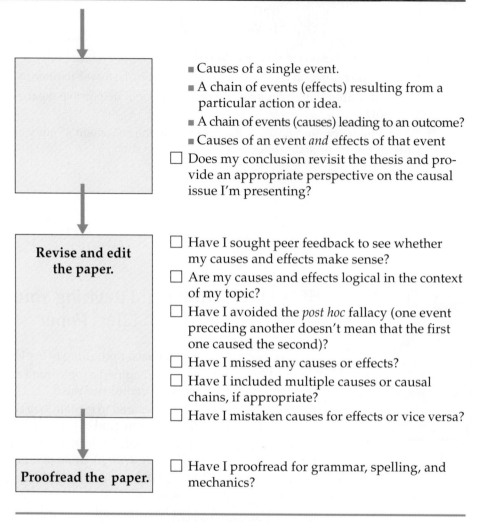

- Causes of a single event.
- A chain of events (effects) resulting from a particular action or idea.
- A chain of events (causes) leading to an outcome?
- Causes of an event *and* effects of that event
☐ Does my conclusion revisit the thesis and provide an appropriate perspective on the causal issue I'm presenting?

Revise and edit the paper.

☐ Have I sought peer feedback to see whether my causes and effects make sense?
☐ Are my causes and effects logical in the context of my topic?
☐ Have I avoided the *post hoc* fallacy (one event preceding another doesn't mean that the first one caused the second)?
☐ Have I missed any causes or effects?
☐ Have I included multiple causes or causal chains, if appropriate?
☐ Have I mistaken causes for effects or vice versa?

Proofread the paper.

☐ Have I proofread for grammar, spelling, and mechanics?

WRITING TOPICS

If you cannot easily decide on a topic for your cause and effect paper, you might want to try one or more of the following suggestions. You can treat most of the subjects as material for a cause-only, effect-only, or cause and effect paper.

1. One of your personality quirks
2. Effects of going to college
3. Why people smoke cigarettes despite their proven dangers
4. A change of mind about something or someone
5. The popularity of Christian bands in mainstream music
6. Results of the 2004 tsunami in Asia
7. Growth or decrease in the popularity of a style of music
8. Growth or decrease in the popularity of a hairstyle
9. Growth or decrease in the popularity of a clothing style

10. Street gangs
11. Why sexism remains a problem
12. Global warming
13. Teaching preschoolers to read
14. Emphasis on computers in American schools
15. Why teenagers drink alcohol
16. Blind dates
17. Excessively strict or lenient parents
18. Internet spam
19. Election fraud
20. World hunger

CROSSCURRENTS

1. Robinson's "Richard Cory" (page 306), Orwell's "A Hanging" (pages 12–16), and Littlebrandt's "Death Is a Personal Matter" (pages 158–160) each treats the issue of death from a different perspective. What social and moral considerations arise in these pieces? What philosophy of living and dying emerges in each?

From IMAGE to WORDS: A Reading and Writing Assignment

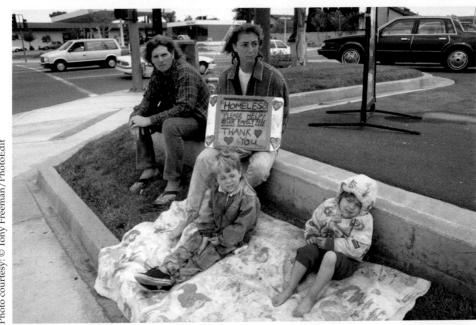

Photo courtesy: © Tony Freeman / PhotoEdit

Look at the photograph above. Write a cause and effect paper that the picture suggests to you. Be sure that your thesis makes some assertion about the topic that you see emerging from the scene. Provide appropriate details to support the causes and (or) effects that you establish.

CHAPTER 14

Definition

- Writing Your Definition Paper
- Student Writing: Formal Definition
- Student Writing: Informal Definition
- Models of Writing
- Readings for Writing
- Reading and Writing About Poetry

From time to time, you may have found yourself in a shouting match with friends over a question such as, which is the all-time great concert group—the Beatles, the Rolling Stones, Queen, or Pink Floyd. Eventually, some wise soul says, "Hey, wait a minute. What's your idea of a great concert group?" The speaker has demanded a **definition** of the term that has sparked the debate. You may find that one person's standard for "great" is how many albums the group sold. Another may appreciate how the group subtly improvises on a theme. And another may insist that "great" means having long-lasting effect on music worldwide. Then you realize, perhaps, either that your respective ideas of a great group are so different that you can't have a discussion or that, once you understand each other's terms, you have no real disagreement.

When writing, you won't have the advantage of another person's asking what you mean. If you want to appear reasonable when you present an idea, you sometimes have to define terms.

Often, a dictionary won't be much help. It may be a good place to start, but at times a dictionary definition won't explain a term fully. Take that word *great*, for example. A dictionary tells you that it means "remarkable or outstanding in magnitude, degree, or extent," and so it does; but how does such a definition help you distinguish between one rock group and another? To do so, you could begin with a dictionary definition, to be sure, but you must let your reader know what you believe the positive or desirable qualities of a rock group are. You must provide an **extended definition**.

As you have no doubt learned on your own, much of your course work—in psychology, history, sociology, biology, and so on—depends on extended definitions. So you know that certain terms, then, require a more elaborate definition than a dictionary gives. The burden is on the writer to explain the meaning of the term. Sometimes in a long paper you have to write an extended definition that may take up one or two paragraphs. Occasionally, a definition can become the paper itself.

The following kinds of terms often need defining:

Words and Terms for Definition

- *Judgmental words*—words that reflect opinions—need definition. Whether subjects being discussed are *good, better, best; bad, worse, worst; beautiful, ugly; friendly, unfriendly; wise, foolish; fair, unfair;* and so on, is a matter of opinion.
- *Specialized terms*—terms with a special meaning to a given group—need definition. Almost every professional or occupational group uses terms that the members of the group understand but that require explanation for those outside the group—for example, *psychosis*, a psychological term; *neoclassicism*, a literary term; *writ*, a legal term; and *gig*, a show-business term.
- *Abstractions*—general words like *love, democracy, justice, freedom,* and *quality*—need definition.
- *Controversial terms* like *male chauvinist, nuclear buildup*, and *affirmative action* need definition.
- *Slang terms* like *bro, phat, cool, the 'hood, bling*, and *hot* may need definition for many audiences.

Writing Your Definition Paper

You can present your extended definition in one of two ways—formally or informally.

Begining a Formal Definition

A **formal definition** contains the three parts of a dictionary definition: (1) the term itself—the word or phrase to be defined; (2) the class—the large group to which the object or concept belongs; and (3) the differentiation—those characteristics that distinguish it from all others in its class.

Term	→	Class	→	Differentiation
A garden		is a small plot of land		used for the cultivation of flowers, vegetables, or fruits.
Beer		is a fermented alcoholic beverage		brewed from malt and flavored with hops.
Lunch		is a meal		eaten at midday.

To write an extended formal definition, you first need to develop a one-sentence definition of the term. Keep the following cautions in mind:

TIPS for Writing One-Sentence Definitions

■ **Make sure to include the class.**   Don't write, "Baseball is when nine players. . . ." Write instead, "Baseball is a *sport* in which nine players. . . ."

■ **Restrict the class.**   Speak of a sonnet not as a kind of literature but as a kind of poem.

■ **Include no important part of the term itself or its derivatives in the class or differentiation.**   Don't say that "a definition is that which defines."

■ **Make certain that the sentence defines and does not simply make a statement about the term.**   "Happiness is a Madonna concert" doesn't have the essential parts of a definition of happiness.

■ **Provide adequate differentiation to clarify the meaning.**   Don't define a traitor as "one who opposes the best interests of his or her country." That definition doesn't exclude the well-meaning person who misunderstands the country's best interests and opposes from ignorance. Try instead, "A traitor is one who opposes the best interests of his or her country with malicious intent."

■ **Don't make the definition too restrictive.**   Don't define a matinee as "a drama presented during the day." That definition doesn't include other forms of entertainment, such as ballets or concerts, which also could be held in daytime.

EXERCISE   Using a dictionary whenever necessary, write one-sentence formal definitions for the following terms.

1. Politics
2. Joy
3. Intelligent design
4. Philosophy
5. Democracy
6. Terrorist
7. Cold fusion
8. Chauvinism
9. Hanukkah
10. Inflation

Drafting Your Formal Definition Paper

Once you have composed a one-sentence formal definition, its three parts can become the major divisions of your paper. The introduction to your paper might contain the term and its one-sentence definition. That sentence could become the thesis for your paper. Or, in addition to providing a one-sentence definition, you could also express an attitude toward the term. In the paper on pages 316–318, student writer Frederick Spense expresses his attitude in this way: "Equality *ought to be* a philosophy and set of laws in which all people are given the same opportunity to achieve their own individual potential."

The next division of your paper could discuss the class, and the final division, the differentiation. In these discussions, you can make your idea clear by using specific details, by making comparisons and using analogies, by giving examples or telling anecdotes, and sometimes by tracing the history of the term. Often you will be able to quote or refer to the definitions others have given the term. This technique is particularly useful if experts disagree over the meaning of the term. An especially effective tool is *exclusion*, showing what the term is *not*:

> *Gourmet* cooking does not mean to me the preparation of food in expensive wines; it does not mean the preparation of exotic dishes like octopus or rattlesnake; it does not mean the smothering of meat with highly caloric sauces. *Gourmet* cooking to me means the preparation of any food—whether black-eyed peas or hollandaise sauce—in such a way that the dish will be as tasty and attractive as it can be made.

In advancing your discussion of class and differentiation, you can use any rhetorical method or combination of methods of development you have studied. In fact, what makes definition such an interesting rhetorical challenge is that you can draw on most of the familiar patterns of essay development. For example, suppose you wanted to define the term *happiness*. You could use a variety of approaches, as indicated here.

Approaches to Your Essay Topic
Defining the Term *Happiness*

Possible approach	**Mode of development**
Provide accurate sensory details to describe the face and actions of a happy person you know.	Description (Chapter 7)
Tell a story about a moment when you were truly happy.	Narration (Chapter 8)
Provide several illustrations (examples) of happiness.	Example (Chapter 9)
Explain how to be happy or unhappy.	Process (Chapter 10)
Compare one state of happiness with another; contrast happiness with sadness.	Comparison–Contrast (Chapter 11)

(Continued)

Divide happy people into groups or categories.	Classification (Chapter 12)
Explain the conditions necessary for true happiness or the outcomes of happiness in a person's life.	Cause and Effect (Chapter 13)
Argue that happiness is not achievable in America today.	Argumentation (Chapter 15)

Writing an Informal Definition Paper

Although many terms lend themselves to the three-part formal definition, some are better explained by **informal definition**. What is a good teacher, for example? or a bad marriage? or an ideal home? Clearly, one can define such topics only in a subjective or personal way; your purpose is to show what the term means to you. In such instances, it is probably wise to avoid a rigid formal definition. Make your conception of the term clear by describing the subject as fully as you can. By the time readers finish the paper, they should understand what the term means to you.

As with formal definitions, you can use any method or combination of methods of development that you have studied to create an informal definition. Examples and anecdotes are especially good for explaining a term. So are comparison, process, classification, and cause and effect. The idea is to use whatever techniques come in handy to put the idea across.

Student Writing: Formal Definition

In the paper that follows, the student writer derives a formal definition of the term *equality* from his reading of "Harrison Bergeron." (Kurt Vonnegut's short story appears later in the chapter, pages 328–332.) Mr. Spense contrasts his understanding of *equality* with that of the futuristic society represented in Vonnegut's story.

Frederick Spense

Everyone Is Equal in the Grave

1   Kurt Vonnegut Jr.'s short story "Harrison Bergeron" contrasts the misunderstanding and perversion of equality with the true meaning of the word. Equality ought to be a philosophy and set of laws in which all people are given the same opportunity to achieve their own

individual potential. In the U.S.A. of 2081, equality has become a philosophy and set of laws in which everyone is forced to be the same.

The Declaration of Independence presents the principle that "all men are created equal," and various laws attempt to put the principle into practice—laws about voting, employment, housing, and so on. "Equal before God and the law" in the second sentence of the story seems to show Vonnegut's approval of this approach. "Equal every which way" is another problem, though, and the story attempts to show that a government that interprets equality in that manner is going to be a slave state.

2

Giving people an equal opportunity to be the best they can be is not the same as forcing people to be like everyone else. Any person who wants to should have the chance to study ballet. That represents equality. Letting poor dancers join the ballet company and "handicapping" good dancers so everyone will be the same is the corruption of equality that has taken place in 2081.

3

Instead of everyone with a good voice having the same chance to become an announcer if he or she wants to, all the announcers in the world of 2081 have speech impediments. Instead of the most skilled technicians competing for jobs on the television crews so that the best person will be chosen, the crews consist of people who cannot even hold cards right side up. Instead of admitting that smart people and dumb people are different even though they have the same worth as human beings, the government installs electronic equipment to prevent the smart people from using their brains for more than a few seconds at a time. Good-looking people wear masks to make them "equal" to ugly people. Strong people wear weights to make them "equal" to weak people.

4

Vonnegut's point is that this is not true equality, but tyranny. It is not just stupid to stifle exceptional people and create a world where being outstanding is a sin, but to do so requires a tremendous government agency whose job is to snoop and to control the smallest aspects of people's private lives. The Constitution has to be amended to make all this possible, and the Handicapper General has the authority to shoot criminals—that is, individuals—on sight.

5

6   Equality is and ought to be one of our most precious ideals. If it ever comes to mean sameness and conformity, it will not really be equality at all, only obedience and regimentation. Equality like that is the equality of the grave.

FOR WRITING OR DISCUSSION

1. What is the thesis of this paper?
2. Does Spense successfully achieve a one-sentence formal definition of the term? If so, what is it?
3. What methods of development does the writer use in advancing his definition? How do they help him make his idea clear?
4. From your reading of Vonnegut's story (pages 328–332), do you believe that the definition of *equality* presented in this paper is one of which Vonnegut would approve? Why, or why not?
5. Write your own definition of the term *equality*. You may draw on "Harrison Berg-eron," some other story, or your own experience.

Student Writing: Informal Definition

In the following student paper, the writer provides fresh insights by informally defining familar words. Study the annotations.

Helen Fleming
The Grinnies

1   Until I was twelve years old, I thought everyone in the world knew about the grinnies, if I thought about the term at all—which is unlikely. After all, everyone in my family used the word quite naturally, and we understood each other. So far as I knew, it was a word like any other word—like *bath*, or *chocolate*, or *homework*. But it was my homework which led to my discovery that *grinnies* was a word not known outside my family.

Introduction provides necessary background as writer presents the term being defined.

2   My last report card had said that I was a "C" student in English, and my parents, both teachers, decided that no child of theirs would be just an average

student of anything. So nightly I spelled words aloud and answered questions about the fine points of grammar. I wrote and rewrote and rewrote every composition until I convinced my mother that I could make no more improvements. And the hard work paid off. One day the teacher returned compositions, and there it was—a big fat, bright red "A" on the top of my paper. Naturally, I was delighted, but I didn't know I was attracting attention until the teacher snapped, "Helen, what *are* you doing?"

Personal experience narrative helps reader see the word "grinnies" in action.

Called suddenly out of my happy thoughts, I said "Oh, I've got the grinnies!" The teacher and my classmates burst into laughter, and then I understood that grinnies were confined to my family. Other people were not so privileged.

3

Transition paragraph links personal narrative with explanations and further examples.

And it is a privilege to have the grinnies, an emotional reaction showing an uncontrollable, spontaneous state of ecstasy. Grinnies appear on the outside as sparkling eyes and a wide, wide smile—not just any smile, but one that shows the teeth and stretches the mouth to its limits. A person experiencing the grinnies appears to be all mouth. On the inside, grinnies are characterized by a feeling of joyful agitation, almost a bubbly sensation. Grinnies usually last just a few seconds, but they can come and go. Sometimes, when life seems just perfect, I have intermittent attacks of the grinnies for a whole day.

4

Formal one-sentence definition, even though the essay itself is an informal *definition.*

Word "And" at beginning of paragraph serves as a transition and helps promote essay coherence.

Further details differentiate the term with precise characteristics.

The term originated in my mother's family. Her younger sister, Rose, who had deep dimples, often expressed her pleasure with such a grin that the dimples appeared to become permanent. When Rose was about four, she started explaining her funny look by saying, "I have the grinnies." The term caught on, and it has been an important word in our family now for two generations.

5

Historical information further explains the term.

The occasion doesn't matter. Anything can bring on the grinnies—just so long as one feels great delight. When my brother finally pumped his bicycle— without training wheels—from our house to the corner and back, he came home with the grinnies. When I was little, my mother's announcement that we would have homemade ice cream for dessert always gave me the grinnies. My

6

More examples to clarify the use of the term.

father had the grinnies when I was valedictorian. Grinnies can be brought on by a good meal, a sense of pride, a new friend, a telephone call from someone special, an accomplishment. Or sometimes one gets the grinnies for no reason at all: just a sudden sense of well-being can bring on a case. Whatever brings them on, an attack of the grinnies is among life's greatest pleasures.

7   In fact, now that I look back on the experience, I feel sorry for my seventh-grade teacher. I think it's a pity that she didn't know the word *grinnies*. It's such a useful term for saying, "I'm really, really pleased!"

Conclusion links to previous paragraph through transition "In fact" and to paragraph 2, contributing to the unity in the essay.

FOR WRITING OR DISCUSSION

1. What is the writer's attitude toward her subject?
2. What is her thesis in the essay? What transitions does the writer use to create coherence?
3. What methods of development does the writer use in defining the term?
4. What examples could you give—other than those used by the writer—of situations that could produce the grinnies?
5. Write an informal definition of a word or term used by some particular group or in a special region of the country. You might select a word like *wannabe, dude, honcho, hack*, or *dweeb*—or another of your own choosing.

Models of Writing

The reading selections that follow provide examples of extended definitions. The first is a humorous take on the ideal job. The second looks at the phenomenon of bloggers. As you study these selections, try to identify the methods of development that help make them effective definitions.

DAVID OWEN

The Perfect Job

1   The perfect job—the one you would have if you could have any job in the world—what would it be?

The most nearly perfect part of any less-than-perfect job is usually the occasional hour in 2
which you are able to pretend that you are doing the job when in fact you are reading a
magazine and eating candy. The rest of the office is throbbing frantically, but you are sitting
quietly at your desk and learning interesting facts about Fergie and that guy who put his wife
in the wood chipper. The perfect job would feel like that, but all the time.

The trouble with less-than-perfect jobs is that they usually don't swoop you up and fling 3
you through your day. That is, you don't very often look up at the clock to find out how
many minutes past eleven it is and discover that it's five and time to go home. That's what
the perfect job would be like. The time would zoom by, the way it does when you are going
through some old boxes and suddenly discover that they are filled with artifacts from the
Pilgrim days.

Well, I've thought about this a lot (while I was supposed to be doing something else), and 4
I've narrowed down my choice of the perfect job to five possibilities:

- Doing an unbelievably great cleanup of my basement, and organizing my workshop so 5
  that I know exactly where everything is, and drawing up a lot of plans to show how I
  might expand my workshop so that it would fill the entire basement instead of only the
  third that it fills now, and buying every conceivable kind of woodworking tool and finding
  exactly the perfect place to keep each one, but never actually getting around to doing any
  woodworking projects.
- Doing the *Times* crossword puzzle and watching MTV while listening to people I knew in 6
  college discuss their marital problems on the other side of a one-way mirror.
- Sorting my children's vast Lego collection—by type, size, and color—into muffin tins and 7
  other containers while my children nearby happily build small vehicles and structures without hitting each other or asking me for something to eat.
- Setting the prison sentences of criminals convicted in highly publicized court cases; making 8
  all parole decisions for these people; receiving daily updates on how they spend their time
  in jail.
- Touring the houses of strangers and looking through their stuff while they're not there. If I 9
  were driving along and happened to see a house that looked interesting, I could pull over
  and let myself in with a set of master keys. If the people happened to be there, I could spray
  them with a harmless paralyzing gas that would prevent them from remembering that I had
  read their diaries and checked to see whether they were making efficient use of their limited
  amount of storage space, which they probably wouldn't have been.

All these jobs, as I see them, would require a full complement of office supplies: every 10
conceivable kind of clip and clasp, name-brand ball-point pens, ungunked-up bottles of correction fluid, ammo-like refills for various desktop mechanisms, and cool, smooth, hard pads
of narrow-lined paper. I guess I would also need a fax machine and a staff of cheerful recent
college graduates eager to do my bidding. Plus a really great benefits program that would pay
not only for doctors and prescription drugs but also for things like deodorant.

Recently I've begun to think that my *real* perfect job would probably consist of all five of my 11
possible perfect jobs, one for each weekday. That way I would never have to lie awake at night
wondering whether sorting my children's Legos would have made me happier than snooping

through people's tax returns. Then, on weekends, I could hang around my house, drinking beer and watching golf tournaments on TV. I would seem to be having a really great time, but in reality I would be counting the hours until Monday and just itching to get back to work.

FOR WRITING OR DISCUSSION

1. How does paragraph 2 establish the humorous context of the essay? What other elements of humor do you find?

2. What important element of the perfect job does Owen establish in paragraph 3? Do you agree that for a job to be perfect, the time ought to "zoom by"? Why, or why not?

3. Outline the five possibilities in Owen's choice of the perfect job. You know that the writer is not serious about these elements. What, then, is he trying to accomplish?

4. Write a definition essay in which you answer the question posed in the first paragraph.

LEV GROSSMAN

Meet Joe Blog

1   A few years ago, Mathew Gross, 32, was a free-lance writer living in tiny Moab, Utah. Rob Malda, 28, was an underperforming undergraduate at a small Christian college in Michigan. Denis Dutton, 60, was a professor of philosophy in faraway Christchurch, New Zealand. Today they are some of the most influential media personalities in the world. You can be one too.

2   Gross, Malda and Dutton aren't rich or famous or even conspicuously good-looking. What they have in common is that they all edit blogs: amateur websites that provide news, information and, above all, opinions to rapidly growing and devoted audiences drawn by nothing more than a shared interest or two and the sheer magnetism of the editor's personality. Over the past five years, blogs have gone from an obscure and, frankly, somewhat nerdy fad to a genuine alternative to mainstream news outlets, a shadow media empire that is rivaling networks and newspapers in power and influence. Which raises the question: Who are these folks anyway? And what exactly are they doing to the established pantheon of American media?

3   Not that long ago, blogs were one of those annoying buzz words that you could safely get away with ignoring. The word blog—it words as both noun and verb—is short for Web log. It was

coined in 1997 to describe a website where you could post daily scribblings, journal-style, about whatever you like—mostly critiquing and linking to other articles online that may have sparked your thinking. Unlike a big media outlet, bloggers focus their efforts on narrow topics, often rising to become de facto watchdogs and self-proclaimed experts. Blogs can be about anything: politics, sex, baseball, haiku, car repair. There are blogs about blogs.

Big whoop, right? But it turns out some people actually have interesting thoughts on a regular basis, and a few of the better blogs began drawing sizable audiences. Blogs multiplied and evolved, slowly becoming conduits for legitimate news and serious thought. In 1999 a few companies began offering free make-your-own-blog software, which turbocharged the phenomenon. By 2002, Pyra Labs, which makes software for creating blogs, claimed 970,000 users.

Most of America couldn't have cared less. Until December 2002, that is, when bloggers staged a dramatic show of force. The occasion was Strom Thurmond's 100th birthday party, during which Trent Lott made what sounded like a nostalgic reference to Thurmond's past segregationist leanings. The mainstream press largely glossed over the incident, but when regular journalists bury the lead, bloggers dig it right back up. "That story got ignored for three, four, five days by big papers and the TV networks while blogs kept it alive," says Joshua Micah Marshall, creator of talkingpointsmemo.com, one of a handful of blogs that stuck with the Lott story.

Mainstream America wasn't listening, but Washington insiders and media honchos read blogs. Three days after the party, the story was on Meet the Press. Four days afterward, Lott made an official apology. After two weeks, Lott was out as Senate majority leader, and blogs had drawn their first blood. Web journalists like Matt Drudge (drudgereport.com) had already demonstrated a certain crude effectiveness—witness l'affaire Lewinsky—but this was something different: bloggers were offering reasoned, forceful arguments that carried weight with the powers that be.

Blogs act like a lens, focusing attention on an issue until it catches fire, but they can also break stories. On April 21, a 34-year-old blogger and writer from Arizona named Russ Kick posted photographs of coffins containing the bodies of soldiers killed in Iraq and Afghanistan and of Columbia astronauts. The military zealously guards images of service members in coffins, but Kick pried the photos free with a Freedom of Information Act (FOIA) request. "I read the news constantly," says Kick, "and when I see a story about the government refusing to relase public documents, I automatically file an FOIA request for them." By April 23 the images had gone from Kick's blog, thememoryhole.org, to the front page of newspapers across the country. Kick was soon getting upwards of 4 million hits a day.

What makes blogs so effective? They're free. They catch people at work, at their desks, when they're alert and thinking and making decision. Blogs are fresh and often seem to be miles ahead of the mainstream news. Bloggers put up new stuff every day, all day, and there are thousands of them. How are you going to keep anything secret from a thousand Russ Kicks? Blogs have voice and personality. They're human. They come to us not from some mediagenic anchorbot on an air-conditioned sound stage, but from an individual. They represent—no, they are—the voice of the little guy.

4

5

6

7

8

9   And the little guy is a lot smarter than big media might have you think. Blogs showcase some of the smartest, sharpest writing being published. Bloggers are unconstrained by such journalistic conventions as good taste, accountability and objectivity—and that can be a good thing. Accusations of media bias are thick on the ground these days, and Americans are tired of it. Blogs don't pretend to be neutral: they're gleefully, unabashedly biased, and that makes them a lot more fun. "Because we're not trying to sell magazines or papers, we can afford to assail out readers," says Andrew Sullivan, a contributor to TIME and the editor of andrewsullivan.com. "I don't have the pressure of an advertising executive telling me to lay off. It's incredibly liberating."

10   Some bloggers earn their bias the hard way—in the trenches. Military bloggers, or mil-bloggers in Net patois, post vivid accounts of their tours of Baghdad, in prose covered in fresh flop sweat and powder burns, illustrated with digital photos. "Jason," a National Guardsman whose blog is called justanothersoldier.com, wrote about wandering though one of Saddam Hussein's empty palaces. And Iraqis have blogs: a Baghdad blogger who goes by Salam Pax (dear_raed.blogspot.com) has parlayed his blog into a book and a movie deal. Vietnam was the first war to be televised; blogs bring Iraq another scary step closer to our living rooms.

11   But blogs are about much more than war and politics. In 1997 Malda went looking for a "site that mixed the latest word about a new sci-fi movie with news about open-source software. I was looking for a site that didn't exist," Malda says, "so I built it." Malda and a handful of co-editors run slashdot.org full time, and he estimates that 300,000 to 500,000 people read the site daily. Six years ago, a philosophy professor in New Zealand named Denis Dutton started the blog Arts & Letters Daily artsandlettersdaily.com to create a website "where people could go daily for a dose of intellectual stimulation." Now the site draws more than 100,000 readers a month. Compare that with, say the *New York Review of Books*, which has a circulation of 115,000. The tail is beginning to wag the blog.

12   Blogs are inverting the cozy media hierarchies of yore. Some bloggers are getting press credentials for this summer's Republican Convention. Three years ago, a 25-year-old Chicagoan named Jessa Crispin started a blog for serious readers called bookslut.com. "We give books a better chance," she says. "*The New York Times Book Review* is so boring. We take each book at face value. There's no politics behind it." Crispin's apartment is overflowing with free books from publishers desperate for a mention. As for the Times, it's scrutinizing the blogging phenomenon for its own purposes. In January the Gray Lady started up Times on the Trail, a campaign-news website with some decidedly bloglike features; it takes the bold step of linking to articles by competing newspapers, for example. "The Times cannot ignore this. I don't think any big media can ignore this," says Len Apcar, editor in chief of the New York Times on the Web.

13   In a way, blogs represent everything the Web was always supposed to be: a mass medium controlled by the masses, in which getting heard depends solely on having something to say and the moxie to say it.

14   Unfortunately, there's downside to this populist sentiment—that is, innocent casualties bloodied by a medium that trades in rumor, gossip and speculation without accountability.

Case in point: Alexandra Polier, better known as the Kerry intern. Rumors of Polier's alleged affair with presidential candidate Senator John Kerry eventually spilled into the blogosphere earlier this year. After Drudge headlined it in February, the blabbing bloggers soon had the attention of tabloid journalists, radio talk-show hosts and cable news anchors. Trouble is, the case was exceedingly thin, and both Kerry and Polier vehemently deny it. Yet the Internet smolders with it to this day.

Some wonder if the backbiting tide won't recede as blogs grow up. The trend now is for more prominent sites to be commercialized. A Manhattan entrepreneur named Nick Denton runs a small stable of bloggers as a business by selling advertising on their sites. So far they aren't showing detectible signs of editorial corruption by their corporate masters—two of Denton's blogs, gawker.com and wonkette.com are among the most corrosively witty sites on the Web—but they've lost their amateur status forever. **15**

We may be in the golden age of blogging, a quirky Camelot moment in Internet history when some guy in his underwear with too much free time can take down a Washington politician. It will be interesting to see what role blogs play in the upcoming election. Blogs can be a great way of communicating, but they can keep people apart too. If I read only those of my choice, precisely tuned to my political biases and you read only yours, we could end up a nation of political solipsists, vacuum sealed in our private feedback loops, never exposed to new arguments, never having to listen to a single word we disagree with. **16**

Howard Dean's campaign blog, run by Mathew Gross, may be the perfect example of both the potential and the pitfalls of high-profile blogging. At its peak, blogforamerica.com drew 100,000 visitors a day, yet the candidate was beaten badly in the primaries. Still, the Dean model isn't going away. When another political blogger, who goes by the nom de blog Atrios, set up a fund-raising link on his site for Kerry, he raised $25,000 in five days. **17**

You can't blog your way into the White House, at least not yet, but blogs are America thinking out loud, talking to itself, and heaven help the candidate who isn't listening. **18**

FOR WRITING OR DISCUSSION

1. What is Grossman trying to define in this essay from *Time* magazine? What is his thesis? What elements of the definition do you find most informative?

2. What, according to the writer, makes blogs so effective?

3. Who are Strom Thurmond and Trent Lott (paragraph 5)? What is "l'affaire Lewinsky?"

4. How does Grossman's intended audience of *Time* magazine readers affect his definition? Comment on the language and style in this regard, especially on elements like "turbocharged the phenomenon" (paragraph 4); "Big whoop, right?" (paragraph 4); "the voice of the little guy" (paragraph 8); "prose covered in fresh slop sweat and powder burns" (paragraph 10). What is the cumulative effect on readers of such words and phrases?

5. Write an essay about some blog that you or someone you know visits—either regularly or from time to time. Why is the blog attractive to you? What purpose does it serve? In what ways does it match or challenge Grossman's definition and analysis?

Readings for Writing

Use these two selections as the basis of a definition paper of your own. The first looks at the meaning of the phrase "person of color" and how it has affected the writer's life. The second is a futuristic short story that deals with the meaning of *equality*, among other themes.

SUNIL GARG

Under My Skin

1   I am a person of color—or at least that is how people often categorize me. Yet what do they mean by that?

2   Certainly, I am brown. My parents emigrated from India in the early 1960's, and I have always thought of myself as Indian-American. But I have never seriously thought of myself as a brown man or as a person of color.

3   I was first confronted with the term when I was accepted to the John F. Kennedy School of Government at Harvard University a few years ago. I received an invitation from the school to attend a special orientation for "students of color." Suddenly, the color of my skin qualified me for special attention.

4   What was the purpose of separating the student body into two groups, whites and those with "color"? Students had not even had the opportunity to introduce themselves on their own terms. By allowing a separate orientation in addition to the general one, the school sent a message to students that color was the one way it had chosen to define the student body.

5   Other students at the Kennedy School explained to me that the term "people of color" includes those who have historically been alienated or oppressed by the Western white world and whose perspectives and cultures have not been properly heard or appreciated.

6   Yet this explanation creates a false relationship between color and culture. Having color does not give anyone a particular culture, nor does having color mean that one's culture or perspective differs from that of whites. I, for instance, identify almost exclusively with Western culture.

People can also become disaffected from American culture because of their religious beliefs, their class, sex or even their weight. Yet the term "people of color" implies that only skin color separates and alienates individuals from society. 7

The term also lumps together the different experiences and challenges facing racial and ethnic groups in the United States. Many times, "people of color" will be used when discussing discrimination, when in fact different groups feel different degrees of discrimination. For instance, a black youth in Harlem has a different experience with racism than does a middle-class Indian-American like myself. 8

By creating this false union among most of the world's population, the term "people of color" also promotes the idea that Western culture and whites are the exercisers of all power and the perpetrators of all evil. One need not be a student of history, however, to understand that racism and oppression are known in almost every nation and that factors beyond color lead men and women to oppress their brethren. 9

I am not denying the existence of racism in America or the importance of skin color in our society. But my fear is that the term "people of color" creates an environment not where cultural diversity is increased, but where alternative perspectives are reduced to tales of racism and victimization. 10

As the ethnic and racial composition of our nation changes substantially, we need to understand and relate to one another, regardless of the color of our skin. 11

We need to find ways to appreciate our country's true diverse perspectives, cultures, knowledge and experiences. This is a far greater challenge, but a necessary one. 12

FOR WRITING OR DISCUSSION

1. What is the main point of the selection? Where does the writer state the thesis? What does the title contribute to the essay? What are the possible meanings of the title?

2. What elements contribute to Garg's definition of the term "person of color"? What does the writer mean by the statement "false union among most of the world's population" (paragraph 9)? What false relation does he see between color and culture? Why might you agree or disagree with him? Do you agree that "factors beyond color" are responsible for racism and oppression? Why or why not?

3. What do you see as the pros and cons of labeling and categorizing people? Is it possible to eliminate labels or to create labels that would not perpetuate stereotypes or the status quo? Is it possible to promote identity awareness without creating divisive separations among groups? Explain your response.

4. Write your own essay in which you defend the term "person of color." Define the term and explain how you think we might use it appropriately. Or, if you prefer, write an essay like Garg's in which you attack the term and its use in our society today.

KURT VONNEGUT JR.
Harrison Bergeron

1   The year was 2081, and everybody was finally equal. They weren't only equal before God and the law. They were equal every which way. Nobody was smarter than anybody else. Nobody was better looking than anybody else. Nobody was stronger or quicker than any-body else. All this equality was due to the 211th, 212th, and 213th Amendments to the Constitution, and to the unceasing vigilance of agents of the United States Handi-capper General.

2   Some things about living still weren't quite right, though. April, for instance, still drove people crazy by not being springtime. And it was in that clammy month that the H-G men took George and Hazel Bergeron's fourteen-year-old son, Harrison, away.

3   It was tragic, all right, but George and Hazel couldn't think about it very hard. Hazel had a perfectly average intelligence, which meant she couldn't think about anything except in short bursts. And George, while his intelligence was way above normal, had a little mental handicap radio in his ear. He was required by law to wear it at all times. It was tuned to a government transmitter. Every twenty seconds or so, the transmitter would send out some sharp noise to keep people like George from taking unfair advantage of their brains.

4   George and Hazel were watching television. There were tears on Hazel's cheeks, but she'd forgotten for the moment what they were about.

5   On the television screen were ballerinas.

6   A buzzer sounded in George's head. His thoughts fled in panic, like bandits from a burglar alarm.

7   "That was a real pretty dance, that dance they just did," said Hazel.

8   "Huh?" said George.

9   "That dance—it was nice," said Hazel.

10   "Yup," said George. He tried to think a little about the ballerinas. They weren't really very good—no better than anybody else would have been, anyway. They were burdened with sashweights and bags of birdshot, and their faces were masked, so that no one, see-ing a free and graceful gesture or a pretty face, would feel like something the cat drug in. George was toying with the vague notion that maybe dancers shouldn't be handi-capped. But he didn't get very far with it before another noise in his ear radio scattered his thoughts.

11   George winced. So did two out of the eight ballerinas.

12   Hazel saw him wince. Having no mental handicap herself, she had to ask George what the latest sound had been.

13   "Sounded like somebody hitting a milk bottle with a ball peen hammer," said George.

14   "I'd think it would be real interesting, hearing all the different sounds," said Hazel, a little envious. "All the things they think up."

15   "Um," said George.

"Only, if I was Handicapper General, you know what I would do?" said Hazel. Hazel, as a matter of fact, bore a strong resemblance to the Handicapper General, a woman named Diana Moon Glampers. "If I was Diana Moon Glampers," said Hazel, "I'd have chimes on Sunday—just chimes. Kind of in honor of religion." 16

"I could think, if it was just chimes," said George. 17

"Well—maybe make 'em real loud," said Hazel. "I think I'd make a good Handicapper General." 18

"Good as anybody else," said George. 19

"Who knows better'n I do what normal is?" said Hazel. 20

"Right," said George. He began to think glimmeringly about his abnormal son who was now in jail, about Harrison, but a twenty-one-gun salute in his head stopped that. 21

"Boy!" said Hazel, "that was a doozy, wasn't it?" 22

It was such a doozy that George was white and trembling, and tears stood on the rims of his red eyes. Two of the eight ballerinas had collapsed to the studio floor, were holding their temples. 23

"All of a sudden you look so tired," said Hazel. "Why don't you stretch out on the sofa, so's you can rest your handicap bag on the pillows, honeybunch." She was referring to the forty-seven pounds of birdshot in a canvas bag, which was padlocked around George's neck. "Go on and rest the bag for a little while," she said. "I don't care if you're not equal to me for a while." 24

George weighed the bag with his hands. "I don't mind it," he said, "I don't notice it anymore. It's just a part of me." 25

"You been so tired lately—kind of wore out," said Hazel. "If there was just some way we could make a little hole in the bottom of the bag, and just take out a few of them lead balls. Just a few." 26

"Two years in prison and two thousand dollars fine for every ball I took out." said George. "I don't call that a bargain." 27

"If you could take a few out when you came home from work," said Hazel. "I mean—you don't compete with anybody around here. You just set around." 28

"If I tried to get away with it," said George, "then other people'd get away with it—and pretty soon we'd be right back to the dark ages again, with everybody competing against everybody else. You wouldn't like that, would you?" 29

"I'd hate it," said Hazel. 30

"There you are," said George. "The minute people start cheating on laws, what do you think happens to society?" 31

If Hazel hadn't been able to come up with an answer to this question, George couldn't have supplied one. A siren was going off in his head. 32

"Reckon it'd fall all apart," said Hazel. 33

"What would?" said George blankly. 34

"Society," said Hazel uncertainly. "Wasn't that what you just said?" 35

"Who knows?" said George. 36

The television program was suddenly interrupted for a news bulletin. It wasn't clear at first as to what the bulletin was about, since the announcer like all announcers, had a serious 37 speech impediment. For about half a minute, and in a state of high excitement, the announcer tried to say, "Ladies and gentlemen—"

38   He finally gave up, handed the bulletin to a ballerina to read.

39   "That's all right—" Hazel said of the announcer, "he tried. That's the big thing. He tried to do the best he could with what God gave him. He should get a nice raise for trying so hard."

40   "Ladies and gentlemen—" said the ballerina, reading the bulletin. She must have been extraordinarily beautiful, because the mask she wore was hideous. And it was easy to see that she was the strongest and most graceful of all the dancers, for her handicap bags were as big as those worn by two-hundred-pound men.

41   And she had to apologize at once for her voice, which was a very unfair voice for a woman to use. Her voice was a warm, luminous, timeless melody. "Excuse me—" she said, and she began again, making her voice absolutely uncompetitive.

42   "Harrison Bergeron, age fourteen," she said in a grackle squawk, "has just escaped from jail, where he was held on suspicion of plotting to overthrow the government. He is a genius and an athlete, is under-handicapped, and should be regarded as extremely dangerous."

43   A police photograph of Harrison Bergeron was flashed on the screen upside down, then sideways, upside down again, then right side up. The picture showed the full length of Harrison against a background calibrated in feet and inches. He was exactly seven feet tall.

44   The rest of Harrison's appearance was Halloween and hardware. Nobody had ever borne heavier handicaps. He had outgrown hindrances faster than the H-G men could think them up. Instead of a little ear radio for a mental handicap, he wore a tremendous pair of earphones, and spectacles with thick wavy lenses. The spectacles were intended to make him not only half blind, but to give him whanging headaches besides.

45   Scrap metal was hung all over him. Ordinarily, there was a certain symmetry, a military neatness to the handicaps issued to strong people, but Harrison looked like a walking junkyard. In the face of life, Harrison carried three hundred pounds.

46   And to offset his good looks, the H-G men required that he wear at all times a red rubber ball for a nose, keep his eyebrows shaved off, and cover his even white teeth with black caps at snaggle-tooth random.

47   "If you see this boy," said the ballerina, "do not—I repeat, do not—try to reason with him."

48   There was a shriek of a door being torn from its hinges.

49   Screams and barking cries of consternation came from the television set. The photograph of Harrison Bergeron on the screen jumped again and again, as though dancing to the tune of an earthquake.

50   George Bergeron correctly identified the earthquake, and well he might have—for many was the time his own home had danced to the same crashing tune. "My God—" said George, "that must be Harrison!"

51   The realization was blasted from his mind instantly by the sound of an automobile collision in his head.

When George could open his eyes again, the photograph of Harrison was gone. A living, breathing Harrison filled the screen.   52

Clanking, clownish, and huge, Harrison stood in the center of the studio. The knob of the uprooted studio door was still in his hand. Ballerinas, technicians, musicians, and announcers cowered on their knees before him, expecting to die.   53

"I am the Emperor!" cried Harrison. "Do you hear! I am the Emperor! Everybody must do what I say at once!" He stamped his foot and the studio shook.   54

"Even as I stand here—" he bellowed, "crippled, hobbled, sickened—I am a greater ruler than any man who ever lived! Now watch me become what I *can* become!"   55

Harrison tore the straps of his handicap harness like wet tissue paper, tore straps guaranteed to support five thousand pounds.   56

Harrison's scrap-iron handicaps crashed to the floor.   57

Harrison thrust his thumbs under the bar of the padlock that secured his head harness. The bar snapped like celery. Harrison smashed his headphones and spectacles against the wall.   58

He flung away his rubber-ball nose, revealed a man that would have awed Thor, the god of thunder.   59

"I shall now select my Empress!" he said, looking down on the cowering people. "Let the first woman who dares rise to her feet claim her mate and her throne!"   60

A moment passed, and then a ballerina arose, swaying like a willow.   61

Harrison plucked the mental handicap from her ear, snapped off her physical handicaps with marvelous delicacy. Last of all, he removed her mask.   62

She was blindingly beautiful.   63

"Now—" said Harrison, taking her hand, "shall we show the people the meaning of the word dance? Music!" he commanded.   64

The musicians scrambled back into their chairs, and Harrison stripped them of their handicaps, too. "Play your best," he told them, "and I'll make you barons and dukes and earls."   65

The music began. It was normal at first—cheap, silly, false. But Harrison snatched two musicians from their chairs, waved them like batons as he sang the music as he wanted it played. He slammed them back into their chairs.   66

The music began again and was much improved.   67

Harrison and his Empress merely listened to the music for a while—listened gravely, as though synchronizing their heartbeats with it.   68

They shifted their weights to their toes.   69

Harrison placed his big hands on the girl's tiny waist, letting her sense the weightlessness that would soon be hers.   70

And then in an explosion of joy and grace, into the air they sprang!   71

Not only were the laws of the land abandoned, but the law of gravity and the laws of motion as well.   72

They reeled, whirled, swiveled, flounced, capered, gamboled, and spun.   73

They leaped like deer on the moon.   74

75   The studio ceiling was thirty feet high, but each leap brought the dancers nearer to it.

76   It became their obvious intention to kiss the ceiling.

77   They kissed it.

78   And then, neutralizing gravity with love and pure will, they remained suspended in air inches below the ceiling, and they kissed each other for a long, long time.

79   It was then that Diana Moon Glampers, the Handicapper General, came into the studio with a double-barreled ten-gauge shotgun. She fired twice, and the Emperor and the Empress were dead before they hit the floor.

80   Diana Moon Glampers loaded the gun again. She aimed it at the musicians and told them they had ten seconds to get their handicaps back on.

81   It was then that the Bergerons' television tube burned out.

82   Hazel turned to comment about the blackout to George. But George had gone out into the kitchen for a can of beer.

83   George came back in with the beer, paused while a handicap signal shook him up. And then he sat down again.

84   "You been crying?" he said to Hazel.

85   "Yup," she said.

86   "What about?" he said.

87   "I forget," she said. "Something real sad on television."

88   "What was it?" he said.

89   "It's all kind of mixed up in my mind," said Hazel.

90   "Forget sad things," said George.

91   "I always do," said Hazel.

92   "That's my girl," said George. He winced. There was the sound of a riveting gun in his head.

93   "Gee—I could tell that one was a doozy," said Hazel.

94   "You can say that again," said George.

95   "Gee—" said Hazel, "I could tell that one was a doozy."

FOR WRITING OR DISCUSSION

1. Vonnegut's story is one of the future in which he looks at trends today that disturb him and asks what life would be like if they continue for a hundred years or so. What other stories, novels, movies, and television programs can you think of that use the same approach?

2. What specifically is the author satirizing in modern America? Do you feel he has good cause to be upset? Why or why not?

3. What would the author feel is a correct definition of *equality*? How would Diana Moon Glampers define *equality*?

4. Why is the name Harrison Bergeron a better choice than a name such as John Smith or Bill Jones?

5. Name the different kinds of handicaps in the story. Does each attempt to solve a different problem?

6. Specifically, what are the bad results of the misunderstanding of equality?

7. What is symbolized by the soaring of Harrison and the ballerina to the ceiling?

8. Does the fact that Harrison declares himself an emperor justify the society's fear of him?

9. Write a paper in which you define *equality*.

Reading and Writing About Poetry

A poet captures the frustrations of unfulfillment in this brief, powerful poem.

LANGSTON HUGHES

Dreams

Hold fast to dreams
For if dreams die
Life is a broken-winged bird
That cannot fly.
Hold fast to dreams   5
For when dreams go
Life is a barren field
Frozen with snow.

FOR WRITING OR DISCUSSION

1. What is the main point of this poem?

2. What does Hughes mean by the first line of the poem? What is the effect of his repeating it in the fifth line?

3. Which of the two metaphors do you find more powerful? (See pages 418–419 for a definition of metaphor.) Or are they both equally strong? Why do you think so?

4. The poem operates through negation—that is, the poet tells us what life would be like without dreams. How do you think Hughes would define *dreams*? or *life with dreams*?

5. Write an essay in which you define *dreams*. Or, you might define *life with dreams* or *life without dreams*. Use metaphors, where appropriate, to add pictorial strength to your paper.

STRATEGY CHECKLIST: Writing and Revising Your Definition Paper

Plan the paper.	☐ Have I selected a word or phrase that lends itself to an extended definition?
	☐ Is the word I've chosen too broad or too narrow, and how can I correct either of these two limitations?
	☐ Have I used one of the prewriting strategies to stimulate my thoughts?
	☐ Have I identified details and examples that support my understanding of the word?
	☐ Have I paid attention to peer comments about my prewriting?
	☐ Have I considered my audience and purpose?
	☐ Have I considered using an outline to plan my presentation?

Write a first draft.	☐ Have I written a thesis that expresses an opinion about the word I am defining?
	☐ For an extended formal definition, have I included a one-sentence definition with three major parts?
	■ Term
	■ Class
	■ Differentiation
	☐ Have I written an introduction that states the term and provides some idea of why I'm choosing to define it?
	☐ Have I considered appropriate strategies to advance my definition?
	■ Description ■ Comparison and contrast
	■ Narration ■ Classification and division
	■ Example ■ Cause and effect
	■ Process
	☐ Have I presented distinctive characteristics of the word in the body paragraphs?
	☐ Does my conclusion revisit the word or phrase, set a new context, or suggest that the reader take some action?

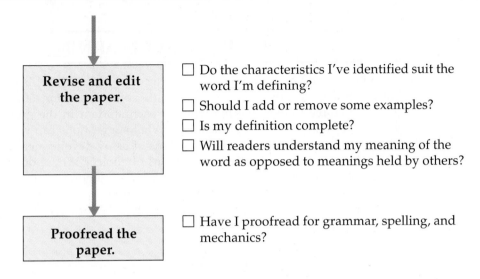

Revise and edit the paper.	☐ Do the characteristics I've identified suit the word I'm defining? ☐ Should I add or remove some examples? ☐ Is my definition complete? ☐ Will readers understand my meaning of the word as opposed to meanings held by others?
Proofread the paper.	☐ Have I proofread for grammar, spelling, and mechanics?

WRITING TOPICS

Consider these words and terms as possible topics for your extended definition paper. Do library or online research, as needed.

1. Evolution
2. Happiness
3. Homelessness
4. Affirmative action
5. Shopping malls
6. Laziness
7. Wealth
8. Leadership
9. Astrology
10. Religion
11. Success
12. Political correctness
13. Depression
14. Hope
15. Virus
16. Friends
17. White-collar crime
18. America
19. "Wannabes"
20. Fun

CROSSCURRENTS

David Owen in "The Perfect Job" (pages 320–322) and Nick Fiscina in "Dad's Disappointment" (pages 128–130) characterize work experiences from completely different perspectives. Write an essay in which you determine the definition of *job* or *work* advocated by the writers and compare and contrast their points of view.

COLLABORATIVE LEARNING

Once you decide on a topic, do prewriting (see pages 39–41) before you draft your definition essay. Come to class with your prewriting efforts and form groups of three to examine the work of each student in the group. Has each writer selected a term rich in meaning? What suggestions can you make about how to develop the thesis? Which patterns of essay development do you think will help each writer best define the word of choice? Where do you think the writer needs to provide details? Is the writer's intended purpose clear? What audience should the essay aim for, in your opinion?

When you produce the draft of your essay, take into account the comments you received from group members.

From **IMAGE** To **WORDS**: A Reading and Writing Assignment

Photography by PE Reed/Photonica/Getly Images

Look at the photograph above. To your way of thinking, what word does the picture serve to define? Select one word or phrase—*happiness*, perhaps, or *tranquility* or *reflection* or *summer*, for example—or some other word of your choosing. Then, write an essay in which you define that word. Draw on elements in the photograph for supporting details. Use your imagination to fill in or develop any details not explicit in the photograph. For instance, you might want to pursue the people's states of mind or fill in concrete sensory details of color, sound, smell, and touch.

For additional writing, reading, and research resources, go to **www. mycomplab.com** <http://www.mycomplab.com/> and choose Skwire/Wiener's *Student's Book of College English*, Twelfth Edition.

CHAPTER 15

Argumentation

- Using Logic
- Writing Your Argumentation Paper
- Student Writing: Argumentation
- Student Writing: Perspectives on Immigrants in America
- Models for Writing
- Readings for Writing
- Researched Student Writing: Argumentation
- Reading and Writing About Poetry

An **argumentation** paper attempts to strengthen or change an attitude of the reader, or to persuade the reader to a particular point of view by means of logic. Although writers of argumentation papers may use emotional appeals, they place their principal faith in appealing to the intellects of their readers.

Argumentation has probably too often appeared in the combative context of a courtroom or debating society: Right and wrong confront each other; one side wins, and one side loses. The victors gloat over the demolished points of their opponents or graciously accept their opponents' concessions of defeat and apologies for being so wrong. Many writers still do strive for total victory of this sort, of course, but argument also can be a matter of bringing opposing parties together, of showing the strengths and weaknesses of all points of view, of building consensus among former enemies. Argumentation can involve making peace as much as waging war.

Using Logic

To check your own logic and that of others, a knowledge of the two kinds of logical thinking, *induction* and *deduction*, and of the errors in logic, the *fallacies*, will be helpful.

Induction

Induction is the process of reasoning from the particular to the general. It is the process of arriving at a general conclusion about all the members of a group or class. Induction is a useful tool because it isn't always practical or possible to check every member of a group before drawing your conclusion. If, for example, you've noticed that for three Fridays in a row, Professor Hadley has given a pop quiz, you may draw the useful conclusion that Professor Hadley is likely to give pop quizzes on Fridays. You don't have to wait until the end of the term to see if you're right.

But induction is useful only if the conclusion about a class is drawn from a fair sampling of that class. What's fair depends on the class. You needn't stick your hand into twenty fires to conclude that fire burns; one or two fires will do. You should sample other classes more broadly. You should draw conclusions about groups of people, for example, from a large representative sampling and even then you should usually qualify statements with words like *tend, may, are likely*, and so on. (See "Hasty Generalization" and "Overgeneralization," page 342; see also Chapter 9, "Example")

Deduction

Deduction is the process of reasoning from the general to the particular. You apply a generalization already established—by yourself or by someone else—to a specific case. Deduction, like induction, is a useful tool. You've concluded, for example, that Professor Hadley is likely to give pop quizzes on Fridays. When your roommate suggests one Friday morning that you cut classes and spend the day in the park, you say, "No, I can't go today. Professor Hadley may give a pop quiz, and my average can't stand a zero." You've applied your generalization (Fridays are likely days for quizzes) to a specific case (this Friday) and just may have assured yourself a passing grade in Professor Hadley's class.

The Syllogism

In its simplest form, the deductive process is stated as a *syllogism*: an argument consisting of a major premise, a minor premise, and a conclusion.

> *Major premise:* Fridays are likely days for pop quizzes.
>
> *Minor premise:* Today is Friday.
>
> *Conclusion:*   Therefore, today is a likely day for a pop quiz.

Perhaps a more sophisticated example is the syllogism implicit in the Declaration of Independence:

> *Major premise:* Rulers who violate basic human rights should be overthrown.
>
> *Minor premise:* King George III has violated basic human rights.
>
> *Conclusion:*   Therefore, King George III should be overthrown.

Syllogisms rarely appear in writing or conversation in their pure three-part form. It is far more common to find enthymemes, condensed syllogisms in which one or more parts are missing, the writer assuming that the missing parts are clearly understood and don't need to be stated directly.

> It's Friday, so I'd better go to Professor Hadley's class. (*Missing premise:* Fridays are likely days for quizzes in Professor Hadley's class.)

I don't trust him because he's sneaky. (*Missing premise*: Sneaky people should not be trusted.)

I hate movies with violence, and this movie is teeming with violence. (*Missing conclusion*: Therefore, I hate this movie.)

Syllogisms are worth serious study primarily because they enable readers and writers to examine the often unstated, and sometimes shaky, assumptions behind otherwise convincing arguments.

For a valid syllogism, both premises must be true. It's hard to imagine a syllogism that begins with the premise "The earth is flat" leading to any valid conclusion. But even if both premises are true, the reasoning process itself may be faulty and the conclusion invalid. Consider this syllogism:

Major premise: English majors read lots of books.

Minor premise: David reads lots of books.

Conclusion: Therefore, David is an English major.

Despite the true premises, the conclusion still doesn't follow. The major premise merely says, "English majors read lots of books"; it says nothing about other people who may also read books. Logically, David may be an English major, but he may also be a merchant marine who spends time on shipboard by reading, an invalid who doesn't enjoy television, a desk clerk whose job is boring, or just someone who likes to read for no particular reason. The logical structure of the argument makes no more sense than this syllogism: Grass is green; her hat is green; therefore, her hat is grass.

Using Induction and Deduction

So far, we have looked at induction and deduction as if the processes were mutually exclusive, but, in practice, they aren't. You will seldom engage in one kind of thought without using the other. When you use induction, you usually have a hunch about what generalization the facts will add up to. If you didn't, you wouldn't have a guideline for handling the facts. Consider, for example, that observation about Professor Hadley's quiz-giving tendency. If you hadn't already suspected that Hadley was a Friday quiz-giver, you might not have noticed that the pop quizzes did occur on Friday. Some deduction, therefore, was involved in the process of reaching the generalization about pop quizzes on Friday.

Similarly, in deductive reasoning you must also use induction. A syllogism is only as valid as both its premises. To ensure sound premises, you must be sure that your evidence is both adequate and fair, and that involves induction. Induction is important, too, when you present your material. Even if yours is the best of syllogisms, you probably won't convince a reader of its worth unless you offer support for it—reasons, statistics, facts, opinions of authorities, examples. The reader's agreement or approval depends on the case you build; it depends on evidence. In the Declaration of Independence, for example, Thomas Jefferson supported his case against George III by citing twenty-eight instances in which the king had violated basic human rights. The instances came from induction.

Avoiding Logical Fallacies

Whether your primary tool is induction or deduction, you need to make certain that the evidence you offer isn't based on errors in logic. In other words, you should avoid the following fallacies.

Post Hoc, Ergo Propter Hoc

This impressive Latin phrase means, "after this, therefore because of this." This fallacy takes for a cause an event that merely happened earlier: For example, *A black cat crossed my path and ten minutes later I broke my ankle; therefore, the black cat caused my broken ankle.* Unless the speaker tripped over the cat, such a statement is as unreasonable as *Night follows day; therefore, day causes night.*

Card Stacking

Card stacking means using only the evidence that supports a thesis and ignoring that which contradicts or weakens it. Card stacking is dishonest and can sometimes do serious damage. Suppose, for instance, that a popular newspaper columnist dislikes the mayor of the city. The columnist could prevent the mayor's reelection simply by emphasizing the administration's mistakes and playing down its accomplishments. Soon, the readers of the newspaper would begin to think of the mayor as a bungler who shouldn't be reelected.

Unfair? Of course. It's also unnecessary. A reasonable thesis doesn't require card stacking. A writer can make concessions and still advance the argument: *Although the mayor has made some attempts to attract convention business, the efforts have been too few and too late,* for example. If a thesis isn't reasonable, if it requires card stacking for support, it probably isn't worth defending and the writer should change it.

Slanting

A variation of card stacking is **slanting**, systematically using words whose connotations suggest extreme approval or disapproval of the subject. A person may be "a bag of bones" or have "a model's figure." In either case, the weight is the same, but one term suggests scorn and the other approval. The conscious use of slanting to sway opinion usually occurs when a writer lacks enough logical evidence to support the thesis. Used this way, it is, like card stacking, quite dishonest. But slanting should not be confused with a writer's legitimate efforts to convey admittedly personal impressions and emotions.

Hasty Generalization

One snowflake doesn't make a blizzard, nor does one experience make a universal law. That one student has cheated on the last five psychology quizzes doesn't mean that all psychology students in the school are cheaters; to say so is to make a **hasty generalization**, to draw a conclusion about a group that is based on insufficient evidence.

Overgeneralization

Overgeneralizations are similar to hasty generalizations. A hasty generalization results from drawing a conclusion about a large number on the basis of very limited evidence. Overgeneralization occurs, regardless of how much "evidence" is available, when one assumes that all members of a group, nationality, race, or sex have the characteristics observed in some members of that group: "all feminists hate housework"; "the English are always cold and reserved"; "never trust a used-car salesperson." Surely it's possible that some feminists like to cook, that some English people are volatile, and that at least one or two used-car salespersons are trustworthy. Words such as *all, never, always, every, true*, and *untrue* are seldom justified when dealing with the complexities of human beings and human institutions. You would do well in writing your papers to qualify potentially troublesome generalizations with words such as *some, seldom, tend, sometimes, frequently, seem, appear, often, perhaps*, and *many*. Both hasty generalizations and overgeneralizations lead to prejudice and superstition and to theses that cannot be developed logically or effectively.

Non Sequitur

Meaning "it does not follow," a ***non sequitur*** is a conclusion that does not follow from the premises. For example:

> I was a volunteer worker this summer so now I am saving to go to medical school.

Usually, *non sequiturs* occur because the writer or speaker neglects to make the connection between the premise and the conclusion clear to readers. In the preceding example, the writer's thinking probably resembles this:

- I worked as a volunteer this summer for an organization that served men and women with serious diseases.
- These people suffered greatly.
- I felt that I was able to bring them some comfort from their pain and that this work gave me great satisfaction.
- I'd like to be able to help ill people.
- Therefore, I am saving to go to medical school so that I can become a physician and bring even more comfort to the sick.

Although the writer sees the connection easily, he has to reveal thought processes so that the audience may also see the connection.

Another kind of *non sequitur* occurs because the writer or speaker draws an incorrect or debatable conclusion:

Jack is 6 feet, 7 inches tall; I want him on my basketball team.

The unstated syllogism that leads to the conclusion is

Successful basketball players tend to be very tall.

Jack is very tall.

Therefore, Jack will be a successful basketball player.

Although both the major premise and the minor premise are true, the conclusion does not necessarily follow. Jack may be so awkward that he trips over his own feet; thus, not all tall people make good basketball players. The writer's conclusion is, therefore, questionable and perhaps should be rejected.

Ignoring the Question

In **ignoring the question**, the writer or speaker deliberately or unintentionally shifts emphasis from the topic under discussion. You can (but should not) ignore a question in several ways.

Ad Hominem Argument

Arguing *ad hominem* (literally, "against the man") means making an irrelevant attack on a person rather than dealing with the actual issue under discussion. Suppose, for example, that Senator Goodfellow, who has admitted to cheating on his income tax for the past five years, proposes a bill for welfare reform. It would be a fallacy to attack the bill by arguing that its proponent is guilty of tax evasion. The bill may be logical, humane, and in the best interest of the country. If it is not, what are its weaknesses? The bill, not Senator Goodfellow's problems with the Internal Revenue Service, should be the subject of discussion.

Not all personal attacks, of course, are necessarily irrelevant. If Senator Goodfellow were seeking reelection, one could logically approve of his ideas and still vote against him because his character defects indicate the danger of trusting him in a position of power and responsibility.

Inexperienced writers sometimes employ the *ad hominem* fallacy in discussing literary works by rejecting a work whose author does not fulfill their idea of a good person:

One cannot be expected to take "Kubla Khan" seriously. Coleridge admitted to writing it after he had taken drugs.

Hemingway was a notorious womanizer. How can we value any of his ideas on morality and fidelity?

Such a practice indicates little understanding of the artistic process or of human nature. Writers, like all people, have human quirks and illnesses; yet such writers have produced inspiring works that affirm the highest values of civilization, and those affirmations deserve consideration. After all, most of us are a mixture of good and evil, wisdom and folly, generosity and greed; if we waited until we found a good idea proposed by a perfect person, we might wait forever.

Straw Man Argument

The writer or speaker attributes to the opposition actions or beliefs of which the opposition is not guilty and then attacks the opposition for those actions or beliefs.

> Parents who boast of never having to spank their children should feel shame instead of pride. Discipline and socially responsible behavior are vitally important, and people who sneer at such things deserve the condemnation of all concerned citizens.

Some parents might very well be able to boast of not having to spank their children and yet also demand of their children discipline and socially responsible behavior.

Begging the Question

The writer or speaker assumes in the thesis something that really needs to be proved.

> Since students learn to write in high school, the college composition course is a waste of time and should be replaced by a more useful and stimulating course.

One who chooses to write a paper with that thesis has the obligation to prove that students do learn how to write in high school—a source of great controversy in all discussions of American education.

Shifting the Burden of Proof

Logic requires that *whoever asserts must prove*. It is not logical to say,

> I believe the flu epidemic was caused by a conspiracy of large drug companies, and you can't prove it wasn't.

For the assertion to be taken seriously, reasonable proof of a conspiracy must be offered.

Circular Argument

Arguing in a circle means simply restating the premise instead of giving a reason for holding the premise.

> I like detective novels because mystery stories always give me great pleasure.

All that sentence says is, "I like detective novels because I like detective novels." Of greater interest would be the characteristics of the detective novels the speaker does like. In other words, one needs a reason for liking detective novels, and to say that one likes them because they give pleasure is not to give a reason. Why do the novels give pleasure? An honest answer to that question will provide a workable thesis and prevent a circular argument.

Either/Or

In the **either/or fallacy**, the writer or speaker suggests that there are only two alternatives when, in fact, there may be more.

> Although I am quite ill, I must turn my term paper in tomorrow, or I will fail the course.

The writer presents only two alternatives; however, it is also possible that the instructor, recognizing the student's illness, might accept a late paper. Of course, if one is cursed with a professor who does not accept late papers, regardless of circumstances, then one actually has only two alternatives, and no fallacy exists.

Argument by Analogy

An **analogy** is an extended comparison. It can clarify a difficult concept or dramatize an abstraction by comparing the unfamiliar with the familiar. But an analogy doesn't prove anything because, regardless of the number of similarities between two things, there are always some differences. One can't assume that because two things are alike in some respects, they are alike in all respects. Consider the following example.

> Learning to write a good essay is like learning to drive a car. Beginning drivers feel overwhelmed by the number of operations they must perform to keep a car moving—controlling the brake and the accelerator, staying in their lane, watching the cars in front of them while keeping an eye on the rear-view mirror. In addition, they must observe all traffic laws. The tasks seem insurmountable. Yet, in time, some of the operations become almost automatic and the drivers relax enough so that they can even look at the scenery now and then. So it is with beginning writers. At first, they wonder how they can make an outline for a paper, write clear topic sentences, develop paragraphs, provide transitions, write good introductions and conclusions, and still observe all the rules of English grammar. As with driving, part of the process eventually becomes automatic, and the writers relax enough to concentrate primarily on the ideas they wish to develop.

The comparison deals only with the similarities of feelings in the two experiences and is a successful analogy because it clarifies the experience of writing for the beginner. But if one extends the comparison to encompass other demands on drivers—checking antifreeze, acquiring new windshield wipers, renewing license plates, repairing flats, maintaining brake fluid—the analogy falls apart.

Historical analogies present a similar problem. We can't assume that because two historical events are alike in some respects, the outcomes will inevitably be the same. You have probably heard the argument that the United States is on the verge of collapse because some conditions here—relaxed sexual mores, widespread demand for immediate pleasure, and political cynicism and corruption—parallel those of the Roman Empire just before its fall. The argument doesn't consider, among other things, that the forms of government differ, that the bases for the economy differ, or that the means of educating the population differ. The two societies are not alike in every respect, and one cannot assume that because one society fell, the other also will fall.

Analogy can be useful for clarifying an idea, but argument by analogy can be dangerous.

EXERCISE   Following are examples of logical fallacies. Read them, and determine what type of fallacy each most strongly represents.

1. I lost my wallet yesterday. I knew that walking under that ladder in the morning would be trouble!
2. Yesterday, my neighbor's sixteen-year-old son zoomed out of the driveway in his new car and barely missed my daughter, who was riding her tricycle on the sidewalk. Last week, a seventeen-year-old girl hit the rear of my car when I had to stop suddenly for a traffic light. When are we going to come to our senses and raise the legal driving age to twenty-one?
3. How can she be guilty of that crime? She has such a lovely family—they go to church regularly and are such friendly people.
4. Of course she's poor. Look at that old torn coat she's wearing!
5. How can Senator O'Malley speak for labor? What does he know about the needs of the average worker? He was born rich.
6. I love visiting Wyoming because I really enjoy traveling out West.
7. We must change this unfair method of closing fire stations.
8. We should either pay our teachers better salaries or admit that we don't care about the quality of our children's education.
9. I don't understand why Abraham Lincoln is considered a great president. He was a warmonger who, by government proclamation, took away the property of a large number of citizens.
10. How do *you* know that life does not exist on other planets?

Writing Your Argumentation Paper

Argumentation papers must draw on controversial subject matter—that is, the possibility for a difference of opinion on the subject must exist. Otherwise, there would be no need to argue. That does not mean, however, that the subject matter need be earthshaking. Writers differ on how to interpret poems or on how to bake cakes. In the sense that the purpose of an argumentation paper is to persuade a reader to a point of view, you have written argumentation papers since you began your study of English composition. In every paper, you have taken a position on a subject and have offered logical reasons for holding that position. Our "Having

Your Say" exercises, appearing frequently throughout the text, further encourage you to write arguments.

Writing a Formal Argument

A formal argumentation paper has its own specific requirements. In a formal argument, the writer should follow certain guidelines.

TIPS   for Writing a Formal Argument

- State the problem or issue, sometimes tracing its causes.
- In some cases, state the possible positions to be taken on the problem.
- State the position that the paper will take.
- Offer supporting detail that the position taken is the reasonable one to hold.
- Anticipate objections to the position and acknowledge or refute them.
- Affirm the position and make a final appeal.

All these requirements are important, but we want especially to note the importance of the next to the last point. Anticipating objections to your position, presenting them in your paper, and admitting or refuting them are key features of the strong argumentative essay.

Developing a Debatable Position

You know all about limiting a topic to suit the time and requirements of the assignment, but in an argumentation paper, there's another key element in regard to selecting your topic. Your topic and thesis must lend themselves to debate. If people can take sides on the issue, you've probably chosen a good topic. Of course, you have to know it well and be able to argue it convincingly. To check on whether your thesis is a good one, always ask yourself this question: Would anyone care to debate it?

Possible Thesis	Is It Debatable?
The scientific community should work hard to find a cure for cancer.	**No.** Who would dispute this statement? It's not a good topic for an argument paper.
We should stop using live animals for scientific testing.	**Yes.** Many disagree and feel that animal testing is essential if we are to make advances in medicine.
Gay couples should have the same marital rights as heterosexual couples.	**Yes.** This is a heated topic in today's society, and many people believe that laws should prevent gay marriage.
People who own pets should clean up their animals' mess from city streets.	**Possibly but not probably.** Few would disagree that someone must clean up after pets; unless the argument is that

	someone other than the owners should address the problem, or that city-dwellers should not be allowed to own pets at all, this is not a viable argument.
We should provide high quality schools for our children.	**No.** No one would debate this assertion.
I believe in a citizen's right not to vote.	**Yes.** Clearly this is a contrarian position, and many people would be happy to debate it.

Student Writing: Argumentation

Examine the following student argumentation papers. The first essay defends a citizen's right not to vote in an election and includes annotations in the margins to demonstrate one student's critical thinking on the essay. The second deals with books and other art. Note the clear statement of thesis and the way the writer deals with opponents to her argument.

Sandra Travis-Edwards

The Right Not to Vote

Introduction: Identifies opposing arguments

1   I believe that the right to vote is one of the most important parts of being an American citizen. Our right to participate in choosing the leaders of our country ensures the continuance of our democratic system, and has protected this democracy and allowed it to flourish over the past two centuries. But, although I believe all this as firmly as it is possible to believe anything, I believe just as strongly in a citizen's right not to vote.

Thesis makes an arguable assertion: People have the right NOT to vote

2   Many people argue that not voting is sheer foolishness. They believe that not voting is a way of avoiding the responsibility of having a political opinion. They say that it is proof that a person has absolutely no interest in politics, and that a person who doesn't vote just doesn't care. While this may often be true, it is not always the case.

More opposing arguments

3   I have chosen not to vote twice in my life, both times for different, yet valid reasons. The first time I chose not to vote was when I was going through a three-year period in which I moved three separate times. I came into one community just in time to register for an extremely important and hotly contested mayoral election. Needless to say I was flooded with canvassers from

Narration with clear chronology

Topic sentence of paragraph 3 with implied link to paragraph 4

Illustration: Writer identifies the first time that she did not vote

various candidates, with flyers on my car's windshield, and with advice from my new neighbors. There were only a few short weeks until the election, and with a new job and a new apartment to get used to, I knew I would never have time to catch up with all the election details I needed. Instead of desperately attempting to become informed about my new neighborhood, its needs, and how each of the many candidates might or might not meet them, I chose not to vote. I believe that when one must choose between casting an ignorant, uninterested vote and casting no vote at all, the latter is the only responsible choice.

The second time I decided not to vote was a little later. I had finally gotten settled in the town which is still my home, and I had had time to get to know the community well enough to be an interested and excited participant in the various elections that had been held since I moved in. The most recent school board election was different, however. I hated the candidates. Everything I saw, heard, and read caused me to distrust their motives, suspect their honesty, and question their competence. The campaign was generally referred to as an attempt to determine the lesser of two evils. I was disgusted, as I believe that voting should be a matter of making a positive choice for a candidate, not being forced to choose between ineptness and idiocy. I chose, once again, not to vote. And when I was asked by anyone—friend, neighbor, or candidate—where my vote would be going, I explained that it would be staying home with me, and I explained why. Sometimes, the action of not voting is a stronger political move than voting is.

The right not to vote is as important as the right to vote. Properly thought out, in situations where it is logically seen to be the best possible option instead of the easy way out of an important responsibility, it can be a way of avoiding casting an ill-informed vote or a way of preserving one's personal integrity and making one's opinions known when faced with a bad slate of candidates.

FOR WRITING OR DISCUSSION

1. Of the two examples of deciding not to vote, which strikes you as more justified? Explain.
2. Does the writer try to consider possible arguments against her position? Are there reasonable and effective arguments that she does not consider? Explain your answer.

Margin notes:

Summary of main point of paragraph: forceful closing

Good phrase: "ineptness and idiocy"

Effective figurative expression: "staying home with me"

Conclusion: when not voting is justified and when not voting is unjustified

Cause and effect: writer explains why she didn't vote

4
"The second time . . .": transition helps achieve unity and coherence by linking topic sentence to previous paragraph

Illustration: another example of when the writer didn't vote, followed by cause and effect analysis

5
Strong transition: connects final paragraph with last sentence of paragraph 4

3. What other situations in addition to those mentioned might support the idea that not voting could be the correct decision?
4. Think of a current or recent candidate or proposed law and write an argumentation paper expressing your support or opposition.

Dennis Rivas
Books Are Not More Valuable than Other Art

1   To some, ours is a lost generation. Television, films, video games and the proliferation of the Internet have herded us all away from the most sacred of entertainment and art forms: the book. Much has been said about this generation's lack of reading. Supposedly this generation is wasting away in front of the television or computer screen, instead of in front of the pages of a nice, thick book. These accusations led me to ask where this veneration of the book came from. In my eyes, it is simply a vehicle for disseminating knowledge just like any other, no better, no worse. The quality of what is written is dictated only by the author. The same applies for movies and television and the various visual media that our technological advances have brought.

2   I am curious why books have been held in such high regard over other media and why so much controversy exists over the fact that this generation reads very little. There are dozens of venues that creative individuals can use to express themselves. The bookish elite don't seem to realize this, so they close their minds and remain aloof. I think I know why this may be the case: simple nostalgia. Perhaps when these individuals were young, they may have read a great piece of literature, let's say *The Adventures of Tom Sawyer*, and it opened their eyes. They instantly became enamored with books. This is a situation many of us can relate to, yearning for the good old days. Nothing in the present ever seems as good as it once was. Ask any book lover why he loves books. He will most likely describe very colorful tales of great stories from the past and how they have influenced life since.

This type of nostalgia is fine. I have nothing against literature and those who enjoy it. But as soon as this person steps on to his high horse and looks down upon those who aren't quite as well-read as he is, there is a problem. Yearning for the good old days can be a problem in a society where technology is ever advancing. The old establishments of self-expression are being replaced. Books, being a part of the old establishment, are becoming obsolete, and for those replete with nostalgia for their favorite tomes, this is unsettling. Those clinging on to the past may not realize that more avenues of artistic self-expression mean greater richness in the types of stories one can tell. This doesn't mean one venue is better than another, it just means one story may be better told in a book and another in film and so on. The story should dictate the medium and not the other way around.

Books and film, among other media, can accomplish much of the same goals depending on how skillful the author is at expressing his vision. Despite this there is a common argument that books can stimulate the imagination in a way visual media never could. The logic is that you only have the words to go on, and so everything visualized is completely fabricated by the mind. However, it is fabricated according to the author's control. The author sets the parameters of what can be imagined. So nothing is completely freely imagined. Just as in film, there remains strict authorial control. We are lead down a path that the author has predetermined. But this, of course, is the point. The author is sharing with us a particular vision. He doesn't want us to deviate from the original story created, as it was created for a purpose.

To that extent, whether the author's chosen medium is a book or a film or a video game is irrelevant. Our imaginative freedom will always be limited when we experience someone else's tale. It has to be in order for the story to be successful. Imagination can still be stimulated by the various media in equally fulfilling ways, but the means for accomplishing this are still different.

There is also criticism of the business side of visual media. In essence, a few conglomerates own all broadcast stations and movie studios. As a result there is little diversity in the content these companies produce, and so we should turn to the written word for salvation. But one must keep in mind that publishing books is also a business, a business not unlike the entertainment industry in its homogeneity of corporations. A handful of publishing houses publish all books in the U.S. Suspicions of too much censorship and corporate control in the entertainment industry could also be extended to the publishing world. The corporations dominating that sector also want to maximize profits and have no problem pandering to the lowest common denominator to do it. Both the entertainment and publishing industries are falling victim to the same problem. No one is better than the other in this regard.

7   Whether you are a book lover, film buff or a video game geek, an important thing to keep in mind is that all these mediums, along with other storytelling and informative media, have the same goal, but they try to accomplish it in different ways. Such diversity is essential in breaking up the monotony of an all-printed or all-cinematic world. Rather than deriding the various media, we should try to appreciate and cultivate the different strengths they bring to the table and the way they enrich the human experience.

FOR WRITING OR DISCUSSION

1. What is the writer's thesis? How does the title reflect it?
2. How accurate is the writer's defense of other media and their ability to "accomplish much of the same goals" as books?
3. Why does the writer use a business-related argument in the essay? How does it contribute to his point?
4. Write an essay called "Books *Are* More Valuable than Other Art" in which you argue the opposite point from Rivas'.

Students Writing: Perspectives on Immigrants in America

In these student essays—editorial columns from different college newspapers—the writers examine immigration issues in America. Answer the questions that follow.

Nick Milano

Citizenship for Christmas

As the Christmas season arrives, stockpiles at food pantries fill up and help at shelters   1
peaks; this time of the year really encourages people to treat others with sincere kindness. In
this spirit, the debate on illegal immigration should be given a second look. From the
moment Columbus stepped onto the shores of Hispaniola to this present day, the Americas,
with the United States as no exception to the rule, have been marred by years of slavery,
manipulation and racism.

The blatant exploitation of Native Americans went hand in hand with the importation of   2
African slaves. The Civil War was followed by more wars with Native Americans and Jim Crow
ruled segregation. The human rights issue that plagues our generation is the treatment of
illegal immigrants. Republicans on the national presidential stage and all across the country
are calling for the construction of a magnificent wall across the border. Debates have seen
other, more peculiar stances taken on the issue.

Mitt Romney and Rudy Giuliani take extreme measures to prove they each treated   3
illegal immigrants worse than the other. But Romney continued to hire a landscaping
company that was caught employing illegal immigrants while he was the governor of
Massachusetts. For a man so gung-ho on tossing illegal immigrants out of the country,
he was reluctant to double check on the men working on his own home. As with a
multitude of other political positions Romney likes to take, it seems he only does so for
the political gains.

Presidential candidate Tom Tancredo has led the charge against illegal immigration with   4
tirades against the refusal of the people to learn English. In the Republican CNN/You Tube
Debate, he refused to even allow for guest workers to come in and help small business
owners who rely on their cheap labor. He claimed that there are plenty of Americans who
would do the work, but for higher wages.

His is a common argument: the illegals are here to steal our jobs! But really, look at   5
the situation logically. There are simple reasons we pay less than two dollars a pound at

the grocery store for apples, bananas, oranges and other fruit and vegetables. The person picking the food is not making minimum wage. He does not have the right to limit himself to a humane 40-hour work week. He does not receive healthcare benefits. He most certainly is not going to collect social security nor retirement benefits from his employer. They sacrifice a great deal, the least of which is their back from the strenuous labor of unskilled jobs.

6   Are they really taking jobs Americans would willingly work?

7   Lost in all the debate over who would treat illegal immigrants the worst is the fact that they are very real people. Granted, they have broken the law by coming to the United States. But for the most part these people embarked on a ruthless journey to the United States in the hopes of giving their children a better shot at life. No doubt there are some who harmed the image of the group as a whole by committing violent crimes or joining gangs like MS-13. Every population has a group who breaks laws and engages in criminal behavior. But just because some Italians may be in La Cosa Nostra, not all Italians engage in bookmaking and drug running.

8   Illegal immigrants who commit violent crimes upon their arrival here should be deported without a second thought. Those who get caught driving drunk should be deported. Those who get caught running with gangs should be sent home. These are simple straightforward guidelines, but it is just too much to stomach when politicians dismiss illegal immigrants merely because they are seeking a new life.

9   It is the Christmas season, a time for reflection on how to better treat people coming here in pursuit of the American Dream. As Mike Huckabee has mentioned time and time again, the United States has a poor history when it comes to human rights and "we're a better country than" one that punishes children. He has made mention of his fear that there are people who want to treat these people poorly because they are different, for racist reasons.

10   The politicians hoping to lead this country into the future better take a step back and consider the motivations for the animosity towards these migrant people merely trying to

better their lives. Is it really because they broke a law by coming to the United States? Can we really blame them for wanting to become part of this great country? The borders must be made secure, but the nation must also embark on a journey towards granting amnesty and citizenship. The United States has a chance to prove it is not a racist country. Let us not allow history to repeat itself yet again. Immigrants leave dire circumstances in the search of a more hopeful future. Who in their shoes would not sacrifice so much for the betterment of their children's lives?

Dan Cunningham

Illegal Immigrants Don't Deserve a License

There is some division on the concept of allowing illegal immigrants to receive driver's licenses. The sub-parties on each side can be classified in one of two groups; idiots and everyone else. Hillary Clinton proudly displayed her ability to not pick a side during one of the primary debates, making her the only common ground between the two groups. Perhaps this stands as common sense, but providing licenses to illegal immigrants is an ineffective safety policy, it is offensive to lower class workers, and it detracts from debates on legitimate immigration policies.

When a citizen passes a driver's exam, he or she is provided with a plastic card with the person's photo on it. There's no magic fairy dust bestowing a better driving ability—just a card. Illegal immigrants that get pulled over for speeding or reckless driving have a lot more to worry about other than not having a license. In fact, all an illegal alien needs is $500 to pay off the charge at the time of being pulled over and he can drive off to break the law even more. In the end, the only safety an immigrant receives from having a license is the ability to act like a citizen in the face of a police officer.

3   Of all policies to help liberalize immigration in the United States, a driver's license is the least significant or effective. A license contains a number, a picture, a name and an address. While immigrants may be absolutely fine with the first three, an address is the most important and incriminating. Any illegal immigrant with half a brain understands that—in the eyes of federal law—they are not wanted. If you live in a country that will cast you away if they find you, there is no reason you would submit accurate data, if any at all, on your whereabouts to any level of government. Then again, if they are foolish enough to submit an accurate address to the DMV, maybe the Republicans are right on trying to send back this generation's wave of illegal immigrants.

4   Consider what a driver's license for illegal immigrants says to the poorest classes of society. This license would be conferred to a group of people who live outside of both the costs and benefits of the government. Illegals do not pay income taxes, they receive free medical care because they are untraceable citizens, and their children can have a free education thanks to the local tax dollars of the working citizens and federal law. This creates a class of citizens that, after factoring in benefits, lives a substantially wealthier life than the lowest quintile of workers. All they have to do to stay that way is not get arrested. To give a license to this group is to validate the support of a black market class on the backs of the hard working taxpayers beneath them. Legitimate policies can deal with the actual problems that illegal immigration causes. The group subverts the government by not having an enforceable tax code and is granted benefits that everyone receives as a result of the Entitlement Era. So, a new policy correcting either of these problems would be optimal in society. There are at least two extreme options that could be considered. The first would be to hire more border patrol and build thicker fences. However, if people want to enter the country badly enough, physical barriers will not stop them. Building walls and fortifying borders are implicitly flawed and will inevitably fail as immigration policy.

5   The second option is to make all of the illegal immigrants into citizens and then enforce the law. This is a simple and favorable concept, but the conservatives seem to feel that this is incredibly dangerous. This would be ironic, seeing as how the current generation's immigrants are

primarily Catholic and voting more conservatively in elections. In fact, in the 2004 election, President Bush received far more support from the Hispanic community than he had four years prior. The onset of a more conservative Hispanic population is strongly correlated to the voter turnout of new immigrants. Even more ironic is the fact that the Democrats are pushing an immigration policy that undermines their long-run success in elections.

Both attrition from immigration and open admittance are extreme long-run goals in policy. Seeing as how those two options are unacceptable to the far left and right, there is a need for a policy that indirectly affects illegal immigrants. The poor need a policy that will put them, economically, on a level plain with those who are here illegally. A driver's license for illegal immigrants serves as a direct statement to the poor that their needs for a better life are less important than those of someone who is not a citizen. Those who supported any policy that would give a license to illegal immigrants should be ashamed of themselves for putting the needs of the black market above the needs of the lower class.

6

Quynh Nguyen
Being a Recent American

My mother, father and older siblings were all born in Vietnam and fled our homeland to the safety of U.S. soil. They were running away from mass murder, starvation and a Communist regime hell-bent on crushing those who opposed them. I'm the first in my family to be born in the United States, so the first and foremost thing my family taught me was to be grateful to be here.

1

All my life I have been told of the hardships of living in Vietnam—that I was lucky to have free education, health care, flushing toilets and running water. Every quarter I have

2

spent playing an arcade game has been tempered with the knowledge that "25 cents could buy an entire bushel of cabbages in Vietnam that would feed a family for two weeks."

3   Imagine growing up feeling guilty for being so darn lucky, so spoiled with the finest amenities the likes of which your ancestors had never imagined. Then try reconciling that guilt with the drive to accomplish great things in college in order to make money to send home and spare family members from poverty.

4   Those expectations make going to college much more complicated than simply finding the major you love. It makes every selfish decision in college, any spare moment spent having fun, every poor grade feel like a wound to the family.

5   It's a common theme I see across students of all ethnicities who come to college—study hard, get a degree and make life better for your family and community. In spite of how pervasive that drive is, I never see this reflected in mainstream college culture. That lack of visibility makes it much harder to talk about the frustrations of reconciling family expectations with personal desires.

6   When we express that frustration, recent-American students like me are encouraged to be "more American." That means dropping the heavy burden of familial expectations and pursuing our personal, most selfish dreams.

7   Our non-immigrant peers have a hard time understanding the nature of self-sacrifice and familial dedication that is the backbone of our upbringing. They also struggle with the idea of ethnic student associations—why the need for ethnic student associations if we're all American and having a White Student Union would be taboo?

8   I have found it difficult to accommodate my culture and background with my identity as an American. In spite of the United States' long history with immigration, U.S. culture has not found a way to embrace other cultures and welcome them into the fold. It is as if maintaining one's ethnicity is inherently un-American, and to forget it completely is the rite of initiation to Americanness.

9   The way I see it, everyone can benefit from the immigration experience, even the mainstream culture. My family has benefited greatly from adopting American values to replace some Vietnamese ones, i.e., feminism and that beating women and children is not OK. I think mainstream U.S. culture could benefit from learning things that my

culture has to offer, like the fact that we Americans are probably the luckiest people on the planet.

I'm grateful, as all of us recent-Americans are, to be here and to experience the freedoms and the rich culture that the United States has to offer. I hope mainstream U.S. culture learns to cherish its immigrants and what we bring to the table (beyond our delicious cuisine).

10

FOR WRITING OR DISCUSSION

1. What is Milano's thesis? Cunningham's? How does Nguyen's thesis add a personal dimension to the topic?

2. Which writer convinces you most on the strength of the writing? How does the writer accomplish this goal? Which details do you find most compelling?

3. On the issues, has Milano convinced you that illegal immigrants are treated badly? Why or why not? How does the word "Christmas" used in the title and the essay strike you?

4. Milano refers to a number of political figures in his essay. Who are they?

5. Has Cunningham convinced you of his argument about immigrants and driver's licenses? Why or why not? What recommendations does he make for addressing the problem? Where in the essay does he indicate any opposing arguments?

6. How does Nguyen accommodate her status as an American and her family's status as Vietnam immigrants? Do you agree with her argument that our "culture has not found a way to embrace other cultures and welcome them into the fold"? How does the writer support this assertion? Which details help you understand her point?

7. Select some aspect of the immigration issue in the United States and write an argumentation essay about it. You may draw on your own experience, your readings, your research, or even on some of the points made in these essays.

Models for Writing

The selections that follow are solid examples of argumentative writing. Drawn from popular periodicals, the pieces demonstrate argumentative writing on serious public issues.

MICHAEL E. LEVIN
The Case for Torture

1   It is generally assumed that torture is impermissible, a throwback to a more brutal age. Enlightened societies reject it outright, and regimes suspected of using it risk the wrath of the United States.

2   I believe this attitude is unwise. There are situations in which torture is not merely permissible but morally mandatory. Moreover, these situations are moving from the realm of imagination to fact.

3   Suppose a terrorist has hidden an atomic bomb on Manhattan Island which will detonate at noon on July 4 unless . . . (here follow the usual demands for money and release of his friends from jail). Suppose, further, that he is caught at 10 a.m. of the fateful day, but—preferring death to failure—won't disclose where the bomb is. What do we do? If we follow due process—wait for his lawyer, arraign him—millions of people will die. If the only way to save those lives is to subject the terrorist to the most excruciating possible pain, what grounds can there be for not doing so? I suggest there are none. In any case, I ask you to face the question with an open mind.

4   Torturing the terrorist is unconstitutional? Probably. But millions of lives surely outweigh constitutionality. Torture is barbaric? Mass murder is far more barbaric. Indeed, letting millions of innocents die in deference to one who flaunts his guilt is moral cowardice, an unwillingness to dirty one's hands. If *you* caught the terrorist, could you sleep nights knowing that millions died because you couldn't bring yourself to apply the electrodes?

5   Once you concede that torture is justified in extreme cases, you have admitted that the decision to use torture is a matter of balancing innocent lives against the means needed to save them. You must now face more realistic cases involving more modest numbers. Someone plants a bomb on a jumbo jet. He alone can disarm it, and his demands cannot be met (or if they can, we refuse to set a precedent by yielding to his threats). Surely we can, we must, do anything to the extortionist to save the passengers. How can we tell 300, or 100, or 10 people who never asked to be put in danger, "I'm sorry, you'll have to die in agony, we just couldn't bring ourselves to. . . ."

6   Here are the results of an informal poll about a third, hypothetical, case. Suppose a terrorist group kidnapped a newborn baby from a hospital. I asked four mothers if they would approve of torturing kidnappers if that were necessary to get their own newborns back. All said yes, the most "liberal" adding that she would administer it herself.

7   I am not advocating torture as punishment. Punishment is addressed to deeds irrevocably past. Rather, I am advocating torture as an acceptable measure for preventing future evils. So understood, it is far less objectionable than many extant punishments. Opponents of the death penalty, for example, are forever insisting that executing a murderer will not bring back his victim (as if the purpose of capital punishment were supposed to be resurrection, not deterrence or retribution). But torture, in the cases described, is intended not to

bring anyone back but to keep innocents from being dispatched. The most powerful argument against using torture as a punishment or to secure confessions is that such practices disregard the rights of the individual. Well, if the individual is all that important—and he is—it is correspondingly important to protect the rights of individuals threatened by terrorists. If life is so valuable that it must never be taken, the lives of the innocents must be saved even at the price of hurting the one who endangers them.

Better precedents for torture are assassination and preemptive attack. No Allied leader would have flinched at assassinating Hitler, had that been possible. (The Allies did assassinate Heydrich.) Americans would be angered to learn that Roosevelt could have had Hitler killed in 1943—thereby shortening the war and saving millions of lives—but refused on moral grounds. Similarly, if nation A learns that nation B is about to launch an unprovoked attack, A has a right to save itself by destroying B's military capability first. In the same way, if the police can by torture save those who would otherwise die at the hands of kidnappers or terrorists, they must.   8

There is an important difference between terrorists and their victims that should mute talk of the terrorists' "rights." The terrorist's victims are at risk unintentionally, not having asked to be endangered. But the terrorist knowingly initiated his actions. Unlike his victims, he volunteered for the risks of his deed. By threatening to kill for profit or idealism, he renounces civilized standards, and he can have no complaint if civilization tries to thwart him by whatever means necessary.   9

Just as torture is justified only to save lives (not extort confessions or recantations), it is justifiably administered only to those *known* to hold innocent lives in their hands. Ah, but how can the authorities ever be sure they have the right malefactor? Isn't there a danger of error and abuse? Won't We turn into Them?   10

Questions like these are disingenuous in a world in which terrorists proclaim themselves and perform for television. The name of their game is public recognition. After all, you can't very well intimidate a government into releasing your freedom fighters unless you announce that it is your group that has seized its embassy. "Clear guilt" is difficult to define, but when 40 million people see a group of masked gunmen seize an airplane on the evening news, there is not much question about who the perpetrators are. There will be hard cases where the situation is murkier. Nonetheless, a line demarcating the legitimate use of torture can be drawn. Torture only the obviously guilty, and only for the sake of saving innocents, and the line between Us and Them will remain clear.   11

There is little danger that the Western democracies will lose their way if they choose to inflict pain as one way of preserving order. Paralysis in the face of evil is the greater danger. Some day soon a terrorist will threaten tens of thousands of lives, and torture will be the only way to save them. We had better start thinking about this.   12

FOR WRITING OR DISCUSSION

1. According to Levin, torture is permissible only in special circumstances. What are those circumstances? In such special circumstances, the author maintains that torture is "not merely permissible but morally mandatory." Explain the difference.

2. The author uses only three major examples to support his thesis. Would the thesis be more convincing with more examples?

3. What principle determines the order in which the three examples are presented?

4. In what ways has Levin influenced your views of torture? Although he wrote this piece long before the fateful attack on New York's World Trade Center on September 11, 2001, how might the events of that day influence people's thinking on the uses of torture? Could Levin's position get out of hand? How?

5. Choose something you would like to see done away with, and write an argumentation paper advocating its legal banning. Some possible topics are cigarettes, alcohol, divorce, *F* grades, seat-belt requirements, and professional boxing.

6. Write an essay called "The Case Against Torture."

JAMES Q. WILSON

Just Take Away Their Guns

1   The President wants still tougher gun control legislation and thinks it will work. The public supports more gun control laws but suspects they won't work. The public is right.

2   Legal restraints on the lawful purchase of guns will have little effect on the illegal use of guns. There are some 200 million guns in private ownership, about one-third of them handguns. Only about 2 percent of the latter are employed to commit crimes. It would take a Draconian, and politically impossible, confiscation of legally purchased guns to make much of a difference in the number used by criminals. Moreover, only about one-sixth of the handguns used by serious criminals are purchased from a gun shop or pawnshop. Most of these handguns are stolen, borrowed, or obtained through private purchases that wouldn't be affected by gun laws.

3   What is worse, any successful effort to shrink the stock of legally purchased guns (or of ammunition) would reduce the capacity of law-abiding people to defend themselves. Gun control advocates scoff at the importance of self-defense, but they are wrong to do so. Based on a household survey, Gary Kleck, a criminologist at Florida State University, has estimated that every year, guns are used—that is, displayed or fired—for defensive purposes more than a million times, not counting their use by the police. If his estimate is correct, this means that the number of people who defend themselves with a gun exceeds the number of arrests for violent crimes and burglaries.

Our goal should not be the disarming of law-abiding citizens. It should be to reduce the number of people who carry guns unlawfully, especially in places—on streets, in taverns—where the mere presence of a gun can increase the hazards we all face. The most effective way to reduce illegal gun-carrying is to encourage the police to take guns away from people who carry them without a permit. This means encouraging the police to make street frisks.

4

The Fourth Amendment to the Constitution bans "unreasonable searches and seizures." In 1968 the Supreme Court decided (*Terry* v. *Ohio*) that a frisk—patting down a person's outer clothing—is proper if the officer has a "reasonable suspicion" that the person is armed and dangerous. If a pat-down reveals an object that might be a gun, the officer can enter the suspect's pocket to remove it. If the gun is being carried illegally, the suspect can be arrested.

5

The reasonable-suspicion test is much less stringent than the probable-cause standard the police must meet in order to make an arrest. A reasonable suspicion, however, is more than just a hunch; it must be supported by specific facts. The courts have held, not always consistently, that these facts include someone acting in a way that leads an experienced officer to conclude criminal activity may be afoot; someone fleeing at the approach of an officer; a person who fits a drug courier profile; a motorist stopped for a traffic violation who has a suspicious bulge in his pocket; a suspect identified by a reliable informant as carrying a gun. The Supreme Court has also upheld frisking people on probation or parole.

6

Some police departments frisk a lot of people, but usually the police frisk rather few, at least for the purpose of detecting illegal guns. In 1992 the police arrested about 240,000 people for illegally possessing or carrying a weapon. This is only about one-fourth as many as were arrested for public drunkenness. The average police officer will make *no* weapons arrests and confiscate *no* guns during any given year. Mark Moore, a professor of public policy at Harvard University, found that most weapons arrests were made because a citizen complained, not because the police were out looking for guns.

7

It is easy to see why. Many cities suffer from a shortage of officers, and even those with ample law-enforcement personnel worry about having their cases thrown out for constitutional reasons or being accused of police harassment. But the risk of violating the Constitution or engaging in actual, as opposed to perceived, harassment can be substantially reduced.

8

Each patrol officer can be given a list of people on probation or parole who live on that officer's beat and be rewarded for making frequent stops to insure that they are not carrying guns. Officers can be trained to recognize the kinds of actions that the Court will accept as providing the "reasonable suspicion" necessary for a stop and frisk. Membership in a gang known for assaults and drug dealing could be made the basis, by statute or Court precedent, for gun frisks.

9

The available evidence supports the claim that self-defense is a legitimate form of deterrence. People who report to the National Crime Survey that they defended themselves with a weapon were less likely to lose property in a robbery or be injured in an assault than those who did not defend themselves. Statistics have shown that would-be burglars are threatened by gun-wielding victims about as many times a year as they are arrested (and much more

10

often than they are sent to prison) and that the chances of a burglar being shot are about the same as his chances of going to jail. Criminals know these facts even if gun control advocates do not and so are less likely to burgle occupied homes in America than occupied ones in Europe, where the residents rarely have guns.

11   Some gun control advocates may concede these points but rejoin that the cost of self-defense is self-injury: Handgun owners are more likely to shoot themselves or their loved ones than a criminal. Not quite. Most gun accidents involve rifles and shotguns, not handguns. Moreover, the rate of fatal gun accidents has been declining while the level of gun ownership has been rising. There are fatal gun accidents just as there are fatal car accidents, but in fewer than 2 percent of the gun fatalities was the victim someone mistaken for an intruder.

12   Those who urge us to forbid or severely restrict the sale of guns ignore these facts. Worse, they adopt a position that is politically absurd. In effect, they say, "Your government, having failed to protect your person and your property from criminal assault, now intends to deprive you of the opportunity to protect yourself."

13   Opponents of gun control make a different mistake. The National Rifle Association and its allies tell us that "guns don't kill, people kill" and urge the Government to punish more severely people who use guns to commit crimes. Locking up criminals does protect society from future crimes, and the prospect of being locked up may deter criminals. But our experience with meting out tougher sentences is mixed. The tougher the prospective sentence the less likely it is to be imposed, or at least to be imposed swiftly. If the Legislature adds on time for crimes committed with a gun, prosecutors often bargain away the add-ons; even when they do not, the judges in many states are reluctant to impose add-ons.

14   Worse, the presence of a gun can contribute to the magnitude of the crime even on the part of those who worry about serving a long prison sentence. Many criminals carry guns not to rob stores but to protect themselves from other armed criminals. Gang violence has become more threatening to bystanders as gang members have begun to arm themselves. People may commit crimes, but guns make some crimes worse. Guns often convert spontaneous outbursts of anger into fatal encounters. When some people carry them on the streets, others will want to carry them to protect themselves, and an urban arms race will be underway.

15   And modern science can be enlisted to help. Metal detectors at airports have reduced the number of airplane bombings and skyjackings to nearly zero. But these detectors only work at very close range. What is needed is a device that will enable the police to detect the presence of a large lump of metal in someone's pocket from a distance of ten or fifteen feet. Receiving such a signal could supply the officer with reasonable grounds for a pat-down. Underemployed nuclear physicists and electronics engineers in the post-cold-war era surely have the talents for designing a better gun detector.

16   Even if we do all these things, there will still be complaints. Innocent people will be stopped. Young black and Hispanic men will probably be stopped more often than older white Anglo males or women of any race. But if we are serious about reducing drive-by shootings, fatal gang wars and lethal quarrels in public places, we must get illegal guns off

the street. We cannot do this by multiplying the forms one fills out at gun shops or by pretending that guns are not a problem until a criminal uses one.

FOR WRITING OR DISCUSSION

1. What is the thesis of Wilson's essay? Where does he state it most directly?

2. What advantage does Wilson see in the police's using the "reasonable-suspicion test" over the "probable-cause standard"?

3. Why does Wilson support the value of self-defense with weapons? What arguments does he provide in opposition to his own point? Why does he use this strategy of presenting opposing arguments?

4. Write an argumentation essay in which you present your own views on gun control and the right to self-defense with weapons. Support your points with evidence drawn from your own experience or from what you have read or heard as part of this ongoing discussion in American society. Make no empty claims: Support your points with clear reasons for your assertions.

MEG GREENFIELD

In Defense of the Animals

I might as well come right out with it: Contrary to some of my most cherished prejudices, the animal-rights people have begun to get to me. I think that in some part of what they say they are right.

I never thought it would come to this. As distinct from the old-style animal rescue, protection, and shelter organizations, the more aggressive newcomers, with their "liberation" of laboratory animals and periodic championship of the claims of animal well-being over human well-being when a choice must be made, have earned a reputation in the world I live in as fanatics and just plain kooks. And even with my own recently (relatively) raised consciousness, there remains a good deal in both their critique and their prescription for the virtuous life that I reject, being not just a practicing carnivore, a wearer of shoe leather, and so forth, but also a supporter of certain indisputably agonizing procedures visited upon innocent animals in the furtherance of human welfare, especially experiments undertaken to improve human health.

So, viewed from the pure position, I am probably only marginally better than the worst of my kind, if that: I don't buy the complete "speciesist" analysis or even the fundamental language of animal "rights" and continue to find a large part of what is done in the name of that cause harmful and extreme. But I also think, patronizing as it must sound, that the zealots are required early on in any movement if it is to succeed in altering the sensibility of the leaden masses, such as me. Eventually they get your attention. And eventually you at least feel obliged to weigh their arguments and think about whether there may not be something there.

4   It is true that this end has often been achieved—as in my case—by means of vivid, cringe-inducing photographs, not by an appeal to reason or values so much as by an assault on squeamishness. From the famous 1970s photo of the newly skinned baby seal to the videos of animals being raised in the most dark, miserable, stunting environment as they are readied for their life's sole fulfillment as frozen patties and cutlets, these sights have had their effect. But we live in a world where the animal protein we eat comes discreetly pre-butchered and prepacked so the original beast and his slaughtering are remote from our consideration, just as our furs come on coat hangers in salons, not on their original propri-etors; and I see nothing wrong with our having to contemplate the often unsettling reality of how we came by the animal products we make use of. Then we can choose what we want to do.

5   The objection to our being confronted with these dramatic, disturbing pictures is first that they tend to provoke a misplaced, uncritical, and highly emotional concern for animal life at the direct expense of a more suitable concern for human suffering. What goes into the animals' account, the reasoning goes, necessarily comes out of ours. But I think it is possible to remain stalwart in your view that the human claim comes first and in your acceptance of the use of ani-mals for human betterment and *still* to believe that there are some human interests that should not take precedence. For we have become far too self-indulgent, hardened, careless, and cruel in the pain we routinely inflict upon these creatures for the most frivolous, unworthy purposes. And I also think that the more justifiable purposes, such as medical research, are shamelessly used as cover for other activities that are wanton.

6   For instance, not all of the painful and crippling experimentation that is undertaken in the lab is being conducted for the sake of medical knowledge or other purposes related to basic human well-being and health. Much of it is being conducted for the sake of super-refinements in the cosmetic and other frill industries, the noble goal being to contrive yet another fragrance or hair tint or commercially competitive variation on all the daft, fizzy, multicolored "personal care" products for the medicine cabinet and dressing table, a firmer-holding hair spray, that sort of thing. In other words, the conscripted, immobilized rabbits and other terrified creatures, who have been locked in boxes from the neck down, only their heads on view, are being sprayed in the eyes with different burning, stinging substances for the sake of adding to our already obscene store of luxuries and utterly super-fluous vanity items.

7   Oddly, we tend to be very sentimental about animals in their idealized, fictional form and largely indifferent to them in realms where our lives actually touch. From time immemorial, humans have romantically attributed to animals their own sensibilities—from Balaam's biblical ass who providently could speak and who got his owner out of harm's way right down to Lassie and the other Hollywood pups who would invariably tip off the good guys that the bad guys

were up to something. So we simulate phony cross-species kinship, pretty well drown in the cuteness of it all—Mickey and Minnie and Porky—and ignore, if we don't actually countenance, the brutish things done in the name of Almighty Hair Spray.

This strikes me as decadent. My problem is that it also causes me to reach a position that is, on its face, philosophically vulnerable, if not absurd—the muddled, middling, inconsistent place where finally you are saying it's all right to kill them for some purposes, but not to hurt them gratuitously in doing it or to make them suffer horribly for one's own trivial whims.   8

I would feel more humiliated to have fetched up on this exposed rock, if I didn't suspect I had so much company. When you see pictures of people laboriously trying to clean the Exxon gunk off of sea otters even knowing that they will only be able to help out a very few, you see this same outlook in action. And I think it *can* be defended. For to me the biggest cop-out is the one that says that if you don't buy the whole absolutist, extreme position it is pointless and even hypocritical to concern yourself with lesser mercies and ameliorations. The pressure of the animal-protection groups has already had some impact in improving the way various creatures are treated by researchers, trainers, and food producers. There is much more in this vein to be done. We are talking about rejecting wanton, pointless cruelty here. The position may be philosophically absurd, but the outcome is the right one.   9

FOR WRITING OR DISCUSSION

1. What is Greenfield's thesis?

2. The writer takes almost half the essay to support a key element in the opposing arguments to her own—that is, she defends the use of animals "in the furtherance of human welfare." Why does she give so much space to the other side of the argument? Does her strategy strengthen or weaken her essay? Explain your response.

3. How does she say she came to her new realization that "some human interests . . . should not take precedence" over animal claims? In what ways might you agree or disagree with her criticism of humans in paragraph 5?

4. How does she defend her unwillingness to support all the claims of animal protection groups?

5. Select a controversial topic—gun control, prayer in the schools, flag-burning, or abortion rights, for example—and write a convincing argumentative essay about how you can accept only partially the arguments on one side of the issue and reject the others.

HAVING YOUR SAY

What is your view of animal rights and experimentation for human benefit? Choose one side of the issue and support it with concrete detail. Be sure to address the opposition's point of view by refuting it, by rejecting it completely, or by accepting only certain elements in the opposition's argument.

Readings for Writing

Note how the visual presentation and the accompanying words make a subtle argument in this cartoon.

JIM BORGMAN
The 1812 Overture

© Reprinted with special permission of King Features Syndicate.

FOR WRITING OR DISCUSSION

1. What is the main point of this cartoon? If Borgman were to write a thesis sentence for it, what do you think the sentence would say?

2. What is the argument, then? Remember that we pointed out in the introduction to this chapter that arguments build on controversial subject matter. What is the controversial subject of this cartoon?

3. How has the cartoonist used humor to make a serious point?

4. Why does Borgman expand the visual scene only in the last frame of the cartoon?

Perspectives on the Death Penalty

In the selections following, you get a glimpse of the arguments in regard to both sides of the death penalty debate. An issue long in the headlines as a defining element of America's political and social policies, the death penalty continues to draw advocates and opponents with every generation. Many arguments are forthright, as in the student essays you will read by Lauren Heist and Alex Shalom, both published in the same student newspaper on the same day. Mark Essig, author of *Edison and the Electric Chair* (2004), looks at the options for executing prisoners on death row and provides a chilling portrait regardless of one's point of view. Finally, Robert Mankoff's cartoon "Good News" is a subtle yet powerful argument for his position.

Which of these selections make the best cases for or against the death penalty, do you think? And why do you think so?

Lauren Heist

Capital Punishment: An Example for Criminals

A child looks around to see if anyone is watching him. When he's sure that the kitchen is empty, he opens up the cookie jar and smuggles a cookie up to his room. When his mother confronts him about the missing cookie, she tells him taking cookies is not very nice and says if he does it again he will be in trouble. A little while later the child sees the cookie jar again. Not seeing anyone around, he again takes a cookie. The mother tells him taking cookies is wrong again but does not punish him. Soon the child learns that because he hasn't gotten in trouble, taking cookies must not be that bad. Because the mother did not follow through on her threat, the child begins to take advantage of the mother, and the child gets away with whatever he wants.

1

2	That is what has happened to our police force today. Criminals do not take the law seriously. They do not fear the government. Criminals are taking advantage of us, and they are getting away with murder, literally.

3	The bottom line is people need to respect the law. Without laws, we would live in anarchy. But too many people feel that they are above the law and it does not apply to them. Because people feel alienated from the bureaucrats who make the laws, they simply choose to ignore the laws.

4	If we want to live in a peaceful society, we must enforce the laws, and that includes using the death penalty. Every criminal who commits a first-degree murder should receive the death penalty. The problem with the way the death penalty is used now is not that it is used too often, but rather that it is not used enough.

5	How many muggers actually think, "Man, I hope I don't get the death penalty," before they decide to hold a gun to the head of a person getting money out of an ATM machine? I can assure you that is not a thought that often crosses their minds. The death penalty is only used in extreme cases for infamous psychopaths and serial killers. The average run-of-the-mill killer can get out of jail in no time flat. If the death penalty were employed more frequently, killers might actually take it into consideration before shooting someone.

6	The most common argument against the death penalty is that it is hypocritical. Critics ask, how can we claim that murder is wrong and then kill the killer? What most critics do not understand is that governments do not live by the same rules that individual people live by. Governments have powers that people do not have because people concede power to the government.

7	For example, governments have the power to confiscate houses by eminent domain if they are in the way of a road that is going to be built. An individual citizen cannot arbitrarily destroy a house or confiscate property, but governments can do these things because people entrust the government to act in the best interest of the majority of its citizens. The government has the right to use the death penalty because it has a responsibility to keep order in the society.

The other argument that people use to oppose the death penalty is that there is always a chance that an innocent person could be executed because the justice system is not perfect. Yes, it is true that the justice system is not entirely foolproof. Nothing is entirely foolproof. The founding fathers tried to ensure that the justice system would be fair by requiring all murder cases to be decided by a jury. People must have faith that their own peers will make fair, logical decisions. In addition, just as critics of the death penalty fear that innocent people might be executed, there is also the possibility that criminals will be set free and will endanger other innocent people. 8

Claiming insanity is no excuse for sparing someone from the death penalty. A murderer is a murderer, no matter who commits it or what mental state they claim to be in at the time. Milwaukee's Jeffrey Dahmer, who killed multiple victims and even admitted to practicing cannibalism, was not sentenced to the death penalty. Instead, he was sentenced to life imprisonment and was killed by a fellow inmate. Why was Dahmer not given the death penalty? Because he was determined to be insane. Susan Smith, the mother who drowned her two young sons in a car, also received life imprisonment instead of the death penalty because she pleaded temporary insanity. People who are clearly guilty of murder should be made examples. If Jeffrey Dahmer and Susan Smith do not receive the death penalty, why would any person ever have to fear the death penalty? 9

Finally, the death penalty should be used more often than it is today because it is economical. Keeping someone in a jail cell for years requires that taxpayers pay for that criminal's food and shelter for the rest of the criminal's life, while he takes up a space that could be used by another criminal. Every day, guilty criminals leave the courthouse and head back out onto the street because the prisons and jails are overcrowded. Meanwhile, 10 other criminals sit on death row, eating up the taxpayers' money and not contributing anything to society.

11   If we want to take this country back from the mobsters and the drug lords and put the power back in the people and the police, we need to use the death penalty. Using the death penalty will not only be economical for all taxpayers, but it will also deter future criminals from killing, which will make us all safer.

Alex Shalom

Abolish the Death Penalty

1   When a convicted murderer's head burst into flames in Florida's electric chair a few weeks ago, reactions varied. The state's Attorney General boasted that, due to problems with the lethal contraption, murderers should be particularly wary if they commit their crimes in Florida because they will suffer greatly before their lives are terminated by the state. Others reacted with disgust and concluded that the United States should abolish the death penalty. The latter is the appropriate response.

2   The U.S. would hardly be breaking ground by abolishing the death penalty. None of the nations of Western Europe practice capital punishment, nor do most of our Latin American neighbors. The reasons for the abolition of the death penalty are many; there are reasons why capital punishment is inherently unjust and there are also reasons why the death penalty, as practiced in the United States, is especially so. I will briefly address both of these categories of reasons. First, however, it will be useful to examine the problems with common justifications for state-sponsored killing.

3   Death penalty proponents generally extend support for capital punishment from both moral and practical perspectives. The pragmatic capital punishment advocates contend that the death penalty deters murder and that it costs less than keeping murderers incarcerated.

The appropriate question, however, should not be whether or not the death penalty deters murder; surely it does. Rather, we should ask whether the death penalty deters murder better than life imprisonment, for no death penalty opponent advocates letting murderers walk free on the street.

Levels of deterrence are difficult to measure, but there are some ways to do so. If one examines the states of Michigan and Illinois—two states with very similar population, land, and demographic make-ups—one discovers something very interesting. Michigan has not executed anyone since it became a state over 150 years ago, while Illinois has actively used the death penalty over the last 20 years. If the death penalty were, in fact, a better deterrent than life imprisonment, then Illinois should have a lower murder rate than Michigan. In reality, Michigan has a lower murder rate than its southwestern neighbor.   4

Though it is ridiculous to put a price on human life, some people argue that because prisons are too costly, murderers should be executed. This is a simplistic answer. While the actual cost of a lethal injection is clearly cheaper than the cost of a lengthy imprisonment, because death is the ultimate punishment, those facing the death penalty are always entitled to many legal appeals. Oftentimes, because those on death row are predominantly indigent, the state is forced to pay for both sides of the appeals process. When the cost of appeals is factored into the equation, it becomes evident that capital punishment is not a cost-effective solution.   5

All facts and figures aside, many people still attempt to justify the continued practice of capital punishment, arguing both that the punishment should fit the crime—that is, "an eye for an eye"—and that the families of the victims deserve the peace of mind of having the murderer killed. Coretta Scott King, who lost both a husband and a mother-in-law to assassination, offers an answer to both of these statements: "I stand firmly and unequivocally opposed to the death penalty for those convicted of capital offenses. An evil deed is not redeemed by an evil deed of retaliation. Justice is never advanced by the taking of a human life. Morality is never upheld by legalized murder."   6

7   In the United States, no crimes other than murder are met with punishments that imitate the crime; they are answered with punishments that fit the crime. The government does not burn the homes of arsonists, nor does it rape rapists. That simply would not make for a just penal system.

8   There is no reason, moral or practical, to support the death penalty; there are, however, several reasons why it should be abolished. Perhaps the best reason is that no system of justice is infallible. As long as a state practices capital punishment, there is always the possibility that an innocent person will be executed. A 1987 study published by the Stanford Law Review showed that, despite our elaborate appeals system, at least 23 innocent people have been executed in the United States in this century.

9   Colonial Massachusetts is possibly best known for the numerous executions of the innocent during the Salem Witch Trials. The judge in many of those cases, Judge Suel, eventually realized the error of his ways. He made a public statement saying that it was wrong to execute the people that he had sentenced to death. I hope no more judges are forced to come to the dreadful conclusion that they are responsible for the murder of an innocent person.

10   Even when the question of innocence does not loom over a judge's head, there are still factors that make the death penalty inequitable and cruelly administered. The death penalty is a racist institution that disproportionately kills the poor. African Americans receive the death penalty somewhat more often than whites. However, the real injustice of capital punishment is that blacks who kill whites are more likely to receive the death penalty than whites who kill blacks. A study presented in front of the Supreme Court showed that murderers whose victims are white are 139 percent more likely to receive the death penalty than if their victim was black. Though it is clearly not the case that the life of a white person is more valuable than that of a black person, this is what our current system of capital punishment is saying.

11   Murderers who are unable to afford to pay for their own defense are far more likely to be executed than those who can afford a lawyer. In Texas, 75 percent of convicted murderers who had court-appointed attorneys received the death penalty, while only 33

of those with private attorneys were killed. According to former Supreme Court Justice Thurgood Marshall, "the burden of capital punishment falls upon the poor, the ignorant, and the underprivileged members of society." This is simply unfair, particularly when lives are at stake.

While the United States does not stand alone in the international community in continuing to practice capital punishment, the other countries that practice it are far from world leaders in the area of human rights. Only five countries execute criminals who committed their crimes while under the age of 18: Yemen, Saudi Arabia, Iran, Pakistan, and the United States. Strange bedfellows, indeed. Much of the rest of the world has realized the inhumanity of capital punishment and abolished it. How many more people will die at the hands of the state before the United States follows suit?   12

MARK ESSIG

Continuing the Search For Kinder Executions

In Tennessee, it is a crime to euthanize a cat with pancuronium bromide, but this doesn't stop the state from using it to execute condemned criminals. Because the drug paralyzes muscles but does not affect nerves, it may leave its victims wide awake but immobilized as they painfully suffocate. So prisoners' advocates and medical experts are now trying to persuade Tennessee—and the nearly 30 other states that use the drug—to choose different poisons for lethal injection, thereby bringing euthanasia protocols for humans in line with those for domestic animals.   1

And so continues the uniquely American habit of tinkering with the machinery of death. For the past century and a half, America's capital punishment debate has resembled a strange game of leapfrog: opponents of the death penalty claim that the current method, whatever it may be, is barbaric, which prompts capital-punishment supporters to refine that method or develop a new one.   2

3   Although 19th-century Americans tended to believe that justice and order demanded the ultimate sanction, they were often shaken by graphic accounts of the pain suffered by hanged men. In 1876, after an especially gruesome hanging, Maine abolished capital punishment. Inspired by this victory, opponents of the death penalty began to emphasize the cruelty of the gallows. But their effort was self-defeating: by claiming that the problem with hanging was the suffering of the condemned, they simply challenged death penalty advocates to find a better way to kill.

4   First came adjustments to the gallows. Hangmen created a formula in which rope length was a function of the prisoner's weight—the heavier the victim, the shorter the drop. But such delicate calculations of anatomy and gravity often failed to add up and many prisoners slowly strangled to death. To dull the pain, Brooklyn officials in 1847 knocked a murderer cold with ether before hanging him, but this simply highlighted the deficiencies of the gallows.

5   Then, in 1889, New York State built the first electric chair, a device championed by Thomas Edison. Edison's advocacy was inspired in part by a wicked plan to hurt his business rival, George Westinghouse—the chair was powered by Westinghouse's alternating current, and Edison hoped consumers would begin to associate AC with danger and death. But Edison had less cynical reasons as well: he was an opponent of the death penalty—"an act of foolish barbarity," he called it—and he believed that electrocution would be less barbaric than the noose. Many others agreed, and eventually 25 states and the District of Columbia installed electric chairs.

6   Electrocution remained the state of the art for three decades, until the public grew dismayed by bungled executions that required several shocks or set the prisoner on fire. Before long there was another scientific option: an airtight chamber filled with poison gas. adopted by Nevada in 1924 and then by 10 more states in the coming decades. Like all complex machines, however, these execution devices were prone to malfunction, and prisoners suffered the consequences.

7   So in 1977 Oklahoma began to poison condemned prisoners with a three-drug cocktail: sodium thiopental (to produce unconsciousness), pancuronium bromide (to paralyze the muscles) and potassium chloride (to stop the heart). Promising a clean, painless death, this protocol quickly gained widespread acceptance.

8   Until now that is. The next step seems obvious: states will adopt a different drug regimen, which, no doubt, will soon gain critics of its own.

9   However, it seems that many death-penalty opponents are realizing that technological leapfrog is a game they can't win, and are opting out of the latest debate. Amnesty international has issued this statement: "The search for a 'humane' way of killing people should be seen for what it is—a search to make executions more palatable." In Nebraska, the only state with the electric chair as its sole method of execution, State Senator Ernie Chambers has vowed to fight any attempt to "make executions easier." He hopes that the United States Supreme Court will one day declare electrocution unconstitutional, leaving Nebraska without a valid execution law.

10   Some of the condemned themselves have even sought a more painful death in order to highlight the hypocrisy of "painless execution." In 2001, John Byrd, a convicted murderer in

Ohio, requested electrocution rather than the needle; when prison workers balked at using the chair, which had been idle for nearly 40 years, the Legislature abolished electrocution and forced Mr. Byrd to die by lethal injection. Earl Bramblett, a Virginia prisoner, had more success in his protest. "I'm not going to lay down on a gurney and have them stick a needle in my arm and make it look like an antiseptic execution," he said, and he died in the electric chair on April 9.

For too long, defenders of capital punishment, fearing that brutal killing methods might provoke public opposition, have found unwitting allies among their adversaries, anxious to relieve the suffering of the condemned. Now penalty opponents are realizing that scientific execution methods, ceaselessly refined, simply mask the barbarity of killing.   11

ROBERT MANKOFF
Good News

"*Good news. Your execution was overturned on appeal.*"

© The New Yorker Collection 1999 Robert Mankoff from cartoonbank.com. All rights reserved.

FOR WRITING OR DISCUSSION

1. What is the thesis of each student's paper? Where does Heist state the thesis most clearly? Shalom?

2. How does each student writer treat the issue of the economics of the death penalty? In what ways do the presentations on the issue deal with opposing points of view? Where else do the writers treat opposing points of view?

3. What is Essig's thesis in "Continuing the Search for Kinder Executions"? In what ways does his closing paragraph suggest a new course of action for opponents of the death penalty? Do you think that such a course would work in reducing the number of supporters?

4. How has Essig used illustration to good advantage in making his argument? Comparison? Which cases do you find most convincing, if any? Why?

5. How has Essig produced a dramatic impact in the last line of the introduction? How does a phrase like "machinery of death" in paragraph 2 affect you as a reader?

6. The death penalty is no laughing matter—yet cartoonist Mankoff has used humor to provide a powerful statement of his position. How does the caption of the cartoon define the artist's argument and his thesis, so to speak? What is the setting of the cartoon, and why is it important? Who is the speaker? How does Mankoff in few words summarize one of the major objections held by those opposing the death penalty? And how does humor contribute to the success of the argument?

7. Identify some other government practice—the taxation system, adoption laws, job protection, wildlife protection, affirmative action, to name just a few of many possibilities—and, after limiting your topic, write a well-reasoned argument, pro or con, that takes a firm position on the issue.

HAVING YOUR SAY

Consider the varied arguments in this section and write your own argumentative essay on the death penalty. You might read or reread George Orwell's essay "A Hanging" (pages 12–16) as another example of writing on capital punishment.

Perspectives on Same-Sex Marriage

In a 6–3 decision in 1996 the United States Supreme Court ruled in *Romer* v. *Evans* that a state government (in this case, Colorado) could not prevent localities from outlawing discrimination against homosexuals. In other words, the famous Equal Protection Clause in the Constitution now specifically covered citizens with gay or lesbian orientations.

In the decade since the Supreme Court decision, relations between same-sex partners have filled the news—and the courts. In particular, and as a result of *Romer* v. *Evans*, gay people and their supporters sought to legalize same-sex marriages. Only the state of Massachusetts, through its Supreme Judicial Court, has made gay marriages legal. In Vermont, same-sex couples have all the rights and benefits of marriage, but the state calls them civil unions rather than marriage. In 2008 the California Supreme Court struck down a law preventing same-sex marriage. And New York state recognizes same-sex marriages performed out of state.

The two essays below both appeared in 1996, soon after the landmark *Romer* v. *Evans* case. Each takes a different stand on the issue of gay marriage, but no matter what the legal future of these unions holds, the essays are good examples of logical arguments with a strong persuasive edge. A cartoon expresses the irony in anti-gay marriage sentiment.

And to bring the arguments to the present, we provide excerpts from two Web sites, both downloaded in 2008, with very strong and opposing beliefs and attitudes about the issue. Finally, a student writer adds his voice to the discussion.

Answer the questions on pages 387–388.

ANDREW SULLIVAN

Let Gays Marry

"A state cannot deem a class of persons a stranger to its laws," declared the Supreme Court last week. It was a monumental statement. Gay men and lesbians, the conservative court said, are no longer strangers in America. They are citizens, entitled, like everyone else, to equal protection—no special rights, but simple equality.

For the first time in Supreme Court history, gay men and women were seen not as some powerful lobby trying to subvert America, but as the people we truly are—the sons and daughters of countless mothers and fathers, with all the weaknesses and strengths and hopes of everybody else. And what we seek is not some special place in America but merely to be a full and equal part of America, to give back to our society without being forced to lie or hide or live as second-class citizens.

That is why marriage is so central to our hopes. People ask us why we want the right to marry, but the answer is obvious. It's the same reason anyone wants the right to marry. At some point in our lives, some of us are lucky enough to meet the person we truly love. And we want to commit to that person in front of our family and country for the rest of our lives. It's the most simple, the most natural, the most human instinct in the world. How could anyone seek to oppose that?

Yes, at first blush, it seems like a radical proposal, but, when you think about it some more, it's actually the opposite. Throughout American history, to be sure, marriage has been between a man and a woman, and in many ways our society is built upon that institution. But none of that need change in the slightest. After all, no one is seeking to take away anybody's right to marry, and no one is seeking to force any church to change any doctrine in any way. Particular religious arguments against same-sex marriage are rightly debated within the churches and faiths themselves. That is not the issue here: There is a separation between church and state in this country. We are only asking that when the government gives out *civil* marriage licenses, those of us who are gay should be treated like anybody else.

5   Of course, some argue that marriage is *by definition* between a man and a woman. But for centuries, marriage was *by definition* a contract in which the wife was her husband's legal property. And we changed that. For centuries, marriage was *by definition* between two people of the same race. And we changed that. We changed these things because we recognized that human dignity is the same whether you are a man or a woman, black or white. And no one has any more of a choice to be gay than to be black or white or male or female.

6   Some say that marriage is only about raising children, but we let childless heterosexual couples be married (Bob and Elizabeth Dole, Pat and Shelley Buchanan, for instance). Why should gay couples be treated differently? Others fear that there is no logical difference between allowing same-sex marriage and sanctioning polygamy and other horrors. But the issue of whether to sanction multiple spouses (gay or straight) is completely separate from whether, in the existing institution between two unrelated adults, the government should discriminate between its citizens.

7   This is, in fact, if only Bill Bennett could see it, a deeply conservative cause. It seeks to change no one else's rights or marriages in any way. It seeks merely to promote monogamy, fidelity and the disciplines of family life among people who have long been cast to the margins of society. And what could be a more conservative project than that? Why indeed would any conservative seek to oppose those very family values for gay people that he or she supports for everybody else? Except, of course, to make gay men and lesbians strangers in their own country, to forbid them ever to come home.

LISA SCHIFFREN

Gay Marriage, an Oxymoron

1   As study after study and victim after victim testify to the social devastation of the sexual revolution, easy divorce and out-of-wedlock motherhood, marriage is fashionable again. And parenthood has transformed many baby boomers into advocates of bourgeois norms.

Indeed, we have come so far that the surprise issue of the political season is whether homosexual "marriage" should be legalized. The Hawaii courts will likely rule that gay marriage is legal, and other states will be required to accept those marriages as valid.

Considering what a momentous change this would be—a radical redefinition of society's most fundamental institution—there has been almost no real debate. This is because the premise is unimaginable to many, and the forces of political correctness have descended on the discussion, raising the cost of opposition. But one may feel the same affection for one's homosexual friends and relatives as for any other, and be genuinely pleased for the happiness they derive from relationships, while opposing gay marriage for principled reasons.

"Same-sex marriage" is inherently incompatible with our culture's understanding of the institution. Marriage is essentially a lifelong compact between a man and woman committed to sexual exclusivity and the creation and nurture of offspring. For most Americans, the marital union—as distinguished from other sexual relationships and legal and economic partnerships—is imbued with an aspect of holiness. Though many of us are uncomfortable using religious language to discuss social and political issues, Judeo-Christian morality informs our view of family life.

Though it is not polite to mention it, what the Judeo-Christian tradition has to say about homosexual unions could not be clearer. In a diverse, open society such as ours, tolerance of homosexuality is a necessity. But for many, its practice depends on a trick of cognitive dissonance that allows people to believe in the Judeo-Christian moral order while accepting, often with genuine regard, the different lives of homosexual acquaintances. That is why, though homosexuals may believe that they are merely seeking a small expansion of the definition of marriage, the majority of Americans perceive this change as a radical deconstruction of the institution.

Some make the conservative argument that making marriage a civil right will bring stability, an end to promiscuity and a sense of fairness to gay men and women. But they miss the point. Society cares about stability in heterosexual unions because it is critical for raising healthy children and transmitting the values that are the basis of our culture.

Whether homosexual relationships endure is of little concern to society. That is also true of most childless marriages, harsh as it is to say. Society has wisely chosen not to differentiate between marriages, because it would require meddling into the motives and desires of everyone who applies for a license.

In traditional marriage, the tie that really binds for life is shared responsibility for the children. (A small fraction of gay couples may choose to raise children together, but such children are offspring of one partner and an outside contributor.) What will keep gay marriages together when individuals tire of each other?

Similarly, the argument that legal marriage will check promiscuity by gay males raises the question of how a "piece of paper" will do what the threat of AIDS has not. Lesbians seem to have little problem with monogamy, or the rest of what constitutes "domestication," despite the absence of official status.

10   Finally, there is the so-called fairness argument. The Government gives tax benefits, inheritance rights and employee benefits only to the married. Again, these financial benefits exist to help couples raise children. Tax reform is an effective way to remove distinctions among earners.

11   If the American people are interested in a radical experiment with same-sex marriages, then subjecting it to the political process is the right route. For a court in Hawaii to assume that it has the power to radically redefine marriage is a stunning abuse of power. To present homosexual marriage as a fait accompli, without national debate, is a serious political error. A society struggling to recover from 30 years of weakened norms and broken families is not likely to respond gently to having an institution central to most people's lives altered.

NOGAYMARRIAGE.COM
Help Save Marriage

NoGayMarriage.com   *L*ink to Us ~ *T*ell-a-Friend

Home   Purpose of Petition   More Information   Make A Donation

Marriage:
One Man . . .
One Woman

Please Help Preserve the Traditional Judeo-Christian Institution of Marriage

Last year, we presented the U.S. Senate with over 2,000,000 petitions of support for the Marriage Protection Amendment. But despite overwhelming public support for the Constitutional amendment, liberals in the Senate filibustered and would not allow a vote on the amendment.

Please sign the petition to the 109th Congress even if you previously signed one to the 108th Congress. AFA will present the petitions to members of Congress.

MILLIONFORMARRIAGE.ORG
Support Marriage Equality for All

HUMAN RIGHTS CAMPAIGN

MILLIONfor**MARRIAGE**.org
mobilizing a million people for the right of EVERY American to get married

SIGN THE PETITION · MAKE A GIFT · TELL YOUR FRIENDS · HRC MARRIAGE CENTER · DOWNLOADS · FAQs · HOME

Support Marriage Equality for ALL!

From coast to coast, we are coming closer to achieving true marriage equality for gay, lesbian, bisexual, and transgender Americans. But we need your help to fight efforts now underway to deny marriage rights to same-sex couples, including state constitutional amendments and federal laws that deny benefits to GLBT couples. Please, sign the Million For Marriage petition below, and be a part of this historic civil rights battle. Gay, straight, married, single... we need everyone who believes in marriage equality to stand up NOW.

1,000,000 **Signatures**
907,875
Petition Signatures as of
today!

Full Petition Text:

I do support the right of every American to marry, including gay, lesbian, bisexual and transgender couples. I believe that marriage and other civil rights protections are essential to making all families safer and more secure.

By signing this petition, I agree to support efforts to make marriage equality a reality in our country, and to oppose any attempts to discriminate against GLBT couples and individuals.

Signed by:
[Your name]
[Your address]

Sign this Petition

Sign Now

First Name:*

Last Name:*

Address Line 1:

Address Line 2:

City:

State/ Province:
--Choose One--

ZIP/Postal Code:

Country:
United States

Cell Phone:
Join HRC's mobile action network:

Email:*

* Required Field

Sign Now

DAN WASSERMAN

All We Want Is a Marriage

© Tribune Media Services, Inc. All Rights Reserved. Reprinted with permission.

Researched Student Writing: Argumentation

Note how this student draws on research to argue his position on same-sex marriage.

Richard Yee

Banning Same-Sex Marriage: An Attack on the American Institution

1   In its relatively short lifetime, the United States of America has faced numerous issues concerning discrimination and equality, conquering differences in race, religion, and gender.

Today, the American people confront yet another field of controversy: sexual orientation. Homosexuality, once considered an unspeakable topic, has gradually found its way into television, cinema, and modern society and presently struggles to find its place in the nation's legal system. Massachusetts and California are currently the only states that allow the marriage of homosexuals; other states prohibit gay marriage or permit only civil unions. A proposed constitutional amendment banning same-sex marriage nationwide is now the subject of heated debate. Advocates are concerned about the protection of tradition and society, but from a legal and ethical standpoint, the proposition is erroneous and unjust. Banning same-sex marriage is unconstitutional, for reasons faulty and unjustifiable, and defeat is necessary to uphold American values.

Proponents of the ban, including President George W. Bush, argue that gay marriage threatens the sanctity of marriage. They claim that marriage is strictly a religious tradition intended to be between a man and a woman, and allowing homosexuals to take part would destroy the sacred institution and eventually society as a whole. Not only is this position a drastic exaggeration, it conflicts with the separation of church and state described in the federal constitution, which ensures the division of religion and government. While marriage may have originated in religion, it has since become a social custom and a basic human right. As Allen Snyder notes, a provision limiting marriage to a group of people on the sole basis of religion would violate the First Amendment (1). Moreover, the notion that gay marriage would lead to the breakdown of marriage and society is a foolish overstatement. Massachusetts and other parts of the world have shown no signs of total destruction since legalizing same-sex marriage. Extending the institution of marriage to homosexuals does not prevent heterosexuals from marrying, nor does it harm the structure of society. Banning it is unconstitutional, and the fears of allowing it are irrational.

Supporters of the amendment also argue that the main purpose of marriage is to encourage procreation, something homosexuals are incapable of. Joanna Grossman counters that, under this definition, opposite-sex couples who are infertile or choose not to have children should not engage in marriage as well (3). Others claim that the best setting for raising children is in a family with opposite-sex parents. However, as

Grossman rebuts, many conventional families consist of neglectful or incompetent parents, and no evidence indicates that a gay couple would be better or worse parents than a straight couple (3). In fact, Andrew Sullivan describes same-sex marriage as "pro-family, uniting those gay family members with their siblings and parents in the unifying ritual of civil marriage" (78). It does not endanger traditional marriage, but rather strengthens it by expanding the institution to encompass additional members. According to Sullivan, homosexuals do not intend to steal or demolish marriage; they only desire to participate in a celebrated practice that calls for "fidelity, responsibility and commitment" (78). Those who suggest gays do not satisfy the qualifications for marriage have apparently forgotten about love, the true reason marriage exists.

4   Yet the ban's greatest problem is not its unconstitutionality or unwarranted motives, but rather its disregard for what America stands for. This nation has strived to promote the equality of opportunity and personal liberty of all, regardless of sex, race, or creed; sexual orientation, a major component of one's individuality, should be no different. It would be un-American to restrict the rights of a particular group of people merely because of who they are. If an act does not harm or negatively affect anyone in any way, then no legitimate reason exists to prohibit it. Hence, forbidding same-sex marriage is a blatant form of discrimination, overlooking widely shared American values. Homosexuals are American citizens and deserve to be treated like American citizens. They have the right to pursue happiness even if the manner in which they do so differs from the social norm. Instead of devising ways to divide America through its differences, a true patriot would unite the nation by embracing its differences. One does not need to agree with or accept homosexuality in order to respect it. By attacking same-sex marriage, one is disrespecting homosexuality as a whole, and, in a way, disrespecting America.

5   Those who oppose gay marriage have made passionate cases from various perspectives, but they all fail under the weight of reason. Limiting marriage for the

purpose of protecting its sanctity is a violation of the federal constitution, and the supposed intentions and objectives of those favoring heterosexuals are close-minded and inconsistent. Giving homosexuals the right to marry poses no threat to heterosexual marriage, nor does it jeopardize the fabric of society. Not only does same-sex marriage benefit society by spreading the joy and obligations of marriage, it is necessary to preserve the fundamental values and beliefs of the nation. As seen in the past, original intentions cease to matter in a continually changing world. What cannot change, however, are the basic principles that make up the foundation of society, and such change is exactly what this constitutional ban will do. What is at stake here is not the institution of marriage, but the institution of America. Denying citizens the right to pursue happiness may not lead to the downfall of civilization, but it would certainly halt centuries of social progress.

Works Cited

Grossman, Joanna. "Are Bans on Same-Sex Marriage Constitutional?" *FindLaw*. Thomson Reuters, 20 Nov. 2003. Web. 18 Jan. 2005.

Snyder, Allen. "Banning Same-Sex Marriage Violates Church-State Separation." *OpEdNews.com*. OpEdNews, 14 Mar. 2004. Web. 18 Jan. 2005.

Sullivan, Andrew. "If at First You Don't Succeed. . . ." *Time* 26 July 2004: 78. Print.

FOR WRITING OR DISCUSSION

1. Sullivan, an openly gay man, writes for periodicals like the *New York Times* and *Newsweek*. Lisa Schiffren, who has written for the *Wall Street Journal* and the *National Review*, was a speechwriter for Vice President Dan Quayle, a Republican conservative, under the George H. Bush administration. How does this information affect your appreciation of the two essays, if at all?

2. How does the title of each essay reinforce the essay's thesis? What is an *oxymoron*, a key word in Schiffren's title?

3. What is the thesis in "Banning Same-Sex Marriage: An Attack on the American Institution" by Richard Yee, the student writer?

4. How do the titles and subtitles in the Web sites reflect their fundamental positions? Which, in your opinion, makes the more powerful appeal? Why do you think so?

5. In "Let Gays Marry," Sullivan mentions the names of several known political leaders. Who are Bob and Elizabeth Dole, Pat and Shelley Buchanan (paragraph 6), and Bill Bennett (paragraph 7)?

6. What reasons does Sullivan provide in support of his argument? Why does he think that the idea of same-sex marriages is not the radical proposal it seems at first? How does Schiffren support her argument? Yee his? How do the words "principled reasons" (paragraph 3) affect the presentation in Schiffren's essay?

7. How do the Web sites support their arguments? For example, what visual images contribute to each site's position? What purpose does the photograph of the bride and groom holding hands serve? The barometer?

8. What is the essential argument of the Wasserman cartoon? How has the artist used irony—indicating one position but meaning the opposite—to good effect here? How does the statement by the gay man in the cartoon reflect core American values? How do you explain the comment by the politician?

9. No doubt you had opinions about same-sex marriage before you examined these selections. Has any of these presentations changed your mind? Has any of the pieces confirmed your original position? Which? Explain your responses. Have the writers or Web sites succeeded in their goals, as far as you yourself are concerned? Why—or how?

10. Write an argumentation essay on same-sex marriages. Where do you stand in the controversy? You may draw on the six selections here to support your point, or you may use personal experience or library or online resources.

HAVING YOUR SAY

What is your view on whether gay people and others of untraditional sexual orientation require special treatment under the law? You might want to read the majority decision written by Justice John Paul Stevens in the *Romer* v. *Evans* case [116 S.Ct. 1620 (1996)], as well as the dissenting opinion by Justice Antonin Scalia.

Reading and Writing About Poetry

Without the apparent strategies familiar to the argumentation essays we've been examining, Emily Dickinson, one of America's prized poets of the nineteenth century, presents a strong argument here about God and religion in her deceptively simple poetic idiom.

EMILY DICKINSON

"Some Keep the Sabbath Going to Church"

Some keep the Sabbath going to Church—
I keep it, staying at Home—
With a Bobolink for a Chorister—
And an Orchard, for a Dome—

Some keep the Sabbath in Surplice—   5
I just wear my Wings—
And instead of tolling the Bell, for Church,
Our little Sexton—sings.

God preaches, a noted Clergyman—
And the sermon is never long,   10
So instead of getting to Heaven, at last—
I'm going, all along.

FOR WRITING OR DISCUSSION

1. What is Dickinson's main point—the argument—in this poem?

2. What comparisons are central to the poem? What is a bobolink? A chorister? How does the poet connect an orchard with a dome? And why mention a dome at all?

3. What is the meaning of the second stanza, lines 5–9?

4. What is the meaning of the last two lines of the poem? In what way do they drive the argument home—that is, make the basic point profoundly and wittily?

5. Write an essay about religion in which you take a position on the value of religious duty (going to church, synagogue, or mosque) as opposed to observing (perhaps even worshiping) the presence of God in informal settings—at home, in the song of birds, in other elements of the natural world.

STRATEGY CHECKLIST: Writing and Revising Your Argumentation Paper

Plan the paper.

☐ Have I identified a topic and a debatable position? Is there clearly one or more positions that might oppose mine?

☐ Have I used prewriting to stimulate my thoughts?

☐ Have I paid attention to peer comments about my prewriting?

☐ Have I weighed my audience and purpose?

☐ Have I done any necessary research at the library and online?

☐ Have I considered using an outline to lay out my argument and the specific details to support it?

Write a first draft.

☐ Have I written a thesis that expresses my position on the debatable topic?

☐ Have I developed an introduction to set the context for my position?

☐ Have I used a tone suitable to my position on the topic?

- Calm and reasonable
- Humorous
- Emotional
- Angry
- Ironic
- Other tone

☐ Have I used appropriate strategies to advance my argument?

- Description
- Comparison and contrast
- Narration
- Classification and division
- Example
- Cause and effect
- Process
- Definition

☐ Have I used induction and deduction to make my points?

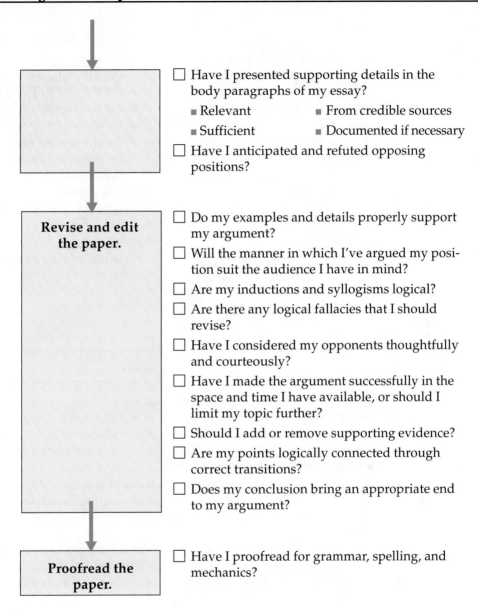

Have I presented supporting details in the body paragraphs of my essay?

- Relevant
- From credible sources
- Sufficient
- Documented if necessary

Have I anticipated and refuted opposing positions?

Revise and edit the paper.

Do my examples and details properly support my argument?

Will the manner in which I've argued my position suit the audience I have in mind?

Are my inductions and syllogisms logical?

Are there any logical fallacies that I should revise?

Have I considered my opponents thoughtfully and courteously?

Have I made the argument successfully in the space and time I have available, or should I limit my topic further?

Should I add or remove supporting evidence?

Are my points logically connected through correct transitions?

Does my conclusion bring an appropriate end to my argument?

Proofread the paper.

Have I proofread for grammar, spelling, and mechanics?

WRITING TOPICS

If you are having difficulty deciding on a topic for your argumentation paper, you might find help simply by choosing one of the following statements and arguing for or against that statement.

1. The media unfairly hound celebrities accused of crimes.
2. The United States government should reinstitute the draft for all men and women eighteen years and older.
3. Reality TV should really be called unreality TV.
4. The sale of tobacco should be made illegal.
5. Among the groups most unfairly discriminated against are overweight people.
6. If we require people to pass a driving test before licensing them to operate a car, we should require people to pass some kind of parenting test before allowing them to have children.
7. Marijuana should be legal for medicinal purposes.
8. As an exercise, swimming far exceeds running as a means to health and fitness.
9. The pollution of the world's oceans is a major threat to humanity.
10. Random drug tests of high school students are a violation of human rights.

CROSSCURRENTS

1. Quynh Nguyen's "Being a Recent American" (pages 357–359) and Esmeralda Santiago's "A Blanco Navidad for New Yorikans" (pages 132–133) provide a personal window on the immigrant experience in America. How would the two writers react to the essays by Nick Milano (pages 353–355) and Dan Cunningham (pages 355–357)?
2. Consider together the arguments in Michael E. Levin's "A Case for Torture" (pages 360–361) and Mark Essig's "Continuing the Search for Kinder Executions" (pages 375–377). If they could meet, what would the two writers say to each other?
3. Both Dennis Rivas in "Books Are Not More Valuable Than Other Art" (pages 350–352) and Caleb Crain in "Twilight of the Books" (pages 194–196) examine the role of books in our modern world, but arrive at completely different conclusions in their arguments. How do the two pieces compare and contrast? If Crain and Rivas could meet, what do you think that they would say to each other?

COLLABORATIVE LEARNING

Bring the drafts of your argumentation essays to class. Form groups of three students to discuss the efforts of group members and to make recommendations for the next draft. Use the "Strategy Checklist: Writing and Revising Your Argumentation Paper" to guide your conversation.

From **IMAGE** to **WORDS**: A Reading and Writing Assignment

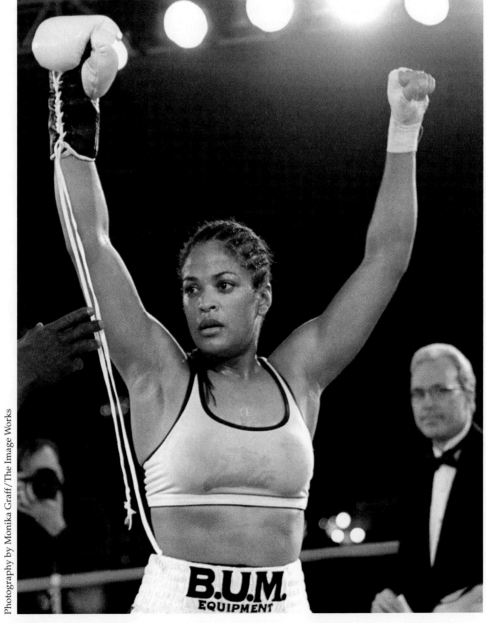

Photography by Monika Graff/The Image Works

The photograph on page 393 captures a scene that has stimulated discussion and argument over the last fifteen years or so. Should women participate in what have been traditionally male-dominated activities? Use the photograph as a springboard for an essay in which you take one side or the other of this argument. Draw on the principles of solid arguments developed in this chapter.

For additional writing, reading, and research resources, go to **www.mycomplab.com** <http://www.mycomplab.com/> and choose Skwire/Wiener's *Student's Book of College English*, Twelfth Edition.

CHAPTER **16**

Mixing Methods of Development

- Developing Your Paper Through Mixed Modes
- Student Writing: Mixing Methods in Developing Your Essay
- Critical Reading: Mixed Methods of Development
- Models of Writing

As you've worked your way through the chapters in this book, you've already seen in practice what we asserted at the outset: Many writing efforts benefit from an intelligent mix of rhetorical methods. Although you've explored the options individually, you've seen that many writers combine rhetorical approaches for maximum effect.

So why, you're no doubt wondering, do we need a separate chapter on using mixed methods in writing? First, the chapter gives you an opportunity to address the topic consciously, not accidentally. We'll point out here through student samples and professional writing and accompanying annotations how and where the writers draw on multiple modes of development to advance their theses. Next, you'll have a chance to think critically about the multiple rhetorical perspectives as they emerge in a particular piece. And finally, you'll have the chance to incorporate mixed methods of development formally in your own writing.

Developing Your Paper Through Mixed Modes

When writing a paper using a variety of rhetorical modes, keep the following four strategies in mind.

 TIPS for Developing a Mixed Modes Essay

- **Choose your topic carefully.** As you plan to write, consider which modes of development might help you best convince your readers. Do you want to write in support of one candidate for office over another? Comparison and contrast clearly would come into play, but, in considering actions taken by each candidate, you might explain the causes and effects of such actions. Drawing on sensory detail to describe the candidates might help you offer snapshots of the personalities with which your readers may be unfamiliar. Do you want to argue for a humane setting for emergency room care in local hospitals? Description would certainly help here, but you might also want to explain the process by which hospital staff admit patients and establish treatment programs or argue for a less-complicated and quicker admissions process.

■ **Be familiar with the demands of the rhetorical strategies that you plan to use.** Recall, for example, the various options available if you want to develop part of your paper with comparison and contrast. Be aware of the various logical fallacies that can trip you up if you're developing your topic in part through argumentation. You should reexamine the Strategy Checklists at the end of each chapter in Part Two. Better yet, reread the chapters that deal with the rhetorical strategies your topic suggests you might use.

■ **Pay particular attention to transitions.**   Developing a coherent paper requires special attention in a mixed modes essay, and you want to be sure to lead the reader carefully from one part of the essay to another. The various elements of your paper must hold together. This does not mean a call for endless *therefores*, *in addition*s, *moreover*s, and the like. It does mean that you should move your reader smoothly from one point to the other by means of logical connections and astute use of the rhetorical modes to make your point successfully. In Brian Jarvis's essay, which you will read here, note how he uses the word *commons* in both the first and second paragraphs. The repetition helps him make a smooth transition from the description in the introduction to his definition of the word as it applies to his school. When he moves to a narrative approach in paragraph 4, he begins with "Ten years ago. . . ." The time reference lends coherence to the essay.

■ **Be reasonable in your choices for developing your essay.**   Because you now understand all the rhetorical options open to you doesn't mean that you have to use them all at once. Your topic and your interest in it should dictate the strategies that will best serve your thesis. In other words, avoid drawing on too many modes of development just for the sake of using them.

Mixing Methods: Looking at Possibilities

Let's examine a topic close up to see how a variety of rhetorical approaches might work together to produce a strong paper.

Suppose you wanted to write about the need to improve voting in your community. These options (and many others, of course) are potentially available, based on your ultimate thesis and purpose.

RHETORICAL STRATEGY	POSSIBLE APPROACH
Description	Describe the broken and hard-to-use voting machines in your community.
Narration	Tell a story about a senior citizen who struggled to cast her vote.
Example	Give several examples of failed voting efforts.
Process	Explain how a local political party tries to get out the vote.
Comparison and contrast	Compare regular balloting and absentee balloting.
Classification and division	Describe the different categories of voters in your community.
Cause and effect	Explain why the voting board has done nothing to improve the ease of voting on election day.
Definition	Define "vote-getting."
Argumentation	Argue that without a proactive government plan to improve voting, elections will never be fair.

Do you see the possibilities? By combining two, perhaps three of these possible approaches, you could produce a paper that uses mixed modes of development. The specifics would depend on your thesis and purpose.

EXERCISE Using the table above, explain how you would use two or more of the rhetorical strategies in an essay on improving local voting in your city or state.

EXERCISE For the topics following identify at least two modes that you could use to develop a paper and explain how you would use them. "Television reruns" is done as an example.

TOPIC	MODES	HOW TO USE
Television reruns	Example	Provide illustrations of popular sitcom reruns.
	Comparison and contrast	Compare one or two old sitcoms and one or two new ones to show change in comedy values.

1. Cell phones
2. Smoking in public
3. Teenage alcohol use
4. Improving the economy
5. Greenhouse gases

Student Writing: Mixing Methods in Developing Your Essay

In this annotated paper by student writer Brian Jarvis, who wrote the essay for *Newsweek*, note the mixed modes of development that support the writer's thesis. Answer the questions after the piece.

Brian Jarvis

Against the Great Divide

1   I always notice one thing when I walk through the commons at my high school: The whites are on one side of the room and the blacks are on the other. When I enter the room, I think I'm at an African nationalist meeting. The atmosphere is lively, the clothes are colorful, the voices are loud, the students are up and about, the language is different, and there's not a white face to be seen. But the moment I cross the invisible line to the other side, I feel I've moved to another country. There are three times as many people, the voices are softer, the clothes more subdued. Everyone's sitting or lying down, and one has as much chance of seeing a black student as a Martian.

Description: Helps establish details of the moment in the introduction to the essay and frames the problem that the writer will address in his paper.

2   The commons is a gathering spot where students relax on benches and talk with friends. They also buy candy and soda, watch TV, and make phone calls. It's a place where all sorts of things happen. But you'll never find a white student and a black student talking to each other.

Note the repetition of the word "commons" here as a transition to the first paragraph, where we read the word for the first time in the essay.

Definition: Jarvis' meaning of "commons."

3   After three years, I still feel uncomfortable when I have to walk through the "black" side to get to class. It's not that any black students threaten or harass me. They just quietly ignore me and look in the other direction, and I do the same. But there's one who sometimes catches my eye, and I can't help feeling awkward when I see him. He was a close friend from childhood.

Ten years ago, we played catch in our backyards, went bike riding, and slept over at one another's houses. By the fifth grade, we went to movies and amusement parks and bunked together at the same summer camps. We met while playing on the same Little League team, though we attended different grade schools. We're both juniors now at the same high school. We usually don't say anything when we see each other, except maybe a polite "Hi" or "Hey." I can't remember the last time we talked on the phone, much less got together outside of school.

Since entering high school, we haven't shared a single class or sport. He plays football, a black-dominated sport, while I play tennis, which is, with rare exception, an all-white team. It's as if fate has kept us apart; though, more likely, it's peer pressure.

In the lunchroom, I sit with my white friends and my childhood friend sits with his black ones. It's the same when we walk through the hallways or sit in the library. If Michael Jackson thinks, "It don't matter if you're black or white," he should visit my high school.

I wonder if proponents of desegregation realized that even if schools were integrated, students would choose to remain apart. It wasn't until 1983 that St. Louis's voluntary city-suburban desegregation program was approved. Today, my school has 25 percent black students. While this has given many young people the chance for a better education, it hasn't brought the two races closer together.

In high school, I've become friends with Vietnamese Americans, Korean Americans, Iranian Americans, Indian Americans, Russian Americans, and exchange students from France and Sweden. The only group that remains at a distance is the African Americans. I've had only a handful of black students in all my classes and only one black teacher (from Haiti).

In its effort to put students through as many academic classes as possible and prepare them for college, my school seems to have overlooked one crucial course: teaching black and white students how to get along, which in my opinion, would be more valuable than all the others. It's not that there haven't

4

Transition: "Ten years ago" helps lend coherence to essay.

Example: From personal experience, the writer presents example of a different relation between blacks and whites from relations identified at the writer's school.

5

Comparison and contrast: In paragraphs 5 and 6, Jarvis shows similarities and differences between friend and him.

6

7

8

9

Cause and effect. Here the writer explains the results of efforts to improve race relations at his high school.

been efforts to improve race relations. Last fall, a group of black and white students established a program called Students Organized Against Racism. But at a recent meeting, SOAR members decided that the separation of blacks and whites was largely voluntary and there was little they could do about it. Another youth group tried to help by moving the soda machine from the "white" side of the commons to the "black" side, so that white students would have to cross the line to get a Coke. But all that's happened is that students buy their sodas, then return to their own territory.

Example: Jarvis proposes a way to improve race relations and draws on examples from personal experience to support his point.

10   Last summer, at a youth camp called Miniwanca in Michigan, I did see black and white teens get along. I don't mean just tolerate one another. I mean play sports together, dance together, walk on the beach together, and become friends. The students came from all races and backgrounds, as well as from overseas. Camp organizers purposely placed me in a cabin and activity group that included whites, blacks, Southerners, Northerners, and foreigners, none of whom I'd met before.

11   For ten days, I became great friends with a group of strangers, at least half of whom were black. One wouldn't know that racism existed at that idyllic place, where we told stories around campfires, acted in plays, and shared our deepest thoughts about AIDS, parents, abortion, and dating. Everyone got along so well there that it was depressing for me to return to high school. But at the same time, it made me hopeful. If black and white teenagers could be friends at leadership camp, couldn't they mix in school as well?

Example: The illustrations continue as the writer first gives examples of joint activities at camp and then suggests ways to get "whites and blacks together as much as possible."

12   Schools need to make it a real priority to involve whites and blacks together as much as possible. This would mean more multicultural activities, mandatory classes that teach black history, and discussions of today's racial controversies. Teachers should mix whites and blacks more in study groups so they have to work together in and out of school. (Students won't do it on their own.) And most important, all students should get a chance to attend a camp like Miniwanca. Maybe the government could find a way to help finance other camps like it.

Conclusion: Provides a bird's-eye view of the problem and the writer's reaction to it.

13   As it is now, black and white teenagers just don't know one another. I think a lot about my friend from childhood—what he does on weekends, what he thinks about college, what he wants to do with his life. I have no answers, and it saddens me.

FOR WRITING OR DISCUSSION

1. What is Jarvis's thesis?
2. What is your reaction to the use of multiple modes of development in this essay?
3. Which details convince you most that the races do not get along harmoniously at Jarvis's school? Jarvis does not report any open conflict. Why, then, is he concerned?
4. Write an argumentative essay about race relations in your school, neighborhood, or place of business.

Critical Reading: Mixed Methods of Development

Experienced writers know that content drives the form of an essay, and they know how to integrate rhetorical strategies to suit their topics and purpose in writing. In the selection below, written by a professor of religion, marginal comments point to elements in the essay that a critical reader might highlight as well as to the varied rhetorical modes the writer draws on. Answer the questions after the selection.

TIMOTHY K. BEAL

Bibles du Jour

"du Jour" is French for "of the day" (e.g., *soup du jour* on restaurant menus).

In introduction, writer immediately sets apart his bible topic from our more familiar understanding of the word "bible" through illustration— i.e., example.

Some historical background puts the topic in perspective, also through rhetorical strategy of example.

1 Today we are witnessing a burgeoning of bibles. Not the kind you read in a synagogue or church, but the kind you read to master Java scripting. Or to get washboard abs. Or to create the perfect window dressing. From *The Internet Bible* to *The Golfer's Bible* to *The Body Sculpting Bible* (his and hers versions) to *The Curtain Bible*, from *The Runner's Bible* to *The Small Game and Varmint Hunter's Bible*, to *Cocktail: The Drinks Bible for the 21st Century*, there's a bible for anyone who wants to do or be anything.

2 Calling these kinds of books bibles is not exactly new. *The Shooter's Bible* (previously *The Stoeger Gun Catalog and Handbook*, subtitled *The World's Standard*), appeared in 1940. But today we find more than ever. By my count, something like one in four books published in America over the past two years with "bible" in the title is this kind of bible. Indeed, you're likely to find more bibles in a bookstore's computer section than in its religion section.

3 Why call these kinds of books bibles? Because it sells, of course. But why? What currency does it give a book to call it a bible? What does this title claim for a book? What does it promise? What does "bible" mean?

Questions establish basic premise of thesis: Readers will expect answers to these questions.

Definition: What is a bible? Writer gives examples of what word means to him.

4 It means *comprehensive*. A book called a bible promises to cover all you need to know and understand about its subject, from A to Z, Genesis to Revelation.

5 It means *authoritative*. A book called a bible claims to be the alpha and the omega, the first and last Word on all things golfing, draping, varmint hunting, whatever, dispensing all the right answers to all the right questions.

6 It means *exclusive*. A book called a bible asserts itself to be the one and only, without serious competition.

7 It means *practical*. A book called a bible promises to serve as a reference manual and a dependable guide for how to proceed on the path you've chosen.

8 And it means *devotional*. A book called a bible treats its subject as something worthy of religious dedication and discipline from practitioners. Its subject literally becomes a religion of the book—*this* book. Take and read.

9 A book called a bible claims to be the one and only book for those who are devoted or who want to be devoted to its subject. Whether or not you know what a turbo charger is, you immediately understand that *Hot Rodder's Bible* is proclaiming itself the ultimate comprehensive authority, guide, and how-to manual for hot-rod devotees. That's what bible means.

10 That's what it means, but in fact there is no one bible, and there never has been. Even before this new generation of bibles came along, religious bibles were legion. The <u>Jewish Bible</u>, or Tanakh, includes the Torah (the first five books, Genesis through Deuteronomy), Neviim (Prophets), and Ketuvim (Writings), in that order. The <u>Protestant Bible</u> includes those same books, but in a different order, as well as the New Testament. The <u>Roman Catholic Bible</u> adds a number of Apocryphal scriptures. And many others reflect the biblical traditions of other forms of Christianity alive and well in America. In addition, <u>numerous translations exist of each of those bibles</u>. And behind each of those translations are literally hundreds of manuscripts written in many different languages and spanning centuries.

True.

Many bibles.

Argumentation: The writer has explained bible as "the one and only book"; now he challenges that idea with religious examples.

11 Neither is any one of the many Jewish and Christian bibles of one voice. Each is the product of multiple oral and literary traditions, multiple voices and pens speaking and writing within many different cultural contexts across hundreds of years. Every one of those bibles is more like a one-volume library than a single book.

Further details to support notion that a bible is not a one-and-only book.

12 <u>As a result no single bible exemplifies our idea of bible-ness</u>. The prototype is a figment of our cultural imagination, revealing not what "the Bible" is but what we think or even wish it to be. *The Fly Fisherman's Bible* is not to fly fishing what "the Bible" is to religion. Rather, it purports to be to fly fishing what we imagine "the Bible" should be to religion.

"Bible-ness"— writer's own invented word. Legitimate? It works!

Transition— summary (see paragraph 10).

13 A century ago, calling such books bibles would have struck most readers as inappropriate, even sacrilegious. Once I thought I had found a remarkably early example: In 1913 Nora Holm published *The Runner's Bible: Compiled and*

Example to support writer's point that current use of word "bible" would have struck most readers in the 1900s as sacrilege.

Annotated for the Reading of Him Who Runs. But lo and behold, the book had nothing to do with breaking a sweat or beating the pavement. It was a Christian "prayer Bible," a compilation of biblical passages accompanied by Holm's devotional commentaries. Her title alludes to the New Testament use of competitive running as a metaphor for the Christian life—running to win "the imperishable" wreath of salvation, as the Apostle Paul puts it.

Paragraph 14, comparison–contrast: The Holm book vs. the Bloom book. Note the differences in the use of "bible" in title of each book.

Holm's book is still in print and is well-known in Christian devotional circles. But these days its publishers must take care to distinguish it from Marc Bloom's better-known *The Runner's Bible* for competitive runners and joggers. Indeed, most readers today would assume that a book called *The Runner's Bible* is for someone who wants to win a 10K, not someone who wants to win the imperishable wreath. The revised subtitle on the 1998 edition of Holm's *Runner's Bible* admits as much: *Spiritual Guidance for People on the Run.*   14

Argumentation — "mainstream American culture is now in many respects postreligious, indeed post-Christian."

Nowadays calling a book about running a bible doesn't strike many of us as inappropriate, let alone sacrilegious. Maybe that's because mainstream American culture is now in many respects post-religious, indeed post-Christian. Images like crosses and Madonnas and terms like "salvation" and "bible" that were once set apart as sacred and handled exclusively within particular religious traditions have crossed over into mainstream consumer culture where they now circulate in countless new ways, primarily to sell stuff. Even those of us who are in fact religious (even Christian) have grown accustomed to seeing such images and words translated into new venues.   15

"Stuff": informal usage.

Example to support idea of flippancy—Madonna and Marilyn Manson, popular culture icons today.

In this light, there *is* a bit of sacrilegious flippancy in calling these kinds of books bibles. Akin to Madonna's and Marilyn Manson's slight smirks as they don holy garb, we pronounce these books bibles with at least some tongue in cheek, aware that we can use the term that way because it has lost its traditional moorings in the sacred and is now floating freely down the mainstream.   16

"sacrilegious flippancy"—interesting phrase.

But might there also be a bit of religious longing here? I have to wonder if the growing market for the new kinds of bibles betrays a bit of nostalgia, even amid the tongue-in-cheek flippancy, for that old-time kind of religious authority that "bible" stands for: a comprehensive, exclusive authority that gives guidance and calls for devotion. I say a bit of nostalgia. Fundamentalism is the name we give to movements ruled by that kind of nostalgia. Most of us know that we can't go back, and that the desire to do so can be a dangerous fantasy.   17

Even when the word "bible" is used casually, betrays nostalgia for old-time religious authority. Note use of cause and effect: Why is the market for new kinds of bibles growing?

Play on words ends piece. "Bible" vs. "biblical proportions." Is this tongue in cheek?

Still, what do we make of the increasing popularity of these newfangled bibles in our brave new postreligious world? One thing is for sure: Tongues in cheeks notwithstanding, a market still exists for authority of biblical proportions.   18

Writer's conclusion extends the argument further: Popularity of "bible" books.

FOR WRITING OR DISCUSSION

1. How does the strategy of illustration serve the introduction? Cause and effect?

2. State the writer's thesis in your own words. How do the questions in paragraph 3 contribute to your understanding of the thesis?

3. Explain the writer's use of argumentation in paragraphs 10 and 15.

4. How do comparison and contrast serve the thesis of the essay?

5. Choose a key word used in many contexts in the way that Beal used the word *bible* to identify different types of books. For example, you may select *star, hero,* or *friend.* Then, define the word in an essay that uses a variety of rhetorical methods. Or, write your own definition of *bible,* also using a mixed modes approach in your paper.

Models of Writing

Use the following selections as a stimulus for your own mixed modes writing and also as a means of examining the interaction among modes that the writers draw on to make their points. Be sure to read critically. Make notes in the margin. (Review pages 5–10.)

HERBERT J. GANS
Fitting the Poor into the Economy

1   The notion of the poor as too lazy or morally deficient to deserve assistance seems to be indestructible. Public policies limit poor people to substandard services and incomes below the subsistence level, and Congress and state legislatures are tightening up even on these miserly allocations—holding those in the "underclass" responsible for their own sorry state. Indeed, labeling the poor as undeserving has lately become politically useful as a justification for the effort to eliminate much of the antipoverty safety net and permit tax cuts for the affluent people who do most of the voting.

2   Such misplaced blame offers mainstream society a convenient evasion of its own responsibility. Blaming poor men and women for not working, for example, takes the onus off both private enterprise and government for failing to supply employment. It is easier to charge poor unmarried mothers with lacking family values than to make sure that there are jobs for them and for the young men who are not marriageable because they are unable to support families.

Technology Review October 1995.

Indeed, the poor make excellent scapegoats for a range of social problems, such as street crime and drug and alcohol addiction. Never mind the reversal of cause and effect that underlies this point of view—for centuries crime, alcoholism, and single motherhood have risen whenever there has not been enough work and income to go around.

The undeserving underclass is also a useful notion for employers as the economy appears to be entering a period of long-term stagnation. Jobs are disappearing—some displaced by labor-saving technologies, others exported to newly industrializing, low-wage countries, others lost as companies "downsize" to face tougher global competition. Indeed, the true rate of unemployment—which includes involuntary part-time workers and long-term "discouraged" workers who have dropped out of the job market altogether—has remained in double digits for more than a generation and no longer seems to drop during times of economic strength. Labeling poor people as lacking the needed work ethic is a politically simple way of shedding them from a labor market that will most likely never need them again.

The most efficient antidote to poverty is not welfare but full employment. In the short run, therefore, today's war against the poor should be replaced with efforts to create jobs for now-surplus workers. New Deal–style programs of large-scale governmental employment, for example, can jump-start a slow economy. Besides being the fastest way to put people to work, a public-works program can improve the country's infrastructure, including highways, buildings, parks, and computer databases.

In addition, private enterprise and government should aim to stimulate the most promising labor-intensive economic activities and stop encouraging new technology that will further destroy jobs—reviving, for example, the practice of making cars and appliances partly by hand. A parallel policy would tax companies for their use of labor-saving technology; the revenues from this tax would pay for alternative jobs for people in occupations that technology renders obsolete. This idea makes good business as well as social sense: human workers are needed as customers for the goods that machines now produce.

To distribute the jobs that do exist among more people, employers could shorten the work day, week, or year. Several large manufacturing companies in Western Europe already use worksharing to create a 35-hour week. Making significant inroads on U.S. joblessness may require reducing the work week to 30 hours.

A more generous welfare system would go a long way toward solving the problems of the remainder: those who cannot work or cannot find jobs. By persisting in the belief that poor people deserve their fate, society can easily justify a paltry and demeaning welfare system that pays recipients only about one-quarter of the median income. A system that paid closer to half the median income, by contrast, would enable those without work to remain full members of society and thus minimize the despair, anger, and various illnesses, as well as premature mortality, distinctive to the poor.

For such antipoverty policies to gain acceptance, mainstream America will have to unlearn the stereotype of poor people as immoral. Most of the poor are just as law-abiding as everyone else. (While a minority of poor people cheat on their welfare applications, an even larger minority of affluent people cheat on their tax returns—yet the notion of undeservingness is never applied to the middle or upper classes.) In admitting that the phenomena now explained as moral dereliction are actually traceable to poverty, Americans will force themselves to find solutions, not scapegoats, to the country's problems.

9   Most of the people assigned to today's undeserving underclass are the first victims of what is already being called the future "jobless economy." In the long run, if the cancer of joblessness spreads more widely among the population, large numbers of the present middle class will have to adapt to the reality that eventually most workers may no longer be employed full time. In that case, more drastic job-creation policies will be needed, including a ban on additional job-destroying technology and the establishment of permanent public employment modeled on the kind now associated with military spending. Worksharing would most likely be based on a 24-hour week.

10   At that point, everyone would in fact be working part time by today's standards, and new ways to maintain standards of living would have to be found. One approach, already being discussed in Europe, is a universal, subsistence-level income grant. This "demogrant," a twenty-first-century version of the $1,000-per-person allotment that presidential candidate George McGovern proposed in 1972, would be taxed away from people still working full time. In any case, private and government agencies should begin now to study what policies might be needed to preserve the American way of life when the full-time job will no longer be around to pay for the American Dream.

11   It is possible, of course, that new sources of economic growth will suddenly develop to revive the full employment and prosperity of the post–World War II decades. And some labor-saving technologies may, in the long run, create more jobs than they destroy; that may well be the case for computers, which have spawned a large sector of the economy. Such happy outcomes cannot be counted on to materialize, however, and there remains the danger that the war on the poor will continue as the politically most convenient path. We will undoubtedly find that when the economy begins to threaten the descendants of today's middle and even affluent classes with becoming poor, and then "undeserving," policies that today seem utopian will be demanded, and quickly.

FOR WRITING OR DISCUSSION

1. What is Gans's thesis in this essay? Where in the essay does he come closest to stating it for the reader?

2. Where does the writer use cause and effect strategies to advance his point?

3. In which paragraphs does Gans use process analysis? Example? Comparison and contrast?

4. Gans says people view the poor as "the undeserving working class." Write an essay called "The Deserving Working Class" and propose strategies for providing the poor with better services or for changing people's views of the poor so that society doesn't blame them for their fates.

RESHMA MEMON YAQUB
You People Did This

As I ran through my neighborhood on the morning of September 11th, in search of my son, who had gone to the park with his baby sitter, I wasn't just afraid of another hijacked plane crashing into us. I was also afraid that someone else would get to my son first, someone wanting revenge against anyone who looks like they're from "that part of the world." Even if he is just one and a half years old.   1

I know I wasn't just afraid that the building where my husband works, a D.C. landmark, might fall on him. I was also afraid that another American might stop him on the street and harass him, or hurt him, demanding to know why "you people" did this. As soon as we heard the news, 7 million American Muslims wondered in terror, "Will America blame me?"   2

When our country is terrorized, American Muslims are victimized twice. First, as Americans, by the madmen who strike at our nation, at our physical, mental and emotional core. Then we're victimized again, as Muslims, by those Americans who believe that all Muslims are somehow accountable for the acts of some madmen, that our faith—that our God, the same peace-loving God worshipped by Jews and Christians—sanctions it.   3

It didn't matter when the federal building in Oklahoma City blew up that a Muslim didn't do it. That a Christian man was responsible for the devastation in Oklahoma City certainly didn't matter to the thugs who terrorized a Muslim woman there, nearly seven months pregnant, by attacking her home, breaking her windows, screaming religious slurs. It didn't matter to them that Sahar Al-Muwsawi, 26, would, as a result, miscarry her baby. That she would bury him in the cold ground, alongside other victims of the Oklahoma City bombing, after naming him Salaam, the Arabic word for "peace."   4

But that travesty and hundreds like it certainly were on my mind that Tuesday morning. And they were reinforced every time a friend called to check on my family and to sadly remind me, "It's over for us. Muslims are done for."   5

Even as we buckled under the same grief that every American was feeling that day, American Muslims had to endure the additional burden of worrying for our own safety, in our own hometowns, far from hijackers and skyscrapers. Shots would be fired into the Islamic Center of Irving, Texas; an Islamic bookstore in Virginia would have bricks thrown through its windows; a bag of pig's blood would be left on the doorstep of an Islamic community center in San Francisco; a mosque near Chicago would be marched on by 300 people shouting racist epithets. A Muslim of Pakistani origin would be gunned down in Dallas; a Sikh man would be shot and killed in Mesa, Arizona (possibly by the same assailant who would go on to spray bullets into the home of a local Afghani family).   6

And those were just the cases that were reported. I know I didn't report it when a ten-year-old neighborhood boy walked by and muttered, "Terrorist," as I got into my car. My neurosurgeon friend didn't report that a nurse at the prominent Washington hospital where they both work had   7

Rolling Stone 25 Oct. 2001.

announced in front of him that all Muslims and Arabs should be rounded up and put into camps, as Japanese were in World War II. My family didn't report that we're sick with worry about my mother-in-law, another sister-in-law and my niece, who are visiting Pakistan, with their return uncertain.

8   In the days to come, in the midst of the darkness, there is some light. A neighbor stops by to tell me that he doesn't think Muslims are responsible for the acts of madmen. Strangers in Starbucks are unusually friendly to me and my son, reaching out as if to say, "We know it's not your fault." The head of a church told me his congregation wants to come and put its arms around us, and to help in any way possible—by cleaning graffiti off a mosque, by hosting our Friday prayers, whatever we needed. President Bush warns Americans not to scapegoat Muslims and Arabs. He even visits a mosque, in a show of solidarity. Congress swiftly passes a resolution to uphold the civil rights of Muslims and Arabs, urging Americans to remain united. Jewish and Christian leaders publicly decry the violence against Muslims. At a mosque in Seattle, Muslim worshippers are greeted by members of other faiths bringing them flowers.

9   There's something America needs to understand about Islam. Like Judaism, like Christianity, Islam doesn't condone terrorism. It doesn't allow it. It doesn't accept it. Yet, somehow, the labels *jihad, holy war* and *suicide martyrs* are still thrown around. In fact, jihad doesn't even mean holy war. It's an Arabic word that means "struggle"—struggle to please God. And suicide itself is a forbidden act in Islam. How could anyone believe that Muslims consider it martyrdom when practiced in combination with killing thousands of innocents? Anyone who claims to commit a politically motivated violent act in the name of Islam has committed a hate crime against the world's 1.2 billion Muslims.

10   It is not jihad to hijack a plane and fly it into a building. But in fact there was jihad done that Tuesday. It was jihad when firemen ran into imploding buildings to rescue people they didn't know. It was jihad when Americans lined up and waited to donate the blood of their own bodies. It was jihad when strangers held and comforted one another in the streets. It was jihad when rescue workers struggled to put America back together, piece by piece.

11   Yes, there were martyrs made that Tuesday. But there were no terrorists among them. There were only Americans, of every race and religion, who, that Tuesday, took death for us.

FOR WRITING OR DISCUSSION

1. What is the meaning of the title? How does it engage the reader to want to read on? How does the first sentence provide the reader with the historical context needed to understand the essay?

2. What is Yaqub's thesis here?

3. How does the writer use quotations to good advantage? For example, what purpose does the quote serve in paragraph 5?

4. How does illustration serve the essay in paragraph 6? Paragraph 8? Paragraph 10? What is the effect on the reader of the accumulation of examples in those paragraphs? Where does Yaqub use comparison and contrast strategies? Cause and effect?

5. What steps would you propose for dealing with terrorism on American soil? Write an essay to address the topic, using a variety of rhetorical strategies.

STRATEGY CHECKLIST: Writing and Revising Your Mixed Modes Paper

Plan the paper.

- [ ] Have I identified a topic that lends itself to development through a variety of rhetorical modes?
- [ ] Have I reviewed the methods of development so that I can use effectively whichever methods work for my topic?
- [ ] Have I used one of the prewriting strategies to stimulate my thoughts?
- [ ] Have I weighed my audience and purpose?
- [ ] Have I considered using an outline to organize my thoughts?

Write a first draft.

- [ ] Have I written a thesis that expresses my opinion about or attitude toward the topic?
- [ ] Have I developed an introduction to set the context for my paper?
- [ ] Have I used appropriate rhetorical modes?
  - Description
  - Narration
  - Example
  - Process
  - Comparison and contrast
  - Classification and division
  - Cause and effect
  - Definition
  - Argumentation
- [ ] Have I integrated the mode strategies appropriately?
- [ ] Have I presented sufficient supporting detail?

Revise and edit the paper.

- [ ] Have I paid attention to peer comments?
- [ ] Do details I've presented support my thesis?
- [ ] Does my use of varied modes reflect what I've learned about them in developing essays?
- [ ] Have I checked carefully for the use—and not overuse—of transitions?
- [ ] Have I made my point successfully in the space and time I have available, or should I limit my topic further?
- [ ] Does my conclusion bring an appropriate end to my paper?

continued

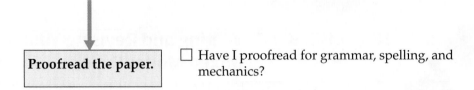

| Proofread the paper. | ☐ Have I proofread for grammar, spelling, and mechanics? |

WRITING TOPICS

These suggestions for topics will help you develop a paper in which you draw on diverse methods of development. Of course, any topic of your own will do nicely as well: The point here is to integrate rhetorical modes so that they help you make your point successfully. An argumentative bent to your paper will help you draw on varied developmental strategies.

1. New Orleans returns
2. Addressing global warming
3. Pollution
4. Love redefined
5. Political corruption
6. Friends and friends
7. Desert war
8. The night sky
9. Going home
10. Bible study
11. City transportation
12. Disciplining children
13. Sports rivalry
14. Consumerism
15. Auto trouble
16. Oceans
17. Confronting terrorism
18. Global warming
19. Prescription drugs
20. Censorship

CROSSCURRENTS

Reread Leo Fasolo's "Life After Death" on pages 233–234 and compare it with Reshma Memon Yaqub's "You People Did This" on pages 407–408. In what ways are they similar, if at all? In what ways are they different? How does the purpose of each piece differ?

COLLABORATIVE LEARNING

Bring to class your draft essays using mixed modes of development. Form groups of three students and read each other's papers, looking particularly at the thesis and how the writer used varied rhetorical strategies to address the topic. Has the writer succeeded in integrating the modes? What suggestions can you make for improvement?

From **IMAGE** to **WORDS**: A Reading and Writing Assignment

© The New Yorker Collection 2005 Roz Chast from cartoonbank.com. All rights reserved.

The quirky cartoonist Roz Chast has highlighted an important issue for today's society: The effects and uses of prescription drugs in our lives. Here, the artist has taken the familiar use of air fresheners and mixed it with three popular tranquilizers or antidepressants to provide a humorous take on our reliance on drugs.

What thoughts do the cartoon and captions stimulate? As you think through the visual image in the context of today's world of easy access to drugs, write an essay about the topic that draws on two or three modes of rhetorical development. State a thesis that emerges from your view of the illustration and provide appropriate supporting details from what you have read and (or) from personal experience.

PART THREE

Special Writing

Special writing situations call for special instructions. Writing on the causes of your decision to go on a diet is far different from writing a paper on the causes of some literary character's actions: Captain Ahab's pursuit of Moby-Dick, for example, or Iago's seemingly motiveless plot against Othello. You may know how to write a well-organized comparison-contrast paper, but writing a personal essay on your reactions to two television sitcoms is far different from writing an essay during a final examination in economics about the arguments for and against lower capital gains taxes.

In Part Three, we provide instruction for dealing with two of the most common kinds of academic writing: literary analysis and essay examinations. In addition, you will find a chapter on business writing, where you will learn about résumés, job application letters, and Internet resources for finding employment.

CHAPTER 17

Literary Analysis

- Writing Your Analysis of Literature
- Student Writing: Literary Analysis
- Readings for Writing

To **analyze** is to study a complex event, thing, or person by examining one or more of its parts and then showing the relationship of each part to the whole. When you receive an assignment such as "Trace the sequence of clues planted by the author so that we have a chance to anticipate the surprise ending in Jackson's 'Charles'" (pages 248–251), you are being asked to write a **literary analysis**. Sometimes instructors assign **explication**, a special form of literary analysis in which short works like poems or stories are examined word by word or paragraph by paragraph to show how each element fits into the general pattern and purpose of the entire work.

Writing Your Analysis of Literature

The following guidelines should help you to deal with literary works. We can't tell you what to say—that will vary with each assignment. It will depend on the material you are analyzing; some subjects offer a great deal of leeway for individual interpretation and insight.

Reading Literature for Analysis

Reading literature for analysis is different from reading for information or for pleasure. Here are some suggestions for reading literary texts (see also Chapter 1, pages 4–33).

TIPS for Reading Literature for Analysis

- **Read the material slowly.** When you need to wade through a pile of junk, fast reading is fine. When you are reading good or great literature, much of which treats complex ideas and emotions, often with complex means of expression, the intelligent approach is to read slowly. Moreover, any analysis involves a close examination of details. Fast reading can give you a general sense of the main points, but it can't prepare you to deal competently with all the concerns of a full-fledged analysis.

■ **Reread.**   When you read a piece for the first time, you're unlikely to have any valid notion of what the author is up to. The author knows how the story or poem is going to end, and the author has been making all sorts of crucial preparations throughout the story to lead into the ending. When you read a selection again, all the ingredients will begin to register in a different way, a way that is emotionally and intellectually impossible to achieve in a first reading. The seemingly separate parts of the story can now come through to you as pieces within a logical pattern. Without a sense of that logical pattern and of how all elements are related to it, your analysis will be weak and incomplete.

■ **Assume that everything is significant.**   In good literature, nothing should be an accident. Each word, each character, each thought, each incident should make a contribution to the total effect the author is trying for. As you think about the material you are going to analyze, keep in mind that *nothing is beneath your notice.* Assume that everything serves a purpose and that you have not reached a full understanding of the story, poem, or play until you see clearly the purpose that everything serves. Read closely, and give serious attention to details. When you get to the writing stage, make liberal use of the details to support your comments. No matter how much actual work you have done, if you do not rely heavily on references to details, your analysis will seem based on vague impressions and snap judgments.

■ **Do not study details out of context.**   Your response to the details of a work—a word, a phrase, a character, an incident—depends on the work as a whole. A sentence like "Mrs. Yee spent twenty minutes arranging the flowers in the vase" could appear in a satire of a neurotic fussbudget or a moving sketch of a mother preparing the house for her child's return from the army. Your analysis or interpretation of the flower arranging must obviously be in harmony with the rest of the work. Keep the intentions of the whole work in mind as you consider the proper approach toward one of its parts.

One more observation: Try not to let your purely personal tastes or prejudices interfere with your responses to the work. An analysis explains what is going on in a piece of literature, not what your own philosophy of life may happen to be.

■ **Forget about "hidden meanings."**   No writer who is any good goes around hiding meanings. Writers have enough trouble expressing them openly. The few writers who do play hide-and-seek with their readers are generally pretentious fakes. In any case, avoid the "hidden meanings" approach to literature. Never use the phrase, as many people do, to refer to an idea or emotion that the author had no intention of concealing but that you just didn't happen to notice on a first reading.

■ **Distinguishing between moral and theme.**   Good literature, in general, is not pure art in the sense that a painting of a pretty landscape is pure art. Most literature attempts far more directly than such paintings to make a comment on life. In considering a story like Edgar Allan Poe's "A Tell-Tale Heart" (pages 430–433), we can and should discuss artistic elements such as plot construction and dialogue, but the story also provides a comment on human nature. If a work has something to say, we must ask ourselves what it is saying as well as how it is saying it.

Skipping the Hunt for Morals

A comment on life, however, is not necessarily a **moral**. In good literature, especially modern literature, it is almost never a moral. This fact confuses many inexperienced readers. For them the question of "what does it mean" or "what does it say" usually implies "what is the moral"—the direct, simple, short statement of a lesson or message to be drawn from the work. When they find no clear moral, they tend to feel cheated or frustrated. Why can't writers just come right out with it and say what they mean? Why are they so fond of hidden meanings (even though we believe that there aren't such things)? Why do they indulge in these mystifying literary games?

There are two ways of answering these questions, one simple and one not so simple. First, morals have a way of being too tidy, too catchy, and dangerously superficial. They are fine in proverbs, children's stories, and five-minute sermons. But literature produced by a thoughtful writer attempts to capture some of the quality of life itself, and the preachy oversimplifications inherent in moralizing spring from distortions of life. *"He who hesitates is lost"; "Life begins at forty"; "It's no use crying over spilt milk"*—this stuff sounds good enough, but we all know that sometimes hesitation is advisable, that a significant life can begin at any age, and that crying over spilt milk has inspired, among many other things, some immortal poetry. When you look for neat little morals in literature, you cheat yourself and you are unfair to the writer. If a writer's comment on life can be summed up in a moral, the odds are that you have wasted your time reading the entire work.

Identifying Themes

As readers and critics we are much better off in dealing with a writer's something-to-say if we think not of the moral but the **theme**. A theme in literature is not a moral, a message, or a piece of advice; rather, it is *the underlying issue, the basic area of permanent human experience treated by the author*. We can say that the theme or themes of *Romeo and Juliet*, for example, are love, and family, and fate, and conflicting loyalties, and reason versus passion. We could add to the list, and a good critic could probably then find a way of linking all the separate themes into one theme that covers them all. The author offers comments on these separate themes by creating certain characters who act in certain ways. Are we really entitled to draw general morals from these themes? Almost certainly not.

Romeo and Juliet are individuals, not representatives of all young lovers. Their families are feuding, as most families are not. The characters in the play face issues that are permanent ingredients of human life and respond to these issues in their own way—and *that* is why the play has something to say, not because it gives us handy hints on how to live our own lives. Discussing the ideas in literature through the concept of *theme* enables us to escape the tyranny of moralizing. It enables writers to be what they are best at being: Writers, not philosophers, prophets, reformers, or know-it-alls.

Interpreting Symbols

What is a symbol? A **symbol** is a person, place, or thing that stands for or strongly suggests something in addition to itself, generally an abstract idea more important than itself. Don't let this definition intimidate you. Symbols are not exotic literary devices that readers have to wrestle with. In fact, the daily, nonliterary lives of readers are filled, quite comfortably and naturally, with more symbols than exist in any book ever written.

A Rolls Royce, for example, is an expensive car manufactured in Britain, but for many people it stands for something else: It is a symbol of success or status or good taste. Our lives are pervaded, perhaps dominated, by symbols. Think about the different symbolic meanings everyone gives to the following: A diamond ring, a new house, money, a police badge, a college diploma, a trip to Europe, a date with a rap star, the Confederate flag, Niagara Falls, a minivan.

Making symbols and reacting to symbols are such basic ingredients of the human mind that we should hardly be astonished to find symbols in literature. Symbols have an extremely practical value to a writer, however. They enable the writer to communicate abstract concepts with the vitality that can come only from specific details. Just as some people may be indifferent to abstract oratory about freedom's being a good thing but deeply moved by a visit to Ground Zero, a reader may be bored by or antagonistic to philosophical assertions about the passing of time but intensely impressed by the specific symbol of a ticking clock in a novel by Faulkner. Symbols of abstract ideas can often have a dramatic impact that the ideas themselves cannot, and sometimes in the hands of a master, symbols can express what might otherwise be almost inexpressible.

Our comments so far have stressed that symbols in literature are not as difficult and mysterious as they are sometimes imagined to be. Dealing with symbols is nevertheless not child's play, and four major traps lie in wait for critics—professionals no less than amateurs.

TIPS for Avoiding Traps Involving Symbols

- **Remember that the symbol stands for or suggests something *in addition to* itself, not *instead of* itself.** The symbolic level of a story or poem should never dwarf the other levels—especially the basic level of people and plot.

■ **Keep in mind that symbols are usually obvious.**   If a critic has to struggle to establish that something functions as a symbol, it probably was not meant to be one. Stick to what the author clearly intends. In Hemingway's *A Farewell to Arms*, one of the characters says repeatedly that she is afraid of the rain because she dreams that it means her death. Then, when she does die and it is indeed raining, we can say that the rain is a symbol of death.

■ **Do not confuse symbols with ordinary significant details.**   A symbol stands for or suggests something substantially different from itself. Rain may symbolize death. A veil may symbolize isolation. Springtime may symbolize youth, rebirth, longing, hope. If a man in a story, however, wipes his running nose with the back of his hand and doesn't cover his mouth when he coughs, we simply know that he has bad manners (in addition to a cold). The way he wipes his nose is not a symbol of bad manners, nor is the way he coughs; they *are* bad manners, details about the character that reveal something about him. A symbol is a person, place, or thing that bears little concrete resemblance to whatever it stands for or suggests; the reader must make a major mental leap to identify the symbol with its meaning. A significant detail about a person, place, or thing, on the other hand, merely conveys more information about or insight into its subject.

■ **Do not be too eager to make a symbol stand for any one thing in particular.** The most effective symbols often are not meant to work that way at all. They *stand for* nothing. They are meant to *suggest*—on an emotional level, at times a virtually subconscious level—a number of elusive concepts. That is precisely why symbols can be so valuable. Herman Melville's white whale in *Moby-Dick*, for example, is surely not meant to symbolize any one idea. The whale becomes such a powerful symbol because it suggests so many ideas: evil, humanity's insignificance, the unchanging order of the universe, nature, God's will, and so on. Symbols are often a great writer's imaginative shortcuts for dealing with the imposing and frightening complexity of life as we know it.

Watching for Metaphors and Similes

Metaphors and similes are the two most common kinds of figurative language or figures of speech. A working definition of **figurative language** is "language that cannot be taken literally." In one way or another, figurative language departs from the conventional meaning and expression of words to bring about special effects, usually emotional. Figurative language is a common ingredient of our speech and writing; it is basic to almost all poetry, far more so than rhyme or meter.

A **simile** is a comparison using the word *like* or *as*.

The lecture was *as* dry as the dust on Grandpa's chicken farm.

All through that dreary summer weekend, we felt *as* if life had turned into a slow-motion movie.

A **metaphor** is a comparison that does without the word *like* or *as*, thus establishing a closer connection between the items compared. It is also helpful, however, to think of a metaphor as a word or phrase that is generally used in one frame of reference but that is shifted to another frame of reference.

> Our lives that dreary summer weekend had turned into a slow-motion movie.

> She had ice water in her veins.

> Bill is the spark plug of his team.

> We thought the new boss was going to be a tiger, but he turned out to be a pussycat.

As indicated by many of the preceding examples, metaphors fill our daily language. A number of them are so familiar that we have to struggle to recognize their metaphorical nature.

the arms of a chair	a wallflower
a clean sweep	the legs of a table
the traffic crawled	the heart of the matter
a poker face	peaches-and-cream complexion

Effective metaphors and similes, when fresh and original, enable writers to stimulate and direct the emotions of their readers, to communicate their own emotions with concrete images rather than flat, abstract statements, and thus to develop stylistic color and excitement. Readers and critics should pay particular attention to **metaphorical patterns**—metaphors sustained and developed through a whole work rather than dropped after one sentence. Many writers consciously use such patterns to achieve greater unity, consistency, and dramatic power, as you have seen in Shakespeare's sonnets (pages 257–258).

Avoiding Common Pitfalls in Literary Analysis

When writing your literary analysis, there are a couple of things you should *not* do, as the following list suggests.

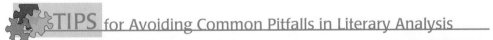

TIPS for Avoiding Common Pitfalls in Literary Analysis

- ■ **Avoid plot summary.** Don't tell the story all over again. Readers may be unaware of any number of subtleties, but you have to assume that they have read the piece, and they know the names of the characters, who's in love with whom, who lives and dies, and so on. You are writing an analysis, not a book report. Note how the student writer of the essay on Shirley Jackson's "Charles" (pages 420–422) doesn't hesitate to give away the surprise ending in her first sentence. Note how she uses all references to events in the story to remind readers of the events and to show how they relate to the thesis of the essay, not to inform readers that the events occurred in the first place.

■ **Do not overuse direct quotations.**   Unless you are writing about an author's style or explaining the meaning of some especially difficult lines, you should be cautious about direct quotations. Rely, for the most part, on references in your own words to the work you are discussing. Advising you to be cautious about direct quotations, however, is not the same as prohibiting them altogether. A well-chosen direct quotation can add a strong dramatic touch to your introduction or conclusion. Moreover, direct quotations can sometimes be valuable if you feel your point might be questionable or controversial. A good general principle is to use your own language unless you have a specific, practical reason for using a direct quotation instead.

Student Writing: Literary Analysis

Now let's look at what happens when a student who is a careful reader and competent writer faces a literary work for analysis.

The following paper analyzes a Shirley Jackson short story that appears in an earlier section of this book (pages 248–251). Harriet McKay's assignment was to "Trace the sequence of clues planted by the author so that we have a chance to anticipate the surprise ending in Jackson's 'Charles.'"

Harriet McKay

The Beginning of the End

1   Until the last sentence of Shirley Jackson's "Charles," I had no idea that Charles, the terror of kindergarten, was an imaginary person created by Laurie and that Charles's little monster antics were really Laurie's own antics. The author fooled me completely, but I have to admit that she played fair. She gave her readers all the clues they needed to make a sensible guess about how the story would end.

2   Laurie's own personality offers one set of clues. Even before classes start, Jackson lets us know that Laurie might have a lot to overcompensate for. His mother has been

dressing him in cute little boy clothes and thinking of him as a "sweet-voiced nursery-school tot." It is at Laurie's own insistence that he begins wearing tough-kid blue jeans. In addition, any boy nicknamed "Laurie" is due for some problems; one doesn't need to be a sexist pig to say that boys named "Laurence" ought to be called "Larry" and that "Laurie," to put it bluntly, is a sissy name. No wonder Laurie goes overboard. He's not a little boy anymore. He has hit the big time in kindergarten, and he begins "swaggering" even before his first class.

Laurie's behavior at home after school starts is another giveaway. Charles may be a monster at school, but Laurie isn't that much better at lunchtime. After only one class, he slams the door, throws his hat on the floor, shouts, speaks "insolently," makes deliberate mistakes in grammar, doesn't look at people when he talks to them but talks to the bread and butter instead, speaks with his mouth full, leaves the table without asking permission and while his father is still talking to him. This is no sweet little tot. His doting parents might try to pin Laurie's behavior on the bad influence of Charles, but that's certainly not the only possible explanation, and that's what doting parents have always tried to do. Besides, it would be stretching things to the limit to imagine that even Charles could have that great an influence after only one morning in the same classroom with him. 3

Still another giveaway is Laurie's explanation for being late. It's impossible to believe that a group of kindergarten kids would voluntarily stay after school to watch a child being punished. Laurie's parents swallow this story so easily that many readers probably didn't notice how fantastic the story really is—but an alert reader would have noticed. 4

The last clue I should have noticed is the way Laurie's parents look forward to the P.T.A. meeting so they can meet Charles's mother. They have been so poised and cool about everything that I really wonder why I did not realize that they would have to be brought down a few pegs at the end of the story. Have they ever made a serious effort to correct their son's bad manners? Have they ever told him to stay 5 away from a rotten kid like Charles? Heavens no, they're much too enlightened. The parents think Charles is amusing, and they can't wait to meet Charles's mother so they can feel superior to her. In simple justice they deserve what they get, and I should have seen it coming.

6   Laurie's personality and behavior, his unbelievable explanation for being late, and his parents' complacency all give readers the clues they need to predict the surprise ending.

FOR WRITING OR DISCUSSION

1. What is the thesis of this paper? Is the thesis stated in one sentence? If so, where?
2. What personality does the writer present to the reader? Is it appropriate to the subject matter?
3. Does the writer omit details from the story that could have strengthened her case?
4. Should the writer have devoted a separate paragraph to the issue of Laurie's lateness? If not, how could the issue have been treated more effectively?
5. Is the last paragraph too short? too abrupt? too dull?
6. Write a brief analysis of this student paper, discussing its strengths and making suggestions for any needed improvements.

EXERCISE   Read or reread the student models "Enough Despair to Go Around" (pages 86–87) by Alan Benjamin and "Two Kinds of Love" (pages 258–260) by Julie Olivera. In what ways do these essays observe the principles of literary analysis that you have studied in this chapter?

Readings for Writing

The short stories that follow should stimulate you to find topics for your own papers of literary analysis. A checklist for writing and revising your literary analysis (pages 433–434) follows the stories. The checklist will help you review the important points in this chapter.

JAMAICA KINCAID

Girl

Wash the white clothes on Monday and put them on the stone heap; wash the color clothes   1
on Tuesday and put them on the clothes-line to dry; don't walk barehead in the hot sun;
cook pumpkin fritters in very hot sweet oil; soak your little cloths right after you take them
off; when buying cotton to make yourself a nice blouse, be sure that it doesn't have gum on
it, because that way it won't hold up well after a wash; soak salt fish overnight before you
cook it; is it true that you sing benna in Sunday school?; always eat your food in such a way
that it won't turn someone else's stomach; on Sundays try to walk like a lady and not like the
slut you are so bent on becoming; don't sing benna in Sunday school; you mustn't speak to
wharf-rat boys, not even to give directions; don't eat fruits on the street—flies will follow
you; *but I don't sing benna on Sundays at all and never in Sunday school*; this is how to sew
on a button; this is how to make a buttonhole for the button you have just sewed on; this is
how to hem a dress when you see the hem coming down and so to prevent yourself from
looking like the slut I know you are so bent on becoming; this is how you iron your father's
khaki shirt so that it doesn't have a crease; this is how you iron your father's khaki pants so
that they don't have a crease; this is how you grow okra—far from the house, because okra
tree harbors red ants; when you are growing dasheen, make sure it gets plenty of water or
else it makes your throat itch when you are eating it; this is how you sweep a corner; this is
how you sweep a whole house; this is how you sweep a yard; this is how you smile to someone you don't like too much; this is how you smile to someone you don't like at all; this is
how you smile to someone you like completely; this is how you set a table for tea; this is
how you set a table for dinner; this is how you set a table for dinner with an important guest;
this is how you set a table for lunch; this is how you set a table for breakfast; this is how to
behave in the presence of men who don't know you very well, and this way they won't recognize immediately the slut I have warned you against becoming; be sure to wash every
day, even if it is with your own spit; don't squat down to play marbles—you are not a boy,
you know; don't pick people's flowers—you might catch something; don't throw stones at
blackbirds, because it might not be a blackbird at all; this is how to make a bread pudding;
this is how to make doukona; this is how to make pepper pot; this is how to make a good
medicine for a cold; this is how to make a good medicine to throw away a child before it
even becomes a child; this is how to catch a fish; this is how to throw back a fish you don't
like, and that way something bad won't fall on you; this is how to bully a man; this is how a
man bullies you; this is how to love a man, and if this doesn't work there are other ways,
and if they don't work don't feel too bad about giving up; this is how to spit up in the air if
you feel like it, and this is how to move quick so that it doesn't fall on you; this is how to
make ends meet; always squeeze bread to make sure it's fresh; *but what if the baker won't
let me feel the bread?*; you mean to say that after all you are really going to be the kind of
woman who the baker won't let near the bread?

FOR WRITING OR DISCUSSION

1. The author was brought up in the West Indies. What elements in the story suggest that the "action" is taking place in the West Indies, or at least in some place other than the United States?

2. Who is the speaker? To whom is the speaker addressing her remarks?

3. What do the italicized words represent?

4. The speaker can correctly be described as a bossy person, a nag, a scold. What evidence suggests that the speaker also has some redeeming, more praiseworthy characteristics?

5. Write a paper contrasting the methods of bringing up children in "Girl" and "Doby's Gone" (next).

ANN PETRY

Doby's Gone

1   When Doby first came into Sue Johnson's life her family were caretakers on a farm way up in New York State. And because Sue had no one else to play with, the Johnsons reluctantly accepted Doby as a member of the family.

2   The spring that Sue was six they moved to Wessex, Connecticut—a small New England town whose neat colonial houses cling to a group of hills overlooking the Connecticut River. All that summer Mrs. Johnson had hoped that Doby would vanish long before Sue entered school in the fall. He would only complicate things in school.

3   For Doby wasn't real. He existed only in Sue's mind. He had been created out of her need for a friend her own age—her own size. And he had gradually become an escape from the very real world that surrounded her. She first started talking about him when she was two and he had been with her ever since. He always sat beside her when she ate and played with her during the day. At night he slept in a chair near her bed so that they awoke at the same time in the morning. A place had to be set for him at mealtime. A seat had to be saved for him on trains and buses.

4   After they moved to Wessex, he was still her constant companion just as he had been when she was three and four and five.

5   On the morning that Sue was to start going to school she said, "Doby has a new pencil, too. And he's got a red plaid shirt just like my dress."

"Why can't Doby stay home?" Mrs. Johnson asked.   6

"Because he goes everywhere I go," Sue said in amazement. "Of course he's going to   7
school. He's going to sit right by me."

Sue watched her mother get up from the breakfast table and then followed her upstairs   8
to the big front bedroom. She saw with surprise that her mother was putting on her going-
out clothes.

"You have to come with me, Mommy?" she asked anxiously. She had wanted to go with   9
Doby. Just the two of them. She had planned every step of the way since the time her mother
told her she would start school in the fall.

"No, I don't have to, but I'm coming just the same. I want to talk to your teacher." Mrs.   10
Johnson fastened her coat and deftly patted a loose strand of hair in place.

Sue looked at her and wondered if the other children's mothers would come to school, too.   11
She certainly hoped so because she wouldn't want to be the only one there who had a mother
with her.

Then she started skipping around the room holding Doby by the hand. Her short black   12
braids jumped as she skipped. The gingham dress she wore was starched so stiffly that the
hemline formed a wide circular frame for her sturdy dark brown legs as she bounced up
and down.

"Ooh," she said suddenly. "Doby pulled off one of my hair ribbons." She reached over and   13
picked it up from the floor and came to stand in front of her mother while the red ribbon was
retied into a crisp bow.

Then she was walking down the street hand in hand with her mother. She held Doby's   14
hand on the other side. She decided it was good her mother had come. It was better that way.
The street would have looked awfully long and awfully big if she and Doby had been by themselves, even though she did know exactly where the school was. Right down the street on this
side. Past the post office and town hall that sat so far back with green lawn in front of them.
Past the town pump and the old white house on the corner, past the big empty lot. And there
was the school.

It had a walk that went straight down between the green grass and was all brown-yellow   15
gravel stuff—coarser than sand. One day she had walked past there with her mother and
stopped to finger the stuff the walk was made of, and her mother had said, "It's gravel." She
remembered how they'd talk about it. "What's gravel?" she asked.

"The stuff in your hand. It's like sand, only coarser. People use it for driveways and walks,"   16
her mother had said.

"Gravel." She liked the sound of the word. It sounded like pebbles. Gravel. Pebble. She   17
said the words over to herself. You gravel and pebble. Pebble said to gravel. She started making up a story. Gravel said to pebble, "You're a pebble," Pebble said back, "You're a gravel."

"Sue, throw it away. It's dirty and your hands are clean," her mother said.   18

She threw it down on the sidewalk. But she kept looking back at it as she walked along.   19
It made a scattered yellow, brown color against the rich brown-black of the dirt-path.

20   She held on to Doby's hand a little more tightly. Now she was actually going to walk up that long gravel walk to the school. She and Doby would play there every day when school was out.

21   The school yard was full of children. Sue hung back a little looking at them. They were playing ball under the big maple trees near the back of the yard. Some small children were squatting near the school building, letting gravel trickle through their fingers.

22   "I want to play, too." She tried to free her hand from her mother's firm grip.

23   "We're going inside to see your teacher first." And her mother went on walking up the school steps holding on to Sue's hand.

24   Sue stared at the children on the steps. "Why are they looking so hard?" she asked.

25   "Probably because you're looking at them so hard. Now come on," and her mother pulled her through the door. The hall inside was dark and very long. A neat white sign over a door to the right said FIRST GRADE in bold black letters.

26   Sue peered inside the room while her mother knocked on the door. A pretty lady with curly yellow hair got up from a desk and invited them in. While the teacher and her mother talked grown-up talk, Sue looked around. She supposed she'd sit at one of those little desks. There were a lot of them and she wondered if there would be a child at each desk. If so then Doby would have to squeeze in beside her.

27   "Sue, you can go outside and play. When the bell rings you must come in," the teacher said.

28   "Yes, teacher," Sue started out the door in a hurry.

29   "My name is Miss Whittier," the teacher said, "You must call me that."

30   "Yes, Miss Whittier. Good-bye, Mommy," she said, and went quickly down the hall and out the door.

31   "Hold my hand, Doby," she said softly under her breath.

32   Now she and Doby would play in the gravel. Squeeze it between their fingers, pat it into shapes like those other children were doing. Her short starched skirt stood out around her legs as she skipped down the steps. She watched the children as long as she could without saying anything.

33   "Can we play, too?" she asked finally.

34   A boy with a freckled face and short stiff red hair looked up at her and frowned. He didn't answer but kept ostentatiously patting at a little mound of gravel.

35   Sue walked over a little closer, holding Doby tightly by the hand. The boy ignored her. A little girl in a blue and white checked dress stuck her tongue out.

36   "Your legs are black," she said suddenly. And then when the others looked up she added, "Why, look, she's black all over. Looky, she's black all over."

37   Sue retreated a step away from the building. The children got up and followed her. She took another backward step and they took two steps forward. The little girl who had stuck her tongue out began a chant, "Look, look. Her legs are black. Her legs are black."

38   The children were all saying it. They formed a ring around her and they were dancing up and down and screaming, "Her legs are black. Her legs are black."

She stood in the middle of the circle completely bewildered. She wanted to go home where it was safe and quiet and where her mother would hold her tight in her arms. She pulled Doby nearer to her. What did they mean her legs were black? Of course they were. Not black but dark brown. Just like these children were white some other children were dark like her. Her mother said so. But her mother hadn't said anyone would make her feel bad about being a different color. She didn't know what to do: so she just stood there watching them come closer and closer to her—their faces red with excitement, their voices hoarse with yelling. 39

Then the school bell rang. And the children suddenly plunged toward the building. She was left alone with Doby. When she walked into the school room she was crying. 40

"Don't you mind, Doby," she whispered. "Don't you mind. I won't let them hurt you." 41

Miss Whittier gave her a seat near the front of the room. Right near her desk. And she smiled at her. Sue smiled back and carefully wiped away the wet on her eyelashes with the back of her hand. She turned and looked around the room. There were no empty seats. Doby would have to stand up. 42

"You stand right close to me and if you get tired just sit on the edge of my seat," she said. 43

She didn't go out for recess. She stayed in and helped Miss Whittier draw on the blackboard with colored chalk—yellow and green and red and purple and brown. Miss Whittier drew the flowers and Sue colored them. She put a small piece of crayon out for Doby to use. And Miss Whittier noticed it. But she didn't say anything, she just smiled. 44

"I love her," Sue thought. "I love my teacher." And then again, "I love Miss Whittier, my teacher." 45

At noon the children followed her halfway home from school. They called after her and she ran so fast and so hard that the pounding in her ears cut off the sound of their voices. 46

"Go faster, Doby," she said. "You have to go faster." And she held his hand and ran until her legs ached. 47

"How was school, Sue?" asked her mother. 48

"It was all right," she said slowly. "I don't think Doby likes it very much. He likes Miss Whittier though." 49

"Do you like her?" 50

"Oh, yes," Sue let her breath come out with a sigh. 51

"Why are you panting like that?" her mother asked. 52

"I ran all the way home," she said. 53

Going back after lunch wasn't so bad. She went right in to Miss Whittier. She didn't stay put in the yard and wait for the bell. 54

When school was out, she decided she'd better hurry right home and maybe the children wouldn't see her. She walked down the gravel path taking quick little looks over her shoulder. No one paid any attention and she was so happy that she gave Doby's hand a squeeze. 55

And then she saw that they were waiting for her right by the vacant lot. She hurried along trying not to hear what they were saying. 56

"My mother says you're a little nigger girl," the boy with the red hair said. 57

And then they began to shout: "Her legs are black. Her legs are black." 58

59   It changed suddenly. "Run. Go ahead and run." She looked over her shoulder. A boy was coming toward her with a long switch in his hand. He raised it in a threatening gesture and she started running.

60   For two days she ran home from school like that. Ran until her short legs felt as though they couldn't move another step.

61   "Sue," her mother asked anxiously, watching her try to catch her breath on the front steps, "what makes you run home from school like this?"

62   "Doby doesn't like the other children very much," she said panting.

63   "Why?"

64   "I don't think they understand about him," she said thoughtfully. "But he loves Miss Whittier."

65   The next day the children waited for her right where the school's gravel walk ended. Sue didn't see them until she was close to them. She was coming slowly down the path hand in hand with Doby trying to see how many of the big pebbles they could step on without stepping on any of the finer, sandier gravel.

66   She was in the middle of the group of children before she realized it. They started off slowly at first. "How do you comb that kind of hair?" "Does that black color wash off?" And then the chant began and it came faster and faster: "Her legs are black. Her legs are black."

67   A little girl reached out and pulled one of Sue's braids. Sue tried to back away and the other children closed in around her. She rubbed the side of her head—it hurt where her hair had been pulled. Someone pushed her. Hard. In the middle of her back. She was suddenly outraged. She planted her feet firmly on the path. She started hitting out with her fists. Kicking. Pulling hair. Tearing at clothing. She reached down and picked up handfuls of gravel and aimed it at eyes and ears and noses.

68   While she was slapping and kicking at the small figures that encircled her she became aware that Doby had gone. For the first time in her life he had left her. He had gone when she started to fight.

69   She went on fighting—scratching and biting and kicking—with such passion and energy that the space around her slowly cleared. The children backed away. And she stood still. She was breathing fast as though she had been running.

70   The children ran off down the street—past the big empty lot, past the old white house with the green shutters. Sue watched them go. She didn't feel victorious. She didn't feel anything except an aching sense of loss. She stood there panting, wondering about Doby.

71   And then, "Doby," she called softly. Then louder, "Doby! Doby! Where are you?"

72   She listened—cocking her head on one side. He didn't answer. And she felt certain he would never be back because he had never left her before. He had gone for good. And she didn't know why. She decided it probably had something to do with growing up. And she looked down at her legs hoping to find they had grown as long as her father's. She saw instead that her dress was torn in three different places, her socks were down around her ankles, there were long angry scratches on her legs and on her arms. She felt for her hair—the red hair ribbons were gone and her braids were coming undone.

She started looking for the hair ribbons. And as she looked she saw that Daisy Bell, the little girl who had stuck her tongue out that first day of school, was leaning against the oak tree at the end of the path.   73

"Come on, let's walk home together," Daisy Bell said matter-of-factly.   74

"All right," Sue said.   75

As they started past the empty lot, she was conscious that someone was tagging along behind them. It was Jimmie Piebald, the boy with the stiff red hair. When she looked back he came up and walked on the other side of her.   76

They walked along in silence until they came to the town pump. They stopped and looked deep down into the well. And spent a long time hallooing down into it and listening delightedly to the hollow funny sound of their voices.   77

It was much later than usual when Sue got home. Daisy Bell and Jimmie walked up to the door with her. Her mother was standing on the front steps waiting for her.   78

"Sue," her mother said in a shocked voice. "What's the matter? What happened to you?"   79

Daisy Bell put her arm around Sue. Jimmie started kicking at some stones in the path.   80

Sue stared at her mother, trying to remember. There was something wrong but she couldn't think what it was. And then it came to her. "Oh," she wailed, "Doby's gone. I can't find him anywhere."   81

FOR WRITING OR DISCUSSION

1. Why does Sue create Doby? Is it normal for a child of Sue's age to create an imaginary playmate, or are we meant to think that Sue may be seriously disturbed mentally?

2. What is Doby a symbol of?

3. Does Miss Whittier know about Doby? Should Miss Whittier have been more aware of the possibilities of Sue's encountering racial prejudice and, if so, have kept a closer eye on her and the other children? Should Sue's mother have alerted her daughter to the possibilities of racial prejudice?

4. What does Sue have to do before she gets the other children's respect?

5. Exactly when does Doby disappear? Why is he most unlikely to return?

6. Write a paper on the issue of illusion versus reality in "Doby's Gone."

HAVING YOUR SAY

What is the state of race relations in American schools today? Could events like those in "Doby's Gone" occur today? Write an argumentative essay to address the issue. Write a thesis that states your opinion; back it up with specific details.

EDGAR ALLAN POE
The Tell-Tale Heart

1   True—nervous—very, very dreadfully nervous I had been and am; but why *will* you say that I am mad? The disease had sharpened my senses—not destroyed—not dulled them. Above all was the sense of hearing acute. I heard all things in the heaven and in the earth. I heard many things in hell. How, then, am I mad? Hearken! and observe how healthily—how calmly I tell you the whole story.

2   It is impossible to say how first the idea entered my brain; but once conceived, it haunted me day and night. Object there was none. Passion there was none. I loved the old man. He had never wronged me. He had never given me insult. For his gold I had no desire. I think it was his eye! yes, it was this! One of his eyes resembled that of a vulture—a pale blue eye, with a film over it. Whenever it fell upon me, my blood ran cold; and so by degrees—very gradually—I made up my mind to take the life of the old man, and thus rid myself of the eye for ever.

3   Now this is the point. You fancy me mad. Madmen know nothing. But you should have seen *me.* You should have seen how wisely I proceeded—with what caution—with what foresight—with what dissimulation I went to work! I was never kinder to the old man than during the whole week before I killed him. And every night, about midnight, I turned the latch of his door and opened it—oh, so gently! And then, when I had made an opening sufficient for my head, I put in a dark lantern, all closed, closed, so that no light shone out, and then I thrust in my head. Oh, you would have laughed to see how cunningly I thrust it in! I moved it slowly—very, very slowly, so that I might not disturb the old man's sleep. It took me an hour to place my whole head within the opening so far that I could see him as he lay upon his bed. Ha!—would a madman have been so wise as this? And then, when my head was well in the room, I undid the lantern cautiously—oh, so cautiously—cautiously (for the hinges creaked)—I undid it just so much that a single thin ray fell upon the vulture eye. And this I did for seven long nights—every night just at midnight—but I found the eye always closed; and so it was impossible to do the work; for it was not the old man who vexed me, but his Evil Eye. And every morning, when the day broke, I went boldly into the chamber, and spoke courageously to him, calling him by name in a hearty tone, and inquiring how he had passed the night. So you see he would have been a very profound old man, indeed, to suspect that every night, just at twelve, I looked in upon him while he slept.

4   Upon the eighth night I was more than usually cautious in opening the door. A watch's minute hand moves more quickly than did mine. Never before that night had I *felt* the extent of my own powers—of my sagacity. I could scarcely contain my feelings of triumph. To think that there I was, opening the door, little by little, and he not even to dream of my secret deeds or thoughts. I fairly chuckled at the idea; and perhaps he heard me; for he moved on the bed suddenly, as if startled. Now you may think that I drew back—but no. His room was as black as pitch with the thick darkness (for the shutters were closed fastened, through fear

of robbers), and so I knew that he could not see the opening of the door, and I kept pushing it on steadily, steadily.

I had my head in, and was about to open the lantern, when my thumb slipped upon the tin fastening, and the old man sprang up in the bed, crying out "Who's there?"   5

I kept quite still and said nothing. For a whole hour I did not move a muscle, and in the meantime I did not hear him lie down. He was still sitting up in the bed listening;—just as I have done, night after night, hearkening to the death watches in the wall.   6

Presently I heard a slight groan, and I knew it was the groan of mortal terror. It was not a groan of pain or of grief—oh, no!—it was the low stifled sound that arises from the bottom of the soul when overcharged with awe. I knew the sound well. Many a night, just at midnight, when all the world slept, it was welled up from my own bosom, deepening, with its dreadful echo, the terrors that distracted me. I say I knew it well. I knew what the old man felt, and pitied him, although I chuckled at heart. I knew that he had been lying awake ever since the first slight noise, when he had turned in the bed. His fears had been ever since growing upon him. He had been trying to fancy them causeless, but could not. He had been saying to himself—"It is nothing but the wind in the chimney—it is only a mouse crossing the floor," or "it is merely a cricket which has made a single chirp." Yes, he has been trying to comfort himself with these suppositions; but he had found all in vain. *All in vain*; because Death, in approaching him, had stalked with his black shadow before him, and enveloped the victim. And it was the mournful influence of the unperceived shadow that caused him to feel—although he neither saw nor heard—to *feel* the presence of my head within the room.   7

When I had waited a long time, very patiently, without hearing him lie down, I resolved to open a little—a very, very little crevice in the lantern. So I opened it—you cannot imagine how stealthily, stealthily, until, at length, a single dim ray, like the thread of a spider, shot from out the crevice and full upon the vulture eye.   8

It was open—wide, wide open—and I grew furious as I gazed upon it. I saw it with perfect distinctness—all a dull blue, with a hideous veil over it that chilled the very marrow in my bones; but I could see nothing else of the old man's face or person: for I had directed the ray as if by instinct, precisely upon the damned spot.   9

And now have I not told you that what you mistake for madness is but overacuteness of the senses!—now, I say, there came to my ears a low, dull, quick sound, such as a watch makes when enveloped in cotton. I knew *that* sound well too. It was the beating of the old man's heart. It increased my fury, as the beating of a drum stimulates the soldier into courage.   10

But even yet I refrained and kept still. I scarcely breathed. I held the lantern motionless. I tried how steadily I could maintain the ray upon the eye. Meantime the hellish tattoo of the heart increased. It grew quicker and quicker, and louder and louder every instant. The old man's terror *must* have been extreme! It grew louder, I say, louder every moment!—do you mark me well? I have told you that I am nervous: so I am. And now at the dead hour of the night, amid the dreadful silence of that old house, so strange a noise as this excited me to uncontrollable terror. Yet, for some minutes longer I refrained and stood still. But the beating grew louder, louder! I thought the heart must burst. And now a new anxiety seized me—the sound would be heard by a neighbor! The old man's hour had come! With a loud yell, I   11 threw open the lantern and leaped into the room. He shrieked once—once only. In an instant I dragged him to the floor, and pulled the heavy bed over him. I then smiled gaily, to defend the deed so far done. But, for many minutes, the heart beat on with a muffled sound. This, however, did not vex me; it would not be heard through the wall. At length it ceased. The old man was dead. I removed the bed and examined the corpse. Yes, he was stone, stone dead. I placed my hand upon the heart and held it there many minutes. There was no pulsation. He was stone dead. His eye would trouble me no more.

12   If still you think me mad, you will think so no longer when I describe the wise precautions I took for the concealment of the body. The night waned and I worked hastily, but in silence. First of all I dismembered the corpse. I cut off the head and the arms and the legs.

13   I then took up three planks from the flooring of the chamber, and deposited all between the scantlings. I then replaced the boards so cleverly, so cunningly, that no human eye—not even *his*—could have detected any thing wrong. There was nothing to wash out—no stain of any kind—no blood-spot whatever. I had been too wary for that. A tub had caught all—ha! ha!

14   When I had made an end of these labors, it was four o'clock—still dark as midnight. As the bell sounded the hour, there came a knocking at the street door. I went down to open it with a light heart—for what had I *now* to fear? There entered three men, who introduced themselves, with perfect suavity, as officers of the police. A shriek had been heard by a neighbor during the night; suspicion of foul play had been aroused; information had been lodged at the police office, and they (the officers) had been deputed to search the premises.

15   I smiled,—for *what* had I to fear? I bade the gentlemen welcome. The shriek, I said, was my own in a dream. The old man, I mentioned, was absent in the country. I took my visitors all over the house. I bade them search—search *well*. I led them, at length, to *his* chamber. I showed them his treasures, secure, undisturbed. In the enthusiasm of my confidence, I brought chairs into the room, and desired them *here* to rest from their fatigues, while I myself, in the wild audacity of my perfect triumph, placed my own seat upon the very spot beneath which reposed the corpse of the victim.

16   The officers were satisfied. My *manner* had convinced them. I was singularly at ease. They sat, and while I answered cheerily, they chatted familiar things. But, ere long, I felt myself getting pale and wished them gone. My head ached, and I fancied a ringing in my ears: but still they sat and still chatted. The ringing became more distinct:—it continued and became more distinct: I talked more freely to get rid of the feeling: but I continued and gained definitiveness—until, at length. I found that the noise was *not* within my ears.

17   No doubt I now grew *very* pale:—but I talked more fluently, and with a heightened voice. Yet the sound increased—and what could I do? It was a *low, dull, quick sound—much such a sound as a watch makes when enveloped in cotton*. I gasped for breath—and yet the officers heard it not. I talked more quickly—more vehemently; but the noise steadily increased. I arose and argued about trifles, in a high key and with violent gesticulations, but the noise steadily increased. Why *would* they not be gone? I paced the floor to and fro with heavy strides, as if excited to fury by the observation of the men—but the noise steadily increased. Oh God! what *could* I do? I foamed—I raved—I swore! I swung the chair upon which I had been sitting, and grated it upon the boards, but the noise arose over all and

continually increased. It grew louder—louder—*louder!* And still the men chatted pleasantly, and smiled. Was it possible they heard not? Almighty God!—no, no! They heard!—they suspected!—they *knew!*—they were making a mockery of my horror!—this I thought, and this I think. But any thing was better than this agony! Any thing was more tolerable than this derision! I could bear those hypocritical smiles no longer! I felt that I must scream or die!—and now—again!—hark! louder! louder! louder! *louder!*—

"Villains!" I shrieked, "dissemble no more! I admit the deed!—tear up the planks!—here, here!—it is the beating of his hideous heart!" 18

FOR WRITING OR DISCUSSION

1. What is the narrator's mental state? How do you know? How does Poe's language help convey the mental state of the narrator?

2. What does the narrator say is the result of his disease? To whom is he speaking?

3. Sound plays an important part in the telling of this story. What images of sound can you identify here? What claim does the narrator make about sound in the first paragraph?

4. What do the frequent repetitions contribute to this story?

5. Do you trust the narrator? Why, or why not? Are his observations reliable?

6. Edgar Allan Poe, who wrote in the nineteenth century ("The Tell-Tale Heart" was published in 1843), continues to be an extremely popular writer. How do you account for his popularity? Write an essay in which you explain, on the basis of this short story, why Poe continues to have a hold on the American imagination.

STRATEGY CHECKLIST: Writing and Revising Your Literary Analysis Paper

Read the literary work.	☐ Have I read the work slowly? Have I reread it?
	☐ Have I read with the assumption that everything is significant?
	☐ Have I concentrated on *theme* rather than *moral*?
	☐ Have I been aware of any use of symbols?
	☐ Have I been alert to the use of metaphors and similes?

continued

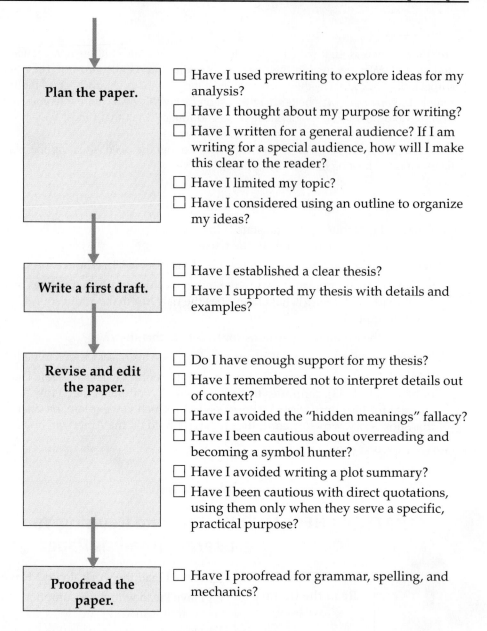

Plan the paper.

☐ Have I used prewriting to explore ideas for my analysis?

☐ Have I thought about my purpose for writing?

☐ Have I written for a general audience? If I am writing for a special audience, how will I make this clear to the reader?

☐ Have I limited my topic?

☐ Have I considered using an outline to organize my ideas?

Write a first draft.

☐ Have I established a clear thesis?

☐ Have I supported my thesis with details and examples?

Revise and edit the paper.

☐ Do I have enough support for my thesis?

☐ Have I remembered not to interpret details out of context?

☐ Have I avoided the "hidden meanings" fallacy?

☐ Have I been cautious about overreading and becoming a symbol hunter?

☐ Have I avoided writing a plot summary?

☐ Have I been cautious with direct quotations, using them only when they serve a specific, practical purpose?

Proofread the paper.

☐ Have I proofread for grammar, spelling, and mechanics?

For additional writing, reading, and research resources, go to **www. mycomplab.com** <http://www.mycomplab.com/> and choose Skwire/Wiener's *Student's Book of College English*, Twelfth Edition.

CHAPTER **18**

Writing Essay Exams

■ Preparing for the Exam
■ Evaluating the Question
■ Planning and Writing
   Your Essay

Essay examinations are an important part of college learning; they provide an excellent gauge of your knowledge of a subject. No doubt you have taken these kinds of tests before: You have one or more questions to answer in an in-class essay of several pages within a defined time frame—usually about an hour.

Essay test questions share a number of qualities that make it possible to generalize about them. This general advice about how to prepare for and take essay exams for all your college courses should help you improve performance.

Preparing for the Exam

To minimize anxiety and to achieve the best results possible on an examination, prepare carefully and well in advance of your test.

If you've paid attention to lectures and class discussions during the semester, you'll have a good sense of your instructor's emphases. Use your lecture notes and review your readings to determine which areas your instructor might target; assume the role of test maker and develop your own essay questions. Use these questions to help you study.

A useful way to begin is to make a table of topics and questions. First, develop a list of the key areas you believe might be covered on the exam. Then alongside the topics, indicate possible questions.

Look at this sample prepared by a student studying for a test on child development.

Table of topics and questions

Topic	Possible essay questions
Physical environment of the fetus	1. How does the physical environment of the fetus contribute to the

psychological development of the child?

2. Discuss the effects of drugs or alcohol on the fetus and explain some of the noticeable psychological results on the newborn.

Prenatal care

1. Explain the steps a caregiver can take to provide appropriate psychological care for the fetus.

2. Define *prenatal* and *neonatal* and give distinguishing characteristics of each.

Psychology of the newborn

1. What can parents do to provide a sound psychological environment for a newborn?

2. What are some possible effects on a child whose basic needs are not met in the first month after birth?

Evaluating the Question

It is very important to know exactly what the exam question is asking so that you can make the required points and provide the necessary detail.

Always read the entire test, and study each essay question carefully. A major complaint from teachers who grade essay exams is that students often do not answer the questions being asked. Read the question with care so that you know precisely what your instructor expects. Essay questions usually contain cue words that signal the specific requirements. You should look for these cue words as you read the question and should develop your responses to address the stated task. The table below lists and explains some cue words and identifies the methods of essay development (explained in Part Two of this book) that you might use to write your answers. Keep in mind that some essay questions will ask for a combination of these methods. And you should refer especially to Chapter 16, "Mixing Modes of Development."

Strategies for Responding to Essay Exam Cue Words

Cue words	What to do	Method of development
Describe, tell, discuss, trace	Give physical characteristics, provide details, indicate sequence, or explain features.	Description Narration
Explain, illustrate, give examples, identify	Make sense or order of, enumerate, or provide details and examples.	Example Definition
How? Explain how, show how, tell how	Explain a process or indicate chronology.	Process
Compare, contrast, compare and contrast	Indicate similarities and (or) differences.	Comparison–contrast
Why, tell why, analyze, explain the results (or effects) of, tell the consequences of	Show the relation between ideas or events; tell how one event influences, causes, or results from another; or draw conclusions.	Cause and effect
Agree or disagree, support, evaluate, judge, defend, argue	Provide logical support for your position on a topic; convince a reader that your position is correct.	Argumentation

The following chart presents, from courses across the disciplines, typical essay examination questions that use some of these cue words.

Typical Essay Exam Questions

Discipline	Essay question
English Literature	Provide examples of Shakespeare's use of animal imagery in *The Tempest* and explain the meaning of several key images.
Biology	Explain the reproductive process of budding in yeast cells.
Sociology	Compare and contrast the conditions in state-run orphanages in California in the nineteenth and twentieth centuries.
Health Care	Terminal illness often has devastating effects on the patient's immediate family. What are some of these effects? How can social service agencies provide support for family members of the terminally ill?
Psychology	Identify three personality disorders and describe the key features of each.
History	Describe the slave trade in America in the eighteenth century.

Planning and Writing Your Essay

Once you examine the question carefully and are confident that you understand the task, take time to plan the essay before you begin writing.

 TIPS for Planning and Writing Your Essay

■ **Assess the expected length and range of your response.**   From the nature of the questions, determine how much you are expected to write. Your teacher may indicate what she expects in the examination questions with statements like "Write a sentence or two" or "Write a paragraph." More often than not, however, you have to infer the length of your expected response. A question worth five or ten points demands a shorter answer—a few sentences or a paragraph, say—than a question worth twenty-five, fifty, or a hundred points.

■ **Use the wording of the essay question to help get you started.**   Essay questions provide information that helps you focus your thinking on the topic. Use some of the language of the question in your response, especially in the introduction to your answer.

   Look again at some of the essay questions from different disciplines just listed and at some possible opening responses to these questions:

Opening Responses to Essay Questions

Essay question	Opening responses that use elements of the questions
Provide examples of Shakespeare's use of animal imagery in *The Tempest* and explain the meaning of several key images.	In *The Tempest* we find many examples of animal imagery, especially regarding the character Caliban.
Explain the reproductive process of budding in yeast cells.	Yeast plants reproduce by a process of budding in which . . .
Terminal illness often has devastating effects on the patient's immediate family. What are some of these effects? How can social service agencies provide support for family members of the terminally ill?	The effects of terminal illness on patients and their families can be devastating, but social service agencies can help by providing a variety of support for individuals and the family as a whole.

■ **Budget your time.** For an hour's exam, reserve about forty-five minutes for writing and about fifteen to twenty minutes for planning, revising, and editing.

■ **Follow the general guidelines for good writing.** You should express your thesis and purpose clearly and should support your assertions with concrete detail. Accuracy, specificity, completeness, and relevance are essential. You will have to draw most details from your lecture and recitation notes as well as from your readings. Although verbatim citations are difficult unless you have a superb memory, you nevertheless should paraphrase key points carefully, identifying sources whenever you can. Write an introduction and a conclusion—brief as time may require them to be. Connect thoughts with necessary transitions within paragraphs; link paragraphs logically within the essay.

■ **Plan your essay carefully and make revisions and editorial changes as needed.** Because of time pressures on an essay examination, you certainly will have to condense the steps we recommended that you take as writers. However, do not ignore basic features of the writing process, especially the prewriting and planning strategies.

Even with the clock ticking, take a few moments to plan. Use the margins or the inside or back cover of your exam booklet to jot down ideas and to develop a scratch outline. When you write, consider the effort as somewhere between a first draft and a revised and edited draft—that is, you cannot write your essay exam on scrap paper and expect to return later to make extensive revisions. Certainly, you must reread your first effort, deleting problematic sections, adding words and sentences, as needed, and fixing errors. Write all additions clearly. Your teacher should be able to follow your marks and directional arrows. Many students skip every other line as they write and leave large top and bottom margins to facilitate changes and insertions. Nevertheless, the press of time will prevent you from rewriting your essay entirely. Don't plan on it. Add key elements that you may have omitted; insert definitions or essential detail; correct mistakes. But unless you are sure that you have sufficient time to recopy a draft, or that your instructor expects a second draft, do not rewrite your essay examination.

STRATEGY CHECKLIST: Taking an Essay Exam

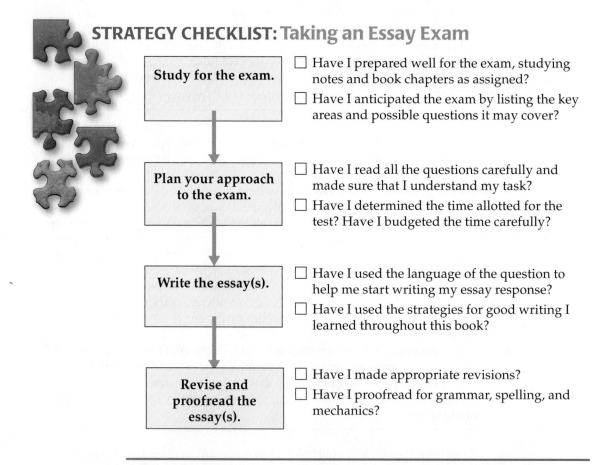

Study for the exam.

☐ Have I prepared well for the exam, studying notes and book chapters as assigned?

☐ Have I anticipated the exam by listing the key areas and possible questions it may cover?

Plan your approach to the exam.

☐ Have I read all the questions carefully and made sure that I understand my task?

☐ Have I determined the time allotted for the test? Have I budgeted the time carefully?

Write the essay(s).

☐ Have I used the language of the question to help me start writing my essay response?

☐ Have I used the strategies for good writing I learned throughout this book?

Revise and proofread the essay(s).

☐ Have I made appropriate revisions?

☐ Have I proofread for grammar, spelling, and mechanics?

For additional writing, reading, and research resources, go to **www. mycomplab.com** <http://www.mycomplab.com/> and choose Skwire/Wiener's *Student's Book of College English*, Twelfth Edition.

CHAPTER 19

Business Writing: An Overview

The writing demands of the business world, complicated by widespread use of word processing programs and other computer aids, build on certain formal conventions. So many misconceptions exist about what constitutes effective writing for a job and on the job that we provide in this overview chapter what we hope will be useful suggestions as you face business writing tasks.

- ■ Writing Inquiry and Complaint Letters
- ■ Addressing an Envelope
- ■ Writing a Letter to Apply for a Job
- ■ Writing Your Résumé
- ■ Writing Memorandums and E-mail

Writing Inquiry and Complaint Letters

Despite the easy access of e-mail (see page 452) and the availability of office phones, cellular phones, and text and voicemail messaging, letters continue to fuel the engine of most businesses. A letter is permanent and won't get wiped away by computer glitches and crashes; it provides an accurate record of transactions; it encourages the building of long-term relations among business partners; and it bears a signature that can carry legal weight. (We must note, however, that e-signatures are now as legal as more traditional "wet" ones.) As communications options expand endlessly, it seems, you often can convey the letter instantly via e-mail or fax, both of which provide quick and easy alternatives to the United States Postal Service and its competitors. Still, you never can go wrong by sending a letter in an envelope with a stamp affixed to it.

Letter of Inquiry

If you write a letter to *inquire* about or *request* something—cancellation of your subscription to *People* magazine, for example, information about the contents of makeup that causes your eyes to tear, or a self-charging mini dust buster that would be great for your dorm room—you want to make your request known as quickly as possible and to back it up with specific and accurate information needed to fulfill your request.

Letter of Complaint

If you write a letter to *complain* about something—incorrect billing for your tuition, for example, the way airline personnel treated you when your flight was cancelled, or the crushed and inedible contents of a box of sourdough pretzels—your objective is to make your complaint known so that the respondent can redress it in some way. Think about what you want in return for your problem and be sure to suggest it in your letter. Your tone in a complaint letter is very important. Be firm and direct but not snide or insulting. Focus on the problem and the resolution; don't condemn the whole company or castigate its leaders. State your charge. Provide all essential details (dates, prices, and place of occurrence as needed) without padding or drama. Remember, you want something in return, and you're writing to someone who may be in a position to give you what you want. Be courteous. Be straightforward. Stick to the facts (see the letter on page 443).

Letter Format

Most business letters follow the **block format**, which word processors now provide automatically as standard, and you can type in information swiftly without worrying about spacing. In the block format, all parts of the letter are flush with the left margin. You separate paragraphs by leaving a blank line between the last line of one paragraph and the first line of the paragraph that comes after it. In the **modified block format**, you indent by 25–30 spaces the inside address, the complimentary close, and the closing instead of placing them flush with the left margin. Note the labeled parts of the block format in the illustration on the following page.

Print your letter on standard, $8\frac{1}{2} \times 11$-inch unlined, heavy bond paper. Unless your letter is really short, use single space, with a blank space between paragraphs. Be sure to proofread your letter very carefully before sending it.

TIPS for Writing and Formatting a Letter

- **Heading.** Type your full street address flush left on the first line of the heading; your city, state, and ZIP code on the next; and the date on the last line. Letter conventions require that you avoid abbreviations (like *St., Ave.,* and *Feb.,* to name a few) except for the name of a state, which should appear in the standard two-letter postal code abbreviation—CA, MD, NY, CO, for example. Do not include your name anywhere in the heading. If you use letterhead stationery—paper that has the company logo and (or) name and the company address printed across the top, bottom, or side—your first typed entry is the date, beneath the letterhead after two or three line spaces.

318 Walker Street
Boulder, CO 10036

Heading: your return address (omit if using letterhead stationery) and date

April 7, 2008

Comma here

Double space

Mr. Steve Kingsbury, General Manager
Customer Service Division
Bose Corporation
The Mountain
Framingham, MA 01701

Inside address

Comma here

Double space

Salutation Dear Mr. Kingsbury: Colon

1-1¼ inch margin

Several months ago I received a gift of your Bose Wave radio, Model AWR1-1W, and have enjoyed using it. But I have encountered two problems for which I would like to request your help.

1¼ inch margin

Double space between body paragraphs

First, I have misplaced the Wave radio remote control unit. It is a thin, black, rectangular object measuring approximately 1-1/2 inches by 3 inches. Apparently it has no model or serial number. Is it possible to replace this item? If so, how much would it cost--and will you accept a credit card or do you require payment by check? How long do you think it would take for me to receive the remote control unit once I place the order? Would there be an extra charge for rapid delivery service?

Body

Double space between body paragraphs

Second, I find that the antenna that accompanies the radio is inadequate for my needs. The antenna is simply a Y-shaped wire that I have spread and attached to the ceiling of my study, which is in the basement of my house. Although there are two windows in the basement, I believe that the radio's location below ground level weakens the transmission of sound. Could you recommend a more powerful antenna that would bring better reception to the room? If so, will you suggest some stores that might carry it? We have a Radio Shack and a Home Depot nearby.

Double space between body paragraphs

I would appreciate a prompt response so that I can enjoy my new radio more fully.

Double space between body paragraphs

Sincerely, Complimentary close

Comma here
Quadruple space

William Cookson Signature

William Cookson Typed name

■ **Inside address.** Space two or three lines (more if you're writing a short letter) beneath the date and type the full name, title, and address of the person you're sending the letter to. Abbreviations such as *Mr., Miss, Mrs., Ms.,* and *Dr.* are acceptable, and you should use them. If you don't know the name of the person you are writing to, it's all right to start the inside address with the person's title or the department you're interested in—for example, *Director of Human Resources* or *Customer Relations Department*. As with the inside address, you want to avoid most abbreviations other than the state and any abbreviation that appears as part of the company name.

If you want to make reference to previous correspondence or documents that will help the reader relate quickly to the issues in your letter, make reference to it a few spaces below the inside address. Type *Re* (an abbreviation for reference) followed by a colon and then indicate the document:

Re: Your letter of December 16, 2008
Re: Invoice Number 67843

■ **Salutation.** In your greeting, after the word *dear*, use the appropriate abbreviation for the person's title followed by the addressee's last name—*Dear Mr. Santiago, Dear Ms. Chin*. If you're writing to more than one person, use the abbreviations from the French: *Messrs.* for the plural of *Monsieur* and *Mmes.* for the plural of *Madame*—*Dear Messrs. Damon and Affleck, Dear Mmes. Schwartz and Murphy*. If you have not included a name in the inside address, do not use the word *dear* in your salutation. Use *Gentlemen, Ladies,* or the combination *Gentlemen/Ladies*. This last combination has supporters among some letter writers, but it is not used widely.

■ **Body.** The body of the letter is the content, the paragraphs in which you make your point. Keep your correspondence to about one page and your paragraphs short. Your letter will no doubt reach the desk of a busy person, and the shorter the letter, the more quickly your point will get across. Make your point concisely and without padding. Civility is essential—the reader of the letter does not have the added advantage of receiving your message with accompanying gestures, intonations, and facial impressions. The words on the page say everything, and you want to be relaxed and informal in your written language (not slangy), but not at the expense of courteous expression. You should avoid stilted (artificially formal and stiff) language and you should prune deadwood carefully. Chapters 22 through 24—that is, all of Part Five, Style, in the *Student's Book of College English*—can help you develop and sustain appropriate letter language and technique.

■ **Complimentary close.** Use one of the following forms, which are most appropriate for and typical of business letters. The complimentary close always begins with a capital letter, ends with a comma, and appears on its own line in the letter.

Sincerely yours, Sincerely, Yours truly,

Leave three or four blank lines for your signature and type your name.

■ **Notations.**   Beneath the signature block you can make notations. If you want to indicate that you are enclosing something with the letter, usually a copy of a prior letter, document, or other reference material, note it beneath the signature as in the instances below.

Enclosures (2)

Encl.: Presbyterian Hospital medical file

If you want to indicate that you're sending a copy of the letter to someone, type the abbreviation *c.* (for copy) followed by the other recipient's name:

c. Mr. Steven Spielberg c. Dr. Ramona Leary

■ **Continuation pages.**   If your letter requires more than one page, do not use letterhead stationery on the second and subsequent pages. Instead, use plain white bond paper. In the block style, flush with the left margin, type the page number, the name of the person you are writing to, and the date.

2

Mr. Steve Kingsbury

April 7, 2008

Addressing an Envelope

Most word processing programs provide an envelope and label option on the toolbar and produce envelopes in appropriate format for postal delivery, extracting the required addresses for the envelope from the letter itself. You must include a return address in the upper left-hand corner of the envelope (not on the back flap). The address in the center of the envelope is the same as the inside address in the letter.

Oscar Sanchez
210 East 64 Street, Apt 24J
New York, NY 10021

Ms. Joyce Haberski, President
Web Designs, Inc.
1520 Commercial Drive
Sacramento, CA 95819

FOLDING A BUSINESS LETTER

Fold your letter neatly in thirds to fit a number 10 size business envelope.

EXERCISE Write a letter of inquiry or complaint to address one of the following situations. Figure out to whom you would write and use that information to construct the inside address and salutation.

1. You want information about a graduate program in physical therapy, including deadlines for applications, course requirements, fellowship availability, and any other related matters.
2. You have had your new automobile in the shop four times in the last two months for transmission problems and still it is not working right. You want a new transmission installed now; the existing transmission cannot be repaired, you believe.
3. You have had no success in raising cucumbers in your garden for the last few summers. They start off all right, but the fruits are distorted and not plentiful, and the foliage turns brown toward mid-season.
4. The bus that takes you from your dorm to the college building for your first class each morning is never on time. Although a schedule is posted, arrival times at your stop are erratic at best, and you have been late to class several times this semester.
5. The food in your college cafeteria is high in fat and sugar, and there are not enough options for people who watch their diet and would choose more healthful foods, such as salads from a salad bar, plain grilled meats or vegetables, and fresh fruit—which seem almost nonexistent.

Writing a Letter to Apply for a Job

Whether you're applying for a part-time job after classes, a two- or three-month summer position, or a full-time job after graduation, the job-seeking letter and accompanying résumé are a vital part of the employment process.

 Many employers now require job candidates to submit all letters and résumés via e-mail. What passes for acceptable writing in informal e-mails to friends and family is thoroughly unacceptable in job applications. Clarity and correctness are essential.

Start prewriting activity by reviewing your education and job history. Your résumé (look ahead to page 451) will help you here. It's all right to stress key features of your résumé, but you want to be sure not to write a job application letter that merely repeats all the information found there. You'll be including your résumé with the letter, so avoid redundancy.

How do you make your letter stand out? Let your personality shine through as you attempt to show the reader your special talents. Use specific examples to indicate relevant experience or to recount an incident that reflects your skills. Avoid the trite and careworn expressions that often infiltrate job letters: "Thank you in advance for your consideration," and "I look forward to hearing from you," and "I would be happy to meet with you at a convenient time," for example. Yes, it's a good idea to try to arrange for an interview, but you gain with a more forceful and direct statement, such as "May I call you next week to set up a meeting?" or "I'll call on Tuesday for an appointment at your convenience."

Many people like to indicate their source of information for the position in the first sentence of their job application letter: "I saw your ad in the employment section of the January 5, 2008, issue of the *New York Times*." "A mutual friend, David Stewart, told me that you are looking for an assistant manager."

The sample letter appearing on page 448 is lucid and concise, yet forceful and infused with the writer's personality. The writer has chosen the block format.

Writing Your Résumé

A résumé is a summary of your education, job history, and accomplishments. Reflect on your past experiences and make a list of anything that seems relevant to displaying your character or giving any other valuable information about yourself. Think about any full- or part-time jobs you have held. Even if they are not in the field you're seeking to pursue, they can indicate ambition, ingenuity, strength of character, degree of responsibility, and so on. Think about honors and awards in school, on the playing field, or in some extra- or cocurricular enterprise. Even extracurricular work at high school, if it shows your skills in a positive light, can add useful information to your résumé.

Start the résumé with your name, address, and telephone number on the top of the page. Include a fax number and (or) an e-mail address, if you have one. Then, you want to establish categories to make it easier for the reader to identify related pieces of information. Some typical categories are *Job Objective,*

201 East 64th Street, Apt. 24J
New York, NY 10021
Phone: (212) 363-9999
E-mail: oscsan@tele.com

April 15, 2008

Key information complete in heading and inside address

Ms. Joyce Haberski, President
Web Designs, Inc.
1520 Commercial Drive
Sacramento, CA 95819

Dear Ms. Haberski:

Salutation: use of Ms. to avoid indicating marital status for woman correspondent

Purpose of letter stated directly and forcefully

I learned from a mutual friend, Brian O'Malley, that your new company is seeking web designers who can help put together commercial web pages for a variety of companies. I'm the person you are looking for. My interests, education, and experience have prepared me well for the job you are trying to fill.

Source of job announcement stated in first sentence

My parents used to joke that even as a child I had bytes along with gray matter in my brain, so tuned into the possibilities of computers was I from a very early age. The keyboard was (and continues to be) my soul mate. Although I wouldn't exactly call myself a computer nerd--I do like other things such as reading mystery novels, playing touch football, and fishing in Folsom Lake not far from our family home in Rancho Cordova--my friends all know that my laptop and I are inseparable. I do love working on the computer and never tire of exploring its potential. In high school I automated the production and design of our school newspaper, Topics Weekly, for which I served as managing editor in my senior year.

Friendly, informal style ("Bytes along with gray matter," "computer nerd"); personal information helps reveal writer's character

Block style followed throughout

After I moved East, I attended Mildred Elley College, where I completed the Associate in Occupational Studies in Informational Technology program and received my O.A.S. degree in 2003. Along with courses in computer repair, programming, and software applications, I studied visual programming, Internet design, and electronic commerce. I worked for two years after graduation at the Wiles Corporation as a Help Desk manager before concluding that I liked the creative side of computer work more than the technical side, and I decided to return to college as a communication arts major.

Essential details from résumé highlighted without restating all points

Key courses identified to suggest essential training for position

As a student at Marymount Manhattan College, I now have many courses in visual design under my belt, and I was fortunate to complete a six-course sequence in the College's Division of Continuing Education, which awarded me a Certificate in Web Design and E-Commerce. As you can see from my enclosed résumé, I will complete my Bachelor of Arts degree this June. I love working with people and, as you can tell, I love working with computers. After an exciting few years in New York City I am eager to return permanently to California, where I was born and where my family lives.

I'll be back home in the Sacramento region after graduation on June 11 and would like very much to meet with you at your convenience soon after. May I call next week to set up an appointment?

Firm yet courteous effort to set up interview

Sincerely yours,

Oscar Sanchez

Oscar Sanchez

Complimentary close and signature

Encl.

Education, Work Experience, Honors and Awards, Personal, and *References*. Set off these categories in boldface type or by underlining them and place them at the left margin. Put relevant information beneath the categories, as shown in the Sanchez résumé on page 451. Use sentence fragments to indicate some of your responsibilities and use lively verbs and verb forms. Writing fragments helps you avoid the redundant "I"—*I* studied this, *I* did that, *I* did something else.

Present relevant information about yourself in each category, as appropriate, following reverse time order—that is, you list the most recent item first. Like the business letter, the résumé should follow accepted formatting conventions, although there is no absolute format that requires strict adherence. You should try to keep your résumé to a single page, if possible. To make the page look more attractive, you might want to vary typeface or type size, but you should resist overdoing design elements on your résumé. Look at the sample (page 451) prepared by Oscar Sanchez, and the accompanying annotations.

 for Preparing a Résumé

- **Reflect on your past accomplishments.** Make a list of any information that's relevant to the type of job you are seeking, including previous work experience, community service, and courses of study that show your preparation for the job.

- **Reflect on your character.** Remember that personal characteristics like self-motivation, willingness to accept responsibility, and organization are qualities that employers look for. List key activities that suggest those and other important character traits.

- **Organize your information.** Create categories for related information; for example, *Education, Work Experience*, and *Personal*.

- **Draft your résumé.** Put your name and contact information at the top. Then draft each section. For work experience and education, present information in reverse time order, most recent first. To save space, use sentence fragments and active verb forms. Use the *Personal* category to highlight special interests and talents. Try to confine your entries to one page.

- **Format and finalize your résumé.** Leave a 1-1/2 inch margin, and type the word *Résumé*, with your name and contact information directly below. Use underlining, boldface, or italics to set off the section headings, but don't be too fancy. Use a standard typeface like *Times New Roman* for the text. If you are preparing a resume to submit to a computerized database, do not use any special type formatting (see page 453). If your résumé runs longer than a page, try to cut it back.

COLLABORATIVE LEARNING

In groups of three people each, exchange letters and résumés. Assume the persona of a job recruiter and, using the job listing to which the letter and resumé respond, tell your classmate what you see as the strengths and weaknesses of his or her submission.

EXERCISE

1. Prepare a résumé that highlights your character, education, and experience. Use the Sanchez résumé and the tips on pages 449–450 as a guide.
2. Check your local newspaper or familiar Web sites for job listings and write a letter applying for some current job that interests you. Attach the job listing with your letter.

Electronic (Digital) Résumés

Your job search may turn up a request for a version of your résumé that an employer can scan into a database. Or, you may wish to send your résumé via e-mail.

In these cases, you need to format your résumé so that it appears in *plain text*. Plain text is text stripped of all special features, such as boldface or italic print, underlining, color, boxes, columns, or graphics of any kind. Only a conventional-width typeface, like *Times New Roman* or *Courier* in 12–14 point font size, is appropriate. Type all entries in a digital format flush with the left margin. If you want to highlight a particular point, use uppercase letters. Use the space bar on your keypad when you need to separate words and letters; do not use the tab button.

Résumés in digital format allow readers to look for key words that match job openings or requirements, so when you respond to a job announcement, use those key words. For example, words like *Webmaster, help desk manager, supervisor, sales representative,* and *management trainee* are self-descriptors easily keyed into a database.

RÉSUMÉ

OSCAR SANCHEZ

Home Address
318 Rose Hill Drive
Rancho Cordova, CA 95822
Phone: (916) 851-2345

Complete, relevant addresses for ease of contact

Campus Address
201 East 64th Street, Apt. 24J
New York, NY 10021
Phone: (212) 363-9999

E-mail: oscsan@tele.com   *E-mail address*

Category "Career Objective" set off in boldface

Career Objective   Web Designer/Web Master

Career objective stated simply and succinctly

Education
2005–2008

Date ranges indicated in chronologically reverse order

Marymount Manhattan College, New York, NY
Bachelor of Arts in Communication Arts
Degree expected: June 2008
Special courses: Advanced Animation, Desktop Video, The Business of Media Arts, Desktop Publishing, Electronic Newswriting
Gradepoint Average in Major: 3.2

Sanchez highlights GPA in major only because it is higher than his cumulative GPA

2000–2003

Mildred Elley College for Careers, Latham, NY
Associate in Occupational Studies in Information Technology (O.A.S.) Degree conferred: June 1998
Special courses: Operating Systems, Software Applications, Introduction to Visual Programming, Electronic Commerce, Internet and Web Page Design

Special education suited to the position

Category "Work Experience" includes full- and part-time work

Work Experience
2003–2005

Wiles Corporation, Brooklyn, NY
As Help Desk Manager, answered questions about and repaired computer failures, installed software programs, fixed faulty programs, and offered ongoing workshops to a staff of 35

Sentence fragments with lively verb forms

Summer 2002 and 2003

The Computer Store, Sacramento, CA
Sold computers, did general troubleshooting for repairs, advised on software purchase

Personal Background

Born in California; grew up in Rancho Cordova (near Sacramento). Moved East in 2000. Interests: Fishing, anything high tech, action films, video arcades, mystery novels, moving back West.

"Personal Background" category provides useful information about applicant

"References" category: reader will know how to get needed references

References   Furnished on request

If you are sending your résumé electronically, embed it in e-mail. Do not send e-mail with your digital résumé as an attachment. Employers fear viruses in attachments and are reluctant to open one from an unsolicited source.

It's always best to follow up an e-mail application and résumé with hard copy sent through the mail.

Look at the résumé in digital format on page 453.

EXERCISE   Prepare your own résumé in electronic (digital) format. Use the sample and the annotations as a guide.

Writing Memorandums and E-mail

The office memorandum (*memo*, for short) is a vital link between and among workers in an institution and provides a formal record of newly initiated activities and requests for information or action. An office manager may write a memo to all her employees about new safety regulations required by the state; a secretary may write to his boss requesting annual leave over Christmas and New Year; and a sales manager may write to a representative requesting explanations of weakening sales for an important product. Some memos are fairly long, but usually the most effective communication in this medium is brief and to the point—and dealing with an explicit topic. Memos never should go to people outside the organization; for such communication you need to write a letter. Look at the annotated memorandum on page 454.

Complementing the paper memorandum and letter as a means of business correspondence, e-mail continues to grow in popularity, and for good reason. It is quick; it is informal; and it can cover wide geographical territories without problems.

E-mail messages should be short and to the point and, despite the informality of the communication, should be error free. Most e-mail providers have built-in spell checks, and at the very least you should run your message through a spell check to prevent errors. Don't assume that e-mail is an open field for bad spelling and grammar; mistakes always diminish the impact of your message in any medium. And don't fall into the trap of inappropriate use: Business e-mail is for doing business. If you want to pass along or receive jokes, local supermarket sales information, concert dates, and so on, be sure that you use your private e-mail account for such purposes, not the account established where you work. Many companies now monitor their employees' e-mail, and you want to be beyond reproach.

SAMPLE OF ELECTRONIC RÉSUMÉ

RÉSUMÉ OF OSCAR SANCHEZ

HOME ADDRESS
318 Rose Hill Drive
Rancho Cordova, CA 95822
Phone: (916) 851-2345

All entries flush left

No italics, underlining, boldface

CAMPUS ADDRESS
201 East 64th Street, Apt. 24J
New York, NY 10021
Phone: (212) 363-9999
E-mail: oscsan@tele.com

Uppercase letters for emphasis

CAREER OBJECTIVE   Web Designer/Web Master   *Key words*

EDUCATION
2005–2008 Marymount Manhattan College, New York, NY.
Bachelor of Arts in Communication Arts. Degree expected:
June 2003. Special courses: Advanced Animation, Desktop
Video, The Business of Media Arts, Desktop Publishing,
Electronic Newswriting.
Gradepoint Average in Major: 3.2

Standard width typeface: 12 point Times New Roman

2000–2003 Mildred Elley College for Careers, Latham, NY.
Associate in Occupational Studies in Information Technology
(O.A.S.). Degree conferred: June 1998. Special courses:
Operating Systems, Software Applications, Introduction to
Visual Programming, Electronic Commerce, Internet and
Web Page Design.

Category "Work Experience" includes full- and part-time work

WORK EXPERIENCE
2003–2005 Wiles Corporation, Brooklyn, NY. As Help Desk
Manager, answered questions about and repaired computer
failures, installed software programs, fixed faulty programs,
and offered ongoing workshops to a staff of 35

Summer 2002 and 2003 The Computer Store, Sacramento,
CA. Sold computers, did general troubleshooting for repairs,
advised on software purchase

Key word: "Help Desk Manager"

PERSONAL BACKGROUND Born in California; grew up in
Rancho Cordova (near Sacramento). Moved East in 2000.
Interests: Fishing, anything high tech, action films, video
arcades, mystery novels, moving back West.

REFERENCES
Furnished on request

Single column

WALDORF CORPORATION
612 Super Highway
Milwaukee, Wisconsin 53201

MEMORANDUM

Date, including
month, day,
and year

Date: October 24, 2008

Person receiving
memorandum

To: Mildred Greenberg-Stevens, Director of Human Resources

Sender's name
and hand-
written initials
(indicating
approval of the
memorandum)

From: Roberta McAlister, Vice President for Administration (RM)

Subject: Day Care Center   Topic of memorandum

Purpose and
desired outcome
stated in the
first paragraph

As you know, many of our employees have asked us to establish a day care center for the children of Waldorf Corporation's workers. I think that this is a good idea, but we have far too little information to recommend the option to our Board of Directors. I have asked Winifred Rollison and Roger Eggers to work along with you in developing a preliminary report that will guide a decision. Please address the following issues:

Standard width
typeface:
12 point Times
New Roman

Double space between paragraphs

- **Space** Where would be the best place to establish a day care center in our building? What area would serve our employees' needs best? How would we create the necessary space?
- **Regulations** What regulations—state, federal, local—exist to guide the construction of a day care center? For example, are we required to reserve a minimum number of square feet; are there special restroom facilities requirements or furniture requirements for the young children?
- **Cost** What would it cost to establish and maintain the day care center? We need to think about supplies and furniture, but also staffing. How much would we have to pay a director? Are there other personnel issues that we have to consider?
- **Need** Just how many Waldorf workers would take advantage of the Center? How many children would we expect to serve each day?

Double space between paragraphs

As you do your research, I'm sure that you will discover other key issues as well; feel free to address them in your report. Please finish your work in a month's time.

Deadline for
completion
of stated task

Thanks very much for agreeing to take this on.

Recipients of
copies of the
memorandum

c. Winifred Rollison, Director of Personnel
   Roger Eggers, Eastern Regional Sales Manager

EXERCISE   Write a memorandum or an e-mail on one of the following issues:

1. Announce to members of your class a trip to a local animal sanctuary; include the purpose of the trip, the day and time, the cost, the person in charge, and any other relevant details.
2. Assume that you are the office manager of an employee pool of twenty-five people and that you are writing to remind your workers of the importance of getting to work and getting to work on time. Sick-day call-ins seem excessive to you. Employees have been clocking in beyond accepted arrival times.
3. Announce to members of your class a series of collaborative study sessions that you're trying to organize in preparation for the biology final.

For additional writing, reading, and research resources, go to **www. mycomplab.com** <http://www.mycomplab.com/> and choose Skwire/Wiener's *Student's Book of College English*, Twelfth Edition.

PART FOUR

Research

Writing a research paper is a rewarding yet highly demanding task for college writers. Teachers in a variety of courses will expect you to research a topic carefully and present your findings in a well-written paper. Yet a successful research paper is much more than a summary of the books and articles you consulted on a topic—it also makes an assertion that is supported by substantive detail from reliable sources.

The two chapters in Part Four take you through the steps necessary to produce research papers for your college courses. In Chapter 20, you'll learn how to choose a subject, how to develop a thesis, and how to start preliminary reading for your research paper. You also will learn how to prepare a working bibliography, how to use online sources, and how to take notes on your reading. You will review as well the important uses of an outline in producing a paper.

In Chapter 21, we point out that necessary to writing a research paper is the ability to document sources accurately and to integrate those sources smoothly with your own writing. You'll see how to quote, summarize, and paraphrase sources. We show two major systems of documentation—one developed by the Modern Language Association (MLA style) and the other developed by the American Psychological Association (APA style). Also included is a sample student research paper on the use of the lie detector in the workplace. The paper has annotations that explain the various features of the work. This model paper can help you write your own paper.

CHAPTER **20**

Doing Research

- ■ Choosing Your Subject
- ■ Developing Your Thesis
- ■ Doing Preliminary Reading
- ■ Preparing Your Preliminary Outline
- ■ Finding Sources and Developing a Working Bibliography
- ■ Taking Notes
- ■ Preparing Your Formal Outline

A research paper (or research essay or library paper or term paper) is a nearly universal assignment in your first-year English course and in many other courses.

Choosing Your Subject

As you think about formulating a subject for your research paper, follow some of the prewriting strategies you explored in Chapter 2. Surf the Web to explore a range of approaches to your subject. Make a rough list. Use free association. Brainstorm on a topic that seems even remotely interesting. Talk at length with roommates, friends, teachers, relatives, employers, coworkers—with anyone who will listen. Watch television talk shows or documentaries related to your subject. Browse in libraries and bookstores. Study newspapers, magazines, and journals; a word or two in a headline or title may catch your eye and get you thinking. Some background reading in a general encyclopedia like the *Encyclopaedia Britannica* may provide a useful overview of your topic.

Once you have even a vague notion of a topic that interests you, think about it for a while. Consider whether it's too broad. Remember the importance of limiting your subject. "Custer's Last Stand" and "The Lizzie Borden Murder Case" might make good papers, but you could not write a good paper of reasonable length on a topic like "Famous Battles" or "Great Trials" because it's too broad.

One final suggestion: Don't be too eager to settle on any single topic immediately. If you have two or three possibilities in mind, so much the better. There may not be as much information available on your first choice as you had hoped, and it's comforting to have something ready to fall back on.

EXERCISE   For the following broad subjects, indicate how you would limit each one to make it suitable for a research paper. Follow the format of the examples.

Broad subject →	**Limited subject**
Communication	The importance of regular conversation with children from six weeks to one year old
The solar system	Current theories on the sun's longevity

Broad subjects

1. Poverty
2. Terrorism
3. Hip-hop music
4. Climate
5. Immigration
6. Campaigning

7. The French underground in World War II
8. Weapons
9. Television programs
10. Software

EXERCISE   Choose a broad subject from the list above or one of your own and limit it for a research paper.

Developing Your Thesis

Virtually every research paper requires that you gather facts and opinions (sometimes conflicting) from a variety of sources and that you organize and present them in your own words and style through your own hard work. Every research paper also requires that you document whatever sources you have used. When you document a source, you tell the reader where you found information taken from someone else's writing. Typical documentation includes the author's name, the title of the selection, and important publication data. You'll read more about documentation in Chapter 21.

However, the most important kind of research paper does more than cite sources—it has as its basis a **thesis**. Most teachers want students to use research in order to develop opinions of their own and to present those opinions in a carefully documented paper. Hence, in a research paper with a thesis, you do extensive investigation to find facts, but you also interpret those facts and you try to persuade the reader that your interpretation or opinion is correct. Rather than merely stating the facts, you use them to support your opinion. The thesis drives the research you present to your readers.

Developing a thesis is critical to writing a successful research paper. This book pays considerable attention to writing a thesis, and you may wish to review the general steps for developing a powerful thesis in Chapter 3.

Your thesis for a research paper will grow and take shape as you investigate your resources. Your research activities almost certainly will cause you to change or modify your original thesis as you progress from prewriting to rough draft to final draft.

For the sample paper "The Banning of the Polygraph," which appears in Chapter 21, student writer Elizabeth Kessler arrived at this thesis sentence after conducting some research on her topic.

Thesis 1

Many employers have used polygraph testing as a means for determining the honesty of future employees.

As Kessler considered this thesis sentence, she realized that it makes a simple assertion of fact but offers no opportunity for interpretation or judgment. She then revised her thesis sentence as follows:

Thesis 2

Supporters and critics battle the merits and drawbacks of lie detector tests.

We see a clear topic statement in this sentence and, on the surface, what seems to be strong opinions about the topic. Yet the more Kessler thought about the topic, the more she realized that her own opinion was absent from the thesis statement. She again had made an assertion of fact: Some people supported the polygraph test and others opposed it. As she pondered the question "How do I feel about using the polygraph test in job-related situations?" and started shaping an early draft, Kessler wrote this thesis sentence:

Thesis 3

My own research indicates that the polygraph test as a condition of employment is highly unfair.

Here Kessler's interpretation of the topic is clear: Required polygraph testing for a job is not fair. As you will see when you examine her paper, as Kessler continued her research, she changed her thesis again.

EXERCISE   Write a tentative thesis for your limited subject. Consider what you will try to assert about your subject. Remember that your thesis may change considerably, especially after you do preliminary (and then sustained) reading and research for your paper.

Doing Preliminary Reading

Once you have an idea of the topic or topics you're interested in, it's time for a close look at reliable Web sites and a trip to the library. Your purpose now is to do some fairly easygoing "reading around." You want to make sure that the subject that seems so interesting when you think about it is still interesting when you read about it. You want to acquire enough of a general perspective on your subject to be able to respond thoughtfully when you begin more serious and detailed reading.

Using General Encyclopedias

Usually, the most sensible place in which to begin reading hard copy is a recent edition of a general encyclopedia, such as the *Encyclopaedia Britannica* or the *Encyclopedia Americana*. The electronic encyclopedia *Encarta* also provides helpful background material. But, be careful about using Wikipedia, an online encyclopedia project written collaboratively by volunteers. Anyone with access to the Web site can edit or change any entry. Contributors' credentials may be suspect. Many entries are accurate; but some critics question its reliability, uneven quality, and inconsistency.

No significant research paper is going to use an encyclopedia article as a major source. The entry can offer only a broad survey of its subject, whereas a research paper explores its subject in depth. At this early stage, however, a broad survey is all you want.

You may be tempted to do your research exclusively on the Internet, which provides endless opportunities for exploring a topic right from your home or dorm room. But at this very early stage of your investigations, you want to resist the temptation to make the Web your only resource. At the outset, you need a clear, *reliable* overview of your topic. You probably know already how much rubbish is floating in cyberspace and how unreliable and downright wicked some sites, chat boxes, blogs, and e-mails are. A good encyclopedia will suggest the appropriate parameters for your research and will help you later in the all-important task of evaluating Internet sources (see pages 26–29). If you are tethered to your computer, however, note that many encyclopedias are available online.

Using Specialized Reference Works

As good as or better than general encyclopedias for preliminary reading are specialized encyclopedias, dictionaries, and other reference works, many of which are updated and revised regularly. For example, if you are writing about an American who is no longer living, the *Dictionary of American Biography* may have an excellent article. The *Dictionary of National Biography* supplies similar information about British men and women who are no longer living. A list of some other specialized reference works follows; check the latest available edition at your library. Your librarian will help you find many of these in online versions so that you can draw on the resources, if you wish, from your computer.

Art

> *Britannica Encyclopaedia of American Art*
> *Encyclopedia of World Art*, 15 vols.
> Bernard S. Myers, ed., *Encyclopedia of Painting*
> *The McGraw-Hill Dictionary of Art*

Business

> Douglas Greenwald, *The McGraw-Hill Dictionary of Modern Economics*
> Glen G. Munn, *Encyclopedia of Banking and Finance*
> Harold S. Sloan and Arnold J. Zurcher, *A Dictionary of Economics*

Education

> *Encyclopedia of Education*, 10 vols.
> *Encyclopedia of Educational Research*

History

> *Dictionary of American History*, 6 vols.
> *The Cambridge Ancient History*, 12 vols.
> *The Cambridge Medieval History*, 8 vols.
> *The Cambridge Modern History*, 14 vols.
> William L. Langer, *An Encyclopedia of World History*

Literature

> Albert C. Baugh, *A Literary History of England*
> John Buchanan-Brown, ed., *Cassell's Encyclopedia of World Literature*
> James D. Hart, *The Oxford Companion to American Literature*
> Phyllis Hartnoll, *The Oxford Companion to the Theatre*
> Paul Harvey, *The Oxford Companion to English Literature*
> Robert Spiller and others, *Literary History of the United States*, 2 vols.
> Roger Whitlow, *Black American Literature*
> Percy Wilson and Bonamy Dobree, *The Oxford History of English Literature*, 12 vols.

Music

> *The New Grove Dictionary of Music and Musicians*, 20 vols.
> *The New Oxford History of Music*, 10 vols.
> Percy A. Scholes, *The Oxford Companion to Music*

Philosophy

> Frederick C. Copleston, *A History of Philosophy*, 8 vols.
> Paul Edwards, ed., *The Encyclopedia of Philosophy*, 4 vols.

Psychology

> H. J. Eysenck and others, *Encyclopedia of Psychology*, 3 vols.
> Robert M. Goldenson, *The Encyclopedia of Human Behavior*, 2 vols.

Religion

> F. L. Cross and Elizabeth A. Livingstone, *The Oxford Dictionary of the Christian Church*
> *The New Catholic Encyclopedia*, 15 vols.
> Geoffrey Parrinder, *A Dictionary of Non-Christian Religions*
> *Encyclopedia Judaica*, 16 vols.

Science

> *The McGraw-Hill Encyclopedia of Science and Technology*, 15 vols.
> *Van Nostrand's Scientific Encyclopedia*

Social Science and Politics

> John P. Davis, ed., *The American Negro Reference Book*
> Barry T. Klein, ed., *Reference Encyclopedia of the American Indian*
> E. R. A. Seligman and Alvin Johnson, eds., *Encyclopedia of the Social Sciences*, 15 vols.
> David L. Sills, ed., *International Encyclopedia of the Social Sciences*, 19 vols.
> Edward C. Smith and Arnold J. Zurcher, eds., *Dictionary of American Politics*

Searching the World Wide Web

As you know, the accessibility of source materials through the World Wide Web has made Internet research not only convenient but also an invaluable supplement to conventional print sources available at your college or neighborhood public library. With the click of a mouse, you can retrieve material from library catalogs and Web sites created by corporations, professional organizations, government agencies, educators, colleges and universities, and too many other possible sources to mention. You can access full texts of books and periodicals, documents, articles and essays, television and radio programs, photographs, songs, symphonies, and cartoons, as well as information and critiques about all of these (and other) materials. If you have a home computer and can sign on to the Internet, you can bring libraries into your living room.

If you've done any research on the Internet, you're probably already familiar with Yahoo! and Google. These search tools are very useful to students preparing a research paper. You access material from these search engines by using a key word or phrase or by identifying a particular subject. The key words that you enter in Yahoo! and Google fit into directories arranged in a hierarchy by the search engines. Each of the search tools, therefore, can provide broad subject directories in response to your key word, and you can explore the directories to find the limited area of your interest. Lists of pertinent Web sites will help you link to information you can explore from a computer.

"Googling" Your Subject

One of your first impulses regarding your research paper will no doubt send you to explore the topic through Google (or Yahoo! or some other search engine) and to identify useful Web sites. We used the key words "Lie Detector" and brought up the first several entries, as shown on page 465.

First, you should note the overwhelming number of potential resources—more than 1.5 million (yes, million!) for someone researching this topic. Next, even on this first page of entries, you face an incredible mix of links to examine for further information. The column to the right with the heading "Sponsored Links" is a list of advertisers, people and companies who pay to have their sites listed and have commercial services to offer. They want you to buy something from them.

As for the other entries, you have to judge the quality of the site before you can rely on it as a valid resource. In some cases you can tell the nature of the site from the descriptions below the highlighted link and can reject any that seem irrelevant to your purpose; or you can go immediately to any that seem useful. In the section of this chapter called "Finding Articles: Periodical Indexes and Databases," we explore some specialized search tools for locating resources in a range of disciplines.

EXERCISE   Check your library for resources, including computer search engines, to use for preliminary reading on your subject. Write the names of three specialized encyclopedias, dictionaries, or other reference works that you use for your preliminary reading.

Preparing Your Preliminary Outline

If all goes well in your preliminary reading, you should be in a position to draw up a **preliminary outline**, or **rough outline**, indicating the major divisions of your paper. You don't need anything elaborate; you will revise and expand the outline as you go along. In the meantime, the preliminary outline enables you to read and take notes as part of a systematic plan. You'll know what information is relevant and irrelevant, what divisions of the paper you need to work on more thoroughly, and so on.

Google search results for "lie detector"

Here is Elizabeth Kessler's rough outline for her research paper:

<u>Topic/Thesis</u>: Polygraph Testing on the Job

1. Cost

2. Reliability

3. Accuracy

4. Relation between guilt and physical measures from test

5. Consequences of test on person's life

This outline, based on preliminary reading, guided Kessler's deeper probing into sources related to her topic and her ultimate writing of drafts for the paper. The outline changed many times—compare it with the items in her formal outline on page 321. At this stage, a preliminary outline is a useful guide to further thinking about your topic.

EXERCISE
Make a rough outline of the major divisions that you now think will structure your paper. Base the outline on your preliminary readings. (Remember: Your outline will most likely change as your research advances.)

Finding Sources and Developing a Working Bibliography

When you complete your rough outline, it's time for serious research and reading, and that brings us to the subject of the bibliography. When you write the final draft of your research paper, you'll have to include a list of works cited, which is an alphabetical list of the books, articles, and other sources that you refer to in the text of your essay. To prepare for that effort, you want to develop a **working bibliography** that records key information about each source. For each book, article, and Web site you find, you will need to note authors' names, titles, and publication data. Since you cannot know in advance which sources will contain useful information, you should record bibliographic information for all of them.

We'll show you the information you will need for your working bibliography later in the chapter, on pages 472–478. Now, let us discuss where you can find books and articles for your essay.

Finding Books: The Library Catalog

Most libraries have turned their paper card catalogs into computerized catalogs. These catalogs list books, reference works, audio and video materials, and periodicals that are available through the library. The library catalog does not list individual articles; for these, you will have to search a periodical index (see pages 467–471).

You can search a library catalog for useful sources by entering key terms. You can search by author's name, by the title of the work, by key words, and by subject. Your search will result in a list of possible titles; to see more about an entry, click on it. This will bring up a screen that shows more detailed information about the work. As an example, when Elizabeth Kessler did research in her public library's online catalog, she first chose to do a key word search using the term "lie detectors," as shown on page 467. When she clicked on the "Search" button, the next screen showed the results for "lie detectors" (see page 468). Kessler thought the first item in the results list, *The Lie Detectors* by Ken Alder, looked promising. She clicked on the title to get more information, as shown in the next screen, the entry for the book (page 469). She noted the call number and went to the stacks to find the book.

Library catalog search page

Finding Articles: Periodical Indexes and Databases

To find magazine or journal articles, you will need to consult **periodical indexes**. Check your own college and public libraries to see which indexes they have in book form and which are online.

The Readers' Guide to Periodical Literature

One of the most frequently used indexes is *The Readers' Guide to Periodical Literature*, an index of articles that have appeared in popular American magazines during any given year since 1900. *The Readers' Guide* appears monthly in pamphlet form and is permanently bound every year. If your subject is a current one, you would, of course, use the most recent *Readers' Guide*. If, however, your subject deals with a particular period in the past, you would want to consult *The Readers' Guide* for the year or years that are appropriate

Library catalog search results for "lie detectors"

for your subject. If, for instance, your subject is the presidency of Franklin Roosevelt, you would consult *The Readers' Guide* for the years 1933–1945, in addition to consulting guides of later years to see how historians evaluate Roosevelt's administration after his death. If your library has a subscription, you can search all issues of *The Readers' Guide* since 1983 online.

The guide has both an author and subject index, but you will probably find it easier to look for subject headings. When you have located the heading or headings you need, you will find listed under the headings all the articles on your subject that have appeared in popular American magazines for the period covered by the particular guide. Because *The Readers' Guide* indexes so much material, the entries must be printed in as little space as possible. That means, for one thing, that many abbreviations appear in each entry. If you do not understand an abbreviation, refer to the keys and explanations of all abbreviations at the beginning of each issue. The need to conserve space also means that the editors do not punctuate titles, dates, and pages. Note the *Readers' Guide* entry under "Lie detectors and detection" that Elizabeth Kessler found (page 470). We've labeled the parts for easy reference.

Library catalog entry for *The Lie Detectors* by Ken Alder

A helpful hint: Don't use *The Readers' Guide* entries as models for entries on your own works cited list (see pages 501–502). Rather, use *The Readers' Guide* to find sources; once you have your sources in hand, copy bibliographic material carefully from the sources themselves and according to the guidelines listed on pages 498–508.

Specialized Periodical Indexes

The Readers' Guide is a good place to start, but it does, after all, index only popular American magazines. For most subjects, you will also want to read articles written by scholars in the field in order to get more specialized information. Almost every academic discipline has one or more journals to which specialists in the field contribute, and you would certainly want to look at their articles. To find them, you would consult the special index and abstracts covering your subject. Most indexes are arranged in the same way as the *The Readers' Guide*, so you will have no difficulty using the special indexes if you have mastered the use of *The Readers' Guide*.

Following is a list of specialized indexes you might want to consult. It is by no means complete, but it will give you some idea of the kinds of indexes available. You can find these and other special indexes in the reference room of the library. Many are now available electronically.

Agriculture Index	*Engineering Index*
Applied Science and Technology	*Environmental Index*
Index	*Humanities Index*, 1974– (called the
Art Index	*Social Science and Humanities*
Biological Abstracts	*Index* from 1965–1973)
Business Periodicals Index	*Index to Legal Periodicals*
Chemical Abstracts	*Music Index*
Computer Abstracts	*The Philosopher's Index*
Criminal Justice Abstracts	*Psychological Abstracts*
Ecology Abstracts	*Religion Index*
Education Index	*Sociological Abstracts*

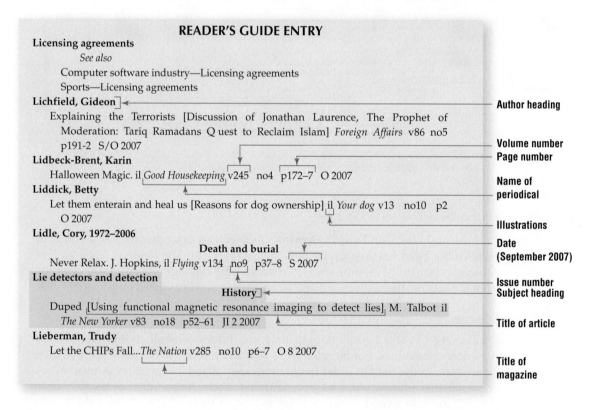

READER'S GUIDE ENTRY

Licensing agreements
See also
Computer software industry—Licensing agreements
Sports—Licensing agreements
Lichfield, Gideon ◄──────────────────────────── **Author heading**
Explaining the Terrorists [Discussion of Jonathan Laurence, The Prophet of
Moderation: Tariq Ramadans Q uest to Reclaim Islam] *Foreign Affairs* v86 no5
p191-2 S/O 2007 ──────────────────────────────── **Volume number**
Lidbeck-Brent, Karin ──────────────────────────── **Page number**
Halloween Magic. il *Good Housekeeping* v245 no4 p172–7 O 2007
Liddick, Betty ──────────────────────────────── **Name of**
Let them enterain and heal us [Reasons for dog ownership] il *Your dog* v13 no10 p2 **periodical**
O 2007
Lidle, Cory, 1972–2006 ──────────────────────────── **Illustrations**
Death and burial ──────────────────────────────── **Date**
Never Relax. J. Hopkins, il *Flying* v134 no9 p37–8 S 2007 **(September 2007)**
Lie detectors and detection
History ◄──────────────────────────────────── **Issue number**
Duped [Using functional magnetic resonance imaging to detect lies], M. Talbot il **Subject heading**
The New Yorker v83 no18 p52–61 Jl 2 2007
Lieberman, Trudy ──────────────────────────────── **Title of article**
Let the CHIPs Fall...*The Nation* v285 no10 p6–7 O 8 2007
── **Title of**
magazine

The Readers' Guide entry for "lie detectors and detection"

Newspaper Indexes

The *New York Times Index* provides a complete listing, by year, of every article
that has appeared in its newspaper. The *Times* has been thoroughly indexed

since 1913. If you need newspaper articles from local papers, you often must page through or scan on microfilm the newspapers issued during the period your subject covers. The *New York Times* Web site provides articles in an extensive database, as does *AP Online* (an electronic source for the Associated Press) and the *Washington Post* Web site. Newspaper databases can provide helpful indexes for articles on key topics.

EXERCISE

List four indexes that you could use to find periodical articles related to your subject. Examine two of these indexes carefully and list several articles from them that seem useful to you as you explore your topic.

Electronic Database Indexes

You've already seen how some libraries use computers to catalog their holdings. Like indexes and catalogs, *databases*—reference lists available on computer—provide extensive bibliographic information for topics in a number of disciplines. Essentially, databases are specialized catalog systems. You can retrieve lists of titles and authors in a variety of subjects covered by the database—and with some databases, such as *Infotrac* and *Ebscohost*, you can use the computer to retrieve the works themselves. At your library you may have to pay a fee for using particular databases.

In the fields of humanities, government, education, science, social science, and business, many computerized libraries use other familiar databases like Lexis/Nexis, DIALOG, Bibliographic Retrieval Services (BRS), and Academic Search Elite. The Educational Research Information Center (ERIC) provides a wide range of information on education. Newspaper Source via EbscoHost provides full text for many U.S. newspapers as well as international newspapers and newswires.

You can search periodical databases by author, title, or subject. Many databases have a list of subject headings that you must use as search terms; others allow you to search by key words. If you are not sure how the database is organized, look for a list of subject headings, or experiment entering key words and then narrowing your search. Your librarian can help you find appropriate subject headings for your research topic.

When Elizabeth Kessler searched the EbscoHost database for her research paper, she first used the key words "lie detectors" (see page 472). EbscoHost returned results along with the option of narrowing the search by subject headings. Kessler first narrowed the search by choosing "lie detectors & detection" and then "employee testing." The first three entries of her final search results appear on page 473. Kessler thought the first item, "Lie Detection and the Polygraph: A Historical Review," would be useful, so she clicked on the title to get the full entry. As you can see on page 474, this entry has full publication information and an abstract (summary) of the article. If Kessler wants to see the whole article, she can click on "PDF Full Text." Not all articles are available in PDF format online; you may have to track down the published journals in the library stacks to see the full articles.

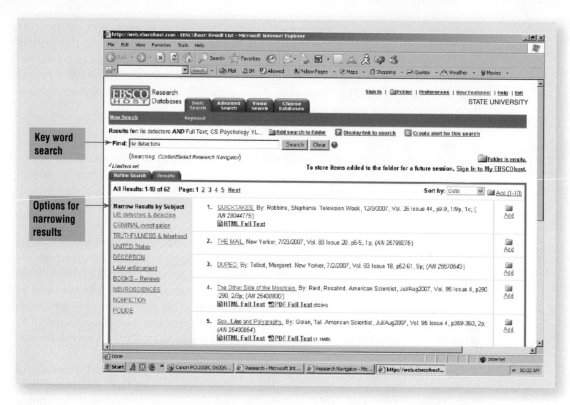

EbscoHost search for key words "lie detector"

Keeping Records for Your Bibliography

As you find each source for your paper, you should record the information you will need to prepare your bibliography (called a Works Cited list in MLA format papers and a References list in APA format papers). There are many ways you can record bibligraphic information. You can use index cards, Word files on a computer, a notebook, or even a software program that prepares citations.

An efficient way to prepare your working bibliography is with **bibliography cards**. For each promising title you find, make out a 3 × 5-inch card. Obviously, you will not use all the sources for which you make cards, but it saves time to make cards for any title that might be useful before you begin your reading. Cards are easy to handle, and they permit you to add new sources and to delete sources that turn out to be useless. Cards can also be alphabetized easily, which will save you time when you make up your final list of works cited.

Whether you use cards or another method, each bibliography record should include all the relevant data that you will need to write a proper entry for your list of works cited. Take time to prepare complete bibliography records as you go along because, again, following the appropriate procedure now will save time

Search narrowed by subject headings

Click on title to see full entry

EbscoHost search results narrowed by subject

and frustration when you write your paper later on. Follow the format of the samples that follow as you prepare your own bibliography records.

Bibliography Records for Books

Bibliography records for books should include the following information. A sample record appears on page 475.

- The author's name
- For an essay, poem, short story, or a play in a collection, the title of the relevant selection, enclosed in quotation marks
- The title of the book
- The city in which the book was published
- The name of the publishing company
- The copyright date
- The complete call number of the book (See the sample catalog entry on page 475.) If you do not have the correct call number, you will not be able to locate the book.
- Edition and revision information, if any

- For multivolume works, the overall number of volumes and the specific number used
- If the book is edited, the editor's name
- If the book is translated, the translator's name

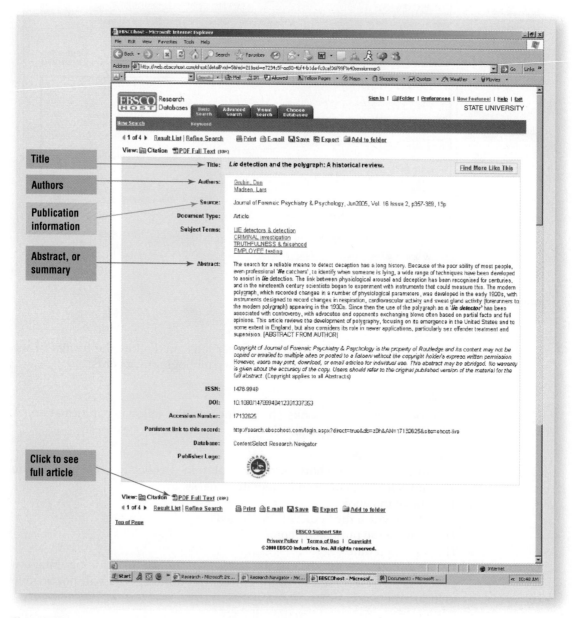

EbscoHost entry for journal article

BIBLIOGRAPHY RECORD FOR A BOOK

Call number ⟶ 363.254 ALD

Author ⟶ Alder, Ken

Title ⟶ *The Lie Detectors: The History of an American Obsession*

Place of publication ⟶ New York

Publisher ⟶ Free Press

Year of publication (copyright date) ⟶ 2007

Medium of publication ⟶ Print

Corresponding MLA citation

in Works Cited list:

Alder, Ken. *The Lie Detectors: The History of an American Obsession*. New York: Free P, 2007. Print.

Look ahead to pages 498–508 for the various works cited formats required for a wide variety of books that you might find in your research. These formats tell you what information to include on your bibliography cards.

Bibliography Records for Periodical Articles

Bibliography records for periodicals should include the following information. A sample record appears on page 476.

- The author's name, if one is given
- The title of the article
- The name of the magazine, journal, or newspaper
- The publication date
- The inclusive page numbers
- For a newspaper, the section number or letter and the edition, when given on the masthead
- For a scholarly journal article, the volume and issue numbers, when given
- For a scholarly journal article from an online database, the database name and date of access
- For APA style citations, record the DOI (digital object identifier) when given

BIBLIOGRAPHY RECORD FOR A JOURNAL ARTICLE
FROM AN ONLINE DATABASE

Authors ⟶ Grubin, Don & Madsen, Lars

Title of article ⟶ "Lie Detection and the Polygraph:
A Historical Review"

Periodical name ⟶ *Journal of Forensic Psychiatry & Psychology*

Date of publication ⟶ June 2005

Volume and issue
numbers ⟶ Vol. 16, Issue 2

Page numbers ⟶ 357–69

Database name ⟶ *ContentSelect Research Navigator*

DOI (needed for APA
style citations) ⟶ 10.1080/14789940412331337353

Medium of publication ⟶ Web

Date accessed ⟶ 17 Mar. 2008

Corresponding MLA citation in Works Cited list:

Grubin, Don, and Lars Madsen. "Lie Detection and the Polygraph: A Historical
Review." *Journal of Forensic Psychiatry and Psychology* 16:2 (2005):
357–69. *ContentSelect Research Navigator*. Web. 17 Mar. 2008.

Pages 501–504 provide examples of the different formats used for citing articles in the list of works cited. Examine these examples carefully as you prepare your bibliography cards.

BIBLIOGRAPHY RECORD FOR WORLD WIDE WEB SOURCE

Author ————————➤ Bonsor, Kevin

Title of article, page,
or document ————————➤ "How Lie Detectors Work"

Web site name ————➤ *HowStuffWorks*

Web site sponsor ————➤ How Stuff Works, Inc.

Date of posting or
copyright ————————➤ 1998-2008

Medium of publication ➤ Web

Date accessed ————————➤ 17 Mar. 2008

URL ————————————➤ www.howstuffworks.com/lie-detector.htm

Corresponding MLA citation in Works Cited list:

Bonsor, Kevin. "How Lie Detectors Work." *HowStuffWorks.* HowStuffWorks,
    1998–2008. Web. 3 Mar. 2008.

Bibliography Records for Worldwide Web Sources

If you are taking material from the general access World Wide Web portion of
the Internet, record information using the format in the sample above. The
following list indicates most parts of an entry for an Internet publication as
well as their order in an entry. Some information you record may not appear
in the works cited entry but will help you find your source again.

- Author's name—or the name of the editor, compiler, or translator
- Document title (article, poem, essay, or other short work) *or* title of posting to
  discussion list or forum (taken from subject line)
- Title of book or periodical, if any
- Name of editor, compiler, or translator of text, if relevant
- Publication information of the print version of the source, if any
- Title of Internet site—online periodical, scholarly project, or personal or pro-
  fessional site (italicized)—or, if a personal or professional site without a title,
  some description such as *Home page*
- Name of site's sponsor
- For an article, volume and issue numbers, or the version number of the
  source if not part of the title

- Date of electronic publication, latest update, or posting
- For a posting to a discussion list or forum, name the list or forum
- Number range or total number of pages, sections, or paragraphs, if numbered
- Medium of publication (Web)
- Date when the researcher accessed the source
- The URL for the source

An important caution: URLs can be long and complicated in their use of letters and symbols. Record them carefully and accurately. Use the copy and paste function in your word processing software to ensure the accuracy of the URL.

EXERCISE Produce a working bibliography by preparing bibliography records for your subject. Record at least ten books, periodicals, World Wide Web, or other sources. Your instructor may wish to examine your bibliography records before you move ahead with your research.

Taking Notes

What do you look for when taking notes? You should look for any fact, idea, or opinion not generally known that appears to relate to your topic. It's easier to take a few extra notes than it is to go back to the library and reread a book or an article or to an electronic source when you discover, after you start writing the paper, that you don't have enough evidence to make a point.

Nevertheless, you should not simply take notes at random. You have begun your research with at least a vague idea of what you want to say. The sooner the idea becomes definite, the more directed and less time-consuming your note taking will become. But don't worry if you find yourself taking many notes from the first sources you read. After all, the subject is fairly new to you, and everything about it may seem important. You should soon get a focus on the material, and then you can become more selective in the notes you take.

When Elizabeth Kessler started taking notes for her paper on polygraph testing (see paper on pages 520–541), she was intrigued at first by the technology of the equipment used to measure physiological changes. Over time this equipment evolved into more and more sophisticated machinery, and Kessler took notes on every aspect of the lie-detecting mechanism itself. But soon she realized that she didn't want to write a paper about the history of lie detector machines. Rather, she wanted to understand the pros and cons of polygraph testing so that she could form her own opinion about the procedure. Kessler's reading and note taking became much more focused at this point. She was able to concentrate on the views of critics and supporters. As her reading advanced further, she discovered that polygraph testing is used in many arenas—police work, government, the armed forces, and job hiring. To manage her subject, Kessler limited it even further by concentrating on lie detector tests and requirements for employment.

Since the advent and development of polygraph testing spans decades, Kessler explored reading from both current sources such as Web sites and an electronic encyclopedia as well as current books and articles and those going back to the 1970s.

Limit your subject and your approach to it as soon as you can, so you can perform the job of note taking efficiently.

Recording Quotations

When you **quote** a source, you use the exact wording from that source to convey facts or ideas contained in it. Quotation marks must enclose the material that you quote. It may be a month or more between the time you take the note and the time you write your paper, and you don't want any uncertainty about which words are yours and which are those of the original author. Many researchers use a special mark—an asterisk, a checkmark, an *X*—in the margin to distinguish their own words from the words of the source. Be certain, too, that you copy the quotation *exactly* as it appears in the original. If the original contains an obvious error, copy the error and follow it with *sic* (the Latin word for "thus") in brackets.

Occasionally, you may want to quote only parts of an entire passage. If you leave out a whole paragraph or more, indicate the omission by placing spaced dots all the way across the note. If you leave out a part of a sentence or one or two sentences, use three spaced dots (an *ellipsis*) to indicate the omission. For an ellipsis within a sentence, use a space before the first period and after the last period as well. If you omit the beginning of a sentence, place the quotation marks before the ellipsis. If you omit the end of a sentence, place the quotation mark after the ellipsis and the end punctuation (period, question mark, or exclamation point).

A few words of caution about using the ellipsis: Never alter the meaning of the original by using an ellipsis. If the original statement reads, "This is not the most exciting movie of the year," using an ellipsis to omit the word *not* would be dishonest. Second, be sure that you still have a complete sentence when you use the ellipsis. Don't omit from the sentence important elements such as subjects and verbs.

When quoting, you may find it necessary to clarify a word or date in the original quotation because you are taking the words out of context. Pronouns, for example, may need clarification. In context, "He suffered extreme hardships" may be perfectly clear. Isolated on a note, however, the pronoun *he* may need to be explained. If you want to insert a word, phrase, or figure into the quotation, do so by putting the information in brackets: "He [Lincoln] suffered extreme hardships." Or the original might read, "in that year, he faced the greatest crisis of his life." The sentence, taken out of context, does not identify the year. You would want to insert it: "in that year [1839], he faced the greatest crisis of his life."

Summarizing and Paraphrasing in Your Notes

Despite this advice on how to use quotations in your research and note taking, you should quote sparingly. In your notes you should summarize or paraphrase most of the original material.

A **summary** is a short restatement of the original source in your own words. A **paraphrase** is a more expanded summary, often contains words taken from the original, and generally follows both the sequence and the logic of the original source. Often, paraphrase and summary work hand in hand. Of course, if you are in a hurry and don't have time to think about the best way to summarize or paraphrase a note, rather than risk plagiarism (see "Avoiding Plagiarism," pages 492–494), do quote the material and later decide how best to convey it in your own words.

When Elizabeth Kessler researched her topic, she found the following passage useful (from page 132 of *Science vs. Crime: The Hunt for Truth* by Eugene B. Block).

Original Source

In the first part of the nineteenth century, Cesare Lombroso pioneered in experiments with the heartbeat as a means of detecting lying, an interesting forerunner of today's polygraph, which has now advanced far beyond the early concepts of the distinguished Italian, utilizing not only heartbeats but changes in respiration and blood pressure to determine the truth or falsity of an answer.

Proud of his success and certain of the soundness of his theories, Lombroso recorded numbers of effective tests, including one concerning a notorious thief whose heartbeat reactions proved him guilty of one crime and innocent of another. It was on the early Lombroso principle that later criminalists like Vollmer, Keeler, and Larson based their developments of the lie detecting machine, but progress was slow and many methods and theories were tried and abandoned.

In her notes, shown below, she recorded the exact words of the original source enclosed in quotation marks. The ellipsis—the three spaced dots following the word *polygraph*—indicates that Kessler omitted a portion of the quote from the original (the words "which has now advanced far beyond the early concepts of the distinguished Italian"). Further, she uses an asterisk to flag concerns that she will consider later on, when she reviews her note cards.

NOTE CONTAINING A DIRECT QUOTATION

Block, Science vs. Crime 132

"In the first part of the nineteenth century, Cesare Lombroso pioneered in experiments with the heartbeat as a means of detecting lying, an interesting forerunner of today's polygraph . . . utilizing not only heartbeats but changes in respiration and blood pressure to determine the truth or falsity of an answer."

*Check earlier work on lie detection. 18th century? earlier?

In a paraphrase of the original source, Kessler uses her own language, blending in some of Block's words and enclosing them in quotation marks.

NOTE CONTAINING A SUMMARY/PARAPHRASE OF THE ORIGINAL MATERIAL

> *Block*, Science vs. Crime 132
>
>   *In the early 1800s, Cesare Lombroso used heartbeats in experiments to detect lies; his work antic-ipated the modern polygraph, which measures heartbeats as well as "changes in respiration and blood pressure to determine the truth or falsity of an answer."*
>
>   *Lombroso's experiments included one on a thief whose heartbeat showed he had committed one crime but not another. Later developments of the polygraph were based on Lombroso's principle.*

Combining paraphrases and direct quotations is a good note-taking strat-egy. It allows you to capture the writer's main idea in your own language and to record some of the writer's own words for possible quotation in your paper.

Disagreements: Distinguishing Between Facts and Opinions

One final warning on note taking: As you take notes, don't assume that just because something is in print, it must be true. Be careful to distinguish between a writer's statement of fact and expression of opinion. There is a world of difference between saying that Aaron Burr was the vice president of the United States and saying that Aaron Burr was a scoundrel. In rare cases in which you note an outright disagreement among authors on matters of fact, slam on your mental brakes and do some checking. One of the standard refer-ence works or encyclopedias might be a good source for resolving such dis-agreements or disputes. When you cannot determine which opinion is correct, acknowledge frankly in your paper the difference of opinion and present both opinions as honestly as possible.

EXERCISE   Take notes as you read your sources. Your instructor may wish to examine your notes for one or more of your readings.

Preparing Your Formal Outline

Start by reading and rereading all your notes carefully. You have accumulated the notes over a period of weeks, and you may not know precisely what material you have gathered.

Making a Slug Outline

Set aside those notes that seem irrelevant to your current idea of the paper. Among those you keep you should see a pattern; you may have several groups of notes with each group relating to a particular aspect of your topic. When you are familiar enough with your notes that you can arrange them in piles according to single headings, you are ready to write a **slug**—that is, a brief heading that indicates the content of each note. Don't try to be creative here and write a different heading for each note; you should have several notes with the same slug.

Because you may change your mind about the point that a particular note should support, it is a good idea to write the slugs in pencil at first. That way you easily can change the slugs until you feel secure about the way the notes should be used. Once you have made a final decision, write a slug in ink in the upper right-hand corner of each note so that it can be seen quickly as you shuffle through your notes.

Some of the slugs that Elizabeth Kessler developed for her paper on polygraph testing include mechanical features, training of examiners, accuracy of readings, and legal support for lie detector tests. These and other slugs on her note cards allowed Kessler to classify her ideas and, ultimately, to produce a formal outline for her paper.

Writing a Formal Outline

If you have succeeded in writing slugs on each note, the outline will almost write itself. Either a topic outline or a sentence outline is acceptable (see Chapter 4). However, if you plan to prove a thesis, it is probably wise to make a sentence outline; doing so will force you to state in a complete thought how each section of your paper contributes to the thesis. Observe all the conventions of good outlining as you write, using the slugs in your notes as rough guides for topics and subtopics. (See the outline on page 521 and the sample paper that follows.) For a long and complex paper, it's usually a good idea to add a category labeled *conclusion* to your formal outline.

Look at the topic outline for Elizabeth Kessler's paper, which appears on the next page. After her thesis statement, which is a complete sentence, note the three major divisions, each labeled with a roman numeral—I, II, III. First-level subdivisions appear beside uppercase letters—A, B, C, and so on. Second-level divisions appear beside arabic numbers—1, 2, 3. Note, too, the full-sentence statement of a conclusion here. Readers of this outline see at a glance where Kessler wants to take her topic. For Kessler herself, the outline served as a starting point for the paragraphs she developed in an early draft. Ultimately, she decided to produce a sentence outline for submission along with her paper (see page 521), and she made a number of changes in the order of the elements and in the language of the various outline points. Like your thesis, your outline will change as your thoughts develop on your topic.

Keep in mind that your formal outline should serve as a guide as you develop and refine the various drafts of your paper. As new ideas develop, change your outline as necessary. If you find yourself drifting away from the topic, use your outline to draw you back.

Topic Outline: Polygraph Testing

<u>Thesis</u>: The polygraph test should not be used as part of employment decisions.

I.   Arguments of polygraph test supporters

    A.   Inexpensive and valid way to identify potential thieves on the job

    B.   Reliable findings

    C.   Well-trained examiners

II. Arguments of those who oppose polygraph tests

    A.   "Toothless" laws

    B.   Examiners poor

    C.   Inaccurate readings

    D.   Physiological displays of guilt not measurable

    E.   Human rights violations

       1. Loss of employment

       2. Invasion of privacy

       3. Reputations destroyed

III. Federal legislation against polygraph testing

    A.   No polygraph screening for employment

    B.   Defined testing procedures

    C.   Employee rights

<u>Conclusion</u>--In spite of a recent national law, polygraph testing should be banned in the workplace.

EXERCISE

1. Compare the formal topic outline with Kessler's preliminary rough outline on page 465. How are they similar? different?
2. Compare the topic outline with the sentence outline (page 521) Kessler ultimately submitted. How are the two outlines alike? different? Why do you think Kessler decided to produce a sentence outline after all?

After you complete your research and note taking, reread your notes carefully and identify a pattern among them. Arrange your notes according to headings and develop a slug outline. (You may find it helpful to review the preliminary outline that you developed for the exercise on page 466.) As you continue planning your paper and writing your drafts, develop a formal outline.

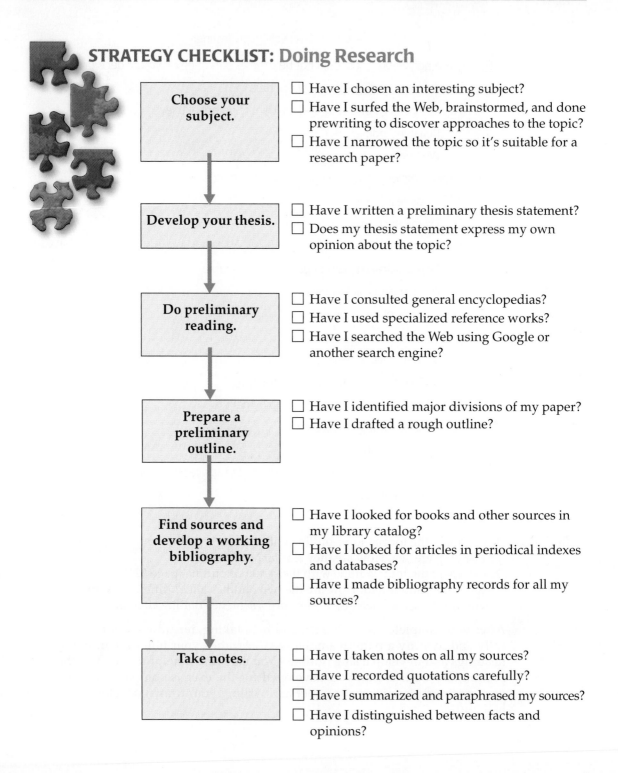

STRATEGY CHECKLIST: Doing Research

Choose your subject.

☐ Have I chosen an interesting subject?
☐ Have I surfed the Web, brainstormed, and done prewriting to discover approaches to the topic?
☐ Have I narrowed the topic so it's suitable for a research paper?

Develop your thesis.

☐ Have I written a preliminary thesis statement?
☐ Does my thesis statement express my own opinion about the topic?

Do preliminary reading.

☐ Have I consulted general encyclopedias?
☐ Have I used specialized reference works?
☐ Have I searched the Web using Google or another search engine?

Prepare a preliminary outline.

☐ Have I identified major divisions of my paper?
☐ Have I drafted a rough outline?

Find sources and develop a working bibliography.

☐ Have I looked for books and other sources in my library catalog?
☐ Have I looked for articles in periodical indexes and databases?
☐ Have I made bibliography records for all my sources?

Take notes.

☐ Have I taken notes on all my sources?
☐ Have I recorded quotations carefully?
☐ Have I summarized and paraphrased my sources?
☐ Have I distinguished between facts and opinions?

Prepare a formal outline.

☐ Have I reviewed my notes and made a slug for each relevant note?

☐ Have I sorted my notes and made a slug outline?

☐ Have I written a formal outline for my paper?

For additional writing, reading, and research resources, go to **www.mycomplab.com** <http://www.mycomplab.com/> and choose Skwire/Wiener's *Student's Book of College English*, Twelfth Edition.

CHAPTER **21**

Writing Your
Research Paper

Writing a research paper involves all the same challenges as writing an essay, and a few additional challenges as well. In writing the paper, you will need to blend quotations and paraphrases of your sources into your own writing, avoid plagiarism, document your sources according to MLA or APA style, and prepare the final copy using conventional MLA or APA formats. We'll begin this chapter with an overview of the research paper writing process and then fill in the details.

Writing Your Research Paper:
An Overview

It's time to set your notes aside, put your outline in front of you, and start writing.

The First Draft

In the first draft, the point is to get your ideas down on paper. Don't worry about grammar or punctuation. Don't try to work in quotations from your sources. You should be familiar enough with the contents of your notes by now to remember the general ideas they contain. Just write.

Subsequent Drafts

Now, write the paper again. Consult your notes to add quotations where appropriate and to fill in facts you might not have remembered when writing the first draft (see pages 39–43). Use blank lines for your draft additions and changes.

You should check your notes, too, to be sure that the facts, ideas, or opinions you have reported are accurate. And, in this second effort, you should make some attempt to correct any grammar or punctuation errors you made in the first draft and to rephrase awkward sentences. Then you should add documentation (see pages 494–508).

Once you have completed this draft, go back through it several times to make certain that you have quoted accurately, that you have documented every source properly, and that you have polished your language as well as you can. Don't hesitate during this process to use scissors and tape or your computer's cut and paste function to add, delete, or shift passages as you go along. If things look too messy for you to read, do another draft of the offending pages—or of the whole paper, if necessary. If you compose your draft on a computer, moving text around will be easy.

Using Explanatory Notes

If you need to explain some point or add information but feel that what you want to say really doesn't fit smoothly into the text of your paper, use a footnote or an endnote. Place a raised number (superscript) after the word where you'd like the reader to consider this additional material. Then, on a separate page called "Notes," use the corresponding number and provide the necessary information. If you use a footnote, place it at the bottom of the page on which your superscript appears.

Look at the next example, from the essay "Nathaniel Hawthorne, Una Hawthorne, and *The Scarlet Letter*," by T. Walter Herbert, Jr.

> It would be an oversimplification to say that Una became merely a creature of her father's imagination, no more than the embodiment of his gender conflicts, as projected onto her. Yet her character, like his, was a cultural construction, and it was one in which Hawthorne had a hand.
>
> This is not the occasion for a detailed treatment of the pattern of solicitude and discipline that the Hawthornes organized about their baby daughter,[3] but crucial issues of the selfhood they sought to impart are disclosed in their naming her Una, after Spenser's maiden of holiness. This decision provoked a controversy among family and friends that illuminates the large cultural processes of gender definition that were then taking place.

> [3]A discussion of Sophia Hawthorne's role in the formation of Una's mental life lies beyond the scope of this essay. Sophia's exceptional response to the emerging norms of gender, the marriage she made to Nathaniel, and her place in the constellation of family relations are complex subjects that bear on this question, which I will treat in a forthcoming book.

The footnote here discusses Sophia's role in Una's mental life—additional information that the writer chose not to include in the text of his essay.

Toward the Final Copy

If you think you have polished the paper as much as you can, make yet another copy, complete with quotations and appropriate documentation (see pages 494–508). Many instructors will not accept a final copy of a paper unless they have seen and approved a draft. If your instructor falls into this category, this draft is the one you should submit. Your instructor will make suggestions, point out stylistic problems, and indicate the parts of your paper that are not developed as fully as they might be. Conscientious students heed their instructors' suggestions and make the appropriate changes on the third draft before preparing the final paper.

Also, before printing your final copy, pay attention to editing details. Proofread carefully. By now you should be familiar with your characteristic errors, and you should comb your paper to find and correct them before submitting your work for evaluation. (See the checklist on pages 120–121 and the discussion of proofreading on pages 119–120.)

Quoting and Paraphrasing Your Sources

Your outline is a kind of X-ray of your awaiting paragraphs—only the bare bones showing. Consider how to flesh out the sentences and develop the paragraphs of your research essay. To support the points made in your paper, you need to quote or paraphrase the information you found in other sources. Most important, however, you need to connect your own writing style smoothly with the comments drawn from other writers.

Quoting an Original Source

Following is a quote from Bennett H. Beach's article "Blood, Sweat and Fears," which appeared in *Time* magazine.

> The FBI uses polygraphs mostly to probe leads and verify specific facts, areas in which, experts concede, the machines are at their best. The agency also employs highly trained examiners, who usually spend half a day on each session (compared with an average of an hour in private industry). Tests given to Jeb Magruder and Gordon Strachan led to evidence of the Watergate cover-up. Right now, Justice Department investigators are using polygraphs extensively in their search for the source of Abscam leaks. Attorney General Benjamin Civiletti has ruled that an "adverse inference" may be drawn if an employee of the FBI or any other part of the Justice Department balks at submitting to the machines.

Assume that you want to use some of this material in your paper. You might want to quote the source exactly—using one or more phrases to several sentences to even the whole paragraph, depending on your purpose. In the following example, note the smooth connection between the student Elizabeth Kessler's words and Beach's words:

> Agencies of the United States government have relied on lie detector tests in important legal matters:
>
> > The FBI uses polygraphs mostly to probe leads and verify specific facts. . . . The agency also employs highly trained examiners, who usually spend half a day on each session. . . . Attorney General Benjamin Civiletti has ruled that an "adverse inference" may be drawn if an employee of the FBI or any other part of the Justice Department balks at submitting to the machines. (Beach 44)

The writer introduces the long supporting quotation with a sentence of her own. The **block format** is used to set off a quotation of four or more typed lines from the text of the essay. The ellipsis (. . .) allows the writer to omit a portion of the quotation. Quotation marks are not used in a block quotation; rather, a ten-space indentation at the left margin sets off the quote. However, when quotation marks appear in the original, as in "adverse inference" in the preceding example, the quotation marks are included in the block quotation as well.

In the following example, Kessler uses shorter quotations from the same source to support her point. However, here the quotations are carefully integrated with the writer's own words and are in each case enclosed by quotation marks.

> Not only does private industry use lie detectors but the federal government does also. "The FBI," reports Beach, "uses polygraphs mostly to probe leads and verify specific facts, areas in which, experts concede, the machines are at their best." To assure a higher degree of accuracy than in other testing situations, no doubt, the FBI "employs highly trained examiners, who usually spend half a day on each session (compared with an average of an hour in private industry)" (44).

Paraphrasing an Original Source

You may also choose to paraphrase the source material. In the following example, Kessler skillfully expresses Beach's point in her own words. Quotation marks surround the phrase "balks at submitting to the machines" because it is quoted from the original source. Note how Kessler attributes the information to Beach and cites the page number for the material she uses.

> As Beach points out, the FBI (as might be expected) uses polygraph testing to aid in major investigations. Yet employees also are expected to take the test. It is clear that the FBI views in a negative light any employee who "balks at submitting to the machines" (44).

Direct Quotations: How Many?

All the rules of good writing that you have learned so far apply to the research paper. But, as you have seen, the research paper presents a special challenge: You must make borrowed material a part of your own statement. You have spent several weeks now taking notes; you have studied them and have decided how to organize them, and that is half the battle. If, however, you simply string quotations together, you will not be writing a research paper; you will be merely transcribing your notes. The paper must be yours—your idea, your organization, and, for the most part, your words. You should use the notes to support your ideas, which means that you should integrate the notes into your own statements. Otherwise, you do not have an honest research paper.

In the following excerpt from a student paper, the writer merely strings quotations together:

> W. E. B. DuBois said in *The Souls of Black Folk* that "the problem of the twentieth century is the problem of the color line" (xiv).
>
> DuBois felt that dreams of opportunities and fulfillment were reserved solely for whites.
>
> DuBois became aware of racial differences at an early age. He related this experience vividly:
>> The shades of the prison-house closed around about us all: the walls strait and stubborn to the whitest, but relentlessly narrow, tall, and unscalable to sons of night who must plod darkly on in resignation, or beat unavailing palms against the stone, or steadily, half hopelessly, watch the streak of blue above. (16)

> When his infant son died, DuBois was depressed, yet he rejoiced because his son would not have to endure life "behind the veil" (155):
>
> > All that day and all that night there sat an awful gladness in my heart— nay blame me not if I see the world thus darkly through the veil, and my soul whispers ever to me, saying "not dead, not dead, but escaped, not bound, but free." No bitter meanness now shall sicken his baby heart till it die a living death, no taunt shall madden his happy boyhood. Fool that I was to think or wish that this little soul should grow choked and deformed within the veil! . . . Well sped, my boy, before the world had dubbed your ambition insolence, had held your ideals unattainable, and taught you to cringe and bow. Better for this nameless void that stops my life than a sea of sorrow for you. (155–56)

The student here has simply copied her notes into the paper. She could make the point more clearly if she phrased it largely in her own words, as in this example:

> W. E. B. DuBois, who said in *The Souls of Black Folk* that "the problem of the twentieth century is the problem of the color line" (xiv), came to believe that dreams of opportunities and fulfillment were reserved solely for whites, and he compared the life of blacks in America with that of prison inmates (16). Indeed, he grew so bitter about the plight of blacks that he rejoiced when his infant son died because the child would never have to experience the prejudice that he had felt (155–56).

In this version, the writer composed a unified paragraph that makes the point clearly without the overuse of quotations. (A good, safe rule of thumb is, unless the subject of your paper is an author's style, quote no more than 10 percent of your paper.) This version shows a much greater mastery of the material than does the first version.

EXERCISE Read the following passage taken from Olivia Judson's essay, "The Selfless Gene" (*Atlantic,* October 2007). Then write two brief paragraphs. In the first, quote directly from the selection. In the second, paraphrase the source.

Many social animals thus live in huge flocks or herds, and not in family groups—or even if the nexus of social life is the family, the family group is itself part of a larger community. In species such as these, social behavior must extend beyond a simple "Be friendly and helpful to your family and hostile to everybody else" approach to the world. At the least, the evolution of social living requires limiting aggression so that neighbors can tolerate each other. And often, the evolution of larger social groupings is accompanied by an increase in the subtlety and complexity of the ways animals get along together.

Consider baboons. Baboons are monkeys, not apes, and are thus not nearly as closely related to us as chimpanzees are. Nonetheless, baboons have evolved complex social lives. They live in troops that can number from as few as eight to as many as 200. Females live with their sisters, mothers, aunts, and infants; males head off to find a new troop at adolescence (around age 4). Big troops typically contain several female family groups, along with some adult males. The relationships between members of a troop are varied and complex. Sometimes two or more males team up to defeat a dominant male in combat. Females often have a number of male "friends" that they associate with (friends may or may not also be sex partners). If a female is attacked or harassed, her friends will come bounding to the rescue; they will also protect her children, play with them, groom them, carry them, and sometimes share food with them. If the mother dies, they may even look after an infant in her place.

Avoiding Plagiarism

Unless the material you borrow is as well known as the Gettysburg Address, when you take facts or ideas from someone else, you must credit the source. Such a statement often frightens students because their first assumption is that they will have to credit almost every sentence in their papers. That is not the case.

You should, of course, give a citation for all direct quotations that are not well known. You should also cite all facts and opinions that are not common knowledge—*even when you have put the facts or opinions into your own words*. Two kinds of facts or opinions come under the heading *common knowledge*: (1) facts everyone in our culture is expected to know (George Washington was the first president of the United States, for example), and (2) facts that are common knowledge in the field you are investigating. Suppose you are writing a paper on Custer's last stand. You might not have known, when you began reading, the name of the Indian tribe that fought Custer and his men. If every source you read, however, says that it was the Sioux tribe, you would not need to give a citation for that fact. Your wide reading lets you know the fact is commonly known to historians. Nor would it be necessary to credit the opinion that Custer blundered; most historians agree that he did. But any theories about why Custer led his men into such a trap should be credited.

If you do not pay careful attention to the techniques of quoting and crediting sources, you run the risk of being accused of plagiarism. **Plagiarism** is the use of facts, opinions, and language taken from another writer without acknowledgment. At its worst, plagiarism is outright theft or cheating: A person has another person write the paper or simply steals a magazine article or section of a book and pretends to have produced a piece of original writing. Far more common is plagiarism in dribs and drabs—a sentence here and there, a paragraph here and there. Nonetheless, small-time theft is still theft, and small-time plagiarism is still plagiarism. For your own safety and self-respect, remember the following rules—not guidelines, *rules*:

- The language in your paper must either be your own or a direct and credited quote from the original source.
- Changing a few words or phrases from another writer's work is not enough to make the writing "your own." Remember rule 1: The writing is either your own or the other person's; there are no in-betweens.
- Documentation acknowledges that the fact or opinion expressed comes from another writer. If the language comes from another writer, quotation marks are necessary in addition to documentation.

Now for a detailed example.

Original Passage

In 1925 Dreiser produced his masterpiece, the massively impressive *An American Tragedy*. By this time—thanks largely to the tireless propagandizing on his behalf by the influential maverick critic H. L. Mencken and by others concerned with a realistic approach to the problems of American life—Dreiser's fame had become secure. He was seen as the most powerful and effective destroyer of the genteel tradition that had dominated popular American fiction in the post–Civil War period, spreading its soft blanket of provincial, sentimental romance over the often ugly realities of life in modern, industrialized, urban America. Certainly there was nothing genteel about Dreiser, either as man or novelist. He was the supreme poet of the squalid, a man who felt the terror, the pity, and the beauty underlying the American dream. With an eye at once ruthless and compassionate, he saw the tragedy inherent in the American success ethic; the soft underbelly, as it were, of the Horatio Alger rags-to-riches myth so appealing to the optimistic American imagination. (Richard Freedman, *The Novel* [New York: Newsweek Books, 1975], 104–05)

Student version	**Comment**
There was nothing genteel about Dreiser, either as man or novelist. He was the supreme poet of the squalid, a man who felt the terror, the pity, and the beauty underlying the American dream.	✗ **Obvious plagiarism.** Student version contains word-for-word repetition without acknowledgment.
There was nothing genteel about Dreiser, either as man or novelist. He was the	✗ **Still plagiarism**. *The documentation alone does not help*. The language is

supreme poet of the squalid, a man who felt the terror, the pity, and the beauty underlying the American dream (Freedman 104).

Nothing was genteel about Dreiser as a man or as a novelist. He was the poet of the squalid and felt that terror, pity, and beauty lurked under the American dream.

"Nothing was genteel about Dreiser as a man or as a novelist. He was the poet of the squalid and felt that terror, pity, and beauty lurked under the American dream" (Freedman 104).

"Certainly there was nothing genteel about Dreiser, either as man or novelist. He was the supreme poet of the squalid, a man who felt the terror, the pity, and the beauty underlying the American dream" (Freedman 104).

By 1925 Dreiser's reputation was firmly established. The reading public viewed Dreiser as one of the main contributors to the downfall of the "genteel tradition" in American literature. Dreiser, "the supreme poet of the squalid," looked beneath the bright surface of American life and values and described the frightening and tragic elements, the "ugly realities," so often overlooked by other writers (Freedman 104).

the original author's, and only quotation marks around the whole passage plus documentation would be correct.

Still plagiarism. The writer has changed or omitted a few words, but by no stretch of the imagination is the student using his or her own language.

Not quite plagiarism, but incorrect and inaccurate. Quotation marks indicate exact repetition of what was originally written. The student, however, has changed some of the original and is not entitled to use quotation marks.

Correct. The quotation marks acknowledge the words of the original writer. The documentation is also needed, of course, to give the reader specific information about the source of the quote.

Correct. The student writer uses his or her own words to summarize most of the original passage. The documentation shows that the ideas expressed come from the original writer, not from the student. The few phrases kept from the original passage are carefully enclosed in quotation marks.

Documenting Sources in the Humanities: MLA Style

The Modern Language Association (MLA) style documentation guidelines presented here follow the *MLA Handbook for Writers of Research Papers*, 7th ed. (2009).

Parenthetical Citations

Documenting or **crediting** or **citing** a source simply means letting the reader know where you found another's quotation, fact, idea, or opinion that appears in your paper. Most current style manuals, including the influential Modern

Language Association's *MLA Handbook for Writers of Research Papers*, Seventh Edition (2009), recommend the efficient method of **parenthetical documentation**.

In this method, the last name of the author and the page number on which the material appears are placed within parentheses immediately after the information or quotation. Or, if you can integrate the author's name conveniently in the text itself, only the page number appears in parentheses. (If you refer to a whole work, however, no page reference is necessary.) Readers interested in finding the work cited then consult the bibliography, titled "Works Cited," at the end of the paper for further information about the source. In parenthetical documentation, footnotes and endnotes are used only to provide additional information or commentary that might otherwise interrupt the flow of the text.

The following examples of parenthetical documentation reflect the Seventh Edition MLA style, used widely in the humanities and in other disciplines as well.

Work by One Author

The most common citation is for a work written by a single author. It contains the author's last name and the page number from which the material is taken, unless the citation is of an entire work.

"The problem of the twentieth century is the problem of the color line"

(DuBois xiv).

Indeed, he grew so bitter about the plight of blacks that he rejoiced when his infant son died because the child would never have to experience the prejudice that he had felt (DuBois 155–56).

In *The Souls of Black Folk*, DuBois shows in dramatic personal terms the effects of prejudice in America.

Work by Two or More Authors

If the work has two or three authors, use the last names of all the authors as they appear on the title page.

If the work has more than three authors, name them all in the order in which they appear on the title page, or use the last name of only the first author and follow the name with *et al.*, the abbreviation for the Latin *et alia*, "and others." Note the period after *al.*, which is an abbreviation for *alia*; and note that no period follows *et* because it is not an abbreviation. (*Et* means *and*.)

A wide range of job opportunities is available to adventurous travelers (Krannich and Krannich 1–3).

The example preceding refers to the book *Jobs for People Who Love to Travel* by Ronald L. Krannich and Caryl Rae Krannich.

Heller, Heller, and Vagnini see carbohydrates as part of a healthy diet (2).

The work cited, *The Carbohydrate Addict's Healthy Heart Program*, is by three authors, Richard F. Heller, Rachael F. Heller, and Frederic J. Vagnini.

Teachers in all courses should determine the writing skill levels of their students (Anderson et al. 4).

Anderson and her coauthors insist that teachers in all courses determine the level of writing skills for their students early in the semester (4).

Anderson and three coauthors wrote *Integrated Skills Reinforcement*. Full references for these books appear on page 499.

More than One Work by the Same Author

He learned as a child that he could be rejected simply because of the color of his skin (DuBois, *Souls* 16).

Because the researcher cites more than one work by DuBois in the paper, an abbreviation of the title, *The Souls of Black Folk*, serves to distinguish this work by DuBois from other works by the same author.

More than One Volume of a Work

Although he had urged conscientious objection during World War I, his views changed gradually, and by 1940, he concluded that he must support the war against the Nazis (Russell 2: 287–88).

The Autobiography of Bertrand Russell has more than one volume; thus, the information cited comes from the second volume, pages 287–288.

Work for Which No Author Is Given

Frequently, the author of a work is not given or is not known. In such a case, do not use the word *anonymous* or its abbreviation, *anon*. Instead, put in parentheses the title or an abbreviated title and the page number, as in this example:

Supporters of the polygraph test point out that to help alleviate possible nervousness, the subject is given access to the questions he will be asked during the test for as long as he desires ("What's It Like" 8).

Information About a Work or Author Already Given in Sentence

Many of your sentences may already contain enough information about a work that the parenthetical documentation can be made even shorter than in the examples given so far.

> W. E. B. DuBois said in *The Souls of Black Folk* that "the problem of the
>
> twentieth century is the problem of the color line" (xiv).

Because the writer names the author and title in the sentence, only the page number appears in parentheses.

The following sentence is from a paper that cites more than one work by DuBois. Since the author's name is used in the sentence, you need not repeat it in the documentation. However, an abbreviated title of the book distinguishes this work by DuBois from other works by the same author.

> W. E. B. DuBois, who believed that "the problem of the twentieth century is the
>
> problem of the color line" (*Souls* xiv), learned as a child that he could be
>
> rejected simply because of the color of his skin.

There are even times when you don't need to use parenthetical documentation. For example, if a writer says, "DuBois devotes his entire *Souls of Black Folk* to the subject," a reader need simply turn to the Works Cited list to find the remaining facts of publication. However, if you need to cite a section of a work, rather than the entire work, use one of the following forms:

> This point has been made before (DuBois 16–156).

> or

> DuBois has made this point before (16–156).

If the section is in a work of more than one volume, you might write

> Russell has detailed the kind of opposition to the war made by pacifists in
>
> England (2: 3–128).

> or

> In the second volume of his work (3–128), Russell has detailed the kind of
>
> opposition to the war made by pacifists in England.

In other words, the more skillfully you construct your sentences, the less information you need to include in your parenthetical documentation.

EXERCISE   Return to the exercise on pages 491–492 and reread the passage. In only one sentence, summarize the passage and provide parenthetical documentation according to the guidelines you just learned.

A List of Works Cited

Parenthetical documentation requires a **list of works cited**, an alphabetical listing of the sources cited in the paper. This list appears on a separate page at the end of the paper and is headed "Works Cited." The list of works cited contains full references to all sources used in the paper.

Different types of sources require somewhat different treatment. The examples that follow are typical MLA-style entries for the list of works cited. For entries that do not appear here, consult the *MLA Handbook for Writers of Research Papers*, 7th ed. (2009), or some other research style manual that your instructor recommends.

Standard Book Entry for the Works Cited List

Book with one author

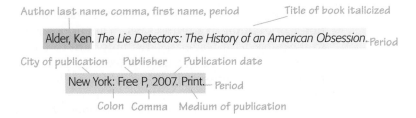

To see where this information comes from, refer to the illustration on page 499. Double-space the entry. Invert the author's name and place a period after it, after the title of the book (which is in italics), and after the publication date. A colon separates the city of publication and the name of the publisher. A comma separates the publisher's name—written in a shortened form (and without *Inc., Company*, and the like) and the year of publication. *Free P* here refers to the Free Press and *Print* is the medium of publication. The first line of the entry begins at the left margin. Indent all subsequent lines of the entry one-half inch from the left.

Other Book Entries for the Works Cited List
Book with two authors

> Haynes, William O., and Rebekah H. Pindzola. *Diagnosis and Evaluation in Speech Pathology*. New York: Allyn, 2007. Print.

Invert only the name of the first author. The order of the names is the same as that on the title page of the original source.

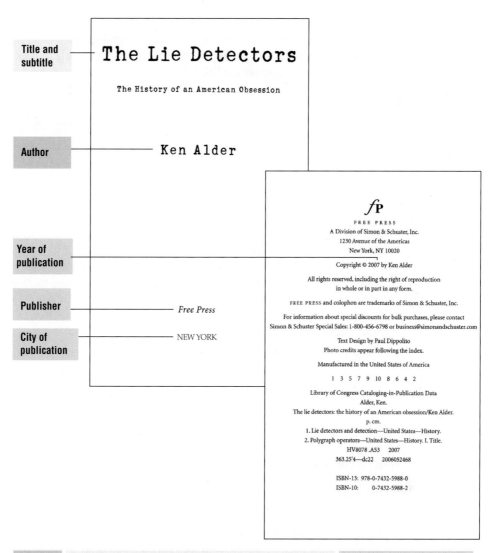

Title and subtitle

The Lie Detectors

The History of an American Obsession

Author

Ken Alder

*f*P

FREE PRESS
A Division of Simon & Schuster, Inc.
1230 Avenue of the Americas
New York, NY 10020

Copyright © 2007 by Ken Alder

All rights reserved, including the right of reproduction
in whole or in part in any form.

FREE PRESS and colophon are trademarks of Simon & Schuster, Inc.

For information about special discounts for bulk purchases, please contact
Simon & Schuster Special Sales: 1-800-456-6798 or business@simonandschuster.com

Text Design by Paul Dippolito
Photo credits appear following the index.

Manufactured in the United States of America

1   3   5   7   9   10   8   6   4   2

Library of Congress Cataloging-in-Publication Data
Alder, Ken.
The lie detectors: the history of an American obsession/Ken Alder.
p. cm.
1. Lie detectors and detection—United States—History.
2. Polygraph operators—United States—History. I. Title.
HV8078 .A53   2007
363.25'4—dc22   2006052468

ISBN-13: 978-0-7432-5988-0
ISBN-10:   0-7432-5988-2

Year of publication

Publisher — *Free Press*

City of publication — NEW YORK

Alder, Ken. *The Lie Detectors: The History of an American Obsession.* New York: Free P, 2007. Print.

Book with three authors

Heller, Richard F., Rachael F. Heller, and Frederic J. Vagnini. *The Carbohydrate Addict's Healthy Heart Program.* New York: Ballantine, 1999. Print.

Book with more than three authors

Anderson, JoAnn Romeo, et al. *Integrated Skills Reinforcement.* New York: Longman, 1983. Print.

You may use the name of the first author only, followed by the notation *et al.,* the Latin abbreviation for "and others." The name given is the first name that appears on the title page. Another option is to provide all names in full in the order in which they appear on the title page.

Anthology

> Wallace, David Foster, and Robert Atwan, eds. *The Best American Essays 2007*. Boston: Houghton, 2007. Print.

The editors collected several essays in this book. The editors' names appear before the title, with the abbreviation *eds.*

Selection in an anthology

> Driscoll, Mary Erina. "Choice, Achievement, and School Community." *School Choice: Examining the Evidence*. Ed. Edith Rasell and Richard Rothstein. Washington: Economic Policy Inst., 1993. 147–72. Print.

The page numbers given at the end of the entry indicate where the essay appears in the anthology. The editors' names appear after the abbreviation *Ed.* ("edited by").

When you use two or more essays from the same collection, you may *cross-reference* them, as in this example:

> Witte, John F. "The Milwaukee Parental Choice Program." Rasell and Rothstein 69–109.

The reference "Rasell and Rothstein" is to the anthology *School Choice: Examining the Evidence*. A citation for the anthology itself must then be included in the Works Cited list.

Special edition of an author's work

> Thoreau, Henry David. *Walden*. Ed. Jeffrey S. Cramer. New Haven: Yale UP, 2006. Print.

Editions other than the first

> Raimes, Ann. *Keys for Writers*. 5th ed. Boston: Houghton, 2008. Print.

For a revised edition, the abbreviation *Rev. ed.* appears after the title.

Translated work

> Tolstoy, Leo. *War and Peace*. 1869. Trans. Richard Pevear and Larissa Volokhonsky. New York: Knopf, 2007. Print.

Multivolume work

> Adams, Wallace E. *The Western World*. 2 vols. New York: Addison, 1968. Print.

Pamphlet

Treat a pamphlet like a book, using the name of the committee or organization that created the pamphlet as the author if no author's name is provided.

Helsinki Summer School 2008. Helsinki: U of Helsinki, 2008. Print.

Selection in an encyclopedia

Kaeliinohomoku, Joanh W. "Hula." *Encyclopedia Americana*. 2006 ed. Print.

It is not necessary to give full publication information for a well-known reference work. If the article is signed only with the initials of the author, the rest of his or her name—the parts usually included in brackets—can be found by consulting the index volume. In some encyclopedias, the full name of the author can be found in the frontmatter section of the encyclopedia.

"Georgetown." *Encyclopaedia Britannica: Micropaedia*. 2007 ed. Print.

When no author is given, the entry begins with the title of the article. *The Encyclopaedia Britannica* has two parts: The *Micropaedia*, which contains short articles on the subject and cross-references to the *Macropaedia*, which contains longer articles on the subject, generally written by important scholars in the field.

Unpublished dissertation

He, Yuemin. "The Exoticized Other: Positive Images of the Chinese in Twentieth-Century American Poetry." Diss. Southern Illinois U at Carbondale, 2004. Print.

Standard Periodical Entry for the Works Cited List

Article with one author

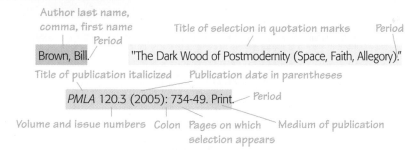

To see where this information comes from, refer to the illustration on page 502.

Like the standard entry for a book, the entry for a journal article contains three major divisions: (1) the author's name, (2) the title of the work, and (3) the publication data. However, for journal articles, both the name of the article (in quotation marks) and the name of the journal (italicized) are included.

Brown, Bill. "The Dark Wood of Postmodernity (Space, Faith, Allegory)." *PMLA* 120.3 (2005): 734–49. Print.

Source information from a journal

As in the example above, many journals use continuous pagination throughout the year—for example, if the first issue ends on page 280, the second issue will begin on page 281. To cite journals that use continuous pagination, place the volume and issue numbers before the year of publication, which is given in parentheses. The month is not needed. A colon precedes the inclusive page numbers on which the selection appears.

Other Periodical Entries for the Works Cited List

Article in a journal that numbers pages in each issue separately

Bernard, Emily. "Fired." *American Scholar* 76.1 (2007): 101–07. Print.

The issue number follows the volume number, and a period separates them (76.1 in the preceding example refers to volume 76, issue 1). If only an issue number appears, include it as you would a volume number.

Selection in a monthly (or bimonthly) magazine

Le Guin, Ursula. "Staying Awake." *Harper's* Feb. 2008: 33–38. Print.

The entry includes the month (abbreviated) instead of a volume number. Only the months May, June, and July are not abbreviated.

Selection in a weekly (or biweekly) magazine

Yousafzai, Sami, and Ron Moreau. "Suicide Offensive." *Newsweek* 3 Apr. 2007: 24–36. Print.

Unsigned selection in a magazine

"The Bible in First Person." *Christian Century* 3 Apr. 2007: 5. Print.

When no author is given, the entry begins with the title of the article. Do not use the word *anonymous* or its abbreviation, *anon.*

Unsigned article in a daily newspaper

"A Suburb Looks Nervously at Its Urban Neighbor." *New York Times* 17 Jan. 2008, late ed.: A20. Print.

Give the name of the newspaper but omit any introductory article, such as *The* from *New York Times* in the example. If the name of the city is part of the title of the newspaper, as in the *New York Times*, italicize it. However, if the name of the city is not part of the newspaper's title, include the city in brackets and do not italicize it: *Star-Ledger* [Newark].

Some newspapers print more than one edition a day, and the contents of the editions may differ. In such cases, include the edition you used. In addition, newspapers often indicate section numbers, and you should include them in the citation. In the preceding example, A20 refers to section A, page 20.

Use a plus sign after the page number when the entire selection does not appear on consecutive pages.

Review in a periodical

Rev. of *Love and War in California*, by Oakley Hall. *New Yorker* 14 May 2007: 149. Print.

Flanagan, Caitlin. "The Age of Innocence." Rev. of *College Girls: Bluestockings, Sex Kittens, and Coeds, Then and Now*, by Lynn Peril. *Atlantic* Apr. 2007: 107–11. Print.

In the first example, the book review is unsigned. In the second, the review is both signed and titled: Flanagan's review of the book *College Girls: Bluestockings, Sex Kittens, and Coeds, Then and Now* is called "The Age of Innocence."

Standard Entry for an Online Source

Source information from an online document

To see where this information comes from, refer to the illustration on page 505.
For Web sources, give as much information as you can, including the original publication information if the source was published elsewhere first. If you cannot find the sponsor or publisher of the site, use *N.p.* (for "No publisher"). If the document does not have a date of posting, use *n.d.* (for "no date"). You do not have to include a URL unless you think readers will have difficulty finding the source by searching. If you must divide a URL at the end of a line, divide it only after a slash mark.

Document within an information database, a scholarly project, or Web site

"Homer." *Encyclopaedia Britannica Online*. Encyclopaedia Britannica, 2007. Web. 18 Feb. 2008.

Webster, Augusta. "A Castway." *Portraits*. London, 1870. *Victorian Women Writers Project*. Ed. Perry Willett. Indiana U, 24 Apr. 1998. Web. 13 Apr. 2008.

Entire Internet site, such as an online scholarly project, information database, or professional or personal site

Willett, Perry, ed. *Victorian Women Writers Project*. Indiana U, 1995-2003. Web. 13 Apr. 2008.

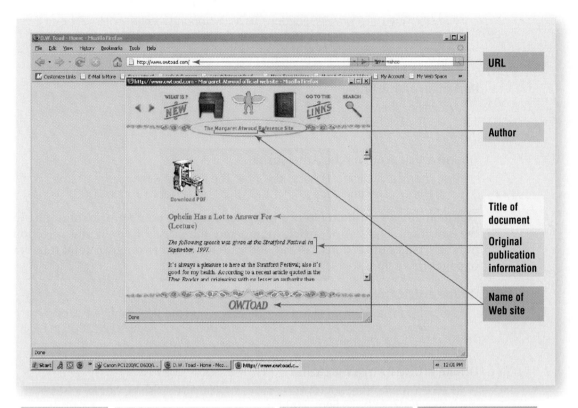

Atwood, Margaret. "Ophelia Has a Lot to Answer For." Stratford Festival, Sept. 1997. *O.W. Toad: The Margaret Atwood Reference Site*. Margaret Atwood, n.d. Web. 18 Mar. 2008. <http://www.owtoad.com>.

Boyle, T. C. Home page. N.p., n.d. Web. 19 June 2007.

CBS.com. CBS, 2007. Web. 23 July 2008.

Home page for a course

Wild, Larry. Theater 241: Stagecraft. Course home page. Dept. of Theater, Northern State U, Fall 2006. Web. 12 Aug 2008.

No component of the entry requires italicizing.

Online book

Anderson, Sherwood. *Winesburg, Ohio*. 1919. *Bartleby.com: Great Books Online*. Bartleby.com, 1999. Web. 11 Dec. 2008.

Webster, Augusta. *Portraits*. London, 1870. *Victorian Women Writers Project*. Ed. Perry Willett. Indiana U, 24 Apr. 1998. Web. 20 Apr. 2008.

The Webster example is a book that is part of a scholarly project.

Part of an online book

Anderson, Sherwood. "Hands." *Winesburg, Ohio*. 1919. *Bartleby.com: Great Books Online*. Bartleby.com, n.d. Web. 9 Oct. 2008.

Online article from a scholarly journal

Rist, Thomas. "Religion, Politics, Revenge: The Dead in Renaissance Drama." *Early Modern Literary Studies* 9.1 (2003): 20 pars. Web. 19 June 2008.

The item *20 pars* in the reference indicates the total number of paragraphs in the selection. The online article numbered the paragraphs. If the selection numbers pages or sections instead, indicate the number range or total number of pages or sections.

Online article from a journal database

Grubin, Don, and Lars Madsen. "Lie Detection and the Polygraph: A Historical Review." *Journal of Forensic Psychiatry and Psychology* 16.2 (2005): 357–69. *ContentSelect Research Navigator*. Web. 17 Mar. 2008.

Online article from a magazine

Bowden, Mark. "The Ploy." *TheAtlantic.com*. Atlantic Publishing Group, 24 May 2007. Web. 19 Sept. 2008.

Online article from a newspaper

Schiesel, Seth, and David Leonhardt. "Justice Dept. Acts to Block Proposed WorldCom-Sprint Deal." *New York Times*. New York Times, 28 June 2000. Web. 19 May 2008.

Online television program

"My Long Goodbye." *Scrubs*. *NBC.com*. WNBC, New York, 5 Apr. 2007. Web. 8 Apr. 2007.

When you watch a program or video or listen to a recording online, the medium of publication is *Web*. See also *Films and television (or radio) programs,* pages 507–508.

Nonperiodical publication on CD–ROM, diskette, or magnetic tape

Mann, Ron. *Emile De Antonio's Painters Painting*. Irvington: Voyager, 1996. CD-ROM.

Selection from a periodically published database on CD-ROM

"Polygraph." *Encarta Reference Lib. 2007*. CD-ROM. Microsoft, 2007.

Item from a personal subscription service

"Circe." *Compton's Encyclopedia Online*. Vers. 2.0. America Online, 1997. Web. 3 Feb. 2006.

E-mail communication

Kane, Joshua. Message to the author. 2 Aug. 2007. E-mail.

Smith, Johnson C. "Re: Critique of Marx's Views." Message to Ramon Vargas-Llosa. 23 June 2000. E-mail.

Wright, John. E-mail interview. 7–9 Apr. 2008.

The Kane entry illustrates an untitled e-mail message sent directly to the writer of the paper at hand; the Smith entry illustrates a titled e-mail message originally sent to someone else. The entry for Wright shows an e-mail interview over a number of days and indicates the inclusive dates.

Online posting to an e-mail discussion list

McCarty, Willard. "Humanist's 20th!" *Humanist Discussion Group*. N.p., 7 May 2007. Web. 28 Jan. 2009. <http://www.digitalhumanities.org/humanist/ Archives/Virginia/v21/0000.html>.

Synchronous communication on a MUD or MOO

Online Forum for Educational MOO Administrators. *LinguaMOO*. N.p., 6 July 1995. Web. 20 June 2005. <http://www.pub.utdallas.edu/~cynthiah/ lingua_archive/edumoo-7-6-95.txt>.

MUD is the acronym for multiuser domain; MOO is the acronym for multiuser domain, object oriented. Both are forums for posting synchronous communication.

Other Types of Works Cited Entries Sources

Recordings, tapes, and compact discs

Groban, Josh. *Noel*. Reprise/WEA, 2007. CD.

The entry includes the name of the artist, the title of the recording, the manufacturer, and the date. The recording is a compact disk. If the piece is in another medium, use *LP* (long-playing record), *Audiocassette*, or *Audiotape* (reel-to-reel tape) at the end of the entry.

Films and television (or radio) programs

The Lives of Others [*Das Leben der Anderen*]. Dir. Florian Henckel von Donnersmarck. Perf. Martina Gedeck, Ulrich Mühe, and Sebastian Koch. Sony, 2007. Film.

"Lillian Gish: The Actor's Life for Me." Narr. Eva Marie Saint. Prod. and dir. Terry Sanders. *American Masters*. PBS. WNET, New York, 11 July 1988. Television.

Cartoons

Smaller, Barbara. Cartoon. *New Yorker* 26 Mar. 2007: 65. Print.

Schulz, Charles. "Peanuts Classic." Comic strip. *Daily News* [New York] 21 Nov. 2005: 43. Print.

Interviews

Fraser, Brendan. Interview. *Tavis Smiley*. PBS. WNET, New York, 16 Jan. 2008. Radio.

Hawke, Ethan. Personal interview. 11 Mar. 2008.

Performances

The Homecoming. By Harold Pinter. Dir. Daniel Sullivan. Perf. Ian McShane, Raul Esparza, and Eve Best. Cort Theatre, New York. 9 Jan. 2008. Performance.

Preparing the Works Cited List

In preparing your list of works cited, follow these guidelines for the correct format.

TIPS   for Preparing the Works Cited List

- **Prepare the list on a separate page headed "Works Cited."** Place the heading about an inch from the top and center it. (Do not underline the heading; use uppercase letters only for the first letter in each word.) The Works Cited page appears at the end of the paper.

- **Double-space before typing the first entry.** Begin each entry flush with the left margin, and indent all other lines of each entry five spaces. Use double-spacing throughout your list of works cited.

- **Arrange the entries alphabetically, according to the authors' last names.** Do not separate books and periodicals. For entries without authors, use the first word in the title (other than *A*, *An*, or *The*) to determine alphabetical order.

- **When you cite two or more books by the same author, arrange them alphabetically by title.** Give the author's full name only in the first entry. In subsequent entries, replace the author's name with three hyphens. For example:

  Geertz, Clifford. *The Interpretation of Cultures*. New York: Basic, 1973. Print.

  ---. *Local Knowledge: Further Essays in Interpretive Anthropology*. New York: Basic, 1983. Print.

See pages 538–541 for a complete, formatted Works Cited list.

EXERCISE   Write entries for a list of works cited according to the MLA-style system of documentation for two sources you will use in your research paper.

Documenting Sources in the Social Sciences: APA Style

Writers in the social sciences use the system of documentation set forth in the *Publication Manual of the American Psychological Association* (APA), Fifth Edition (2001) and the *APA Style Guide to Electronic References* (2007). Since your instructors in psychology, sociology, and other courses may require you to follow APA guidelines, you should be familiar with this system. Like the MLA style, **APA-style documentation** uses parenthetical citations supported by a separate list of sources headed "References," which appears at the end of the research paper.

Parenthetical Citations

A typical APA-style text citation includes the author's name and the date of publication, separated by a comma.

> Lower species of animals use only a few signs in their communication systems. For example, the rhesus monkey uses only about 37 different signals (Wilson, 1972).

As with MLA-style documentation, the APA system aims to integrate references smoothly with the text of the paper. Here are some further examples:

> In 1972 Wilson showed that the rhesus monkey uses only about 37 different signals in its communication system.
>
> According to Wilson (1972), rhesus monkeys use only 37 signals. Communication systems that rely on only a few signs are typical of lower animal species.

When quoting a passage from a source, the page number on which the passage appears follows the publication date. Note the required use of the abbreviations *pp.* for "pages" and *p.* for "page." Separate the date and the page information by a comma.

> Creative people use divergent thinking to their advantage and "prefer complexity and some degree of apparent imbalance in phenomena" (Barron, 1963, pp. 208–209).

When citing more than one work by the same author published in the same year, use an *a* after the date for the first publication, a *b* after the date for the second, and so on. The citations on the references list should also include these letters. In the following example, the reference is to the second 1971 article by Schacter, "Some Extraordinary Facts About Obese Humans and Rats." This reference is marked *b* on the references list. Schacter's first 1971 article, "Eat, Eat," would be marked *a* on the references list (see page 513).

> Researchers have identified important similarities for obesity in rats and humans
>
> (Schacter, 1971b).

The examples that follow show how to cite multiple authors in the APA system. Note that the ampersand (&) replaces the word *and* between authors' names in the parenthetical citation (see the first example). If the authors' names are not given parenthetically, as in the second example, use the word *and*.

> Famous studies of the chimpanzee Washoe demonstrated that animals other
>
> than humans could learn and use language (Gardner & Gardner, 1969).

> Rumbaugh, Gill, and von Glaserfeld (1973) studied the language skills of the
>
> chimpanzee Pan.

When citing works by three or more authors, use all authors' names (followed by the date) for the first reference, but in the second and subsequent text references use the abbreviation *et al.* after the first author's name.

> Rumbaugh et al. (1973) have documented certain levels of reading and the
>
> ability to complete sentences among chimpanzees.

 Return to pages 489–491. Revise any two MLA-style citations there so that they reflect the APA style of parenthetical citation.

A List of APA References

APA-style documentation requires that a list of the references cited in the paper appear on a separate page at the end. The heading "References" is typed at the top of the page and is not underlined (see page 513). Titles of books, newspapers, journals, and magazines appear in italics. On the following pages are sample references in the APA format.

Standard Book Entries for the References List
Book with one author

Book with two or more authors

Hick, S. F., & McNutt, J. G. (2002). *Advocacy, activism, and the Internet*. Chicago: Lyceum.

Standard Periodical Entry for the References List

APA style requires italics, not underlining for book and periodical titles.

Article in a journal that numbers the pages in each issue separately

Lanza, R. (2007). A new theory of the universe. *American Scholar, 76*(2), 18–33.

The notation refers to volume 76, issue 2.

Article in a monthly (or bimonthly) magazine

> Cannon, C. M. (2007, January/February). Untruth and consequences. *The Atlantic, 299*, 56–67.

In a monthly or bimonthly magazine, the month of publication is given after the year in parentheses. A comma separates the year and the month. The volume number follows the magazine title. Use the abbreviation *p.* for page and *pp.* for pages only for newspaper entries.

Article in a daily newspaper

> Isaacs, N. (2007, April 5). Exercisers slow it down with Qigong. *The New York Times*, p. G1.

Electronic Sources

> Hinshelwood, R. O. (2007). Intolerance and the intolerable: The case of racism. *Journal for the Psychoanalysis of Culture and Society, 12*(1), 1–20. Retrieved from http://palgrave-journals.com/pcs/journal/v12/n1/full /2100103a.html

> Dyer, J., & Findlay, B. (2007). Psychocardiology: Advancing the assessment and treatment of heart patients. *E-Journal of Applied Psychology, 3*(2), 3–12. Retrieved from http://ojs.lib.swin.edu.au/index.php/ejap/article /view/88/120

> Sengupta, S. (2008, January 17). Push for education yields little for India's poor. *The New York Times*. Retrieved from http://www.nytimes.com

> Grubin, D., & Madsen, L. (2005). Lie detection and the polygraph: A historical review. *Journal of Forensic Psychiatry & Psychology, 16*(2), 357–369. doi: 10.1080/14789940412331337353

Use the models above to develop citations for a range of electronic sources that you might cite in a paper. Note that in APA style, the words "Retrieved from" precede the URL and a period does not appear at the end of the URL. If you need to break a URL from one line to the next, break *before* the slash (/) or other major puncuation mark, but break *after* the double slash (//). Dates of retrieval appear only if you reference a draft version of the article; final versions of articles require no retrieval dates in the citation. Finally, if an article is assigned a digital object identifier (DOI) in a database, as in the Grubin entry above, use this number in place of database names and URLs.

The *APA Style Guide to Electronic References* (2007) provides more information and a comprehensive collection of sample references for electronic sources.

Preparing Your APA References List

If your instructor asks you to prepare your paper in APA format, here is a sample references list for you to examine and some tips for preparing the references list.

References

Bernard, E. (2005). Teaching the n-word. *American Scholar, 74*(2),
46–49.

Chase, A. (2000, June). Harvard and the making of the Unabomber.
Atlantic, 282, 41–65.

Gardner, R. A., & Gardner, B. T. (1969). Teaching sign language
to a chimpanzee. *Science, 165*, 664–672.

Lanza, R. (2007). A new theory of the universe. *American Scholar,
74*(2), 18–33.

Schacter, S. (1971a, November). Eat, eat. *Psychology Today, 5*,
44–47, 78–79.

Schacter, S. (1971b). Some extraordinary facts about obese
humans and rats. *American Psychologist, 26*, 129–144.

Trussoni, D. (2006). *Falling through the earth: A memoir.*
New York: Henry Holt.

TIPS for Preparing an APA References List

■ **Type the heading "References" at the top of a new page.** On a separate page that will appear at the end of the paper, type the heading centered on the line. Do not underline it; do not enclose it in quotation marks. List all the sources cited in the text. Double-space from the heading to the first entry.

■ **Arrange all entries alphabetically.** Without separating books from periodicals, arrange all entries alphabetically according to the author's last name (or, according to publication dates—earliest to most recent—for works by the same author).

■ **Double-space within and between all entries.**

■ **The first line of each entry is flush with the left margin.** Indent second and subsequent lines of each entry five spaces.

■ **Number the References page.**

Be sure to check the APA Web site <http://www.apastyle.org/elecref.html> for more information about APA style requirements.

EXERCISE Select four bibliography notes (two for books, two for periodicals) that you prepared for your research paper and write an APA-style references list for them.

Preparing Your Manuscript

Before you begin to prepare your final copy, make sure your printer has ink or toner and is in good working order. Since you have put so much work into writing the paper, you don't want to spoil the final product by presenting your instructor with a hard-to-read, smudged copy. Avoid unusual typefaces like script or italic. On a computer, Times New Roman is standard for formal documents. Set the type size at 10- or 12-point.

Good bond paper gives a more attractive appearance than less expensive types. White, 8½ × 11-inch, twenty-pound bond paper is usually recommended. Avoid using erasable paper because it smudges and will not take corrections made in ink. If you type and do not like to erase or have difficulty erasing neatly, use a correction tab to remove errors. If you use a computer, you'll find corrections easy to make, but don't neglect to reread your paper carefully before you submit it. (Also see pages 42–43 on writing with a computer.) Check for careless errors like unnecessary spaces and repeated words. Follow these guidelines as you prepare the final copy:

TIPS for Preparing the Final Copy

- **Double-space.** Double-space the paper throughout, including long quotations and notes, except as indicated in the following discussion of margins.

- **Use one-inch margins.** Leave margins of one inch at the top, bottom, and both sides of the text. If you are not using a title page, type the centered title two inches from the top of the page, and double-space between the title and the first line of the text. Indent the first word of each paragraph five spaces from the left margin. Indent a block quotation ten spaces from the left margin.

- **Format the title.** MLA guidelines call for a heading on the first page instead of a separate title page. The writer's name, instructor's name, course number, and date appear flush left on the first manuscript page, spaced as shown in the example on page 515.

   However, many instructors prefer a title page, especially if an outline or table of contents precedes the first page of text. If your instructor calls for a

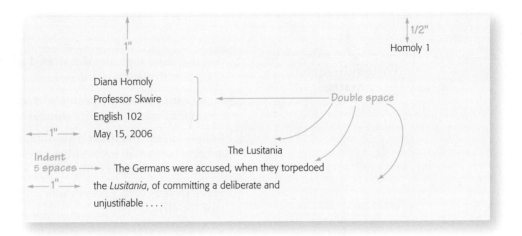

title page, it should contain the title of your paper, your name, the course name and number, the name of your instructor, and the date. Neatly center this information on the page, as shown on page 520.

Whichever form you use, remember that you should never put your own title in quotation marks, underline it, or capitalize it in full. Underline words in the title only if you would underline them in the text also.

■ **Pagination.** Number all pages consecutively (except the title page and any prefatory material) in the upper-right-hand corner. Just type the number; don't punctuate it with a period, hyphens, or parentheses. In addition to putting the number in the upper-right-hand corner, you may also want to type your name right before the page number to ensure against misplaced pages. (See the pagination of "The Banning of the Polygraph," page 521, for example.) Number prefatory materials, such as your outline, acknowledgments, or preface, with lowercase roman numerals—i, ii, and so on.

STRATEGY CHECKLIST: Writing Your Research Paper

Note: This checklist begins with the first draft. For a research and planning Strategy Checklist, see Chapter 20.

Write the first draft.	☐ Is my thesis clear and limited? Does it state or suggest an interpretation or judgment on the topic? ☐ Does the body of the paper develop the thesis?

continued

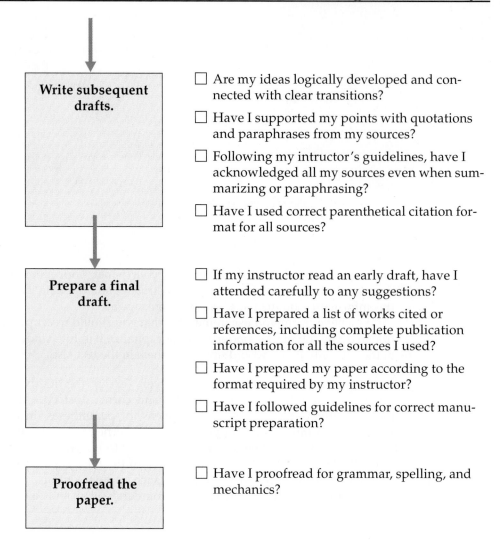

Write subsequent drafts.

☐ Are my ideas logically developed and connected with clear transitions?

☐ Have I supported my points with quotations and paraphrases from my sources?

☐ Following my intructor's guidelines, have I acknowledged all my sources even when summarizing or paraphrasing?

☐ Have I used correct parenthetical citation format for all sources?

Prepare a final draft.

☐ If my instructor read an early draft, have I attended carefully to any suggestions?

☐ Have I prepared a list of works cited or references, including complete publication information for all the sources I used?

☐ Have I prepared my paper according to the format required by my instructor?

☐ Have I followed guidelines for correct manuscript preparation?

Proofread the paper.

☐ Have I proofread for grammar, spelling, and mechanics?

EXERCISE　　Using your formal outline as your guide, write the necessary drafts of your research paper. Document all sources. Prepare a list of works cited. Be sure to study the student sample and the accompanying commentary on the following pages.

Frequently Asked Questions About Writing Research Papers

How do I find a good topic?

As with any paper, identify areas that interest you. Baseball? Fashion? TV programming? Prewrite. Browse your library's catalog. Surf the Web. Rent movies and watch relevant TV. Talk to friends, teachers, coworkers, family. Think about your topic.

When I have decided on a topic, what do I do next?

Limit your topic so that it is suitable for a research paper of the scope and length defined by your instructor. *Baseball* might become *how Hollywood presents baseball heroes in film; TV programming* might become *violence in television cartoons for children* (see pages 34–36).

How do I develop a thesis for my topic?

Once you have limited your topic by browsing and discussing your ideas, you must make some assertion about your topic, and that will be your tentative thesis (see pages 53–54). Each thesis below grew from the limited topics above:

- Hollywood films idealize baseball heroes, who never correspond in fact to the real troubled athletes playing the game.
- Students of the media may disagree on the long-term effects of TV violence on children, but the graphic images of brutality in popular cartoons cause deep psychological problems for young viewers.

Expect to revise your thesis many times as your research progresses and your ideas take shape.

How do I begin my reseach?

Develop a general perspective on your topic by relaxed "reading around." Look up your topic in a recent edition of a general or specialized encyclopedia (see pages 461–463). Use library catalogs; browse bookshelves; use search engines to identify Web sources that might stimulate your thinking at this stage simply by their names or home pages.

What if I can't find any good sources?

Talk to a librarian. Talk to your teacher. Talk to classmates.

How can I organize my thoughts at this point?
Develop an informal outline (see pages 72–74) to help you read and take notes in a systematic way.

How do I identify the sources of my quotes and paraphrases?
Most papers for English courses require documentation in the MLA style (see pages 494–508). Name your source exactly and provide some identifying information in the body of the paper as you present quotes or paraphrases, and name your source more completely in a list of works cited at the end of your paper (see page 508).

What documentation style do I use for writing social science papers?
Use the format described in the *Publication Manual of the American Psychological Association* (see pages 509–513) and the *APA Style Guide to Electronic References*.

How do I do the kind of serious research that will help me write about my topic?
Read selections from books you've identified. To find current periodical selections (an important source of current information), use *The Reader's Guide*, newspaper indexes, or other periodical indexes useful to your topic (see pages 467–471). Do an electronic search (see pages 463–464). Read reliable Web sources carefully (see pages 26–29).

How do I record information?
Reproduce information carefully and use quotation marks on your research notes around *anything* you copy word for word from a source. Separate your own thoughts carefully from quotes. (Use special marking or another color ink.) Use ellipses (spaced dots) to indicate words you've left out of a quote (see page 479). Use paraphrasing and write summaries to record most of the information you're extracting from your readings (see pages 479–481).

Once I start accumulating notes from my reading, how can I organize them when I'm ready to write my paper?
Give each note a topic slug and then stet the notes by topic. Make an outline. (See Chapter 4 as well as pages 481–482.) Develop a sentence outline.

What if my teacher doesn't require an outline?
You probably should do one anyway, just to make sure that you're organizing the points in your paper logically.

How do I actually use someone else's words or ideas in my own paragraphs?
Learn to integrate smoothly any quotations you take from sources, use quotation marks where needed, and cite the sources correctly (see pages 488–492). If

you paraphrase, make sure that it's clear—through correct citation—which thoughts are yours and which are those of your source. Use quotation marks around any set of words within your paraphrase that come directly from the source. Ignoring citation risks plagiarism, a very serious offense (see pages 492–494).

How many quotations should I use in my paper?
Be careful not simply to string quotations together as you write your paper. Use quotes to support your ideas, which means that you have to integrate the quotes into your own statements. Often paraphrasing makes the point as well as lengthy quotes (see pages 490–491).

Sample MLA-Style Research Paper

The following sample research paper shows how one student, Elizabeth Kessler, managed to blend a variety of elements successfully. The commentary that appears on the pages facing the paper highlights its key features and calls attention to special issues. The paper uses MLA-style documentation.

TITLE PAGE, IF REQUIRED

Title begins one-third down page.

The Banning of the Polygraph

← *Double-space between the title and the next line.*

by

Elizabeth Kessler

English 102, Section 18

Professor D. Skwire

15 January 2009

Writer's name, course and section, instructor's name, and date of submission are all double-spaced.

OUTLINE, IF REQUIRED   Kessler   i

*Formal sentence outline
observes format described
in Chapter 4.*

Outline

<u>Thesis</u>: The polygraph test as an element in employment decisions   *Final thesis*
should be banned.

First major I.   Those who argue in favor of the polygraph feel it should
division   be used as a criterion for employment.

A. Supporters claim that the examiners are adequately
trained.   *First-*
level
B. Supporters claim that polygraph findings are reliable.   *subdivisions*
C. Supporters argue that it is an inexpensive and effective
method to avoid hiring potential thieves.

II. Those who oppose the polygraph test correctly believe it
should not be used as a criterion for employment.

A. Opponents believe the examiners are uneven in quality.
B. Opponents believe the readings are not accurate.
C. Opponents believe there is no clear-cut physiological
indication of guilt.
D. Opponents believe the laws regarding the use of the
polygraph are "toothless."
E. Opponents believe the test violates basic human rights.
1. The test can lead to loss of employment and damage   *Second-level*
to reputation.   *subdivisions*
2. The test is an invasion of privacy.

III. The 1988 Polygraph Protection Act restricts lie detector use.

<u>Conclusion</u>: Despite legislation restricting polygraph use nationally,   *Conclusion*
continuing abuses and potential abuses in the future argue forcefully
against the lie detector test in the workplace.

■ 1

■ 2
■ 3
■ 4

The polygraph (lie detector) monitors physiological change[1] in a person's blood pressure, pulse rate, breathing, and skin conductivity (Beach 44). The subject, while attached to the polygraph machine, must respond to a series of questions to measure the person's honesty. Any great physiological change during a particular question is said to indicate deception (Inbaw 44). Employers use polygraphs

■ 5

to weed out dishonest or prospective employees and "as a means of curbing employee thefts, a multibillion-dollar-a-year headache" (Gugas 6). After twenty years, the use of the machine had increased tenfold: By the 1980s, two million Americans a year were tested. "By then," writes Ken Alder, "one-fourth of all U.S. firms used the technique for preemployment screening or systematic checkups on honesty" (254). Banks, police departments, and guard agencies have made similar demands ("Tests Untrustworthy" 16).

■ 6

Despite wide use much debate surrounds testing. Supporters praise it, it is true.[2] Yet critics argue strongly against its use. Merely a machine, the polygraph simply "picks up a person's emotional reactions to questions by measuring breathing, sweating responses, and blood pressure." One psychiatrist insists that "there is no such

■ 7

thing as a lie detector" ("Truth" 76). A syndicated columnist reminded readers of the "foolishness of dependence" on the

■ 8

polygraph (Safire A39). Indeed, on the evidence, one must agree with the 1988 Employee Polygraph Protection Act, which attempts to ban the polygraph test as a criterion for most employment. Lie

■ 9

detectors have no place in the work environment.

Those who favor the polygraph test claim that it is accurate because those who administer it are adequately trained. The examiner "must be consistently objective and should be thoroughly

■ 1 The page number appears in the upper right-hand corner of each page of the paper. Some writers also include their last name before the page number, as Kessler does. Type the page number (and your name, if you choose to include it here) one-half inch from the top of the page.

■ 2 Begin the first paragraph about two inches from the top of the page.

■ 3 The raised numerals 1 and 2 correspond to notes 1 and 2 on page 1 of the research paper. Such notes provide explanatory information that doesn't fit smoothly into the paper.

■ 4 The parenthetical citation (Beach 44) refers to a work fully named with all the appropriate publishing data in the list of works cited (see page 10 of the research paper). No comma separates the author's name and the page number. No abbreviation for *page* or *pages* is used. Kessler cites Beach because she paraphrased the definition of the polygraph from him.

■ 5 Quotation marks surround the words beginning with *as* and ending with *headache* because Kessler copied the statement word for word from Gugas's book *The Silent Witness* (see page 10 for the complete citation). Here is part of the paragraph as it appears in Gugas; note how Kessler extracted only the small piece that would serve her purpose.

> Business and industry use the polygraph examination widely in screening job applicants and as a means of curbing employee thefts, a multibillion-dollar-a-year headache. Our Army, Navy, Air Force, and Marines all use polygraph testing. I myself set up the lie-detector program for the Criminal Investigation Department of the Marine Corps when I was a Marine Major. . . .

■ 6 Note how the introduction calls attention to both supporters and critics of polygraph testing. The paper itself expands on these issues.

■ 7 The citation ("Truth" 76) indicates that the quotation appears on page 76 of an unsigned piece. Kessler shortened the full title "The Truth About Lie Detectors, Says David Lykken, Is That They Can't Detect a Lie." See the list of works cited on page 11.

■ 8 The citation (Safire A39) refers to a column in section A, page 39 of the *New York Times*. The complete reference appears in the list of works cited on page 11 of Kessler's paper.

■ 9 The thesis sentence states the topic, following logically from the points raised in the introduction. Kessler's thesis makes a forceful assertion: Keep polygraphs out of the workplace.

Kessler 2

■ 10 trained in scientific interrogation to reduce the inherent human error" ("Polygraph"). In fact, many states demand education and other requirements for the licensing of polygraph examiners

■ 11 ("In Ohio" F4). Because nervousness may bring about the same emotional responses as deception, which may lead to false readings, these examiners, it is said, are trained extensively in psychology and physiology. The training supposedly enables the examiner to distinguish between nervousness and actual deception ("What's It Like" F8). Supporters of the test believe that the training

■ 12 equips examiners to make accurate distinctions.

Advocates of the polygraph also claim that its findings are reliable. Using control questions, an examiner can determine a person's normal emotional reaction. By establishing a normal response, the examiner then can detect deception, which reveals itself in an abnormal

■ 13 response (Inbaw 44). Supporters of the test point out that to reduce nervousness, the subject has access to the questions on the test for as long as he desires ("What's It Like" F8). Thus, the ability to detect and relieve nervousness should lead to accurate readings.

Supporters of the polygraph further argue that it is "a valuable

■ 14 tool for an employer in . . . investigating workplace crime" ("How to Comply" 36). Each year theft exceeds twenty billion dollars (Beach 44). To help decrease this amount, the employers enlist the aid of the polygraph. According to the National Association of Convenience Stores, the use of the polygraph can reduce employee theft by as

■ 15 much as 50 percent (Flaherty 31). Interestingly, at numerous Chicago banks during the 1930s, employees who failed lie detector tests and remained on the payroll became "The banks' most honest

■ 16 employees. . . . The lie detector become [sic] a psychological deterrent as much as a catcher of thieves" (Alder 124).

■10 Kessler cites a quotation from another electronic source. The "Polygraph" piece appears in *Encarta*, an encyclopedia on CD-ROM. See page 11 of the research paper for the exact source.

■11 "In Ohio" is a shortened title for "In Ohio, Anyone May Run Lie Detector," which refers to an unsigned article that Kessler identifies fully in the list of works cited. The full title appears in the works cited list on page 10.

■12 The closing sentences sum up the main issue developed in each paragraph. In the second paragraph, last sentence, the word *thus* connects the closing sentence logically with the ideas that precede it.

■13 Here Kessler uses an important strategy in writing arguments: She presents her opponents' views clearly and fairly. She herself does not approve of polygraph testing, but she does not ignore the issues put forth by those who support the test. The paragraph expands on point I. B. in Kessler's outline on page i.

■14 The ellipsis points (three spaced periods) indicate that Kessler omitted from the quotation the words she felt were not relevant. As indicated on the list of works cited, the source is an article called "How to Comply with the Polygraph Law," which appeared in *Nation's Business*. (See full details on the list of works cited on page 10.) If the original source itself contains an ellipsis, place brackets around the ellipsis you have inserted to distinguish it from the ellipsis in your source. Kessler remembered to use a space before and after the three spaced periods.

■15 The statistical data are impressive. Even though Kessler is arguing a point opposite to what she believes, she marshalls substantial evidence to show the other side of the issue. To help readers draw thoughtful conclusions on their own, writers should present opposing arguments fairly.

■16 The Latin abbreviation *sic* means "thus" or "so." It tells readers that Kessler knows that the correct verb form here is past tense—*became*, not *become*—but that she is reporting the text exactly as it appeared in Alder's book, with the error intact.

Kessler 3

■ 17

Supporters argue, too, that the polygraph test is much quicker, more efficient, and less expensive than background checking. As Beach indicates, using the polygraph costs about $35 to $150; doing a background check on a potential employee costs significantly more, an average of $300 (44).

And, of course, federal support for polygraph testing has added validity to their use. Agencies of the United States government have relied on lie detector tests in important legal matters:

■ 18

> The FBI uses polygraphs mostly to probe leads and verify specific facts. . . . The agency also employs highly trained examiners, who usually spend half a day on each session. . . . an "adverse inference" may be drawn if an employee of the FBI or any other part of the Justice Department balks at submitting to the machines. (Beach 44)

■ 19

The supporters of the polygraph believe its efficiency and low cost justify its use.

Those who favor the polygraph in the workplace, then, argue that adequately trained examiners produce reliable findings at low cost. These are strong arguments. However, those who oppose the test question the claims made by its supporters, and they are right to do so.

■ 20

■ 21

Despite assertions that examiners are adequately trained to distinguish among physiological responses, Beach points out that opponents to the test have called attention to regular reports by employees that examiners browbeat them during polygraph testing (44). And "about 90% of the damaging reports made to employers are based not on physiological reactions but on the examiners'

■17 Here Kessler integrates into her sentence the name of the author whose work she paraphrases. The parenthetical reference (44) tells readers the page number in Beach's article "Blood, Sweat, and Fears," which Kessler paraphrased. The full citation appears on page 10 of Kessler's paper. Note throughout this paragraph the consistent use of numbers, all written as numerals. See pages 630–631.

■18 Kessler sets off this quotation ten spaces from the left margin because it takes more than four lines. The parenthetical citation of Beach comes after the last line of the quotation. See page 488 for the complete paragraph as it appears in Beach's article.

■19 The transitional paragraph neatly connects the two major sections of the essay. In the first part of the paragraph, Kessler summarizes the issues advanced by polygraph test supporters. The word *then* in the first sentence connects the ideas expressed here with the preceding paragraphs. With the word *however*, Kessler signals her opposition to the strong arguments put forth by those who support the test. Notice how the last sentence connects to the thesis sentence on page 1 of the research paper.

■20 Kessler shows why she believes that the training of polygraph examiners is uneven. Readers must weigh the assertions in this paragraph against the arguments by those who say that examiners are well trained.

■21 Kessler has paraphrased the statement for which she credits Beach. Here is the selection exactly as it appears in Beach's article:

> Lie detector tests, either to screen job applicants or to uncover theft by employees, have become big business: hundreds of thousands are given each year, and the number is rising steadily. But despite technical improvements in the equipment, the accuracy of the results is often open to question, and there are persistent reports of browbeating by examiners. . . .

Even though she uses her own language to restate Beach, Kessler attributes the source of her ideas with the page reference (44). The author's name appears in the sentence; hence, it is excluded from the parenthetical citation.

Kessler 4

assumptions, or on incriminating confessions made during an interview" ("Truth" 76). These findings suggest that the quality of operators in the polygraph industry is uneven at best.

Furthermore, critics say that the test is accurate only 60 to 75 percent of the time, and many variants have never been checked for validity ("Tests Untrustworthy" 16). Error is more likely to occur when a truthful person is shown to be deceptive (Beach 44). The opposition argues that readings do not always indicate deception and that people who do not believe that the machine can detect dishonesty feel no stress when lying: Therefore, no great physiological response will

■ 22

indicate deception on the readings (Flaherty 32). Clinical tests suggest that tranquilizers can reduce the physiological response that accompanies deception (Ward et al. 74). Also, those who are "really

■ 23

clever . . . can fool the machines" ("Rights Abuse" 10).

When seven FBI agents with access to high-secret information failed polygraph tests not long ago, the director at that time, Robert S. Mueller III, said the failed polygraphs did not automatically mean that the agents were suspected of spying. He said that "a follow-up investigation could exonerate" all the employees (Johnston, A18).

■ 24

So much for accuracy! One must question the value of readings that may be unreliable.

■ 25

Nor does a clear-cut physiological indication of guilt seem to be as certain as supporters of the test claim. Often, heightened feelings bring about physiological responses that are similar to those caused by deception. According to David Lykken, a psychiatrist and professor of psychology, people who run a special risk include those who get upset if someone accuses them of something they did not do, those with short tempers, and those who tend to feel guilty

■22 Flaherty and Ward are sources for the paraphrases included in this paragraph. See the list of works cited on pages 10 and 11 of the paper for the complete citations.

■23 Kessler uses ellipses to indicate that she has left out words in this quotation taken from an editorial, called "Rights Abuse," in the *Christian Science Monitor*. (See reference in Works Cited list, page 11.)

■24 Kessler uses a sentence fragment as an exclamation ("So much for accuracy!") to make a sharp commentary on the meaning of Mueller's statement. Once again, she offers her own opinion, based on an element in her research.

■25 This paragraph develops point II. C. in the outline (page i). The transition *nor* connects the ideas of this paragraph to those in the paragraph before it.

Kessler 5

anyway. Lykken believes that the polygraph machine detects not only the physiological responses that accompany lying but also the nervousness people feel when strapped to a machine. The polygraph confuses guilt with fear, anger, and other emotions that can alter heart rate, breathing, and perspiration. Each person varies in physiological responses to these emotions ("Truth" 79).

■ 26

Moreover, until now, polygraph laws tended to be "toothless." Some laws prohibit requiring present or prospective employees to submit to a polygraph; however, businesses are still free to make the request (Flaherty 34). Private companies can advertise job-related lie-detection services even now. One company, for example, asserts that its polygraph test . . . "is a valuable 'investigative tool'" for ongoing questions about economic loss and that its expert examiners "can help 'clear' loyal staff members while resolving open issues during a non-accusatory interview and examination process" (Dallas Polygraph

■ 27

Services). If a current or prospective employee refuses to take the test, employers may interpret the refusal as an admission of guilt ("Truth" 79). In fact, refusal may mean the loss of a job (Beach 44).

■ 28

This is unfair: The burden lies entirely on the employee's shoulders. Further, some laws free only present, not prospective employees from a polygraph test. Finally, the fines and jail terms for violating these laws rarely have risen above misdemeanor level. Fines, which seldom exceed $1,000, do not hinder "deep-pocketed" employers from using the polygraph (Flaherty 34). Such laws, test opponents argue, have not protected employees.

One must also consider the problem of human rights violation ("In Ohio" F4). Especially in regard to criminal cases, some sociologists and experts in theology say that polygraph testing "unjustly robs

■ 26 This paragraph develops point II. D. in the outline.

■ 27 The information about the company comes from the company's Web site. Kessler provides the full Internet source on her list of works cited, page 10. "Dallas Polygraph Services" is the name of the page she used from the Web site http://dallaspolygraph.com.

■ 28 Kessler reflects on her findings, inserting her own opinion on the information she presents. Writers of research papers should do more than simply summarize, paraphrase, or quote acknowledged experts.

Kessler 6

■ 29

suspects of their innermost secrets." Courts have ruled that the test illegally forces people to testify against themselves (Block 131). Several experts claim that the lie detector, with all its apparatus, constitutes a "modern third degree" and may intimidate a subject into blurting out a false confession before the test begins (Beach 44). They argue, also, that an unfavorable reading, whether accurate or not, could result in damage to an employee's reputation and the inability to obtain new employment, especially since, in many states, a person must sign a form before taking the test that allows any individual access to the test results ("Personal Rights Issue" 7). Thus, one can, in effect, be found guilty and be punished—having committed no crime— without the traditional protections of presumption of innocence until guilt is proved, trial by jury, and the right to confront accusers. Finally, many employers see in the polygraph an opportunity to force their values and ideas on employees (Flaherty 30). The polygraph test, then, can be an infringement on individual rights.

■ 30

A further infringement on individual rights, according to opponents of the test, is invasion of privacy. Many examiners have probed into personal affairs of those being tested (Beach 44). The examiners ask questions pertaining to political, sexual, and union matters. Mike Tiner of the Union of Food and Commercial Workers reported that in the 1980s questions involving political, sexual, and union matters were definitely on the increase (Beach 44). As a result, many large non-governmental employers avoid polygraph testing. A retired director of personnel at Schlumberger Limited, a large multinational corporation, believes that potential employees would prefer to work in organizations that valued "personal impressions and evaluations of candidates rather than the 'answer'

■29 Kessler smoothly integrates the quote from Block with her own language. Look at the statement from Block, then at the note Kessler prepared, as she read the source material.

> Some sociologists and theologians question the fairness of the lie detector, arguing that it unjustly robs suspects of their innermost secrets, and some courts have held that to some extent it illegally compels defendants to testify against themselves. Yet modern police authorities insist that many baffling cases have been solved only because such a test, taken voluntarily by a suspect, has proved scientifically that he or she lied in answering key questions pertinent to the case.

Block, Science vs. Crime, 131

"Some sociologists and theologians question the fairness of the lie detector, arguing that it unjustly robs suspects of their innermost secrets, and some courts have held that to some extent it illegally compels defendants to testify against themselves."

Police say, however, that polygraphs help solve puzzling cases by giving scientific proof of lying.

*Focus here is on criminal cases.

Kessler has copied one sentence exactly and has enclosed it in quotation marks on her note card. She has also paraphrased the rest of the paragraph—the sentence starting with the words *Police say* on the notes. In addition, she has written a brief note to herself on the card—the sentence beginning with the word *Focus*. She uses an asterisk to highlight the statement as her own, so that she will not mistakenly attribute it to Block when she reviews the note cards later on and chooses information to include in her essay.

When Kessler draws on the material from this note card to make her point in the paper, she uses only one part of the quotation from Block. Kessler paraphrases the portion of the quote that reads "and some courts have held that to some extent it illegally compels defendants to testify against themselves." In her paper, this part of the quote becomes "Courts have ruled that the test illegally forces people to testify against themselves (Block 131)." The parenthetical documentation tells readers that both the quote and the paraphrase are from Block.

■30 Note the smooth transition. Kessler writes "A further infringement on individual rights," repeating exactly a phrase from the last sentence of the previous paragraph, adding the word "further." This paragraph develops point II. E. 2. in the outline.

■ 31

provided by a machine" (Alexander). Invasions of privacy are violations of constitutional rights and should not be tolerated.

■ 32

      Fortunately, the government heeded the chorus of voices against the lie detector over the years. In 1988, Congress passed the Polygraph Protection Act, which, according to an article called "How to Comply with the Polygraph Law" in *Nation's Business,* finally prohibits

■ 33

polygraphs to "screen job applicants or investigate employees . . ." (36). The law defines proper testing procedures and gives employees a wide range of rights, including notice in advance of the time and place of the examination, its scope, and the reasons the employer has for suspecting the employee in some specific incident "involving economic loss or injury to the business" (36). In addition, the law spells out "procedural requirements" with guidelines for the examiners' qualifications. Some good sense has prevailed here; many workers now have protection against offensive testing.

■ 34

      Yet despite restrictions in the 1988 law, many civil rights advocates are still unhappy. In fact, some are vicious in their attack against polygraph use. *AntiPolygraph.org* argues that "Our government's stubborn reliance on this pseudoscience poses clear and present danger: make-believe science yields make-believe security." Advertising claims like those of the James W. Bassett Company in 2008 have not abated ("Polygraph Testing Services"). The legal system in the past has not protected employees well against abusive polygraph testing, and one must reserve judgment about how long-term enforcement will support the federal law. The polygraph Protection Act allows too many exceptions, particularly the "reasonable suspicion" feature. Employers bent on using the test no doubt can develop charges of suspicion against employees

▪ 31 The citation ("Alexander") is to another electronic source, this one an e-mail Kessler received from a former multinational corporate employee. See page 10 for the full citation of this e-mail.

▪ 32 Kessler draws to a close by bringing the topic up to date in light of current law. She treats fairly the positive provisions of the new bill, even though they might challenge her own position. This paragraph expands on point III in Kessler's outline.

▪ 33 Note punctuation with ellipsis at the end of a sentence. Three spaced periods indicate an omission at the end of the *Nation's Business* quote. The parenthetical reference here follows the quotation mark after the ellipsis; a sentence period follows the final parenthesis.

▪ 34 The opening sentence of the conclusion reestablishes one of the basic themes of the paper—the ongoing debate about polygraph testing. Kessler here states strongly her own opinions, raising again what she sees as the key issues in the dispute—the test's unreliability and its encroachment on civil rights. She provides a powerful quotation from an established Web site (*AntiPolygraph.org*) to debunk lie detection as a science. Her conclusion does not simply restate the essential points of the paper, nor is it a shorter version of the introduction. Rather, Kessler uses the conclusion to reassert her own beliefs sharply and clearly.

Kessler 8

they dislike. Additionally, federal, state, and local governments are exempt from the law, as are several private-sector employers, including security companies and many drug companies. Ultimately, the poor accuracy record of the tests in general condemns them, no matter how much they are restricted. As a result of these weaknesses in the law and of other major issues, polygraphs should have no place in any employee judgments.

■ 35   Notes

¹These physiological changes in the body functions are measured by the use of special apparatus: a rubber tube placed around the chest, a pressurized cuff around one arm, and several sensors taped to the skin (Dunn 85).

■ 36   ²Although efforts to detect lies go back to ancient times, the modern history of polygraph testing starts with Cesare Lombroso and his experiments with human heartbeats. After him, Hugo Munsterberg, "Harvard's pioneer in criminal psychology" (Block 132), advanced efforts to develop a reliable lie detector. In 1920, criminologists August Vollmer, John A. Larson, and Leonardo Keller developed a machine that could record "on paper with up-and-down lines a subject's changes in heartbeat, blood pressure, and respiration under steady questioning" (134).

■ 35 Note 1 refers to the superscript[1] on page 1 of Kessler's paper. It adds information that is not essential to the paper but that is nonetheless instrumental in helping readers understand how the polygraph equipment may be used. Kessler does not want to focus on the mechanical features of the polygraph in the text of her paper, which concentrates on the unfairness of using the device.

Indicate the note number as a superscript; indent five spaces and double-space all lines of the note. Place the notes on a separate page headed "Notes," typed one inch from the top and centered. The Notes page appears directly before the Works Cited page. (Your instructor may prefer that you type footnotes at the bottom of the page on which the superscript appears in the text.)

■ 35 Note 2 refers to the superscript[2] on page 1 of the paper.

Kessler 10

■ 36   Works Cited

■ 37   Alder, Ken. *The Lie Detectors: A History of an American*
          Obsession. New York: Free P, 2007. Print.

■ 38   Alexander, Arthur. "Re: Polygraph Examinations in Employment."
          Message to the author. 15 Oct. 2008. E-mail.

■ 39   *AntiPolygraph.org*. Antipolygraph.org, 2007. Web. 15 Nov. 2008.

■ 40   Beach, Bennet H. "Blood, Sweat and Fears." *Time* 8 Sept.
          1980: 44. Print.

          Block, Eugene B. *Science vs. Crime: The Evolution of the Police*
          Lab. San Francisco: Cragmont, 1979. Print.

■ 41   "Dallas Polygraph Services." *DallasPolygraph.com*. Michael D. Park
          and Associates Polygraph, 2007. Web. 12 Oct. 2008.

          Dunn, Donald. "When a Lie Detector Test Is Part of the Job Inter-
          view." *Business Week* 27 July 1981: 85–86. Print.

          Flaherty, Francis. "Truth Technology." *Progressive* June 1982: 30–35.
          Print.

■ 42   Gugas, Chris. *The Silent Witness: A Polygraphist's Casebook*.
          Englewood Cliffs: Prentice, 1979. Print.

          "How to Comply with the Polygraph Law." *Nation's Business*
          Dec. 1989: 36–37. Print.

■ 43   "In Ohio, Anyone May Run Lie Detector." *Dayton Daily News*
          31 Mar. 1982: F4. Print.

          Inbaw, Fred. "Polygraph Test." *Encyclopedia Americana*. 1993 ed.
          Print.

■ 44   Johnston, David. "Seven F.B.I. Employees Fail Polygraph Tests for
          Security." *New York Times* 4 Apr. 2002, late ed.: A18. Print.

■ 36 The references appear on a separate page headed "Works Cited" and are listed alphabetically by the authors' last names (or, if the work is unsigned, by the first key word in the title). Put the heading "Works Cited" about an inch from the top of the page. Center it. Do not separate entries for books, periodicals, and Web sources.

■ 37 This is an entry for a book with one author. If a reference runs to a second line, indent it five spaces. *P* is an acceptable abbreviation for *Press*.

■ 38 The reference is to an electronic source, an e-mail Kessler received from a retired director of personnel (see page 539 of the paper itself).

■ 39 The reference is to a Web site accessed by the writer through a Google search. AntiPolygraph.org is "dedicated to the abolishment of polygraph testing." The name of the site is italicized. The year 2007 indicates the online publication date; *15 Nov. 2008* is the date Kessler accessed the material online.

■ 40 The reference is to an article in a weekly periodical.

■ 41 The reference is to another electronic source, a Web site called *Dallaspolygraph.com*. Michael D. Park and Associates Polygraph is the site's sponsor. *Dallaspolygraph.com* is a commercial site that strongly supports the use of polygraph testing. Note how Kessler has balanced her electronic sources here. See notes 38 and 39 above.

■ 42 This is another standard entry for a book. *Prentice* is an acceptable abbreviation for Prentice Hall, the publisher.

■ 43 Because this newspaper article is unsigned, Kessler alphabetizes it according to the word *In*, the first word in the title.

■ 44 The entry is standard for a signed article in a daily newspaper. David Johnston is the reporter whose name appears in the byline. The item *A18* means that the article appears in section A, page 18, of the newspaper. The notation *late ed.* after the date indicates the particular edition in which the article appeared. (Different editions of a newspaper often contain different material.) Note the comma before the specified edition.

Kessler 11

"Lie Detectors Raise Personal Rights Issue." *Dayton Daily News*
29 Mar. 1982: F6–8. Print.

"Lie Detector Tests Untrustworthy." *USA Today* Feb. 1981: 16. Print.

"Polygraph." *Microsoft Encarta Premium 2008*. CD-ROM. Microsoft,
2008.

"Polygraph Testing Services." *Theftstopper.com.* James W. Bassett,
2008. Web. 18 Oct. 2008.

■45   "Rights Abuse." Editorial. *Christian Science Monitor* 20 Oct.
1999: 10. Print.

Safire, William. "Lying 'Lie Detectors.'" *New York Times* 10 Oct.
2002, late ed.: A39. Print.

■46   "The Truth about Lie Detectors, Says David Lykken, Is That They
Can't Detect a Lie." *People* 11 May 1981: 75+. Print.

■47   Ward, William, et al. "Meprobamate Reduces Accuracy of Physiological Detection of Deception." *Science* 3 Apr. 1981:
73–74. Print.

"What's It Like to Take a Lie Detector Test?" *Law and Order*
[Columbia] 5 July 1981: F7–8. Print.

■ **45** Kessler indicates that this source is an editorial with the word *Editorial* right after the title of the selection.

■ **46** This article from a weekly magazine appears on interrupted pages; the selection starts on page 75 and continues on pages 76 and 79. The pages on which the selection continues do not appear in the citation.

■ **47** Since there are more than three authors for this magazine article—William Ward, Emily Carota Orne, Mary R. Cook, and Martin T. Orne—the citation names only the first author, followed by the Latin abbreviation *et al.*, meaning "and others." However, you may choose to give all names in full in the order in which they appear. Invert only the names of the first author, placing the last name first. For all other authors in a multiple author citation, place the first name before the surname.

For additional writing, reading, and research resources, go to **www. mycomplab. com** <http://www.mycomplab.com/> and choose Skwire/Wiener's *Student's Book of College English*, Twelfth Edition.

PART FIVE

Style

Writing a well-organized essay is one thing. Writing a well-organized *good* essay is another, more complicated thing. Thousands of rusty filing cabinets and dusty shelves are filled with perfectly well-organized writings that got their authors nothing but bored and irritated readers—not to mention poor grades. These writings all had a thesis; they all supported the thesis; they all had an introduction, a body, and a conclusion. The paragraphs in these writings all had topic sentences, and the topic sentences were all connected to the thesis. In short, these writings followed all the directions and advice that this book has given so far. So what went wrong?

The answer to that begins with another question. Do we waste time praising a relative's remodeled home because the sofa is in the living room and the stove in the kitchen? We all know that if the sofa had been in the bathroom and the stove on top of the coffee table, we'd be faced with a disaster, but we generally take logical organization for granted. In a reasonably well-organized piece of writing the reader simply assumes the structure is satisfying and then concentrates on other matters. The reader is right, too. Few homeowners have ever received compliments for putting the bed in the bedroom, and few writers have ever been praised for their superb mastery of topic sentences.

When we do praise writers, we generally praise them because they know how to work with words. We may think we liked a particular story or article because its ideas were powerful and interesting, but it was the words that *made* the ideas powerful and interesting. Good writers can fascinate us with instructions on how to use automobile directional signals. Poor writers can bore us with passionate love letters. Bear in mind, too, that good writers are almost never just born that way. Their writing skill is the result of intelligent tinkering and careful revision, not of magic.

Part Five, then, discusses ways of refining your use of language. We concentrate here not on grammar and organization but on **style**—not just how to write *correctly* but how to write *well*.

CHAPTER 22

Proper Words in Proper Places

- Denotation and Connotation
- Abstract Writing and Concrete Writing

Jonathan Swift, the author of *Gulliver's Travels*, once defined good style as "proper words in proper places." Gustave Flaubert, the great French novelist, felt that the writer's craft was embodied in the quest for *le seul mot juste*, "the single right word." Nearly all writers can learn to hit the right word simply by becoming more alert to the possibilities of language and the need for thoughtful revision.

Denotation and Connotation

Traditionally, the most logical way to begin thinking about right and wrong words is through the distinction between denotation and connotation:

- The **denotation** of a word is its explicit, surface meaning, its bare "dictionary meaning."
- The **connotation** of a word is its implicit meaning, the meaning derived from the emotions associated with the word in people's minds.

Words like *Las Vegas* or *Ireland*, for example, simply denote a particular city or country—a mere geographical location—but for many people, they also have an emotional significance that has nothing to do with geography. The connotative meanings of a word do not always appear in a dictionary, but they are as vital a part of the word's full meaning as are denotations.

The Importance of Connotation

Let's take a simple example. Suppose you are the head of a successful advertising agency, and a major motor corporation wants you to handle the campaign introducing a new car. Would you recommend calling the car the Giraffe, the Porcupine, or the Hawk?

We all probably agree that among Giraffe, Porcupine, and Hawk, the last name is the only reasonable choice for the new car. For most people, the idea of a hawk carries with it connotations of power, speed, and perhaps freedom and beauty. These are concepts that motivate people who buy cars, no matter how loudly they may claim that their sole interests are economy and "just transportation." Consider the animal names in use for car models and notice how many connote power, speed, or both: Bronco, Mustang, Jaguar, Rabbit, Thunderbird, Firebird, Ram. The name Hawk, then, has certain connotations that might be helpful in marketing the car.

What are the connotations of the name Giraffe? Most of us would probably think of tremendous—even absurd—size, and of something that basically looks funny, although giraffes are actually capable of running extremely fast. What about Porcupine? When the average person bothers to think about porcupines at all, the connotations are likely to be of pesky creatures that sensible folks try to stay away from. People respond to the connotations of words, and it is hard to conceive of finding many car buyers for the Giraffe or the Porcupine.

Word Sensitivity

Developing a sensitivity to the connotations of words, then, is an invaluable asset for all writers. The right word will be the one with the right connotations—the connotations that most precisely reflect the writer's intended meaning and produce the desired reaction from the writer's audience. Was the person who had too much to drink *inebriated, intoxicated, drunk, looped, smashed, tipsy, high, crocked, pickled, loaded*, or *blotto*? Was the overweight person *plump, fat, pudgy, obese, chubby, portly, chunky, corpulent, stout*, or *stocky*? Few greater compliments can be paid to writers than to say that they have a knack for choosing the right words. That knack does not come simply from having a large vocabulary. Rather, it comes mainly from thinking about the fine distinctions in connotation that separate words with similar denotation. It comes from never automatically assuming that the first word that springs to mind is the right one. And it comes from careful revision and never being too happy with one's choice of words too soon.

EXERCISE   Rearrange each group of words by connotation, from the least favorable term to the most favorable. In many cases, opinions will differ; there are few purely right and purely wrong answers.

1. unromantic, realistic, pragmatic, hardheaded
2. thin, skinny, slender, bony, emaciated
3. weep, cry, blubber, bawl
4. squabble, disagreement, quarrel, brawl
5. knowledgeable, bright, shrewd, smart, brainy

6. pretty, gorgeous, lovely, stunning, beautiful
7. miserable, blue, depressed, sad, unhappy
8. look, ogle, stare, glower, gaze
9. strut, swagger, stride, pace
10. gripe, complain, squawk, bellyache

EXERCISE All the words in parentheses make sense in the sentences that follow. How does the meaning of the sentence change, depending on which word you use?

1. The minister strikes me as (an idealist, a dreamer).
2. The criticisms of the new health care proposal are mostly (uninformed, foolish, idiotic).
3. We have (loud, raucous, noisy) neighbors.
4. The salesperson at the bookstore seemed (reserved, aloof).
5. The astronauts' mission was (challenging, laborious).
6. I was (apprehensive, terrified) about beginning a new career.
7. My grandfather says that as a young man he (loved, adored) Marilyn Monroe.
8. He was as smart as (a fox, a trained dog in a circus, Albert Einstein).
9. Congresswoman Saunders is a gifted (speaker, talker, orator).
10. Sometimes (solitude, loneliness, isolation) can be good for the soul.
11. The football team was (beaten badly, humiliated).
12. Meeting people from other countries can be (broadening, educational).
13. Dinner had been delayed, and I felt truly (famished, hungry, ravenous).
14. Next to the little boy, the Great Dane looked (huge, immense).
15. The brush fires (damaged, devastated) much of the landscape.

Abstract Writing and Concrete Writing

Although the distinction between denotation and connotation is valuable to writers, it is sometimes easier to see the immediate, practical consequences to a writer's quest for the right word in the distinction between abstract writing and concrete writing:

- **Abstract writing** is writing that lacks specific details and is filled with vague, indefinite words and broad, general statements.
- **Concrete writing** is characterized by specific details and specific language.

Every piece of writing needs generalizations, of course, and vague words such as *nice* and *interesting* can be useful. But writing that is dominated by such words is abstract writing, and abstract writing is the main cause of bored readers. It is often a reflection of lazy or careless thinking. It can interfere with full communication of meaning. It prevents many students from developing their writing adequately ("I've already said all I have to say. How am I supposed to get 300 more words on this subject?").

Consider the following examples of abstract and concrete writing.

Abstract $\longrightarrow$	Concrete
Too much poverty exists in this country.	I see one-third of a nation ill-housed, ill-clad, ill-nourished.
Mr. Jones is a tough grader.	Mr. Jones flunked 75 percent of his class and gave no higher than a C to the students who passed.
Computers now execute many of the tasks that only humans could do many years ago.	Today's technology allows computers to perform tasks like processing banking transactions, obtaining research from thousands of sources, and sending information overseas.
The story is quite amusing in places, but basically is very serious.	Underneath the slapstick humor, the story presents a bitter attack on materialism and snobbishness.
Religious faith is important, but practical considerations are also important.	Trust in God, and keep your powder dry.

Nothing is technically wrong with all these examples of abstract writing, but we need only compare them to the rewritten concrete versions to see their basic inadequacy. They convey less information. They are less interesting. They have less impact. There is nothing wrong with them except that they could be much better.

Using Specific Details

The use of specific details is the most direct way to avoid abstract writing. Unfortunately, much of the material we read every day is abstract: flabby, dull, vague, and essentially meaningless. Like hot air, it lacks real body, real substance. The sports columnist writes, "The team should do better this year," and leaves it at that, instead of adding, "It should finish in third or fourth place and even has a fighting chance for the pennant." The teacher writes an angry letter saying, "This school ignores all vital needs of the faculty," and sounds like just another crank unless the letter goes on and points to *specific* needs that have in fact been ignored.

Student writing—from essay exams to themes in composition courses— would improve considerably if students paid more attention to eliminating excessive abstractions and adding specific details. Our use of language, not to mention our level of thought, would probably improve a hundredfold if we established an informal rule:

> *Never* make an unsupported general statement, a general statement not backed up by specific details.

This rule sounds easy enough, but it means what it says. It means a writer should never try to get by with sentences such as, "The day was too hot"; "The hero of the story was very ambitious"; "The administration is corrupt"; "The Industrial Revolution brought about many changes." These sentences are neither ungrammatical nor necessarily incorrect in what they say, but without specific details they are worthless. "The day was too hot" is uninteresting and unpersuasive. *Back it up.* The reader should know that the temperature was 93 degrees, that Bill's sweaty glasses kept slipping off his nose, that a cocker spaniel who had managed to find a spot of shade was too exhausted and miserable to bother brushing away the flies. Whatever the piece of writing—a letter of application for a job, an analysis of a short story, a final exam in history— specific details give the writing life and conviction that abstractions alone can never achieve.

One more point about specific details: Within reason, *the more specific the better*. As long as the detail is relevant—as long, that is, as it supports the generalization and is not instantly obvious as too trivial for consideration—the writer is unlikely to go wrong by being too specific. On a history exam, a student may generalize, "In the Revolutionary War, the Americans had many difficulties." As specific support for that statement, the student may go on to write, "The number of Tories was quite large." But better in all respects would be, "Tories numbered as much as 30 percent of the population." Eventually, it is true, one can defeat one's purpose; it would be a mistake to give the reader the names and addresses of all the Tories during the Revolutionary War. The writing would then become so overwhelmed by specifics that the major point would be lost. Elementary common sense is usually the best guide in preventing that kind of mistake, and in actual practice few student writers run up against the problem of being too specific.

To summarize: Support all your generalizations with relevant, specific details. Remember that, within reason, the more specific the details, the better the writing.

Abstract (weak)

The telephone is a great scientific achievement, but it can also be a great inconvenience. Who could begin to count the number of times that phone calls have come from unwelcome people or on unwelcome occasions? Telephones make me nervous.

More specific (better)

The telephone is a great scientific achievement, but it can also be a great pain. I get calls from bill collectors, hurt relatives, salespeople, charities, and angry neighbors.

The calls always seem to come at the worst times, too. They've interrupted my meals, my baths, my parties, my sleep. I couldn't get along without telephones, but sometimes they make me a nervous wreck.

Still more specific (much better)

The telephone is a great scientific achievement, but it can also be a great big headache. More often than not, that cheery ringing in my ears brings messages from the Ace Bill Collecting Agency, my mother (who is feeling snubbed for the fourth time that week), salespersons of encyclopedias and magazines, solicitors for the Police Officers' Ball and Disease of the Month Foundation, and neighbors complaining about my dog. That's not to mention frequent wrong numbers—usually for someone named "Arnie." The calls always seem to come at the worst times, too. They've interrupted steak dinners, hot tubs, Friday night parties, and Saturday morning sleep-ins. There's no escape. Sometimes I wonder if there are any telephones in padded cells.

EXERCISE Invent two or three specific details to back up each of the following generalizations. Use your imagination. Remember, the more specific the better. Don't settle for a detail like "He reads many books" to support the statement "My teacher is very intellectual."

1. Some television commercials are extremely entertaining.
2. Some television commercials are extremely irritating.
3. Most people are foolish about their own health.
4. After enough time goes by, anything can become a bore.
5. Thunder showers are dangerous.
6. It's hard to keep up with Gretchen.
7. When it comes to driving, slowpokes are as bad as speed demons.
8. Iraqis are trying to build a democracy in their country.
9. A photograph can capture the emotions of a moment.
10. Going on a picnic is asking for trouble.

Using Specific Words and Phrases

Writers who apply seriously our "the more specific the better" rule will find not only that their writing has more impact and meaning but also that their style as a whole—their use of language—has started to change significantly. Specific details in themselves are not a guarantee of good writing. Something has to happen to the language, too. The words with which a writer presents specific detail must *themselves* be specific. In fact, through using **specific words**, a good writer can make even the most tiresomely familiar abstractions take on new life.

For most writers, the biggest challenge is learning to recognize when a particular word or phrase is not specific enough, and why. Often the first word that pops into our heads doesn't really work as effectively as it should. "He smiled," for example, may seem the natural way to describe a common facial expression. But have we truly conveyed the exact expression we are trying to write about? Wouldn't our readers get a clearer picture of the face we have in mind if we tried to pin down the word that best describes *this* smile: He grinned? smirked? sneered? leered? simpered? turned up the corners of his mouth? smiled half-heartedly? smiled broadly? Once we develop the habit of checking our original word choices carefully, making sure we've come as close to our precise meaning as possible, our style will become at once more specific and more colorful. Revision, as you have seen throughout this book, then, is not an inconvenience; it's an essential tool of the trade.

Nobody, it is true, will ever be ridiculed or exposed to public disgrace for writing, "She went to the door." But surely our readers deserve to be told, and surely we should want them to know, if she ran or walked or strolled or strutted or shuffled or limped or stumbled or sauntered or trotted or tiptoed to that door. Only one abstract word needs to be changed here, but the person who habitually recognizes that abstract word, refuses to let it pass, and selects a specific word to replace it is no longer just someone who writes, but a *writer*.

Using specific words is a different matter from supporting generalizations with details, though specific words may sometimes help give us a more detailed picture. Selecting specific words is primarily a means of expression, a way of putting things, a style. "He wore a hat" becomes, "His top hat tilted jauntily over one eyebrow." We are not backing up a previous statement about someone's clothing preferences here—we are making a statement that has a specific meaning in and of itself. Together, specific details and specific words are the primary means of eliminating boring and dreary abstractions from our writing.

EXERCISE

In the sentences that follow, the italicized words or phrases are abstract and dull. Find a specific word or short phrase that can substitute for the abstract one without changing the meaning of the sentence.

1. The *car moved slowly* down the road.
2. The *pet* was *poorly trained*.
3. My aunt *made a nice profit* on *that investment*.
4. The guest brought a *small gift* for the party's *host*.
5. My parents gave me a *nice watch* for the *great event*.
6. The articles in that *publication* discussed very *timely issues*.
7. Unless you make *payment promptly*, we will take *legal action*.
8. The *school official* commented that *technology* is a valuable tool in education.
9. *Traveling by air* makes me *slightly uncomfortable*.
10. I planted some *beautiful flowers outside*.

Using Comparisons

Another way of avoiding abstract writing and increasing the liveliness of concrete writing is to use effective figures of speech, particularly **comparisons** (see pages 418–419 for a discussion of metaphors and similes). Sometimes a writer may have a hard time coming up with a forceful substitute for a humdrum expression like "it was very easy." There are plenty of synonyms for "very easy," of course, but the writer's best bet might be a comparison: "It was as easy as (*or* It was so easy it was like) drinking a second glass of beer," or like "splattering toothpaste on the bathroom mirror," or like "forgetting the car keys." Good comparisons are attention-getters. They can add a helpful spark to otherwise pedestrian writing.

Two cautions are in order. First, use comparisons in moderation. The more comparisons a piece of writing contains, the less impact each one is likely to have. Second, and more important, avoid the routine, trite comparisons that fill our language. Don't write "it was as easy as pie" or "It was as easy as taking candy from a baby." Try to be fresh and different. Rather than be trite, avoid comparisons altogether.

Make sure, too, that you phrase your comparisons correctly, whether you are using them for lively specific detail or as a simple means of making a point—"Alice is smarter than Sally," for example. But beware of illogical sentences like those that follow.

Incorrect ——————▶	**Improved**
Some of these horror stories are very similar to Edgar Allan Poe. [Intending to compare the horror stories of one author to the horror stories of another author, the writer instead compares the horror stories of one author to another author.]	Some of these horror stories are very similar to Edgar Allan Poe's. *or* Some of these horror stories are very similar to those of Edgar Allan Poe.
His appetite was as huge as a pig.	His appetite was a huge as a pig's. *or* His appetite was as huge as that of a pig. *or* His appetite was as huge as a pig's appetite.
The new supermarket's prices are higher than the competition.	The new supermarket's prices are higher than the competition's. *or* The new supermarket's prices are higher than those of the competition.

Another kind of illogical comparison unintentionally excludes an item of comparison from the group that it belongs to through the omission of the word *other*.

Incorrect ⟶	Improved
Lincoln had more detailed knowledge of the Bible than any American president.	Lincoln had more detailed knowledge of the Bible than any other American president.
My high school paid less attention to sports than any school in the city.	My high school paid less attention to sports than any other school in the city.

Sometimes, too, improper phrasing can result in confusion. What did the writers of these sentences want to say?

I like him more than you.	Did the writer mean "I like him more than you like him" or "I like him more than I like you"?
Hemingway is more indebted to Mark Twain than anyone else.	Did the writer mean "Hemingway is more indebted to Mark Twain than to anyone else" or "Hemingway is more indebted to Mark Twain than anyone else is"?

EXERCISE Make up *two* logical phrases to complete each of the following comparisons. Be prepared to tell which of your phrases is better and why.

1. I have no more chance of passing this course than . . .
2. My brother is more dependable than . . .
3. The congressman's explanation was as plausible as . . .
4. If you'd buy an insurance policy from him, you're the kind of person who . . .
5. I haven't had a more hectic day since . . .
6. The National Parks are as majestic as . . .
7. The police officers chased the speeding car like . . .
8. The burning sun made my skin feel like . . .
9. Waiting in line is more boring than . . .
10. I trust her so much that I would . . .

EXERCISE Rephrase the following sentences where necessary.

1. The judge was less harsh on me than my friend.
2. Eminem's music was more relevant to our lives than Elvis Presley.

3. Legalized abortions arouse stronger emotions than any controversial issue.
4. The way he talks is like my teacher.
5. I prefer 7-Up commercials to Coke.
6. Our gross national product is substantially larger than Germany.
7. *South Pacific* has a better score than any Broadway musical.
8. The incumbent's campaign is more radical than her opponent.
9. This soap opera has more agony per character than any show on television.
10. The fans swarmed around the rock star like bees to honey.
11. The administration's proposal for reducing the deficit is less drastic than the opposition.
12. Andrew, I love you more than any man.
13. Ricardo liked the *paella* more than his brother.
14. The leopard is more beautiful and more powerful than any animal.
15. My medical plan is better than my sister's.

For additional writing, reading, and research resources, go to **www. mycomplab. com** <http://www.mycomplab.com/> and choose Skwire/Wiener's *Student's Book of College English*, Twelfth Edition.

CHAPTER 23

Effective Sentences

- Wordiness and Economy
- Passive and Active Verbs
- Faulty Parallelism
- Faulty Subordination and Sentence Combining
- Sentence Monotory and Variety

The stylistic considerations we have discussed so far—denotation and connotation, specific details, specific language—require decisions about individual words. In this chapter we consider elements of style more closely related to entire sentences and groups of sentences than to single words.

Wordiness and Economy

Many human individuals use more words in their sentences than are absolutely necessary and essential to express the thoughts and ideas that they (the human individuals) are attempting to communicate. They repeat the same thing constantly and say the same thing over and over again. Sometimes instead of actually repeating themselves they merely substitute various and sundry long phrases for a simple word due to the fact that it is their opinion that readers will be impressed by this writing method of procedure. But in the modern contemporary world of today, good writing should never be wordy. It should be economical—that is, it should say what it has to say, and then stop, cease, and desist.

In case you haven't noticed, the sentences you just read violate all of their own good advice. They contain numerous examples of wordiness: "human individuals" instead of "people," "thoughts and ideas" instead of "thoughts" *or* "ideas," "due to the fact that" instead of "because," "it is their opinion" instead of "they think." We could cut these sentences to half their length without losing anything but a mass of nonfunctioning words:

Many people use more words than are necessary to express their thoughts. They repeat the same things constantly or substitute long phrases for a simple word because they want to impress their readers. But good writing should never be wordy: It should say what it has to say, and then stop.

Wordiness is a major writing problem. It is hard to avoid because it can turn up for any number of reasons, and writers usually don't realize that they are being wordy. Nobody wants to be a windbag, yet unneeded words sneak into nearly everyone's writing.

Before discussing the different kinds of wordiness, we should clear up one point: Wordiness results from using words that don't do anything—it has no direct connection to the number of words. A poor writer can produce a wordy paragraph on the meaning of freedom; a good writer can produce a whole book on the same subject that is not wordy. If the words contribute to the effect the writer wants, if eliminating any of them would sacrifice something valuable, then the writer is *not* being wordy. Only when words can be eliminated without any harm being done do we find real wordiness.

There are four major sources of wordiness: deadwood, pointless repetition of meaning, inadequate clause cutting, and delay of subject.

Cutting Deadwood

Some words are like dead wood on a tree or bush—unless you remove them, they sap the strength of the healthy words around them. Moreover, an attentive writer can remove **deadwood** with little or no tampering with the rest of the sentence, as in the examples that follow.

Deadwood ⟶	Improved
His hair was red in color.	His hair was red.
Pollution conditions that exist in our cities is disgraceful.	Pollution in our cities is disgraceful.
The building has a height of 934 feet.	The building rises 934 feet.
She was in a depressed state of mind.	She was depressed.
Disneyland struck us as a fascinating kind of place.	Disneyland struck us as fascinating.
In this day and age we live in, people seem totally apathetic about everything.	People today seem totally apathetic.
The hero of the story was an individual in the high-income bracket.	The hero of the story was wealthy.
The validity of such statements should not be adhered to.	Such statements are invalid.
He spoke to her in a harsh manner.	He spoke to her harshly.
I am going to major in the field of sociology.	I plan to major in sociology.

The character had a hard type of decision to make.	The character had a hard decision to make.
Because of the fact that my teacher disliked me, he gave me a bad grade.	Because my teacher disliked me, he gave me a bad grade.
Sometimes the moral of a story is a very important factor.	Sometimes the moral of a story is very important.
The story "Silent Snow, Secret Snow," written by the author Conrad Aiken, is a story with an unhappy ending.	"Silent Snow, Secret Snow" by Conrad Aiken is a story with an unhappy ending.

Deadwood infiltrates nearly everyone's first draft, but there is no room for these tiresome words-without-purpose in a finished composition. As a general rule, it is safe to assume that if words can be removed without harming anything—as in the preceding examples—they should be removed.

Avoiding Pointless Repetition of Meaning

Pointless repetition of meaning is a special kind of deadwood. Aside from adding useless words, such repetition reflects writers' lack of confidence in themselves—their fear that their point will not be clear unless they make it twice. Unfortunately, this overemphasis usually suggests sloppy thinking to the reader, rather than a desire for accuracy.

Pointless repetition ⟶	Improved
The film was very interesting and fascinating.	The film was fascinating.
Our streams are filthy and dirty.	Our streams are filthy.
This approach could end in a catastrophic conclusion.	This approach could end catastrophically.
The author gives examples of different and varied criticisms of the novel.	The author gives examples of different criticisms of the novel.
To begin with, in the first place, the story has terrific suspense.	In the first place, the story has terrific suspense.
Some early critics of Jonathan Swift called him an insane madman suffering from the symptoms of mental disease.	Some early critics of Jonathan Swift called him insane.
There is no question about the worth and value of an education.	There is no question about the value of an education.
He has no emotional feelings.	He has no feelings.

Each and every person ought to read a newspaper.	Everyone ought to read a newspaper.
The new administration will make the exact same mistake as the old one.	The new administration will make the same mistake as the old one.

EXERCISE Point out any instances of deadwood and pointless repetition in the following sentences.

1. At this point in time, we have no travel plans.
2. In my opinion, I think depression is a terrible kind of illness.
3. We have ignored and neglected the basic fundamental essentials for too long a period of time.
4. Men and women of both sexes must join the combat to fight for a better world.
5. Rebecca Lobo is an individual who excels in the area of basketball.
6. Sleepy and tired, he looked drained and exhausted.
7. A healthful lifestyle can help prevent many different kinds of diseases and illnesses.
8. As far as jewelry is concerned, my favorite jewelry is a simple string of pearls.
9. With bright, vivid colors and hues, Georgia O'Keefe made American modern painting a beautiful kind of art.
10. I pledge to oppose the forces of godless atheism and disloyal treason.

Cutting Wordy Clauses

One of the most effective ways of reducing wordiness is to cut a cumbersome clause into a shorter phrase or, if possible, a single word. This **clause cutting** can result in a tighter, more economical structure, with the phrase or word more firmly incorporated into the sentence than the original clause ever was.

Wordy clause $\longrightarrow$	Improved
The woman who had red hair was afraid.	The red-haired woman was afraid.
Some of the students who were more enthusiastic wrote an extra paper.	Some of the more enthusiastic students wrote an extra paper.
The story was very exciting. It was all about ghosts.	The ghost story was very exciting.
Alexander the Great was a man who tried to conquer the world.	Alexander the Great tried to conquer the world.
The applause, which sounded like a thunderclap, shook the auditorium.	The applause shook the auditorium like a thunderclap.

No one who has a child of his or her own can fail to appreciate the charm of this poem.	No parent can fail to appreciate the charm of this poem.
Passionate love is a feeling that has inspired many great writers and artists.	Passionate love has inspired many great writers and artists.

Avoiding Delay of Subject

The phrases *there is, there has, it is,* and *it has*—in all tenses—are frequent causes of wordiness. Nothing is wrong with these phrases in themselves; they are necessary parts of the language, and some thoughts might be inexpressible without them. Too often, however, they are used carelessly and delay a sentence or clause from getting down to business. In the following examples, the original sentences begin with words that have no more purpose than the throat-clearing noises made by a speaker before a talk. The revised sentences begin with important words, words that communicate the central concern of each sentence.

Wordy delay ⟶	Improved
There are too many people who care only for themselves.	Too many people care only for themselves.
It has often been commented on by great philosophers that philosophy solves nothing.	Great philosophers have often commented that philosophy solves nothing.
There have been a number of conflicting studies made of urban problems.	A number of conflicting studies have been made of urban problems.
It was on December 7, 1941, that the Japanese attacked the U.S. fleet at Pearl Harbor.	On December 7, 1941, the Japanese attacked the U.S. fleet at Pearl Harbor.
It is a fact that there has been a great increase in sensationalism in the theater.	Sensationalism in the theater has greatly increased.

EXERCISE   Rewrite these sentences to make them more economical, cutting clauses and eliminating wordy delay of subject wherever possible.

1. The man who lives next door to me walks his two poodles every morning that it is cool and sunny.
2. There have been many complicated plans that have been proposed to reduce the number of nuclear weapons that are stationed in Europe.
3. Many people who frequently travel by plane may experience some delays, which are caused by new airport security measures recently put in place.

4. The idea of a guaranteed annual wage is a notion that conflicts with many traditional middle-class values.

5. Another time, when he was shown the list of the names of the officers who had been appointed to serve under him at the Battle of Waterloo, the Duke commented, "I don't know if they will frighten the French, but, by Gad, they terrify me!"

6. People who do not know any better unthinkingly use chemicals that can be harmful to health on their backyard flowers and vegetables.

7. There has been much disagreement among people who produce television programs about giving shows ratings to tell audiences which are programs that contain violence and explicit subject matter.

8. People who play practical jokes are people who are basically insecure.

9. Cars that are made in Germany do not have the reputation for good workmanship that they used to have.

10. It was an agonizingly difficult decision to make.

Passive and Active Verbs

In most English sentences, the subject performs an action.

> John likes this poem.
> The critic saw the movie.
> The senator is going to vote for the bill.

The verb in such sentences is said to be in the **active voice**. The active voice is direct, clear, and concise; in most sentences, it is what we expect.

Too often, however, instead of using the active voice, writers substitute the more stilted **passive voice**. A verb in the passive voice combines a form of *to be* with the past participle of the verb: *is given, has been delivered, was mailed*. Thus, instead of *acting*, the subject of the sentence is *acted upon*.

> This poem is liked by John.
> The movie was seen by the critic.
> The bill is going to be voted for by the senator.

Compared to the active voice, the passive is generally awkward, exceedingly formal, and wordy. It is better to write "This paper will analyze the story" than "The story will be analyzed in this paper." It is better to write "My sociology teacher offered some challenging insights into contemporary problems" than "Some challenging insights into contemporary problems were offered by my sociology teacher."

On occasion, the passive voice doesn't sound bad, of course. Such occasions may arise when the actor is unknown, insignificant, or nonexistent, or when a deliberately impersonal tone is required. Don't be afraid of the passive when it seems normal and unforced—as in the last part of the preceding sentence—but always be alert to its dangers. When you use the passive voice, you should always have a reason for choosing it over the active voice.

Here are a few examples of perfectly acceptable passives:

The game was delayed because of rain.
The eighteenth century has been called the Age of Enlightenment.
Your prompt attention to this request for payment will be appreciated.

EXERCISE Change the passive voice to the active voice wherever appropriate in the following sentences.

1. Fewer novels are being read by teenagers these days.
2. At the corner restaurant, all of the tacos are freshly made each day.
3. The director was convicted of embezzling funds and using the money for herself.
4. The doctor was advised to get malpractice insurance.
5. The doctor was advised to get malpractice insurance by his lawyer.
6. Don't believe everything that you are told.
7. The victim was pronounced dead on arrival by the coroner.
8. The causes of greenhouse emissions are being studied by researchers at major universities.
9. Your child should be hugged and kissed by you frequently.
10. Rare old maps were stolen from a Connecticut library.
11. Legislation to raise taxes is being considered in a joint meeting of the House and Senate.
12. Two suspects were interrogated by Officer Chan.
13. The ball was hit into the bleachers, where it conked an unsuspecting hot dog vendor on the head and he was rushed to the hospital.
14. The course syllabus was handed out by Professor Sharp and was read by all of the students.
15. Omar's punishment is being discussed by his parents.

Faulty Parallelism

What Is Parallelism?

Essentially, **parallelism** means expressing ideas and facts of equal (or coordinate or "parallel") importance in the same grammatical form. We do it all the time, almost unconsciously.

The store was filled with *chairs, tables, sofas,* and *lamps.*	(a group of four nouns)
He *came home, ate dinner,* and *went to bed.*	(three verb phrases)
You can get there by *car, bus,* or *plane.*	(three nouns)
I thought the climactic episode in the story was *shocking, offbeat,* and *amusing.*	(three adjectives)

Parallel grammatical structure reinforces a writer's thoughts by stressing the parallel importance of the various sentence elements, and so makes life easier for the reader. Many of the most famous phrases in our language draw strength in part from effective use of parallelism:

. . . *life, liberty,* and the *pursuit* of happiness.	(group of three nouns)
. . . *of the people, by the people,* and *for the people.*	(three prepositional phrases)
Love me or *leave me.*	(two imperatives)
Early *to bed* and early *to rise* / Makes a man *healthy,* and *wealthy,* and *wise.*	(two infinitives/three adjectives)
I come *to bury Caesar,* not *to praise him.*	(two infinitives with objects)
I came, I saw, I conquered.	(three independent clauses)
Better be *safe* than *sorry.*	(two adjectives)

Avoiding Faulty Parallelism

Now notice how faulty parallelism or lack of parallelism can sabotage a sentence.

Incorrect ⟶	Correct
You can get there by *car, bus,* or *fly.* (noun, noun, verb)	You can get there by *car, bus,* or *plane.* (noun, noun, noun)
I thought the climactic episode in the story was *shocking, offbeat,* and *I found it very amusing.* (adjective, adjective, independent clause)	I thought the climactic episode in the story was *shocking, offbeat,* and very *amusing.* (adjective, adjective, adjective)
She *liked* people and *was liked* by people. (active voice, passive voice)	She *liked* people and people *liked* her. (active voice, active voice)
The teacher told us *to work* fast and *that we should write* on only one side of the paper. (infinitive, clause)	The teacher told us *to work* fast and *to write* on only one side of the paper. (infinitive, infinitive)

Descriptive words added to some of the parallel elements do not break the basic parallelism and can be valuable in avoiding monotony.

Judith had *brains, talent*, and an extremely charming *personality*.	(still parallel: a group of three nouns, even though one is modified by an adjective, and the adjective is modified by an adverb)
The man owned a *mansion* and a fine *collection* of modern etchings.	(still parallel: two nouns, even though one of them is modified by an adjective and followed by a prepositional phrase)
The baby has now learned how to *whimper, shriek, yell* loudly, and *cry* its head off.	(still parallel: four infinitives, even though one is modified by an adverb and one is followed by an object)

Parallelism, then, is an indispensable aid to style and meaning, but keep in mind that its value is limited to cases in which the various elements are of equal importance. If we try to parallel unequal elements, we can wind up with startling calamities, unless we are being intentionally humorous:

She had wealth, vitality, sophistication, and a short nose.
My friend John is a revolutionary activist and a former Cub Scout.
We must all work together to eliminate war, disease, hunger, and dirty movies.

EXERCISE Which of the following sentences use faulty parallelism? Which use parallelism correctly? Which use inappropriate parallelism? Make corrections in the sentences that need them.

1. She enjoys running, mountain climbing, and the movies.
2. Some day I will go bungee jumping, parasailing, and buy a boat.
3. The principal said the main issues were discipline, academic achievement, and good attendance at the pep rally.
4. Percy Bysshe Shelley wrote some of the greatest poems in the English language, lived a spectacularly scandalous private life, and had a weird middle name.
5. Steven Yip's résumé shows that he is hardworking, responsible, and an experienced manager.
6. Alfred Hitchcock had a nearly unbroken record of directing films that were suspenseful, original, and great successes.
7. Magazines, newspapers, and reading books are some possible pastimes when you have to wait to see the doctor.
8. Portuguese *Fado* music touches the heart, stirs the mind, and captures the trials of love.

9. My sister's doctor told her to eat a lot of leafy vegetables, fruits, and not to smoke.
10. Faith, hope, and charity are three classic virtues.

Faulty Subordination and Sentence Combining

Which of the following observations on that great new epic movie, *The Return of the Hideous Vampire*, is likely to be most significant?

It was produced by Paramount.
It is one of the best horror movies of the last ten years.
It was filmed in Technicolor.

Which of these facts about Earnest N. Dogood deserves the most emphasis?

He is a Republican.
He has announced his candidacy for president of the United States.
He is a senator.

The answers are obvious; in both cases, the second item is the one you should have chosen. Neither set of statements provides parallel thoughts—because ideas and facts are not all created equal. Treating each set of items as parallel in a sentence, giving equal weight to each fact, would create a monotonous stream of unfiltered data.

A skillful writer will **subordinate** some of those facts, arranging the sentence or paragraph so that some parts are clearly secondary to others. This process is sometimes called **sentence combining**.

Look again at the beginning of this section on subordination above. We have three pieces of information about a movie. The writer with no sense of subordination merely smacks down each point as it comes to mind, without attempting to differentiate between major and minor items, giving each item a sentence to itself.

The Return of the Hideous Vampire was produced by Paramount. It is one of the best horror movies of the last ten years. It was filmed in Technicolor.

By contrast, with proper subordination the writer collects the three related observations, reserves the independent clause for the most important one, and tucks away the rest in a less conspicuous place.

The Return of the Hideous Vampire, a Technicolor film produced by Paramount, is one of the best horror movies of the last ten years.

We can see the same principle at work with the sentences about Earnest N. Dogood that also begin this section.

Unsubordinated ⟶	**Subordinated**
Earnest N. Dogood is a Republican. He has announced his candidacy for president of the United States. He is a senator.	Senator Earnest N. Dogood, a Republican, has announced his candidacy for president of the United States.

Remember that related ideas can often be combined in a way that shows their relations more clearly. Remember, too, that an independent clause, whether it stands alone as a single sentence or is incorporated into a complex sentence, is a loud cry for attention and should generally be saved for matters of importance.

Here are a few examples of how subordination can improve writing:

Unsubordinated ⟶	**Subordinated**
Jane is a wonderful person. She is very shy. She is extremely kind to everybody.	Although very shy, Jane is a wonderful person who is extremely kind to everybody.
	or
	Although she is a wonderful person who is extremely kind to everybody, Jane is very shy.
This play explores the fate of love in a mechanized society. It is highly symbolic, and it has two acts.	This highly symbolic play of two acts explores the fate of love in a mechanized society.
Professor Jones is terribly sarcastic. He is also a tough grader. It is true that he knows his subject. Most students dislike him, however.	Despite Professor Jones's knowledge of his subject, most students dislike him because of his terrible sarcasm and tough grading.

EXERCISE   Rewrite the following sentences, making effective use of subordination.

1. Some scientists are skeptical about life on other planets. Astronomers calculate that there are many Earth-like planets. Some evidence exists that microbes once survived on Mars.
2. He is an ignorant young man. He is boorish. He is ugly. He is cheap. Why did I say "yes" when he asked me to go to the party?
3. Cape Cod is crowded. It's overcommercialized. It's expensive. I love it.
4. The nuclear age is in its seventh decade. We should reevaluate atomic energy. People are very emotional about it.

5. Jill was going up the hill to fetch a pail of water, and Jack was helping her. Then Jack fell down.

6. Bicycle riding is an exhilarating and challenging sport. It is also great exercise. It tones muscles. It builds stamina.

7. It was sad to hear him say such harsh things about poor people. He had once been poor himself.

8. My uncle will never give up his dream of making a killing on the stock market. All his investments have been bad so far, and people laugh at him constantly.

9. Good writing does not happen by accident. Inexperienced writers believe in inspiration. Professionals know that good writing requires hard work.

10. Everything I like to eat is fattening. Everything I like to eat is also unhealthy. I know I should eat more salads and fresh vegetables. I hate them, however. I don't think I will ever be able to change.

11. "Ping-Pong" is a childish name for a real sport. It shows that most Americans look down on it. The grown-up name is "table tennis." It is a sport that is taken seriously almost everywhere else in the world, and it is played with great skill and ferocity.

12. My mother is a bundle of nerves. My mother is afraid of dark rooms. She also fears insects. Some of her other fears are directed toward heights, dogs, door-to-door salespeople, and doctors.

13. Watching golf on television is silly. You can't see anything. The tiny golf balls are invisible as they fly through the air. It's boring, too.

14. Most Texans know what to do in case of a tornado. They have endured more tornadoes in the last forty years than any other state.

15. Sara just got a golden Labrador retriever. He is the color of honey. He is just ten weeks old. He is not yet trained. Sara thinks he knows his name already since he runs to her when she calls, "Tyler!"

Sentence Monotony and Variety

Readers frequently find themselves struggling to concentrate on a string of sentences even though nothing obvious seems to be wrong. Sentence by sentence, in fact, the author may be writing perfectly well. Put the sentences together, though, and monotony sets in. The monotony can usually be attributed either to a series of sentences that are all, or nearly all, of the same *length* or the same *structure*.

Varying Sentence Length

Sentences come short, medium, and long—and the simple principle for effective writing is to try for variety. Don't take this principle more rigidly than it's intended. Don't assume, for instance, that every single short sentence must be followed by a long one, and vice versa. A string of short or long sentences can sometimes be effective, providing that it is eventually followed by a sentence that varies the pattern. Common sense and alertness will tell you when variety is needed. Just remember that too many sentences of the same length bunched together can create a monotonous style and a restless reader.

Monotonous ———————————➤	**Improved**
He told us the car got good mileage. He said the tires were excellent. The engine was supposed to be quiet. The transmission was supposed to be smooth. He stressed that the brake linings still had plenty of wear. Everything he said was a lie.	He told us the car got good mileage and that it had excellent tires, a quiet engine, a smooth transmission, and sound brake linings. In other words, he lied.
I thought the course was going to be easy, but I was wrong, because after a two-week sickness early in the term I could never find the time to catch up with the assignments, and I kept getting poor grades. I wish I had had the foresight to see what was coming and had taken the initiative either to drop the course or to ask the teacher for an incomplete, but pride or vanity kept me plugging away, and nothing did any good.	I thought the course was going to be easy, but I was wrong. After a two-week sickness early in the term, I could never find the time to catch up with the assignments, and I kept getting poor grades. Why didn't I drop? Why didn't I ask for an incomplete? If I'd known for sure what was coming, I probably would have done one or the other. Pride or vanity kept me plugging away, however, and nothing did any good.

Varying Sentence Structure

Regardless of sentence length, a group of sentences can become monotonous if each sentence uses the same basic structure. All the sentences may begin with a present participle (-*ing* endings), for example, or the first word of each sentence may always be the subject of the sentence, or the first word may never be the subject. Perhaps every sentence turns out to be a compound sentence (two or more independent clauses) or a complex sentence (one independent clause and one or more dependent clauses).

Now forget about the grammatical terms. Remember only that there are many different ways of structuring a sentence, and wise writers never limit themselves to one method. Variety is again the key.

Monotonous ———————————➤	**Improved**
Entering the personnel manager's office, Bill wanted to make a good impression. Smiling, he shook hands. Sitting down, he tried not to fidget. Answering the questions politely, he	Entering the personnel manager's office, Bill wanted to make a good impression. He smiled, shook hands, and tried not to fidget when he sat down. He answered questions

kept his voice low and forced himself not to say "uh." Being desperate for a job, he had to be at his best. Wondering if his desperation showed, he decided to risk a little joke.

Red wine goes best with meat, and white wine goes best with fish. Red wine should be served at room temperature, and white wine should be chilled. Red wine should usually be opened about a half hour before serving, and the accumulated gases should be allowed to escape from the bottle. These rules are not meaningless customs, but they are proven by centuries of experience, and they improve the taste of the food as well as the wine.

politely, keeping his voice low and forcing himself not to say "uh." Bill was desperate for a job. He had to be at his best. Wondering if his desperation showed, he decided to risk a little joke.

Red wine goes best with meat, and white wine goes best with fish. Unlike white wine, which should be served chilled, red wine should be served at room temperature. Red wine also benefits from being opened about a half hour before serving to allow the accumulated gases to escape from the bottle. Proven by experience, these rules improve the taste of the food as well as the wine. They are not meaningless customs.

EXERCISE   The following groups of sentences are monotonous. Rewrite them to add greater variety in sentence length and structure.

1. Tired and bored, I gazed vacantly out the window. Energetic and powerful, a robin dug for worms. Cheerful and bright, a cardinal chirped melodiously in a treetop. Ashamed and humbled, I watched their total involvement in life.
2. Certificates of deposit from local banks are insured by a federal agency, so they are extremely safe investments, but your money is tied up in them for long periods of time unless you are willing to accept stiff penalties for early withdrawal, and they also do not always pay particularly high rates of interest. You may find it more beneficial to invest in a conservative mutual fund specializing in government bonds, which will give you great safety, too, but it also offers excellent returns on your money and permits you to withdraw money by check any time you wish.
3. Eager to begin their vacation, the family loaded the minivan. Filled with enthusiasm, they drove for twenty-five minutes. Shocked by the sudden failure of the engine, they pulled the car to the side of Interstate 90. Horrified at their poor planning, they realized they had forgotten to fill the tank with gas.
4. Going shopping with my sister is lots of fun. Walking around the mall, we go into almost every store. Making decisions is easier with her along, too. Keeping each other from buying useless or silly items is part of our game plan.
5. Recycling cans, glass, paper, and plastic is very important for the human race because if we keep making more trash we will run out of places to put it, and then we will suffocate ourselves and our planet under piles of junk. Don't let this happen because it would be a terrible tragedy, and all we have to do to prevent it is remember to recycle.

CHAPTER **24**

Additional Style Problems and Solutions

- Triteness
- Euphemisms
- Repetition, Good and Bad
- Slang
- Fancy Writing
- Sexist Language
- Miscellaneous Do's and Don'ts

We discussed individual word choices in Chapter 22 and effective sentences in Chapter 23. In a sense, style has to be a matter of words and sentences, of course, but some issues are best approached from a wider perspective. Writers who frequently use trite expressions or sexist language, for example, are not merely creating ineffective sentences but are creating an image of themselves in the reader's mind that can have a far more devastating impact than a wordy phrase or an error in parallelism. Writers who overindulge themselves in showing off large vocabularies or familiarity with current slang can antagonize a reader and risk ruining a whole essay. In this chapter, we define and describe these problems and others that are most likely to arise so that you can either avoid them completely or recognize and correct them if they do appear in your writing. We also explain which of these stylistic elements can serve a valid purpose when used consciously and carefully.

Triteness

A **trite expression**, or **cliché**, is a word or phrase that has become worn out through overuse. Many trite expressions may once have been original and even brilliant, but through constant repetition they have lost whatever impact they once had. If a writer uses many trite expressions, a reader may be tempted to assume that the thoughts are as secondhand as the language.

Triteness generally calls attention to itself in some way. Words like *the, a, man, woman, come, go* are not trite even though we tend to use them all the time, because they are simple, direct, and unself-conscious. Trite expressions seem, on the surface, to convey a thought or feeling particularly well, and people who haven't read enough to recognize them sometimes think them clever, or elegant, or lively. Experienced readers, however, interpret them for what they usually are—evidence of a writer's laziness and lack of imagination.

The best way to handle triteness is to eliminate it. Apologetic little quotation marks do not help. If the writer has been trite, quotation marks call even more attention to the fault and let the reader know that the triteness was no accident.

The following list contains a number of trite expressions. Avoid them. Choose ten from the list and try to think of original and effective ways to express the same ideas.

Trite Expressions

more fun than a barrel of monkeys	dumb as an ox
worth its weight in gold	meaningful dialog
over the hill	turned on
stop on a dime	red as a rose
fresh as a daisy	tired but happy
happy as a lark	a good time was had by all
hard as nails	white as snow
have someone in a corner	black as pitch
make a long story short	put it in a nutshell
no use crying over spilled milk	Mother Nature
a penny saved is a penny earned	Father Time
cool as a cucumber	spread like wildfire
pretty as a picture	the crack of dawn
in the pink	spring chicken
hale and hearty	dog-eat-dog
apple-pie order	survival of the fittest
under the weather	every cloud has a silver lining
devil-may-care attitude	sick as a dog
go at it tooth and nail	work like a dog
generation gap	easy as pie
broaden one's horizons	sweet as sugar
peer pressure	quick as a wink
do unto others	quick as a flash
flat as a pancake	greased lightning
tender loving care	a matter of life and death

sly as a fox	male chauvinist pig
stubborn as a mule	a bolt from the blue
rat race	father of his country
Old Glory	signed, sealed, and delivered
trial and error	open-and-shut case
struggle for existence	flash in the pan
the bigger they are, the harder they fall	babe in the woods
sad but true	not a cloud in the sky
south of the border	feathered friends
armed to the teeth	slow as molasses
lean and lanky	do your own thing
flattery will get you nowhere	last but not least

In addition to these phrases, we express some familiar—and important—ideas in the same language so often that the ideas themselves seem trite unless we word them differently. No matter how much we believe in the need for stable human relations, we are not going to get very excited when someone tells us "People must learn to get along with one another." If we are presenting one of these ideas, we must express it in a dramatic, forceful way, or at least show that we do not regard it as a profound new insight. Here is a partial list of such potentially trite ideas:

Trite Ideas

The older generation has made a mess of things.
A good marriage involves more than sex.
Getting to know people of different backgrounds is a good thing.
College is more difficult than high school.
Pollution is a major problem in the United States.
Education is necessary for many jobs.
We live in a technological society.
This problem could have been avoided by better communication.
This problem will be solved by better communication.
We need to think more about people who are less fortunate.
It is possible to have different opinions about a poem.
Nature is beautiful.
Adults have more responsibilities than children.
This issue is very complicated.

Euphemisms

A **euphemism** is a word or phrase used as a polite substitute for a more natural but less refined word or phrase. Euphemisms can be handy to have around, especially in social situations. For example, chances are that the parents of Suzy or Jerry will be more comfortable to hear that their child is "not working up to full capacity" than to be told that their child is "lazy."

As a rule, though, you should avoid euphemisms, especially in your writing. They generally seem pretentious, fussy, and old-fashioned. The natural, honest word is usually the best one, so long as honesty is not confused with exhibitionistic crudeness or vulgarity. In most cases, then, avoid writing both "He passed on to a better world" and "He croaked." Try instead "He died."

Euphemisms ⟶	Direct language
low-income individual	poor person
urban poverty area	slum
sanitation worker	trash collector
custodian *or* superintendent	janitor
mortician *or* funeral director	undertaker
conflict	war
distortion of the facts	lie
casualties	dead and wounded
senior citizen	old person
powder one's nose	go to the bathroom
financially embarrassed	in debt
reconditioned	used
to pass on	to die

EXERCISE Locate the trite expressions and euphemisms in the following sentences and suggest alternatives.

1. He had once established a meaningful relation with a member of the fair sex, but time flies, and she moved on to greener pastures.
2. When the senior citizen stepped into the street and began walking as slow as molasses, I had to stop my car on a dime to avoid an unfortunate incident.
3. Excessive ingestion can significantly increase adipose tissue.
4. The army executed a strategic withdrawal.

5. It made my blood boil to hear that officers of the law were accused of assaulting an unarmed gentleman who was as helpless as a kitten.
6. Mr. Abdul's immediate superior told him that his services would no longer be required.
7. Mrs. Chung's recent generous donations to various philanthropic organizations suggested that she was rolling in dough.
8. The unruly child screamed like a banshee and ran around like a bull in a china shop, his face turning beet red and his hair sticking up in all directions.
9. Gina's hair is jet black, her skin is smooth as silk, and her evening gown fits her like a glove, but she doesn't hold a candle to my betrothed.
10. The firms need some new blood, so they will employ several up-and-coming young lawyers.

Repetition, Good and Bad

Repetition can help or hurt your writing depending on how you use it. When used to add clarity or dramatic impact, repetition is a major stylistic resource. At other times, however, repetition can interfere with good style, and writers need to be aware of its dangers.

Repetition for Clarity

Repetition can help to clarify meaning and get the writer and reader from one sentence or clause to another. One of the simplest and most valuable transitional devices for a writer is the repetition of a key word or phrase, sometimes in slightly altered form, from a preceding sentence or clause:

> Five drug *companies* have been accused of misleading advertising. The first of these *companies* is. . . .

> Critics tend to make too much of a fuss about *symbols*. *Symbols* are not obscure artistic tricks. Our own daily lives are filled with *symbols*.

Repetition for Impact

Repetition can often add effective dramatic impact, as in the following examples.

> We've shrugged at scandals. We've shrugged at violence. We've shrugged at overpopulation and pollution and discrimination. Now it's time to stop shrugging.

> When she lost her husband, she lost her friend, lost her lover, lost her confidant. She lost everything that had given meaning to her life.

> The decision must be made this week—not this year, not this month, not early next week, but this week.

If not handled skillfully and tastefully, repetition for impact can also lead to foolish emotionalism or unnecessary stress on the obvious:

> Must cruel developers have their way forever? What of the flowers? What of the trees? What of the grass? What of the homeless birds and squirrels and bunnies?

> There is too much violence on television. Bang, bang, bang, bang, bang—that's all we ever hear. Bang, bang, bang.

Undesirable Repetition of Meaning

Avoid restating a point that is already sufficiently clear. For example:

> The American flag is red, white, and blue *in color*.

> She was remarkably beautiful. *She was, in fact, quite exceptionally good-looking*.

> The effect *and outcome* of all this was most unfortunate.

> In today's *modern contemporary* world. . . .

(See the discussion of wordiness in Chapter 23, pages 554–556.)

Undesirable Repetition of the Same Word

Although repetition of a word or word form can help to clarify a point or serve as a transitional device, if used too often it can become monotonous and irritating. This is especially true if the word itself is not crucial to the meaning of the passage; words such as *very, really*, and *interesting* are major offenders.

> I am *very* pleased to be here on this *very* distinguished occasion. Your *very* kind remarks and your *very* generous gift have left me *very* much at a loss for words, but *very* deeply appreciative.

> I *really* enjoyed reading this story. It was a *really* exciting story with *real* people in *real* situations. The suspense was *really* terrific.

Beware of using different forms of the same word through carelessness. The result can be an awkward and confusing sentence.

> We had a *wonderful* time seeing the *wonders* of Florida.

> The *beauties* of Shakespeare's sonnets are outstandingly *beautiful*.

> People must be made more *aware* of the need for increased *awareness* of our environment.

Undesirable Repetition of Sounds

Save rhymes for poetry. Avoid horrors like these:

> The condemnation of the administration was brought about by its own lack of ability and student hostility.

> The church is reexamining its position on the condition of the mission.

Go easy on **alliteration**, the repetition of sounds at the beginning of words. Every once in a while, alliteration can be effective, but when a writer is obviously pouring it on, the results are silly at best.

We must toss these sneering, snickering, swindling swine out of office.

The orchestra's bold blowing of the brasses thrilled me to the bottom of my being.

EXERCISE Point out any undesirable repetition in the following sentences and make the necessary corrections.

1. Endless streams of tourists threaten to ruin our state's rivers, brooks, and streams.
2. Let's not bring up that argument anymore. Let's never discuss it again.
3. Despite efforts to forget, I find that the mind will remind us of our errors.
4. I am sure that avarice adds fuel to his already active aspirations for advancement.
5. I asked her to marry me, and she said yes. She said yes!
6. A burglar stole Mrs. Plutocratz's jewelry and mink stole.
7. The carpenter has such energy and drive that it's a pleasure just to watch him drive a nail into a piece of wood.
8. At this point in time I am looking for an assistant.
9. Bill Hawkins was a tragic figure—tragic in school, tragic in business, tragic in marriage, tragic in life.
10. Angela Donaldson's dreadful, disastrous decision still depresses and dismays her devoted fans.
11. The president squandered and foolishly spent the company's money until he had to declare bankruptcy.
12. I love you, my love, with a love that surpasses the love of all the greatest lovers in history.
13. The fantastic fragrance of the field filled with wildflowers made me feel faint.
14. It seems that Professor Reames had great dreams.
15. Miles Davis was a jazz musician with great musical talent.

Slang

A carefully chosen, appropriate **slang** expression can sometimes add interest and liveliness to writing. Slang can help to establish a humorous or casual tone.

More significantly, in a few cases, it can suggest an attitude or a shade of meaning that a more conventional expression could not.

By and large, however, slang is inappropriate for the comparatively formal, analytical writing that college courses most often demand. But when you feel sure that a slang expression can genuinely communicate something you could not otherwise convey as well, don't be afraid to use it. When you do use it, avoid the coy quotation marks that some writers put around slang to show that they are really sophisticated people who could use more formal language if they wanted to. Good slang should seem natural, and if it is natural, it doesn't need quotes.

> Once thought of as the intellectual leader of a generation, Thompson turned out to be just another jerk with the gift of gab.
>
> Billed as a luxury resort, the hotel was a high-priced dump.

Be careful about using slang, however. Don't use it to show how up-to-date you are; slang changes so fast that what seemed current yesterday is often embarrassingly old-fashioned tomorrow. Don't use slang to show your reader what a folksy person you are; that technique almost always fails. Avoid crude sentences like these:

> In *Hamlet*, Hamlet's girlfriend, Ophelia, goes nuts.
>
> This profound political allegory really turned me on.
>
> Albert Einstein was one of the big brains of the twentieth century.

Fancy Writing

For every writer who uses slang to show off, there are probably a dozen who show off by habitually using big or unfamiliar words. A large vocabulary is an asset for any writer, of course, but that fancy word or phrase should be used only when it adds something valuable to tone or meaning that a more familiar word or phrase could not add. If the familiar word will do the job as well, use it; the unfamiliar word will seem stilted and pretentious. (See the discussion of jargon on page 580.)

Fancy ⟶	Improved
Many of our new buildings suffer from inadequate fenestration.	Many of our new buildings have too few windows.
They raised their hands in the time-honored gesture of respect to the emblem of their nation's sovereignty	They saluted their country's flag.
Charles Dickens's novelistic achievements are veritably unrivaled in English letters.	Charles Dickens wrote better novels than any other English writer.

Be particularly careful about mixing slang and fancy writing unless you are deliberately trying for a humorous effect. Tuxedos and sweatshirts are both wearable articles of clothing, but they do not go well together.

Poor mix	⟶	Improved
Also listed as available options on this formidable contender for car-of-the-year honors are cruise control, power sunroof, tape deck, and zillions of other gizmos.		Also listed as available options on this formidable contender for car-of-the-year honors are cruise control, power sunroof, tape deck, and a host of other luxuries.
With its vulgarity masquerading as wit, its tired stereotypes masquerading as characters, and its disjointed episodes masquerading as plot, this new play is totally yucky.		With its vulgarity masquerading as wit, its tired stereotypes masquerading as characters, and its disjointed episodes masquerading as plot, this new play is a dismal failure.

EXERCISE Correct any inappropriate use of slang or fancy writing in the following sentences.

1. The cacophony emanating from the foyer indicated to us an altercation among our offspring.
2. Good writers eschew prolixity.
3. Through all the vicissitudes of life, Benjamin Franklin kept his cool.
4. Little Billy became lachrymose when his mother turned off the boob tube.
5. Many liberal policy makers concur with welfare recipients who express sentiments indicating their desire to obtain employment as long as it isn't flipping burgers at some burger joint.
6. The mobster's hortatory remarks were intended to placate his minions but only exacerbated long-simmering tensions.
7. My previous employer was a birdbrain.
8. My colleague's perpetual obsequiousness makes me want to crack up.
9. The vocalist's melodious utterances lulled me into a slumber.
10. Geometry is difficult, but interesting. Algebra is the pits.

Sexist Language

Sexist language is language that displays prejudice and stereotyped thinking about the roles, character, and worth of both sexes, though women have most frequently been its victims. Avoiding sexist language is a moral issue, of course—the sexist bigot is no more appealing than the racial, religious, or ethnic bigot. It is also a stylistic issue because language reflects social realities, and habits of language may continue long after the social realities have changed. Sexist language is sometimes more the product of habit than of intention.

To prevent or eliminate sexist language, pay particular attention to the following suggestions.

 TIPS for Avoiding Sexist Language

- **Avoid stereotypes in occupations.** The notion of distinctive man's work and woman's work has by and large become outdated.

Sexist language ——————→	Improved
A nuclear physicist needs to take his environmental responsibilities seriously.	Nuclear physicists need to take their environmental responsibilities seriously.
Adele is hoping to become a policeman.	Adele is hoping to become a police officer.
Carla Rodriguez is an outstanding lady doctor.	Carla Rodriguez is an outstanding doctor.
Our file clerk quit yesterday, and we need a new woman for the job.	Our file clerk quit yesterday, and we need to find someone new for the job.

- **Avoid stereotypes in character and social behavior.** Not all women giggle, gossip, and want to have babies any more than all men swear, drink beer, and overdose on football.

Sexist language ——————→	Improved
A good cook always seems to have a secret recipe for her Thanksgiving stuffing.	A good cook always seems to have a secret recipe for Thanksgiving stuffing.
Her woman's heart melted when she saw her new grandson.	Her heart melted when she saw her new grandson.

- **Avoid insulting and condescending language.** Some sexist words are obvious insults and easy enough to recognize: *babes, dames, dolls, broads,* and the like. Other words and phrases masquerade as affectionate tributes or compliments but can, in fact, be extremely patronizing: *the fair sex, the gentle sex, my better half, girl* (when used to describe a grown woman), and so on. Avoid both types.

Sexist language ——————→	Improved
When Jenny left the company, it was hard to find another girl to replace her.	When Jenny left the company, it was hard to find anyone to replace her.
My aunt was thoughtful, helpful, and compassionate—a truly gracious lady.	My aunt was thoughtful, helpful, and compassionate—a truly outstanding person.

■ Avoid using *man*, *men*, and *mankind* as synonyms for *humanity*, *people*, and *the human race.*

Sexist language ⟶	Improved
Man's future is uncertain.	Humanity's future is uncertain.
Men must first learn to love themselves before they can love anyone else.	People must first learn to love themselves before they can love anyone else.
Are you telling me that mankind is on the brink of doom? What else is new?	Are you telling me that the human race is on the brink of doom? What else is new?

■ Avoid using the pronoun *he* when sex is unknown or irrelevant.

Sexist language ⟶	Improved
We need a person who can offer a few hours of his time each week.	We need a person who can offer a few hours of time each week.
A liar needs to make sure that he has a good memory.	Liars need to make sure that they have good memories.

(For a more detailed discussion of nonsexist pronoun use, see page 633 of the Handbook and page 686 of the Glossary.)

EXERCISE Rewrite the following sentences to eliminate sexist language.

1. After moving from her neighborhood of the past twenty-five years, Julie most missed the girls' nights out every Tuesday.
2. Anyone who owns an ATM card, an EZ-pass, or a computer may have his right to privacy violate.
3. A collegiate athlete must be able to manage his time well.
4. Marjorie Small is a fully ordained lady minister.
5. A parent concerned about her child's progress in school should first arrange for a conference with her child's teacher.
6. With both of them working, they thought they were at last in a position to pay for a cleaning lady.
7. Forget about elections and wars. The fate of man is determined more by climate than by anything else.
8. Alan so urgently needs a male authority figure to enforce discipline and teach him right from wrong.
9. She shouldn't let these disappointments bother her pretty little head. All she really needs is a good cry.
10. Schoolwork thrives on parental interest. Make sure to keep in touch with your children's teacher and show her that you care.
11. Every company should have a day for fathers to bring their daughters to work with them.

12. Stand by your man, little lady.
13. Our postal service has become most erratic. I'm not sure that mailmen still take pride in their work.
14. Almost no young clerk at a malfunctioning supermarket cash register nowadays seems capable of figuring out for herself how to make change.
15. Mothers who attend PTA meetings may feel more involved in their children's education.

Miscellaneous Do's and Don'ts

Some special stylistic problems common to classroom writing don't fit conveniently under any of the main labels, so we've included brief comments about them here.

 TIPS for Writing in an Academic Style

- **Don't write a personal letter to your instructor.**

  This assignment at first confused me, but after several cups of coffee, I began to get an idea: I remembered that last week you said something about certain kinds of literature depending on formal patterns, and I think I've come up with an interesting notion about the two stories we just read. See what you think.

If that paragraph were read by anyone other than the teacher or the members of the class that discussed the stories, it would make almost no sense. What difference does it make to a general reader—or teacher—how much coffee the student drank? What assignment does the student refer to? What stories did the class just read?

- **Don't make formal announcements of what you are going to do.**

  In this paper I am going to prove that, far from being ignored, the elderly have received special privileges for decades.

  The thesis that I shall attempt to establish in this paper is that crime rates have gone down because of broad social patterns, not because of better police work.

It's distracting and unnecessary to begin a paper with a trumpet fanfare. Don't tell the reader what you are going to do. Get down to business and do it.

  Far from being ignored, the elderly have received special privileges for decades.

  Crime rates have gone down because of broad social patterns, not because of better police work.

- **Avoid a speechmaking tone.**

  In conclusion, let me simply say that. . . .

  With your permission, I'd like to make a few observations on that point.

Such sentences introduce an irritating artificial quality into written English.

■ **Don't shilly-shally.**

> In my opinion, the Industrial Revolution was a major chapter in the history of civilization.

> I think that Dr. Watson is childishly impressed by Sherlock Holmes.

Go easy on terms such as *in my opinion, I think*, and the like. An apologetic or uncertain tone suggests that you do not have faith in your ideas, and if you do not believe in what you say, your audience probably won't either. Of course, you would not state a personal theory as a universal truth; but don't weaken solid ideas by shilly-shallying, and don't expect an *in my opinion* to make a shaky idea more acceptable.

■ **Don't bluster.**

> Anyone but an idiot can see that Hughes's poem protests the treatment of African Americans.

> Legalized prostitution is opposed mainly by neurotic hypocrites and religious nuts.

Blustering is the opposite of shilly-shallying. Its effect on an intelligent audience is just as negative.

■ **Be careful about using the word *you* as an indefinite pronoun.**

> Even though you are a drug addict, you are not necessarily an evil person.

> Your constant arguments with your parents are part of the process of growing up.

You is the pronoun of direct address. In this book, for example, we, the authors, write to you, the students in a composition course, and thus address you directly. But in writing aimed at a general audience, it is preferable to use the indefinite pronouns *anyone, one, each, either, neither, another, anybody, someone, somebody, everyone, everybody*, and *nobody*. And *you* cannot be substituted for *the speaker, the character, the average citizen, people, the student, the author, the reader*, and so on. Since you cannot be sure of the age, class, sex, or living conditions of your readers, you will not want to chance offending or unintentionally amusing them by attributing to them attitudes, strengths, vices, or talents they may not possess.

> Drug addicts are not necessarily evil.

> Constant arguments with parents are part of the process of growing up.

■ **Define unfamiliar terms.**   This advice is especially important in any paper on technical subjects. An audience of nonspecialists can be expected to have the general knowledge of educated citizens, but nothing more. Avoid **jargon**— the special language of particular professions and activities—whenever you can. When you can't, see to it that your reader understands you. A paper on automobile repairs, for instance, would need to define terms such as *universal joint* and *differential*. A paper on legal problems would need to define *tort* and *writ of mandamus*. A paper on finance would need to define *cash flow* and *price-earnings ratio*.

EXERCISE   Comment on the stylistic problems in each of the following sentences, and rewrite the sentences where necessary.

1. Your ugly buck teeth can now be corrected more quickly and economically than was once the case.
2. This paper will demonstrate that Beyoncé is more than just a pretty face.
3. Cobalt treatment engendered remission.
4. In my opinion, I believe that George W. Bush will go down in history as an extremely controversial president.
5. Writing this comparison–contrast paper involved less drudgery than I first thought it would.
6. Any intelligent person knows that seatbelt laws violate your right to privacy.
7. Recent government funding cuts mean that you may no longer be able to feed your hungry children.
8. Thus the poem clearly shows, in my humble opinion, that Dickinson was a shrewd observer.
9. I feel that it will be many years before experts know exactly how anesthetics operate on the body.
10. It is patently obvious that radicals of any sort are lunatics.
11. The focus of this paper will be the explanation of the pros and cons of nuclear power.
12. The caesura in the fourth stanza of the sestina is effected by the poet's scrupulous diction.
13. Sitting here, crouched before my laptop, I wonder how to begin this essay.
14. A Shakespearean sonnet is, I think, easier to write than a Petrarchan.
15. This novel, in my mind, is a very important work of fiction, and I'm sure you will agree.

For additional writing, reading, and research resources, go to **www. mycomplab. com** <http://www.mycomplab.com/> and choose Skwire/Wiener's *Student's Book of College English*, Twelfth Edition.

PART SIX

Handbook, Glossary, and ESL Pointers

Part Six is a quick guide to basic writing skills. Use it to check on grammatical points, to answer simple questions that may occur to you while writing or revising, to correct any mechanical errors that your instructor finds in your work, and to guide you in appropriate word choice. Most English teachers assume that you have already mastered the basics, and your instructor probably will devote only limited classroom time to mechanics. It is your responsibility to make your papers grammatically correct. This Handbook, the Glossary, and ESL Pointers can help you do that.

Both the Handbook and the Glossary follow an alphabetical arrangement. The Handbook presents the most common areas of trouble: comma splices, fragmentary sentences, and so on. You will find a number of exercises on more difficult points so that you can test your understanding of them. The Glossary of Problem Words explains specific words and phrases that frequently confuse writers. ESL Pointers: Tips for Non-Native Writers addresses major areas of difficulty for English Language Learners writing in English for their courses.

After you complete the exercises, take the Self Tests as they appear throughout Part Six. Check your answers to the Self Tests on pages 715–721.

We have tried to keep our explanations as free as possible of specialized grammatical terminology. When such terminology is necessary, we have strived to make our explanations self-contained. For example, in our treatment of adjective–adverb confusion, we work definitions of adjectives and adverbs into the discussion. Some separate definitions have proven essential, however, and it's wasteful to define overwhelmingly common terms such as *subject, noun*, and *verb* every time we mention them. Definitions of such common terms appear alphabetically in the Handbook.

Handbook

Abbreviations.   As a rule, avoid abbreviations.

Wrong	**Right**
NYC and other municipalities can cure their financial ills only by aid from the federal gov't.	New York City and other municipalities can cure their financial ills only by aid from the federal government.
Thanksgiving comes on the fourth Thurs. of Nov.	Thanksgiving comes on the fourth Thursday of November.
I had trouble finding the proper st. & had to ask a taxi driver for directions.	I had trouble finding the proper street and had to ask a taxi driver for directions.

Even when abbreviations are permissible, it is nearly always acceptable in standard English to spell a word in its entirety; therefore, when in doubt, spell it out.

However, in cases like the following, abbreviations are required or preferred. In general, the trend in abbreviations is not to use periods after letters or spaces between letters, especially when all letters of an abbreviation are capital letters (FBI, CD-ROM, NY).

- *Standard forms of address.* Before a person's name, it is standard usage to write *Mr., Mrs., Ms., Dr.,* or *St.* (for Saint, not street).
- *Titles.* If both a person's surname (last) and given name (first) or initials are used, then it is acceptable to write *Rev., Hon., Prof., Sen.*

  Rev. John Yip, Prof. A. J. Carr (but not Rev. Yip or Prof. Carr)

- *Degrees.* After a name, abbreviate academic degrees, *Jr.,* and *Sr.* Academic degrees may also be abbreviated when used by themselves.

  Marion Jonas, MD
  He is now studying for a BA after completing his AAS degree.

- *Organizations.* The names of many organizations and some countries are commonly abbreviated, without periods.

NATO   NAACP   OPEC   UN   USA   AFL-CIO   MLA

- *Other*. Traditional footnote references and bibliographical terms (many no longer in common use) are nearly always abbreviated, as are a few familiar words.

etc.	pp. 137–40
ibid.	vol.
et al.	TNT
p. 23	DNA

EXERCISE   Replace unnecessary abbreviations in the following sentences.

1. After the Aug. 2005 hurricane Katrina hit New Orleans, the La. gov't provided $$ and drs.
2. Many U.S. airlines have flights from L.A. to N.Y.
3. Mr. Dowd always complains that there is nothing to watch on t.v. on Tues. nights.

SELF TEST: Abbreviations

Replace unnecessary abbreviations in the following sentences.

1. Dr. Rauch's daughter got her MBA at a university in PA.
2. The firm's offices moved last Dec. from Spring St. to Valley Rd.
3. The FBI raided his co.'s quarters in L.A., Calif.
4. My bro. & sister left town on Thurs.
5. The rev. worked for the NAACP & held a special Xmas service for gov't workers who hold PhD degrees.

Adjective-Adverb Confusion

Adjectives modify nouns.

Getting a diploma takes *hard* work.

The boxer's *left* jab is his *strongest* weapon.

The *better* team won.

The porridge was *hot*.

Adverbs modify verbs, adjectives, or other adverbs.

We walked *carefully*.

ad

Foolishly, we kept arguing until midnight.

The porridge was *very* hot.

The doctor had to cut *quite* deeply.

Form most adverbs by adding *-ly* to adjectives:

Adjective	Adverb
nice	nicely
strong	strongly
poor	poorly

When an adjective already ends in *y* or *ly*, you may have to change the *y* to an *i* before adding the adverbial *-ly* ending. A few of the resulting adverbs may sound so awkward that an adverbial phrase is the preferred form.

Adjective	Adverb
pretty	prettily
messy	messily
nasty	nastily

but

Adjective	Adverbial Phrase
friendly	in a friendly way
lovely	in a lovely way
heavenly	in a heavenly way

A few adjectives and adverbs are identical in form:

Adjective:	He is a *better* person for the experience.
	Fast drivers are dangerous drivers.
Adverb:	He did *better* than I.
	I can type *fast*.

Some words are adverbs in themselves—adverbs to start with—and do not spring from adjectives: *very, quite, rather, somewhat*. Other adverbs are irregular; the adjective *good*, for example, is expressed as an adverb by the word *well*.

Adjective:	He was a *good* worker.
Adverb:	He did the work *well*.

Confusion of adjectives and adverbs is among the most common grammatical errors and is likely to turn up from one of the following causes.

■ *Misuse of an adjective to modify a verb.*

Wrong	Right
I wish she acted *different*.	I wish she acted *differently*.
Bill did *good* on his examination.	Bill did *well* on his examination.
Let's speak *direct* to each other.	Let's speak *directly* to each other.

■ *Misuse of an adjective to modify an adverb or other adjective.*

Wrong	Right
The price was *sure* very expensive.	The price was *surely* very expensive.
The patient is *considerable* worse today.	The patient is *considerably* worse today.
My teacher is *real* strict.	My teacher is *really* strict.

■ *Misuse of an adverb after a linking verb.* The correct modifier after a linking verb is an adjective. The single most common linking verb is *to be (am, is, are, was, were, will be*, and so on). Verbs dealing with the senses—sight, touch, taste, smell, hearing—are often used as linking verbs: *feel, look, sound, taste, appear.* Other verbs frequently serving as linking verbs are *get, seem, remain, become.* (See also *good, well* in the Glossary.)

Wrong	Right
The music sounds *beautifully*.	The music sounds *beautiful*.
The food tastes *badly*.	The food tastes *bad*.

Some verbs, including many of those just listed, may be used as transitive or intransitive verbs, as well as linking verbs. In such cases, note how an adjective or adverb determines meaning.

I smell bad. (I need to buy deodorant.)

I smell badly. (My sinuses are stuffed up.)

He looks evil. (He looks like a wicked person.)

He looks evilly. (His glances are frightening.)

I feel terrible. (I am depressed or in ill health.)

I feel terribly. (My sense of touch has deserted me.)

EXERCISE Choose the correct adjective or adverb in the following sentences.

1. If you act (quick, quickly), you will receive a free bonus gift.
2. Thunder rattled (angry, angrily) in the hills.
3. Some frozen foods are (real, really) tasty.

4. The international news sounds (explosive, explosively).
5. If you speak (hasty, hastily), you may repent (hasty, hastily).
6. Feeling (thirsty, thirstily), he drank (noisy, noisily).
7. Driving too (slow, slowly) can cause as many accidents as driving too (fast, fastly).
8. Writing (concise, concisely) helps to prove a point more (effective, effectively).
9. Though he appeared (calm, calmly) his heart thumped (rapid, rapidly).
10. My sister looks (splendid, splendidly) in her new three-piece suit.

EXERCISE   Find the errors in the following paragraphs.

1. My Florida vacation went terrible! It rained the entire time I was there. I had planned to get a suntan, go snorkeling, and hopefully see some dolphins, but all my plans went sourly. Instead, I wandered unhappy through the hotel hallways, wishing I had stayed at home. The worst part of all was that the sun shone down brilliant as I boarded the plane to go home.

2. You can make linguine with clam sauce much more easy than you might expect. Prepare the linguine as you would normally. Then, fry some onions and garlic in butter. Add the juice from a can of clams and a little parsley and simmer the mixture gentle. Add the clams and, after they have heated, mix the linguine in real good. This dish tastes great with a little Parmesan cheese.

3. A curving path wound through the forest. Carlos and Bryna walked down it slow, admiring the scenery and enjoying the cool shade. They spotted a doe and her fawn hiding among the trees. They moved closer, but the animals ran away too quick to follow.

SELF TEST: Correct Adjectives and Adverbs

Select the correct word from parentheses.

1. Speaking (personal, personally), I think the coach is the only real problem the team has.
2. All our products are (fresh, freshly) baked each day.
3. Juan drove home (quick, quickly) to see if his son was still not feeling (good, well).
4. As (near, nearly) as I can determine, the first job offer seems the best.
5. Far from being a snob, Mario is a (real, really) fine person once you get to know him.
6. The cat scaled the huge oak (real, really) (quick, quickly).
7. Professor Wilson is an excellent teacher and writes (beautiful, beautifully), too.

   8. The twins always looked (similar, similarly) in their matching clothes.

   9. Tara's supervisor felt (bad, badly) about snapping at Tara for no reason.

  10. The fans yelled so (loud, loudly) that the gym echoed.

Adjectives, comparative and superlative forms. See *Comparative and superlative forms.*

Adjectives, coordinate. See *Comma, E.*

Adverbs. See *Adjective–adverb confusion.*

Adverbs, comparative and superlative forms. See *Comparative and superlative forms.*

Agreement. See *Pronoun agreement; Subject–verb agreement.*

Antecedent. The noun or pronoun to which a pronoun refers.

> *Richard Yee* left *his* lunch at home.
> Here, the pronoun *his* refers to its noun antecedent, *Richard Yee.*

Apostrophe. Use the apostrophe to form contractions, plurals, and possessives.

- *Contractions.* In contractions, the apostrophe indicates that a letter or letters have been left out.

   it is = it's   she is = she's   who is = who's   you will = you'll

   let us = let's   you are = you're   do not = don't   she would = she'd

- *Plurals.* Use the *'s* to form the plural of letters: *a*'s, *x*'s, *B*'s, *C*'s. You need only an *s* to form the plurals of abbreviations and numbers.

   the 1930s   the &s (*or* the &'s)   two *c*'s in *occupy*

   DAs   POWs

- *Possessives.* Use an apostrophe to form the possessive of nouns and indefinite pronouns. The first task is to determine whether you need a possessive apostrophe. If you do, the second task is to use it correctly.

    Difficulties for many people begin with the confusion of speaking with writing. In speech, *cats, cat's,* and *cats'* all sound identical. The meanings are all different, however, and in writing, those differences show up immediately. *Cats* is a simple plural—add an *s* to the singular without the use of an apostrophe.

   The cats howled all night.

   Purring is a way cats have of showing affection.

Cat's is a possessive singular, another way of expressing the thought *of the cat.* *Cats'* is a possessive plural, another way of expressing the thought *of the cats.* Note the simplicity of determining whether a word with a possessive apostrophe is singular or plural: Just look at the part of the word *before the apostrophe.*

Singular	**Plural**
cat's claws	cats' claws
machine's speed	machines' speed
Mr. Smith's home	the Smiths' home

Note, too, that in a phrase like *of the cats*, the word *of* takes care of the idea of possession, and no apostrophe is used.

Possessives with *of* **(no apostrophe)**	**Possessives with apostrophes**
The claws of a cat are sharp.	A cat's claws are sharp.
The name of my cat is Tigger.	My cat's name is Tigger.
The hunting abilities of cats are well known.	Cats' hunting abilities are well known.
The mysterious glow in the eyes of cats can be frightening.	The mysterious glow in cats' eyes can be frightening.

One more observation is necessary. Possessive pronouns—*my, mine, our, ours, your, yours, his, her, hers, its, their, theirs*—are already possessive in themselves and *never take apostrophes.*

When a possessive apostrophe is required, the rules are relatively simple.

1. Singular or plural nouns that do not end in *-s* form their possessives by adding *'s.*

Ivan's car	Arlene's book	Women's Liberation
the teacher's notes	New York's mayor	children's games

2. Plural nouns that end in *-s* form their possessives by adding only an apostrophe:

the students' teacher	Californians' freeways
oil companies' profits	the two boys' mother
automobiles' engines	the two teachers' classes

3. Singular nouns that end in *-s* ordinarily form their possessives by adding *'s.* Some writers make exceptions of words that already have so many *s* or *z* sounds in them (for example, *Massachusetts, Jesus*) that pronunciation of a final *'s* could create awkward hissings and buzzings. You can form the possessive of such words by adding only an apostrophe. Both methods

are correct, and writers can use their own judgment as long as they are consistent.

the octopus's tentacles   the press's responsibilities

Dickens's novels   the business's profits

Charles's bowling ball   Jesus's disciples (*or* Jesus' disciples)

Mr. Jones's new roof   Moses's journey (*or* Moses' journey)

4. Indefinite pronouns form their possessives by adding *'s*:

   nobody's fool   someone's knock

   anyone's guess   everybody's business

5. In the case of joint possession—possession by two or more—the possessive is formed by adding an apostrophe or *'s*, as appropriate, to the last noun:

   the girls and boys' school   Jill and Bob's car

   NOTE: To show individual possession, write "Jill's and Bob's cars" and "the girls' and boys' schools." Here Jill has a car and Bob has a car, the girls have a school and the boys have a school.

EXERCISE   Rewrite the following phrases to form possessives, using only an apostrophe (') or an apostrophe plus the letter *s* (*'s*) as appropriate.

   1. The wail of the saxophone
   2. The wail of the saxophones
   3. The president of the country
   4. The presidents of the countries
   5. The checking account of Mr. James
   6. The checking account of the Jameses
   7. The suspense of the story
   8. The suspense of the stories
   9. The leaves of the birch tree
   10. The leaves of the birch trees
   11. The choice of the person
   12. The choice of the people
   13. The mother of Sarah and Jess
   14. The mothers of Sarah and Jess (*two mothers—individual possession*)
   15. The title of the book

EXERCISE   In the following sentences, decide which of the italicized words ending in *-s* are simple plurals or verbs and which are possessives. Then make the necessary corrections and be prepared to explain them.

1. *Managements problems* with the *unions* derive more from *misunderstandings* than from genuine conflicts of interest.
2. The *prison guards* ignored the *inmates complaints* about their *cells* filthy *conditions.*
3. *Joggings* appeal *eludes* me. There must be less boring exercises.
4. That ancient *trees* gnarled *branches* only add to *its* beauty.
5. Your behavior is worse than *theirs; yours* can't be excused by your *fathers* neglect.
6. The *Lees* joined the *Sepulvedas* for dinner at *Psaros* Restaurant.
7. The *actors* constant bickering forced the *shows producers* to choose which one of the *performers* would leave.
8. After *years* of happiness, *Frances* and *Roberts* marriage is on the *rocks.*
9. Many of our *universes* greatest *mysteries,* like the *causes* of aging and the *reasons* we need sleep, have baffled the *worlds scientists* for *centuries.*
10. *Hundreds* of *customers complaints* filled the *companys* mail room.

SELF TEST: Apostrophe Use

Correct any errors.

1. The girls hat's are more colorful than your's.
2. Investors' began to worry that the company's stock price's would fall dramatically and its' profits' disappear.
3. Our neighbors houses are much more modern than our's.
4. Clinical trial's of the pharmaceutical company's new vaccine begin next week.
5. Sheet's and towel's are on sale this week at Ross' Home Furnishing Store.
6. The boy's basketball rolled under their Uncle Manuels' van.
7. Before we move in, we will decide which room will be our's, which will be your's, and which will be Miguel's.
8. My brothers ferocious German shepherd tore a hole with his sharp teeth in the mail carriers' bag.
9. Spiro's sisters wedding is in two weeks, but most of the bridesmaid's dresses' are still not ready.
10. Five of the student's test scores were misplaced, but your's and Giovanni's were not among them.

Appositive.   See *Comma, F.*

Block quotations.   See *Quotation marks.*

Brackets.   Use brackets ([ ]) to enclose comments or added information that you have inserted into a direct quotation. Do not use parentheses instead of brackets

[ ]

because the reader will assume that the inserted material is part of the original quotation.

> "While influenced by moral considerations, Lincoln signed it [the Emancipation Proclamation] primarily to further the war effort."

> "The music column had the altogether intimidating title of *Hemidemisemiquavers* [sixty-fourth notes]."

Capital letters. Use a capital letter for the first word of a sentence or direct quotation, the first word and all important words of titles, the first word and all nouns of a salutation, the first word of a complimentary close, some pronouns, and all proper nouns—the names of particular persons, places, or things.

■ *The first word of a sentence or direct quotation.*

> A popular early television show featured a detective whose most characteristic line was, "We just want the facts, ma'am."

■ *The first and all important words of titles of books, movies, radio and television programs, songs, magazines, plays, short stories, poems, essays, and chapters.* Unimportant words (for example, *a, an, and, the*) and prepositions (e.g., *of, in, to, with, about*) are not capitalized unless they are the first word.

> *A Streetcar Named Desire* [play]   "Ode to a Nightingale" [poem]
>
> *Time* [magazine]   "Gifts" [essay]
>
> *Roget's College Thesaurus* [book]   "Basin Street Blues" [song]

■ *The first word and all nouns of a salutation.*

> Dear Sir: My dear Ms. Hunt: Dear Bill,

■ *The first word of a complimentary close.*

> Sincerely yours,   Yours truly,

■ *Some pronouns.*
  1. First-person singular: *I.*
  2. References to the Judeo-Christian Deity, where necessary to avoid confusion:

> God told Moses that he must carry out His commandments.

■ *Proper nouns.*
  1. Names and titles of persons and groups of persons:
     a. Persons: Martin Luther King Jr., President George W. Bush, Oprah, Hillary Rodham Clinton
     b. Races, nationalities, and religions: Caucasian, Chinese, Catholic (but *black, white*).
     c. Groups, organizations, and departments: League of Women Voters, Ford Motor Company, United States Senate, Department of Agriculture.
     d. Particular deities: God, Allah, Buddha, Zeus.

Cap

2. Names of particular places:
    a. Cities, counties, states, and countries: Cleveland, Cuyahoga County, Ohio, United States of America.
    b. Particular geographical regions: Europe, Pacific Northwest, the South.
    c. Streets: East Ninth Street, El Cajon Avenue.
    d. Buildings: Empire State Building, Union Terminal.
    e. Heavenly bodies (except the sun and moon): Mars, Milky Way, Andromeda, Alpha Centauri.

3. Names of particular things:
    a. Days and months: Friday, August.
    b. Holidays: Easter, May Day.
    c. Historical events and periods: the Civil War, the Middle Ages.
    d. School courses: Biology 101, History 102 (but "a *history* course").
    e. Languages: English, Russian.
    f. Schools: Cornell University, Walt Whitman High School (but "I graduated from *high school*").
    g. Brands: Buick, Peter Pan Peanut Butter (but "I had a *peanut butter* sandwich for lunch").

EXERCISE   Capitalize words as needed in the following sentences.

1. my best subject in high school was mathematics, but my tenth grade english teacher really taught me to enjoy classics like *jane eyre* and *the grapes of wrath.*
2. every saturday in july the arthur taylor jazz quartet performs concerts in grant park.
3. my friend suzy yip swoons when josh groban sings "to where you are."
4. ellen hasn't decided whether to spend christmas in chicago with her grandparents or in seattle with her aunt felice and uncle gregg.
5. mr. tanner's third graders at pine street elementary school planted daffodils in the park in honor of mother's day.
6. according to the food and drug administration, genetically altered crops are entirely safe.
7. drive south on sumpter street and park across from home depot, the largest store in our town.
8. director steven spielberg won wide acclaim for *saving private ryan, schindler's list,* and *munich.*
9. have you seen the two-headed turtle at the nature museum in charlotte, north carolina?
10. painting 101 will meet on tuesdays and thursdays beginning this fall.

SELF TEST: Capital Letters

Correct any errors in capitalization in the following sentences.

1. please park your car facing west on marquette lane South.
2. the carson middle school's marching band raises money each year for a trip to montreal.
3. some Doctors feel that taking fever-reducing medicines like tylenol is unnecessary, and that low fevers actually can help the body.
4. when suzanne traveled to the south, she tasted crawfish for the first time.
5. do you think that the new york giats can win the super bowl again?
6. we'll leave for florida on the friday after thanksgiving.
7. anika speaks four languages: english, french, german, and spanish.
8. the Golden Retriever darted back and forth from the water's edge to his Owner, wagging his tail playfully and barking at the Sunbathers on crawford beach.
9. we will have our next cub scout meeting at the springfield civic center.
10. the Portrait of princess diana at the national portrait gallery in london seems to attract more viewers than any other Picture in the gallery.

Clause.   A group of words with a subject and predicate. A clause can be independent or dependent. An *independent clause* stands alone as a separate sentence.

Maria went home.

A *dependent clause* cannot stand alone; rather, it must depend on an independent clause to complete its meaning.

After I came home, I took a nap.

The man *who lived next door* died.

Collective nouns.   See *Subject–verb agreement*.

Colon.   A colon (:) commonly appears after a clause introducing a list or description, between hours and minutes, in the salutation of a formal letter, between biblical chapter and verse numbers, and between the title and subtitle of a book. Less commonly, a colon may separate independent clauses and appear before quotations.

■ *List*. A colon appears between a general statement and a list or description that follows:

We shall never again find the equals of the famous three *B*'s of music: Bach, Beethoven, and Brahms.

He plans to take five courses: history, English, psychology, French, and physical education.

NOTE: A colon should appear after a complete statement. Do not use a colon after a form of the verb to be (*be, am, is, are, was, were, been*, etc.) or after a preposition.

Wrong	**Right**
Perennial contenders for the NFL championship are: San Francisco, New England, Dallas, and Buffalo.	Several teams are perennial contenders for the NFL championship: San Francisco, New England, Dallas, and Buffalo.

or

Perennial contenders for the NFL championship are San Francisco, New England, Dallas, and Buffalo.

- *Time*. When recording a specific time in numerals, use a colon between hours and minutes:

8:00 p.m.   8:10 a.m.

- *Salutation*. In formal letter writing, use a colon after the salutation:

Dear Ms. Johnson: Dear Sir:

- *Biblical references*. To separate chapter from verse, use a colon:

Genesis 1:8 (chapter 1, verse 8)

- *Title and subtitle*. A colon separates the title and subtitle of a book:

Johnson's Dictionary: A Modern Selection

- *Independent clauses*. A colon may appear between independent clauses when the second clause explains the first:

They reared their children on one principle, and one principle only: Do unto others what they would like to do unto you—and do it first.

- *Quotations*. A colon sometimes introduces a short quotation and often introduces a long block quotation:

Whenever I try to diet, I am reminded of the bitter truth of Oscar Wilde's epigram: "I can resist everything but temptation."

In commenting on his function as a writer, Joseph Conrad put every writer's dream into words:

> My task which I am trying to achieve is, by the power of the written word to make you hear, to make you feel—it is, before all, to make you *see*. That—and no more, and it is everything. If I succeed, you shall find there

according to your deserts: encouragement, consolation, fear, charm—all you demand—and, perhaps, also that glimpse of truth for which you have forgotten to ask.

NOTE: No quotation marks surround a long block quotation.

EXERCISE   Correct any errors by adding or removing colons.

1. The conference will resume at 200 p.m.
2. My heroes have always been: Albert Einstein and Martin Luther King Jr.
3. We brought several board games Monopoly, Scrabble, and Sorry.
4. Professor Barkley's voice was calm and her eyes were kind, but her message was clear if you don't take the class seriously, you will get a poor grade.

SELF TEST: Colons

Correct any errors by adding or removing colons. One sentence is already correct.

1. Sponsored public service announcements achieve two goals they deliver important messages and create goodwill for the advertisers.
2. Karl's new job brought him to cities he had never visited, like: Milan, London, Santiago, and Tokyo.
3. Because my father is always looking at his watch, for Father's Day I bought him the book *Keeping Watch A History of American Time*.
4. Gina's delectable brownies are the perfect dessert: sweet, rich, gooey, and chocolatey.
5. I hate to admit it, but my mother's favorite saying was true "Give some people an inch, and they'll take a mile."

Commas.   Using a comma correctly is almost never a matter of taste or inspiration. It is even less a matter of following the ancient junior high school formula of tossing in a comma "to indicate a pause." Different people pause for breath and emphasis in different places, and nearly *every* mark of punctuation indicates some kind of pause—periods, semicolons, and dashes no less than commas. When errors in comma usage occur, they are most often the result of the writer's being comma-happy—putting in too many commas. Our basic rule, then, is *never use a comma unless you know it is necessary*. A comma is necessary in the following cases:

- Between elements in a list or series
- Between independent clauses joined by *and, but, or, nor, for, yet, so*
- After introductory elements

- Before and after interrupting elements
- Between coordinate adjectives
- Before and after nonrestrictive elements
- Before and after phrases that express a contrast
- Before and after words of direct address, interjections, and *yes* and *no*
- Between certain words to prevent misreading
- In conventional elements such as dates, numbers, addresses, titles, correspondence, and direct quotations

A. *Series.* Separate three or more items in a list or series by commas for the sake of clarity.

The potential buyer should take special care to inspect the roof, basement, and ceilings.

Make sure you read parts one, two, and three before completing the assignment.

The three novels in Dos Passos's *USA* trilogy are *The 42nd Parallel*, *Nineteen Nineteen*, and *The Big Money*.

NOTE: In all three examples, the comma before *and* is optional. Most experienced writers use the comma, however, because it reinforces the idea of a series in the reader's mind.

B. *Independent clauses.* Two independent clauses (a group of words that can stand alone as a complete sentence) joined by a coordinating conjunction—*and, but, or, nor, for, yet, so*—require a comma *before* the conjunction:

Barack Obama fought hard for votes, and he impressed people all over the country.

Each writing assignment requires a different kind of organization, but each may require a different length.

Use no comma if there is only one independent clause:

Barack Obama fought hard for votes and impressed people all over the country.

Each writing assignment requires a different kind of organization and may require a different length.

EXERCISE Add or remove commas as needed in the following sentences. Some sentences may be correct.

1. I decided against taking the new job yet I suspected I would always be grateful for the offer.
2. Marie knew that the book would sell but never dreamed of its record-breaking success.
3. I have traveled extensively throughout the United States but I have never been abroad.

4. The manager told the division heads that they must all work together or she would fire them all separately.

5. Hand-held phones are smaller than ever, and provide more, and more services than in the past.

6. Nothing made any sense in my income tax forms so I decided I needed to consult an accountant.

7. Florida held its 2008 Presidential primary in January and the Democratic National Committee punished the state by disallowing its delegates.

8. Martin was restless and he thought about giving Pamela a call.

9. Martin was restless and thought about giving Pamela a call.

10. The English partly destroyed the Spanish Armada, but the weather played an even larger destructive role.

SELF TEST: Commas in Series and Clauses

Add or remove commas as needed in the following sentences. Some sentences are correct.

1. I continue to receive the newspaper yet I never have time to read it.

2. We did not use our digital camera but we did scan our vacation photos onto the computer.

3. Doug went to the mall, and then to the movies.

4. José, ran fifteen yards, and scored a touchdown.

5. Ice cream is better than nothing, but a hot fudge sundae is better than anything.

6. Marry me for, I love you.

7. College is lots of fun and lots of work.

8. Becoming a pilot was Carla's dream yet she was afraid to fly.

9. The head of this department must have creativity ingenuity and reliability.

10. Ruth read *Interview with a Vampire* and watched *Dracula* on television for she was too scared to sleep.

C. *Introductory elements.* In general, use a comma after an introductory element:

Because the students were having trouble with commas, they read the section on punctuation.

In good writing, there are few punctuation errors.

The italicized parts of these two sentences are introductory elements. When the introductory element is extremely short—one word, for example—you can omit the comma if the meaning remains clear: "*Soon* the term will end."

Poor	**Correct**
Because this is an introductory element it should have a comma after it.	Because this is an introductory element, it should have a comma after it.
Despite the best efforts of both parties no agreement was reached.	Despite the best efforts of both parties, no agreement was reached.
Never having seen her before I expected the worst.	Never having seen her before, I expected the worst.
As soon as he had showered he went straight to bed.	As soon as he had showered, he went straight to bed.

However, if the introductory element is moved so that it appears *after* the independent clause (and thus no longer introduces anything), do not use a comma:

No agreement was reached despite the best efforts of both parties.

He went straight to bed as soon as he had showered.

EXERCISE

Insert a comma after the introductory element as needed.

1. Finished at last with work she looked forward to an evening on the town.
2. Because Carmela forgot to set her alarm she missed her nine o'clock appointment.
3. Having decided that both sides had presented excellent cases I then concluded that my only reasonable vote was an abstention.
4. To learn more about Cuba we attended a lecture at our local community college.
5. After a long introductory clause or phrase use a comma.
6. Use a comma after a long introductory clause or phrase.
7. Now I feel better prepared.
8. Considering my shortcomings I have been luckier than I deserve.
9. Bored and disgusted with the ball game I thought bitterly that there were some peanut vendors in the stands who were better athletes than anyone on the field.
10. Whenever I hear someone suggest that love is the answer to our problems I wonder why love has usually made me miserable.

SELF TEST: Commas and Introductory Elements

Insert commas as needed in the following sentences.

1. At the Land Rover Driving School students learn to control their four-wheel-drive vehicles on unpaved roads.

2. Our eyes were bleary and our knees were shaky after we spent the entire day watching cartoons.

3. During the past twenty years in the army Emily has learned many things.

4. Watching the circus, eating cotton candy, and drinking lemonade Freddy was happier than he had ever been.

5. Soon recycling will be so much a part of our lives that we will not even notice its minor inconveniences.

6. Having prepared the fish perfectly the chef tossed several sprigs of parsley on top of it for decoration.

7. Tomorrow Pedro will be ready for work.

8. After a long and difficult day at work Natalie enjoyed a five-mile jog.

9. You must do some research on the company before you go there for an interview.

10. After finishing the whole assignment he suddenly realized he'd done the wrong exercises.

D. *Interrupting elements.* A comma should be used before and after an interrupting element. Interrupting elements, while often needed for clarity and continuity, are those that break the flow of words in the main thought of a sentence or clause. In the previous sentence, *while often needed for clarity or continuity* is an interrupting element. Some writers find it helpful to think of interrupting elements as asides to the audience or parenthetical insertions. Interrupting elements may be words such as *indeed, however, too, also, consequently, therefore, moreover, nevertheless* and phrases such as *as the author says, of course, after all, for example, in fact, on the other hand.*

Wrong	**Right**
Suppose for example that you decide to write about your own life.	Suppose, for example, that you decide to write about your own life.
We must bear in mind too that even the best system is imperfect.	We must bear in mind, too, that even the best system is imperfect.
Punctuation as we can see is not exactly fun.	Punctuation, as we can see, is not exactly fun.
The only thing wrong with youth according to George Bernard Shaw is that it is wasted on the young.	The only thing wrong with youth, according to George Bernard Shaw, is that it is wasted on the young.
His pledges for the future however could not make me forget his broken promises of the past.	His pledges for the future, however, could not make me forget his broken promises of the past.

E. *Coordinating adjectives.* Use a comma to separate coordinating adjectives—adjectives of equal rank—that come before the nouns they modify.

Wrong	Right
This poet uses concrete believable images.	This poet uses concrete, believable images.
Her warm enthusiastic energetic behavior was often mistaken for pushiness.	Her warm, enthusiastic, energetic behavior was often mistaken for pushiness.

You can identify coordinating adjectives in two ways: (1) the word *and* may be used to join them (concrete *and* believable, warm *and* enthusiastic *and* energetic) or (2) they may be reversed (believable, concrete; enthusiastic, energetic, warm). Compare these examples to "This poet uses several concrete images." We cannot say "several and concrete" or "concrete several." Therefore, we do not use a comma between them. Note, too, that if the coordinate adjectives had originally been joined by *and*, no commas would have been necessary: "Her warm *and* enthusiastic *and* energetic behavior was often mistaken for pushiness."

EXERCISE   Add commas as needed around the interrupting elements and between the coordinating adjectives in the following sentences. Also remove any incorrectly placed commas. Some sentences may be correct.

1. The student's sincere deep apology fell on deaf ears.
2. The teacher's apology I am sorry to say seemed less sincere.
3. Protracted, municipal efforts to expand the airport, are at a standstill.
4. The mayor keeps insisting however that efforts will continue.
5. Drinking a glass of cool refreshing water can energize you.
6. Always make certain, in addition, to check your manuscript for careless errors.
7. Dogs too can get sunburns.
8. The so-called, good, old days were often actually bad, old days.
9. Turner's theory to put it bluntly was wrong.
10. Her inherent bad vertebral structure inhibited her career as a gymnast.

SELF TEST: Commas and Interrupting Elements

Insert commas as required in the following sentences. Remove any unnecessary commas. One sentence is correct.

1. The days of wild, violent video games as any fan knows are just beginning!
2. Preventative care for an automobile to be sure is worthwhile.
3. Don't let those sweet and of course meaningless smiles deceive you.
4. The administration's basic, economic problem I believe is unfair taxation.
5. The outlook for the future, according to Secretary Miller, is not as bad as most columnists seem to think.

6. Teenagers' bedrooms tend to be chaotic, rumpus rooms in short pig sties.

7. There are effective ways she insisted to perform better under pressure.

8. My fundamental, monetary difficulty is that I'm broke.

9. The cat in Dad's opinion is nothing but a sweet, cuddly pain in the neck.

10. Early Gothic novels therefore are basically silly, overwritten romances.

F. *Nonrestrictive elements.* A comma should be used before and after a nonrestrictive element.

Nonrestrictive modifiers. Commas are used before and after nonrestrictive modifiers. A nonrestrictive modifier gives additional information about the noun it modifies but is not necessary to identify or define that noun:

The Empire State Building, *which I visited last year*, is a most impressive sight.

My father, *who has worked in a steel foundry for thirty years*, has made many sacrifices for me.

A *restrictive modifier* is not set off by commas. It is a necessary part of the meaning of the noun it modifies:

A person *who is always late for appointments* may have serious psychological problems.

The novel *that Professor Higgins praised so highly* is very disappointing.

People *who live in glass houses* shouldn't throw stones.

Many jobs *for highly skilled technicians* are still available.

Proper punctuation of restrictive and nonrestrictive modifiers often can affect meaning:

The sofa, with those huge armrests, is an eyesore.	(The writer sees just one sofa. The nonrestrictive modifier merely conveys more information about it.)
The sofa with those huge armrests is an eyesore.	(The writer sees more than one sofa. The restrictive modifier is necessary to distinguish this sofa from the others.)

A special type of nonrestrictive element is called the *appositive*—a word or group of words that means the same thing as the element that precedes it. In the sentence, "Joseph Terrell, *mayor of Greenville*, will speak at graduation," the italicized phrase is an appositive—that is, it has the same basic meaning as the first element, *Joseph Terrell*. The rules governing the punctuation of modifiers also govern the punctuation of appositives.

Nonrestrictive appositives. Commas are used before and after nonrestrictive appositives. A nonrestrictive appositive gives additional information about the noun it follows but is not necessary to identify that noun:

Ms. Susan Swattem, *my high school mathematics teacher*, was the meanest person in town.

Thomas Jefferson, *third president of the United States*, also founded the University of Virginia.

A *restrictive appositive* is not set off by commas. It is necessary to identify the noun it follows:

The expression *hitch your wagon to a star* was first used by Emerson.

He spoke to Susan *my sister*, not Susan *my wife*.

As with modifiers, proper punctuation of nonrestrictive and restrictive appositives often can affect meaning.

My brother, George, is a kindly soul.	(The writer has only one brother, so the word *brother* is sufficient identification. *George* is nonrestrictive.)
My brother George is a kindly soul.	(The writer has more than one brother, so the name of the specific brother is a necessary part of the meaning. *George* is restrictive.)

EXERCISE   Add commas where necessary to set off the nonrestrictive elements in the following sentences. Also remove any commas that have been incorrectly placed. Some sentences may be correct.

1. Anyone who hates loud music cannot appreciate a Metallica concert.
2. The Smurfs, elflike blue creatures of spectacular cuteness, won the hearts of America's children during the early 1980s.
3. A person who cares about the future cannot be indifferent to the proliferation of nuclear weapons.
4. The highway repair project which the department scheduled for completion in two years now will need double that time to be completed.
5. The film that my cousin Stefan loved, bored me so much, that I fell asleep.
6. Albert Einstein that legendary figure of modern science was a notable underachiever during his school days.
7. Exxon which is the largest oil company in the world used to be known as Standard Oil Company of New Jersey.
8. The man who picked up the packages for the old woman had his wallet stolen when he bent over.
9. Harold Arlen who wrote such songs as "Stormy Weather" and "Let's Fall in Love" also composed the classic score for the film *The Wizard of Oz*.
10. The star of *High School Musical*, Zac Efron who has an unbelieveable following among teenage girls appeals to many adult women too.

SELF TEST: Commas and Nonrestrictive Elements

Set off nonrestrictive elements with commas in the following sentences. Remove any unnecessary commas. Some sentences are correct.

1. A college student, who doesn't have the sense to study, may not have the sense to belong in college.
2. The Republican candidate who promised to cut taxes defeated the Democrat in last night's election.
3. Nobody who dislikes bubble gum can be trusted.
4. A person, who dislikes dogs and children, can't be all bad.
5. Bill Gates the founder of Microsoft is considered one of the most intelligent people in America.
6. People, who are early to bed and early to rise, may be healthy, wealthy, and wise, but they certainly are dull!
7. Some women feel that soap operas which rarely reflect their own lives are romantic and daring.
8. People who are lonely may seem aloof and proud.
9. Maya Angelou who wrote *I Know Why the Caged Bird Sings* is quite eloquent.
10. That which we most desire may be that which we least require.

G. *Contrast.* Commas should be used to set off phrases expressing a contrast.

   She told him to deliver the furniture on Wednesday, not Tuesday.

   Hard work, not noble daydreams, is what I believe in.

   The money did not bring hope, but anxiety.

   NOTE: The comma can sometimes be omitted before contrasting phrases beginning with *but*: "We have nothing to fear *but* fear itself."

H. *Direct address, interjections,* yes *and* no. Commas separate words and phrases of direct address, interjections, and the words *yes* and *no* from the rest of the sentence.

   1. *Direct address:*

      I tell you, ladies and gentlemen, that this strategy will not work.

      Jim, you're still not following the instructions.

   2. *Interjections:*

      Well, it appears that the committee has finally issued its report.

      Oh, I'd say the new car should arrive in about three weeks.

Although commas are generally used with mild interjections, more dramatic interjections may take exclamation points:

Well! It was the worst mess I'd ever seen.

Oh! How could she have made such a contemptible remark?

3. *Yes* and *no*:

Yes, I plan to vote for Ruppert.

I have to tell you plainly that, no, I cannot support your proposal.

I. *Misreading.* Apart from any more specific rules, commas are sometimes necessary to prevent misreading. Without commas, the following examples would be likely to stop readers in midsentence and send them back to the beginning.

Confusing	Correct
High above the trees swayed in the wind.	High above, the trees swayed in the wind.
At the same time John and Arnold were making their plans.	At the same time, John and Arnold were making their plans.
Hugging and kissing my half-smashed relatives celebrated the wedding.	Hugging and kissing, my half-smashed relatives celebrated the wedding.

J. *Conventions.* Use commas in such conventional elements as dates, numbers, addresses, titles, correspondence, and direct quotations.

1. *Dates.* Commas separate the day of the month and the year:

April 24, 1938   January 5, 1967

If you write only the month and year, you can omit the comma:

April 1938   *or*   April, 1938

If the year is used in midsentence with the day of the month, follow it by a comma. With the month only, you may omit the comma:

World War II began for the United States on December 7, 1941, at Pearl Harbor.

World War II began for the United States in December 1941 at Pearl Harbor.

World War II began for the United States in December, 1941, at Pearl Harbor.

In works cited entries, use European or miltary date order, where no commas are necessary (see pages 498–508):

7 December 1941

15 March 2008

2. *Numbers.* Use commas to group numbers of more than three digits to the left of the decimal point:

   $5,280.00   751,672.357   5,429,000   5,280

   However, commas are not used for page numbers, addresses, or years:

   page 4233   1236 Madison Ave.   1989

3. *Addresses.* Use commas to separate towns, cities, counties, states, and districts:

   Cleveland, Ohio

   Brooklyn, Kings County, New York

   Washington, D.C.

   NOTE: Do not use a comma to separate the ZIP code from the state.

   Pasadena, California   91106

4. *Titles.* A comma often separates a title from a name that precedes it:

   Harold Unger, MD   Julia Harding, PhD

5. *Correspondence.* Use a comma after the salutation in informal letters and after the complimentary close:

   Dear John,   Dear Jane,

   Respectfully yours,   Sincerely yours,

6. *Direct quotations.* See *Quotation Marks.*

EXERCISE   Insert commas as needed in the following sentences. Remove any unnecessary commas.

1. My brother Choon, was born in Shanghai China on September 8 1958.
2. Yes I do hope that my activism will help change government policies.
3. Emily is this your sweater?
4. At the moment, we are compiling, a guest list for our New Year's Eve bash.
5. Savoring each delicious bite she wanted the meal to go on forever.
6. Below the bridge looked like a tiny road as our plane gained height.
7. Apply sunscreen liberally and spend your summer romping in the sun not indoors cringing from the discomfort of sunburn.
8. Susan's reaction, was one not of outrage but of resignation.
9. Beginning July 12 2009 we will accept applications for the position of Assistant Director of the Milton School.
10. You must understand my friend that this is not easy for me.

SELF TEST: Commas: Other Uses

Insert commas as needed in the following sentences. Remove any unnecessary commas. One sentence is correct.

1. Yes dear I did call your sister yesterday.
2. A preschooler's spinning of tall tales is part of the development of intellect not a purposeful attempt to deceive.
3. The keynote speaker at Memorial Hospital's next benefit dinner will be Sally Johnson MD.
4. No, there are not any written instructions for these next two projects.
5. My letter dated March 17 2009 explains in detail my strategies for expanding our human resources department.
6. Facing the crowd together the band members felt confident and self-assured.
7. Annette when do you plan to return to Detroit?
8. Oh I am beginning to feel so frustrated by your selfishness.
9. A song from the movie *Rent*, refers to a year as 525600 minutes.
10. Kent Hoffman PhD is an associate professor at Thomas Jefferson University in Philadelphia Pennsylvania.

CS

Comma splice. Often considered a special kind of *run-on sentence* (for which the Handbook provides a separate entry), a *comma splice* is a punctuation error that occurs when two independent clauses are joined only by a comma. You can correct a comma splice by (1) using both a comma and a coordinating conjunction or (2) replacing the comma with a semicolon or a period.

There are only seven coordinating conjunctions: *and, but, or, nor, for, yet*, and *so*. When you use these between independent clauses, in formal usage, precede them by a comma.

Wrong	**Right**
The boy had been physically disabled since infancy, he still tried to excel in everything he did.	The boy had been physically disabled since infancy, but he still tried to excel in everything he did.
	or
	The boy had been physically disabled since infancy; he still tried to excel in everything he did.
	or
	The boy had been physically disabled since infancy. He still tried to excel in everything he did.

Each writing assignment requires a different kind of organization, each may be a different length.	Each writing assignment requires a different kind of organization, and each may be a different length.

or

Each writing assignment requires a different kind of organization; each may be a different length.

or

Each writing assignment requires a different kind of organization. Each may be a different length.

It is often tempting to use words such as *however, therefore, nevertheless, indeed,* and *moreover* after a comma to join independent clauses. Don't! The only words following a comma that can join two independent clauses are the seven coordinating conjunctions.

Wrong	**Right**
We started with high hopes, however, we were disappointed.	We started with high hopes; however, we were disappointed.
She had been hurt many times, nevertheless, she always seemed cheerful.	She had been hurt many times; nevertheless, she always seemed cheerful.

Although any choice among coordinating conjunctions, semicolons, and periods will be technically correct, the best choice often depends on complex issues of style and thought. If the independent clauses under consideration are surrounded by long sentences, for example, the writer might choose to break the monotony with a period, thus creating two short sentences. If the independent clauses are surrounded by short sentences, the writer can sometimes achieve variety by creating a long sentence with a coordinating conjunction or semicolon. In addition, the more closely connected the thoughts in two independent clauses, the more likely the writer will be to show that connection by using a coordinating conjunction or semicolon. In such cases, two separate sentences would indicate too great a separation of thought. Obviously, no easy rules work here, and the writer's intentions have to be the main guide.

A somewhat more sophisticated way to correct a comma splice is often the best way: Since the comma splice is created by connecting two independent clauses with a comma, change one of the independent clauses into a phrase or dependent clause. Notice how this technique works with the preceding sample sentences.

Physically disabled from infancy, the boy still tried to excel in everything he did.

Although he had been physically disabled from infancy, the boy still tried to excel in everything he did.

While each writing assignment requires a different kind of organization, each may be a different length.

We started with high hopes but were disappointed.

Despite her being hurt many times, she always seemed cheerful.

NOTE: Comma splices can be acceptable in standard English when each clause is unusually short and when the thought of the whole sentence expresses an ongoing process.

I came, I saw, I conquered.

Throughout the interview, she squirmed, she stammered, she blushed.

EXERCISE   Rewrite the following sentences, correcting the comma splices where necessary. Some sentences are correct.

1. General Electric is a widely diversified company, it makes everything from light bulbs to airplane engines, refrigerators to medical scanning devices.
2. It is allergy season again, I can't stop sneezing from the pollen and ragweed.
3. Trash talk is a disgrace to professional sports, therefore it should be outlawed.
4. Although I am no cook myself, I love to study the gourmet recipes.
5. Fear can prevent a person from acting, hate, on the other hand, will often cause action.
6. She was a human being: she was born, she lived, she suffered, she died.
7. Nothing matters more than your own personal integrity, never surrender your principles.
8. Most daytime talk shows allow people to air their dirty laundry in public, however, *The View* contains relevant topics for intelligent viewers.
9. Do not join two sentences with just a comma, use a comma and a conjunction, a semicolon, or a period to separate sentences.
10. My uncle believes that loyalty is rarely rewarded as much as it should be in the business world, he tells me therefore, not to be afraid or ashamed of changing jobs.

EXERCISE   Correct the comma splices in the following paragraphs.

1. Desperately searching the kitchen for something to eat, I found nothing. A little milk, some leftover macaroni, and one beet were the only things in the refrigerator, I saw that the situation was hopeless, I knew I would starve. In my anguish I thought about competing with the puppy for his food, but that seemed a little extreme. There was no escape, I would have to shop.
2. Air travel gets more and more expensive and less and less comfortable all the time, moreover, in order to give travelers in first class more room, airlines have moved the less expensive seats even closer together. This

change leaves travelers almost no leg room at all, it's ridiculous. Even a short flight leaves one with numb feet and aching knees. Unless airlines make considerable improvements, they may find that people are choosing slower, but more comfortable, ways to travel.

3. The children ran wild through the neighborhood that summer they chased each other up and down the streets on roller skates, skateboards, and bicycles. Their games of tag engulfed block after block in the town. It was glorious. It seemed as if the long, sunny days would never end, school would never start. But the weather began to cool, and the leaves began to change. Back to school they went. The streets were quiet and a little lonely without them.

SELF TEST: Comma Splices

Correct the comma splices in the following sentences. Some sentences are correct.

1. Some appetite-suppressing pills are now off the market, research found that they can cause heart problems.
2. The Olympic Games are supposed to promote international harmony, but they often appear to do the opposite.
3. Nothing can make Arthur change his mind, he can make a mule look cooperative.
4. Many mail-order companies sell their customer lists, then we receive hundreds of unsolicited offers each year.
5. After fifty pages, the book had failed to interest me, therefore, I finally decided to give up.
6. I used to write comma splices all the time, Dad taught me how to find and correct them.
7. Lawrence and Paolo spent too many nights at the bars, they looked tired and ill, they were a real mess.
8. She is a fantastic driver and a good mechanic; however, she can never remember where she parked her car.
9. Teenage Mutant Ninja Turtles were silly, childish, and too violent, nevertheless, the kids loved them.
10. Last winter we went sledding, we ice skated, and we went on sleigh rides.

Comparative and superlative forms. Comparative forms of adjectives and adverbs are used to compare or contrast groups of two—and only two. The comparative form of regular adjectives is formed by adding *-er* to the ending of the adjective or by using the word *more* before the adjective: *nicer, sweeter, more dramatic, more beautiful.* (Some adjectives are irregular: The comparative of *good* is *better*; the comparative of *bad* is *worse.*) The comparative form of adverbs is formed by using *more* before the adverb: *more nicely, more sweetly, more dramatically, more beautifully.*

Superlative forms of adjectives and adverbs compare or contrast groups of three or more. The superlative form of regular adjectives is formed by adding *-est* to the ending of the adjective or by using the word *most* before the adjective: *nicest, sweetest, most dramatic, most beautiful.* (Some adjectives are irregular: The superlative of *good* is *best*; the superlative of *bad* is *worst*.) The superlative form of adverbs uses *most* before the adverb: *most nicely, most sweetly, most dramatically, most beautifully.*

In summary, comparative forms apply to two, and superlative forms apply to more than two.

Wrong	Right
If I had to choose between Reese Witherspoon and Renee Zellweger, I would have to say that Witherspoon is the *best* actor.	If I had to choose between Reese Witherspoon and Renee Zellweger, I would have to say that Witherspoon is the *better* actor.
The high school girl and the junior high school girl competed on the parallel bars. The junior high school girl was given the *higher* scores.	The high school girl and the junior high school girl competed on the parallel bars. The junior high school girl was given the *highest* scores.
I like many people, but I like Betsy *more.*	I like many people, but I like Betsy *most.*
Although my first and second themes both required hard work, I wrote the second *most* easily.	Although my first and second themes both required hard work, I wrote the second *more* easily.

EXERCISE   Correct any errors in comparative and superlative forms. Some sentences are correct.

1. Comparing travel by cars to travel by planes, I enjoy cars most.
2. Rockefellers and Kennedys are both rich, but Rockefellers are probably richer.
3. The new Corvette is the most beautiful car I have ever seen.
4. Jenny won first prize for her watercolor landscape, but Elizabeth's painting was better.
5. One needs both love and friendship in marriage. Friendship could easily be the most important.
6. Among all my friends, I believe Karen is the one more likely to help in a crisis.
7. Though I adore both chocolate and strawberry ice cream, I enjoy strawberry the most.
8. At the moment, I feel more inclined toward a career in medicine than in law.

9. Most complicated choices depend on luck as well as on intelligence.

10. Dreiser was a great writer in many respects, but of all the giants of American literature he probably had less basic talent.

EXERCISE Correct any errors in comparative and superlative forms in the following paragraphs.

1. Hansel and Gretel stopped just outside the gingerbread house. It was the most wonderful thing they had ever seen. Every bit of the house was made out of something delicious: candy, cookies, or cake. The children were very hungry, and the house smelled very good. They decided to break off small pieces to eat. Hansel was oldest, so he went first.

2. My mother and father shop very differently. Mom goes out for an entire day, looks in every store, and sometimes comes home with nothing. She shops to see what is available and to think about what she might want to buy. Dad goes out for twenty minutes, shops in one place, and always brings home what he set out to buy. He shops for one reason: He needs something. Dad is certainly more efficient, but Mom probably has the most fun.

3. Writing business letters can be very difficult. It is a real challenge to find the appropriate tone. One must be formal yet friendly, brief yet thorough. Even the more experienced writers may have great trouble composing a really good business letter. Perhaps this widespread difficulty is the reason that form letters have become so popular.

SELF TEST: Comparatives and Superlatives

Correct any errors in comparative and superlative forms. Some sentences are correct.

1. She said that if she had to choose between Jake Gyllenhaal and Matt Damon, she would be the most luckiest woman alive.

2. I have visited many national parks, and Bryce Canyon is the more spectacular.

3. Which of the seven dwarfs do you think is the more amusing?

4. He is most at home in front of an audience than alone in his room.

5. Tilda Swinton is a talented actor but Laura Linney is the best of the two.

6. This has been the worst trip ever.

7. Orange may be the less flattering of the two colors, but it is the cheapest.

8. Good nutrition requires balanced meals and self-control. Which is hardest?

9. My grandmother's quilt is one of her most prized possessions.

10. At this point, it would be more better to run away than to fight.

Comparisons.   Comparisons must be both logical and complete.

- *Logical.* Do not compare items that are not related. For example, you would not compare horses to safety pins because they have nothing in common. Not all illogical comparisons are this obvious, however, since it is usually the phrasing rather than the thought behind it that is at fault.

Wrong	**Right**
His appetite is as huge as a pig. (Here the comparison is between *appetite* and *pig*.)	His appetite is as huge as a pig's. *or* His appetite is as huge as a pig's appetite. *or* His appetite is as huge as that of a pig.
Mark Twain is more amusing than any American writer. (Here Mark Twain is excluded from the group that he belongs to.)	Mark Twain is more amusing than any other American writer.

- *Complete.* A comparison must be complete; that is, the items being compared must be clear, and both items must be stated.

1. Clarity:

   Poor: I like him more than you.

   Right: I like him more than I like you.

                  or

                  I like him more than you like him.

2. Both items stated:

   Poor: Old Reliable Bank has higher interest rates. (Higher than it had before? Higher than other banks have? Higher on deposits or higher on loans?)

   Right: Old Reliable Bank has higher interest rates on savings accounts than any other bank in the city.

(For further discussion of comparisons, see Chapter 22, pages 551–553.)

comp

EXERCISE Correct any faulty comparisons in the following sentences.

1. President George W. Bush's political philosophy is not too unlike his father.
2. Hitchcock's *Psycho* is still the most frightening movie.
3. I like meeting strangers more than my husband.
4. Her marks were higher than anyone in the class.
5. My new television's reception is better than my old TV.
6. *Hamlet* is more interesting than any play ever written.
7. His great big sad eyes are like a cocker spaniel.
8. Curious, bouncy, and not too bright, he was as out of place at the meeting as a kangaroo.
9. Wah Lee's kitchen is cleaner than his sister.
10. Stephen Hawking can explain physics better than any scientist today.

SELF TEST: Faulty Comparisons

Revise the faulty comparisons in the following sentences. One sentence is correct.

1. Mai Ling says she likes you better than any of her friends.
2. Cal Ripkin Jr.'s record for consecutive games played is better than any other baseball player in history.
3. The graceful line of neck and throat resembles a swan.
4. Nobody's acting is better than Jack Nicholson.
5. Miss Rochester had the best rating.
6. Dr. Raj is better with children than any pediatrician.
7. My feet are bigger than my sister.
8. His hand felt as cold and flabby as a week-old fish.
9. This poetry is better than any of Lord Byron.
10. McDonald's hamburgers are better than Burger King.

Complement. Usually a noun, pronoun, or adjective that follows a linking verb and is necessary for logical completion of the predicate.

Marilyn Monroe was an *actor*.

Who are *you*?

That proposal seems *sensible*.

Compound subjects. See *Subject–verb agreement*.

Conjunction. A word used to join parts of sentences or clauses. *Coordinating conjunctions* (joining words or clauses of equal importance) are *and, but, or, nor,* *for, yet, so; subordinating conjunctions* (linking dependent and independent clauses) are *because, while, when, although, until, after,* and so on.

Conjunctions, coordinating.   See *Comma, B; Comma splice.*

Conjunctions, subordinating.   See *Fragmentary sentences.*

Coordinating adjectives.   See *Comma, E.*

Coordinating conjunctions.   See *Comma, B; Comma splice.*

Dangling modifier.   See *Modifiers.*

Dash.   A dash (—) serves to emphasize a parenthetical or otherwise nonessential word or phrase. It can also highlight an afterthought or separate a list or series from the rest of the sentence. An introductory list or series may be separated by a dash from the rest of the sentence if it is summarized by a word that serves as the subject of the sentence.

■ *Parenthetical word or phrase.*

   Only when politicians are exposed to temptation—and rest assured they are almost always so exposed—can we determine their real worth as human beings.

■ *Afterthought.*

   The only person who understood the talk was the speaker—and I have my doubts about her.

■ *List or series.*

   The great French Impressionists—Manet, Monet, Renoir—virtually invented a new way of looking at the world.

   The Scarlet Letter, Moby-Dick, Walden, Leaves of Grass, Uncle Tom's Cabin—these American classics were all published during the incredible five-year span of 1850–1855.

   NOTE: Use dashes sparingly, or they lose their force. Do not confuse a dash with a hyphen (see *Hyphen*). In typing, indicate a dash by striking the hyphen key twice (--), leaving no space between the dash and the two words it separates.

Dependent clause.   See *Clause.*

Direct object.   See *Object.*

Double negative. Always incorrect in standard English, a double negative is the use of two negative terms to express only one negative idea. Remember that in addition to obvious negative terms such as *no, not,* and *nothing,* the words *hardly* and *scarcely* are also considered negatives.

Wrong	**Right**
I don't have no memory of last night.	I don't have any memory of last night.
	or
	I have no memory of last night.
For truly religious people, money cannot mean nothing of value.	For truly religious people, money cannot mean anything of value.
	or
	For truly religious people, money can mean nothing of value.
His mother couldn't hardly express her feelings of pride at his graduation.	His mother could hardly express her feelings of pride at his graduation.
Our troubles had not scarcely begun.	Our troubles had scarcely begun.

Ellipsis. An ellipsis (. . .) shows omission of one or more words from quoted material. If the ellipsis occurs at the end of a sentence, four spaced dots are used; one dot is the period for the sentence.

Original	**Use of ellipsis**
"The connotation of a word is its implicit meaning, the meaning derived from the atmosphere, the vibrations, the emotions that we associate with the word."	"The connotation of a word is its implicit meaning, . . .the emotions that we associate with the word."
"We had a drought in 1988 and major floods in 1989. Statistics can be deceptive. The two-year statistics for rainfall look totally normal, but the reality was wildly abnormal."	"We had a drought in 1988 and major floods in 1989. . . .The two-year statistics for rainfall look totally normal, but the reality was wildly abnormal."

End marks. The three end marks are the period, question mark, and exclamation point.

- *Period.* A period is used at the end of complete sentences, after abbreviations, and in fractions expressed as decimals.

1. *Sentences*. If a complete sentence makes a statement, use a period at the end:

   Please give unused clothing to the Salvation Army.

   Place pole *B* against slot *C* and insert bolt *D*.

   The class wants to know when the paper is due.

2. *Abbreviations*. Use a period after some abbreviations:

   Mr. R. P. Reddish   Mt. Everest   p.m.

   NOTE: A period is not used in abbreviations such as UNESCO, NAACP, FCC, MLA, and AARP. See *Abbreviations*.

3. *Decimals*. Use a period before a fraction written as a decimal.

   $\frac{1}{4} = 0.25$ $\frac{1}{20} = 0.05$

   NOTE: If you use a decimal point to indicate money, you also need a dollar sign: $5.25.

■ *Question mark*. A question mark indicates a direct question or a doubtful date or figure.

1. *Direct question*. Use a question mark at the end of a direct question. Do not use a question mark with indirect questions such as "They asked when the paper was due."

   When is the paper due?

   Did the teacher say when the paper is due?

   You need to use a question mark when only the last part of a sentence asks a question, and when a quotation that asks a question is contained within a larger sentence.

   I know I should go to college, but where will I get the money for tuition?

   The student asked, "When is the paper due?"

   After asking, "When is the paper due?" the student left the room.

   NOTE: In the last example, the question mark replaces the usual comma inside the quotation.

2. *Doubtful date or figure*. After a doubtful date or figure, use a question mark in parentheses. This does not mean that if you are giving an approximate date or figure you should use a question mark. Use it only if the accuracy of the date or figure is doubtful.

   The newspaper reported that the government said it cost $310 (?) to send a person to the moon. (Here a question mark is appropriate because it is doubtful if $310 is the figure. Perhaps there has been a misprint in the paper.)

Chaucer was born in 1340 (?) and died in 1400. (Here historians know when Chaucer died but are doubtful of exactly when he was born, even though most evidence points to 1340. If historians were completely unsure, they would simply write, "Chaucer was born in the mid-1300s and died in 1400.")

A question mark in parentheses should never be used to indicate humor or sarcasm. It is awkward and childish to write, "He was a good (?) teacher," or, "After much debate and cynical compromise, the legislature approved a satisfactory (?) state budget."

■ *Exclamation point.* An exclamation point is used at the end of emphatic or exclamatory words, phrases, and sentences. In formal writing, exclamation points are rare. They most often occur in dialog, and even there they should be used sparingly lest their effect be lost.

1. *Word or phrase:*

   My God! Is the paper due today?

   No! You cannot copy my exam.

2. *Sentence:*

   The school burned down!

   Stop talking!

   NOTE: Comic book devices such as !?! or !! should be avoided. Words, not the symbols after them, should carry the primary meaning.

EXERCISE Add periods, question marks, and exclamation points as needed in the following sentences.

1. Every newspaper delivery driver must have dependable transportation and a reliable backup driver
2. Who will wait in line for tickets to the charity concert
3. Ling wondered if her fax machine was malfunctioning again
4. Last May I got a job with a nonprofit consumer advocacy organization based in Washington, DC
5. Did you know that a ten-foot high razor wire fence surrounds Melilla on the coast of Morocco
6. The receptionist asked when I could come in for an interview
7. "Why do you insist on taking my things without asking" she demanded angrily
8. I believe that we must hold HMOs accountable for any decisions that affect patients' health
9. The candidate claims that he favors hate-crimes legislation, but why did he never propose such legislation when he was a congressman
10. Don't you think it's time you moved into your own apartment

SELF TEST: End Marks

Correct any mistakes in the use of end marks in the following sentences. Some sentences contain more than one mistake.

1. "How can you write an essay on a book you've never read," she asked?
2. Elba wondered why it took six months for her new sofa to arrive?
3. The climate at the summit of Mt. Washington is extremely volatile and unpredictable!
4. I know that my petunias get plenty of sun, so why are they dying.
5. Oh, no. I've lost my keys again.
6. Clive asked himself how much he really enjoyed golf?
7. The city bus will take you to the ML Grieg Library.
8. The speakers asked the state, local, and federal governments to cooperate with private organizations on environmental preservation?
9. Get me out of here right now.
10. Why can't we all just get along.

frag

Exclamation point.   See *End marks*.

Fragmentary sentences.   A fragmentary sentence (also called a sentence fragment) is a grammatically incomplete statement punctuated as if it were a complete sentence. It is one of the most common basic writing errors.

     To avoid a sentence fragment, make sure that your sentence contains at least one independent clause. If it does not contain an independent clause, it is a fragment.

     Here are some examples of sentences with the independent clause italicized; sometimes the independent clause is the whole sentence, and sometimes the independent clause is part of a larger sentence.

Jack and Jill went up the hill.

He sees.

If you don't stop bothering me, *I'll phone the police.*

Tomorrow at the latest, *we'll have to call a special meeting.*

He straightened his tie before he entered the room.

Discovering that she had lost her mother, *the little girl started to cry.*

An *independent clause* is a group of words that contain a subject and verb and express a complete thought. This traditional definition is beyond criticism except that it can lead to messy discussions about the philosophical nature of a complete thought. You can avoid such discussions by concentrating on the practical reasons for a missing independent clause. There are three major reasons: omission of subject or verb, confusion of verb derivatives (verbals) with verbs, and confusion of a dependent clause with an independent clause.

- *Omission of subject or verb.* This is the simplest kind of fragment to spot:

  There are many events that take place on campus. *Such as plays, concerts, and innumerable other activities.*

  My father finally answered me. *Nastily and negatively.*

  Mr. Jones has plenty of interests to keep himself busy. *Nagging, scolding, snooping, and drinking.*

  The new department head had a brand-new pain in the neck. *In addition to the old ones.*

  We had many blessings. *Like love, nature, family, God, and television.*

  These fragments should be obvious even without the italics, and the remedies should be just as obvious. Simple changes in punctuation will solve the problems. Here are the same sentences with the fragments eliminated:

  There are many events that take place on campus, such as plays, concerts, and innumerable other activities.

  My father finally answered me nastily and negatively.

  Mr. Jones has plenty of interests to keep himself busy: nagging, scolding, snooping, and drinking.

  The new department head had a brand-new pain in the neck in addition to the old ones.

  We had many blessings, like love, nature, family, God, and television.

- *Confusion of verb derivatives (verbals) with verbs.* Verbals are words derived from verbs. Unlike verbs, they cannot function by themselves as the predicate of a sentence. Infinitive forms are verbals (*to do, to see, to walk*). So are gerunds and present participles (*-ing* endings: *doing, seeing, walking*). Study the italicized sentence fragments that follow.

  I decided to take her to the game. *Susan enjoying football with a passion.*

  Nobody ought to vote. *The government being corrupt.*

  We should take pleasure in the little things. *A boy petting his dog. Lovers holding hands. Soft clouds moving overhead.*

  To *make the world a better place. To help people be happy.* These are my goals.

  In the last example, the fragments lack subjects as well as verbs and can readily be identified. Inexperienced writers, however, looking at the fragments in the first three examples, see a subject and what appears to be a verb.

They assume, consequently, that the words make up an independent clause. They are wrong. A present participle by itself cannot serve as a verb, and an independent clause must have a verb. Study these corrected versions of the fragments.

I decided to take her to the game. Susan has been enjoying football with a passion.

Nobody ought to vote. The government is corrupt.

We should take pleasure in the little things: a boy petting his dog, lovers holding hands, soft clouds moving overhead.

I want to make the world a better place. I want to make people happy. These are my goals.

■ *Confusion of a dependent (subordinate) clause with an independent clause.* All clauses contain a subject and a verb. Unlike an independent clause, however, a *dependent* or *subordinate clause* does not express a complete thought and therefore cannot function as a sentence. A subordinate clause at the beginning of a sentence must always be followed by an independent clause. A subordinate clause at the end of a sentence must always be preceded by an independent clause. Fortunately, subordinate clauses can be readily identified if you remember that *they always begin with subordinating conjunctions*—a much easier approach than trying to figure out whether your sentence conveys a complete thought. Here, in alphabetical order, is a list of the subordinating conjunctions you are most likely to encounter. Whenever one of these words immediately precedes a clause (subject + verb), that clause becomes a subordinate clause and cannot stand alone as a complete sentence.

after	as soon as	even though	provided that	unless
although	as though	how	since	until
as	because	if	so that	whenever
as if	before	in order that	than	wherever
as long as	even if	once	though	while

NOTE: Except when used as question words, *who, which, when,* and *where* also introduce a subordinate clause.

In the left-hand column below, examples of subordinate clauses used as sentence fragments are italicized. In the right-hand column, italics indicate corrections to repair these sentence fragments.

Fragments	**Corrected**
If I ever see home again.	If I ever see home again, *I'll be surprised.*
Keats was a great poet. *Because he was inspired.*	*Keats was a great poet because* he was inspired.

I will never apologize. *Unless you really insist.*	*I will never apologize unless* you really insist.
Provided that the contract is carried out within thirty days.	Provided that the contract is carried out within thirty days, *we will not sue.*
This is the person who will be our next governor. *Who will lend this state to a better tomorrow.*	*This is the person who will be our next governor, who* will lead this state to a better tomorrow.

The major difficulty anyone is likely to have with sentence fragments is in identifying them. They are usually easy to correct. Sentence fragments occur, in many cases, because of a misunderstanding of complex grammatical issues, but they can almost always be corrected with elementary revisions in punctuation.

Sentence fragments should nearly always be avoided. In rare situations, they can sometimes be justified, especially if the writer wants a sudden dramatic effect.

I shall never consent to this law. Never!

Death to the tyrant!

Scared? I was terrified.

Lost. Alone in the big city. Worried. The boy struggled to keep from crying.

EXERCISE Some of the following are sentence fragments. Rewrite them to form complete sentences. You may have to supply additional information.

1. Trying to follow Professor Garcia's lecture.
2. After majoring in English at the University of Southern California.
3. Who will send the invitations?
4. Although I admired her greatly and thought she deserved a chance.
5. Dressed in jeans and a torn tee shirt.
6. Because the senator planned to pursue some other interests.
7. Although improving many people's appearance, contact lenses are far less convenient than traditional eyeglasses.
8. To make a long story short.
9. To mention just a few items of relatively minor importance.
10. A person who can approach problems with a unique combination of vision and practicality.
11. Unless we all work together for a better world, we may have no world at all.
12. Who was that masked man?
13. Until the orchestra plays more popular selections.
14. Angry and screaming at the top of their lungs.

15. In addition to dwindling market share, mounting losses, and falling stock prices.

EXERCISE   Find and correct the sentence fragments in the following paragraphs.

1. Yu-lin had several errands to run that afternoon. Going to the shoe repair store, stopping off at the bank, and dropping off a few books at the library. He had no idea if he could finish in time. Thinking carefully, he made a plan. He would stop at the bank, then pick up his shoes. And then drive all the way across town to the library. If he drove quickly and didn't get stopped by any red lights, he could be home in time to start supper and do a few loads of laundry.

2. Scrabble is a game that requires intelligence, skills, and almost infinite patience. A single game can take as long as three hours and can get very dull at times. While you wait for your opponent to think of a word. There isn't much for you to do but look at the ceiling, try to remember how to spell *syzygy*, and hope that your opponent doesn't play a word in the space you hope to use. Beyond these few diversions, all you can do is wait. And wait.

3. My favorite way to spend an evening. To curl up on the couch with a big bowl of popcorn and watch old movies. Black-and-white movies are best. I munch my popcorn and let myself get pulled into a fantasy. Where people have doormen, where everyone wears hats and gloves, where chivalry is not dead. Romance, too. I love the movies where the hero and heroine fall desperately and hopelessly in love. Films like that are always wonderfully sad and romantic, and if I cry, the popcorn just gets a little extra salt. Of course, I also like the old comedies and suspense thrillers. There's just no way for me to go wrong with a night filled with comfort, snack food, and entertainment.

SELF TEST: Fragments

Find and correct the fragments in the following sentences. More than one option exists for correcting the fragments.

1. Americans celebrate Flag Day on June 14. To salute a flag that was stitched in 1776. And has bound the nation together ever since.

2. After Celeste's five-year-old daughter split her lip. On a metal shovel at the playground. The distraught mother decided that playgrounds are just too dangerous.

3. Barking and wagging her tail furiously. My golden retriever welcomed me home. After a grueling day at the office. I really needed her affection.

4. It was the perfect day for a barbeque. Sunny, breezy, and warm.

5. Living on a farm isn't easy. So much work to do beginning at dawn. Milking cows. Collecting eggs. Caring for all the animals.

6. Mrs. Scott always acts aloof towards us. If she even acknowledges us at all. As if we aren't good enough. Because our home isn't as large as hers.

7. A representative for Chevrolet says that the company's new pickup combines several important attributes. Ruggedness, versatility, and personal comfort.

8. The panelists at the business symposium wrestled with a difficult question. Whether technology and the Internet have left small businesses behind.

9. Wind gusts can cause serious problems for firefighters. Struggling to keep a fire under control.

10. When you make your own car payments. When you pay rent. And when you earn a paycheck. That's when I will consider you a responsible adult.

Fused sentence.   See *Run-on sentence.*

Hyphen.   A hyphen (-) is used to form some compound words and to divide words at the end of a line.

■ *Compound words.*

1. As a general rule, you should consult a recent dictionary to check the use of the hyphen in compound words. Many such words that were once hyphenated are now combined. The following are some compound words that are still hyphenated:

   mother-in-law   court-martial

   knee-deep   water-cooled

2. All numbers from twenty-one to ninety-nine (except multiples of ten) are hyphenated:

   forty-three   one hundred fifty-six

3. A hyphen joins two or more words that form an adjective before a noun:

   a well-known teacher   a first-rate performance

   but   *but*

   The teacher is well known.   The performance was first rate.

■ *Divided words.* Divide words at the end of a line by consulting a dictionary and following accepted syllabication. A one-syllable word cannot be divided. In addition, a single letter cannot be separated from the rest of the word; for example, *a-bout* for *about* would be incorrect. The hyphen should come at the very end of the line, not at the beginning of the next line.

Independent clause.   See *Clause.*

Indirect question.   See *End marks.*

Infinitive.   Simple form of a verb preceded by the word *to*—for example, *to come, to go.*

Intransitive verb.   See *Verb.*

Italics (underlining).   In handwriting, underlining represents printed italics. The rules for underlining and italics are the same. Underline or italicize titles of complete works; most foreign words and phrases; words used emphatically; and letters, words, and phrases pointed to as such. If you are preparing an essay based on MLA or APA style, use italics.

> Handwritten:
>
> I love <u>Star Wars</u>.
>
> Print generated:
>
> I love *Star Wars*.
>
> *NOTE:* When a word or phrase that would usually be italicized appears in a section of text that is already italicized, the word or phrase is typed or written with no italics.

- *Titles of complete works.*

  1. Books: *The Great Gatsby, Paradise Lost, The Hitchhiker's Guide to the Galaxy*

  2. Newspapers and magazines: *New York Times, Chicago Tribune, Newsweek*

  3. Plays and movies: *A Raisin in the Sun, Macbeth, Jarhead, Sleepless in Seattle*

Enclose the titles of poems in quotation marks, except for book-length poems such as Milton's *Paradise Lost* and Homer's *Iliad.* Use quotation marks to enclose the titles of small units contained within larger units—such as chapters in books, selections in anthologies, articles or short stories in magazines, and individual episodes of a television series. (See *Quotation marks.*)

- *Foreign words and phrases not assimilated into English.*

vaya con Diós	*paisano*	*auf Wiedersehen*

  but

cliché	genre	laissez-faire	taco

■ *Words used emphatically.*

Ask me, but don't *tell* me.

Under *no* circumstances can we permit this to happen.

She didn't really know *everything*, although it seemed that way.

Except in special situations, good word choice and careful phrasing are far more effective than italicizing or underlining to show emphasis.

■ *Letters, words, and phrases pointed to as such.*

Do not use words such as *however* and *therefore* as coordinating conjunctions.

The letter *x* is often used in algebra.

The phrase *on the other hand* anticipates contrast.

A *proton* is a positively charged particle in the nucleus of an atom.

Check with your instructor about his or her preference for italics or underlining.

Linking verb.   See *Verb; Adjective–adverb confusion.*

Misplaced modifier.   See *Modifiers.*

Modifiers.   The most frequent errors involving modifiers are dangling modifiers and misplaced modifiers.

■ *Dangling modifiers. A dangling modifier* is a group of words, often found at the beginning of a sentence, that do not refer to anything in the sentence or that seem to refer to a word to which the dangler is not logically related. Dangling modifiers usually include some form of a verb that has no subject, either implied or stated. This construction results in statements that are sometimes humorous and always illogical. To correct a dangling modifier, either change the modifier into a subordinate clause, or change the main clause so that the modifier logically relates to a word in it. On occasion, you may have to change both clauses.

dm

Incorrect	Correct
Climbing the mountain, the sunset blazed with a brilliant red and orange. (This sentence says that the sunset is climbing the mountain.)	As we were climbing the mountain, the sunset blazed with a brilliant red and orange. (Subordinate clause) *or* Climbing the mountain, we saw the sunset blazing with a brilliant red and orange. (Main clause)

After looking in several stores, the book was found. (In this sentence, the book is looking in several stores.)

After looking in several stores, we found the book.

To become an accurate speller, a dictionary is very helpful. (In this sentence, the dictionary is becoming an accurate speller.)

If you want to become an accurate speller, a dictionary is very helpful.

or

To become an accurate speller, you should use a dictionary.

While talking and not paying attention, the teacher gave the class an assignment. (This sentence says that the teacher is talking and not paying attention while giving an assignment. If that is what the writer meant, then this sentence is correct. If, however, the writer meant that the class was talking and not paying attention, then it is incorrect.)

While the class was talking and not paying attention, the teacher gave an assignment.

or

While talking and not paying attention, the class was given an assignment by the teacher.

mm

■ *Misplaced modifiers.* Since part of the meaning of the English language depends on word order—some other languages depend mostly on word endings—you must make sure that phrases serving as modifiers and adverbs such as *only, always, almost, hardly,* and *nearly* are placed in the position that will make the sentence mean what you intend. *Misplaced modifiers,* unlike dangling modifiers, can almost always be corrected simply by changing their positions.

1. Phrases serving as modifiers:

    The teacher found the book for the student in the library.

    This sentence indicates that the student was in the library. If, however, the writer meant that the book was found in the library, then the modifier *in the library* is misplaced. The sentence should read:

    In the library, the teacher found the book for the student.

        The writer of the following sentence seems to be saying that the college is near the lake:

    His parents met his friend from the college near the lake.

    If, however, the writer meant that the meeting took place near the lake, the modifier is misplaced and the sentence should read:

    Near the lake, his parents met his friend from the college.

2. Adverbs like *only, always, almost, hardly* and *nearly* usually qualify the word that comes after them. Therefore, the position of these words depends on what the writer wishes to say.

The adverb *only* is a notorious troublemaker. Observe how the sentence *"I want a son"* changes meaning significantly with the change in position of *only*:

I *only* want a son.	(I don't yearn for or long for a son; I only want one.)
I want *only* a son.	(I have no other wants.)
I want an *only* son.	(One son is as many as I want.)
I want a son *only*.	(I do not want a daughter.)

EXERCISE Rewrite the following sentences as necessary to correct any dangling or misplaced modifiers.

1. Racing down the street, our books fell out of the bag.
2. My history professor spoke passionately about the evils of cheating on Tuesday.
3. Carve the roast after standing at room temperature for a few minutes.
4. I baked special cookies for the minister with chocolate chips.
5. The quarterback was removed from the game before he was permanently injured by the coach.
6. Singing in a soft voice, the acoustical system made it possible for all to hear.
7. Erica bikes well on the mountain trails with powerful leg muscles.
8. Running toward second base, we saw the runner make a daring slide.
9. Juan wants Judy to love him badly.
10. While driving through Yosemite, a bear stopped our car.

EXERCISE Correct any dangling or misplaced modifiers in the following paragraphs.

1. The weather was beautiful that day, and everyone tried to make the most of it. The park was filled with people playing catch, flying kites, or simply lying in the grass and soaking up the sun. Chirping happily in the trees, numerous picnickers were entertained by choruses of birds. Swimming was a popular way to spend the day, too. The river overflowed with kids of all ages taking their last summer swim.
2. Everyone knew the house was haunted. Looming ominously in the distance, it overshadowed the whole town. No one had been inside for years. Everyone had been afraid since that fateful day when, shrieking and hollering, the house was rapidly vacated by the family that owned it. They all

said they had seen a ghost in frightened voices. No one believed them, not at first. Then, the noises began.

3. Football fans sometimes seem a little crazy to the rest of the world. They love their teams so much and want them to win so badly that these fans will do just about anything. Cleveland is just one example. Wearing dog masks, barking, and throwing dog bones at the opposition, the town goes wild. All of this silliness springs not from insanity, but from love and devotion. It's just the fans' way of saying, "We're behind you all the way. Win one for us!"

SELF TEST: Dangling and Misplaced Modifiers

Correct the misplaced modifiers in the following sentences. One sentence is correct.

1. Nailed to the fence, Walter noticed a "No Trespassing" sign.
2. My parrot landed gracefully on my shoulder with ruffled feathers.
3. Barking wildly and nipping at an old woman's heels, I thought the dog had gone mad.
4. Plucking the delicate petals, the children smiled secretly as they felt the autumn breeze.
5. Watching the horror film, Esteban got a terrible pain from the gruesome scene in his stomach.
6. Chomping loudly and belching, we were appalled at Uncle Ray's terrible table manners.
7. Unable to sleep, the warm milk soothed Sam so that he was able to relax.
8. I like to watch television doing my ironing.
9. Michelle was told never to speak to strangers by her mother.
10. Golden brown and juicy, I thought the turkey looked delicious.

Modifiers, nonrestrictive.   See *Comma, F.*

Modifiers, restrictive.   See *Comma, F.*

Nonrestrictive modifiers.   See *Comma, F.*

Noun.   Traditionally defined as the name of a person, place, thing, or concept, nouns are generally used as the subject, object, or complement of a sentence: *Roosevelt, Bill, accountant, California, Lake Ontario, Boulder Dam, desk, car, freedom, love.*

Numerals.

■ *Numerals are used to indicate dates, times, percentages, money, street numbers, and page references.*

On January 21, 2003, at 5:00 a.m., a fire broke out at 552 East 52nd Street, and before the Fire Department brought the flames under control, the fire had destroyed 75 percent of the building.

■ *In other cases, if a number is one or two words, spell it out; if it is over two words, use the numeral.*

In the big contest forty-five young boys won ribbons. William ate 152 hot dogs.

■ *Opt for ease and consistency when you refer to different numbers in one sentence.*

In the big contests yesterday 45 young boys won ribbons and William ate 152 hot dogs in 2 minutes.

■ *Spell out all numbers that begin a sentence.*

Four thugs assaulted an old woman last night.

Three hundred thirty-one traffic deaths happened nationwide during the Labor Day weekend.

Object.   The person, place, or thing that receives the action of a verb, or the noun or pronoun after a preposition.

George shot *Joe*.

Florence kissed *him*.

All motives are suspect to *them*.

You'll find your *gloves* in the car.

Parallelism.   Express ideas and facts of equal importance in the same grammatical form. See pages 560–562 for a fuller treatment of parallelism.

Parentheses.   Parentheses can enclose incidental comments, provide explanatory details, sometimes set off numerals that accompany the points of a paper, and enclose source information in research papers. In largely outdated citation formats, parentheses enclose information in footnotes. In many cases, parentheses serve to mark afterthoughts that probably should have been incorporated into the writing elsewhere. Use parentheses sparingly.

■ *Incidental comments.*

The movie *The Killers* (its plot had little resemblance to Hemingway's short story) won an award.

■ *Explanation of details.*

The cornucopia (the horn of plenty) is a Thanksgiving symbol.

■ *Enumerated points.*

This essay has four main pieces of advice: (1) know your professors as people, (2) attend college-sponsored events, (3) attend student-sponsored events, and (4) use the library.

■ *Source material.*

[1]Peter Straub, *Shadowland* (New York: Coward, 1980), 10. (Straub 10.)

Passive voice.   See *Voice*. Also see Chapter 23, pages 559–560.

Period.   See *End marks*.

Person.   The form of pronouns and verbs that indicates the speaker (*first person*), the person or thing spoken to (*second person*), or the person or thing spoken about (*third person*).

	Pronoun	Verb
First person	I, we	go
Second person	you	go
Third person	he, she, it	goes
	they	go

Possessives.   See *Apostrophe*.

Predicate.   The part of a clause that tells what the subject does, or what is being done to the subject.

Sal *went home.*

The child *will be punished.*

See also *Subject*.

Preposition.   A connecting word such as *in, by, from, on, to,* or *with* that shows the relation of a noun or a pronoun to another element in a sentence.

The man *with* the gun shot the deer.

Pronoun.   A word that takes the place of a noun. It may be personal (*I, you, he, she, it, we, they, me, him, her*), possessive (*my, mine, your, yours, his*), reflexive or intensive (*myself, yourself, herself*), relative (*who, which, that*), interrogative (*who, which, what*), or indefinite (*anyone, somebody, nothing*).

Pronoun agreement.   A pronoun must agree with its antecedent both in gender (masculine, feminine, or neuter) and number (singular or plural). The antecedent of a pronoun is the word or words to which the pronoun refers. For example, in the sentence "Jason lost his book," the pronoun *his* refers to the antecedent *Jason.* Another example is "Jason could not find his book. He had lost it." In the second sentence, there are two pronouns—*he* and *it.* The antecedent of *he* is *Jason,* and

agr

the antecedent of *it* is *book*. With the exception of constructions such as *it is nearly eight o'clock*, in which *it* has no antecedent, all pronouns should have antecedents.

■ *Gender*. When the gender of a singular antecedent is unknown, irrelevant, or general (as in *student* or *person*, for example), be sure to avoid sexist language. The traditional rule calling for the masculine pronoun to take precedence in such situations is now outdated and has been rejected by all or nearly all publishers of books, magazines, and newspapers as well as English instructors.

> **sexist**

If the singular antecedent is retained, sexist language can be avoided by using a form of *he or she*, though this phrasing can often be awkward and excessively formal.

A student needs to turn in his or her work on time.

A person who truly likes others will find that others will like him or her.

The most effective way of avoiding sexist language is usually to change the singular antecedent to plural.

Students must turn in their work on time.

People who truly like others will find that others will like them.

(See *he, his, him, himself* in the Glossary, and pages 576–578 in Chapter 24.)

■ *Number*. Most pronoun agreement errors occur when the pronoun does not agree with its antecedent in number. If the antecedent is singular, the pronoun must be singular; if the antecedent is plural, the pronoun must be plural.

1. *Indefinite pronouns*. Words like *anybody, somebody, everybody, nobody,* and *each* are always singular. Others like *few* and *many* are always plural. Indefinite pronouns such as *all, any, most,* and *more* can be either singular or plural, depending on the object of the preposition that follows them: "All of my concern is justified"; but, "All of my concerns are justified."

Incorrect:	Everybody missed the deadline for turning in their paper.
	Each employee was told that they represented the company, not just themselves.
Correct:	Everybody missed the deadline for turning in his or her paper.
	Each employee was told that he or she represented the company, not just himself or herself.

NOTE: Overuse of the *he or she* approach can lead to awkwardness. It's a good idea to see if changing to a plural antecedent can create a more effective sentence.

All the students missed the deadline for turning in their papers.

The employees were told that they represented the company, not just themselves.

2. *Collective nouns.* Some singular nouns refer to more than one thing: *group, youth, family, jury,* and *audience,* for example. If the noun acts as a unit, it takes a singular pronoun. If the individuals within the unit act separately, the noun takes a plural pronoun.

The jury reached *its* decision.

The jury divided bitterly on *their* decision.

The audience rose to *its* feet to show *its* approval.

The audience straggled to *their* seats through the entire first act.

3. *Antecedents joined by* either . . . or *and* neither . . . nor. When two antecedents are joined by *either . . . or* or *neither . . . nor*, the pronoun agrees with the antecedent closer to it:

Either Ruby or Jan lost *her* album.

Either the mother or the daughters lost *their* albums.

Either the daughters or the mother lost *her* album.

Neither the boys nor the girls lost *their* albums.

4. *Compound antecedents.* Except when the words function as a single unit—such as in "Macaroni and cheese *is* my favorite dish"—antecedents joined by *and* take a plural pronoun:

The owl and the pussycat shook *their* heads sadly.

EXERCISE   Correct any errors in pronoun agreement in the following sentences.

1. No one at the meeting knew what they might expect the mayor to say.
2. Everyone remembered their lines in last night's performance.
3. Both my brother and my sister brought their children to the party.
4. Every student needs to understand the importance of coming to their classes on time.
5. The crowd of sport fans shouted their disapproval of the umpire's decision.
6. Everybody I know talks about their birthplace with great affection, but almost nobody ever goes back.
7. Neither Win Hou nor his brother Shing wore their jacket, though the air was chilly.

8. All of the soup was tainted, so they were recalled by the manufacturer.
9. Either the boss or the workers will have to make up his mind about medical benefits.
10. The team celebrated their victory.

EXERCISE   Correct any pronoun agreement errors in the following paragraphs.

1. At the end of the show we will have a curtain call and a company bow. The chorus will bow first. Then, the supporting cast will take their bows in a group. The two leads will meet center stage and receive their applause. Finally, everyone will take their neighbors' hands and the entire company will bow together. Please, don't forget to bow quickly and smile.

2. The jury debated for a long time. Could they convict this man of murder? Such a conviction would mean at least life imprisonment, if not the death penalty. Were they positive he was guilty? For five hours the jury argued among themselves. Finally, a verdict was reached. Together, the jury filed back into the courtroom and prepared to give the decision they had reached.

3. Going to the laundromat is no fun at all. It takes forever, and inconsiderate people make it take even longer. There is always someone who has saved up his laundry for an entire year and is using five washers and six dryers. People with less laundry have to wait hours for an empty machine. Then there are the kids who have never done laundry before. They wash their socks and their underwear with their blue jeans and complain when their whites get dingy. The rest of us have to wait while these fools relaunder all their clothes. I am so tired of it all that I just might start doing my laundry in my dishwasher.

SELF TEST: Pronoun Agreement

Correct pronoun agreement errors in the following sentences. Some sentences are correct.

1. Everyone must have their passport and birth certificate if they want to cross the border.
2. The screaming citizenry shouted rude slogans at their disgraced former ruler.
3. Either Delia or her sisters will have to give up her turn in the front seat.
4. One of the Gomez brothers leaned back casually, carefully straightening their shirtsleeves.
5. No one but Erhan will have their license revoked.
6. Neither Greg nor Marcia can find her textbook.
7. Every chef knows they must work with extremely sharp knives.
8. None of it was finished, so they were set aside for a while.

9. A patient with damage to the part of the brain called the hippocampus may remember only events from before his injury.
10. Emma and John opened the champagne and poured some into their glasses.

Pronoun case.   *Pronoun case* refers to the change in form of pronouns that corresponds with their grammatical function. There are three cases, and their names are self-explanatory: *subjective* (when the pronoun acts as a subject), *objective* (when the pronoun acts as an object), and *possessive* (when the pronoun acts to show possession). Following is a list of case changes for the most common pronouns:

Subjective	Objective	Possessive
I	me	my, mine
you	you	your, yours
he	him	his
she	her	her, hers
it	it	its
we	us	our, ours
they	them	their, theirs
who	whom	whose

- *Compound subjects and objects (subjects and objects connected by* and). Do not be misled by a compound subject or object. Use the pronoun case that shows the pronoun's grammatical role.

Wrong	Right
My father scolded Jim and *I.*	My father scolded Jim and *me.*
Betty and *her* had many good times.	Betty and *she* had many good times.

A simple test for getting the right word is to eliminate one of the compound terms and see which pronoun works better. No one would write "My father scolded I"—so "My father scolded me" is correct. No one would write "Her had many good times"—so "She had many good times" is correct.

- *Object of a preposition.* In a prepositional phrase, any pronoun after the preposition always takes the objective case.

Wrong	Right
This match is just between you and *I.*	This match is just between you and *me.*
I went to the movies with Ramona and *she.*	I went to the movies with Ramona and *her.*
This present is for John and *he.*	This present is for John and *him.*

■ *After forms of* to be: (is, am, are, was, were, has been, had been, might be, will be, *etc.*). A pronoun after forms of *to be* is always in the subjective case. This rule still applies rigorously in formal written English. It is frequently ignored in informal English and has all but disappeared from most conversation.

It was she.

This is he.

The winners will be they.

■ *After* as *and* than. In comparisons with *as* and *than*, mentally add a verb to the pronoun to determine which pronoun is correct. Should you write, for example, "Bill is smarter than I," or, "Bill is smarter than me"? Simply complete the construction with the "understood" verb. You could write, "Bill is smarter than I am," but not, "Bill is smarter than me am." Therefore, "Bill is smarter than I" is correct.

Wrong	Right
I am just as good as *them*.	I am just as good as *they*.
Her mother had more ambition than *her*.	Her mother had more ambition than *she*.
Bill liked her more than *I*.	Bill liked her more than *me*. (Meaning *Bill liked her more than he liked me*.)
Bill liked her more than *me*.	Bill liked her more than *I*. (Meaning *Bill liked her more than I liked her*.)

■ We *or* us *followed by a noun*. Use *we* if the noun is a subject, *us* if the noun is an object. If ever in doubt, mentally eliminate the noun and see which pronoun sounds right. Should you write, for example, "The professor had us students over to his house" or "The professor had we students over to his house"? Mentally eliminate *students*. No one would write "The professor had we over to his house," so *us* is correct.

Wrong	Right
After the final exam, *us* students were exhausted.	After the final exam, *we* students were exhausted.
The company's reply to *we* consumers was almost totally negative.	The company's reply to *us* consumers was almost totally negative.

■ *Gerunds*. A gerund is an *-ing* verb form that functions as a noun. In "Swimming used to be my favorite sport," *swimming* is a gerund. A pronoun before a gerund takes the possessive case.

Wrong	Right
Us nagging him did no good.	*Our* nagging him did no good.

His parents do not understand *him* reading so poorly.

His parents do not understand *his* reading so poorly.

Them believing what she says does not mean that she is telling the truth.

Their believing what she says does not mean that she is telling the truth.

■ *Who and whom.* See the Glossary, pages 703–705.

EXERCISE Choose the correct pronoun in each of the following sentences. Be prepared to explain your choice.

1. He cared about money every bit as much as (I, me), but he was a more successful hypocrite than (I, me).
2. For (he and she, him and her), divorce might have been the only practical choice.
3. Will you accompany Sally and (I, me) to the movies?
4. (She, Her) and I took the same courses last semester.
5. (Him, His) lying has become part of his character.
6. (He and I, Him and me) decided that we would adopt a beagle from our local shelter.
7. I honestly don't know what he expects (we, us) poor students to do.
8. The judge then assessed an additional fine for (them, their) resisting arrest.
9. The winning contestants were no brighter or quicker than (I, me).
10. Bennett hated Stephen and (she, her) with a jealous passion.

EXERCISE Find and correct any errors in pronoun case in the following paragraphs.

1. Jack Fitzwilliam, master thief, strolled calmly down the street. In his pockets were the diamonds and pearls that, until recently, had been the sacred treasure of the Montgomery family. Now they were Jack's. He knew the police were only moments behind him. However, with his false beard and moustache, he had no fear of being recognized, and if he ran from the police they might think of him running as an admission of guilt.
2. Just between you and I, I've never been very fond of Ann Pickett. It's not that she's cruel or nasty; we just have so little in common. For some reason, we are always expected to be best friends and exchange cozy confidences. To me, that is unthinkable. We just never have anything to talk about.
3. We are tired of this abuse, and we just won't take it any longer. Us poor kids do all the work around here. We mow the lawn, take out the trash, do the dishes, feed and walk the dogs, fold the laundry, and wash windows. You adults just sit around and do nothing. When are you going to start taking some responsibility for yourselves? When are you going to become mature and capable? We're tired of waiting. Us kids are on strike.

SELF TEST: Pronoun Case

Select the correct pronoun in the following sentences.

1. (She, Her) and her three cats boarded the plane.
2. There's no question that I'm taller than (she, her).
3. Discouraged and crestfallen, Brett and (I, me) slowly returned home.
4. Our aged music professor, a once-famous contralto, can still sing better than any of (we, us) students.
5. He gave the money to Woo Chai and (I, me).
6. (Us, We) consumers are tired of being tricked by false advertising.
7. I know so little about politics that (me, my) running for political positions makes no sense.
8. It was a secret between (he and she, him and her), but the whole world knew about it by sunset.
9. The attorney best suited for this complicated case is (she, her).
10. The people who are latest to the party will be (they, them).

Pronoun reference. A pronoun must not only agree with its antecedent, but that antecedent must be clear as well. An ambiguous antecedent is as bad as no antecedent at all. Generally, two types of ambiguity occur: a pronoun with two or more possible antecedents, and one pronoun referring to different antecedents.

- *Two or more possible antecedents.* In the sentence, "When Stanton visited the mayor, he said that he hoped his successor could work with him," the pronouns *he, his,* and *him* can refer to either the mayor or Stanton. This problem can be avoided by making the antecedent clear: "When Stanton visited the mayor, Stanton said that he hoped his successor could work with the mayor." Here the pronouns *he* and *his* clearly refer to Stanton. Be particularly careful of the potential ambiguity in vague use of the word *this*.

Ambiguous	Improved
I received an *F* in the course and had to take it over again. This was very unfair. (Was the *F* unfair or having to take the course again? Were both unfair?)	I received an *F* in the course and had to take it over again. This grade was very unfair.
Young people are unhappy today and are demanding change. This is a healthy thing. (What is healthy—being unhappy, demanding change, or both?)	Young people are unhappy today and are demanding change. This demand is a healthy thing.

ref

■ *One pronoun referring to different antecedents.* "Mark received an *F* on his term paper and had to write a revision of it. It took a long time because it had many errors." In these sentences, the first *it* refers to the paper, the second to the revision, and the third to the paper. A reader could easily become confused by these sentences. In that case, simply replacing the pronouns with their antecedents would solve the problem: "Mark received an *F* on his term paper and had to write a revision of it. The revision took a long time because the paper had many errors."

EXERCISE Rewrite the following sentences by correcting any errors in pronoun reference. Some sentences are correct.

1. Scuba diving and snorkeling are very popular in Palau, but it can be dangerous.
2. The fans cheered the performers hysterically, and they didn't leave the hall for another hour.
3. The students left the rooms in their usual order.
4. Jim told his father that he ought to put his funds into a money-market account.
5. Anita Sanchez inspected the carburetor and distributor. It needed several adjustments.
6. Emma's coach told her that she needed to see some more plays before she could leave for the day.
7. Zoe received her citizenship papers and registered to vote. This made her very happy.
8. The animals clawed and rattled their cages. They were filthy and their stench was horrifying.
9. The prosecutor disagreed with the judge. He felt he was guilty.
10. His final grades were an *A* and a *C*. This really saved him.

EXERCISE Find and correct the pronoun reference errors in the following paragraphs.

1. The old Road Runner and Coyote cartoons are popular with just about all children. The shows have no plot to speak of, just lots of random silliness. This is what makes them so much fun for kids to watch. It's always amazing to see the endless schemes the Coyote will use to try to catch the Road Runner, and it's even more fun to try to guess how it will fail. These cartoons certainly aren't edifying or educational, but it's so much fun that no child really minds.
2. Sir William Gilbert and Sir Arthur Sullivan are famous for writing some of the greatest operettas in the history of music. Although the two men never got along personally (perhaps because of his infamous temper), their words and music blended harmoniously. Extremely popular, if slightly shocking in their time, Gilbert and Sullivan's operettas are just as

popular today. Everyone from the Met to the smallest community theater has a Gilbert and Sullivan show in their repertoire. *Topsy Turvey*, a successful film, made the two writers come alive for audiences. They still dazzle with their words and music.

3. A three-year-old's idea of the perfect lunch is a peanut butter and jelly sandwich. Do not, however, make the mistake of thinking you can slap a little PB and J on some bread, toss it to a kid, and be left in peace. Three-year-olds are picky. They must be made to precise specifications or they won't eat them. Use white bread, the squishier the better. Little kids don't eat whole wheat. Use creamy peanut butter, not chunky. Little kids don't like food with texture. Use grape jelly. Don't mess with exotic alternatives. Little kids can't say *marmalade* and won't eat it. Cut the sandwich into four triangles; remove the crusts; serve; and breathe a sigh of relief.

SELF TEST: Pronoun Reference

Correct errors in pronoun reference in the following sentences. One sentence is correct.

1. The novelist admitted to plagiarizing his rival's work, but all he said was that he was very upset by his actions.
2. The cold wind gave life to the newspaper as it swept along the street and skimmed the pavement.
3. The tortillas annoyed the weekly patrons. They were dry and unappealing.
4. Even the most talented performers can practice for years and still make mistakes. This can be discouraging.
5. Ingrid told Anne that her tights had a run.
6. Sandy and Bill attempted to read the signs, but they were too mixed up.
7. George Washington supposedly chopped down a cherry tree and never told a lie. Can this be true?
8. The teachers had the students get ready for recess. They couldn't wait to get out to the playground.
9. This examination is an absolute outrage, and we complained to the dean about it.
10. The musicians carefully cleaned their instruments, and then they were stored in their cases for the night.

Question marks. See *End marks.*

Questions, indirect. See *End marks.*

Quotation marks. Quotation marks are used to indicate material taken word for word from another source; to mark the title of a poem, song, short story, essay, and any part of a longer work; and to point out words used in a special sense—words set apart for emphasis and special consideration, slang and collo-quial expressions, derisively used words.

- *Direct quotations.* Quotation marks indicate what someone else has said in speech or writing:

  The mayor said, "The city is in serious financial trouble if the new city income tax does not pass."

  "No man is an island," John Donne once wrote.

  "The world," said the senator, "is growing smaller and smaller."

  If there is a quotation within a quotation, use single marks for the second quote:

  The mother commented wryly, "I wonder if Dr. Spock and the other great authorities on bringing up kids have ever seen you, calm as can be, say, 'I don't wanna.'"

  Observe the following rules in punctuation of direct quotations.

  1. *Block quotation.* If a direct quotation other than dialog is more than four lines long, it should be blocked. Block quotations *do not* take quotation marks and are indented ten spaces from the left margin.

     > In the section of the text on quotation marks, the authors make the following observation:
     >
     > > Use quotation marks to indicate material taken word for word from another source; to mark the title of a poem, song, short story, essay, and any part of a longer work; and to point out words used in a special sense—words set apart for emphasis and special consideration, slang and colloquial expressions, derisively used words.

  2. *Periods and commas.* Periods and commas at the end of quotations always go inside the quotation marks.

     "The city will be in serious financial trouble if the city income tax does not pass," said the mayor.

     The film was widely considered pornographic although to describe it, the producer used the word "art."

  3. *Other punctuation.* An exclamation point or question mark goes inside the quotation marks if it is part of the quotation. If it is part of a longer statement, it goes outside the quotation marks.

     The student asked, "Is this paper due Friday?"

     Did Robert Frost write "Mending Wall"?

     A colon or a semicolon always goes outside the quotation mark.

The text says, "A colon or a semicolon always goes outside the quotation marks"; this rule is simple.

■ *Titles.* Use quotation marks to indicate the title of a work—a poem, a song, a short story, a chapter, an essay—that is part of a larger whole, or a short unit in itself.

John Collier wrote the short story "The Chaser."

The chapter is called "Stylistic Problems and Their Solutions."

■ *Words used in a special sense.* Quotation marks are sometimes put around words used in a special sense, but these quotation marks are often overused. Pay close attention to the cautionary statements that accompany the following examples.

1. *Words used as words.*

   I can never tell the difference between "affect" and "effect."

   "Really" and "very" are frequently overused words.

   Underlining or italicizing is usually preferable to quotation marks in sentences of this kind. (See *Italics.*)

2. *Words used as slang and colloquial expressions.*

   The speaker gave me good "vibes."

   I wonder what's on the "tube."

   This usage is almost always undesirable. (See Chapter 24, pages 574–575.)

3. *Words used derisively.* The use of quotation marks to indicate sarcasm or derision is generally a primitive means of showing feelings and, as a rule, should be avoided:

   The "performance" was a collection of amateurish blunders.

   This "dormitory" is unfit for human habitation.

EXERCISE Add quotation marks (or italics: See pages 626–627) as needed in the following sentences. In some cases you will need to add capitals and commas as well.

1. Coach Sharif reminded us I expect all of my players to remain prepared and flexible, including those of you who may be on the bench.
2. Did you read The Da Vinci Code?
3. Though he hasn't repaid the $50 he borrowed, using the word crook to describe him is much too harsh.
4. The teacher reminded her kindergarten class, don't forget that Officer Torres said, Always hold a grown-up's hand when you cross the street.
5. We'll never forget the cheers of joy when Professor Kwan said, Tomorrow's test is cancelled.

6. Eric Carle's The Very Hungry Caterpillar is a longtime favorite storybook for many children.

7. The more my neighbor referred to her party as her soireé, the less I wanted to attend it.

8. Jermaine wondered why the map didn't show the fork in the road that he had just reached.

9. A Midsummer Night's Dream is Shakespeare's most hilarious comedy.

10. The Secretary of Labor said learning about safety may be the most important lesson of a teen's summer job.

SELF TEST: Quotation Marks

Insert quotation marks and make any necessary changes in punctuation and capitalization in the following sentences.

1. Our local children's theater group is doing a choral reading of The Raven by Edgar Allan Poe.

2. I'm sure the referee said strike, Ginger insisted.

3. How many times a day do you think your mother said in a minute when you were a child?

4. I'm out of the Olympics, the disappointed skater announced after her third foot injury.

5. My friend urged me to read a pamphlet called Your Guide Through Life's Financial Decisions.

6. The student asked anxiously will we have some time to review the material before the exam?

7. Kids should work very hard during the year and then have a break for time with their parents and activities like camps and jobs the former Education Secretary stated.

8. The command of algebraic skills wrote Professor Small gives students confidence when attacking difficult problems.

9. Spider venom is a gold mine of pharmacological tools, the neuroscientist explained.

10. Have you chosen a running mate the reporters asked the presidential candidate.

ro/fs

Run-on sentence.   A *run-on sentence* or *fused sentence* is two or more sentences written as one, with no punctuation between them. It is most commonly corrected by rewriting the run-on sentence as separate sentences, by placing a semicolon between the sentences, or by placing a comma and a coordinating conjunction between the sentences. A comma alone would create a comma splice, often considered a special kind of run-on sentence. (See *Comma splice*.)

Incorrect	Correct
This rule sounds easy enough putting it into practice is not so easy.	This rule sounds easy enough. Putting it into practice is not so easy.
	or
	This rule sounds easy enough; putting it into practice is not so easy.
	or
	This rule sounds easy enough, but putting it into practice is not so easy.

EXERCISE Correct the following run-on sentences by using a comma and a coordinating conjunction (*and, but, or, nor, for, yet, so*), a semicolon, or a period.

1. The music of Queen is still popular I didn't realize that the group boasts the longest running fan club in history.
2. It is possible to "zap" almost anything in a microwave, however roasts still require conventional cooking.
3. The fear of being buried alive is universal the fear may first have been expressed in writing by Poe.
4. Make sure you separate sentences with a conjunction, a semicolon, or a period never just run them together.
5. Drunk drivers are dangerous they killed thousands of people last year.
6. Many houses have hidden defects for example, the plumbing may be bad.
7. Medical literature lists more than three hundred causes for hiccups so-called everyday hiccups can result from inhaling too much air, eating spicy foods, and drinking too rapidly, among other causes.
8. It's all very well to say that we need new carpeting it's just that we don't have the funds.
9. Your new sweater is lovely I think that the color is perfect.
10. Waking early has never agreed with me it leaves me sulky and disagreeable.
11. A knowledge of classical mythology is a valuable part of anyone's educational background it can not only add a spark to one's own writing but can enable one to get more out of one's reading.
12. I don't know how anyone can possibly dislike chocolate it's my favorite food.
13. My sister can't sit still for more than a few minutes she can barely sit through her favorite sitcom she certainly can't concentrate on a novel.
14. They boarded the airplane with a sense of fear and trepidation then they noticed the pilot was reading an instruction book.
15. Spinach is the best vegetable Popeye claimed it gave him his incredible strength.

SELF TEST: Run-On Sentences

Insert the appropriate punctuation to correct the following run-on sentences.

1. Hundreds of bicyclists will participate in an exciting event this Sunday it is the county's fourth annual Mountain Bike Festival cyclists begin and end at the county park in Kent.

2. My aunt has a recipe for delicious chocolate chip cookies however she guards a secret ingredient it is oatmeal.

3. The candidate is considering very carefully his pick for vice president a crucial consideration is to find a reliable team player.

4. This dorm room is tiny how can anyone expect two people to live here?

5. Many of America's river communities face a common challenge soon they must balance the search for prosperity with the need to preserve their natural resources.

6. Darryl walked the dog then he fed her.

7. I love to go to the movies I often like the popcorn better than the films.

8. Immigrants continue to make our country great they take many jobs that businesses cannot fill.

9. I saw *No Country for Old Men* it was bloodier than I had thought.

10. Phish began to play suddenly the audience jumped up and cheered.

Semicolon.   Use a semicolon between two independent clauses when the coordinating conjunction has been left out and between separate elements in a list or series when the elements contain punctuation within themselves.

- *Between independent clauses.*

    Stating the problem is simple enough; solving it is the tough part.

    Roberta wasn't precisely sure what the bearded stranger wanted; all she knew was that he made her nervous.

    Observe that in both of these cases a coordinating conjunction preceded by a comma could be used to replace the semicolon. Under no circumstances could a comma alone be used between these independent clauses. In order to use a comma, you must also have a coordinating conjunction (*and, but, or, nor, for, yet, so*) between independent clauses. (See *Comma splice.*)

- *Between separate elements that contain commas in a list or series.*

    The following American cities have grown enormously in recent years: Houston, Texas; Dallas, Texas; Phoenix, Arizona; and Denver, Colorado.

Sentence.   A group of words beginning with a capital letter and ending with a period, question mark, or exclamation point that contains at least one independent clause.

Birds sing.

Do birds sing?

Shut up, all you birds!

(See *Clause; Predicate; Subject*.)

Shifts in time and person.   Do not unnecessarily shift from one tense to another (past to present, present to future, and so on) or from one person to another (*he* to *you, one* to *I*).

shift

■ *Tense shifts*. If you begin writing in a particular tense, do not shift to another
unless a change in time is logically necessary. The following paragraph
breaks this rule:

> In William Carlos Williams's "The Use of Force," a doctor *was called* to examine a
> young girl. The doctor *was concerned* about diphtheria and *needs* to examine the
> girl's throat. The girl *is* terrified and *begins* to resist. As her resistance *continues*, the
> doctor *is compelled* to use more and more physical force. Though he *knows* the force
> *is* necessary, the doctor, to his horror, *found* that he *enjoyed* it and really *wanted* to
> hurt the girl.

Here the writer starts in the past tense (*was called, was concerned*), shifts to the
present tense (*needs, is, begins, continues, is compelled, knows, is*), and then
shifts back to the past tense (*found, enjoyed, wanted*). Why? There is no reason.
No change in time is needed. If writers view the events of a story as happening in the present, they should use the present tense consistently. Writers
could also view the events as past actions—over and completed—and write
entirely in the past tense. In either case, writers should decide which view
they prefer and stick to it throughout.

All verbs in present tense

In William Carlos Williams's "The
Use of Force," a doctor *is called* to
examine a young girl. The doctor *is
concerned* about diphtheria and *needs*
to examine the girl's throat. The girl *is*
terrified and *begins* to resist. As her
resistance *continues*, the doctor *is
compelled* to use more and more
physical force. Though he *knows* the
force *is* necessary, the doctor, to his
horror, *finds* that he *enjoys* it and really
wants to hurt the girl.

All verbs in past tense

In William Carlos Williams's "The Use of
Force," a doctor *was called* to examine a
young girl. The doctor *was concerned*
about diphtheria and *needed* to examine
the girl's throat. The girl *was* terrified
and *began* to resist. As her resistance
continued, the doctor *was compelled*
to use more and more physical force.
Though he *knew* the force was necessary,
the doctor, to his horror, *found* that he
enjoyed it and really *wanted* to hurt
the girl.

■ *Shifts in person*. Write from a consistent point of view, making sure that any
change in person is logically justified. If, for example, you begin expressing
your thoughts in the third person (*he, she, it, they, one, the reader, the student,
people*, and so on), avoid sudden shifts to the first person (*I, we*) or to the

second person (*you*). Similarly, avoid sudden shifts from third- or first-person singular to third- or first-person plural.

Poor	**Improved**
Most *average citizens* think *they* are in favor of a clean environment, but *you* may change *your* mind when *you* find out what it will cost. (Shift from third person *average citizens* and *they* to second person *you, your*.)	Most *average citizens* think *they* are in favor of a clean environment, but *they* may change *their* minds when *they* find out what it will cost.
The teenager resents the way *he* is being stereotyped. *We're* as different among *ourselves* as any other group in the population. *They* are tired of being viewed as a collection of finger-snapping freaks who say "cool" all the time. (Shift from third-person singular *teenager* and *he* to first-person plural *we* to third-person plural *they*.)	*Teenagers* resent the way *they* are being stereotyped. *They* are as different among *themselves* as any other group in the population. *They* are tired of being viewed as a collection of finger-snapping freaks who say "cool" all the time.
Readers will find this suspense-filled mystery irresistible, just as *they* have found P. D. James's previous efforts. *You* should have a real battle keeping *yourself* from looking ahead to the last page. (Shift from third-person *readers* and *they* to second-person *you, yourself*.)	*Readers* will find this suspense-filled mystery irresistible, just as *they* have found P. D. James's previous efforts. *They* should have a real battle keeping *themselves* from looking ahead to the last page.
One wonders what is going on at City Hall. *We* have put up with flooded basements and lame excuses long enough. (Shift from third-person *one* to first-person *we*.)	*We* wonder what is going on at City Hall. *We* have put up with flooded basements and lame excuses long enough.

EXERCISE Correct any illogical shifts in tense or person in the following sentences.

1. You can never tell when one needs a friend's help.
2. Chapter 1 introduces us to a scientist who is devoted to making the world a safer place. In Chapter 2, the scientist turned into a werewolf.
3. Teenage parents get the worst of both worlds. We didn't have the temperament or finances for adulthood, and we had too many responsibilities to enjoy what remained of our youth.
4. The two thugs drive up to the door of the diner. They walk in, sit down, and pick up a menu. They look at Nick coldly. "What's the name of this dump?" they asked.

5. You need to be careful about shopping at discount stores. First, a person needs to check the quality as well as the price. Even cheap is too expensive if your purchase self-destructs after a few days.

6. Many of John Grisham's books involve a lawyer who became disillusioned with the judicial system or who is forced to give up a position as an attorney.

7. The snow is falling, and we were getting ready for another winter.

8. The company is going to introduce its new line of luxury cars this weekend. We decided two years ago that we would have to be represented at the high end of the market to stay fully competitive.

9. A person who is contemplating buying a new washing machine must take into account your types of clothing and your washing habits.

10. Finding a one hundred dollar bill in the park was a problem. My girlfriend wants to give it to charity. I wanted to turn it in to the ranger.

SELF TEST: Shifts in Person or Tense

Change any inappropriate shifts in tense or person in the following sentences.

1. Switching tenses was a big problem. It is not an easy habit to break.

2. Mark Twain said, "Be good, and you will be lonesome." He also says that the reports of his death are greatly exaggerated.

3. Thousands of registered voters forget to cast their votes at election time. You should be proud of your voice and proud to use it.

4. Verb tenses make me tense. They made my best friend cranky, too.

5. My pen is running out of ink, and I will get another when the ink was completely gone.

6. Contact lenses are less convenient than glasses, but many people thought that contacts were more attractive.

7. Karin crept softly up the stairs, and then she peers around the corner to see if the coast is clear.

8. The tennis champion raced across the court and, with a desperate sweep of his outstretched racket, he slams the ball out of his opponent's reach.

9. One has no choice but to square your shoulders and clean the oven.

10. Learning to write well takes time and practice and took lots of hard work.

Spelling.   Poor spelling can seriously damage an otherwise fine paper. Faced with any significant number of spelling errors, readers cannot maintain their original confidence in the writer's thoughtfulness and skill.

    The one spelling rule every writer needs to know is very simple: *Use a dictionary.* Rules for spelling specific words and groups of words almost always have exceptions and are difficult to learn and remember. Good spellers, almost without excep-

sp

tion, turn out to be people who read a great deal and who have the dictionary habit, not people who have memorized spelling rules. The most important spelling rule, then, as well as the quickest and easiest one, is use the dictionary.

Yet, it can sometimes be handy to have available a list of frequently misspelled words. For quick reference, we include such a list. Note that words spelled the same as parts of longer words are not usually listed separately: for example, the list has *accidentally* but not *accident*, *acquaintance* but not *acquaint*.

Frequently misspelled words

absence	arithmetic	commission	disastrous
accidentally	ascend	committee	discipline
accommodate	athletic	comparative	dissatisfied
accumulate	attendance	compelled	dormitory
achievement	balance	conceivable	effect
acquaintance	batallion	conferred	eighth
acquire	beginning	conscience*	eligible
acquitted	belief	conscientious*	eliminate
advice*	believe	conscious*	embarrass
advise*	beneficial	control	eminent
all right	benefited	controversial	encouragement
amateur	boundaries	controversy	encouraging
among	Britain	criticize	environment
analysis	business	deferred	equipped
analyze	calendar	definitely	especially
annual	candidate	definition	exaggerate
apartment	category	describe	excellence
apparatus	cemetery	description	exhilarate
apparent	changeable	desperate	existence
appearance	changing	dictionary	existent
arctic	choose	dining	experience
arguing	chose	disappearance	explanation
argument	coming	disappoint	familiar

*See the Glossary.

fascinate	laboratory	particular	prophecy (noun)
February	laid	pastime	prophesy (verb)
fiery	led	performance	pursue
foreign	lightning	permissible	quantity
formerly	loneliness	perseverance	quiet*
forty	lose	personal*	quite*
fourth	losing	personnel*	quizzes
frantically	maintenance	perspiration	recede
generally	maneuver	physical	receive
government	manufacture	picnicking	receiving
grammar	marriage	possession	recommend
grandeur	mathematics	possibility	reference
grievous	maybe	possible	referring
height	mere	practically	repetition
heroes	miniature	precede*	restaurant
hindrance	mischievous	precedence	rhythm
hoping	mysterious	preference	ridiculous
humorous	necessary	preferred	sacrifice
hypocrisy	ninety	prejudice	sacrilegious
hypocrite	noticeable	preparation	salary
immediately	occasionally	prevalent	schedule
incidentally	occurred	principal*	seize
incredible	occurrence	principle*	sense
independence	omitted	privilege	separate
inevitable	opinion	probably	separation
intellectual	opportunity	procedure	sergeant
intelligence	optimistic	proceed*	severely
interesting	paid	profession	shining
irresistible	parallel	professor	siege
judgment	paralysis	prominent	similar
knowledge	paralyze	pronunciation	sophomore

*See the Glossary.

Frequently misspelled words   (continued)

specifically	surprise	tragedy	usually
specimen	technique	transferring	village
stationary*	temperamental	tries	villain
stationery*	tendency	truly	weather
statue	than, then*	tyranny	weird
studying	their, they're, there*	unanimous	whether
succeed	thorough	undoubtedly	whether
succession	through	unnecessary	woman, women
supersede	to, too, two*	until	writing

*See the Glossary.

EXERCISE   Correct the misspelled words in the following sentences. Numbers in parentheses indicate the number of incorrectly spelled words.

1. In February he generaly feels disatisfied with the whether. (3)
2. When you are referring to the commission on attendance, don't exagerate their excellence. (1)
3. You can succeed at writting if you persue your goal to elemente grammar errors. (3)
4. Ocasionally a beleif can controll your existance and sieze your good sense. (5)
5. I usualy recomend that you truely seperate the salery issue from the more intresting challanges you will face by working in a foreign country. (7)

SELF TEST: Spelling

Find the incorrectly spelled word in each of the following groups.

1. atheletic	advice	too	quantity	statue
2. marriage	opinion	village	lose	buisiness
3. wisdom	prefered	belief	surprise	convince
4. fortunate	friend	ocurred	distance	again
5. minute	opposite	interruption	sargeant	people
6. offended	assured	exellent	neither	encouragement
7. reccommend	coming	height	villain	beyond
8. maybe	niece	breakfast	ambulance	fourty

9. cemetery	jewlery	among	losing	succeed
10. president	balance	recede	tries	arguement

Subject.   A word, phrase, or clause that names the person, place, thing, or idea that the sentence is about. (See also *Predicate*.)

Sal went home.

The president's *speech* was heard by 100,000 people.

Subject–verb agreement.   A verb must agree with its subject in number and person. This rule has most practical meaning only in the present tense; in other tenses, the verb forms generally remain the same regardless of number or person. (The exception is in the past tense of *to be*; in that instance the verb forms do change: *I was, you were, he was, we were, they were.*)

In the present tense, the third-person singular verb usually differs from the others—most often because an *-s* or *-es* is added to the verb stem. A third-person singular verb is the verb that goes with the pronouns *he, she*, and *it* and with any singular noun.

to dream

	Singular	**Plural**
First person	I dream	we dream
Second person	you dream	you dream
Third person	he $\left.\begin{array}{l}\text{he}\\\text{she}\\\text{it}\end{array}\right\}$ dreams	they dream

The lovers *dream* of a long and happy future together.

The lover *dreams* of his sweetheart every night.

People often *dream* about falling from great heights.

Jennifer *dreams* about being buried alive.

to miss

	Singular	**Plural**
First person	I miss	we miss
Second person	you miss	you miss
Third person	$\left.\begin{array}{l}\text{he}\\\text{she}\\\text{it}\end{array}\right\}$ misses	they miss

The children *miss* their father more than they thought they would.

The child *misses* her friends.

The commuters *miss* the bus almost every morning.

The left fielder *misses* more than his share of easy fly balls.

Even with highly irregular verbs, the third-person singular in the present tense takes a special form (always with an *-s* at the end).

to be

	Singular	**Plural**
First person	I am	we are
Second person	you are	you are
Third person	he she } is it	they are

to have

	Singular	**Plural**
First person	I have	we have
Second person	you have	you have
Third person	he she } has it	they have

The clowns *are* happy.

Erica *is* sad.

The Joneses *have* a lovely new home.

Mr. Jones *has* a lot to learn.

The few cases in which a present tense verb in the third-person singular has the same form as in the other persons come naturally to almost every writer and speaker: *he can, he may, he might,* and so on.

Once a writer realizes the difference between third-person singular and other verb forms, the only problem is likely to be deciding which form to use in a few tricky situations.

- *Compound subjects.* If the subject is compound (joined by *and*), the verb is plural unless the two words function as a single unit—"Pork and beans *is* an easy dish to prepare," for example—or unless the two words refer to a single person, as in "My cook and bottle washer *has* left me" (one person performed both jobs).

Wrong	**Right**
Writing and reading *is* necessary for success in college.	Writing and reading *are* necessary for success in college.
The introduction and conclusion *does* not appear in an outline.	The introduction and conclusion *do* not appear in an outline.

- *Neither . . . nor, either . . . or, nor, or.* If two subjects are joined by any of these terms, the verb agrees with the closer subject.

Wrong	**Right**
Neither the students nor the teacher *are* correct.	Neither the students nor the teacher *is* correct.
Either the supporting details or the thesis statement *are* wrong.	Either the supporting details or the thesis statement *is* wrong.
Snowstorms or rain *cause* accidents.	Snowstorms or rain *causes* accidents.
Rain or snowstorms *causes* accidents.	Rain or snowstorms *cause* accidents.

- *Time, money, weight.* Words that state an amount (time, money, weight) have a singular verb when they are considered as a unit even if they are plural in form.

Wrong	**Right**
Two semesters *are* really a short time.	Two semesters *is* really a short time.
Five dollars *are* a modest fee for credit by examination.	Five dollars *is* a modest fee for credit by examination.
Five kilos of soybeans *are* about eleven pounds.	Five kilos of soybeans *is* about eleven pounds.

- *Titles.* Titles of songs, plays, movies, novels, or articles always have singular verbs, even if the titles are plural in form.

Wrong	**Right**
The Wings of the Dove were made into a movie.	*The Wings of the Dove was* made into a movie.
"The Novels of Early America" *were* published in *American Literature*.	"The Novels of Early America" *was* published in *American Literature*.

- *Collective nouns.* Collective nouns such as *family, audience, jury*, and *class* have singular verbs when they are considered as a unified group. If the individuals within the unit act separately, the verb will be plural.

Wrong	**Right**
The family *plan* a vacation.	The family *plans* a vacation.
The jury *is* divided on the verdict.	The jury *are* divided on the verdict.

The audience *are* going to give this show a standing ovation.

The audience *is* going to give this show a standing ovation.

The audience *is* divided in their opinion of the show.

The audience *are* divided in their opinion of the show.

- *Indefinite pronouns*. Indefinite pronouns such as *one, no one, someone, everyone, none, anyone, somebody, anybody, everybody, each, neither,* and *either* take singular verbs:

Wrong	**Right**
None of the ideas *are* correct.	None of the ideas *is* correct.
Each of the students *have* the time to study.	Each of the students *has* the time to study.
Either *are* a valid choice.	Either *is* a valid choice.

- *Intervening elements*. No matter how many words, phrases, or clauses separate a subject from its verb, the verb must still agree with the subject in number.

1. Separated by words:

   Wrong: Many state capitals—Carson City, Augusta, Jefferson City, Olympia—*is* only small towns.

   Right: Many state capitals—Carson City, Augusta, Jefferson City, Olympia—*are* only small towns.

   Here the plural *capitals*, not the singular *Olympia*, is the subject.

2. Separated by phrases:

   Wrong: A crate of oranges *are* expensive.

   Right: A crate of oranges *is* expensive.

   Here *crate*, not *oranges*, is the subject.

   Wrong: Agreement of subjects with their verbs *are* important.

   Right: Agreement of subjects with their verbs *is* important.

   Here *agreement*, not *subjects* or *verbs*, is the subject.

3. Separated by clauses:

   Wrong: Reading well, which is one of the necessary academic skills, *make* studying easier.

   Right: Reading well, which is one of the necessary academic skills, *makes* studying easier.

Here *reading*, not *skills*, is the subject.

- *Reversed position.* If the subject comes after the verb, the verb must still agree with the subject.

  1. *There.* If a sentence begins with *there* and is followed by some form of *to be* (*is, are, was, were,* etc.), the number of *be* is determined by the subject. *There* is never the subject (except in a sentence like this one).

     Wrong: There *is* five students in this class.

     Right: There *are* five students in this class.

     Here *students* is the subject, and it is plural. Therefore, the verb must be plural.

  2. *Prepositional phrases.* Sometimes a writer begins a sentence with a prepositional phrase followed by a verb and then the subject. The verb must still agree with the subject.

     Wrong: Throughout a grammar book *appears* many helpful writing hints.

     Right: Throughout a grammar book *appear* many helpful writing hints.

     Here *hints*, not *book,* is the subject.

EXERCISES   Correct any subject–verb agreement errors in the following sentences. Some sentences are correct.

1. Every pair of glasses Rosa owns are scratched.
2. The twists and turns of international espionage are the main themes of the novels of Alan Durst.
3. My school, as well as hundreds of others all over the country, are trying to tighten academic standards.
4. Disagreement among highly trained economists about budgetary deficits of hundreds of millions of dollars are causing the public to become more confused every day.
5. Neither John nor Esteban have enough money to buy textbooks.
6. Peeling all of those nasty carrots are making me sick.
7. Each of the celebrities' houses are more extravagant than the next.
8. Federal judges and the president constitute the judicial and executive branches of government.
9. The heavenly fragrance of the roses and gardenias were my reward for having coaxed them into bloom.
10. Although I can't see the bells, their clanging and chiming rouses me from my idle daydreams.

EXERCISE Find and correct any subject–verb agreement errors in the following paragraphs.

1. Lobsters are great for a special dinner, but you have to work for what you eat. You'll need to crack the claws of your lobster with a pair of nut-crackers, which are the only tool for the task. Once the claws are cracked, you can pull out the meat with a nutpick. After consuming the claws, you will want to attack the tail, the smaller legs, and the actual body of the lobster. Proper consumption requires experience gained only through years of practice. So, if you're a first-timer, bring a veteran along for guidance.

2. Balancing checkbooks aren't really very difficult. Problems arise only because of carelessness or inattention. Forgetting to note the amount and number of each check that has been written, neglecting to write down automatic teller transactions, and assuming that bank statements are always correct are major causes of checkbook imbalances. All that are required for balanced checkbooks is attention. Pay attention to every transaction, and write everything down immediately. Assuming that things can be taken care of later will result in checkbook chaos.

3. In fairy tales, the beautiful princess was always locked up in some high stone tower. She didn't do much. She didn't say much. She just waited to be rescued. I want to know why the princesses never bothered to try to escape. Were they too stupid? Were they too weak? I bet that half of the tower doors were left unlocked, and that those two dragons guarding the gate was no more than baby dragons. Any princess worth her salt would have tried to escape. Why didn't a single one even consider it?

SELF TEST: Subject–Verb Agreement

Correct the errors in subject–verb agreement in the following sentences.

1. Neither the train nor the bus are air conditioned.
2. There is many ways to catch fish.
3. A meal of rice and beans are quite nutritious.
4. Each of the game show contestants are required to answer twelve questions correctly.
5. The winning team plan to celebrate its victory at the local pizza parlor.
6. *The Savages* are winning prizes for its star Philip Seymour Hoffman.
7. Three days were too long for me to be apart from my daughters.
8. Seven dollars are all you spent on your date?
9. Every family in those apartment buildings are living in squalor.
10. None of the wildfires are showing any sign of abating.

Subjunctive mood. Once far more common in English than it is now, the subjunctive mood is still sometimes used to express "conditions contrary to fact"—hypothetical conditions, conditions not yet brought about, suppositional ideas, and the like. In the subjunctive, the verb form is usually plural even though the subject is singular.

She wished she *were* here.

If I *were* you, I would turn down the latest offer.

I move that the chairperson *declare* the meeting adjourned.

He looked as if he *were* going to be sick.

Subordinating conjunctions.   See *Fragmentary sentences*.

Subordination.   The most important idea in a sentence should be in an independent clause. Lesser ideas, explanations, qualifying material, and illustrations should be in subordinate clauses or phrases. (See also Chapter 23, pages 563–564.)

sub

Poor	Improved
John is a wonderful person. He is very shy. He is extremely kind to everybody.	Although very shy, John is a wonderful person who is extremely kind to everybody. (The main idea is that John is a wonderful person.)
	or
	Although he is a wonderful person who is extremely kind to everybody, John is very shy. (The main idea is that John is very shy.)
Professor Jones is terribly sarcastic. He is also a tough grader. It is true that he knows his subject. Most students dislike him, however.	Despite Professor Jones's knowledge of his subject, most students dislike him because of his terrible sarcasm and tough grading.
I am going to start on my new job, and I am very optimistic.	I am very optimistic about starting on my new job.

Superlative forms.   See *Comparative and superlative forms*.

Tense shifts.   See *Shifts in time and person*.

Titles, punctuation of.   See *Italics; Quotation marks*.

Transitive verb.   See *Verb*.

Underlining.   See *Italics*.

Verb.   A word that expresses an action, an occurrence, or a state of being. Verbs may be divided into three classes: *transitive verbs*, which require objects to complete their meaning (Mary *admires* him); *intransitive verbs*, which are com-

vb

plete in themselves (John *trembled*); and *linking verbs*, which join a subject to its complement (Phyllis *is* a beauty; Their actions *were* cowardly).

In sentences, a complete verb often consists of a *main verb* (marked in grammatical abbreviation as MV) and a *helping verb* (HV). Sometimes a complete verb is a single-word verb. Helping verbs, or auxiliaries, work along with principal parts or other verb forms (like present participles, the *-ing* form of a verb) to express appropriate action.

Helping Verbs

be	are	does	**might**	**should**
being	was	has	**must**	**will**
been	were	have	**can**	**would**
is	do	had	**could**	
am	did	**may**	**shall**	

The nine helping verbs in boldface print—*must, may, can, shall, will, might, could, would*, and *should*—constitute an important subgroup of helping verbs, called modals. Modals tell what the writer believes about the action and express probability, ability, or need or obligation. (She *may drive* the motorcycle; She *can drive* the motorcycle; She *must drive* the motorcycle.)

Verbs: principal parts. The form of most verbs changes according to which tense is being used, and to get the correct form a writer needs to know the principal parts of each verb. There are generally considered to be three principal parts: the *stem* or *infinitive* (the stem is the present tense form of the verb, and the infinitive is the stem preceded by *to*), the *past tense*, and the *past participle*. The past participle is the form used with helping verbs in perfect tenses (*I have seen, I had seen, I will have seen*) and in the passive voice (*I am seen, I was seen, I will be seen, I have been seen*), and in modal verb structures (*I can see, I should see, I may see*).

The principal parts of *regular verbs* are formed by adding *-ed* or *-d* to the stem: *rush, rushed, rushed; love, loved, loved; drag, dragged, dragged*. The past tense and past participle of regular verbs are always the same.

The principal parts of *irregular verbs* need to be learned separately—and even for the most experienced writer sometimes require checking in a dictionary or handbook. For quick reference, here is an alphabetical list of the principal parts of the most common irregular verbs.

Stem	Past tense	Past participle
arise	arose	arisen
be	was	been
bear	bore	borne, born
begin	began	begun

bind	bound	bound
blow	blew	blown
break	broke	broken
bring	brought	brought
burst	burst	burst
buy	bought	bought
catch	caught	caught
choose	chose	chosen
come	came	come
creep	crept	crept
deal	dealt	dealt
dig	dug	dug
dive	dived, dove	dived
do	did	done
draw	drew	drawn
drink	drank	drunk
drive	drove	driven
eat	ate	eaten
fall	fell	fallen
flee	fled	fled
fly	flew	flown
forbid	forbad, forbade	forbidden
freeze	froze	frozen
give	gave	given
go	went	gone
grow	grew	grown
hang	hung	hung
hang (execute)	hanged	hanged
know	knew	known
lay	laid	laid
lead	led	led
lend	lent	lent

lie	lay	lain
lose	lost	lost
mean	meant	meant
ride	rode	ridden
ring	rang	rung
rise	rose	risen
run	ran	run
see	saw	seen
seek	sought	sought
send	sent	sent
shake	shook	shaken
shine	shone, shined	shone, shined
shrink	shrank	shrunk
sing	sang	sung
sink	sank, sunk	sunk
sleep	slept	slept
sneak	sneaked	sneaked
speak	spoke	spoken
spin	spun	spun
spit	spat	spat
spread	spread	spread
steal	stole	stolen
stink	stank	stunk
swear	swore	sworn
swim	swam	swum
swing	swung	swung
take	took	taken
teach	taught	taught
tear	tore	torn
thrive	thrived, throve	thrived, thriven
throw	threw	thrown
wear	wore	worn

| weep | wept | wept |
| write | wrote | written |

Confusion of the past tense and past participle of irregular verbs is a frequent cause of writing errors. Remember that the past participle is the correct form after *has*, *have*, and *had*.

Wrong	**Right**
The mountaineers *had froze* to death.	The mountaineers *had frozen* to death.
The sprinter *has* just *broke* another track record.	The sprinter *has* just *broken* another track record.
I *begun* the book yesterday.	I *began* the book yesterday.
We *seen* that movie when it first came out.	We *saw* that movie when it first came out.

EXERCISE Correct any errors in verb form in the following sentences.

1. The police finally apprehended Gus. He had stole his last Ferrari.
2. They flown nonstop around the world. Now they begun nonstop appearances on television.
3. I have wrote on this painful subject before, but your negligence has drove me to distraction.
4. The phone must have rang thirty times last night.
5. I have swore on the altar of the gods to do my duty even unto death.
6. Yesterday Priscilla swum thirty laps. Her recovery seems complete.
7. The eagle flown away over the tall pines.
8. The quarterback had threw the ball at least fifty yards down the field.
9. The wide receiver had blew another great opportunity and snuck away before the crowds attacked him.
10. My mother insisted that she had wore that winter coat for the last time.

EXERCISE Find and correct any errors in verb form in the following paragraphs.

1. Ella loved watching her older sisters get ready to go out at night. It was always fun to watch women who were working all day transform themselves into beautiful butterflies. They were so quick to change, too! Off came the dingy work clothes and the everyday shoes and socks, and on went the delicate dresses, tiny dance slippers, and silky stockings. Suddenly, her sisters weren't the people she fighted with over the telephone and the bathroom. They were beautiful, elegant, sweet-smelling strangers.
2. Every once in a while, monks who worked on transcribing manuscripts couldn't resist adding their own words to the books they were copying.

Because transcribing was hard, dull, and tiring work, the words the monks added were often words of complaint. Scribbled in the margins of some old books are messages praying that the work day would end soon, or saying that the monks would have froze to death without a miracle. Sometimes these marginal notes are more interesting than the books that hold them. The notes are a window into the monks' lives and a way for modern readers to personalize the Middle Ages.

3. It was a creepy kind of night. The wind blown fiercely through the streets. We shivered in our flimsy Halloween costumes. We weren't scared, of course. We were too old to be scared. If we walked a little more quickly and clung more closely than usual, it was for warmth, not protection. The moon shined down from behind the clouds. It gave a softened light. We admired it, picked up our candy bags, and continued down the block.

SELF TEST: Verb Form

Correct any verb form errors in the following sentences. Some sentences are correct.

1. Angela would've went to the park if she hadn't arose feeling sick.
2. They couldn't possibly have stole that much money.
3. The whale had spat Jonah out onto dry land.
4. Sharon swore she had lain the photographs on the table.
5. Joe had drank too much and felt ill for the rest of the night.
6. Honey, I shrunk the kids!
7. The movie *The Ox-Bow Incident* is about a group of men who have hung three innocent people.
8. I fell in love, and it seemed the sun shined brighter than before.
9. J. C. swum until her fingers begun to wrinkle from the water.
10. Alice had fell down the rabbit hole for a long time before she began to worry.

Verbs: tenses. What is the difference between *I eat* and *I am eating*? What is the difference between *I passed* and *I have passed*? Most verbs can be expressed in any tense, and the many different tenses enable the writer to present fine shades of meaning with great accuracy.

There are six tenses. Most verbs can take either the *active voice* or the *passive voice* in any tense (see pages 668–669). To make matters even more varied, *progressive constructions* can be used for all tenses of active verbs and some tenses of passive verbs.

to save

Tenses	Active voice	Progressive
Present	I save	I am saving
Past	I saved	I was saving

Future	I will (*or* shall) save	I will be saving
Present perfect	I have saved	I have been saving
Past perfect	I had saved	I had been saving
Future perfect	I will (*or* shall) have saved	I will have been saving

Passive voice

Present	I am saved	I am being saved
Past	I was saved	I was being saved
Future	I will (*or* shall) be saved	
Present perfect	I have been saved	
Past perfect	I had been saved	
Future perfect	I will (*or* shall) have been saved	

to drive

Tenses	Active voice	Progressive
Present	I drive	I am driving
Past	I drove	I was driving
Future	I will drive	I will be driving
Present perfect	I have driven	I have been driving
Past perfect	I had driven	I had been driving
Future perfect	I will have driven	I will have been driving

Passive voice

Present	I am driven	I am being driven
Past	I was driven	I was being driven
Future	I will be driven	
Present perfect	I have been driven	
Past perfect	I had been driven	
Future perfect	I will have been driven	

A. *Present tense.* The present tense indicates present action, of course, especially continuing or habitual action:

I *save* ten dollars every week.

I *eat* a good breakfast each morning.

She *drives* carefully.

The present is also used to express permanent facts and general truths, and is usually the preferred tense for discussing literary actions:

The speed of light *is* faster than the speed of sound.

Truth *is* stranger than fiction.

In *The Great Gatsby*, all the events *take* place during the 1920s.

Nick Carraway *is* the only character in the novel who *understands* Gatsby.

The present can even be called upon to deal with future action.

Tomorrow she *drives* to the convention.

The *present progressive* indicates actions occurring—actions "in progress"—at the specific instant referred to.

I *am eating* a good breakfast, and I do not want to be interrupted.

She *is driving* too fast for these icy roads.

The same principle of action in progress at the time applies to all progressive tenses:

Past Progressive:	The criminal *was shaving* when the police arrested him.
Future Progressive:	At this time next week, I *will be surfing* in Hawaii.

B. *Past tense.* The past tense describes previous actions, generally actions over and done with:

The lifeguard *saved* two children last week.

She *drove* to Florida three years ago.

C. *Future tense.* The future tense describes actions after the present:

From now on, I *will save* fifteen dollars every week.

Marlene says that her in-laws *will drive* her to drink.

D. *Present perfect tense.* The present perfect tense (*have* or *has* plus the past participle) refers to past actions, generally of the fairly recent past, that still go on or have bearing on the present:

I *have saved* over one thousand dollars so far.

She *has driven* this short route to work many times.

The preceding sentences expressed in the simple past would suggest different meanings. "I saved over one thousand dollars" would suggest that the saving has now stopped. "She drove this short route to work many times" would suggest that some other route is now being used.

E. *Past perfect tense.* The past perfect tense (*had* plus the past participle) is employed for actions previous to the simple past—"more past than past."

The lifeguard saved two children last week and *had saved* three adults the week before.

She *had driven* to Florida three years ago, so she felt quite confident about making the trip again.

F. *Future perfect tense.* The future perfect tense (*will have* or *shall have* plus the past participle) expresses action that will be completed before some future time:

By this time next year, I *will have saved* two thousand dollars.

When she gets to Florida, she *will have driven* through three time zones.

The proper sequence of tenses within a sentence or series of sentences when different verbs refer to different time periods is an important consideration for all writers. The simple rule that verb tenses need to express precisely the intended period of time is not always simple to apply to one's own writing.

Improper sequence	**Correct sequence**
The witness *told* [past] the court that on the night of the crime he *saw* [past] the accused break the window of the liquor store.	The witness *told* [past] the court that on the night of the crime he *had seen* [past perfect] the accused break the window of the liquor store. (The past perfect *had seen* refers to events "more past than past.")
When I *will get* [future] to the lake, you *will* already *be* [future] there for two weeks.	When I *will get* [future] to the lake, you *will* already *have been* [future perfect] there for two weeks. (The future perfect *will have been* refers to events that will be completed before some future time.)
Although the coach *has set* [present perfect] new curfew hours, the players still *have refused* [present perfect] to comply.	Although the coach *has set* [present perfect] new curfew hours, the players still *refuse* [present] to comply. (The coach's rules were set a while ago. The present tense *refuse* is necessary to show that the players' refusal to follow the rules is current.)

EXERCISE Make any necessary corrections in verb tenses in the following sentences.

1. The candidate had promised that she will never increase taxes, but she did.
2. The doctor says that when he first saw the patient, the patient was suffering for two weeks with severe migraine headaches.

3. When the book will be released, the competition will already be on sale for a month.
4. Lei Feng saved half of each paycheck for two years, but then he had blown it all on one trip to the casino.
5. Soledad has taken all the abuse she can. She felt a legal separation was the only course open to her.
6. Brian still says that he really loves her, but Joan had declared that he has said that many times before.
7. The long-awaited report is going to be printed next week. It will have shown a long pattern of misappropriation of public funds.
8. At the hearings, the admiral insisted he did not receive any warning of the enemy attack.
9. When I will finally visit England, all my friends will be there dozens of times.
10. I did not want my nephew to play that horrible music again. I heard it many times before.

SELF TEST: Verb Tense

Correct the verb tense errors in the following sentences. Some sentences are correct.

1. If only she had admitted her guilt at the beginning, her sentence would be reduced.
2. David did not do it anymore. He did it too many times for too many years.
3. By the time the party had begun we will have just left our house.
4. When you slowpokes will have arrived, we will have been there for hours.
5. If you took the high road, and I took the low road, who would get to Scotland first?
6. Pedro combed his hair, brushed his teeth, and went to bed.
7. We had not tasted the main course before our plates have been whisked away.
8. Simone always knows all the news. She knows it all tomorrow, too.
9. When this machine is in working order, it will have enabled Dr. Doom to control the planet.
10. When Carlos and Marsha first met, Marsha had been crossing the street.

Voice. The quality of a verb that tells whether the subject *acts* or is *acted upon*. A verb is in the *active voice* when its subject does the acting, and in the *passive voice* when its subject is acted upon.

Active:	The Senate passed the new law.
Passive:	The new law was passed by the Senate.

Wordiness.   *Wordiness* means using more words than are necessary. Wordiness never makes writing clearer, more convincing, more interesting, or more graceful—just longer. Be sure to examine your work for wordiness before turning it in. (For exercises and more detailed information, see Chapter 23.)

wordy

Glossary of Problem Words

A, an. Use *a* when the next word begins with a consonant sound. Use *an* when the next word begins with a vowel sound.

    a book   an urgent request

    a rotten apple   an added attraction

Note that it is the sound that counts, not the actual letter.

    a hasty decision   an unusual picture

    an hour   a usual routine

Accept, except. *Accept* is a verb meaning "to receive, to agree to, to answer affirmatively." *Except* is usually a preposition meaning "excluding." It is also used infrequently as a verb meaning "to exclude."

    I accepted the parcel from the mail carrier.

    Senator Jones hoped they would accept his apology.

    I liked everything about the concert except the music.

    I except you from my criticism.

Adapt, adept, adopt. *Adapt* means "change or adjust in order to make more suitable or in order to deal with new conditions." *Adept* means "skillful, handy, good at." *Adopt* means "take or use as one's own" or "endorse."

    The dinosaur was unable to adapt to changes in its environment.

    The new textbook was an adaptation of the earlier edition.

    Bill has always been adept at carpentry.

    They had to wait six years before they could adopt a child.

    The Senate adopted the new resolution.

Adolescence, adolescents. *Adolescence* refers to the teenage years. *Adolescents* are teenagers.

    My adolescence was marked by religious questioning, parental snooping, and skin problems.

    Adolescents pay outrageous rates for automobile insurance because, as a group, they have outrageous numbers of accidents.

Adverse, averse to. *Adverse* means "hostile, difficult, unfavorable." *Averse to* refers to someone's being unwilling or reluctant.

> Adverse weather conditions have tormented farmers for the past decade.

> John has always been averse to accepting other people's ideas.

Advice, advise. *Advice* is a noun. *Advise* is a verb.

> My advice to you is to leave well enough alone.

> I advise you to leave well enough alone.

Affect, effect. If you are looking for a noun, the word you want is almost certainly *effect*, meaning "result." The noun *affect* is generally restricted to technical discussions of psychology, where it means "an emotion" or "a stimulus to an emotion." If you are looking for a verb, the word you want is probably *affect*, meaning "impress, influence." The verb *effect* is comparatively uncommon; it means "bring about, accomplish, produce."

> Many of our welfare programs have not had beneficial effects.

> This song always affects me powerfully.

> The crowd was not affected by the plea to disband.

> We hope this new program will effect a whole new atmosphere on campus.

> Pete's affect was always sullen and perverse.

Affective, effective. The word you are after is almost certainly *effective*, meaning "having an effect on" or "turning out well." *Affective* is a fairly technical term from psychology and semantics meaning "emotional" or "influencing emotions."

> Only time will tell if Federal Reserve policy is effective.

> The affective qualities of sound are difficult to evaluate in laboratory conditions.

Aggravate. The original meaning of *aggravate* is "worsen" or "intensify." The more common meaning of "irritate" or "annoy" is also acceptable in all but the fussiest formal writing.

Ain't. *Ain't* should never be used in written English except in humor or dialog. Use of the phrase *ain't I*, when asking a question in conversational English, is undesirable, as is the supposedly elegant but totally ungrammatical *aren't I*. *Am I not* is grammatically correct, but awkward and stuffy. The best solution to the problem is to avoid it by expressing the thought differently.

All ready, already. *Already* means "previously" or "by the designated time." *All ready* means "all set, all prepared."

Professor Wills has already told us that twice.

The plane is already overdue.

The meal was all ready by six o'clock.

All right, alright. *Alright* is often considered nonstandard English. It is good policy to use *all right* instead.

All together, altogether. *All together* means "joined in a group." *Altogether* means "thoroughly" or "totally."

For once, the citizens are all together on an important issue.

The character's motivations are altogether obscure.

Allusion, illusion. An *allusion* is "an indirect mention or reference," often literary or historical. The verb form is *allude.* An *illusion* is "an idea not in accord with reality."

The nominating speech alluded to every American hero from Jack Armstrong to Neil Armstrong.

The patient suffered from the illusion that he was Napoleon.

A lot of. This phrase is more appropriate in conversation than in general written English. Use it sparingly. Remember that *a lot* is *two* words. Do not confuse it with *allot,* meaning "to give out" or "apportion."

Alright. See *All right, alright.*

Altogether. See *All together, altogether.*

A.M., a.m., P.M., p.m. These are Latinate abbreviations used with time; A.M. means *ante meridiem* (before noon); P.M. means *post meridiem* (after noon). Either capitals or lowercase letters are acceptable, but you should not alternate between the two in any one piece of writing. Always precede these abbreviations with specific numbers. Don't use "in the morning," "in the afternoon," or "in the evening" along with these abbreviations. Use one or the other.

Wrong: Her office hours start at 7:00 A.M. in the morning.

           Pick me up at 6:15 P.M. in the evening.

           We expect her sometime in the a.m.

Right: Her office hours start at 7:00 A.M. *or* Her office hours start at 7:00 in the morning.

           Pick me up at 6:15 P.M. *or* Pick me up at 6:15 in the evening.

           We expect her sometime in the morning.

Among, between.   Use *between* when dealing with two units. Use *among* with more than two.

Wrong: The company president had to make an arbitrary decision among the two outstanding candidates for promotion.

Tension has always existed between my mother, my father, and me.

Right: The company president had to make an arbitrary decision between the two outstanding candidates for promotion.

Tension has always existed among my mother, my father, and me.

Amount, number.   Use *amount* to refer to quantities that cannot be counted. Use *number* for quantities that can be counted.

No amount of persuasion will convince the voters to approve the new levy, though the mayor has tried a number of times.

An.   See *A, an*.

And etc.   *Etc.* is an abbreviation of *et cetera*, meaning "and so forth" or "and other things." Using the word *and* in addition to *etc.* is therefore repetitious and incorrect. See *Etc*.

Anxious, eager.   *Anxious* suggests worry or fear, as in anxiety. *Eager* suggests enthusiasm.

Wrong: I am so anxious to see you again at our reunion next week.

Right: I am so eager to see you again at our reunion next week.

Wrong: The whole town waited anxiously for the triumphant hockey team.

Right: The whole town waited eagerly to greet the triumphant hockey team.

Anyone, any one.   Use *anyone* when you mean anybody at all. Use *any one* when you are considering separately or singling out each person or thing within a group.

Anyone can learn how to do simple electrical wiring.

Any one of these paintings is worth a small fortune.

The same principle applies to *everyone, every one* and *someone, some one*.

Anyways.   Not standard written English. Use *anyway*.

As.   Do not use *as* as a substitute for *because* or *since*.

Poor: I was late for my appointment as I missed the bus.

As I am a shy person, I find it hard to make new friends.

Better: I was late for my appointment because I missed the bus.

Since I am a shy person, I find it hard to make new friends.

As far as.   This phrase should be followed by a noun and a verb. Without the verb, it is incomplete.

Poor: As far as religion, I believe in complete freedom.

Better: As far as religion is concerned, I believe in complete freedom.

Askance.   This word is an adverb meaning "suspiciously, disapprovingly"—used for looks, glances, and the like. It should never be used as a noun.

Wrong: The sportswriters looked with askance at the coach's optimistic prediction.

Right: The sportswriters looked askance at the coach's optimistic prediction.

Aspect.   An overused, pseudoscholarly word. Try to avoid it wherever possible. Where you feel you must use it, try to preserve the concept of *looking* as part of the implicit meaning of the word.

We viewed the problem in all its aspects.

As to.   Stuffy. Change to *about*.

Poor: We need to talk more as to our late deliveries.

Better: We need to talk more about our late deliveries.

Averse to.   See *Adverse, averse to.*

Awful.   The original meaning of *awful* is "awe-inspiring, arousing emotions of fear." Some people insist that this is still its only valid meaning. We see nothing wrong, however, when it is also used to mean "extremely bad, ugly, unpleasant." The word *dreadful* has evolved in the same way, and we know of no objections to that word. See *Awfully.*

Awfully.   Does not mean "very."

Poor: He's an awfully nice person.

          I'm awfully impressed by what you said.

Better: He's a very nice person.

          I'm impressed with what you said.

A while, awhile.   *A while* is a noun. *Awhile* is an adverb.

I thought I saw her a while ago.

Take it easy for a while.

Success comes only to those who are prepared to wait awhile.

Bad, badly.   *Bad* is the adjective, *badly* the adverb. In some sentences, the verbs *look*, *feel*, and *seem* function as linking verbs and must be followed by the adjectival form.

I play badly.

but

I feel bad.

She looks bad.

The idea seems bad.

Watch the location of *badly* when you use it to mean "very much." It can often be misread as having its more familiar meaning, and comic disaster can occur.

Incorrect: I want to act badly.

                 He wanted her to love him badly.

Be.   Not standard written English in constructions like *I be going* and *They be ready*. Use *I am going* or *They are ready* instead.

Being as, being as how, being that.   Not standard written English. Use *because* or *since*.

Beside, besides.   *Beside* means "alongside of." It can also mean "other than" or "aside from."

He pulled in beside the Buick.

Your last statement is beside the point.

Besides means "in addition to" or "moreover."

I'm starting to discover that I'll need something besides a big smile to get ahead.

Besides, I'm not sure I really liked the dress in the first place.

Between.   See *Among, between*.

Brake, break.   *Brake*, whether a verb or noun, has to do with stopping a vehicle or other piece of machinery. For additional meanings, see a dictionary.

Frantically, he slammed on the brake.

She braked her car to a complete stop.

Break, whether a verb or noun, has many meanings, most commonly "to destroy, damage, exceed, interrupt." The simple past is *broke*; the past participle is *broken*.

Porcelain can break, so be careful.

Her left arm was broken.

Hank Aaron broke Babe Ruth's home-run record.

The committee took a ten-minute break.

The attempted jail break was unsuccessful.

The brake of the school bus has been broken.

Breath, breathe.   *Breath* is a noun. *Breathe* is a verb.

His statement is like a breath of fresh air.

The soprano drew a deep breath.

In some cities it can be dangerous to breathe the air.

The soprano breathes deeply.

But however, but nevertheless, but yet.   All these phrases are guilty of pointless repetition of meaning. Rewriting helps the logic and eliminates wordiness.

Poor: Inflation is horrible, but however, the remedies are sometimes even more horrible.

She loved her husband, but yet she feared him.

Failure may be inevitable, but nevertheless we will do our best.

Better: Inflation is horrible, but the remedies are sometimes even more horrible.

Inflation is horrible; however, the remedies are sometimes even more horrible.

She loved her husband, yet she feared him.

Failure may be inevitable, but we will do our best.

But that, but what.   Not standard written English. Use *that*.

Wrong: I don't question but that you have good intentions.

I don't question but what you have good intentions.

Right: I don't question that you have good intentions.

Can, may.   In formal English questions, *can* asks if the ability is there, and *may* asks if the permission is there.

Can your baby speak yet?

May I intrude on your conversation? (Not *can*—anyone with a voice has the ability to intrude.)

Outside of formal contexts, few people worry about the distinction.

Can't hardly.   A double negative. Use *can hardly*.

Can't help but.   Wordy and repetitious. Avoid this phrase in written English.

Poor: I can't help but worry about what winter will do to my old car.

Better: I can't help worrying about what winter will do to my old car.

Capital, capitol.   *Capital* refers to money, uppercase letters, and cities that are seats of government. A *capitol* is a building in which major legislative bodies meet. With an uppercase *C*, *Capitol* refers to the building in Washington, DC.

Investments in Compucorp, though highly speculative, offer excellent opportunities for capital gains.

The poet e. e. cummings had an aversion to capital letters.

Madison is the capital of Wisconsin.

Madison's capitol closely resembles the Capitol in Washington, DC.

Casual, causal. These lookalike words are often misread. *Casual* means "informal" or "unplanned." *Causal* means "having to do with a cause," "constituting a cause," and so on.

Bill is entirely too casual about his financial future.

Karen understands the causal connection between cigarettes and lung disease, but she keeps smoking anyway.

Censor, censure. *Censor*, as a verb, means "to examine mail, art, etc., to see if it should be made public," or "to cut out, ban." As a noun, *censor* means "a person engaged in censoring." *Censure* can be a verb or noun meaning "condemn" or "condemnation," "criticize adversely" or "adverse criticism."

Parts of the movie have been censored.

The prison censor examines all mail.

The Citizens Committee recently censured the mayor.

Dickens's deathbed scenes have long been singled out for censure.

Center around. Since a center is a single point in the middle of something, *center around* is an illogical phrase. Use *center on* instead.

The discussion centered on ways to increase productivity in the coming year.

Cite, site, sight. *Cite*, a verb, means "mention." *Site*, a noun, means "location." *Sight*, also a noun, means something viewed, the ability to see, or the foreseeable future.

He cited many examples to prove his point.

The site of a new housing project has been debated for more than a year.

In her feather hat and seashell earrings, she was quite a sight!

There's no cure in sight for advanced stages of brain cancer.

Climactic, climatic. *Climactic* is the adjectival form of *climax*.

The hero's death is the climactic moment of the story.

Climatic is the adjectival form of *climate*.

Climatic conditions in the Dakotas go from one extreme to the other.

Complected. Not standard English. *Complexioned* is preferable, but it's better to reword your sentence so you can avoid using either term.

> *Acceptable:*   He was a light-complexioned man.
>
> *Better:*   He had very fair skin.

Complement, compliment. The verb *complement* means "to complete" or "bring to perfection." The noun *complement* means "the full amount." *Compliment* means "praise" (noun or verb).

> Cheese and wine complement each other.
>
> The ship had its required complement of officers.
>
> I don't appreciate insincere compliments.
>
> Don't compliment me unless you mean it.

Compose, comprise. *Compose* means "to make up, to constitute."

> Thirteen separate colonies composed the original United States.

Comprise means "to be made up of, to encompass."

> The original United States comprised thirteen separate colonies.

If the distinction between these two words gives you trouble, forget about *comprise* and use *is composed of* instead.

Conscience, conscientious, conscious. *Conscience* is the inner voice that tells us right from wrong. *Conscientious* means "painstaking, scrupulous, ruled by conscience," as in *conscientious objector*. *Conscious* means "aware."

> No one should ask you to act against your conscience.
>
> I've tried to do this work as conscientiously as possible.
>
> Jerry became conscious of a subtle change in Mary's attitude.

Console, consul, council, counsel. *Console:* As a verb (accent on second syllable)—"to sympathize with, to comfort." As a noun (accent on first syllable)—"a radio, phonograph, or television cabinet, usually a combination, resting directly on the floor"; also "a small compartment, as found in an automobile between bucket seats"; for other meanings, see a dictionary.

Consul: A representative of a nation, stationed in a foreign city, whose job is to look after the nation's citizens and business interests.

Council: A governing body or an advisory group.

Counsel: As a verb—"to advise, to recommend." As a noun—"advice, recommendation, exchange of ideas."

I could find no words to console the grieving widow.

I've lived with this portable stereo too long. I want a console.

The French consul will answer any of your questions on import duties.

The council met last week in a special emergency session.

The tax expert counseled him on medical deductions.

Sarah knew she could rely on her father's friendly counsel.

Contemptible, contemptuous. Use *contemptible* to describe something or someone deserving of scorn. Use *contemptuous* to describe the expression of scorn.

Few crimes are more contemptible than child abuse.

Instead of shaking hands, she thumbed her nose and stuck out her tongue. Her contemptuous attitude was clear.

Continual, continuous. *Continuous* means "completely uninterrupted, without any pause."

The continuous noise at the party next door kept us awake.

The patient received continuous round-the-clock care.

Continual means "frequently repeated, but with interruptions or pauses."

He had a bad cold and blew his nose continually.

She changed jobs continually.

Costume, custom. *Costume* refers to style of dress. *Custom* refers to conventional practice. See a dictionary for other meanings.

He decided to wear a pirate's costume to the masquerade.

Trick or treat is an old Halloween custom.

Could care less. See *Couldn't care less*.

Couldn't care less. Means "utterly indifferent to." The phrase *could care less* is sometimes mistakenly used to mean the same thing. It does not mean the same thing; it makes no sense at all.

Wrong: I could care less about her opinion of me.

Right: I couldn't care less about her opinion of me.

Couldn't hardly. See *Can't hardly* and *not hardly*.

Could of, should of, would of. Not standard written English. Use *could have, should have, would have.*

Council.   See *Console, consul, council, counsel.*

Counsel.   See *Console, consul, council, counsel.*

Credible, creditable, credulous.   *Credible* means "believable." *Creditable* means "worthy of praise." *Credulous* means "gullible, foolishly believing."

    Their lame excuses were not credible.

    Adam's behavior since his parole has been creditable.

    She's so credulous she still believes that the stork brings babies.

Criterion.   This word (plural: *criteria*) is overused and frequently stuffy. Use *standard*, instead.

Cute.   An overused word. Avoid it wherever possible in written English.

Data.   Technically, a plural word, the singular form of which is *datum*. The word's Latin origins, however, have nothing to do with its current usage. We believe that *data* can be treated as singular in all levels of English—and probably should be.

    Correct: This data is accurate and helpful.

    Correct (but very formal):   These data are accurate and helpful.

Decompose, discompose.   *Decompose* means "to rot or break into separate parts." *Discompose* means "disturb, fluster, unsettle."

    When the police found the body, it had already begun to decompose.

    His drunken foolishness discomposed all of us.

Definitely.   Nothing is wrong with this word except that it is used far too often (and often misspelled) to add vague emphasis to weak thoughts and weak words.

Detract, distract.   *Detract* means "belittle." *Distract* means "divert, confuse."

    Almost everyone tries to detract from television's real accomplishments.

    A mosquito kept distracting her attention.

Device, devise.   *Device* is a noun meaning, among other things, "mechanism" or "special effect." *Devise* is a verb meaning "to invent" or "to plot."

    The safety pin is a simple but extraordinarily clever device.

    The person who devised the safety pin is one of humanity's minor benefactors.

Dialog.   Alternative spelling for *dialogue*. In general, save this word for references to conversation in literary works.

No creative writing class can give a writer an ear for good dialog.

Proper punctuation of dialog requires knowledge of many seemingly trivial details.

Some critics assert that Eugene O'Neill's plays have many great speeches but almost no believable dialogue.

Martin Buber, the great twentieth-century theologian, expanded the meaning of *dialog* to refer to an intense, intimate relationship that can sometimes take place between God and human beings. Buber's influence, unfortunately, has led many people who should know better to corrupt the term into a pretentious, sometimes self-serving, synonym for normal conversation. Avoid this usage.

> *Poor:* At its meeting last week, the committee engaged in effective dialog.
>
> The Singles Club provides its members with many opportunities for meaningful dialog.

As if that corruption were not enough, the word has been virtually destroyed through its faddish use as a verb. *Dialog* is not a verb in standard written English. Never use it that way.

> *Wrong:* We dialogued about politics until two in the morning.
>
> Professor Biggs said that she enjoyed dialoging with her students after class.

Different than, different to. *Different from* is preferable in all circumstances.

Discompose. See *Decompose, discompose.*

Discreet, discrete. *Discreet* means "tactful," "reserved." *Discrete* means "separate," "distinct."

Discreet silence is sometimes the most effective reply to an insult.

Rising interest rates have several discrete effects on the economy.

Disinterested, uninterested. Don't confuse these words. *Disinterested* means "impartial, unbiased." *Uninterested* means "bored, indifferent." An audience is uninterested in a poor play. A disinterested judge is necessary for a fair trial.

Disorientate, disorientated. Awkward variations of *disorient* and *disoriented.*

Distract. See *Detract, distract.*

Each. Takes a singular verb and a singular pronoun. See *He, his, him, himself.*

Each breed of dog has its own virtues.

Each dancer was told to practice her bows.

Each of the Cleveland Indians is taking his turn at batting practice.

Eager.   See *Anxious, eager*.

Economic, economical.   Use *economic* for references to business, finance, the science of economics, and so on. *Economical* means "inexpensive" or "thrifty."

> Economic conditions are improving in the textile industry.
>
> The economical shopper looks hard for bargains.

Effect.   See *Affect, effect*.

Effective.   See *Affective, effective*.

Either.   Use *either* only when dealing with two units.

> *Wrong:*   Either the Republican, the Democrat, or the Independent will be elected.
>
> *Right:*   Either Elaine or Tom will get the job.

When *either* is the subject, it takes a singular verb and pronoun.

> The men are both qualified. Either is ready to give his best.

See *Neither*.

Elicit, illicit.   *Elicit* means "to draw out." *Illicit* means "improper" or "prohibited."

> The interviewer was unable to elicit a direct answer.
>
> Where would our modern novelists turn if they were suddenly prohibited from writing about illicit romance?

Eminent, imminent. *Eminent* means "distinguished" or "noteworthy." *Imminent* means "about to happen."

> The eminent speaker delivered a disappointing address.
>
> After years of frustration, a peace treaty is imminent.

Ensure, insure.   Both words are often used interchangeably, but use *insure* for references to financial guarantees against loss of life, health, and property.

> The new screens should ensure that insects stay outside where they belong.
>
> Authorities say that if you insure your home or apartment, you should take photographs of all your most valuable possessions.
>
> Our state has just made it mandatory for motorists to insure their own vehicles.

Equally as.   Not a standard English phrase. Eliminate the *as* or substitute *just as*.

> *Poor:*   My grades were equally as good.
>
>   The style was equally as important as the plot.

> *Better:* My grades were equally good.
>
> The style was just as important as the plot.

Etc. Abbreviation of *et cetera* (Latin for "and so forth," "and other things"). Except where brevity is a major concern, as in this glossary, avoid *etc.* It tends to convey the impression that the writer doesn't want to be bothered with being accurate and specific. See *And etc.*

Every. This adjective makes the noun it modifies take a singular verb and a singular pronoun. See *He, his, him, himself.*

> Every woman leader needs to learn how to deal with the prejudices of her male counterparts.
>
> Every Denver Bronco is required to report his weight upon arrival at training camp.
>
> Every idea has been put into its proper place in the outline.

Every day, everyday. *Every day* is the common phrase used for references to time.

> He loved her so much that he wanted to see her every day.
>
> Every day that we went to the pond that summer, we saw new signs of pollution.

Everyday is an adjective meaning "normal, ordinary, routine."

> After the interview, Bill looked forward to changing into his everyday clothes.
>
> The everyday lives of many everyday people are filled with fears, tensions, and the potential for tragedy.

Everyone, every one. See *Anyone, any one.*

Except. See *Accept, except.*

Expand, expend. *Expand* means "to increase, enlarge, fill out." *Expend* means "to spend, use up."

> The company needs to expand its share of the market.
>
> The student fell asleep during the final examination because he had expended all his energy in studying.

Explicit, implicit. *Explicit* means "stated or shown directly." *Implicit* means "implied, not stated or shown directly."

> Cheryl's mother gave explicit instructions to be home before dark.
>
> Even by current standards, the movie goes to extremes in its explicit presentation of sex.

My wife and I have an implicit understanding that the first one who can't stand the dirt any longer is the one who does the dishes.

The diplomatic phrasing does not hide the implicit threat of war.

Facet.   An overused, pseudoscholarly word. Avoid it wherever possible.

Farther, further.   Use *farther* for geographic distance, *further* for everything else.

Allentown is five miles farther down the road.

Further changes improved the curriculum.

Jim kissed her, but they were further apart than ever.

We need to go further into the subject.

Faze, phase.   *Faze* means "disconcert, fluster."

Critical sneers will not faze a great artist.

Phase means "a stage in development." It is an overused word. Limit it to contexts in which the passage of time is especially significant.

Poor: One phase of the team's failure is poor hitting.

Better: The history of the team can be divided into three phases.

Fellow.   As an adjective, *fellow* means "being in the same situation" or "having the same ideas." Make sure you do not use it to modify a noun that already implies that meaning.

Wrong: My fellow colleagues have been hasty.

Right: My fellow workers and I voted to strike.

Fewer, less.   Use *fewer* for references to amounts that can be counted individually, item by item. Use *less* for general amounts or amounts that cannot be counted or measured.

Joe earned fewer dollars this year than he did five years ago.

Joe made less money this year than he did five years ago.

Figurative, figuratively.   See *Literal, literally*.

Flaunt, flout.   *Flaunt* means "show off arrogantly or conspicuously." *Flout* means "treat scornfully, show contempt," mostly in attitudes toward morality, social customs, traditions.

They lost no opportunity to flaunt their newfound wealth.

Those hoodlums flout all the basic decencies and then complain that we misunderstand them.

Foreword, forward. A *foreword* is a preface or introduction. *Forward* is the opposite of backward. It can also mean "bold" or "impertinent."

> The only interesting part of the entire book was the foreword.

> Our mistakes are part of history. We must now look forward.

> Amy's old-fashioned grandfather told her that she was a forward hussy.

Formally, formerly. *Formally* means "in a formal manner." *Formerly* means "in the past."

> We dressed formally for Pedro and Olga's wedding.

> People formerly thought that the automobile would become just another fad.

Former. Means "the first of two." Don't use *former* when dealing with more than two items or persons.

> *Wrong:* Grant, McKinley, and Harding were poor presidents. The former was the poorest.
>
> *Right:* Grant, McKinley, and Harding were poor presidents. The first was the poorest.
>
> Grant and McKinley were poor presidents. The former was the poorer.

See *Latter*.

Further. See *Farther, further*.

Good, well. The adjective *good* modifies a noun. The adverb *well* modifies a verb, adjective, or other adverb.

> Mary was a *good speaker*.

> She *spoke well*.

> The speech *went well*.

After a linking verb, always use *good*. Common linking verbs are *to be* (in all forms and tenses—*am, is, are, was, were, have been, has been, had been, would be, will be*, and so on), *feel, look, sound, taste, appear, smell*, and the like.

> Her voice sounded good.

> The speech was good.

> Mary felt good.

See the discussion of adjective–adverb confusion, pages 585–587.

Hanged, hung. Both are past participles of *hang*; technically, they are interchangeable. Traditionally, however, *hanged* is reserved for references to executions and *hung* is used everywhere else.

The spy was hanged the next morning.

All the pictures hung crookedly.

He, his, him, himself.   English has no distinct singular pronoun to refer to both sexes. In the past, the masculine pronoun was used to refer to a singular subject of either sex or when sex was irrelevant or unknown.

The used-car buyer needs to be careful. In fact, *he* can hardly be too careful, for many dealers are waiting for the opportunity to swindle *him*.

Each citizen can make *his* choice known on Election Day.

Everybody should protect *himself* from the dangers of alcoholism.

However, increased sensitivity to sexist language (see pages 576–578) has caused this usage to disappear from contemporary published writing. The easiest and most common way to avoid sexist language is to change singular phrasing to plural whenever possible.

Used-car buyers need to be careful. In fact, *they* can hardly be too careful, for many dealers are waiting for the opportunity to swindle *them*.

All citizens can make *their* choice known on Election Day.

People should protect *themselves* from the dangers of alcoholism.

Rephrase sentences that do not lend themselves to a plural approach should be rephrased. See *He/she, his/her, him/her, he or she, his or hers, him or her*.

He/she, his/her, him/her, he or she, his or hers, him or her.   Though often convenient and sometimes indispensable, these efforts to achieve sexual equality in language are usually best saved for legal contracts. The phrasing is generally strained and pompous. Use a plural subject and pronoun whenever possible, or recast the sentence to eliminate sexist language (see pages 576–578).

Poor: Everyone needs to make early plans for his/her career.

In cases of fatal illness, should a patient be told the truth about what is wrong with him or her?

Better: People should make early plans for their careers.

In cases of fatal illness, should patients be told the truth about what is wrong with them?

Hoard, horde.   *Hoard* is a verb meaning "amass" or a noun meaning "a large, hidden supply." *Horde* is a large throng or crowd.

As rumors of war increased, some citizens began to hoard food.

The old man's hoard of gold was concealed beneath the floorboards.

The horde of locusts totally destroyed last year's grain crop.

Hopefully. *Hopefully* is an adverb, which means that it modifies and usually appears next to or close to a verb, adjective, or another adverb.

> The farmers searched hopefully for a sign of rain.
>
> Hopefully, the children ran down the stairs on Christmas morning.

Hopefully does *not* mean "I hope, he hopes, it is hoped that. . . ." Avoid using it in sentences like the following:

> Hopefully, we can deal with this mess next weekend.
>
> The new driver's training program, hopefully, will cut down on traffic fatalities.

In fairness, so many educated writers and speakers mishandle *hopefully* that the incorrect usage is likely to worm its way into standard English someday.

Human, humane. *Humane* means "kind, benevolent." *Human* means "pertaining to *man-* and *womankind.*"

> Humane treatment of prisoners is all too rare.
>
> The human condition is frail at best.

I, me. *I* functions as the subject of a sentence or clause, and as a complement in the extremely formal but grammatically correct *It is I. Me* is the object of a verb or preposition.

> He gave the book to me.
>
> He gave me the business.
>
> For me, nothing can beat a steak and French fries.
>
> Why does she like me so much?

To determine which word to use in sentences like "Nobody is more enthusiastic than I" or "Nobody is more enthusiastic than me," simply complete the sentences with a verb and see which makes sense.

> *Wrong:*   Nobody is more enthusiastic than me (am).
>
> *Right:*   Nobody is more enthusiastic than I (am).

Idea, ideal. An *idea* is a concept or notion. An *ideal* is a model of perfection. As an adjective, *ideal* means "perfect."

> A new idea for solving the problem suddenly occurred to Linda.
>
> Lofty ideals need to be tempered by common sense.
>
> Ideal children exist only in books.

Illicit. See *Elicit, illicit.*

Illusion. See *Allusion, illusion.*

Imminent.   See *Eminent, imminent.*

Implicit.   See *Explicit, implicit.*

Imply, infer.   To *imply* means "to suggest or hint at something without specifically stating it."

> The dean implied that the demonstrators would be punished.
>
> The editorial implies that our public officials have taken bribes.

To *infer* means "to draw a conclusion."

> I inferred from her standoffish attitude that she disliked me.
>
> The newspaper wants its readers to infer that our public officials have taken bribes.

Incredible, incredulous.   *Incredible* means "unbelievable." *Incredulous* means "unconvinced, nonbelieving."

> The witness gave evidence that was utterly incredible.
>
> I was incredulous at hearing those absurd lies.

Indict.   To *indict* means "to charge with a crime." It does not mean to arrest or to convict.

> The grand jury indicted Fields on a gambling charge.

Individual.   Often contributes to stuffiness and wordiness.

> *Bad:*   He was a remarkable individual.
>
> *Better:* He was a remarkable man.
>
> *Best:*   He was remarkable.

Infer.   See *Imply, infer.*

Inferior than.   Not standard English. Use *inferior to.*

Ingenious, ingenuous.   *Ingenious* means "clever." *Ingenuous* means "naive, open."

> Sherlock Holmes was an ingenious detective.
>
> Nothing could rival the ingenuous appeal of the little child's eyes.

The noun forms are *ingenuity, ingenuousness.*

In reference to.   Stuffy business English. Use *about.*

In spite of.   *In spite* is two separate words.

Insure.   See *Ensure, insure.*

Inter-, intra-. *Inter-* is a prefix meaning "between different groups." *Intra-* is a prefix meaning "within the same group."

Ohio State and Michigan fought bitterly for intercollegiate football supremacy.

The English faculty needs a new department head who can control intradepartmental bickering.

Irregardless. Not standard English. The proper word is *regardless.*

Irrelevant, irreverent. *Irrelevant* means "not related to the subject." *Irreverent* means "scornful, lacking respect."

Your criticisms sound impressive but are really irrelevant.

America could use some of Mark Twain's irreverent wit today.

Confusion of these words may be responsible for the frequent mispronunciation of *irrelevant* as *irrevelant.*

Its, it's. *Its* is the possessive of *it. It's* is the contraction for *it is.*

The cat licked its paws. It's a wonderfully clean animal.

Its' is not a word. It does not exist in current usage, and it never has.

Job. Frequently overused in student writing. *Job* is probably most effective when reserved for simple references to employment for wages.

Poor: Shakespeare does a great job of showing Hamlet's conflicting emotions.

Better: Our economy needs to create more jobs.

Kind of. Means what it says—"a type of, a variety of." It does *not* mean "somewhat" or "rather" except in the most informal writing.

Poor: She was kind of eccentric.

I was kind of curious about his answer.

Better: He suffered from an obscure kind of tropic fever.

She had a kind of honest stubbornness that could be very appealing.

Latter. Means "the second of two." Don't use *latter* when dealing with more than two items or people.

Wrong: Washington, Jefferson, and Lincoln were great presidents. The latter was the greatest.

Right: Washington, Jefferson, and Lincoln were great presidents. The last was the greatest.

Washington and Lincoln were great presidents. The latter was the greater.

See *Former.*

Lay, lie.   *Lay* is a transitive verb. It always takes an object *or* is expressed in the passive voice.

Present	Past	Past participle	Present participle
lay	laid	laid	laying

Lie is an intransitive verb. It never takes an object and never is expressed in the passive voice. This problem-causing *lie*, by the way, means "recline," not "fib."

Present	Past	Past participle	Present participle
lie	lay	lain	lying

I lay my burden down forever.

The hen laid six eggs yesterday.

The mason has laid all the bricks.

Our plans have been laid aside.

The porter is laying down our suitcases.

Now I am going to lie down.

Yesterday he lay awake for five hours.

The refuse has lain there for weeks.

Homeless people are lying on the park benches.

Lead, led.   As a noun, *lead* has various meanings (and pronunciations).

The student had no lead for his pencil.

The reporter wanted a good lead for her story.

Which athlete is in the lead?

The past of the verb *lead* is *led*.

The declarer always leads in bridge.

I led an ace instead of a deuce.

Is it possible to lead without making enemies?

Grant led the Union to triumph at Vicksburg.

Leave, let.   *Leave* means "to depart." *Let* means "to allow, permit."

Wrong: Leave us look more closely at this sonnet.

Right: Let us look more closely at this sonnet.

Lend, loan.   *Lend* is a verb; *loan* is a noun.

Jack was kind enough to lend me ten dollars.

High interest rates have interfered with loans.

Less.   See *Fewer, less.*

Liable, libel.   *Liable* means "likely to" or "legally obligated." *Libel* is an unjust written statement exposing someone to public contempt.

> After a few drinks, that man is liable to do anything.
>
> The owner of the dog was liable for damages.
>
> Senator Green sued the newspaper for libel.

Libel, slander.   *Libel* is written injustice. *Slander* is spoken injustice.

Like, as.   In agonizing over whether to use *like* or *as* (sometimes *as if*), look first at the words that follow. If the words make up a clause (subject plus verb) use *as*; if not, use *like*.

> Even philosophers can sometimes act like fools.
>
> Even philosophers can sometimes act as fools would act.
>
> The painting made the sunset look like a double-cheese pizza.
>
> The painting made the sunset look as if it were a double-cheese pizza.
>
> My boss treated me like dirt.
>
> My boss treated me as if I were dirt.

This rule is not foolproof, but it will solve most practical problems. *Like* in place of *as* is now fairly well accepted outside of formal written English.

Literal, literally.   These terms mean "in actual fact, according to the precise meaning of the words." Some people use *literal, literally* when they mean the opposite: *figurative, figuratively.*

> *Wrong:*   He literally made a monkey of himself.
>
> Some of our councilmen are literal vultures.
>
> I literally fly off the handle when I see children mistreated.
>
> *Right:*   The doctor said Karen's jealousy had literally made her ill.
>
> We were so lost that we literally did not know north from south.
>
> A literal translation from German to English rarely makes any sense.

Loan.   See *Lend, loan.*

Loath, loathe.   *Loath* is an adjective meaning "reluctant." *Loathe* is a verb meaning "hate."

> I am loath to express the full intensity of my feelings.
>
> I loathe people who use old-fashioned words like *loath.*

Loose, lose.   *Loose* is the opposite of *tight. Lose* means "to misplace."

Mad.   Use *mad* in written English to mean "insane," not "angry."

> *Poor:*   Please don't be mad at me.
>
> *Better:*   Shakespeare tends to be sympathetic to his mad characters.
>
>   The current trade policy is utterly mad.

Majority, plurality.   A candidate who has a *majority* has more than half of the total votes. A candidate who has a *plurality* has won the election but received less than half the total votes.

Masochist.   See *Sadist, masochist.*

Massage, message.   A *massage* makes muscles feel better. A *message* is a communication.

May.   See *Can, may.*

May be, maybe.   *May be* is a verb form meaning "could be, can be." *Maybe* is an adverb meaning "perhaps."

> I may be wrong, but I feel that *Light in August* is Faulkner's finest novel.
>
> Maybe we ought to start all over again.

Me.   See *I, me.*

Medal, metal, mettle.   A *medal* is awarded to heroes and other celebrities. *Metal* is a substance such as iron or copper. *Mettle* refers to stamina, enthusiasm, vigorous spirit.

> The American team won most of its Olympic medals in swimming.
>
> Future metal exploration may take place beneath the sea.
>
> Until the Normandy invasion, Eisenhower had not really proved his mettle.

Medium.   An overused word in discussing communications. The plural of *medium* is *media*. See a dictionary for its many meanings.

Mighty.   Use *mighty* to mean "powerful" or "huge." Do *not* use it as a substitute for *very*.

> *Poor:*   I was mighty pleased to meet you.
>
> *Better:*   I was very pleased to meet you.

Moral, morale.   *Moral*, as an adjective, means "having to do with ethics" or "honorable, decent, upright." As a noun, it means "lesson, precept, teaching." *Morale* refers to one's state of mind or spirit.

Not all moral issues are simple cases of right and wrong.

The story has a profound moral.

The new coach tried to improve the team's morale.

More, most. Use *more* when two things are being compared. For any number over two, use *most*.

Between Sally and Phyllis, Sally was the more talented.

Of all my teachers, Mr. Frederic was the most inspired.

Never use *most* as a synonym for *almost*.

Wrong: Most everyone showed up at the party.

           I'll be home most any time tomorrow.

Mr., Mrs., Miss, Ms.   These titles should not be used in referring to figures from the historical, cultural, and scientific past. With living figures, the titles should be used in moderation; the better known the person, the less need for the title.

Poor: Mr. John Adams was the second president of the United States.

          Mr. Nathaniel Hawthorne wrote *The Scarlet Letter*.

          Mr. Yeltsin's speech received worldwide press coverage.

Better: John Adams was the second president of the United States.

          Nathaniel Hawthorne wrote *The Scarlet Letter*.

          Yeltsin's speech received worldwide press coverage.

Ms.   Now standard usage as a title for women, though *Miss* and *Mrs.* are still used.

Myself.   Use *myself* to reinforce and stress the pronoun *I*, not as a replacement for it or the word *me*.

Wrong: Make an appointment with José and myself next week.

Right: I myself made that fudge.

Natural.   Means "unartificial," among other things. It is overused as a term of vague praise. It might be applied to someone's voice or manner, but it sounds absurd in a sentence like this:

Brand X eyelashes will give you that natural look.

Neither.   Use only when dealing with *two* units.

Wrong: I like neither collies nor poodles nor dachshunds.

Right: I like neither dogs nor cats.

When *neither* is the subject, it takes a singular verb and pronoun.

> Both nations are responsible. Neither is doing its best for the environment.

See *Either*.

Nice.   An overused word, generally too vague in meaning to have much value. Try to find more specific substitutes.

None.   Means "no one" or "not one" and takes a singular verb and pronoun.

> None of these women understands that she is a public servant.

> None of those men is willing to accept his responsibilities.

Not hardly.   A double negative. Not standard English. Use *hardly*.

> *Wrong:*   He couldn't hardly see his hand in front of his face.

> *Right:*   He could hardly see his hand in front of his face.

Number.   See *Amount, number*.

Oftentimes.   Wordy and pointless version of *often*.

Only.   A tricky word in some sentences. Make sure that it modifies what you really want it to.

> *Poor:*   I only felt a little unhappy. (Only *felt?* Are we meant to assume that the writer did not consciously *think* this way?)
>
> I only asked for a chance to explain. (Are we meant to assume that the writer did not insist on or strongly desire that chance?)
>
> *Better:*   I felt only a little unhappy.
>
> I asked only for a chance to explain.

Orientate, orientated.   Awkward variations of *orient* and *oriented*.

Passed, past.   *Passed* is the past participle of pass. *Past* is used mainly as an adjective or a noun. Never use *passed* as an adjective or noun.

> We passed them on the highway.

> Valerie had a mysterious past.

> History is the study of past events.

Patience, patients.   *Patience* has to do with not being in a hurry. *Patients* are people seeking medical care or under medical attention.

> We expect the delivery tomorrow; our patience is almost at an end.

> The patients nervously waited in the doctor's office.

Perpetrate, perpetuate.   *Perpetrate* means "to commit an evil, offensive, or stupid act." *Perpetuate* means "to preserve forever."

> He perpetrated a colossal blunder.

> We resolved to perpetuate the ideals our leader stood for.

Persecute, prosecute.   *Persecute* means "to oppress or pick on unjustly." *Prosecute* means "to carry forward to conclusion or bring court proceedings against."

> Persecuting religious and racial minorities is an ongoing folly of the human race.

> The general believes that the war must be prosecuted intensely.

> We must prosecute those charged with crimes as rapidly as possible.

Personal, personnel.   *Personal* is an adjective meaning "private, individual." *Personnel* is a noun referring to the people employed in an organization. It can also refer to a department in the organization that oversees employee-based issues such as hiring and firing, morale, and processing of claims for benefits.

> My love life is too personal for me to discuss.

> There is no point to arguing about matters of personal taste.

> The company's personnel increased more than 10 percent in the past year.

> Address all inquiries to the Personnel Department.

Perspective, prospective.   *Perspective* has various meanings, most commonly "the logically correct relationships between the parts of something and the whole" or "the drawing techniques that give the illusion of space or depth." *Prospective* means "likely to become" or "likely to happen."

> Inflation is not our only problem; we need to keep the economy in perspective.

> Medieval painting reveals an almost complete indifference to perspective.

> The prospective jurors waited nervously for their names to be called.

> None of the prospective benefits of the merger ever materialized.

Phase.   See *Faze, phase.*

Phenomenon.   Singular; the standard plural form is *phenomena.*

Plurality.   See *Majority, plurality.*

Plus.   Do not use *plus* between clauses as a substitute for *and.*

> *Poor:*   I had to buy groceries, plus I had to study for a test.
> *Better:*   I had to buy groceries, and I had to study for a test.

Precede, proceed. *Precede* means "to go before." *Proceed* means "to go on." See a dictionary for other meanings.

> Years of struggle and poverty preceded her current success.
>
> Let us proceed with our original plans.

Prejudice, prejudiced. *Prejudice* is ordinarily used as a noun. *Prejudiced* is an adjective.

> *Wrong:*   John is prejudice.
>
>   The neighborhood is filled with prejudice people.
>
> *Right:*   John is prejudiced.
>
>   Legislation alone cannot eliminate prejudice.

Prescribe, proscribe. *Prescribe* means "to order, recommend, write a prescription." *Proscribe* means "to forbid." See other meanings in a dictionary.

> The committee prescribed a statewide income tax.
>
> The authorities proscribe peddling without a license.

Prescription. *Prescription* is often misspelled "perscription"—there is no such word.

Principal, principle. As an adjective, *principal* means "foremost, chief, main." As a noun, it can refer to a leading person (as of a school) or the amount owed on a loan exclusive of interest. For other meanings see a dictionary. *Principle* is a noun meaning "a fundamental doctrine, law, or code of conduct."

> The principal conflict in the novel was between the heroine's conscious and subconscious desires.
>
> For the third time that week, Jeff was summoned to the principal's office.
>
> The interest on a twenty-five- or thirty-year mortgage often exceeds the principal.
>
> Be guided by one principle: "Know thyself."
>
> The candidate is a woman of high principles.

Prioritize. This overused word is often a pretentious and awkward substitute for *set up priorities*.

Pronunciation. Note the spelling. There is no such word as *pronounciation*.

Quiet, quite, quit. *Quiet* means "silence, to become silent, to make silent." *Quite* means "rather" or "completely," in addition to its informal use in expressions like "quite a guy." *Quit* means to stop, to terminate.

The parents pleaded for a moment of peace and quiet.

Throughout the concert, I tried to quiet the people behind me.

April was quite cold this year.

When the job was quite finished, Mary felt like sleeping for a week.

Quit looking at me as if I did something wrong.

Did you quit your job yesterday?

Raise, rise. *Raise* is a transitive verb. *Rise* is an intransitive verb and never takes an object.

I always rise at 8:00 a.m.

The farmer raises corn and wheat.

Rationalize. This word is most effective when used to mean "think up excuses for." It can also mean "to reason," but in this sense it is just a stuffy word for a simple idea. The noun form is *rationalization*.

The gangster tried to rationalize his behavior by insisting that his mother had not loved him.

All these rationalizations conceal the unpleasant truth.

Really. An overused word. It is especially weak in written English when it serves as a synonym for *very* or *extremely*.

Poor: We saw a really nice sunset.

That was a really big show.

When you do use *really*, try to preserve its actual meaning, stressing what is *real* as opposed to what is false or mistaken.

The noises were really caused by mice, not ghosts.

He may have been acquitted through lack of evidence, but everyone knew that Bronson was really guilty.

Reason is because. Awkward and repetitious. Use *reason is that*. Even this phrase is awkward and should be used sparingly. Never repeat *is* as many speakers and writers do.

Wrong: The reason is is that . . . .

Poor: His reason for jilting her was because his parents disapproved of older women.

Better: His reason for jilting her was that his parents disapproved of older women.

Even better: He jilted her because his parents disapproved of older women.

Relevant.   An overused word, frequently relied on to express shallow thought: "Literature is not relevant to our needs," for example. See *Irrelevant, irreverent* for note on pronunciation.

Respectfully, respectively.   *Respectfully* means "with respect." *Respectively* means "each in the order named."

> Everyone likes to be treated respectfully.

> The speaker discussed education, medical research, and defense spending, respectively.

Sadist, masochist.   A *sadist* enjoys hurting living creatures. A *masochist* enjoys being hurt.

Seeing as how.   Not standard English. Use *since* or *because.*

Seldom ever.   *Ever* is unnecessary in this phrase. Avoid it.

> *Poor:*   He was seldom ever angry.

> *Better:*   He was seldom angry.

Sensual, sensuous.   *Sensuous* is the usually positive word referring to physical pleasure. The negative word is *sensual*, suggesting gross overindulgence in physical sensations.

> Jane felt that a hot tub and a cold martini were among life's great sensuous delights.

> Two years of unlimited sensual abandon were directly responsible for Ben's early death.

Set, sit.   To *set* means "to place" or "to put." A dictionary gives dozens of other meanings as well. Our main concern is that *set* does not mean *sit* or *sat*.

> Set the table.

> We sat at the table. (*Not* "We set at the table.")

> Set down that chair.

> Sit down in that chair. (*Not* "Set down in that chair.")

Shall, will.   Elaborate rules differentiate between these words. Few people understand the rules, and no one remembers them. Our advice on this subject is to use *will* all the time except when *shall* obviously sounds more natural, as in some questions and traditional phrases. Examples: "Shall we dance?" "We shall overcome."

Share.   *Share* is an excellent word to indicate what generous children do with candy bars and what generous adults do with their last five dollars. In recent years, the word has sometimes been abused as a pretentious and sentimental synonym for *show* or *tell about*.

> *Poor:*   Joan shared her snapshots of her summer vacation with us.
>
> *Better:*   Joan showed us her snapshots of her summer vacation.
>
> *Poor:*   I asked him to share his innermost thoughts with me.
>
> *Better:*   I asked him to tell me his innermost thoughts.

Shone, shown.   *Shone* is the alternate past tense and past participle of *shine*. Same as *shined*. *Shown* is the alternate past participle of *show*. Same as *showed*.

> The sun shone brightly.
>
> More shocking films are being shown than ever before.

Should of.   See *Could of, should of, would of*.

Sic.   Means *thus* or *so* in Latin. *Sic* is used in brackets within quoted material to indicate that an obvious error or absurdity was actually written that way in the original.

> The author tells us, "President Harold [sic] Truman pulled one of the biggest political upsets of the century."

Site.   See *Cite, site*.

Slander.   See *Libel, slander*.

So.   When *so* is used for emphasis, the full thought often needs to be completed by a clause. See *Such*.

> *Poor:*   The coffee was so sweet.
>
>   My sister is so smart.
>
> *Right:*   The coffee was so sweet that it was undrinkable.
>
>   My sister is so smart that she does my homework for me every night.

So-called.   This word has a specific meaning. Use *so-called* to complain about something that has been incorrectly or inaccurately named. Do not use it as a simple synonym for *undesirable* or *unpleasant*.

> *Wrong:*   These so-called jet planes make too much noise.
>
>   She wore a so-called wig.
>
> *Right:*   Many of our so-called radicals are quite timid and conservative.
>
>   These so-called luxury homes are really just mass-produced bungalows.

Someone, some one. See *Anyone, any one.*

Somewheres. Not standard English. Use *somewhere.*

Sort of. Means "a type of, a variety of." Do not use as a substitute for *somewhat* or *rather.* See *Kind of.*

Stationary, stationery. *Stationary* means "unmoving, unchanging." *Stationery* is paper for letter writing.

Story. A *story* is a piece of short prose fiction. Do not use the word when referring to essays and articles, poems, plays, and novels. Remember, too, that the action in any work of literature is *plot*, not story.

Such. When *such* is used for emphasis to mean "so much" or "so great," the full thought usually needs to be completed by a clause. See *So.*

    Poor: He was such a wicked man.

            We had such fun at the picnic.

    Right: He was such a wicked man that everyone feared him.

            We had such fun at the picnic, we had to force ourselves to go home.

Supposed to. Don't forget the *d* in *supposed.*

    This poem is supposed (not *suppose*) to be one of the greatest ever written.

    The students are supposed (not *suppose*) to have a pep rally tomorrow night.

Sure and. *Sure to* is preferable in writing.

    Poor: Be sure and cancel newspaper deliveries before leaving for vacation.

    Better: Be sure to cancel newspaper deliveries before leaving for vacation.

Than, then. *Than* is the word for expressing comparisons and exceptions. *Then* is the word for all other uses.

    Florida is more humid than California.

    At first Roberta thought the story was funny. Then she realized its underlying seriousness.

Their, they're, there. *Their* is the possessive form of *they.*

    They took their seats.

They're is the contraction of *they are.*

    The defensive linemen say they're going to do better next week.

For all other situations, the correct word is *there.*

They.   Often used vaguely and meaninglessly, as in "They don't make things the way they used to," or "They really ought to do something about safety." Nowhere is the use of they more meaningless and weird than when applied to an individual writer. *Never* write:

> This was an excellent mystery. They certainly fooled me with the solution.

> I think it was sad that they had Othello die at the end of the play.

This, these.   Frequent problem-producers when used imprecisely. Make certain that no confusion or vagueness is possible. To be on the safe side, many writers make a habit of following *this* and *these* with a noun that clarifies the reference: "this idea, these suggestions, this comment."

Through, thru.   *Through* is the standard spelling except, perhaps, on road signs where space and reading time merit special consideration.

> We drove straight through to Buffalo.

> Thru Traffic Keep Left.

Thusly.   Not standard English. Use *thus*.

To, too, two.   *To* is the familiar preposition used in diverse ways. *Too* means "also" or "excessively." *Two* is the number.

Try and.   Acceptable in conversation, but undesirable in print. Use *try to*.

> *Poor:*   We must all try and improve our environment.

> *Better:*   We must all try to improve our environment.

Type of.   This phrase frequently contributes to wordiness.

> *Wordy:*   He was an interesting type of artist.
>
>   I enjoy a suspenseful type of novel.

> *Better:*   He was an interesting artist.
>
>   I enjoy a suspenseful novel.

Under way.   Two words, except in special technical fields.

Uninterested.   See *Disinterested, uninterested*.

Unique.   This word means "one of a kind"; it cannot be made stronger than it already is, nor can it be qualified. Do not write "very unique, more unique, less unique, somewhat unique, rather unique, fairly unique."

Used to.   Don't forget the *d* in *used*.

> I used (not *use*) to like the tales of Jules Verne.
>
> We are used (not *use*) to this kind of treatment.

Vain, vane, vein.   *Vain* refers to vanity or futility. *Vane* is most commonly another word for "weathervane." *Vein* is a blood vessel but has many figurative meanings as well.

> Jim is so vain that he dyes the gray hairs on his chest.
>
> Betty's efforts to control her temper were mostly in vain.
>
> You can recognize the house by the rooster vane near the chimney.
>
> The vein carries blood to the heart.
>
> Beneath the teasing runs a vein of deep tenderness.
>
> At first the miners thought they had found a vein of gold.

Very.   One of the most overused words in the language. Try to find one *exact* word for what you want to say instead of automatically using *very* to intensify the meaning of an imprecise, commonplace word.

very bright	*could be*	radiant
very bad	*could be*	terrible
very sad	*could be*	pathetic, depressed
very happy	*could be*	overjoyed, delighted

Weather, whether.   *Weather* has to do with climate. *Whether* has to do with choices and alternative possibilities.

> The dark clouds indicate that the weather may soon change.
>
> Anita needs to decide whether to accept the most recent job offer.
>
> I can never recall whether the bank is closed on Monday or Wednesday.

When.   In using this word, make sure it refers to *time*, as in "It was ten years ago when we first fell in love."

> *Wrong:*   Basketball is when five men on opposing teams . . .
>
> *Right:*   Basketball is a game in which five men on opposing teams . . .
>
> *Wrong:*   New York is when the Democratic Convention was held.
>
> *Right:*   New York is where the Democratic Convention was held.

Where.   In using this word, make sure it refers to *place*, as in "This is the house where I used to live."

Wrong: I am interested in seeing the movie where the motorcycle gang takes over the town.

Right: I'm interested in seeing the movie in which the motorcycle gang takes over the town.

Wrong: The class is studying the time where the Industrial Revolution was beginning.

Right: The class is studying the time when the Industrial Revolution was beginning.

Where . . . at, where . . . to.   The *at* and the *to* are unnecessary. They show how wordiness can often sneak into our writing almost subconsciously.

Poor: Where are you staying at?

           Where is he going to?

Better: Where are you staying?

           Where is he going?

Whether or not.   The one word *whether* means the same as *whether or not*, and is therefore preferable.

Poor: We wondered whether or not it would snow.

Better: We wondered whether it would snow.

Who, that, which.   Use *who* or *that* for people, preferably *who*, never *which*. Use *which* or *that* for things, preferably *that*, never *who*.

Keats is one of many great writers who died at an early age.

There's the woman that I was telling you about.

Podunk is a town that people always ridicule.

The play which we are now studying is incredibly difficult.

Who, whom.   Although the distinction between *who* and *whom* is no longer a major issue in the conversation of many educated speakers and in much informal writing, formal English still fusses about these words—and perhaps your instructor does, too. We first discuss the traditional rules; then we consider more casual approaches.

■ Formal English requires *who* to serve as the *subject* of verbs in dependent clauses:

He is a fine man who loves his family.

She is a person who should go far in this company.

I dislike people who can't take a joke.

Formal English uses *whom* as the *object* in dependent clauses:

> The drunk driver whom Officer Jerome had ticketed last night turned out to be Judge Furness.

> The teacher whom I feared so greatly last term has now become a good friend.

Note that it is the role played by *who* or *whom* in the *dependent clause* that determines which word is right; don't be distracted by the connections that *who* or *whom* may appear to have with other parts of the sentence. In cases of doubt, a sometimes effective tactic is to substitute *he, she, they* or *him, her, them* for the word in question and see which makes better sense. If *he, she, they* works, use *who*. If *him, her, them* works, use *whom*.

> I dislike people (who, whom) can't take a joke.

Take the dependent clause (*who, whom*) *can't take a joke*. Clearly, *they can't take a joke* works, and *them can't take a joke* does not work. Use *who*.

> The drunk driver (who, whom) Officer Jerome had ticketed last night turned out to be Judge Furness.

Take the dependent clause (*who, whom*) *Officer Jerome had ticketed last night. Officer Jerome had ticketed him last night* makes sense; *Officer Jerome had ticketed he last night* does not make sense. Use *whom*.

Special problems pop up when words intervene between *who* or *whom* and its verb. Don't be misled by expressions like *I think, they say, it seems, she feels*, and so on. These expressions should be thought of as interrupting words and do not affect the basic grammar of the clause.

> The minority leader is the man who I think should be the next president. (*Who* is the subject of *should be*.)

> No artist who he said was brilliant ever impressed us. (*Who* is the subject of *was*.)

■ Through the years, the complex traditional rules have confused many people, and we've tried to explore only the most frequent complexities. As teachers, we confess that we feel distinctly uncomfortable when the old rules are broken. We also confess, however, that Theodore Bernstein, late stylist-in-chief of the *New York Times*, makes a strong case in declaring that the rules are more trouble than they are worth. Check with your own instructor, and then consider the following guidelines and shortcuts:

1. Immediately after a preposition, use *whom*.

> He asked to whom I had been speaking.

> This is the person in whom we must place our trust.

2. At other times, use *who*.

> In my home, it's the man who does the cooking.

> Fred Smiley is the man who Ethel chose.

3. If *who* sounds "wrong" or unnatural, or if you are in a situation that demands formal writing and feel uncertain about the formal rules (the sample sentence about Fred and Ethel breaks the rules), try to eliminate the problem with one of these techniques:

   a. Change *who* or *whom* to *that.*

      Fred Smiley is the man that Ethel chose.

   b. Remove *who* or *whom.*

      Fred Smiley is the man Ethel chose.

Who's, whose.   *Who's* is a contraction of *who is* or *who has. Whose* is the possessive form of *who.*

   Who's going to get the promotion?

   Fenton is a man who's been in and out of jail all his life.

   Whose reputation shall we attack today?

   Kennedy was a president whose place in history is assured.

Will.   See *Shall, will.*

Would of.   See *Could of, should of, would of.*

Your, you're.   *Your* is the possessive form of *you. You're* means "you are."

   You're certain to get caught in rush-hour traffic.

   All of your suggestions are excellent.

   Your attitude shows that you're not truly interested.

EXERCISE   Make any changes necessary to correct the following sentences containing problem words. Numbers in parentheses refer to the number of errors in each item.

   1. She should of left the cite earlier but refused to except her own advise. (4)
   2. Miss Chien was unaccustomed to receiving complements on her wardrobe from her kindergarten students, but however, she excepted this complement gracefully anyways. (5)
   3. Given a choice between chicken, fish, or beef, I usually pick fish, being that its so healthful. (3)
   4. My nephew literally drives me up a wall when he repeatedly asks whether or not we're going to the park. (2)
   5. The whether this winter has been awfully bitter, so I'm glad I bought alot of wool sweaters, heavy pants, and etc. (4)
   6. The cable television network announced that it's restructuring now underway would center around integrating its t.v. and Internet operations to insure quality service. (4)

7. Maria was all together alright this a.m. but by evening she felt so badly she couldn't hardly breath. (6)
8. I could care less as to her advise anyways. (4)
9. The reason she disliked him was because he was equally as vein as his boss, the principle. (4)
10. Hopefully next year there will be less people sent to prison seeing as how the nation's prison population is so high. (3)

SELF TEST: Problem Words

Correct any incorrect words in the following phrases and sentences.

1. can't hardly talk
2. an exciting type of film
3. drive thru the park
4. a more unique idea
5. Did you except her suggestion?
6. between you, Chung Woo, and me
7. mighty tasty enchilada
8. Pedro and myself made a crumb cake.
9. I like neither dogs, cats, nor birds as pets.
10. suppose to leave early
11. keep quite in the church
12. over their
13. disinterested in the speaker's lecture
14. ate less M & Ms
15. hung the murderer
16. leave us study the homework
17. laid in the sun at the pool
18. a lose knot
19. paid her a complement
20. different than her friend

ESL Pointers: Tips for Non-Native Writers

Speakers of other languages bring to the study of English a range of knowledge and skills linked to the grammar system of their native tongues. Although many grammatical systems have similar features, learning to read and write in a new language has many challenges. Reading and writing English to meet the demands of an academic community are not easy even for native speakers. Those who learn English as a second or third language must deal with a number of common issues, and these next few pages attempt to address some of the most important ones. We have built instruction around basic parts of speech and fundamental concepts in grammar, many of which you saw in Part Six.

Verbs and Helping Verbs, Including Modals

English verbs, as in other languages, have several forms—called the **principal parts** of verbs (see pages 660–664)—that work independently or cooperatively with familiar helping verbs (also called **auxiliary verbs** or simply **auxiliaries**). The infinitive *to be* is highly irregular and appears below the main examples for *to look* and *to speak*.

Summary Checklist: Principal Parts and Auxiliaries for Three Sample Verbs

Infinitive—the base form of the verb (always includes the word *to*)	Present tense form (infinitive without the word *to*)	Past tense	Past participle (used with helping verbs to form perfect tenses and passive voice)	Present participle (used with helping verbs to form progressive tenses)
to look [Regular verb]	I **look** He, she, it **looks** You, they **look**	I **looked**	I **have looked** He, she, it **has looked** You, we, they **have looked**	I am **looking** He, she, it **is looking** You, we, they **are looking** I, he, she, it **was looking** You, we, they **were looking**
to speak [Irregular verb]	I **speak** He, she, it **speaks** You, they **speak**	I **spoke**	I **have spoken** He, she, it **has spoken** You, we, they **have spoken** The words **were spoken**	I am **speaking** He, she, it **is speaking** You, we, they **are speaking** I, he, she, it **was speaking** You, they **were speaking**
to be [Irregular verb]	I **am** He, she, it **is** You, they **are**	I, he, she, it **was** You, they **were**	I **have been** He, she, it **has been** You, we, they **have been**	I am **being** He, she, it **is being** You, we, they **are being** I, he, she, it **was being** You, we, they **were being**

A subgroup of helping verbs, called **modals**, also works with principal parts of verbs (see pages 659–660). Because the modals do not identify actual events—you remember that they indicate probability, ability, or need or obligation—they can cause confusion.

Follow these guidelines for using helping verbs, including modals.

Using Helping Verbs and Modals with Principal Parts of Verbs

■ Use *has, have, had* with the past participle to form the perfect tenses: *has driven; has eaten; has, have been.* Do not use these helping verbs with the infinitive (or base form) of the verb:

Incorrect: He has speak. They have look.

Correct: He has spoken. They have looked.

■ Use the modals with the infinitive (or base form) of the verb: *can run, should rest, might be.*

Incorrect: He can speaking. They should looks.

Correct: He can speak. They should look.

■ Use *do, does,* and *did* with the infinitive (or base form) of the verb. Modals include *do begin, does work, did fly.*

Incorrect: I do speaks. She does speaking. They did looked.

Correct: I do speak. She does speak. They did look.

■ Use the various forms of the verb *to be* with present or past participles, depending on your intended meaning:

Present participles: **am** running, **is** singing, **are** laughing, **was** working, **were** studying. Verbs that express states of being (*appear, become, be, believe, seem*), sensory awareness (*feel, hear, see, smell, taste*), and emotion or feeling (*dislike, hate, imagine, intend, know, like, prefer, realize, suppose, think, understand, want, desire, wish, wonder*) do *not* usually appear in the progressive tenses. (There are some exceptions.)

Incorrect: The chili was tasting bad.

        Liu and Cal are appearing ready.

        The professor is preferring my answer.

Correct: The chili tasted bad.

        Liu and Cal appear ready.

        The professor prefers my answer.

Past participles: **is** produced, **was** forbidden, **were** frozen. With the *to be* verb, past participles form the passive voice. Do not use the simple past form of the verb to form the passive voice. (In general, you should avoid the passive voice in writing and use the active voice instead. See pages 668–669.)

Incorrect: The important words were spoke.

        The door was close to the visitors.

Correct: The important words were spoken.

        The door was closed to the visitors.

Phrasal Verbs

Some verbs in English combine with prepositions (see page 713) and sometimes adverbs (see page 587) to form **phrasal verbs**. Phrasal verbs are two- and three-word expressions, generally with a new and different meaning from the original verb's meaning.

Verb:	He *ran* down the street. [*Ran* here means moved quickly.]
Phrasal Verb:	He *ran into* his former girlfriend. [*Ran into* means met unexpectedly.]
Phrasal Verb:	She *ran out of* patience. [*Ran out of* means came to an end, finished.]
Verb:	Juanita *kept* the book. [*Kept* here means held on to or set aside.]
Phrasal Verb:	Juanita *kept off* the grass. [*Kept off* means avoided, did not touch.]
Phrasal Verb:	Juanita *kept to* her story. [*Kept to* means did not change.]

Phrasal verbs play an important part in daily conversation and informal writing, and although they appear less frequently in academic writing, you need to learn them. As common idiomatic expressions, they contribute to your fluency and confidence as an English language user.

Tips and Pointers for Phrasal Verbs

■ You can separate the parts of some phrasal verbs, but not others. There is no general rule.

Separate:	*Take out* the garbage.	*Take* the garbage *out*.
	Tear the wallpaper *down*.	*Tear down* the wallpaper.
Do Not Separate:	*Keep up* with your sister. NOT Keep with your sister up.	
	Look after the child. NOT Look the child after.	

■ Place a pronoun object between the words of phrasal verbs you can separate:

The police *took* **him** *away*. NOT The police took away him.

■ You usually have the option of placing a phrase object between the words of or after a separable phrasal verb.

The police *took* **the criminal** *away*. The police *took away* the **criminal**.

■ When the object is a *clause*, do not place the clause so it separates the parts of a phrasal verb.

Incorrect: The police took the criminal who had escaped them for years away.

Correct: The police took away the criminal who had escaped them for years.

■ Here are some familiar phrasal verbs. You should not separate the phrasal verbs that appear in boldface print:

ask out	**go over**	fill out, fill up, fill in	make up (with), make over
break up (with), break down	**grow up**	find out	run out (of), run

bring up, bring about	hand in, hand over, hand out		over, **run across, run into**
call back, call off, call in	keep out, keep off, **keep up with**	**get along with,** get back, get away,	**speak to, speak with**
drop off, drop in, **drop out (of)**	leave out	get in, get out, get on **get off**	turn in, turn on, turn off, turn down wake up
figure out	look around, look up, look over, **look after, look into, look out for**		

Nouns: Countable and Uncountable

Some English nouns—words for things, people, places, or ideas—cannot be counted separately and, almost invariably, cannot show plurality. Other nouns can be counted separately.

Examples of Nouns You Cannot Count

Sports, games, and other activities	football, checkers, homework, studying, reading, soccer,
Languages	Spanish, Chinese, Vietnamese, Creole
Courses and study fields	History, biology, math, psychology
Foods	Bok choy, lettuce, pork, spaghetti, milk
Liquids, particles, grains, powders, gases	Coffee, water, dust, sand, sugar, air, oxygen, fog, steam, water
Natural events	Rain, weather, lightning, sunshine, gravity
Abstract ideas and emotions	Beauty, fun, peace, hatred, truth, information, fear
Other uncountable nouns	Luggage, money, furniture, news information, clothing, equipment, vocabulary, mail, jewelry

Remember, you can't make most of these uncountable nouns plural.

Incorrect: Our furnitures finally arrived.
Correct: Our furniture finally arrived.

Incorrect: Our luggages broke on our trip.
Correct: Our luggage broke on our trip.

You can use most of these uncountable nouns with words or phrases that do indicate separate units (these phrases are called *partitives*): *piece of* pie, *slice of* bread, *quart of* milk, for example. Even when the partitive is plural, keep the uncountable noun singular.

Incorrect: We ate four pieces of pies.
Correct: We ate four pieces of pie.

Incorrect: We drank three glasses of milks.
Correct: We drank three glasses of milk.

The Articles *a, an,* and *the*

- Avoid using the **indefinite article** *a* or *an* with most noncount nouns.

  Incorrect: A luggage is on the airport scale.
  Correct: Luggage is on the airport scale.

- Use the **definite article** *the* or the word *some* when the uncountable noun has an explicit identity known to your reader.

  Incorrect: I saw a lightning last night.
  Correct: I saw some lightning last night.
                I saw the lightning last night.

- Use *a* before words that start with a consonant sound and *an* before words that start with a vowel sound. With words beginning with the letter *h*, use *a* before a consonant sound (*a* ham sandwich) and *an* before a vowel sound (*an* hour).

  a pencil   an apple

  a union   an express train

  a year ago an age ago

- The articles *a* and *an* do not work successfully with all nouns. With singular countable nouns, use the indefinite articles *a* or *an* only when you don't iden-tify which particular one you mean. Use the definite article *the* when you specify which one among several.

  Maria bought *a* dress for her daughter. [one dress among several]

  He dropped *an* egg on the floor. [no particular egg]

  Maria bought *the* dress for her daughter. [the reader knows which dress]

  He dropped *the* egg on the floor. [a particular egg that the reader knows about]

- Be sure not to leave out the articles.

  Incorrect: Maria bought dress for her daughter.

- Use the definite article *the* if you repeat a noun you already have mentioned.

  Carlos gave *milk* to William's baby. *The* milk was warm and sweet.

- Use the definite article *the* to identify a unique event, occasion, or other one-of-a-kind reference.

  The Declaration of Independence was signed in 1776 on a day we now celebrate as *the* Fourth of July.

When Not to Use the Definite Article *The*

- **Most geographical places**: Europe, Fifth Avenue, Texas, Bismarck, Italy, Mount Rushmore, Lake Como, South America, Jamaica
- **Names of people**: John F. Kennedy, Madonna
- **Academic subjects and languages**: algebra, French, sociology
- **Holidays**: Christmas, Thanksgiving, Veteran's Day
- **Businesses, stores, universities, and colleges**: IBM, Wal-Mart, Cisco Systems, Princeton University, LaGuardia Community College
- **Exceptions**: Use the definite article *the* for oceans, deserts, and mountain ranges (the Gobi Desert, the Rockies); geographical regions (the Western Hemisphere, the Far East, the Great Lakes); rivers, gulfs, and canals (the Hudson River, the Gulf of Tunis, the Suez Canal)

Prepositions

Prepositions are words that show relations between other words and function with those words in prepositional phrases. As modifiers, prepositional phrases tell when (*in* the morning), where (*on* the boat), or how (*by* airplane). English has many prepositions; some common prepositions are *above, about, after, against, along, among, at, because of, before, behind, below, between, by, by means of, except (for), from, in, in addition to, inside, into, near, next to, on, off, out, past, through, to, toward, until, up, upon, with*, and *without*. The uses of *in, at*, and *on* can seem complicated to speakers of other languages. And many prepositions are part of idiomatic expressions whose meanings you simply must memorize in order to use correctly.

Using *in, at,* and *on*

Use *in:*

- to show time in a year, a month, or period

  in 2004   in March   in a week's time   in the evening

- to show certain places that are usually parts of larger entities

  in your basement   in the refrigerator   in Miami   in Hollywood

Use *at:*

- to identify a specific location

  at the dentist's   at the supermarket

- to indicate a specific time period

  at two o'clock   at noon   at 1:00 a.m.   at lunch

Use *on:*

- to indicate a specific day or date

  on July 5   on Wednesday   on your day off

- to refer to a surface

  on the desk   on Route 66   on the street

EXERCISE Correct any errors that you find in the following sentences. Numbers in parentheses indicate the number of errors in each sentence.

1. He has try to keep up his friend with in their jogging every morning. (2)
2. David Kee's luggages had break when he flown from LA to Chicago in bad weathers. (4)
3. They were have funs in Wilson College along the Fifth Avenue in the downtown San Francisco. (4)
4. Loiza arrive to the supermarket to buy a sugar at Wednesday in the March of last year. (5)
5. Mayor did speaks, and he went the budget items over for audience. (4)
6. Alphonso was wanting cold drink in July afternoon, as he was appearing tired in the Yellowstone National Park. (5)
7. The children were dress up when they seen a elephant at zoo relaxing in a sunshine. (5)
8. Waters in the glasses were froze at refrigerator. (5)
9. At wrong stop she got the bus off and had look around for taxi. (4)
10. David had ask the girl who was smiling to him out on date. (3)
11. Mustafa and Lila did begins dating and they were wanting to go movies on the Saturday night. (4)
12. My teacher was disliking my report on the Europe where I spoke my grandmother to after very long time. (4)
13. In the October the weathers had turning very cold. (3)
14. Augusta has went to bakery for two loaf of breads. (4)
15. She have work at the IBM where she manage shippings department. (4)

SELF TEST: ESL Problems

Correct the errors in the following sentences. Numbers in parentheses indicate the number of errors in each sentence.

1. Betty Fong had broke plate to floor when she hear a lightning the last night. (7)
2. Professor can speaking Russian but do uses language only at class in the Webster Community College. (5)
3. My uncle was wanting visit museum but main door was close after the five o'clock. (6)
4. She have go the test over many the times, but at Saturday on Chicago, classmates were hold study session in public library. (9)
5. "Look child after," she had scream to friend Beverley, "or he can fallen big puddle into and can getting very wet." (8)

Answer Key to Self Tests

Abbreviations, Page 585

1. Dr. Rausch's daughter got her MBA at a university in Pennsylvania.
2. The firm's offices moved last December from Spring Street to Valley Road.
3. The FBI raided his company's quarters in Los Angeles, California.
4. My brother and sister left town on Thursday.
5. The reverend worked for the NAACP and held a special Christmas service for government workers who hold PhD degrees.

Correct Adjectives and Adverbs, Page 588

1. personally
2. freshly
3. quickly, well
4. nearly
5. really

6. really, quickly
7. beautifully
8. similar
9. bad
10. loudly

Apostrophe Use, Page 592

1. girls' hats; yours
2. Investors; prices; its profits
3. neighbors'; ours
4. trials
5. Sheets; towels; Ross's (or Ross')

6. boys'; Manuel's
7. ours; yours
8. brother's; carrier's
9. sister's; bridesmaids' dresses
10. students'; yours

Capital Letters, Page 595

1. Please park your car facing west on Marquette Lane South.
2. The Carson Middle School's marching band raises money each year for a trip to Montreal.
3. Some doctors feel that taking fever-reducing medicines like Tylenol is unnecessary, and that low fevers actually can help the body.
4. When Suzanne traveled to the South, she tasted crawfish for the first time.
5. Do you think that the New York Giants can win the Super Bowl again?
6. We'll leave for Florida on the Friday after Thanksgiving.
7. Anika speaks four languages: English, French, German, and Spanish.
8. The golden retriever darted back and forth from the water's edge to his owner, wagging his tail playfully and barking at the sunbathers on Crawford Beach.
9. We will have our next Cub Scout meeting at the Springfield Civic Center.
10. The portrait of Princess Diana at the National Portrait Gallery in London seems to attract more viewers than any other picture in the gallery.

Colons, Page 597

1. Sponsored public service announcements achieve two goals: they deliver important messages and create good will for the advertisers.
2. Karl's new job brought him to cities he had never visited, like Milan, London, Santiago, and Tokyo.
3. Because my father is always looking at his watch, for Father's Day I bought him the book *Keeping Watch: A History of American Time.*

4. Correct.

5. I hate to admit it, but my mother's favorite saying was true: "Give some people an inch, and they'll take a mile."

Commas In Series and Clauses, Page 599

1. I continue to receive the newspaper, yet . . .

2. We did not use our digital camera, but . . .

3. Doug went to the mall and . . .

4. José ran fifteen yards and scored a touchdown.

5. Correct.

6. Marry me, for I love you.

7. Correct.

8. Becoming a pilot was Carla's dream, yet . . .

9. . . . creativity, ingenuity, and reliability.

10. Ruth read *Interview with a Vampire* and watched *Dracula* on television, for . . .

Commas and Introductory Elements, Pages 600–601

1. At the Land Rover Driving School, students learn to control their four-wheel-drive vehicles on unpaved roads.

2. No commas needed.

3. During the past twenty years in the army, Emily has learned many things.

4. Watching the circus, eating cotton candy, and drinking lemonade, Freddy was happier than he had ever been.

5. No commas needed.

6. Having prepared the fish perfectly, the chef tossed several sprigs of parsley on top of it for decoration.

7. No commas needed.

8. After a long and difficult day at work, Natalie enjoyed a five-mile jog.

9. No commas needed.

10. After finishing the whole assignment, he suddenly realized he'd done the wrong exercises.

Commas and Interrupting Elements, Pages 602–603

1. The days of wild, violent video games, as any fan knows, are just beginning!

2. Preventative care for an automobile, to be sure, is worthwhile.

3. Don't let those sweet, and, of course, meaningless smiles deceive you.

4. The administration's basic economic problem, I believe, is unfair taxation.

5. Correct.

6. Teenagers' bedrooms tend to be chaotic rumpus rooms, in short, pig sties.

7. There are effective ways, she insisted, to perform better under pressure.

8. My fundamental monetary difficulty is that I'm broke.

9. The cat, in Dad's opinion, is nothing but a sweet, cuddly pain in the neck.

10. Early Gothic novels, therefore, are basically silly, overwritten romances.

Commas and Nonrestrictive Elements, Page 605

1. A college student who doesn't have the sense to study may not have the sense to belong in college.

2. The Republican candidate, who promised to cut taxes, defeated the Democrat in last night's election.

3. Correct.

4. A person who dislikes dogs and children can't be all bad.

5. Bill Gates, the founder of Microsoft, is considered one of the most intelligent people in America.

6. People who are early to bed and early to rise may be healthy, wealthy, and wise, but they certainly are dull!

7. Some women feel that soap operas, which rarely reflect their own lives, are romantic and daring.

8. Correct.

9. Maya Angelou, who wrote *I Know Why the Caged Bird Sings*, is quite eloquent.

10. Correct.

Commas: Other Uses, Page 608

1. Yes, dear, I did call your sister yesterday.
2. A preschooler's spinning of tall tales is part of the development of intellect, not a purposeful attempt to deceive.
3. The keynote speaker at Memorial Hospital's next benefit dinner will be Sally Johnson, MD.
4. Correct.
5. My letter, dated March 17, 2009, explains in detail my strategies for expanding our human resources department.
6. Facing the crowd together, the band members felt confident and self-assured.
7. Annette, when do you plan to return to Detroit?
8. Oh, I am beginning to feel so frustrated by your selfishness.
9. A song from the movie *Rent* refers to a year as 525,600 minutes.
10. Kent Hoffman, PhD, is an associate professor at Thomas Jefferson University in Philadelphia, Pennsylvania.

Comma Splices, Page 611

1. Some appetite-suppressing pills are now off the market because research found that they can cause heart problems. (or, ". . . the market. Research found. . .".)
2. Correct.
3. Nothing can make Arthur change his mind; he can make a mule look cooperative. (or " . . . mind. He. . . ".)
4. Many mail-order companies sell their customer lists. Then, we receive hundreds of unsolicited offers each year.
5. After fifty pages, the book had failed to interest me; therefore, I finally decided to give up. (or " . . . me. Therefore. . . ".)
6. I used to write comma splices all the time, but Dad taught me how to find and correct them. (or " . . . time. Dad. . . ".)
7. Lawrence and Paolo spent too many nights at the bars. They looked tired and ill; they were a real mess. (other options exist)
8. Correct.
9. Teenage Mutant Ninja Turtles were silly, childish, and too violent. The kids loved them. (or " . . . violent; nevertheless. . . ". A period after *violent* and a capital N in *nevertheless* is also acceptable.)
10. Correct.

Comparatives and Superlatives, Page 613

1. She said that if she had to choose between Jake Gyllenhaal and Matt Damon, she would be the luckiest woman alive.
2. I have visited many national parks, and Bryce Canyon is the most spectacular.
3. Which of the seven dwarfs do you think is the most amusing?
4. He is more at home in front of an audience than alone in his room.
5. Tilda Swinton is a talented actor, but Laura Linney is the better of the two.
6. Correct.
7. Orange may be the less flattering of the two colors, but it is the cheaper.
8. Good nutrition requires balanced meals and self-control. Which is harder?
9. Correct.
10. At this point, it would be better to run away than to fight.

Faulty Comparisons, Page 615

1. Mai Ling says she likes you better than she likes any of her other friends OR Mai Ling says she likes you better than any of her friends do.
2. Cal Ripkin Jr.'s record for consecutive games played is better than any other baseball player's in history.
3. The graceful line of neck and throat resembles that of a swan.

4. Nobody's acting is better than Jack Nicholson's.

5. Miss Rochester had the best rating of all the contestants. [or of any other group]

6. Dr. Raj is better with children than any other pediatrician.

7. My feet are bigger than my sister's OR My feet are bigger than those of my sister.

8. Correct.

9. This poetry is better than any of Lord Byron's.

10. McDonald's hamburgers are better than Burger King's OR McDonald's hamburgers are better than those of Burger King.

End Marks, Page 620

1. "How can you write an essay on a book you've never read?" she asked.

2. Elba wondered why it took six months for her new sofa to arrive.

3. The climate at the summit of Mt. Washington is extremely volatile and unpredictable.

4. I know that my petunias get plenty of sun, so why are they dying?

5. Oh, no! I've lost my keys again.

6. Clive asked himself how much he really enjoyed golf.

7. The city bus will take you to the M.L. Grieg Library.

8. The speakers asked the state, local, and federal governments to cooperate with private organizations on environmental preservation.

9. Get me out of here right now!

10. Why can't we all just get along?

Fragments, Pages 624–625 (Suggested Responses)

1. Americans celebrate Flag Day on June 14 to salute a flag that was stitched in 1776 and has bound the nation together ever since.

2. After Celeste's five-year-old daughter split her lip on a metal shovel at the playground, the distraught mother decided that playgrounds are just too dangerous.

3. Barking and wagging her tail furiously, my golden retriever welcomed me home. After a grueling day at the office, I really needed her affection.

4. It was the perfect day for a barbeque: sunny, breezy, and warm.

5. Living on a farm isn't easy because there is so much work to do. Beginning at dawn we are milking cows, collecting eggs, and caring for all of the animals.

6. Mrs. Scott always acts aloof towards us, if she even acknowledges us at all. It's as if we aren't good enough because our home isn't as large as hers.

7. A representative for Chevrolet says that the company's new pickup combines several important attributes, such as ruggedness, versatility, and personal comfort.

8. The panelists at the business symposium wrestled with a difficult question: Have technology and the Internet left small businesses behind?

9. Wind gusts can cause serious problems for firefighters struggling to keep a fire under control.

10. I will consider you a responsible adult when you make your own car payments, when you pay rent, and when you earn a paycheck.

Dangling and Misplaced Modifiers, Page 630
(Suggested Responses)

1. Walter noticed a "No Trespassing" sign nailed to the fence.

2. With ruffled feathers, my parrot landed gracefully on my shoulder.

3. I thought the dog that was barking wildly and nipping at an old woman's heels had gone mad.

4. Correct.

5. Watching the horror film, Esteban got a terrible pain in his stomach from the gruesome scene.

6. Hearing him chomping loudly and belching, we were appalled at Uncle Ray's terrible table manners.

7. Unable to sleep, Sam drank warm milk so that he was able to relax.

8. I like to watch television while doing my ironing.

9. Michele was told by her mother never to speak to strangers.

10. I thought the golden brown and juicy turkey looked delicious.

Pronoun Agreement, Pages 635–636 (Suggested Responses)

1. All travelers must have their passports and birth certificates if they want to cross the border OR To cross the border, everyone must have a passport and birth certificate.
2. Correct.
3. Either Delia or her sisters will have to give up their turn in the front seat.
4. One of the Gomez brothers leaned back casually, carefully straightening his shirtsleeves.
5. Only Erhan will have his license revoked.
6. Correct.
7. All chefs know they must work with extremely sharp knives.
8. None of it was finished, so it was set aside for a while.
9. Correct.
10. Correct.

Pronoun Case, Page 639

1. She	3. I	5. me	7. my	9. she
2. she	4. us	6. We	8. him and her	10. they

Pronoun Reference, Page 641 (Suggested Responses)

1. The novelist admitted to plagiarizing his rival's work but all the guilty man said was that he was very upset by his own actions OR The novelist admitted to plagiarizing his rival's work, but all his rival said was that he was very upset by his competitor's actions.
2. Sweeping along the street and skimming the pavement, the cold wind gave life to the newspaper OR The cold wind gave life to the newspaper that swept along the street and skimmed the pavement.
3. The weekly patrons complained about the dry and unappealing tortillas.
4. Even the most talented performers can practice for years and still make discouraging mistakes.
5. Ingrid told Anne that Anne's tights had a run OR "My tights have a run," Ingrid said to Anne.
6. Sandy and Bill attempted to read the signs but the wording was too mixed up.
7. George Washington supposedly chopped down a cherry tree and never told a lie. Can these things be true?
8. The teachers had the students get ready for recess. The kids couldn't wait to get out to the playground.
9. Correct.
10. The musicians carefully cleaned their instruments and then stored them in their cases for the night.

Quotation Marks, Page 644

1. Our local children's theater group is doing a choral reading of "The Raven," by Edgar Allan Poe.
2. "I'm sure the referee said, 'Strike,'" Ginger insisted.
3. How many times a day do you think your mother said, "In a minute!" when you were a child?
4. "I'm out of the Olympics," the disappointed skater announced after her third foot injury.
5. My friend urged me to read a pamphlet called "Your Guide Through Life's Financial Decisions."
6. The student asked anxiously, "Will we have some time to review the material before the exam?"
7. "Kids should work very hard during the year and then have a break for time with their parents and activities like camps and jobs," the former Education Secretary stated.
8. "The command of algebraic skills," wrote Professor Small, "gives students confidence when attacking difficult problems."
9. "Spider venom is a gold mine of pharmacological tools," the neuroscientist explained.
10. "Have you chosen a running mate?" the reporters asked the presidential candidate.

Run-on Sentences, Page 646 (Suggested Responses)

1. Hundreds of bicyclists will participate in an exciting event this Sunday. It is the county's fourth annual Mountain Bike Festival. Cyclists begin and end at the county park in Kent.
2. My aunt has a recipe for delicious chocolate chip cookies. However, she guards the secret ingredient. It is oatmeal.
3. The candidate is considering very carefully his pick for vice president. A crucial consideration is to find a reliable team player.
4. This dorm room is tiny. How can anyone expect two people to live here?
5. Many of America's river communities face a common challenge. Soon they must balance the search for prosperity with the need to preserve their natural resources.
6. Darryl walked the dog, and then he fed her.
7. I love to go to the movies, but I often like the popcorn better than the films.
8. Immigrants continue to make our country great; they take many jobs that businesses cannot fill.
9. I saw *No Country for Old Men* and it was bloodier than I had thought.
10. Phish began to play. Suddenly, the audience jumped up and cheered.

Shifts in Person or Tense, Page 649 (Suggested Responses)

1. Switching tenses is a big problem. It is not an easy habit to break.
2. Mark Twain said, "Be good, and you will be lonesome." He also said that the reports of his death were greatly exaggerated.
3. Thousands of registered voters forget to cast their votes at election time. Those voters should be proud of their voices and proud to use them.
4. Verb tenses make me tense. They make my best friend cranky, too.
5. My pen is running out of ink, and I will get another when the ink is completely gone.
6. Contact lenses are less convenient than glasses, but many people think that contacts are more attractive.
7. Karin crept softly up the stairs, and then she peered around the corner to see if the coast was clear.
8. The tennis champion raced across the court and, with a desperate sweep of his outstretched racket, he slammed the ball out of his opponent's reach.
9. One has no choice but to square one's shoulders and clean the oven.
10. Learning to write well takes time and practice and lots of hard work.

Spelling, Pages 652–653

1. athletic   **3.** preferred   **5.** sergeant   **7.** recommend   **9.** jewelry
2. business   **4.** occurred   **6.** excellent   **8.** forty   **10.** argument

Subject–Verb Agreement, Page 658

1. Neither the train nor the bus is air conditioned.
2. There are many ways to catch fish.
3. A meal of rice and beans is quite nutritious.
4. Each of the game show contestants is required to answer twelve questions correctly.
5. The winning team plans to celebrate its victory at the local pizza parlor.
6. *The Savages* is winning prizes for its star Philip Seymour Hoffman.
7. Three days was too long for me to be apart from my daughters.
8. Seven dollars is all you spent on your date?
9. Every family in those apartment buildings is living in squalor.
10. None of the wildfires is showing any sign of abating.

Verb Form, Page 664

1. Angela would have gone to the park if she hadn't arisen feeling sick.
2. They couldn't possibly have stolen that much money.
3. Correct.
4. Sharon swore she had laid the photographs on the table.
5. Joe had drunk too much and felt ill for the rest of the night.
6. Honey, I shrank the kids!
7. The movie *The Ox-Bow Incident* is about a group of men who have hanged three innocent people.
8. Correct.
9. J.C. swam until her fingers began to wrinkle from the water.
10. Alice had fallen down the rabbit hole for a long time before she began to worry.

Verb Tense, Page 668

1. If only she had admitted her guilt at the beginning, her sentence would have been reduced.
2. David did not do it anymore. He had done it too many times for too many years.
3. By the time the party has begun we will have just left our house.
4. When you slowpokes arrive, we will have been there for hours.
5. Correct.
6. Correct.
7. We had not tasted the main course before our plates had been whisked away.
8. Simone always knows all the news. She will know it all tomorrow, too.
9. When this machine is in working order, it will enable Dr. Doom to control the planet.
10. When Carlos and Marsha first met, Marsha was crossing the street.

Problem Words, Page 706

1. can hardly talk
2. an exciting film
3. drive through the park
4. a unique idea
5. Did you accept her suggestion?
6. among you, Chung Woo, and me
7. very tasty enchilada
8. Pedro and I made a crumb cake
9. I do not like dogs, cats, or birds as pets OR I like neither dogs nor cats as pets.
10. supposed to leave early
11. keep quiet in the church
12. over there
13. uninterested in the speaker's lecture
14. ate fewer M&Ms
15. hanged the murderer
16. let us study the homework
17. lay in the sun at the pool
18. a loose knot
19. paid her a compliment
20. different from her friend

ESL Problems, Page 714

1. Betty Fong had broken a plate on the floor when she heard lightning last night.
2. The professor can speak Russian but uses the language only in class at Webster Community College.
3. My uncle wanted to visit the museum, but the main door was closed after five o'clock.
4. She had gone over the test many times, but on Saturday in Chicago, classmates were holding a study session in the public library.
5. "Look after the child," she had screamed to her friend Beverley, "or he can fall into a big puddle and can get very wet."

Credits

Pages 8–9: Downes, Lawrence, "The Shy Egg-Stealing Neighbor You Didn't Know You Had" by Lawrence Downes from *The New York Times*, November 6, 2005, © 2005 The New York Times. All rights reserved. Used by permission and protected by the Copyright Laws of the United States. The printing, copying, redistribution, or retransmission of the Material without express written permission is prohibited.

Pages 12–16: Orwell, George, "A Hanging" from *Shooting an Elephant and Other Essays*, by George Orwell, copyright 1950 by Harcourt, Inc. and renewed 1979 by Sonia Brownell Orwell, reprinted by permission of Houghton Mifflin Harcourt Publishing Company; "A Hanging" by George Orwell (Copyright © George Orwell, 1931) by permission of Bill Hamilton as the Literary Executor of the Estate of the Late Sonia Brownell Orwell and Secker & Warburg Ltd. and A. M. Heath & Co., Ltd.

Pages 30–32: Caldwell, Christopher, "Shopping" by Christopher Caldwell from *The New York Times*, December 23, 2007, © 2007 The New York Times. All rights reserved. Used by permission and protected by the Copyright Laws of the United States. The printing, copying, redistribution, or retransmission of the Material without express written permission is prohibited.

Pages 63–65: Kristof, Nicholas D., "Love and Race" by Nicholas D. Kristof from *The New York Times*, December 6, 2002, © 2002 The New York Times. All rights reserved. Used by permission and protected by the Copyright Laws of the United States. The printing, copying, redistribution, or retransmission of the Material without express written permission is prohibited.

Pages 65–66: Hughes, Langston, "Salvation" from *The Big Sea* by Langston Hughes. Copyright 1940 by Langston Hughes. Copyright renewed © 1968 by Arna Bontemps and George Houston Bass. Reprinted by permission of Hill and Wang, a division of Farrar, Straus, and Giroux, LLC. and Harold Ober Associates.

Pages 67–70: Cox, Michael and Richard Alm, "Scientists Are Made, Not Born" by W. Michael Cox and Richard Alm. Originally appeared in *The New York Times*, February 28, 2005. Reprinted by permission of the authors.

Ch 3 Shoup, Donald, "Gone Parkin'" by Donald Shoup from *The New York Times*, March 29, 2007, © 2007 The New York Times. All rights reserved. Used by permission and protected by the Copyright Laws of the United States. The printing, copying, redistribution, or retransmission of the Material without express written permission is prohibited.

Pages 132–133: Santiago, Esmeralda, "A Blanco Navidad for New Yorikans" by Esmeralda Santiago from *The New York Times*, December 19, 1999, © 1999 The New York Times. All rights reserved. Used by permission and protected by the Copyright Laws of the United States. The printing, copying, redistribution, or retransmission of the Material without express written permission is prohibited.

Pages 134–135: Angell, Roger, "On the Ball" from *Five Seasons* by Roger Angell. Copyright © 1977 by Roger Angell. Reprinted by permission of International Creative Management.

Pages 135–137: Didion, Joan, "Marrying Absurd" from *Slouching Towards Bethlehem* by Joan Didion. Copyright © 1966, 1968, renewed 1996 by Joan Didion. Reprinted by permission of Farrar, Straus, and Giroux, LLC.

Pages 138–139: Feagler, Dick, "America Loses if It Loses Willie" by Dick Feagler from *The Plain Dealer,* April 11, 1994. Copyright © 1994 by Plain Dealer Publishing Company (Cleveland, OH). Reproduced with permission of Plain Dealer Publishing Company in the format Textbook and Other via Copyright Clearance Center.

Pages 142: Strand, Mark, "Black Sea" from *Man and Camel* by Mark Strand, copyright © 2006 by Mark Strand. Used by permission of Alfred A. Knopf, a division of Random House, Inc.

Pages 140–141: Kingston, Maxine Hong, from *The Woman Warrior* by Maxine Hong Kingston, copyright © 1975, 1976 by Maxine Hong Kingston. Used by permission of Alfred A. Knopf, a division of Random House, Inc.

Pages 155–157: Jackson, David Lee, "My Father's House" by Jarrett David Lee Jackson. Used by permission of the author.

Pages 158–160: Littlebrandt, Carol, "Death Is a Personal Matter" by Carol Littlebrandt, originally published in *Newsweek,* January 12, 1976, under the name of Carol K. Gross.

Pages 161–163: Gomez, Rogelio R., "Foul Shots" by Rogelio R. Gomez, *The New York Times Magazine,* October 13, 1991.

Pages 163–166: Sarris, Greg, "You Don't Look Indian" by Greg Sarris, originally appeared as "Battling Illegitimacy: Some Words Against the Darkness" in *Sequoia,* Vol. 33, No. 2, Winter 1970. Reprinted by permission of the author.

Pages 167–168: Chopin, Kate, "Story of an Hour" by Kate Chopin, 1894.

Pages 169–170: Cullen, Ida M., "Incidents" from *On These I Stand* by Ida M. Cullen. Copyright © 1947 by Harper & Bros, NY, renewed 1975 by Ida M. Cullen. Copyrights held by Amistad Research Center, Tulane University, administered by Thompson and Thompson, Brooklyn, NY.

Page 177: Abramsky, Sasha, from "When They Get Out" by Sasha Abramsky in *Atlantic Monthly,* June 1999. Reprinted by permission of the author.

Pages 187–188: Klikenborg, Verlyn, "Inside the Mind's Eye: A Network to Highways " by Verlyn Klikenborg from *The New York Times,* November 29, 2004, © 2004 *The New York Times*. All rights reserved. Used by permission and protected by the Copyright Laws of the United States. The printing, copying, redistribution, or retransmission of the Material without express written permission is prohibited.

Pages 189–190: Updike, John, "A Childhood Transgression", from *More Matter: Essays and Criticism* by John Updike, copyright © 1999 by John Updike. Used by permission of Alfred A. Knopf, a division of Random House, Inc

Pages 191–193: Ehrenreich, Barbara, "What I've Learned from Men" by Barbara Ehrenreich, *Ms.* magazine.Reprinted by permission of *Ms.* magazine, © 1985.

Pages 194–196: Crain, Caleb, first published in *The New Yorker,* December 24, 2007, © 2007 by Caleb Crain, reprinted with permission from The Wylie Agency, Inc.

Pages 196–198: Brady, Judy, "I Want a Wife" by Judy Brady, 1990. Reprinted by permission of the author.

Page 199: Millay, Edna St. Vincent, "Lament" from *Collected Poems,* Harper & Row, 1948. Reprinted by permission of the Edna St. Vincent Millay Society.

Pages 209–212: Folikoue, Ayoko, "Installation: Umbrellas Spread Across the Landscape." Reprinted by permission of the author.

Pages 214–216: Kaufmann, R. R., "How to Survive a Hotel Fire."

Pages 216–219: Kalish, Mildred Armstrong, "Wash Day" from *Little Heathens: Hard Times and High Spirits on an Iowa Farm During the Great Depression* by Mildred Armstrong Kalish, copyright © 2007 by Mildred Armstrong Kalish. Used by permission of Bantam Books, a division of Random House, Inc.

Pages 220–223: Giovanni, Nikki, "Campus Racism" from *Racism 101* by Nikki Giovanni. Copyright © 1994 by Nikki Giovanni. Reprinted by permission of HarperCollins Publishers.

Pages 223–225: Douglas, Susan, "Remote Control: How to Raise a Media Skeptic" by Susan Douglas from the *Utne Reader,* January/February 1997. Reprinted by permission of the author.

Pages 225–226: Frost, Robert, "Fire and Ice," 1920.

Pages 239–241: Twain, Mark, "The Professional."

Pages 241–242: Zinsser, William, "Speaking of Writing" from "The Transaction" in *On Writing Well, Seventh Edition*, by William K. Zinsser. Copyright © 1976, 1980, 1985, 1988, 1990, 1994, 1998, 2001, 2006 by William K. Zinsser. Reprinted by permission of the author.

Pages 243–245: Britt, Suzanne, "The Lean and Hungry Look" by Suzanne Britt from *Newsweek*, October 9, 1978. Reprinted by permission of the author.

Pages 245–248: Caton, Bruce, "Grant and Lee: A Study in Contrasts" by Bruce Caton. Reprinted by permission of the United States Capitol Historical Society.

Pages 248–251: Jackson, Shirley, "Charles" from *The Lottery and Other Stories* by Shirley Jackson. Copyright © 1948, 1949 by Shirley Jackson. Copyright © renewed 1976, 1977 by Laurence Hyman, Barry Hyman, Mrs. Sarah Webster and Mrs. Joanne Schnurer. Reprinted by permission of Farrar, Straus and Giroux, LLC.

Pages 252–254: Saki (H. H. Munro), "The Open Window."

Page 255: Marijuana Policy Project homepage reprinted by permission.

Pages 272–273: Sandberg, Jared, "A Brief, Handy Guide to Those Odd Birds in the Upper Branches" by Jared Sandberg, *The Wall Street Journal*, 2003. Reprinted with permission of The Wall Street Journal, copyright © 2003 Dow Jones & Company, Inc. All Rights Reserved Worldwide.

Pages 274–276: Holt, John, "Three Kinds of Disciplines" from *Freedom and Beyond* by John Holt, 1995. Reprinted by permission of Heinemann.

Pages 277–278: Sen, Amartya, "A World Not Neatly Divided" by Amartya Sen. Originally appeared in *The New York Times*, November 23, 2001. Reprinted by permission of the author.

Pages 279–282: Sunstein, Cass R., "How Polarizing Is the Internet?" by Cass R. Sunstein from *The Chronicle of Higher Education*, Vol. 54, Issue 16, December 14, 2007. Used by permission of the author.

Pages 282–283: Frost, Robert, "The Rose Family" from *The Poetry of Robert Frost* edited by Edward Connery Lathem. Copyright 1928, 1969 by Henry Holt and Company. Copyright 1956 by Robert Frost. Reprinted by permission of Henry Holt and Company, LLC.

Pages 303–304: Staples, Brent, "What Adolescents Miss When We Let Them Grow Up in Cyberspace" by Brent Staples from *The New York Times*, May 9, 2005, © 2005 The New York Times. All rights reserved. Used by permission and protected by the Copyright Laws of the United States. The printing, copying, redistribution, or retransmission of the Material without express written permission is prohibited.

Pages 291–295: Cutts, Keely, "Wolves in Yellowstone" from *Stick and Stones: And Other Student Essays*, edited by Lawrence Barkley, Rise B. Axelrod, and Charles R. Cooper. Copyright © 2004 Bedford/St. Martin's. Reproduced by permission of Bedford/St. Martin's.

Pages 296–298: Tucker, Carll, "On Splitting" by Carll Tucker, *Saturday Review*, January 21, 1978. Reprinted by permission of the author.

Pages 298–299: Sivanand, Mohan, "Why I Write Wrong" by Mohan Sivanand, *Reader's Digest*, April 2000. Copyright © 2000 by The Reader's Digest Association, Inc. Reprinted with permission from Reader's Digest.

Pages 300–302: Sachs, Tony and Sal Nunziato, "Spinning Into Oblivion" from *The New York Times*, April 5, 2007, © 2007 The New York Times. All rights reserved. Used by permission and protected by the Copyright Laws of the United States. The printing, copying, redistribution, or retransmission of the Material without express written permission is prohibited.

Page 306: Robinson, Edwin Arlington, "Richard Cory" from *The Second Book of Verse*, 1922.

Pages 320–322: Owen, David, "The Perfect Job" from *Atlantic Monthly*, March 1990. Reprinted by permission of the author.

Pages 322–325: Grossman, Lev, "Meet Joe Blog" from *Time*, June 13, 2004. Used by permission.

Pages 326–327: Garg, Sunil, "Under My Skin" from *The New York Times*, September 7, 1996. Used by permission of the author.

Pages 328–332: Vonnegut, Kurt Jr., "Harrison Bergeron" from *Welcome to the Monkey House* by Kurt Vonnegut, Jr., copyright © 1961 by Kurt Vonnegut, Jr. Used by permission of Dell Publishing, a division of Random House, Inc.

Page 333: Hughes, Langston, "Dreams" from *The Collected Poems of Langston Hughes,* edited by Arnold Rampersad with David Roessel, Associate Editor, copyright © 1994 by The Estate of Langston Hughes. Used by permission of Alfred A. Knopf, a division of Random House, Inc. and Harold Ober Associates.

Pages 350–352: Rivas, Dennis, "Books Are Not More Valuable Than Art" by Dennis Rivas from *The Daily Campus,* November 8, 2007. Reprinted by permission.

Pages 353–355: Milano, Nick, "Citizenship for Christmas" in *Massachusetts Daily Collegian,* December 13, 2007. Used by permission.

Pages 355–357: Cunningham, Dan, "Illegal Immigrants Don't Deserve a License" from *The Daily Campus,* December 6, 2007. Reprinted by permission.

Pages 357–359: Nguyen, Quynh, "Being a Recent American" from Minnesota Daily, November 21, 2007. Used by permission.

Pages 360–361: Levin, Michael, "The Case for Torture" in *Newsweek,* June 1982. Reprinted by permission of the author.

Pages 362–365: Wilson, James Q., "Just Take Away Their Guns" from *The New York Times Magazine,* March 20, 1994. Reprinted by permission of the author.

Pages 365–367: Greenfield, Meg, "In Defense of the Animals" from *Newsweek,* April 17, 1989. Reprinted by permission of the author's literary executor.

Pages 375–377: Essig, Mark, "Continuing the Search for Kinder Executions" from *The New York Times,* October 21, 2003, © 2003 The New York Times. All rights reserved. Used by permission and protected by the Copyright Laws of the United States. The printing, copying, redistribution, or retransmission of the Material without express written permission is prohibited.

Pages 379–380: Sullivan, Andrew, "Let Gays Marry" by Andrew Sullivan from *Newsweek,* June 3, 1996, © 1996 *Newsweek.* All rights reserved. Used by permission and protected by the Copyright Laws of the United States. The printing, copying, redistribution, or retransmission of the material without express written permission is prohibited.

Pages 380–382: Shiffren, Lisa, "Gay Marriage, an Oxymoron" originally appeared in *The New York Times,* May 23, 1996. Reprinted by permission of the author.

Page 382: NoGayMarriage.com homepage reprinted with permission from the American Family Association.

Page 383: Million for Marriage.com homepage. Copyright © 2006 Human Rights Campaign. Reprinted by permission.

Pages 384–387: Yee, Richard, "Banning Same-Sex Marriage: An Attack on the American Institution." Copyright © 2007 by Richard Yee. Used by permission of the author.

Page 389: Dickinson, Emily, "Some keep the Sabbath going to church," reprinted by permission of the publishers and Trustees of Amherst College from *The Poems of Emily Dickinson,* Thomas H. Johnson, ed., Cambridge, Mass.: The Belknap Press of Harvard University Press, copyright © 1951, 1955, 1979, 1983 by the President and Fellows of Harvard College.

Pages 401–403: Beal, Timothy, "Bibles du Jour" from *Chronicle of Higher Education,* July 26, 2002. Reprinted by permission of the author.

Pages 404–406: Gans, Herbert J., "Fitting the Poor into the Economy" from *Technology Review,* October 1995. Reprinted by permission of the author.

Pages 407–408: Yaqub, Reshma Memon, "You People Did This" from *Rolling Stone,* October 25, 2001. Copyright © Rolling Stone LLC 2001. All Rights Reserved. Reprinted by Permisison.

Pages 423–424: Kincaid, Jamaica,"Girl" from *At the Bottom of the River.* Copyright © 1978, 1983 by Jamaica Kincaid. Reprinted by permission of Farrar, Straus and Giroux, LLC. and The Wylie Agency, Inc.

Pages 424–429: Petry, Ann, "Doby's Gone." Reprinted by the permission of Russell & Volkening as agents for the author. Copyright © 1944 by Ann Petry, renewed 1972 Ann Petry. Originally appeared in *Phylon*, 1944.

Pages 430–433: Poe, Edgar Allan, "The Tell-Tale Heart."

Page 470: Figure 20.3, from *Reader's Guide to Periodical Literature*. Reproduced with the permission of the H. W. Wilson Company.

Page 472: Figure 20.4a, screen capture of EBSCO search for key words "lie detector" courtesy of EBSCO.

Page 473: Figure 20.4b, screen capture of EBSCO search results narrowed by subject headings courtesy of EBSCO.

Page 474: Figure 20.4c, abstract of "Lie Detection and the Polygraph: A Historical Review" by Don Grubin and Lars Madsen from *Journal of Forensic Psychiatry & Psychology*, June 2005, Vol. 16, Issue 2, as it appears on EBSCO database. Courtesy of Taylor and Francis and EBSCO.

Page 492: Judson, Olivia, "The Selfless Game." Copyright © 2007 by Olivia Judson. Originally appeared in *The Atlantic* (October 2007). Reprinted by permission of Georges Borchardt, Inc., on behalf of the author.

Page 499: Figure 21.1, from *The Lie Detectors: The History of an American Obsession* by Ken Alder. Copyright © 2007 by Ken Alder. Reproduced by permission of The Free Press, a Division of Simon & Schuster Adult Publishing Group. All rights reserved.

Page 502: Figure 21.2, reprinted by permission of the Modern Language Association of America from the title page and "The Dark Wood of Postmodernity (Space, Faith, Allegory)" by Bill Brown, *PMLA*, May 2005: 734.

Page 505: Figure 21.3, screen capture from www.owtoad.com, © O. W. Toad Ltd.

Index

Correction Symbols and Abbreviations

Your instructor may use these symbols and abbreviations on your papers. Page numbers refer you to appropriate sections of the text.

ab	Incorrect abbreviation (584–585)		**sp**	Spelling error (649–652)
abst	Too abstract (546–552)		**sub**	Faulty subordination (563–564, 659)
ad	Adjective, adverb confusion (585–587)		**trans**	Transition (103–106)
agr	Subject–verb agreement (653–658) or pronoun agreement (632–634)		**var**	Sentence variety (565–567)
			vb	Error in verb form (659–663)
			vt	Error in verb tense (664–668)
awk	Awkward style		**wc**	Poor word choice: see dictionary or Glossary (670–706)
cap	Capitalize (593–594)			
ca	Pronoun case (636–638)		**wordy**	Wordiness (669)
comp	Faulty comparison (551–552, 614)		**wr**	Write out whole word (584–585) or spell out numeral (630–631)
cs	Comma splice (608–610)			
dm	Dangling modifier (627–628)		**ww**	Wrong word: see dictionary or Glossary (670–706)
esl	English as a Second Language issue (707–714)		⊙	Insert period (617–618);
frag	Fragmentary sentence (620–624)		?	Question mark (617–618);
fs	Fused sentence or run-on sentence (644–645)		!	Exclamation point (619)
			⸲	Insert comma (597–607)
glos	See Glossary (670–706)		;	Insert semicolon (646)
gr	Obvious error in grammar		:	Insert colon (595–597)
lev	Inappropriate level of usage: too colloquial (574–575) or too fancy (575–576)		""	Insert quotation marks (641–643)
			'	Insert apostrophe (589–591)
			-	Insert hyphen (625)
log	Faulty logic (341–343)		...	Insert ellipsis (617);
mm	Misplaced modifier (628–629)		()	Parentheses (634–635);
pass	Awkward use of passive verb (559–560, 668–669)		[]	Brackets (592–593); Dash (606)
			ital	Use italics (underlining) (626–627)
p	Error in punctuation		//	Faulty parallelism (560–562)
ref	Faulty pronoun reference (639–641)		|	Separate letters or words
rep	Undesirable repetition of meaning (573), words (573), or sounds (573–574)		⌣	Bring together letters or words
			¶	Start new paragraph
			No ¶	No paragraph
ro	Run-on sentence or fused sentence (644–646)		~	Transpose letters or words
			/	Do not capitalize (593–594)
sexist	Sexist language (576–578)		˘	Careless error
shift	Illogical shift in tense or person (647–649)		?	Illegible or meaning unclear
			ꝶ	Delete

Guide to the Handbook and Glossary

Handbook

The Handbook provides practical guidance on grammar, punctuation, and mechanics.

Consult the appropriate text pages for discussion, explanation, and practice exercises.

Grammar

Punctuation and Mechanics

Apostrophe

Comma

Other Punctuation Marks

Mechanics

Glossary of Problem Words

The Glossary of Problem Words explains specific words and phrases that frequently confuse writers. The Glossary begins on page 670. Some commonly consulted Glossary entries follow for easy reference.